Louisiana Legal Ethics

STANDARDS AND COMMENTARY

EDITED AND ANNOTATED BY

Dane S. Ciolino

ALVIN R. CHRISTOVICH PROFESSOR OF LAW
LOYOLA UNIVERSITY NEW ORLEANS COLLEGE OF LAW

2018

Dane S. Ciolino, *Louisiana Legal Ethics: Standards and Commentary* (2018).

Version 1.0.

Copyright © 2018 by Dane S. Ciolino. All rights reserved.

ISBN-13: 978-1983486661

ISBN-10: 1983486663

Available for purchase from www.lalegalethics.org and from Amazon.com. Also available on Kindle and other e-reader devices.

Printed in the United States of America by CreateSpace, an Amazon.com Company.

Nothing in this book is to be considered as the rendering of legal advice for specific cases. Readers are responsible for obtaining such advice from their own legal counsel. The author and printer intend for this book to be used only for educational and informational purposes.

The views expressed in this book are those of the author alone and not of Loyola University New Orleans College of Law.

All American Bar Association materials, including materials created by divisions and sections thereof, are used by permission. Copyright in all such materials is owned exclusively by the American Bar Association. In addition, each "Background" section of the rules discussed in the chapter entitled "Louisiana Rules of Professional Conduct" quotes materials prepared by the ABA Ethics 2000 Commission for the ABA House of Delegates. These materials are cited as "ABA Ethics 2000 Commission Revision Notes to Model Rule x (2002)." No claim of original authorship is made as to these or any other ABA materials.

This book should be cited as Dane S. Ciolino, *Louisiana Legal Ethics: Standards and Commentary* (2018).

Table of Contents

About the Book

Louisiana Legal Ethics: Standards and Commentary (2018) contains (1) the full text of the Louisiana Rules of Professional Conduct, (2) "background" information about the adoption of each rule by the Louisiana Supreme Court, (3) related ABA resources, including comments to the corresponding ABA model rule, and (4) annotations discussing Louisiana case law, administrative decisions and other authorities relevant to each rule. It also contains selected "professionalism" materials and practice materials.

Dane S. Ciolino edits and annotates this book. He serves as the Alvin R. Christovich Distinguished Professor of Law at Loyola University New Orleans College of Law. His current scholarly and teaching interests at Loyola include Professional Responsibility, Evidence, Advocacy, and Criminal Law.

Professor Ciolino graduated *cum laude* from Rhodes College in 1985, and *magna cum laude* from Tulane Law School in 1988, where he was inducted into Order of the Coif and selected as Editor in Chief of the *Tulane Law Review*. After graduation, he clerked for the United States District Court, Eastern District of Louisiana, and practiced law at Cravath, Swaine & Moore LLP, in New York City, and Stone Pigman Walther Wittmann LLC, in New Orleans.

He has served as reporter to the Louisiana State Bar Association Ethics 2000 Committee, as chairperson of a Louisiana Attorney Disciplinary Board Hearing Committee, as Chair of the Lawyer Disciplinary Committee of the United States District Court for the Eastern District of Louisiana, and as a member of various Louisiana State Bar Association committees including the Professionalism Committee, the Lawyer & Judicial Codes of Conduct Committee, and the Ethics Advisory Service Committee. He also serves as general counsel to the Ethics Review Board of the City of New Orleans. His weblog, Louisiana Legal Ethics, is located at www.lalegalethics.org.

Professor Ciolino engages in a limited law practice and in law-related consulting, principally in the areas of legal ethics, lawyer discipline, judicial discipline, governmental ethics, and federal criminal law. He represents clients in disciplinary matters before the Louisiana Supreme Court, the Louisiana Attorney Disciplinary Board, and the Louisiana Judiciary Commission. He also handles legal malpractice cases, lawyer disqualification motions, and lawyer fee disputes. Finally, he consults and serves as an expert witness in the fields of legal ethics, legal fees, and the standards of care and conduct governing lawyers.

Professor Ciolino can be reached by telephone at (504) 975-3263, and by email at dane@daneciolino.com. For additional biographical information, visit www.daneciolino.com.

This book is available for purchase at www.lalegalethics.org and at Amazon.com.

Thanks to Prof. Ciolino's Loyola University New Orleans College of Law students for their editing and research work on the 2018 edition as part of the Lawyering III class during the fall semester of 2017. Thanks to Claire Zeringue for serving as the research assistant on this edition. Continuing thanks to Jae A. Donnelly for her extensive editorial and artistic contributions to the original edition, and particularly, for her cover artwork.

Dane S. Ciolino
Metairie, Louisiana
January 2018

Introductory Materials
Historical Background of Louisiana Rules of Professional Conduct

Although Louisiana courts have long exercised their inherent power to regulate a lawyer practicing before them, the use of uniform standards to evaluate lawyer conduct is a relatively modern development.[1] In the earliest reported case of lawyer discipline in Louisiana, the Superior Court of the Territory of Orleans in 1810 struck the name of Pierre Dormenon from the roll of attorneys.[2] After hearing testimony from "men of veracity," the court found that disbarment was warranted because Mr. Dormenon, "wearing a scarf . . . marched at the head of the brigands" during a 1793 slave revolt in Santo Domingo.[3] Similarly, the Louisiana Supreme Court imposed a twelve-month suspension on Michel De Armas for using "arrogant and indecorous language" in a brief, which the court held, "the law forbids us to suffer."[4] In disciplining a lawyer for apparently self-evident wrongdoing, the court did not labor to find whether either lawyer violated any applicable standard of conduct governing members of the bar. Given that no such standards existed, this should come as no surprise.

In 1899, the LSBA undertook the first effort to codify the principles governing lawyering in Louisiana. In so doing, Louisiana diverged from the lawyer codes then in place in most other states,[5] and instead, based its new code on a seventeenth century oath for advocates from the Swiss Canton of Geneva.[6] Although denominated by the LSBA as a "Code of

---

[1]Excerpted from Dane S. Ciolino, *Lawyer Ethics Reform in Perspective: a Look at the Louisiana Rules of Professional Conduct Before and after Ethics 2000*, 65 La. L. Rev. 535, 538-48 (2005).

[2]*Dormenon's Case*, 1 Mart. (o.s.) 129 (La. 1810).

[3]*See id.* at 130, 131. Two years later, the court readmitted Dormenon after he was elected to the Louisiana House of Representatives and cleared by that body of wrongdoing in connection with the slave revolt. *See Dormenon's Case*, 2 Mart. (o.s.) 305, 306 (La. 1812).

[4]*See Michel De Armas' Case*, 10 Mart. (o.s.) 123 (La. 1821).

[5]*See* Report of the Comm. on Code of Prof'l Ethics, 31 ABA Rep. 678 (1907) ("With the exception of the Louisiana Code, all the State Bar Associations Codes are formulated, almost totidem verbis, upon that of Alabama . . . .").

[6]*See* Henry S. Drinker, *Legal Ethics* 23 (1954); *see also* Ellen S. Podgor, *Criminal Misconduct: Ethical Rule Usage Leads to Regulation of the Legal Profession*, 61 Temple L.R. 1323, 1325 n.17 (1988); Peter A. Joy, *Making Ethics Opinions Meaningful: Toward More Effective Regulation of Lawyers' Conduct*, 15 Geo. J. Legal Ethics 313, 322 n.30 (2002). Three other states, namely California, Oregon and Washington, had also based their lawyer ethics codes on the Swiss advocate's oath. *See* Drinker, *supra*. Moreover, the oath had previously been translated and reprinted in New York's 1850 Field Code of Procedure.

Ethics," this enumeration of broad principles read more like a pledge than a disciplinary code.[7] For example, the Code declared that it was the "duty" of a Louisiana lawyer to "maintain the respect due to courts of justice and judicial officers," to "employ . . . such means only as are consistent with truth," to "maintain inviolate the confidence, and at every peril to ourselves, to preserve the secrets of our clients," and to "abstain from all offensive personalities," among other things.[8]

ABA CANONS OF ETHICS

Shortly after the LSBA adopted this code, the ABA formed a committee in 1905 to consider the "advisability and practicability" of creating its own.[9] In short order, the committee decided that an ethics code was in fact advisable and practicable, and then set out to collect all of the existing codes, including the LSBA 1899 Code of Ethics.[10] Ultimately, the committee concluded its work, and the ABA adopted its 1908 Canons of Ethics.[11] Although history has given the Canons mixed reviews,[12] they mark the beginning of the ABA's preeminence in the field of lawyer regulation.[13]

See James M. Altman, Considering the A.B.A.'s 1908 Canons of Ethics, 71 Fordham L.R. 2395, 2422 n.171 (2003). The Swiss lawyers' oath dates from 1683. *See* Center Update, 9 Prof. Lawyer 15, 18 (1998).

[7]*See* Altman, *supra*, at 2422 n.171.

[8]*See* La. State Bar Ass'n, Report of the Louisiana State Bar Association 1898–1899, Charter of 1899, art. II, at 20 (1899). In adopting the Swiss advocates' oath, the LSBA added an eighth canon not found in the Swiss source, namely, the duty to "live uprightly; and in our persons, to justify before men the dignity, honor and integrity of a great and noble profession." *See id.* ¶ 8.

[9]*See* Drinker, *supra*, at 24.

[10]The LSBA Code of Ethics was attached as Appendix C to the ABA committee's report. *See* ABA, Report of the Thirtieth Annual Meeting at 714 (1907); Altman, *supra*, at 2422, n.171; *see also* Carol Rice Andrews, The First Amendment Problem with the Motive Restrictions in the Rules of Professional Conduct, 24 J. Legal Prof. 13, 20 n.23 (2000) (discussing ABA committee's consideration of the Swiss lawyers' oath).

[11]*See id.*; *see generally* Altman, *supra*; Charles W. Wolfram, Modern Legal Ethics § 2.6.2, at 53 (1986).

[12]One prominent commentator has noted that the Canons attracted little professional, public, or scholarly attention in their day. *See* Wolfram, *supra*, at 54. For a discussion of the Canons and its critics, *see generally* Altman, *supra*.

[13]*See, e.g.*, Wolfram, *supra*, § 2.6.2, at 56 ("The significance of the Canons, aside from their historical importance as an episode in bar regulation, is that they served as the forerunner to the 1969 Code and the 1983 Model Rules.").

After the ABA enacted the 1908 Canons, Louisiana became one of the first states to adopt them. At its 1910 meeting in Baton Rouge, the LSBA adopted all thirty-two canons without revision.[14] Thereafter, Louisiana courts and lawyers slowly began to cite to the Canons as authoritative statements of the principles of lawyering.[15] Such citations, however, were infrequent. Moreover, confusion remained among members of the Louisiana bar as to the standards governing their conduct. For example, during an LSBA meeting in 1926, a well-intentioned delegate from New Orleans offered a resolution calling for "a revision and restatement of the present code of ethics of this Association, to the end that the same may be made more comprehensive and specific."[16] The president of the LSBA responded by asking the delegate if he was aware "that the present code of ethics is the canon of ethics of the American Bar Association." The delegate responded as follows:

> Mr. F.B. Freeland (Orleans): No, I was not cognizant of that fact; but I looked at the charter of the Association and found there what appears to be the code of ethics for the Association, and I was not cognizant of the fact that the canons of the American Bar Association were our code of ethics. In fact, that is the main idea I had in mind. If that is the fact, then I most cheerfully withdraw my motion.
>
> President Herold: I am so informed by the Secretary.[17]

In the years following adoption of the Canons, the ABA continually revised and supplemented them. For example, the ABA revised the Canons in 1928, 1933, 1937, 1940, 1942, 1943, and 1951.[18] The LSBA kept pace with these changes, first by simply adopting verbatim the ABA's revisions, and later, by selectively picking, choosing, and amending the ABA's standards. For example, in 1929, the LSBA Charter formally adopted the "Canons of Ethics of The American Bar Association in effect January 1, 1929" as "the Code of Ethics of this Association."[19] However, the charter also opened the door for more

---

[14]*See* La. State Bar Ass'n, Report of the Louisiana State Bar Association for 1910 at 208 (1910).

[15]*See LSBA v. Wheeler*, 243 La. 618, 638 n.12, 145 So. 2d 774, 781 n.12 (1962); *LSBA v. Sackett*, 234 La. 762, 764–65, 101 So. 2d 661, 662 (1958); *Macaluso v. Succession of Marinoni*, 184 La. 1052, 1053, 168 So. 296, 296 (1936); *Gilmore v. Gasquet*, 178 La. 437, 442, 151 So. 763, 764 (1933); *Foundation Fin. Co. v. Robbins*, 179 La. 259, 269, 153 So. 833, 836 (1934).

[16]*See* La. State Bar Ass'n, Report of the Louisiana State Bar Association for 1926 at 199 (1926) (resolution of Mr. F.B. Freeland (Orleans)).

[17]*Id.*

[18]*See, e.g.,* Drinker, *supra*, at 25-26.

[19]La. State Bar Ass'n, Report of the Louisiana State Bar Association for 1929 at 219 (1929) (reprinting Article III of Charter of the Louisiana State Bar Association).

selective adoption by providing that "[t]he Association shall have the right at any general meeting, by resolution, to alter or amend said Code and to adopt additional canons of ethics, without the necessity of amending the charter."[20] Indeed, by the early 1940s, the LSBA was liberally diverging from the ABA Canons on matters of form and substance.[21]

ABA MODEL CODE OF PROFESSIONAL RESPONSIBILITY

Louisiana's increasing divergence from the aging ABA Canons reflected a more widespread dissatisfaction with the Canons' vague and imprecise standards. Such discontent led the ABA to appoint a committee in 1964 to reevaluate the Canons.[22] After working for more than four years, the committee proposed, and the ABA adopted, its Model Code of Professional Responsibility in 1969.

Unlike the 1908 Canons that preceded it, the 1969 Model Code consisted of "three separate but interrelated parts: Canons, Ethical Considerations, and Disciplinary Rules."[23] The Canons were "statements of axiomatic norms" expected of a lawyer.[24] The Ethical Considerations were "aspirational in character" and represented "the objectives toward which every member of the profession should strive."[25] Finally, the Disciplinary Rules were "mandatory in character" and set forth the "minimum level of conduct below which no lawyer [could] fall without being subject to disciplinary action."[26]

The 1969 Code was quickly and widely accepted around the nation, with Louisiana at the forefront of the wave of adoptions.[27] During its April 1970 meeting, the LSBA passed a resolution to submit the issue of adoption of the ABA Code to its general membership. That summer, the referendum passed, and the Code was adopted.[28]

---

[20]La. State Bar Ass'n, Report of the Louisiana State Bar Association for 1929 at 219 (1929) (reprinting Article III of Charter of the Louisiana State Bar Association).

[21]See La. State Bar Ass'n, Report of the Louisiana State Bar Association for 1941 at 117-25 (1942) (diverging from ABA on Cannons 7, 11, 12, 27, 31, 33, 34, 37, and 39, among others).

[22]See Wolfram, *supra*, § 2.6.3, at 56.

[23]See ABA Model Code of Prof'l Resp. Prelim. Statement (1969).

[24]*Id.*

[25]*Id.*

[26]*Id.*

[27]See Wolfram, *supra*, § 2.6.3, at 56 ("[t]he 1969 Code was an impressive and quick success..."); Monroe H. Freedman & Abbe Smith, Understanding Lawyers' Ethics § 1.03, at 5 (2d ed. 2002) (noting that "[t]he Model Code was quickly adopted, with some variations of substance, by virtually all jurisdictions.").

[28]See A. Leon Hebert, Professional Responsibility, 19 La. Bar J. 199, 199 (1971).

ABA MODEL RULES OF PROFESSIONAL CONDUCT

Despite the Model Code's widespread acceptance by the states, enthusiasm for it quickly waned. Critics assailed it as unconstitutional, unresponsive to the realities of modern practice, unhelpful to solo and transactional lawyers, and internally incoherent.[29] As a result of this mounting criticism, deconstruction of the Model Code began just eight years after its adoption when the ABA formed the "Kutak Commission" in 1977. After re-evaluating the Model Code, the Kutak Commission eventually jettisoned its hortatory Canons and Ethical Considerations and replaced them with a single set of black-letter "Rules" setting forth minimally-acceptable standards of conduct. In adopting these proposals in 1983 as the "Model Rules of Professional Conduct," the ABA "completed the transformation from the vague and largely inspirational Canons to an expressly legalistic rule-based ethics regime."[30]

Louisiana set out to consider adopting the ABA's newly-minted Model Rules. At the request of Louisiana Supreme Court Chief Justice John A. Dixon, Jr., the LSBA formed a "Task Force to Evaluate the American Bar Association's Model Rules of Professional Conduct."[31] Although some apparently believed there was no need to replace the then-existing Louisiana Code of Professional Responsibility, the five members of the Task Force eventually undertook to do just that, perhaps as a result of "pressure from the American Bar Association" and the persuasiveness of the "suggestion" from the Louisiana Supreme Court that it do so.[32] Ultimately, the Task Force tweaked and modified the ABA Model Rules in a number of respects and then issued a decidedly lukewarm report giving the LSBA House of Delegates the option of either adopting and recommending the Model Rules "in the form and content proposed in this report and not as originally adopted by the American Bar Association," or retaining the "present Code of Professional Responsibility."[33] In November 1985, the House chose the first option and approved the Task Force's modified version of the ABA Model Rules.[34] After considering the Task Force's recommendations and reconciling several issues of form and substance, the

---

[29] *See, e.g.*, Wolfram, *supra*, § 2.6.4, at 60; Freedman & Smith, *supra*, § 1.03, at 5 (characterizing the Code as "incoherent, inconsistent and unconstitutional").

[30] Joy, *supra*, at 328.

[31] *See generally* N. Gregory Smith, *Missed Opportunities: Louisiana's Version of the Rules of Professional Conduct*, 61 La. L. Rev. 1, 7-18 (2000) (discussing the history of Louisiana's adoption of the 1983 ABA Model Rules).

[32] *See id.* at 8-9 (citing Report and Recommendation of the Task Force to Evaluate the American Bar Association's Model Rules of Professional Conduct at 42 (Nov. 1985); Letter from John A. Dixon to Louis D. Smith (Sep. 27, 1983)).

[33] *See id.* at 10.

[34] *See id.* at 14 (citing Letter, Thomas O. Collins, Jr., to Louisiana Supreme Court (Nov. 25, 1986)).

Louisiana Supreme Court enacted the Louisiana Rules of Professional Conduct and made them effective on January 1, 1987.[35]

ETHICS 2000 COMMITTEE

The years following the adoption of the Rules of Professional Conduct brought much change to the practice of law. Throughout the nation, the proliferation of lawyer advertising, mass tort lawsuits, lawyer referral services, alternative dispute resolution, interstate practice, and Internet advice called into question the adequacy of the ABA's model standards, despite nearly thirty amendments in the years following 1983.[36] As a result, in 1997 the American Bar Association determined yet again that the time had come to reconsider its model standards. In that year, ABA president Jerome J. Shestack formed the Commission on Evaluation of the Rules of Professional Conduct and charged it to reevaluate the 1983 Model Rules.[37] Many commentators hoped that the Commission, later known as the "ABA Ethics 2000 Commission,[38] would "not just examine [the Model Rules] of conduct but help bring us to a higher moral ground."[39]

The Commission's early work plan, published in 1998,[40] ambitiously organized its work into three "tracks" of different priorities.[41] Despite these ambitious plans, the

---

[35]*See id.* at 16-17; Warren L. Mengis, Developments in the Law, 1986–1987: Professional Responsibility, 48 La. L. Rev. 437, 437 (1987).

[36]*See* Am. Bar Ass'n, Annotated Model Rules of Professional Conduct vii (5th ed. 2003).

[37]Debra Baker, Ethics 2000 Marches On: Reviewers of Lawyer Conduct Rule on Schedule to Issue Report, A.B.A. J., Apr. 1999, at 85; James Podgers, Model Rules Get the Once-Over: Ethics 2000 Project Launches Review of ABA Professionalism Standards, A.B.A. J., Dec. 1997, at 90; Steven C. Krane, Ethics 2000: What Might Have Been, 3 Prof. Lawyer 2 (1999); Robert A. Stein, Updating Our Ethics Rules, A.B.A. J., Aug. 1998, at 106.

[38]The Commission was comprised of thirteen members chaired by E. Norman Veasey (Chief Justice, Delaware Supreme Court), and was served by two reporters, Professors Nancy J. Moore and Carl A. Pierce.

[39]*See* Steven Keeva, Professionalism Tops Shestack Agenda: Diversity, LSC, Other Issues Promise to Crowd the Presidential Plate, Too, A.B.A. J., Oct. 1997, at 96.

[40]*See* Ctr. for Prof'l Resp., Am. Bar Ass'n, Ethics 2000 Commission Work Plan (1998), available at http://www.abanet.org/cpr/e2kworkplan.htm.

[41]In track one, the commission targeted a number of rules for immediate reconsideration, including Rules 1.1, 1.6, 1.7, 1.8, 1.9-1.12, 2.2, 4.2 and 8.4. In track two, the Commission identified the following rules and issues as "most in need of fixing": Rules 1.2, 3.3, 1.14, 1.15, 3.4, 1.5, 1.13, 3.5, 3.8, and the Preamble and Scope. Furthermore, the Commission placed on track two the consideration of the following potential new rules: a "new rule on duties to prospective clients"; a "new rule covering systems for law practice (accounting, conflict checks, docket-management)"; a "new rule on discipline for law firms"; and, a "new rule on a lawyer representing fiduciaries." Finally, in track three the Commission

Commission's actual work was more measured. Rather than charting an entirely new course, the Commission decided that "it would follow a presumptive rule of making no change [to the ABA Model Rules] unless it is substantively necessary."[42] The Commission's initial report, which was denominated Report 401, proposed significant but not sweeping revisions.[43] The Report was first considered by the ABA House of Delegates during its annual meeting in Chicago during the summer of 2001. The House later adopted the Report, with revisions, during its mid-year meeting in 2002.[44]

In addition to the changes in lawyering that prompted the ABA's Ethics 2000 initiative at the national level, developments closer to home drove reform initiatives in Louisiana as well. For example, the increasingly vigilant enforcement of ethical norms by the Louisiana Office of Disciplinary Counsel—facilitated in large part by a 1990 restructuring of the disciplinary process and a significant increase in enforcement funding through controversial lawyer assessments—accentuated the call for reform in Louisiana. As a result, in late 1999 the Louisiana State Bar Association created the LSBA Ethics 2000 Committee[45] and appointed members drawn from diverse geographic areas and practice settings, including two judges, three previous LSBA presidents, a law professor, two chairpersons of the Louisiana Attorney Disciplinary Board, the Chief Disciplinary

---

grouped for consideration the following "subject areas that are increasingly important in the future of law practice and implicate multiple rules": a lawyer acting as a dispute resolution neutral; lawyer representing clients in ADR; lawyer handling class actions; aggregate settlements; lawyer referrals; client-law firm networking; internet advice; internet advertising; misdirected communications; email encrypting; lawyer screens; electronic access to client files; lawyer hotlines; internet advice; regulation of nonlawyer assistants; pro se help services; research firms; and, lawyer relationships with intermediary organizations, among others. *Id.*

[42]*See* ABA Ethics 2000 Comm'n Meeting Minutes, Sept. 27-28, 1998, available at http://www.abanet.org/cpr/e2k/092798mtg.html. These minutes, and other current and historical ABA Ethics 2000 Commission materials are available on the website of the Ethics 2000 Commission. *See* Ctr. For Prof'l Resp., Am. Bar. Ass'n, at http://www.abanet.org/cpr/ethics2k.html.

[43]The Commission's report was revised and resubmitted to the House in March 2001. In addition to the commission Report, a "Minority Report" was submitted to the House of Delegates. The principal author of this report was commission member Lawrence J. Fox of Philadelphia. Lawrence J. Fox, Minority Report, available at http://www.abanet.org/cpr/e2k-dissent.html.

[44]*E.g.*, Carol R. Andrews, *Standards of Conduct for Lawyers: An 800-Year Evolution*, 57 S.M.U. L. Rev. 1385, 1385 n. 2 (2004).

[45]*See* Letter from Robert E. Guillory, Jr., President, LSBA (Dec. 9, 1999).

Counsel, respondents' counsel, and a liaison to the Louisiana Supreme Court.[46] The Committee's charge was threefold: (1) to monitor and study the ongoing work of the American Bar Association Ethics 2000 Commission; (2) to conduct a comprehensive review of the Louisiana Rules of Professional Conduct; and (3) to recommend rule changes to the LSBA House of Delegates and, ultimately, the Louisiana Supreme Court.[47]

The Committee's work began in 1999. To define the nature and scope of its efforts, the Committee made a number of preliminary determinations that shaped its deliberations. First, the Committee decided that it would not propose adoption of the "Comments" to the ABA Model Rules. Although the Comments provide very useful guidance to courts and practitioners, the ABA has never intended them to serve as black-letter standards.[48] Indeed, they are replete with hortatory provisions that would engender issues of notice and due process if employed as standards for discipline.[49]

In addition, debate on the Comments to each Model Rule would have consumed a prohibitive amount of Committee time. Moreover, although some Committee members argued for adoption of the Comments simply to make them available to Louisiana judges and lawyers, Louisiana courts already use the Comments to interpret black-letter provisions of the Louisiana Rules.[50] Finally, because the LSBA and the ABA have made the

---

[46]The Committee was comprised of the following LSBA members: Harry S. Hardin, III, Chair; Christine Lipsey, Vice-Chair; Professor Dane S. Ciolino, Reporter; Kim M. Boyle; Connor B. Eglin; Orlando N. Hamilton, Jr.; Judge Carolyn W. Gill-Jefferson; Harvey J. Lewis; Charles B. Plattsmier; Judge Harry Randow; Michael H. Rubin; Marta-Ann Schnabel; Joseph L. Shea, Jr.; Richard C. Stanley; Timothy F. Averill, Supreme Court Liaison; E. Phelps Gay, Board Liaison.

[47]*See generally* Dane S. Ciolino, Re-Evaluating Our Rules of Professional Conduct, 48 La. Bar J. 18 (2000).

[48]The ABA Model Rules specifically provide that "[t]he Comment accompanying each Rule explains and illustrates the meaning and purpose of the Rule. . . . The Comments are intended as guides to interpretation, but the text of each Rule is authoritative." *See* Model Rules of Prof'l Conduct Scope ¶ 21. In addition, some of the Comments are intended merely "to alert lawyers to their responsibilities under . . . other law." *See id.* ¶ 15. Such informal "alerts" would be out of place in a disciplinary code.

[49]As Professor Smith put it: "There are statements in the comments . . . that are more than guides to interpretation. They amount to hidden substantive rules. This is not exactly an ideal state of affairs. In some circumstances, a lawyer might be faced with discipline based upon an obligation that is unexpectedly articulate in a comment instead of in the text of the rules." *See* Smith, *supra* note 31, at 68. Because Louisiana has not adopted the Comments, he notes that this "risk would be remote in Louisiana." *See id.*

[50]*See, e.g., In re Grevemberg,* 838 So. 2d 1283 (La. 2003) (citing ABA Comments to Model Rule 1.8(c)); *Walker v. DOTD,* 817 So. 2d 57, 63 (La. 2002) (citing ABA Comments to Model Rule 1.11); *In re Watley,* 802 So. 2d 593, 597 (La. 2001) (citing ABA Comments to

Comments readily accessible on the Internet, Westlaw, and in hard-copy publications, the issue of access was less compelling than it perhaps had been in the past.[51]

Second, the Committee decided that it would not deviate from the language of the ABA Model Rules unless there was a compelling reason for doing so. The Committee believed that greater consistency with the ABA's model standards would provide more resources to Louisiana lawyers and judges interpreting the Louisiana counterparts. For example, consistency would allow Louisiana practitioners to utilize legal ethics case law developed in other jurisdictions. Furthermore, consistency would make the commentary on the Model Rules published in law reviews, treatises, the ABA's Comments, and the working papers of the ABA Ethics 2000 Commission relevant and useful here. Finally, many members of the Committee believed that greater consistency with the ABA Model Rules would ease the burden of justifying the Committee's proposals to the court and thus increase the chances of adoption.[52]

Third, the Committee decided that it would not propose revisions to rules upon which the Louisiana Supreme Court had acted recently. For example, in the not-so-distant past, the court considered and revised the rules on lawyer advertising and solicitation, as well as those on the sale of a law practice.[53] The Committee believed that it would be premature to revise such recently-considered provisions.

The Committee labored diligently from 1999 until 2003. It held twenty-four Committee meetings. It disseminated its meeting minutes, work product, and preliminary drafts through the LSBA's Internet web site, and it actively sought and received suggestions from

---

Model Rule 5.4); *see also* Smith, *supra*, at 33 (noting that Louisiana courts "have implicitly and explicitly acknowledged" the value of the ABA Comments).

[51]Many of these same considerations led the 1984 Louisiana Task Force to Evaluate the American Bar Association's Model Rules of Professional Conduct to reach the same conclusion. Professor Smith notes that the Task Force declined to adopt the Comments to the 1983 Model Rules (1) because it did not want to get "bogged down in disputes over language or concepts" in the Comments; (2) because it wanted to avoid conflicts between modified black-letter rules and unmodified Comments; and, (3) because adoption of the ABA Comments was not necessary in order to make them available to Louisiana practitioners. *See* Smith, *supra*, at 12-13.

[52]Moreover, greater consistency with the law governing lawyers in Louisiana's sister states furthers the presumably important goal of facilitating interstate commerce. *See* Voltaire, 7 Oeuvres de Voltaire, Dialogues 5 (1838) (complaining that the law in pre-revolutionary France required "change legal systems as often as you change horses") (quoted in Shael Herman, The Louisiana Civil Code: A European Legacy for the United States 12 (1993)).

[53]*See* Smith, *supra*.

local bar associations, specialty bar associations, lawyers, judges, and lay persons throughout the state by conducting CLE seminars, symposia, and nine public hearings.[54]

After completing its work, the Committee submitted a final report to the LSBA House of Delegates in December 2002.[55] On January 25, 2003, the LSBA House of Delegates debated the Committee's report and unanimously approved it after modifying a handful of rules.[56] LSBA president Larry Feldman thereafter forwarded the resolution to the Louisiana Supreme Court.[57] Following a meeting with members of the Committee in May 2003, the court requested additional clarification as to a few proposals.[58] Ultimately, the court

---

[54]Many of these hearings were well attended by lawyers as a result of the availability of free continuing legal education attendance credit. Only a few members of the general public attended the hearings. One demanded to know why the Pope was not included in the revision process.

[55]*See* LSBA Ethics 2000 Final Recommendations (Dec. 2002).

[56]*See* Minutes of the House of Delegates of the Louisiana State Bar Association at 8-12 (Jan. 25, 2003); *id.* at 12 ("The resolution as amended was unanimously approved."); *see generally* Marta-Ann Schnabel, House of Delegates Passes New Rules of Professional Conduct, 50 La. Bar J. 437, 437 (2003). For example, the House of Delegates adopted floor amendments (1) deleting language from Rule 6.1 encouraging a lawyer to make economic contributions to pro bono organizations, (2) adding "religious . . . views" to the list of client views that a lawyer does not endorse by representation, and most importantly, (3) replacing the expansive lawyer misconduct reporting rule proposed by the LSBA Ethics 2000 Committee with Model Rule 8.3. *See id.*

[57]*See* Letter from Larry Feldman, Jr., to Pascal F. Calogero, Jr. (Feb. 18, 2003) (enclosing "[a]pproval of resolution (as amended) from LSBA Ethics 2000 Committee proposing amendment to the Louisiana Rules of Professional Conduct").

[58]*See* Letter from Chief Justice Pascal F. Calogero, Jr. to Harry S. Hardin, III (Oct. 29, 2003). More particularly, the court sought additional information regarding proposed Rules 1.5(e) (division of fees), 1.7 (concurrent conflicts), 1.8(g) aggregate settlements), 1.8(j) (sexual relations with clients), 1.13 (organizational clients), 4.2(b) (contact with represented persons), 5.4 (sharing of legal fees with nonprofit organizations), 5.5 (unauthorized practice of law), 6.1 (pro bono service), 7.4 (specialization), 7.6 (pay-to-play), 8.3 (reporting professional misconduct), 8.4(g) (threatening criminal or disciplinary charges), and 8.5 (jurisdiction and choice of law). The LSBA Ethics 2000 Committee responded to the court's requests on November 20, 2003. *See* Letter from Harry S. Hardin, III, to Pascal F. Calogero, Jr. (Nov. 20, 2003) (attaching "Memorandum from the LSBA Ethics 2000 Committee to the Louisiana Supreme Court in Response to the court's October 29, 2003 Letter").

enacted the revised Louisiana Rules of Professional Conduct on January 20, 2004, and made them effective on March 1, 2004.[59]

RECENT AMENDMENTS TO THE LOUISIANA RULES OF PROFESSIONAL CONDUCT

After the sweeping rule changes made in 2004, the Louisiana Supreme Court has periodically amended the Louisiana Rules of Professional Conduct. The court adopted some of these amendments in response to requests by the Louisiana State Bar Association, and some in response to changes to the ABA Model Rules of Professional Conduct. Some of the more significant amendments are discussed below.

In 2005, the court amended Rules 5.5 and 8.5 to adopt revisions to the 2002 Model Rules of Professional Conduct proposed by the ABA's Commission on Multijurisdictional Practice. These amendments became effective on April 1, 2005.

Between 2008 and 2011, the Louisiana Supreme Court adopted (and partially retracted after federal litigation) major amendments to Rule 7, regarding lawyer advertising.

In 2015, the court amended Rules 1.6 to adopt a new paragraph, denominated as Louisiana Rule 1.6(b)(7), permitting a lawyer to disclose confidential information to the extent the lawyer "reasonably believes necessary": "(7) to detect and resolve conflicts of interest between lawyers in different firms, but only if the revealed information would not

---

[59] *See* Order of January 20, 2004 (La. Jan. 21, 2004) ("Article XVI of the Articles of Incorporation of the Louisiana State Bar Association be and is hereby repealed and re-enacted to read as follows . . . ."). Note that pursuant to the Local Rules of all of the United States District Courts in Louisiana, these rules are also applicable to lawyers practicing in federal courts situated in this state. *See* Unif. Local Rules of La. U.S. Dist. Cts. Rule 83.2.4 E&M ("This court hereby adopts the Rules of Professional Conduct of the Louisiana State Bar Association, as hereafter may be amended from time to time by the Louisiana Supreme Court, except as otherwise provided by a specific rule or general order of a court."); *id.* 83.2.4 W ("This court hereby adopts the Rules of Professional Conduct of the Louisiana State Bar Association, as hereafter may be amended from time to time by the Louisiana Supreme Court, except as otherwise provided by a specific rule of the courts."); *see also Parker v. Rowan Cos., Inc.*, No. Civ. A. 03-0545, 2003 WL 22852218 (E.D. La. 2003) (Vance, J.) ("The United States District Court for the Eastern District of Louisiana has adopted the Rules of Professional Conduct adopted by the Supreme Court of the State of Louisiana for its Rules of Disciplinary Enforcement."). Note, however, that federal courts, as a matter of federal law, can and do look to other standards for guidance as well. *See Parker*, 2003 WL 22852218, at *2 ("The ethical canons that are relevant to this Court's opinion include (1) the local rules for the Eastern District of Louisiana, (2) the ABA's Model Rules of Professional Conduct, (3) the ABA's Model Code of Professional Responsibility, and (4) the Louisiana State rules of conduct.") (citing *Horaist v. Doctor's Hosp. of Opelousas*, 255 F.3d 261, 266 (5th Cir. 2001); *FDIC v. U.S. Fire Ins. Co.*, 50 F.3d 1304, 1311-12 (5th Cir. 1995)).

compromise the attorney-client privilege or otherwise prejudice the client." In adopting this amendment, the court made the Louisiana rule similar to the corresponding ABA Model Rule. The ABA adopted similar language because sometimes a lawyer may need to disclose potential conflicts when the lawyer is considering associating with a new firm, or when law firms are considering a merger. See ABA Model Rules of Prof'l Conduct r. 1.6 cmt. 13. In reality, Louisiana lawyers changing or joining firms have long made these disclosures without this express authorization.

In 2015, the court adopted a new paragraph, denominated as Rule 1.6(c), that provides as follows: "A lawyer shall make reasonable efforts to prevent the inadvertent or unauthorized disclosure of, or unauthorized access to, information relating to the representation of a client." Although this is a new amendment, the Louisiana Rules have always required a lawyer to be "competent" and to preserve confidential information. To competently preserve confidential information, lawyers presumably have always been required to exercise reasonable care in this regard. Therefore, this rule does not impose a new obligation.

In 2015, the Louisiana Supreme Court adopted a Louisiana State Bar Association recommendation to amend Rule 1.15 to require periodic reconciliations of client trust accounts. See La. Sup. Ct. Order of Jan. 13, 2015. The order provides as follows: "The following sentence shall be added to the end of Rule 1.15(f): "A lawyer shall subject all client trust accounts to a reconciliation process at least quarterly,1 and shall maintain records of the reconciliation as mandated by this rule."

In 2016, the Louisiana Supreme Court adopted a revised version of ABA Model Rule 1.17 permitting the sale of a law practice.

In 2017, the court made no amendments to the Louisiana Rules of Professional Conduct.

2017 LOUISIANA LEGAL ETHICS YEAR IN REVIEW

Here are the top ten developments in Louisiana legal ethics in 2017, and a few cases and rule-making efforts to watch in 2018.

1. LSBA DECLINES TO RECOMMEND ANTI-DISCRIMINATION RULE

On November 27, 2017, the LSBA Rules of Professional Conduct Committee reported that it would make "no recommendation" regarding the adoption of a rule prohibiting discrimination and harassment in conduct related to the practice of law.

In 2016, the ABA amended Model Rule 8.4 to include a broad anti-discrimination and anti-harassment provision, and three revised comments. The amendment added a new paragraph (g) to the black-letter of Rule 8.4: "It is professional misconduct for a lawyer to: . . . (g) engage in conduct that the lawyer knows or reasonably should know is harassment or discrimination on the basis of race, sex, religion, national origin, ethnicity, disability, age, sexual orientation, gender identity, marital status or socioeconomic status in conduct related to the practice of law." See ABA Revised Resolution 109 (adopted Aug. 8, 2016).

Although the LSBA committee's chairperson noted that "it is difficult to summarize the rationale of the lengthy debate in its entirety, the primary arguments made by those opposing the rule" were as follows:

- Existing rules permit ODC to prosecute much of the conduct that would be covered by the proposed rule, "thus making it unnecessary."

- The proposed rule contains ambiguous terms that could engender litigation and create uncertainty.

- The proposed rule may be unconstitutional.

2. LSBA PROPOSES SWEEPING NEW RULE ON FIXED FEES

Under existing law, a lawyer earns a fixed fee at the commencement of the representation. As a result, current Louisiana Rule of Professional Conduct 1.5(f)(2), permits a lawyer to deposit a fixed fee into the lawyer's operating account—or to spend the funds—upon receipt.

The obligation to refund an unearned portion of a fixed fee after payment has caused problems in practice. The Client Assistance Fund and the Office of Disciplinary Counsel have reported instances in which a lawyer has died prior to completing the work promised. They have also reported instances in which a client has fired a deadbeat lawyer after paying a fixed fee. In such cases, the client's request for a post-discharge refund all too often has been met with this reply: "Sorry, the money's all gone."

Because of these problems, on November 21, 2017, the LSBA Rules of Professional Conduct Committee proposed a sweeping revision to the rules governing fixed-fees. *See* Stanley Letter to LASC (Nov. 21, 2017). Among other things, the committee's new proposal:

- Recommends a revision to Rule 1.5(a) that expressly prohibits the designation of any payment (of fees or costs) as "nonrefundable." *Id.*

- Recommends a revision to Rule 1.5(f)(2) that would require fixed-fee and minimum-fee agreements to be "set forth with specificity in a writing signed by the client," and that would require the lawyer to provide a copy of the signed agreement to the client. *Id.*

- Recommends a revision to Rule 1.5(f)(2) that would require fixed fee and minimum fee payments to be "placed in the lawyer's trust account until earned." However, it would permit the lawyer, "with the informed consent of the client," to "set reasonable milestones occurring during the representation to allow these funds to be transferred from the trust account to the operating account as fees are earned." Such transfers would be permissible "without further authorization from the client for each transfer," subject to "periodic accounting in writing to the client for these funds as is reasonable under the circumstances." *Id.*

3. LSBA PROPOSES WRITING REQUIREMENT FOR ALL FEE AGREEMENTS

Under existing Louisiana law, only contingent fee agreements must be in writing. *See* Louisiana Rules of Prof'l Conduct r. 1.5(c) (providing that "[a] contingent fee agreement shall be in a writing signed by the client"). As to all other types of fee agreements—including hourly-fee agreements and fixed-fee agreements—no writing requirement exists, although the rules suggest that written fee agreements are "preferable." *See id.* r. 1.5(b) (providing that the rate of the fee "shall be communicated to the client, preferably in writing").

This will change, however, if the Louisiana Supreme Court adopts a recent proposal from the LSBA Rules of Professional Conduct Committee. On November 21, 2017, the committee proposed a revision to Rule 1.5(b) that would require all fee agreements to be in writing:

> (b) The scope of the representation and the basis or rate of the fee and expenses for which the client will be responsible shall be communicated to the client, preferably in a writing approved bv the client, before or within a reasonable time after commencing the representation, except when the lawyer will charge a regularly represented client on the same basis or rate. Any changes in the basis or rate of the fee or expenses shall also be communicated to the client in writing within a reasonable time.

See Stanley Letter to LASC (Nov. 21, 2017).[60]

4. PROSECUTOR'S ETHICAL DUTY TO DISCLOSE EXCULPATORY INFORMATION IS COEXTENSIVE WITH CONSTITUTIONAL DUTY

On October 18, 2017, the Louisiana Supreme Court resolved an unsettled question as to whether a prosecutor's "ethical" duty to disclose exculpatory evidence under Louisiana Rule of Professional Conduct 3.8(d) is broader than the similar constitutional duty under *Brady v. Maryland* (U.S. 1963). In an opinion written by Justice Crichton, the court determined that the duties "are coextensive." *See In re Ronald Seastrunk*, No. 2017-B-0178 (La. Oct. 18, 2017).

The court's decision in *Seastrunk* rejected the expansion of Louisiana Rule 3.8(d) beyond the limits of *Brady*, which would have been bad policy. Although a minority of states[61] impose a broader "ethical" obligation to disclose exculpatory information, doing so in Louisiana would have subjected prosecutors to unwarranted discipline. Among other problems, untethering Rule 3.8(d) from *Brady* and the Louisiana Rules of Criminal

---

[60] Note that this is part of a sweeping proposal by the LSBA Rules of Professional Conduct Committee relating to fixed fees. *See* Dane S. Ciolino, *LSBA Proposes Sweeping New Rule on Fixed Fees*, Louisiana Legal Ethics Blog (Dec. 3, 2017).

[61] *In re Larsen*, No. 20140535, 2016 WL 3369545 (Utah 2016); *In re Disciplinary Action Against Feland*, 820 N.W.2d 672 (N.D. 2012); ABA Formal Op. 09-454 (2009).

Procedure[62] would have exposed prosecutors to discipline for simply complying with federal constitutional law and state statutory law. Disconnecting Rule 3.8(d) and *Brady* would have transformed routine discovery disputes into disciplinary actions. Imposing discipline on a prosecutor for failing to turn over information that is absolutely inconsequential would have been pointless and unfair. For that reason, the *Seastrunk* opinion correctly brings Louisiana into line with a majority of states.[63]

5. FAILURE TO PAY LITIGATION-RELATED EXPENSES CAN BE DISCIPLINARY MISCONDUCT

The Office of Disciplinary Counsel traditionally does not allow itself to be used as a collection agent for the vendors and creditors of lawyers. In so doing, the office has relied on the Louisiana Supreme Court's 2003 decision in *In re Bilbe*, 841 So. 2d 729 (La. 2003). In that case, the hearing committee opined that "the failure to pay an invoice of a court reporter does not constitute action that is prejudicial to the administration of justice[64] even though Respondent has no justification for not paying the invoice." Otherwise, the disciplinary counsel "would become a collection agency for creditors of attorneys." *Id.* at 736.

On January 9, 2017, however, the Louisiana Supreme Court reinstated a disciplinary investigation that was closed by ODC arising out of a lawyer's failure to pay unspecified litigation expenses:

> Based on our review of the record, we find the disciplinary board was arbitrary and capricious in dismissing the complaint. This court's opinion in *In re Bilbe*, 02-1740 (La. 2/7/03), 841 So. 2d 729, is limited to the unique facts presented and does not stand for the blanket proposition that an attorney's failure to pay litigation-related expenses can never constitute conduct prejudicial to the administration of justice.

See In re Appeal of Decision of the Disciplinary Board, 208 So. 3d 370 (La. 2017). As a result, the court remanded the matter to ODC "to conduct further investigation and to institute formal charges, if appropriate." *Id.*

Let us all hope that this does not portend the conversion of ODC into a bill-collection agency. In the meantime, don't crumple up that expert's invoice.

---

[62] *See* La. Code Crim. P. art. 723(B) (requiring disclosure of "any evidence constitutionally required to be disclosed pursuant to *Brady v. Maryland*, 373 U.S. 83 (1963) and its progeny").

[63] *See State ex rel. Okla. Bar Ass'n v. Ward*, 353 P.3d 509 (Okla. 2015); *Disciplinary Counsel v. Kellogg-Martin*, 923 N.E.2d 125 (Ohio 2010); *United States v. Weiss*, No. 05-CR-179-B, 2006 WL 1752373 (D. Colo. June 21, 2006); *In re Attorney C*, 47 P.3d 1167 (Colo. 2002)

[64] Louisiana Rule 8.4(d) prohibits "conduct that is prejudicial to the administration of justice." *See* La. Rules of Prof'l Conduct r. 8.4(d).

6. ABA ISSUES OPINION ON SECURING ELECTRONIC COMMUNICATIONS

On May 22, 2017, the ABA Standing Committee on Ethics and Professional Responsibility issued a new formal opinion on Securing Communication of Protected Client Information. *See* ABA Formal Op. 477R (May 22, 2017). In so doing, the committee updated a 1999 opinion on the topic because "the role and risks of technology in the practice of law have evolved" over time.

The regulatory framework governing a lawyer's use of electronic technology for communication is built on reasonableness. A lawyer must be competent by exercising the knowledge, skill, thoroughness, and preparation "reasonably necessary" for the representation. *See* ABA Model Rules of Prof'l Conduct r. 1.1. Further, a lawyer must use "reasonable efforts" to prevent the inadvertent or unauthorized disclosure of client information. *See id.* r. 1.6(c). To comply with these standards, a lawyer must keep "abreast of knowledge of the benefits and risks associated with relevant technology." *See* ABA Model Rules of Prof'l Conduct r. 1.1 cmt. 8. What is "reasonable," of course, changes with the circumstances. Among the factors a lawyer should consider in handling electronic information are the following:

- the sensitivity of the information;
- the likelihood of disclosure if additional safeguards are not employed;
- the cost of employing additional safeguards;
- the difficulty of implementing the safeguards; and,
- the extent to which the safeguards adversely affect the lawyer's ability to represent clients.

See ABA Model Rules of Prof'l Conduct r. 1.6 cmt. 18. Given these indeterminate standards, what's a lawyer to do? The opinion offers some helpful advice.

7. USE OF FAKE SUBPOENAS BY NEW ORLEANS AREA PROSECUTORS

In April 2017, *The Lens* began to expose the use of fake subpoenas by prosecutors in Orleans Parish, Jefferson Parish, and St. Tammany Parish. *See* Charles Maldonado, *Orleans Parish Prosecutors are Using Fake Subpoenas to Pressure Witnesses to Talk to Them* (Apr. 26, 2017); Charles Maldonado, *Jefferson Parish Prosecutors Used Fake Subpoenas Similar to Those in New Orleans* (Apr. 27, 2017); Charles Maldonado, *Notices Sent to Witnesses on North Shore Weren't Called Subpoenas, But They Looked Real Enough* (May 19, 2017). These "subpoenas," issued without court approval, summoned recipients to the prosecutors' offices for interviews on threat of "fine and imprisonment" for "failure to obey."

It is inappropriate for the district attorney's office to falsely declare that such documents are "subpoenas" and to state that disregarding them can be punishable by fine or imprisonment. These statements are "false statements of material fact or law to a third person," and may violate Louisiana Rule of Professional Conduct 4.1(a).

8. ABA ISSUES OPINION ON "GENERALLY KNOWN" EXCEPTION TO USING FORMER-CLIENT INFORMATION

Both the ABA Model Rules of Professional Conduct and the corresponding Louisiana Rules broadly prohibit a lawyer from revealing former-client confidences. A lawyer may do so rarely and then only when a specific exception in the rule governing existing-client confidentiality[65] applies.

The rules, however, permit more liberal use of former-client confidences. Model Rule 1.9(c)(1) and Louisiana Rule 1.9(c)(1) permit a lawyer to use confidential information if it does no harm to a former client. Moreover, the rules permit use of such information to the disadvantage of a former client "when the information has become generally known." *See* ABA Formal Op. No. 479 (Dec. 15, 2017).

But confusion exists as to just when information is "generally known." Some lawyers believe, incorrectly, that information is "generally known" when it is a matter of public record or when it is publicly accessible. On the contrary, "the fact that the information may have been discussed in open court, or may be available in court records, in public libraries, or in other public repositories does not, standing alone, mean that the information is generally known for Model Rule 1.9(c)(1)." Indeed, "[i]nformation that is publicly available is not necessarily generally known." *See id.* at 5.

Formal Opinion 479 attempts to clear up this confusion and to craft a "workable definition" of the generally-known standard. To this end, the opinion defines two circumstances under which information is "generally known."

First, information is "generally known" when it is "widely recognized by members of the public in the relevant geographic area." *Id.* Such wide recognition—or "public notoriety"—can result from "publicity through traditional media sources, such as newspapers, magazines, radio, or television; through publication on internet web sites; or through social media." *Id.*

Second, information is "generally known" when it is "widely recognized in the former client's industry, profession, or trade." Such recognition can exist if the information "is announced, discussed, or identified in what reasonable members of the industry, profession, or trade would consider a leading print or online publication or other resource in the particular field. Information may be widely recognized within a former client's industry, profession, or trade without being widely recognized by the public." *Id.*

9. U.S. SUPREME COURT TO HEAR LOUISIANA CASE ON AUTHORITY OF LAWYER TO CONCEDE CLIENT'S GUILT IN DEATH PENALTY CASE

On September 28, 2017, the United States Supreme Court granted certiorari in *McCoy v. Louisiana*, No. 16-8255 to decide whether it is ineffective assistance of counsel under the Sixth Amendment for defense counsel in a capital case to concede guilt over the defendant's objections and protestations of innocence.

---

[65] *See* La. Rules of Prof'l Conduct r. 1.6 (2004).

McCoy was convicted of first-degree murder in Bossier Parish for killing his estranged wife's son, mother, and step-father. During opening statements in the guilt phase of McCoy's trial in 2011, McCoy's lawyer explicitly and repeatedly conceded that McCoy had murdered the three deceased: "I'm telling you, Mr. McCoy committed these crimes." McCoy was convicted and sentenced to death. The Supreme Court has ordered briefing and will consider the matter at oral argument in January 2018.

10. ABA COMMITTEE PROPOSES OVERHAUL OF LAWYER ADVERTISING RULES

On December 21, 2017, the ABA Standing Committee on Ethics and Professional Responsibility issued a working draft of proposed amendments to the lawyer-advertising provisions of the ABA Model Rules of Professional Conduct. *See* ABA Standing Cmte. on Ethics and Prof'l Responsibility, *Working Draft of Proposed Amendments to Model Rules* 7.1-7.5 (Dec. 21, 2017). In a memorandum accompanying the draft, the committee noted that its proposals are intended to "streamline and simplify" the rules and to permit lawyers "to use new technologies that can inform consumers accurately and efficiently about the availability of legal services." *See* Barbara S. Gillers, *Memorandum in Support of Working Draft of Proposed Amendments to ABA Model Rules of Prof'l Conduct on Lawyer Advertising* at 2 (Dec. 21, 2017). The committee recommends the following:

- Combining and consolidating existing rules into a single prohibition against false and misleading communications (including standards governing firm names and designations).

- Changing provisions that now call for publication of a lawyer's "office address" to instead call for "contact information," to recognize "technological advances" as to how a lawyer can be contacted.

- Permitting lawyers to give "nominal thank you gifts" to those who refer clients.

- Permitting live person-to-person solicitation of "experienced users of the type of legal services involved for business matters."

- Eliminating the labeling requirement ("ADVERTISEMENT") for targeted mailings, but prohibit such mailings that are misleading, involve coercion, duress or harassment.

Id.

The committee has circulated its proposals to state bar associations, the Conference of Chief Justices, the National Organization of Bar Counsel, and the Association of Professional Responsibility Lawyers. It will accept public comment at the ABA midyear meeting in Vancouver in February 2018, and then publish final proposals in spring 2018. Ultimately, the committee hopes to put the proposals up for a vote at the ABA House of Delegates meeting in August 2018.

In 2008, the Louisiana Supreme Court adopted some of the most complex and indecipherable advertising rules in the country. Have these rules—which were the subject of costly federal litigation ultimately funded by us (Louisiana lawyers)—proven to be worth it? To rip off an old campaign speech, it might be well if we would ask ourselves this: Are we better off now than we were eight years ago? Are prospective clients better informed? Are lawyers' advertisements "better"? Are Louisiana lawyers more respected?

The answer to all of these questions is "no." As APRL, other state bar associations, and now the ABA have begun to recognize, lawyer-advertising regulations should simply ensure that lawyers don't deceive or coerce prospective clients. Those laudable goals are best accomplished with simple rules prohibiting false and misleading communications, and prohibiting in-person solicitation. For that reason, the labyrinthine regulations contained in the current Louisiana rules should be reworked.

ABA Model Rules Preface, Preamble and Scope

PREFACE

For more than ninety years, the American Bar Association has provided leadership in legal ethics and professional responsibility through the adoption of professional standards that serve as models of the regulatory law governing the legal profession.

On August 27, 1908, the Association adopted the original Canons of Professional Ethics. These were based principally on the Code of Ethics adopted by the Alabama Bar Association in 1887, which in turn had been borrowed largely from the lectures of Judge George Sharswood, published in 1854 as Professional Ethics, and from the fifty resolutions included in David Hoffman's A Course of Legal Study (2d ed. 1836). Piecemeal amendments to the Canons occasionally followed.

In 1913, the Standing Committee on Professional Ethics of the American Bar Association was established to keep the Association informed about state and local bar activities concerning professional ethics. In 1919 the name of the Committee was changed to the Committee on Professional Ethics and Grievances; its role was expanded in 1922 to include issuing opinions "concerning professional conduct, and particularly concerning the application of the tenets of ethics thereto." In 1958 the Committee on Professional Ethics and Grievances was separated into two committees: a Committee on Professional Grievances, with authority to review issues of professional misconduct, and a Committee on Professional Ethics with responsibility to express its opinion concerning proper professional and judicial conduct. The Committee on Professional Grievances was discontinued in 1971. The name of the Committee on Professional Ethics was changed to the Committee on Ethics and Professional Responsibility in 1971 and remains so.

In 1964, at the request of President Lewis F. Powell Jr., the House of Delegates of the American Bar Association created a Special Committee on Evaluation of Ethical Standards (the "Wright Committee") to assess whether changes should be made in the then-current Canons of Professional Ethics. In response, the Committee produced the Model Code of Professional Responsibility. The Model Code was adopted by the House of Delegates on August 12, 1969, and subsequently by the vast majority of state and federal jurisdictions.

In 1977, the American Bar Association created the Commission on Evaluation of Professional Standards to undertake a comprehensive rethinking of the ethical premises and problems of the legal profession. Upon evaluating the Model Code and determining that amendment of the Code would not achieve a comprehensive statement of the law governing the legal profession, the Commission commenced a six-year study and drafting process that produced the Model Rules of Professional Conduct. The Model Rules were adopted by the House of Delegates of the American Bar Association on August 2, 1983. At the time this edition went to press, all but eight of the jurisdictions had adopted new professional standards based on these Model Rules.

Between 1983 and 2002, the House amended the Rules and Comments on fourteen different occasions. In 1997, the American Bar Association created the Commission on Evaluation of the Rules of Professional Conduct ("Ethics 2000 Commission") to comprehensively review the Model Rules and propose amendments as deemed appropriate. On February 5, 2002 the House of Delegates adopted a series of amendments that arose from this process.

In 2000, the American Bar Association created the Commission on Multijurisdictional Practice to research, study and report on the application of current ethics and bar admission rules to the multijurisdictional practice of law. On August 12, 2002 the House of Delegates adopted amendments to Rules 5.5 and 8.5 as a result of the Commission's work and recommendations.

The American Bar Association continues to pursue its goal of assuring the highest standards of professional competence and ethical conduct. The Standing Committee on Ethics and Professional Responsibility, charged with interpreting the professional standards of the Association and recommending appropriate amendments and clarifications, issues opinions interpreting the Model Rules of Professional Conduct and the Code of Judicial Conduct. The opinions of the Committee are published by the American Bar Association in a series of hard bound volumes containing opinions from 1924 through 1998 and the current loose-leaf subscription service, *Recent Ethics Opinions*, starting in 1999.

Requests that the Committee issue opinions on particular questions of professional and judicial conduct should be directed to the American Bar Association, Center for Professional Responsibility, 321 North Clark Street, Chicago, Illinois 60654.

PREAMBLE: A LAWYER'S RESPONSIBILITIES

[1] A lawyer, as a member of the legal profession, is a representative of clients, an officer of the legal system and a public citizen having special responsibility for the quality of justice.

[2] As a representative of clients, a lawyer performs various functions. As advisor, a lawyer provides a client with an informed understanding of the client's legal rights and obligations and explains their practical implications. As advocate, a lawyer zealously asserts the client's position under the rules of the adversary system. As negotiator, a lawyer seeks a result advantageous to the client but consistent with requirements of honest dealings with others. As an evaluator, a lawyer acts by examining a client's legal affairs and reporting about them to the client or to others.

[3] In addition to these representational functions, a lawyer may serve as a third-party neutral, a nonrepresentational role helping the parties to resolve a dispute or other matter. Some of these Rules apply directly to lawyers who are or have served as third-party neutrals. See, e.g., Rules 1.12 and 2.4. In addition, there are Rules that apply to lawyers who are not active in the practice of law or to practicing lawyers even when they are acting in a nonprofessional capacity. For example, a lawyer who commits fraud in the conduct of a business is subject to discipline for engaging in conduct involving dishonesty, fraud, deceit or misrepresentation. See Rule 8.4.

[4] In all professional functions a lawyer should be competent, prompt and diligent. A lawyer should maintain communication with a client concerning the representation. A

lawyer should keep in confidence information relating to representation of a client except so far as disclosure is required or permitted by the Rules of Professional Conduct or other law.

[5] A lawyer's conduct should conform to the requirements of the law, both in professional service to clients and in the lawyer's business and personal affairs. A lawyer should use the law's procedures only for legitimate purposes and not to harass or intimidate others. A lawyer should demonstrate respect for the legal system and for those who serve it, including judges, other lawyers and public officials. While it is a lawyer's duty, when necessary, to challenge the rectitude of official action, it is also a lawyer's duty to uphold legal process.

[6] As a public citizen, a lawyer should seek improvement of the law, access to the legal system, the administration of justice and the quality of service rendered by the legal profession. As a member of a learned profession, a lawyer should cultivate knowledge of the law beyond its use for clients, employ that knowledge in reform of the law and work to strengthen legal education. In addition, a lawyer should further the public's understanding of and confidence in the rule of law and the justice system because legal institutions in a constitutional democracy depend on popular participation and support to maintain their authority. A lawyer should be mindful of deficiencies in the administration of justice and of the fact that the poor, and sometimes persons who are not poor, cannot afford adequate legal assistance. Therefore, all lawyers should devote professional time and resources and use civic influence to ensure equal access to our system of justice for all those who because of economic or social barriers cannot afford or secure adequate legal counsel. A lawyer should aid the legal profession in pursuing these objectives and should help the bar regulate itself in the public interest.

[7] Many of a lawyer's professional responsibilities are prescribed in the Rules of Professional Conduct, as well as substantive and procedural law. However, a lawyer is also guided by personal conscience and the approbation of professional peers. A lawyer should strive to attain the highest level of skill, to improve the law and the legal profession and to exemplify the legal profession's ideals of public service.

[8] A lawyer's responsibilities as a representative of clients, an officer of the legal system and a public citizen are usually harmonious. Thus, when an opposing party is well represented, a lawyer can be a zealous advocate on behalf of a client and at the same time assume that justice is being done. So also, a lawyer can be sure that preserving client confidences ordinarily serves the public interest because people are more likely to seek legal advice, and thereby heed their legal obligations, when they know their communications will be private.

[9] In the nature of law practice, however, conflicting responsibilities are encountered. Virtually all difficult ethical problems arise from conflict between a lawyer's responsibilities to clients, to the legal system and to the lawyer's own interest in remaining an ethical person while earning a satisfactory living. The Rules of Professional Conduct often prescribe terms for resolving such conflicts. Within the framework of these Rules, however, many difficult issues of professional discretion can arise. Such issues must be

resolved through the exercise of sensitive professional and moral judgment guided by the basic principles underlying the Rules. These principles include the lawyer's obligation zealously to protect and pursue a client's legitimate interests, within the bounds of the law, while maintaining a professional, courteous and civil attitude toward all persons involved in the legal system.

[10] The legal profession is largely self-governing. Although other professions also have been granted powers of self-government, the legal profession is unique in this respect because of the close relationship between the profession and the processes of government and law enforcement. This connection is manifested in the fact that ultimate authority over the legal profession is vested largely in the courts.

[11] To the extent that lawyers meet the obligations of their professional calling, the occasion for government regulation is obviated. Self-regulation also helps maintain the legal profession's independence from government domination. An independent legal profession is an important force in preserving government under law, for abuse of legal authority is more readily challenged by a profession whose members are not dependent on government for the right to practice.

[12] The legal profession's relative autonomy carries with it special responsibilities of self-government. The profession has a responsibility to assure that its regulations are conceived in the public interest and not in furtherance of parochial or self-interested concerns of the bar. Every lawyer is responsible for observance of the Rules of Professional Conduct. A lawyer should also aid in securing their observance by other lawyers. Neglect of these responsibilities compromises the independence of the profession and the public interest which it serves.

[13] Lawyers play a vital role in the preservation of society. The fulfillment of this role requires an understanding by lawyers of their relationship to our legal system. The Rules of Professional Conduct, when properly applied, serve to define that relationship.

SCOPE

[14] The Rules of Professional Conduct are rules of reason. They should be interpreted with reference to the purposes of legal representation and of the law itself. Some of the Rules are imperatives, cast in the terms "shall" or "shall not." These define proper conduct for purposes of professional discipline. Others, generally cast in the term "may," are permissive and define areas under the Rules in which the lawyer has discretion to exercise professional judgment. No disciplinary action should be taken when the lawyer chooses not to act or acts within the bounds of such discretion. Other Rules define the nature of relationships between the lawyer and others. The Rules are thus partly obligatory and disciplinary and partly constitutive and descriptive in that they define a lawyer's professional role. Many of the Comments use the term "should." Comments do not add obligations to the Rules but provide guidance for practicing in compliance with the Rules.

[15] The Rules presuppose a larger legal context shaping the lawyer's role. That context includes court rules and statutes relating to matters of licensure, laws defining specific

obligations of lawyers and substantive and procedural law in general. The Comments are sometimes used to alert lawyers to their responsibilities under such other law.

[16] Compliance with the Rules, as with all law in an open society, depends primarily upon understanding and voluntary compliance, secondarily upon reinforcement by peer and public opinion and finally, when necessary, upon enforcement through disciplinary proceedings. The Rules do not, however, exhaust the moral and ethical considerations that should inform a lawyer, for no worthwhile human activity can be completely defined by legal rules. The Rules simply provide a framework for the ethical practice of law.

[17] Furthermore, for purposes of determining the lawyer's authority and responsibility, principles of substantive law external to these Rules determine whether a client-lawyer relationship exists. Most of the duties flowing from the client-lawyer relationship attach only after the client has requested the lawyer to render legal services and the lawyer has agreed to do so. But there are some duties, such as that of confidentiality under Rule 1.6, that attach when the lawyer agrees to consider whether a client-lawyer relationship shall be established. See Rule 1.18. Whether a client-lawyer relationship exists for any specific purpose can depend on the circumstances and may be a question of fact.

[18] Under various legal provisions, including constitutional, statutory and common law, the responsibilities of government lawyers may include authority concerning legal matters that ordinarily reposes in the client in private client-lawyer relationships. For example, a lawyer for a government agency may have authority on behalf of the government to decide upon settlement or whether to appeal from an adverse judgment. Such authority in various respects is generally vested in the attorney general and the state's attorney in state government, and their federal counterparts, and the same may be true of other government law officers. Also, lawyers under the supervision of these officers may be authorized to represent several government agencies in intragovernmental legal controversies in circumstances where a private lawyer could not represent multiple private clients. These Rules do not abrogate any such authority.

[19] Failure to comply with an obligation or prohibition imposed by a Rule is a basis for invoking the disciplinary process. The Rules presuppose that disciplinary assessment of a lawyer's conduct will be made on the basis of the facts and circumstances as they existed at the time of the conduct in question and in recognition of the fact that a lawyer often has to act upon uncertain or incomplete evidence of the situation. Moreover, the Rules presuppose that whether or not discipline should be imposed for a violation, and the severity of a sanction, depend on all the circumstances, such as the willfulness and seriousness of the violation, extenuating factors and whether there have been previous violations.

[20] Violation of a Rule should not itself give rise to a cause of action against a lawyer nor should it create any presumption in such a case that a legal duty has been breached. In addition, violation of a Rule does not necessarily warrant any other nondisciplinary remedy, such as disqualification of a lawyer in pending litigation. The Rules are designed to provide guidance to lawyers and to provide a structure for regulating conduct through disciplinary agencies. They are not designed to be a basis for civil liability. Furthermore,

the purpose of the Rules can be subverted when they are invoked by opposing parties as procedural weapons. The fact that a Rule is a just basis for a lawyer's self-assessment, or for sanctioning a lawyer under the administration of a disciplinary authority, does not imply that an antagonist in a collateral proceeding or transaction has standing to seek enforcement of the Rule. Nevertheless, since the Rules do establish standards of conduct by lawyers, a lawyer's violation of a Rule may be evidence of breach of the applicable standard of conduct.

[21] The Comment accompanying each Rule explains and illustrates the meaning and purpose of the Rule. The Preamble and this note on Scope provide general orientation. The Comments are intended as guides to interpretation, but the text of each Rule is authoritative.

Louisiana Rules of Professional Conduct
Article 1. Client-Lawyer Relationship

RULE 1.0. TERMINOLOGY

(a) "Belief" or "believes" denotes that the person involved actually supposed the fact in question to be true. A person's belief may be inferred from circumstances.

(b) "Confirmed in writing," when used in reference to the informed consent of a person, denotes informed consent that is given in writing by the person or a writing that a lawyer promptly transmits to the person confirming an oral informed consent. See paragraph (e) for the definition of "informed consent." If it is not feasible to obtain or transmit the writing at the time the person gives informed consent, then the lawyer must obtain or transmit it within a reasonable time thereafter.

(c) "Firm" or "law firm" denotes a lawyer or lawyers in a law partnership, professional corporation, sole proprietorship or other association authorized to practice law; or lawyers employed in a legal services organization or the legal department of a corporation or other organization.

(d) "Fraud" or "fraudulent" denotes conduct that is fraudulent under the substantive or procedural law of the applicable jurisdiction and has a purpose to deceive.

(e) "Informed consent" denotes the agreement by a person to a proposed course of conduct after the lawyer has communicated adequate information and explanation about the material risks of and reasonably available alternatives to the proposed course of conduct.

(f) "Knowingly," "known," or "knows" denotes actual knowledge of the fact in question. A person's knowledge may be inferred from circumstances.

(g) "Partner" denotes a member of a partnership, a shareholder in a law firm organized as a professional corporation, or a member of an association authorized to practice law.

(h) "Reasonable" or "reasonably" when used in relation to conduct by a lawyer denotes the conduct of a reasonably prudent and competent lawyer.

(i) "Reasonable belief" or "reasonably believes" when used in reference to a lawyer denotes that the lawyer believes the matter in question and that the circumstances are such that the belief is reasonable.

(j) "Reasonably should know" when used in reference to a lawyer denotes that a lawyer of reasonable prudence and competence would ascertain the matter in question.

(k) "Screened" denotes the isolation of a lawyer from any participation in a matter through the timely imposition of procedures within a firm that are reasonably adequate under the circumstances to protect information that the isolated lawyer is obligated to protect under these Rules or other law.

(l) "Substantial" when used in reference to degree or extent denotes a material matter of clear and weighty importance.

(m) "Tribunal" denotes a court, an arbitrator in a binding arbitration proceeding or a legislative body, administrative agency or other body acting in an adjudicative capacity. A legislative body, administrative agency or other body acts in an adjudicative capacity when a neutral official, after the presentation of evidence or legal argument by a party or parties, will render a binding legal judgment directly affecting a party's interests in a particular matter.

(n) "Writing" or "written" denotes a tangible or electronic record of a communication or representation, including handwriting, typewriting, printing, photostating, photography, audio or videorecording and electronic communications. A "signed" writing includes an electronic sound, symbol or process attached to or logically associated with a writing and executed or adopted by a person with the intent to sign the writing.

BACKGROUND

The Louisiana Supreme Court adopted this rule on January 20, 2004. It became effective on March 1, 2004, and has not been amended since. This rule is identical to ABA Model Rule of Professional Conduct 1.0 (2002), except for paragraph (n) (ABA revision in 2012 replaced "e-mail" with "electronic communications."

Prior to 2002, Louisiana, like most other states, never adopted the "Terminology" provision of the ABA Model Rules because the ABA provision had no rule number. In 2002, the ABA removed the stand-alone Terminology section from the Model Rules and created a new Rule 1.0 to give the defined terms greater prominence and to permit the use of Comments to explicate further some of the provisions. *See* ABA Ethics 2000 Commission Revision Notes to Model Rule 1.0 (2002).

"Informed Consent." In 2002, the ABA substituted the term "informed consent" for the pre-2002 term "consent after consultation." The ABA believed that the term "consultation" was not well understood and did not sufficiently indicate the extent to which clients had to be given adequate information and explanation in order to make reasonably informed decisions. The ABA believed that the term "informed consent," which is familiar from its use in other contexts, is more likely to convey to lawyers what is required under the Rules. No change in substance was intended. *See id.*

"Firm." In 2002, the ABA clarified (in comments to ABA Rule 1.0) that legal departments of government entities are included within the definition of "firm." The ABA also included a reference to "other association authorized to practice law" to encompass lawyers practicing in limited liability entities. However, it intended no change in substance. *See id.*

"Fraud." In 2002, the ABA redefined the term "fraud" because it was concerned that the pre-2002 definition was ambiguous since it did not clearly state whether, in addition to the intent to deceive, the conduct in question had to be fraudulent under applicable substantive or procedural law. The ABA was concerned that under the prior definition conduct could be considered "fraudulent" merely because it involved an intention to deceive, even though it did not violate any other law. The ABA clarified in Model Rule 1.0 that in order for conduct to be "fraudulent," it must be fraudulent under applicable substantive or procedural law. *See id.*

"Writing." In 2002, the ABA defined "signed" to include methods intended as the equivalent of a traditional signature. This electronic signature provision was modeled on the Uniform Electronic Transactions Act. *See id.*

"Screened." In 2002, the ABA defined "screened" to include a requirement that the lawyer be "timely" isolated from participation in the matter. The ABA believed that the timeliness requirement is so important that it included the timeliness requirement in the text of Rules 1.11, 1.12 and 1.18. *See* ABA Ethics 2000 Commission Revision Notes to Model Rule 1.11 (2002).

COMMENTS TO ABA MODEL RULE 1.0
Confirmed in Writing

[1] If it is not feasible to obtain or transmit a written confirmation at the time the client gives informed consent, then the lawyer must obtain or transmit it within a reasonable time thereafter. If a lawyer has obtained a client's informed consent, the lawyer may act in reliance on that consent so long as it is confirmed in writing within a reasonable time thereafter.

Firm

[2] Whether two or more lawyers constitute a firm within paragraph (c) can depend on the specific facts. For example, two practitioners who share office space and occasionally consult or assist each other ordinarily would not be regarded as constituting a firm. However, if they present themselves to the public in a way that suggests that they are a firm or conduct themselves as a firm, they should be regarded as a firm for purposes of the Rules. The terms of any formal agreement between associated lawyers are relevant in determining whether they are a firm, as is the fact that they have mutual access to information concerning the clients they serve. Furthermore, it is relevant in doubtful cases to consider the underlying purpose of the Rule that is involved. A group of lawyers could be regarded as a firm for purposes of the Rule that the same lawyer should not represent opposing parties in litigation, while it might not be so regarded for purposes of the Rule that information acquired by one lawyer is attributed to another.

[3] With respect to the law department of an organization, including the government, there is ordinarily no question that the members of the department constitute a firm within the meaning of the Rules of Professional Conduct. There can be uncertainty, however, as to the identity of the client. For example, it may not be clear whether the law department of a corporation represents a subsidiary or an affiliated corporation, as well as the corporation by which the members of the department are directly employed. A similar question can arise concerning an unincorporated association and its local affiliates.

[4] Similar questions can also arise with respect to lawyers in legal aid and legal services organizations. Depending upon the structure of the organization, the entire organization or different components of it may constitute a firm or firms for purposes of these Rules.

Fraud

[5] When used in these Rules, the terms "fraud" or "fraudulent" refer to conduct that is characterized as such under the substantive or procedural law of the applicable jurisdiction and has a purpose to deceive. This does not include merely negligent misrepresentation or negligent failure to apprise another of relevant information. For purposes of these Rules, it is not necessary that anyone has suffered damages or relied on the misrepresentation or failure to inform.

Informed Consent

[6] Many of the Rules of Professional Conduct require the lawyer to obtain the informed consent of a client or other person (*e.g.*, a former client or, under certain circumstances, a prospective client) before accepting or continuing representation or pursuing a course of conduct. *See, e.g.*, Rules 1.2(c), 1.6(a) and 1.7(b). The communication necessary to obtain such consent will vary according to the Rule involved and the circumstances giving rise to the need to obtain informed consent. The lawyer must make reasonable efforts to ensure that the client or other person possesses information reasonably adequate to make an informed decision. Ordinarily, this will require communication that includes a disclosure of the facts and circumstances giving rise to the situation, any explanation reasonably necessary to inform the client or other person of the material advantages and disadvantages of the proposed course of conduct and a discussion of the client's or other

person's options and alternatives. In some circumstances it may be appropriate for a lawyer to advise a client or other person to seek the advice of other counsel. A lawyer need not inform a client or other person of facts or implications already known to the client or other person; nevertheless, a lawyer who does not personally inform the client or other person assumes the risk that the client or other person is inadequately informed and the consent is invalid. In determining whether the information and explanation provided are reasonably adequate, relevant factors include whether the client or other person is experienced in legal matters generally and in making decisions of the type involved, and whether the client or other person is independently represented by other counsel in giving the consent. Normally, such persons need less information and explanation than others, and generally a client or other person who is independently represented by other counsel in giving the consent should be assumed to have given informed consent.

[7] Obtaining informed consent will usually require an affirmative response by the client or other person. In general, a lawyer may not assume consent from a client's or other person's silence. Consent may be inferred, however, from the conduct of a client or other person who has reasonably adequate information about the matter. A number of Rules require that a person's consent be confirmed in writing. *See* Rules 1.7(b) and 1.9(a). For a definition of "writing" and "confirmed in writing," see paragraphs (n) and (b). Other Rules require that a client's consent be obtained in a writing signed by the client. *See, e.g.,* Rules 1.8(a) and (g). For a definition of "signed," see paragraph (n).

Screened

[8] This definition applies to situations where screening of a personally disqualified lawyer is permitted to remove imputation of a conflict of interest under Rules 1.10, 1.11, 1.12 or 1.18.

[9] The purpose of screening is to assure the affected parties that confidential information known by the personally disqualified lawyer remains protected. The personally disqualified lawyer should acknowledge the obligation not to communicate with any of the other lawyers in the firm with respect to the matter. Similarly, other lawyers in the firm who are working on the matter should be informed that the screening is in place and that they may not communicate with the personally disqualified lawyer with respect to the matter. Additional screening measures that are appropriate for the particular matter will depend on the circumstances. To implement, reinforce and remind all affected lawyers of the presence of the screening, it may be appropriate for the firm to undertake such procedures as a written undertaking by the screened lawyer to avoid any communication with other firm personnel and any contact with any firm files or other information, including information in electronic form, relating to the matter, written notice and instructions to all other firm personnel forbidding any communication with the screened lawyer relating to the matter, denial of access by the screened lawyer to firm files or other information, including information in electronic form, relating to the matter and periodic reminders of the screen to the screened lawyer and all other firm personnel.

[10] In order to be effective, screening measures must be implemented as soon as practical after a lawyer or law firm knows or reasonably should know that there is a need for screening.

ANNOTATIONS
Firm

As to indigent defenders' offices in Louisiana, the Louisiana Supreme Court has held as follows:

> Generally, under our jurisprudence, "Indigent Defender Boards are ... treated as the equivalent of private law firms to effectuate a defendant's Sixth Amendment right to effective assistance of conflict-free counsel and the ethical obligation of an attorney associated with other lawyers in a firm to avoid representing a client 'when any one of them practicing alone would be prohibited from doing so . . . .' La. Rules of Professional Responsibility, Rule 1.10(a)."

State v. Garcia, 108 So. 3d 1, 28 (La. 2012) (citing *State v. Connolly*, 930 So. 2d 951, 954 n.1 (La. 2006); *State v. McNeal*, 594 So. 2d 876 (La.1992). However, the court in *Garcia* suggested that lawyers employed as "independent contractors" are not members of the "firm." *Id.* at 29. This should be considered a fact-specific holding in the *Garcia* case and not a general holding. Whether a lawyer is a member of a "firm" should not turn on whether the lawyer is labeled a "partner," "employee" or "independent contractor." The analysis should be a functional and practical one that considers the lawyer's access to confidential information, and the sharing of information among other lawyers with whom the lawyer is associated in the practice of law.

Fraud

Consistent with paragraph (d) of this rule, the term "fraud" is defined in the Louisiana Civil Code to include only intentional affirmative misrepresentations or suppressions of the truth—not merely negligent ones:

> Fraud is a misrepresentation or a suppression of the truth made with the intention either to obtain an unjust advantage for one party or to cause a loss or inconvenience to the other. Fraud may also result from silence or inaction.

La. Civ. Code Ann. art. 1953.

Informed Consent

The comments to the Model Rules state that whether a client is "experienced in legal matters generally and in making decisions of the type involved" is a factor relevant to evaluating informed consent. *See* ABA Model Rules of Prof'l Conduct r. 1.0 cmt. 6 (2002). The Louisiana Supreme Court in *Hodges v. Reasonover*, 103 So. 3d 1069, 1078 (La. 2012), however, held that the "sophistication" of the client is an irrelevant factor in evaluating informed consent:

We decline to find the extent of an attorney's fiduciary duty depends on the sophistication of the client. To do so would create two classes of clients and implicitly hold that well-educated, business-savvy clients are somehow less deserving of an attorney's full candor and loyalty. This rule would be directly contrary to the high ethical standards set forth in the Rules of Professional Conduct and repugnant to Louisiana public policy.

Therefore, a Louisiana lawyer should provide full and extensive disclosure in all cases in which the lawyer seeks informed consent—irrespective of the sophistication of the client.

RULE 1.1. COMPETENCE

(a) A lawyer shall provide competent representation to a client. Competent representation requires the legal knowledge, skill, thoroughness and preparation reasonably necessary for the representation.

(b) A lawyer is required to comply with the minimum requirements of continuing legal education as prescribed by Louisiana Supreme Court rule.

(c) A lawyer is required to comply with all of the requirements of the Supreme Court's rules regarding annual registration, including payment of Bar dues, payment of the disciplinary assessment, timely notification of changes of address, and proper disclosure of trust account information or any changes therein.

BACKGROUND

The Louisiana Supreme Court amended this rule on March 29, 2006. It became effective, as amended, on April 15, 2006.

MODEL RULE COMPARISON

This rule is substantially similar to ABA Model Rule of Professional Conduct 1.1 (2002). Paragraph (a) is identical to the Model Rule. Paragraph (b) is not included in the ABA Model Rule, but is included in the Louisiana rule so that members of the Louisiana bar who fail to comply with mandatory continuing legal education requirements can be subjected to professional discipline under this rule and Rule 8.4(a). Paragraph (c) is not included in the ABA Model Rule, but was added to the Louisiana rule effective April 15, 2006 to subject a lawyer to discipline who fails to comply with annual registration requirements.

COMMENTS TO ABA MODEL RULE 1.1

Legal Knowledge and Skill

[1] In determining whether a lawyer employs the requisite knowledge and skill in a particular matter, relevant factors include the relative complexity and specialized nature of the matter, the lawyer's general experience, the lawyer's training and experience in the field in question, the preparation and study the lawyer is able to give the matter and whether it is feasible to refer the matter to, or associate or consult with, a lawyer of established competence in the field in question. In many instances, the required proficiency is that of a general practitioner. Expertise in a particular field of law may be required in some circumstances.

[2] A lawyer need not necessarily have special training or prior experience to handle legal problems of a type with which the lawyer is unfamiliar. A newly admitted lawyer can be as

competent as a practitioner with long experience. Some important legal skills, such as the analysis of precedent, the evaluation of evidence and legal drafting, are required in all legal problems. Perhaps the most fundamental legal skill consists of determining what kind of legal problems a situation may involve, a skill that necessarily transcends any particular specialized knowledge. A lawyer can provide adequate representation in a wholly novel field through necessary study. Competent representation can also be provided through the association of a lawyer of established competence in the field in question.

[3] In an emergency a lawyer may give advice or assistance in a matter in which the lawyer does not have the skill ordinarily required where referral to or consultation or association with another lawyer would be impractical. Even in an emergency, however, assistance should be limited to that reasonably necessary in the circumstances, for ill-considered action under emergency conditions can jeopardize the client's interest.

[4] A lawyer may accept representation where the requisite level of competence can be achieved by reasonable preparation. This applies as well to a lawyer who is appointed as counsel for an unrepresented person. *See* also Rule 6.2.

Thoroughness and Preparation
[5] Competent handling of a particular matter includes inquiry into and analysis of the factual and legal elements of the problem, and use of methods and procedures meeting the standards of competent practitioners. It also includes adequate preparation. The required attention and preparation are determined in part by what is at stake; major litigation and complex transactions ordinarily require more extensive treatment than matters of lesser complexity and consequence. An agreement between the lawyer and the client regarding the scope of the representation may limit the matters for which the lawyer is responsible. *See* Rule 1.2(c).

Retaining or Contracting with Other Lawyers
[6] Before a lawyer retains or contracts with other lawyers outside the lawyer's own firm to provide or assist in the provision of legal services to a client, the lawyer should ordinarily obtain informed consent from the client and must reasonably believe that the other lawyers' services will contribute to the competent and ethical representation of the client. *See* also Rules 1.2 (allocation of authority), 1.4 (communication with client), 1.5(e) (fee sharing), 1.6 (confidentiality), and 5.5(a) (unauthorized practice of law). The reasonableness of the decision to retain or contract with other lawyers outside the lawyer's own firm will depend upon the circumstances, including the education, experience and reputation of the nonfirm lawyers; the nature of the services assigned to the nonfirm lawyers; and the legal protections, professional conduct rules, and ethical environments of the jurisdictions in which the services will be performed, particularly relating to confidential information.

[7] When lawyers from more than one law firm are providing legal services to the client on a particular matter, the lawyers ordinarily should consult with each other and the client about the scope of their respective representations and the allocation of responsibility among them. *See* Rule 1.2. When making allocations of responsibility in a matter pending

before a tribunal, lawyers and parties may have additional obligations that are a matter of law beyond the scope of these Rules.

Maintaining Competence

[8] To maintain the requisite knowledge and skill, a lawyer should keep abreast of changes in the law and its practice, including the benefits and risks associated with relevant technology, engage in continuing study and education and comply with all continuing legal education requirements to which the lawyer is subject.

ANNOTATIONS

Generally

The most fundamental obligation that a lawyer owes to a client is the duty to handle the client's matter competently. *See generally* Restatement (Third) of the Law Governing Lawyers § 16(2) (2000). Incompetent lawyering can lead not only to discipline[66] for violating Rule 1.1, *see, e.g., In re Lee*, 85 So. 3d 74, 79 (La. 2012) (suspending a lawyer for two years for failure to understand basic succession law and for lacking thoroughness and preparation); *In re Young*, 849 So. 2d 25, 30 (La. 2003) (disciplining a lawyer for failure to prepare for criminal trial), but also to delictual liability for professional malpractice. In 2007, the Louisiana Supreme Court disciplined a lawyer under Rule 1.1(a) for incompetently investing a client's funds. *In re Pharr*, 950 So. 2d 636, 640-41 (2007) (holding that although the lawyer did not intentionally harm the client's financial interests, the lawyer's fiscal mismanagement was "the product of incompetence"). An improper disbursement of client funds can violate Rule 1.1(a). *See In re Thomas*, 74 So. 3d 695, 699-701 (La. 2011) (noting that the lawyer's inability to adequately disburse funds for a client's debt demonstrated incompetence). *In re Gilbert*, 185 So. 3d 734 (La. 2016) (lawyer disbarred for engaging in comingling of client funds, neglecting legal matters, failing to effectively communicate with the clients and failing to withdraw from representation); *State v. Singleton*, 2015-1099 (La. Ct. App. 4th Cir. May 25, 2016) (finding that the public defender and lawyer had good cause to withdraw from representation because competent representation of the client would be impossible due to the shrinking budget for public defenders and increasing caseload); *In re Conry*, 158 So. 3d 786 (La. 2015) (lawyer claimed lawyer's inexperience in the practice of law caused mismanagement of the practice and argued ADHD was a cause of this, however, the committee found a pattern of misconduct and recommended disbarment, which the court agreed was warranted); *In re Cade*, 166 So. 3d 243 (La. 2015) (lawyer failed to diligently work on client's personal injury case, resulting in dismissal with prejudice; lawyer's license was suspended for one year, with six months deferred); *In re Mendy*, 217 So. 3d 260 (La. 2016) (lawyer disbarred for neglecting

---

[66] In most cases, discipline imposed for violations of Rule 1.1 stems from the lawyer's failure to thoroughly prepare and prosecute a matter rather than from the lawyer's lack of "knowledge" or "skill." For this reason, disciplinary actions brought under this rule are often accompanied with alleged violations of Rule 1.3 (diligence). *See, e.g, In re Mendy*, 81 So. 3d 650 (La. 2012); *In re Andrus*, 814 So. 2d 1283 (La. 2002); *In re Landry*, 728 So. 2d 833 (La. 1999); *In re Grady*, 731 So. 2d 878 (La. 1999).

legal matters, failing to return unearned fees, and failing to cooperate with ODC investigations).

Delictual Liability for Malpractice
ELEMENTS

A plaintiff establishes legal malpractice under Louisiana law through proof (1) that there was a lawyer-client relationship, (2) that the lawyer was negligent, and (3) that the plaintiff suffered a loss caused by that negligence. *See, e.g., Costello v. Hardy*, 864 So. 2d 129, 138 (La. 2004); *Waste Mgmt. of Louisiana, LLC v. Penn-Am. Ins. Co.*, 110 So. 3d 200, 203 (La. Ct. App. 3 Cir. 2013),*Whittington v. Kelly*, 917 So. 2d 688, 692 (La. Ct. App. 2nd Cir. 2005), *Broadscape.com, Inc. v. Jones, Walker, Waechter, Poitevant, Carrere & Denegre, L.L.P.*, 866 So. 2d 1085, 1088 (La. Ct. App. 4th Cir. 2004); *Kosak v. Trestman*, 864 So. 2d 214, 218 (La. Ct. App. 4th Cir. 2003); *Spicer v. Gambel*, 789 So. 2d 741, 744 (La. Ct. App. 4th Cir. 2001); *Spellman v. Bizal*, 755 So. 2d 1013, 1017 (La. Ct. App. 4th Cir. 2000);*Johnson v. Tschirn*, 746 So. 2d 629, 631-32 (La. Ct. App. 4th Cir. 1999); *Francois v. Reed*, 714 So. 2d 228, 229-30 (La. Ct. App. 1st Cir. 1998); *Butler v. Chuzi*, 687 So. 2d 605, 606-07 (La. Ct. App. 4th Cir. 1997); *Finkelstein v. Collier*, 636 So. 2d 1053, 1058 (La. Ct. App. 5th Cir. 1994); *Dier v. Hamilton*, 501 So. 2d 1059, 1061 (La. Ct. App. 2d Cir. 1987). *See generally* Warren L. Mengis, *Professional Responsibility*, 46 La. L. Rev. 637, 642 (1986).

To prove the existence of a lawyer-client relationship (prong one), the plaintiff must establish that he or she sought and received advice and assistance from the defendant-lawyer in matters pertinent to the lawyer's profession. *See State v. Green*, 493 So. 2d 1178, 1180-81 (La. 1986). "What is critical . . . is [that] a person must seek legal advice from [a lawyer] acting in his capacity as such." *Id.*; *see also LaNasa v. Fortier*, 553 So. 2d 1022, 1023-24 (La. Ct. App. 4th Cir. 1989). The Louisiana Supreme Court has stated that the Restatement (Third) of the Law Governing Lawyers § 14 provides some guidance in determining when a lawyer-client relationship arises. *In re Austin*, 943 So. 2d 341, 347 (La. 2006). The Restatement provides:

> A relationship of client and lawyer arises when:
>
> (1) a person manifests to a lawyer the person's intent that the lawyer provide legal services for the person; and either
>
> (a) the lawyer manifests to the person consent to do so; or
>
> (b) the lawyer fails to manifest lack of consent to do so, and the lawyer knows or reasonably should know that the person reasonably relies on the lawyer to provide the services; or
>
> (2) a tribunal with power to do so appoints the lawyer to provide the services.

Restatement (Third) of the Law Governing Lawyers § 14 (2000). Importantly, privity of contract is not necessary in establishing the existence of a lawyer-client relationship. *Smith v. Patout*, 956 So. 2d 689, 691 (La. Ct. App. 3d Cir. 2007) (holding that a lawyer who signed several documents for a client had "clearly" agreed to represent the client's interests and thus, owed a fiduciary duty to him).

To prove negligence (prong two), the plaintiff must establish both the applicable duty of care and a breach of that duty. *See, e.g., Geiserman v. MacDonald*, 893 F.2d 787, 793 (5th Cir. 1990); *Ault v. Bradley*, 564 So. 2d 374, 379 (La. Ct. App. 1st Cir. 1990), writ denied, 569 So. 2d 967 (La. 1990). A Louisiana lawyer owes a client the duty "to exercise at least that degree of care, skill, and diligence which is exercised by prudent practicing attorneys in his locality." *Ramp v. St. Paul Fire & Marine Ins. Co.*, 269 So. 2d 239, 244 (La. 1972); *see also Jenkins v. St. Paul Fire & Marine Ins. Co.*, 422 So. 2d 1109 (La. 1982); *Leonard v. Reeves*, 82 So. 3d 1250, 1257 (La. Ct. App. 1 Cir. 2012) (noting that the "legal standard of care may vary depending upon the particular circumstances of the [attorney-client] relationship"); *Sherwin-Williams Co. v. First La. Constr., Inc.*, 915 So. 2d 841, 844-45 (La. Ct. App. 1st Cir. 2005); *Burris v. Vinet*, 664 So. 2d 1225, 1229 (La. Ct. App. 1st Cir. 1995); *Leonard v. Stephens*, 588 So. 2d 1300, 1304 (La. Ct. App. 2d Cir. 1991); *Nelson v. Waldrup*, 565 So. 2d 1078, 1079 (La. Ct. App. 4th Cir. 1990); *Reed v. Verwoerdt*, 490 So. 2d 421, 427 (La. Ct. App. 5th Cir. 1986). However, a lawyer is "not required to exercise perfect judgment in every instance." *See Reeves*, 82 So. 3d 1250, 1257; *Spellman v. Bizal*, 755 So. 2d 1013, 1017 (La. Ct. App. 4th Cir. 2000). A plaintiff typically establishes the applicable standard of care through expert testimony from a lawyer familiar with law practice in the relevant locale. *See Geiserman*, 893 F.2d at 791 (quoting 2 R. Mallen & J. Smith, *Legal Malpractice* § 27.15, at 667, 668-69 (4th ed. 1995)); *Dixon v. Perlman*, 528 So. 2d 637, 642 (La. Ct. App. 2d Cir. 1988) (noting that expert testimony will usually, but not always be required); *see also Reed*, 490 So. 2d at 427 (requiring expert testimony); *Stephens*, 588 So. 2d at 1304; *Morgan v. Campbell, Campbell & Johnson*, 561 So. 2d 926, 929 (La. Ct. App. 2d Cir. 1990); *Houillon v. Powers & Nass*, 530 So. 2d 680, 681-82 (La. Ct. App. 4th Cir. 1988). Similarly, whether the defendant-lawyer breached the applicable standard is "a fact specific question and must ordinarily be established through expert . . . testimony."[67] *Dickey v. Baptist Mem. Hosp. N. Miss.*, 146 F.3d 262, 265 (5th Cir. 1998) (discussing the establishment of the applicable standard of care in a medical malpractice case). However, in cases of "obvious negligence, the court may, without expert testimony, take judicial notice of a legal duty which was breached by an attorney." *Nelson*, 565 So. 2d at 1079 (citing *Ramp*, 269 So. 2d at 239); *see also MB Indus., LLC v. CNA Ins. Co.*, 74 So. 3d 1173, 1185 (La. 2011) (recognizing no need for expert testimony when it was clear the "defendant attorney committed 'gross error'"); *Geiserman v. MacDonald*, 893 F.2d 787, 793-94 (5th Cir. 1990) (stating that expert testimony may not be required in cases of "egregious negligence"); *Morgan*, 561 So. 2d at 929 (finding that expert testimony is not required in cases involving an obvious breach of the duty of care); *Dixon*, 528 So. 2d at 642 (concluding that expert testimony may not be required when the trial court is "familiar with the standards of practice in its community").

---

[67] For a case finding that a lawyer did not breach any applicable standard of care, see *Spellman v. Bizal*, 755 So. 2d 1013 (La. Ct. App. 4th Cir. 2000) (no breach for withdrawing as counsel of record when no motions pending and no trial date set).

Once the plaintiff-client has proven the existence of a lawyer-client relationship (prong one), and that the lawyer's conduct was negligent (prong two), the client has established a prima facie case that the lawyer's conduct caused the client to suffer some loss (prong three). Thereafter, the burden "shifts to the defendant attorney to prove that the client could not have succeeded on the original claim." *See, e.g., Johnson v. Tschirn*, 746 So. 2d 629, 632 (La. Ct. App. 4th Cir. 1999) (internal quotation omitted) (citing *Nelson v. Waldrup*, 565 So. 2d 1078 (La. Ct. App. 4th Cir. 1990); *Jenkins v. St. Paul Fire & Marine Ins. Co.*, 422 So. 2d 1109 (La. 1982)). The law shifts the burden in this manner because it presumes that the defendant-lawyer would not have handled the client's claim if it were completely devoid of merit.[68] For this reason, the client is not required to prove that the negligence caused him to lose his underlying case by trying a "case within a case." *See Jenkins*, 422 So. 2d at 1110; *Dier v. Hamilton*, 501 So. 2d 1059, 1061 (La. Ct. App. 2d Cir. 1987). On the contrary, the defendant-lawyer must go forward with evidence that the client would have lost[69] notwithstanding the lawyer's impropriety or negligence. *See Jenkins*, 422 So. 2d at 1110.

RELEVANCE OF VIOLATION OF A RULE OF PROFESSIONAL CONDUCT

Whether a lawyer's violation of a rule of professional conduct is relevant to a claim for malpractice is a controversial issue. The "Scope" section of the ABA Model Rules of Professional Conduct states that "[t]he Rules are designed to provide guidance to lawyers and to provide a structure for regulating conduct through disciplinary agencies. They are not designed to be a basis for civil liability." Model Rules of Professional Conduct Scope ¶ [20] (2002). Notwithstanding this statement, most jurisdictions permit experts to consider a disciplinary rule in "understanding and applying" the applicable standard of care if the rule is designed to protect the plaintiff and is relevant to the claim. *See* Restatement (Third) of the Law Governing Lawyers § 52(2) (2000); Note, *The Evidentiary Use of the Ethics Codes in Legal Malpractice: Erasing a Double Standard*, 109 Harv. L. Rev. 1102, 1119 (1996) (arguing that the "logic, feasibility, [and] functional value" warrant applying the Model Rules to the malpractice context); Model Rules of Professional Conduct Scope ¶ [20] (2002) (conceding that "since the Rules do establish standards of conduct by lawyers, a lawyer's violation of a Rule may be evidence of breach of the applicable standard of conduct").

Unconstrained by the limiting language in the "Scope" section of the ABA Model Rules, Louisiana courts consider the Louisiana Rules of Professional Conduct to have the full

---

[68] The Fourth Circuit has held that "[t]he inference of causation of damages can easily be made in cases where the attorney enters into a 'relationship' with a client on the premise that the client has a valid cause of action, or on a contingency fee basis." *Broadscape.com*, 866 So. 2d at 1089 (La. Ct. App. 4th Cir. 2004).

[69] Put another way, a lawyer's malpractice is a cause in fact of damage to his client when proper performance by the lawyer would have prevented the harm. *See Schwehm v. Jones*, 872 So. 2d 1140 (La. Ct. App. 1st Cir. 2004); *see also Ault v. Bradley*, 564 So. 2d 374, 379 (La. Ct. App. 1st Cir. 1990).

force and effect of substantive law. *See, e.g., Dazet Mortgage Solutions LLC v. Faia*, 116 So. 3d 711, 716 (La. App. Ct. 5th Cir. 2013); *In re Huddleston*, 655 So. 2d 416, 422 (La. Ct. App. 5th Cir. 1995); *Soderquist v. Kramer*, 595 So. 2d 825, 829 (La. Ct. App. 2d Cir. 1992). Thus, the Louisiana Rules of Professional Conduct create legal duties that are enforceable against a Louisiana lawyer in malpractice actions. *See Schlesinger v. Herzog*, 672 So. 2d 701, 707 (La. Ct. App. 4th Cir. 1996) (holding that the Rules of Professional Conduct "have the force and effect of substantive law" and transform ethical issues into legal duties); *Dier v. Hamilton*, 501 So. 2d 1059, 1061 (La. Ct. App. 2d Cir. 1987) (holding that alleged violation of Louisiana ethics rules on conflicts of interest established prima facie case of professional impropriety for purposes of legal malpractice action). However, liability based on such a rule-based duty turns on whether the rule in question exists to protect the plaintiff from the particular harm suffered. *See, e.g., Smith v. Haynsworth, Marion, McKay & Geurard*, 472 S.E.2d 612, 613-15 (S.C. 1996); *see also Gresham v. Davenport*, 537 So. 2d 1144, 1147 (La. 1989); *Tassin v. State Farm Ins. Co.*, 692 So. 2d 604, 608 (La. Ct. App. 3d Cir. 1997). The duty of competence prescribed by Rule 1.1 clearly is intended to protect clients.

Prescription and Preemption of Lawyer Malpractice Claims

Louisiana Revised Statutes section 9:5605[70] sets forth a prescriptive[71] period of one year for all legal malpractice claims against a Louisiana lawyer: "No action for damages against any attorney at law duly admitted to practice in this state . . . whether based upon tort, or breach of contract, or otherwise . . . shall be brought unless filed in a court of competent jurisdiction and proper venue within one year from the date of the alleged act, omission, or neglect, or within one year from the date that the alleged act, omission, or neglect is discovered or should have been discovered . . . ." La. Rev. Stat. Ann. § 9:5605(A). Actions for malpractice are also subject to a three-year preemptive[72] period: "[E]ven as to actions filed within one year from the date of such discovery, in all events such actions shall be filed at the latest within three years from the date of the alleged act, omission, or neglect." *Id.* The Louisiana Supreme Court has held that:

> The 'date of discovery' from which prescription or peremption begins
> to run is the date on which a reasonable man in the position of the
> plaintiff has, or should have, either actual or constructive knowledge of

---

[70] "[T]he prescriptive and peremptive period" for all legal malpractice claims against Louisiana lawyers "shall be governed exclusively by this section." *See* La. Rev. Stat. Ann. § 9:5605(C) (emphasis added).

[71] There is caselaw in Louisiana holding that the one-year period set forth in section 9:5605 is actually a peremptive period rather than a prescriptive period. For an exhaustive discussion of this issue, *see Dauterive Contractors, Inc. v. Landry & Watkins*, 811 So. 2d 1242, 1252 (La. Ct. App. 3d Cir. 2002) ("We hold that both the one-year and three-year periods are peremptive and are subject to all rules governing peremption.").

[72] Note that the peremptive period does not apply "in cases of fraud, as defined in Civil Code Article 1953." La. Rev. Stat. Ann. § 9:5605(E); *see also infra*.

> the damage, the delict, and the relationship between them sufficient to indicate to a reasonable person he is the victim of a tort and to state a cause of action against the defendant. Put more simply, the date of discovery is the date the negligence was discovered or should have been discovered by a reasonable person in the plaintiff's position.

Teague v. St. Paul Fire & Marine Ins. Co., 974 So. 2d 1266, 1275 (La. 2008) (citations omitted).

CONTINUOUS REPRESENTATION AND *CONTRA NON VALENTEM*

The contra non valentem doctrine and continuous representation rule do not suspend or interrupt the peremptive periods set forth in section 9:5605. In *Hendrick v. ABC Ins. Co.*, 787 So. 2d 283 (La. 2001), the Louisiana Supreme Court held as follows:

> The attorney-client relationship is built on trust[,] and the continuous representation rule as encompassed by *contra non valentem* seeks to protect clients who rely on that trust and fail to file legal malpractice suits against their attorneys within the appropriate prescriptive period. *Contra non valentem* does not suspend prescription when a litigant is perfectly able to bring his claim, but fails to do so. When a client does not innocently trust and rely upon his attorney, but rather actively questions his attorney's performance, the client may be denied the safe harbor of *contra non valentem* if equity and justice do not demand its application.

Id. at 293. However, this opinion did not specifically address whether the continuous-representation rule applied to the period set forth in section 9:5605. *See id.* at 289-93. *See, e.g., Reeder v. North*, 701 So. 2d 1291 (La. 1997); *Pena v. Williams*, 867 So. 2d 801 (2004) (La. Ct. App. 4th Cir. 2004); *Atkinson v. LeBlanc*, 860 So. 2d 60 (La. Ct. App. 5th Cir. 2003). In 2012, the Louisiana Supreme Court in *Jenkins v. Starn*, 85 So. 3d 612 (La. 2012), squarely held that the continuous-representation rule does not suspend or interrupt the peremptive period set forth in La. R.S. 9:5605(B). *Id.* at 626.

FRAUD BY THE LAWYER

The peremptive periods set forth in the Louisiana Revised Statutes "shall not apply in cases of fraud, as defined in Civil Code Article 1953." *Id.* § 9:5605(E). For this exception to apply, however, the plaintiff must "state a cause of action for fraud" in his petition by alleging "both a misrepresentation, suppression, or omission of true information and the intent to obtain an unjust advantage or to cause damage or inconvenience to another." *Fenner v. DeSalvo*, 826 So. 2d 39, 44 (La. Ct. App. 4th Cir. 2002). Thus, this exception does not apply if the plaintiff simply recites the word "fraud" in his petition without more particular allegations. *See id.* As to whether the fraud exception in subsection E applies to the statute's one-year period, three-year period, or both, *see Dauterive*, 811 So. 2d at 1252-53.

In *Lomont v. Myer-Bennett*, 172 So. 3d 620 (La. 2015), the Louisiana Supreme Court expanded the scope of this "fraud exception" in three significant respects. First, the court overruled prior caselaw holding that "post-malpractice actions consisting of fraudulent concealment cannot amount to fraud." Said the court:

> [U]nder the clear wording of the statute and the Code article, any action consisting of "a misrepresentation or a suppression of the truth made with the intention either to obtain an unjust advantage for one party or to cause a loss or inconvenience to the other" will prohibit application of the peremptive period. Concealment of malpractice to avoid a malpractice claim conforms to this definition. It would be absurd to interpret the statute to exclude fraudulent concealment of the malpractice. There is no support for an interpretation that would allow attorneys to engage in concealment of malpractice until the three-year peremptive period has expired.

Id. at 10.

Second, the court held that "fraud" sufficient to halt the running of peremption can arise simply from a lawyer's silence in the wake of an act of malpractice. Because Louisiana Rule of Professional Conduct 1.4 requires a lawyer to keep the client "reasonably informed," a lawyer's failure to notify the client of the lawyer's own malpractice can constitute a fraudulent act sufficient to trigger the exception. *See id*. at 19.

Third, the court held that when a lawyer fraudulently conceals an act of malpractice, that fraudulent concealment serves to prevent the running of any peremptive or prescriptive periods until the client becomes "aware of the deception" and learns of the possible malpractice claim. *See id*. at 26.

As a practical matter, the *Lomont* decision portends a significant expansion of liability for legal malpractice in Louisiana. Historically, courts have dismissed a large percentage of legal malpractice claims due to peremption. In the wake of *Lamont*, however, the "fraud" exception may stop the running of peremption only in those (few) malpractice cases in which the lawyer has expressly informed the client in writing of the act of malpractice.

Limitation of Malpractice Liability and Structured Settlements

Under Louisiana Revised Statutes § 37:222(A), "[a]n attorney who acts in good faith shall not be liable for any loss or damages as a result of any act or omission in negotiating or recommending a structured settlement of a claim or the particular mechanism or entity for the funding thereof or in depositing or investing settlement funds in a particular entity, unless the loss or damage was caused by his willful or wanton misconduct." Under this provision, "'[g]ood faith' is presumed to exist when the attorney recommends or negotiates, invests, or deposits funds with an entity which is funded, guaranteed, or bonded by an insurance company which, at the time of such act, had a minimum rating of 'A+9' or 'Double A', or an equivalent thereof, according to standard rating practices in the insurance industry." *La. Rev. Stat. Ann*. § 37:222(B)(2).

Malpractice in Criminal Defense Practice

A cause of action for legal malpractice against a criminal defense lawyer exists even prior to final disposition of the underlying criminal case. Therefore, a potential plaintiff need not–and should not–delay filing such a claim until all writ applications and post-conviction proceedings have been exhausted. *See Augman v. Colwart*, 874 So. 2d 191, 194 (La. Ct. App. 1st Cir. 2004) ("[T]he date of the negligent act itself, not the judgment giving definitive effect to that act, triggers the one-year and three-year periods.").

The caseload of criminal defense counsel should not, "by reason of its excessive size or complexity, interfere[] with providing quality representation, endanger[] a client's interest in independent, thorough, or speedy representation, or [have] a significant potential to lead to the breach of professional obligations." ABA Stds. Relating to the Admin. of Crim. Justice–The Def. Function std. 4–1.8(a).

In providing reasonably adequate death-penalty representation, capital defense counsel should consult and consider the ABA Guidelines for the Appointment and Performance of Defense Counsel in Death Penalty Cases. The United States Supreme Court, however, has made clear that these standards are "guides to what reasonableness means, not its definition." *E.g., Bobby v. Van Hook*, 558 U.S. 4, 8 (2009) (internal quotations omitted).

Mandatory Continuing Legal Education

A Louisiana lawyer must attend a total of twelve and one-half hours of qualified continuing legal education classes each year, unless a specific exception or exemption applies. Of these twelve and one-half hours, one hour must concern ethics and one must concern professionalism. *See* La. Sup. Ct. R. XXX(3)(a) & 3(c). The Louisiana Supreme Court has been relatively harsh in disciplining lawyers who do not comply with MCLE and dues-paying obligations in a timely manner. For example, in *In re McCarthy* the court suspended a lawyer for six months for failing to complete mandatory continuing legal education, failing to timely pay his annual bar dues and prior disciplinary assessment, and subsequently practicing law during these periods of ineligibility. 972 So. 2d 1143, 1144 (La. 2008). Likewise, in *In re Moeller* the court suspended a lawyer for a significant period of time for long history of noncompliance with MCLE requirements and dues payments. 111 So. 3d 325, 327-28 (La. 2013) (noting that it was of no consequence that no actual harm occurred); *In re Teissier*, 171 So. 3d 906 (La. 2015) (lawyer failed to comply with mandatory continuing legal education requirements, and to pay bar dues and disciplinary assessment).

No Duty to Carry Legal Malpractice Insurance

The Louisiana Supreme Court does not require Louisiana lawyers to carry malpractice insurance or to disclose whether they do so. In 2004, the American Bar Association adopted a "Model Rule on Insurance Disclosure." *See* ABA Model Rule on Insurance Disclosure (Aug. 10, 2004). The purpose of the model court rule was to provide potential clients with access to information to make "an informed decision about whether to hire a particular lawyer." *Id.* This model rule requires each licensed lawyer to certify "whether the lawyer is currently covered by professional liability insurance," and "whether the lawyer intends to maintain insurance during the period of time the lawyer is engaged in the private practice of law." The rule exempts any lawyer employed as "a full-time government lawyer" or employed "by an organizational client." *Id.*

Since 2004, several states have adopted an insurance disclosure requirement by mandating disclosure either on bar-registration statements (18 states) or directly to potential clients (7 states); six states have rejected the ABA model rule (Arkansas, Connecticut, Florida, Kentucky, North Carolina, and Texas); and one state requires its lawyers to carry legal malpractice insurance (Oregon). *See* ABA Standing Committee on Client Protection, State Implementation of ABA Model Court Rule on Insurance Disclosure (updated Apr. 6, 2015).

Although Louisiana lawyers are not required to carry malpractice insurance, it is readily available. The Louisiana State Bar Association's endorsed insurance program is administered by Gilsbar (incidentally, the name "Gilsbar" is an acronym that stands for *Group Insurance Louisiana State BAR*). For more information on this program, visit the LSBA website.

Technological Competence
In 2012, the ABA adopted an amendment to ABA Model Rule of Professional Responsibility 1.1, comment 8, noting that "a lawyer should keep abreast of changes in the law and its practice, including the benefits and risks associated with relevant technology . . . ." *See* ABA, Commission on Ethics 20/20 Resolution 105A (August 2012). Thus, a Louisiana lawyer should acquire and maintain a minimum level of competency with the use of modern technology, including the use of email for lawyer-client and lawyer-lawyer communication, creating PDF files, searching and advising clients about social media, and using online resources for legal research and fact investigation.

A cautionary tale from Florida[73] demonstrates why a competent lawyer who uses email—and all should—must understand the considerable risks associated with automatic, background spam filtering. A lawyer should never trust a spam filter. Instead, a lawyer should routinely scan the lawyer's spam inbox to look for improperly classified communications.

Mandatory CLE Credit for Pro Bono Service
Effective May 1, 2015, the Louisiana Supreme Court Rules for Continuing Legal Education to grant up to three hours of mandatory continuing legal education credit for pro bono legal work:

> Credit may also be earned through providing uncompensated pro bono legal representation to an indigent or near indigent client or clients. To be eligible for credit, the matter must have been assigned to the Member by a court, a bar association, or a legal services or pro bono organization that has as its primary purpose the furnishing of such pro bono legal services and that has filed a statement with the Louisiana

---

[73] *See Emerald Coast Utilities Authority v. Bear Marcus Pointe, LLC,* Case No. 1D15-5714 (Fla 1st DCA 2017).

Committee on MCLE. A Member providing such pro bono legal representation shall receive one (1) hour of CLE credit for each five (5) hours of pro bono representation, up to a maximum of three (3) hours of CLE credit for each calendar year. To receive credit, the Member shall submit MCLE Form 6 ("Application for CLE Credit for Pro Bono Services").

See La. Sup. Ct. Rule XXX, Rule 3, Regulation 3.21.

Discipline

When a lawyer's incompetence causes injury or potential injury to a client, the following sanctions are generally appropriate: *disbarment,* when the lawyer does not understand "the most fundamental legal doctrines or procedures"; *suspension,* when the lawyer engages in an area of practice in which the lawyer knows he is not competent; and, *reprimand,* when the lawyer either fails to understand relevant legal doctrines or procedures, or is negligent in determining whether he is competent to handle a legal matter. ABA Stds. for Imposing Lawyer Sanctions stds. 4.51-4.53 (1992). If a lawyer's incompetence causes little or no actual or potential injury to a client, *admonition* is generally the appropriate sanction when the lawyer engages in an isolated instance of negligence in determining whether he or she is competent to handle a legal matter. *Id.* Std. 4.54.

The Louisiana Supreme Court has noted that "a short suspension is the appropriate discipline for failure to render competent representation." *In re Downing,* 930 So. 2d 897, 904 (La. 2006) (citing *In re Young,* 849 So. 2d 25 (La. 2003)). The Louisiana Supreme Court has also held that although a lawyer's state of mind is not a defense to incompetence, it is a relevant factor in determining an appropriate sanction. *In re Pharr,* 950 So. 2d 636, 641 (La. 2007) (holding disbarment would be unduly punitive where the lawyer did not intend to harm a client's financial interests and where the lawyer entered into a consent judgment to compensate the client's losses).

RULE 1.2. SCOPE OF REPRESENTATION AND ALLOCATION OF AUTHORITY BETWEEN CLIENT AND LAWYER.

(a) Subject to the provisions of Rule 1.16 and to paragraphs (c) and (d) of this Rule, a lawyer shall abide by a client's decisions concerning the objectives of representation, and, as required by Rule 1.4, shall consult with the client as to the means by which they are to be pursued. A lawyer may take such action on behalf of the client as is impliedly authorized to carry out the representation. A lawyer shall abide by a client's decision whether to settle a matter. In a criminal case, the lawyer shall abide by the client's decision, after consultation with the lawyer, as to a plea to be entered, whether to waive jury trial and whether the client will testify.

(b) A lawyer's representation of a client, including representation by appointment, does not constitute an endorsement of the client's political, religious, economic, social or moral views or activities.

(c) A lawyer may limit the scope of the representation if the limitation is reasonable under the circumstances and the client gives informed consent.

(d) A lawyer shall not counsel a client to engage, or assist a client, in conduct that the lawyer knows is criminal or fraudulent, but a lawyer may discuss the legal consequences of any proposed course of conduct with a client and may counsel or assist a client to make a good faith effort to determine the validity, scope, meaning or application of the law.

BACKGROUND

The Louisiana Supreme Court adopted this rule on January 20, 2004. It became effective on March 1, 2004, and has not been amended since. This rule is identical to the ABA Model Rules of Professional Conduct 1.2 (2002), except for two minor substantive changes.

First, paragraph (a) contains the language "[s]ubject to the provisions of Rule 1.16." (The ABA Model Rule does not cross-reference Rule 1.16.) The LSBA proposed this revision to clarify that a lawyer who disagrees with a client's decisions concerning the objectives of representation may withdraw, must withdraw, or may be required to continue the representation, as permitted or required by Rule 1.16.

Second, the LSBA recommended, and the court adopted, the inclusion of "religious . . . views" in paragraph (b). This insertion, made through a floor amendment during the LSBA House of Delegates meeting in January 2003, clarifies that a lawyer does not endorse the religious views of their clients merely by representing them.

Paragraph (a): Implied Authority to Act

The ABA added a sentence to paragraph (a) of the corresponding Model Rule to clarify that "[a] lawyer may take such action on behalf of the client as is impliedly authorized to carry out the representation." It also added a new Comment 2 that addresses the resolution of disagreements with clients about the means to be used to accomplish the client's objectives. *See* ABA Ethics 2000 Commission Revision Notes to Model Rule 1.2 (2002). The new sentence in paragraph (a) parallels the reference in Model Rule 1.6(a) to the lawyer's implied authority to reveal information relating to the representation. The scope of the lawyer's implied authority is to be determined by reference to the law of agency. The ABA Ethics 2000 Commission believed that this formulation struck the right balance between respect for the lawyer's expertise and the preservation of the client's autonomy by allowing the lawyer to exercise professional discretion on behalf of the client, subject to consultation with the client as required by Rule 1.4(a)(2), but leaving open the possibility that a client might revoke such implied authority. *See id.*

Paragraph (a): Duty to Abide by Client Instructions

Other than acknowledging the power of the client to revoke a lawyer's implied authority, the ABA Ethics 2000 Commission did not attempt to specify the lawyer's duties when the lawyer and client disagree about the means to be used to accomplish the client's objectives. As explained in Comment 2, the Commission believed that disagreements between a lawyer and client about means must be worked out by the lawyer and client within a framework defined by the law of agency, the right of the client to discharge the lawyer, and the right of the lawyer to withdraw from the representation if the lawyer has a fundamental disagreement with the client. *See id.*

Paragraph (c): Limited-Scope Representations

The ABA Ethics 2000 Commission modified paragraph (c) to more clearly permit, but also to more specifically regulate, agreements by which a lawyer limits the scope of the representation to be provided to a client. Although a lawyer enters into such agreements in a variety of practice settings, this proposal in part was intended to provide a framework within which a lawyer may expand access to legal services by providing limited but nonetheless valuable legal service to low or moderate-income persons who otherwise would be unable to obtain counsel. *See id.*

Furthermore, paragraph (c) specifically precludes a limited representation that would not be "reasonable under the circumstances." Comment 7 to the Model Rule discusses this limitation. In cases in which the limitation is reasonable, the client must give informed consent as defined in Rule 1.0(e). Because a useful limited representation may be provided over the telephone or in other situations in which obtaining a written consent would not be feasible, the proposal does not require that the client's informed consent be confirmed in writing. Comment 8, however, reminds a lawyer who is charging a fee for a limited representation that a specification of the scope of the representation will normally be a necessary part of the lawyer's written communication with the client pursuant to Model Rule 1.5(b). *See id.*

COMMENTS TO ABA MODEL RULE 1.2
Allocation of Authority between Client and Lawyer

[1] Paragraph (a) confers upon the client the ultimate authority to determine the purposes to be served by legal representation, within the limits imposed by law and the lawyer's professional obligations. The decisions specified in paragraph (a), such as whether to settle a civil matter, must also be made by the client. *See* Rule 1.4(a)(1) for the lawyer's duty to communicate with the client about such decisions. With respect to the means by which the client's objectives are to be pursued, the lawyer shall consult with the client as required by Rule 1.4(a)(2) and may take such action as is impliedly authorized to carry out the representation.

[2] On occasion, however, a lawyer and a client may disagree about the means to be used to accomplish the client's objectives. Clients normally defer to the special knowledge and skill of their lawyer with respect to the means to be used to accomplish their objectives, particularly with respect to technical, legal and tactical matters. Conversely, lawyers usually defer to the client regarding such questions as the expense to be incurred and concern for third persons who might be adversely affected. Because of the varied nature of the matters about which a lawyer and client might disagree and because the actions in question may implicate the interests of a tribunal or other persons, this Rule does not prescribe how such disagreements are to be resolved. Other law, however, may be applicable and should be consulted by the lawyer. The lawyer should also consult with the client and seek a mutually acceptable resolution of the disagreement. If such efforts are unavailing and the lawyer has a fundamental disagreement with the client, the lawyer may withdraw from the representation. *See* Rule 1.16(b)(4). Conversely, the client may resolve the disagreement by discharging the lawyer. *See* Rule 1.16(a)(3).

[3] At the outset of a representation, the client may authorize the lawyer to take specific action on the client's behalf without further consultation. Absent a material change in circumstances and subject to Rule 1.4, a lawyer may rely on such an advance authorization. The client may, however, revoke such authority at any time.

[4] In a case in which the client appears to be suffering diminished capacity, the lawyer's duty to abide by the client's decisions is to be guided by reference to Rule 1.14.

Independence from Client's Views or Activities

[5] Legal representation should not be denied to people who are unable to afford legal services, or whose cause is controversial or the subject of popular disapproval. By the same token, representing a client does not constitute approval of the client's views or activities.

Agreements Limiting Scope of Representation

[6] The scope of services to be provided by a lawyer may be limited by agreement with the client or by the terms under which the lawyer's services are made available to the client. When a lawyer has been retained by an insurer to represent an insured, for example, the

representation may be limited to matters related to the insurance coverage. A limited representation may be appropriate because the client has limited objectives for the representation. In addition, the terms upon which representation is undertaken may exclude specific means that might otherwise be used to accomplish the client's objectives. Such limitations may exclude actions that the client thinks are too costly or that the lawyer regards as repugnant or imprudent.

[7] Although this Rule affords the lawyer and client substantial latitude to limit the representation, the limitation must be reasonable under the circumstances. If, for example, a client's objective is limited to securing general information about the law the client needs in order to handle a common and typically uncomplicated legal problem, the lawyer and client may agree that the lawyer's services will be limited to a brief telephone consultation. Such a limitation, however, would not be reasonable if the time allotted was not sufficient to yield advice upon which the client could rely. Although an agreement for a limited representation does not exempt a lawyer from the duty to provide competent representation, the limitation is a factor to be considered when determining the legal knowledge, skill, thoroughness and preparation reasonably necessary for the representation. See Rule 1.1.

[8] All agreements concerning a lawyer's representation of a client must accord with the Rules of Professional Conduct and other law. See, e.g., Rules 1.1, 1.8 and 5.6.

Criminal, Fraudulent and Prohibited Transactions
[9] Paragraph (d) prohibits a lawyer from knowingly counseling or assisting a client to commit a crime or fraud. This prohibition, however, does not preclude the lawyer from giving an honest opinion about the actual consequences that appear likely to result from a client's conduct. Nor does the fact that a client uses advice in a course of action that is criminal or fraudulent of itself make a lawyer a party to the course of action. There is a critical distinction between presenting an analysis of legal aspects of questionable conduct and recommending the means by which a crime or fraud might be committed with impunity.

[10] When the client's course of action has already begun and is continuing, the lawyer's responsibility is especially delicate. The lawyer is required to avoid assisting the client, for example, by drafting or delivering documents that the lawyer knows are fraudulent or by suggesting how the wrongdoing might be concealed. A lawyer may not continue assisting a client in conduct that the lawyer originally supposed was legally proper but then discovers is criminal or fraudulent. The lawyer must, therefore, withdraw from the representation of the client in the matter. See Rule 1.16(a). In some cases, withdrawal alone might be insufficient. It may be necessary for the lawyer to give notice of the fact of withdrawal and to disaffirm any opinion, document, affirmation or the like. See Rule 4.1.

[11] Where the client is a fiduciary, the lawyer may be charged with special obligations in dealings with a beneficiary.

[12] Paragraph (d) applies whether or not the defrauded party is a party to the transaction. Hence, a lawyer must not participate in a transaction to effectuate criminal or fraudulent

avoidance of tax liability. Paragraph (d) does not preclude undertaking a criminal defense incident to a general retainer for legal services to a lawful enterprise. The last clause of paragraph (d) recognizes that determining the validity or interpretation of a statute or regulation may require a course of action involving disobedience of the statute or regulation or of the interpretation placed upon it by governmental authorities.

[13] If a lawyer comes to know or reasonably should know that a client expects assistance not permitted by the Rules of Professional Conduct or other law or if the lawyer intends to act contrary to the client's instructions, the lawyer must consult with the client regarding the limitations on the lawyer's conduct. See Rule 1.4(a)(5).

ANNOTATIONS
Formation of Lawyer-Client Relationship

The relationship of lawyer-client is formed contractually and "results only from a clear and express agreement between the parties." *See Spicer v. Gambel*, 789 So. 2d 741, 744 (La. Ct. App. 4th Cir. 2001) (citing *Keller v. LeBlanc*, 368 So. 2d 193 (La. Ct. App. 1st Cir. 1979)); *see also Weinstein v. Weinstein*, 62 So. 3d 878, 882 (La. Ct. App. 3rd Cir. 2011). A plaintiff can prove formation of this relationship by showing that he sought "advice and assistance" from the lawyer "in matters pertinent to [the lawyer's] profession," or by showing that an "agreement of representation has been made under conditions acceptable to both parties." *See Spicer*, 789 So. 2d at 744 (citing *State v. Green*, 493 So. 2d 1178 (La. 1986); *Weinstein*, 62 So. 3d at 882; *Lirette v. Roe*, 631 So. 2d 503 (La. Ct. App. 4th Cir. 1994)).

The existence of an attorney-client relationship turns largely on the client's subjective belief that such a relationship exists. *See, e.g., In re LeBlanc*, 884 So. 2d 552, 557 (La. 2004); *In re Jackson*, 842 So. 2d 359, 362 (La. 2003); *In re Jones*, 779 So. 2d 712, 714 n.3 (La. 2001); *LSBA v. Bosworth*, 481 So. 2d 567 (La. 1986); *St. Paul Fire & Marine Ins. Co. v. GAB Robins N. Am., Inc.*, 999 So. 2d 72, 77 (La. App. Ct. 4th Cir. 2008); *Francois v. Reed*, 714 So. 2d 228 (La. Ct. App. 1st Cir. 1998); *see also Tristem, Ltd. v. City of New Orleans*, 2003 WL 22852214 *1 (E.D. La. 2003). However, a client's subjective belief must be based on facts known to the lawyer which put the lawyer on reasonable notice that the client may harbor such a belief.[74] For example, if a person seeks legal services from a lawyer, a lawyer-client relationship is formed if either the lawyer consents to provide legal services, or fails expressly to decline the representation under circumstances where the lawyer knows or should know that the person reasonably relies on the lawyer to provide the services. See, e.g., Restatement (Third) of the Law Governing Lawyers § 14(1) (2000).

In evaluating whether a lawyer-client relationship exists, the Louisiana Supreme Court has relied upon the standards set forth in the Restatement (Third) the Law Governing Lawyers. *See In re Austin*, 943 So. 2d 341, 347 (La. 2006) (quoting Restatement (Third) of

---

[74] For cases in which courts have declined to find the existence of an attorney-client relationship, see *Lirette v. Roe*, 631 So. 2d 503, 506 (La. Ct. App. 4th Cir. 1994) (finding no relationship formed "in the absence of any initial communication, either verbal, written or otherwise"); *Spicer v. Gambel*, 789 So. 2d 741, 744-45 (La. Ct. App. 4th Cir. 2001) (finding no relationship formed by merely filing motion for extension of time for potential client).

the Law Governing Lawyers § 14 (2000)); *Scranton v. Ashley Ann Energy*, L.L.C., 91 So. 3d 1174, 1181 n.12 (La. Ct. App. 2nd Cir. 2012). Under the Restatement, a relationship of lawyer and client arises when (a) a person manifests to a lawyer the person's intent that the lawyer provide legal services for that person; and either, (a) the lawyer manifests to the person consent to do so; or (b) the lawyer fails to manifest lack of consent to do so, and the lawyer knows or reasonably should know that the person reasonably relies on the lawyer to provide the services." *See Austin*, 943 So. 2d at 347.

Lawyer-Client Agreements

The Louisiana Rules do not require that all lawyer-client agreements be reduced to writing. Rather, the Rules require signed writings only for contingent fee arrangements. *See* Louisiana Rule 1.5. However, a lawyer should require the client to sign an engagement agreement prior to commencing work. For model lawyer-client agreements (including, among other agreements and provisions, an hourly-fee agreement and a draft arbitration clause), see the table of contents of this book.

Limiting the Scope of a Lawyer's Representation

Under the Louisiana Rules of Professional Conduct, a lawyer "may limit the scope of the representation" if the client consents. *See* La. Rules of Prof'l Conduct r. 1.2(c) (2004); Restatement (Third) of the Law Governing Lawyers § 19(1) (2000). For example, a lawyer who represents an employee injured on the job may agree to handle a products-liability case against the manufacturer of the machine that caused the injury, but decline to handle the worker's compensation matter against the client's employer. Or, a family lawyer who represents a divorcing spouse may agree to handle a community property partition, but decline to handle a custody dispute.

Although permissible, the limitation must be "reasonable under the circumstances," and the client must provide "informed consent." *See* Rule 1.2(c). The prerequisite of informed consent to a limited representation "is required so that the client will understand the dangers that may be inherent in contracting for limited legal services." *Okla. Bar Ass'n v. Green*, 936 P.2d 947, 955 (Okla. 1997); *see also In re Maternowski*, 674 N.E.2d 1287, 1291 (Ind. 1996) ("[M]eaningful consent to a limitation on the lawyer's scope of representation must be based on full, objective disclosure and unbiased advice").

In the matter of *In re Zuber*, 101 So. 3d 29 (La. 2012), the Louisiana Supreme Court considered this rule in the context of an insurance-defense lawyer who agreed to represent the insured—a physician in a medical malpractice case—but who limited the scope of his representation by taking settlement direction only from the insurance company (in accordance with the plain language of the insured's contract of insurance). Under these circumstances, the court suggested the following:

> A prudent lawyer hired by an insurer to defend an insured will communicate with the insured concerning the limits of the representation at the earliest practicable time. For example, basic information concerning the nature of the representation and the insurer's right to control the defense and settlement under the

> insurance contract reasonably could be incorporated as part of any routine notice to the insured that the lawyer has been retained by the insurer to represent him.

Zuber, 101 So. 3d at 34 (citing ABA Formal Ethics Op. 96-403 (1996)). Thereafter, during the course of the limited scope representation, "the lawyer should make efforts to keep the insured reasonably apprised of developments in the case." *Id.* at 35 (citing *Mitchum v. Hudgens*, 533 So. 2d 194, 202 (Ala. 1988)).

Unfortunately, Zuber did not discuss the limited scope of his representation with his physician client. However, the court decided to give Zuber a break: "[G]iven the lack of controlling jurisprudence at the time of respondents' actions in this case and considering the totality of the circumstances, we decline to find clear and convincing evidence of any violation of the Rules of Professional Conduct on their part. Accordingly, we will dismiss the formal charges." *Id.* Future lawyers will not be so lucky:

> [W]e take this opportunity to make it clear to respondents and all members of the bar that limited representation situations are fraught with potential dangers to all parties, as readily illustrated by the instant case. Henceforth, lawyers should be scrupulous in adherence to their obligations under Rule 1.2 to ensure that all clients in such a relationship are fully apprised of the nature of the representation and indicate consent by accepting the defense. Such communications will ensure that the client's rights are protected and minimize any potential for future disagreement over the nature of the representation.

Id. at 35.

Local-Counsel Arrangements

Difficult issues relating to the scope of a lawyer's representation arise in the context of a Louisiana lawyer acting as "local counsel" for an out-of-state lawyer in a matter pending in a Louisiana court. The term "local counsel" is one that is susceptible of a wide range of meanings. A lawyer acting as "local counsel" performs primarily ministerial functions, while another lawyer is actively involved in handling the matter. For this reason, a lawyer serving as "local counsel" should, at the commencement of the representation, identify the client and carefully define the lawyer's role in the matter. To do so adequately, the lawyer should consult with both the out-of-state lawyer and the client. Once the lawyer's role is understood by all, the lawyer should have all interested persons sign a written representation agreement detailing the responsibilities that the lawyer is undertaking as "local counsel." For a case illustrating the perils associated with undertaking a local counsel arrangement, see *Curb Records, Inc. v. Adams & Reese, L.L.P.*, 1998 U.S. Dist. Lexis 3311 (E.D. La. Mar. 18, 1998), *rev'd*, 203 F.3d 828 (5th Cir. 1999).

Assisting Client with Crime or Fraud

The black-letter law set forth in this rule is seemingly straightforward. Although a lawyer cannot knowingly help a client commit a crime or perpetrate a fraud, a lawyer is permitted to discuss the legal consequences of "any" proposed course of conduct that the client may be considering. However, discerning the difference between facilitating unlawful conduct and providing permissible legal advice can be problematic in practice. Whether the lawyer has crossed the line, at least for purposes of professional discipline, can turn on the lawyer's intent in providing the advice in question. For example, if the lawyer offers advice for the purpose of dissuading a client from violating the law, it is unlikely that the lawyer would be disciplined if the client subsequently used the advice to further malevolent ends. *See* Restatement (Third) of the Law Governing Lawyers § 94(2) (2000) & cmt. c. Likewise, whether the lawyer has crossed the line, again for purposes of professional discipline, can turn on the lawyer's degree of certainty that the client actually intends to use the legal advice to further an unlawful scheme. A mere suspicion on the part of the lawyer that the client may have such designs should not be enough to warrant discipline. *See id.* cmt. g.

Assisting Client with Marijuana Distribution Authorized by State Law

In May 2016, Louisiana became the twenty-fifth state to adopt legislation permitting the cultivation, distribution, and use of medical marijuana. LSU and Southern University are gearing up their grow houses and cultivation facilities. Will Louisiana lawyers be able to provide them with legal advice to further their efforts?

The problem is this: marijuana distribution remains a crime under federal law. Louisiana Rule of Professional Conduct 1.2(d) prohibits a lawyer from counseling a client to engage, or assisting a client, "in conduct that the lawyer knows is criminal." *See* La. Rules of Prof'l Cond. R. 1.2(d). While the rule allows a lawyer to discuss the "legal consequences" of any proposed course of conduct and to make a "good faith effort to determine the validity, scope, meaning or application of the law," *id.*, it simply does not allow a lawyer to assist a drug-distribution operation by, for example, drafting contracts with vendors, transporters, suppliers, and the like.

On November 2, 2016, the Louisiana State Bar Association Rule of Professional Conduct Committee debated the issue and declined to recommend an amendment to the Louisiana rules that would have permitted lawyers to give legal advice to LSU and Southern regarding marijuana cultivation and distribution. In so doing, the committee respected the basic federalism principle of supremacy embodied in Article VI § 2 of the United States Constitution. Indeed, if the State of Louisiana were to permit racial discrimination in the workplace in violation of federal civil rights laws, the rules would not allow a lawyer to advise a restaurant as to how to refuse to hire African-American waiters. Allowing advice regarding illicit marijuana cultivation and distribution would have been just as unacceptable in our federal system.

Settlement Authority

The law presumes that a lawyer has authority to engage in settlement negotiations on behalf of a client. *See, e.g., Williams v. Williams*, No. 2006-CA-0358, 2007 WL 441360, at *7 (La. Ct. App. 1st Cir. 2007), remanded by *Williams v. Williams*, 970 So. 2d 633 (La. App. 1st Cir 2007); *Grimes v. Ciba-Geigy Corp.*, 684 So. 2d 1159, 1160 (La. Ct. App. 1st Cir. 1996); *Singleton v. Bunge Corp.*, 364 So. 2d 1321, 1325 (La. Ct. App. 4th Cir. 1978). However, a lawyer has absolutely no authority to settle a matter without express client authority. *See* La. Civ. Code art. 2997(5) (requiring express authority for mandatary to "[e]nter into a compromise or refer a matter to arbitration"); *see also In re Beal*, 117 So. 3d 501, 503 (La. 2013); *In re Schnyder*, 918 So. 2d 455, 460 (La. 2006); *Grimes*, 684 So. 2d at 1160; *Fredric Hayes, Inc. v. Rollins*, 435 So. 2d 1151 (La. Ct. App. 3d Cir. 1983); *Thornton v. Willis*, 106 So. 2d 337, 340 (La. Ct. App. 2d Cir. 1958) (holding that even though a settlement was entered into by a lawyer in the "utmost good faith," the client was not bound because the lawyer did not have express or implied authority to do so); *see also* Restatement (Third) of the Law Governing Lawyers § 22(1) (2000). Moreover, a lawyer may not sue a client to recover a contingent fee based on a settlement offer that the client imprudently declined to accept. *See Culpepper & Carroll, PLLC v. Cole*, 929 So. 2d 1224, 1227 (La. 2006) ("regardless of the wisdom of Mr. Cole's decision, his refusal to accept the settlement was binding on [the lawyer]").

Criminal Practice

Under the ABA Standards Relating to the Administration of Criminal Justice, the accused has the ultimate right to make the following decisions: what pleas to enter; whether to accept a plea agreement; whether to waive a jury trial; whether to testify; and, whether to appeal. *See* ABA Stds. Relating to the Admin. of Crim. Justice–The Def. Function std. 4–5.2(a); *see also* Restatement (Third) of the Law Governing Lawyers § 22(1) (2000). However, "strategic and tactical decisions" should be made by the defense lawyer, after consultation with the client to the extent that it is "feasible and appropriate." ABA Stds. Relating to the Admin. Of Crim. Justice—The Def. Function std. 4–5.2(b). Such "strategic and tactical" decisions include determining which witnesses to call, whether and how to conduct cross-examination, which jurors to accept or strike, which motions should be made, and what evidence should be introduced. *Id.*

A lawyer should not attempt to resolve a criminal case by negotiating with a complaining witness to "drop charges" in exchange for money. In *In re Sharp*, 802 So. 2d 588 (La. 2001), a lawyer was suspended for violating Rule 1.2 for assisting his client "in a scheme to induce the victim in the underlying criminal proceeding to drop the criminal charges in exchange for payment of money." *See id.* at 592.

Disciplinary Sanctions

The applicable ABA Standard for Imposing Lawyer Sanctions for violations of Rule 1.2 is Standard 4.4 (lack of diligence). *See infra* Annotations to Rules 1.3 and 6.1 (false statements, fraud and misrepresentation); Annotations to Rules 3.3-3.4. *See* ABA Stds. for Imposing Lawyer Sanctions appx. 1 (1992).

RULE 1.3. DILIGENCE

> **A lawyer shall act with reasonable diligence and promptness in representing a client.**

BACKGROUND

The Louisiana Supreme Court readopted this rule on January 20, 2004. It became effective on March 1, 2004, and has not been amended since. This rule is identical to ABA Model Rules of Prof'l Conduct r. 1.3 (2002).

COMMENTS TO ABA MODEL RULE 1.3

[1] A lawyer should pursue a matter on behalf of a client despite opposition, obstruction or personal inconvenience to the lawyer, and take whatever lawful and ethical measures are required to vindicate a client's cause or endeavor. A lawyer must also act with commitment and dedication to the interests of the client and with zeal in advocacy upon the client's behalf. A lawyer is not bound, however, to press for every advantage that might be realized for a client. For example, a lawyer may have authority to exercise professional discretion in determining the means by which a matter should be pursued. See Rule 1.2. The lawyer's duty to act with reasonable diligence does not require the use of offensive tactics or preclude the treating of all persons involved in the legal process with courtesy and respect.

[2] A lawyer's work load must be controlled so that each matter can be handled competently.

[3] Perhaps no professional shortcoming is more widely resented than procrastination. A client's interests often can be adversely affected by the passage of time or the change of conditions; in extreme instances, as when a lawyer overlooks a statute of limitations, the client's legal position may be destroyed. Even when the client's interests are not affected in substance, however, unreasonable delay can cause a client needless anxiety and undermine confidence in the lawyer's trustworthiness. A lawyer's duty to act with reasonable promptness, however, does not preclude the lawyer from agreeing to a reasonable request for a postponement that will not prejudice the lawyer's client.

[4] Unless the relationship is terminated as provided in Rule 1.16, a lawyer should carry through to conclusion all matters undertaken for a client. If a lawyer's employment is limited to a specific matter, the relationship terminates when the matter has been resolved. If a lawyer has served a client over a substantial period in a variety of matters, the client sometimes may assume that the lawyer will continue to serve on a continuing basis unless the lawyer gives notice of withdrawal. Doubt about whether a client-lawyer relationship still exists should be clarified by the lawyer, preferably in writing, so that the client will not mistakenly suppose the lawyer is looking after the client's affairs when the lawyer has ceased to do so. For example, if a lawyer has handled a judicial or administrative proceeding that produced a result adverse to the client and the lawyer and the client have not agreed that the lawyer will handle the matter on appeal, the lawyer must consult with the client about the possibility of appeal before relinquishing responsibility for the matter. See Rule 1.4(a)(2). Whether the lawyer is obligated to prosecute the appeal for the client

depends on the scope of the representation the lawyer has agreed to provide to the client. See Rule 1.2.

[5] To prevent neglect of client matters in the event of a sole practitioner's death or disability, the duty of diligence may require that each sole practitioner prepare a plan, in conformity with applicable rules, that designates another competent lawyer to review client files, notify each client of the lawyer's death or disability, and determine whether there is a need for immediate protective action. Cf. Rule 28 of the American Bar Association Model Rules for Lawyer Disciplinary Enforcement (providing for court appointment of a lawyer to inventory files and take other protective action in absence of a plan providing for another lawyer to protect the interests of the clients of a deceased or disabled lawyer).

ANNOTATIONS
Diligence and Zeal
This rule nominally replaces the lawyer's obligation to represent a client "zealously"– which was previously set forth in Canon 7 of the former Louisiana Code of Professional Responsibility–with an obligation to act diligently and promptly. Nevertheless, a Louisiana lawyer often justifies the lawyer's professional conduct by reference to the perceived obligation to represent clients zealously. Moreover, the official comments to ABA Model Rule 1.3 state that a lawyer should act with "commitment and dedication to the interests of the client and with zeal in advocacy on the client's behalf." *See* ABA Model Rules of Prof'l Conduct r 1.3 cmt. 1 (2002). Thus, while the duty of "zealous representation," per se, does not appear in the current Louisiana Rules of Professional Conduct, it is a phrase often used by Louisiana lawyers. (Unfortunately, a lawyer may invoke the refrain of "zealous representation" in an effort to justify unprofessional and uncivil conduct.); *In re Hollis*, 201 So. 3d 891 (La. 2016) (lawyer was found to have violated Rule 1.3 by neglecting a legal matter and allowing the client's claim prescribe).

Common Violations
The Louisiana Office of Disciplinary Counsel alleges violations of this rule in a significant percentage of the cases it prosecutes. A lawyer commits infractions of this rule when they negligently or intentionally ignore matters that warrant attention. Such inattention may result in a matter taking an unreasonably long period of time to be resolved. *See In re Schaefer*, 895 So. 2d 1289 (La. 1999); *see also In re Beck*, 109 So. 3d 897, 905 (La. 2013); *In re Roberson*, 19 So. 3d 1186, 2009-1353 (La. 2009) (lawyer's lack of diligence caused client's matter to be dismissed). Moreover, inattention may cause a matter to prescribe prior to the filing of suit. *See, e.g., In re Broussard*, 26 So. 3d 131, 132 (La. 2010); *In re Williams-Bensaadat*, 964 So. 2d 317 (La. 2007); *In re Jackson*, 842 So. 2d 359 (La. 2003); *In re Thompson*, 712 So. 2d 72 (La. 1998); *In re Yaeger*, 698 So. 2d 951 (La. 1997). A lawyer also commits infractions of this rule when the lawyer abandons the practice of law without making adequate arrangements to protect the interests of the lawyer's clients. *See In re Boyer*, 26 So. 3d 139, 140-44 (La. 2010); *In re Pharr*, 950 So. 2d 636, 639-640 (La. 2007) (holding that a lawyer violated Rule 1.3 by failing to act with the diligence necessary to preserve the client's funds); *see also In re Bivins*, 724 So. 2d 198 (La. 1998). To avoid

diligence-related problems, a lawyer should implement office practices and procedures to ensure that critical deadlines are properly calendared, active files are periodically reviewed, and all clients are regularly informed about the progress of their matters. Furthermore, a lawyer should do the following:

- Regularly review files.
- Use electronic to-do lists with automatic email, text message and pop-up reminders.
- Consider adopting workflow procedures like David Allen's *Getting Things Done* method, among many others.
- Don't procrastinate.

Relationship to Other Rules

A lawyer's duty of diligence is closely related to the duties of competence and communication. Indeed, many disciplinary actions prosecuted by the Louisiana Office of Disciplinary Counsel for alleged violations of this rule have been joined with alleged violations of Rule 1.1 (competence) and Rule 1.4 (communication). A lawyer who became aware of violations of the duty of diligence and who then attempted to settle a resulting potential malpractice claim violated Rule 1.8. *See, e.g., In re Dunn*, 98 So. 3d 289, 295 (La. 2012); *In re Thompson*, 712 So. 2d 72 (La. 1998). *In re Bullock*, 187 So. 3d 986 (La. 2016) (lawyer suspended because she did not file a wrongful death lawsuit to prevent claim from prescribing); *In re Mendy*, 217 So. 3d 260 (La. 2016) (disbarment for lack of diligence and other misconduct); *In re Brown*, 189 So. 3d 387 (La. 2016) (permanent disbarment for failing to remit settlement funds to clients, failing to pay third parties, and converting fees to the lawyer's own use after neglecting legal matters, failing to communicate with clients, and engaging in criminal conduct).

Criminal Practice

Both prosecutors and defense counsel have an obligation to promptly and diligently resolve criminal matters. A prosecutor should "avoid unnecessary delay in the disposition of cases," act with "reasonable diligence and promptness in prosecuting an accused," and not "intentionally use procedural devices for delay for which there is no legitimate basis." *See* ABA Stds. Relating to the Admin. of Crim. Justice–The Def. Function std. 3-2.9. Furthermore, a prosecutor should be "punctual in attendance in court" and in the filing of all papers. *Id.* A defense lawyer likewise should "act with reasonable diligence and promptness in representing a client," "avoid unnecessary delay," and be "punctual" in court and in the filing of papers. *See id.* std. 4-1.3; *see also In re Vix*, 11 So. 3d 1090 (La. 2009) (suspending a criminal defense lawyer for two years for repeatedly failing to file briefs for numerous clients; all but three months of suspension deferred because the lawyer resolved most of the issues that led to the misconduct, i.e. refunding fees and resigning as counsel).

Disciplinary Sanctions

When a lawyer's lack of diligence causes injury or potential injury to a client, the following sanctions are generally appropriate: *disbarment*, when the lawyer abandons the practice, knowingly fails to perform services for a client, or engages in a pattern of neglect with respect to client matters, and causes serious or potentially serious injury to a client; *suspension*, when the lawyer knowingly fails to perform services for a client or engages in a pattern of neglect, and causes injury or potential injury to a client;[75] *reprimand*, when the lawyer is negligent and does not act with reasonable diligence in representing a client, and causes injury or potential injury to a client; and *admonition*, when the lawyer is negligent and does not act with reasonable diligence in representing a client, and causes little or no actual or potential injury to a client. *See* ABA Stds. for Imposing Lawyer Sanctions std. 4.4 (1992). However, in extreme cases "involving numerous instances of neglect, failure to communicate with clients, and failure to cooperate with the ODC," the appropriate disciplinary sanctions may range from "lengthy suspensions to disbarment." *In re Brancato*, 932 So. 2d 651, 659 (La. 2006) (disbarring a criminal defense lawyer for accepting representation of clients, performing minimal legal work, failing to communicate with clients, and ultimately abandoning legal matters and the lawyer's clients, several of whom were incarcerated).

---

[75] The Louisiana Supreme Court has held that the "baseline sanction" for lack of diligence, neglect of matters and failure to communicate is "suspension from the practice of law." *See In re Phelps*, 827 So. 2d 1140, 1143 (La. 2002).

RULE 1.4. COMMUNICATION

(a) A lawyer shall:

(1) promptly inform the client of any decision or circumstance with respect to which the client's informed consent, as defined in Rule 1.0(e), is required by these Rules;

(2) reasonably consult with the client about the means by which the client's objectives are to be accomplished;

(3) keep the client reasonably informed about the status of the matter;

(4) promptly comply with reasonable requests for information; and

(5) consult with the client about any relevant limitation on the lawyer's conduct when the lawyer knows that the client expects assistance not permitted by the Rules of Professional Conduct or other law.

(b) The lawyer shall give the client sufficient information to participate intelligently in decisions concerning the objectives of the representation and the means by which they are to be pursued.

(c) A lawyer who provides any form of financial assistance to a client during the course of a representation shall, prior to providing such financial assistance, inform the client in writing of the terms and conditions under which such financial assistance is made, including but not limited to, repayment obligations, the imposition and rate of interest or other charges, and the scope and limitations imposed upon lawyers providing financial assistance as set forth in Rule 1.8(e).

BACKGROUND

The Louisiana Supreme Court adopted this rule on January 20, 2004. It became effective on March 1, 2004. The court amended this rule in 2006 to add paragraph (c), which implements amendments to Rule 1.8(e) restricting the ability of a lawyer to provide financial assistance to a client.

Paragraph (a) of this rule is identical to the ABA Model Rule of Professional Conduct 1.4(a) (2002).

Paragraph (b) of this rule differs from Model Rule 1.4(b). The Louisiana rule provides that the lawyer shall give the client "sufficient information to participate intelligently in decisions concerning the objectives of the representation and the means by which they are to be pursued," while the ABA counterpart provides that the lawyer "shall explain a matter to the extent reasonably necessary to permit the client to make informed decisions regarding the representation." *Compare* La. Rules of Prof'l Conduct r. 1.4(b) (2004) *with* Model Rules of Prof'l Conduct r. 1.4(b). The LSBA Ethics 2000 Committee recommended divergence from the ABA rule to clarify that, in accord with Rule 1.2, both lawyer and client have a role to play in making decisions concerning the representation. However, the Committee intended no major substantive difference from the ABA rule.

Paragraph (c) of this rule is not included in ABA Model Rule 1.4.

Louisiana Revision Notes

Prior to the 2004 revision of the rule, paragraph (b) of the Louisiana rule provided that a lawyer was required to communicate with his client only "to the extent the client is willing and able to do so." *See* La. Rules of Prof'l Conduct r. 1.4 (1987). The LSBA Ethics 2000 Committee recommended deleting the language because it could be misinterpreted to suggest that a lawyer need not communicate with a client who is either "unwilling" or "unable" to speak with the lawyer. As to the "unwilling" client, the lawyer and client presumably would have serious issues that must be resolved under Rules 1.2 and 1.16 rather than by this rule. As to the "unable" client, the lawyer should consult Rule 1.14 rather than simply proceeding without communication.

ABA Revision Notes

The ABA revised Model Rule 1.4 to consolidate all rules imposing a general duty to communicate with a client within a single rule. In addition, the ABA added the word "reasonably" to paragraph (a)(2) to preclude a reading of the rule that would always require consultation in advance of the lawyer taking any action on behalf of the client, even when such action is impliedly authorized under Rule 1.2(a). *See* ABA Ethics 2000 Commission Revision Notes to Model Rule 1.4 (2002).

COMMENTS TO ABA MODEL RULE 1.4
Generally

[1] Reasonable communication between the lawyer and the client is necessary for the client effectively to participate in the representation.

Communicating with Client

[2] If these Rules require that a particular decision about the representation be made by the client, paragraph (a)(1) requires that the lawyer promptly consult with and secure the client's consent prior to taking action unless prior discussions with the client have resolved what action the client wants the lawyer to take. For example, a lawyer who receives from opposing counsel an offer of settlement in a civil controversy or a proffered plea bargain in a criminal case must promptly inform the client of its substance unless the client has previously indicated that the proposal will be acceptable or unacceptable or has authorized the lawyer to accept or to reject the offer. See Rule 1.2(a).

[3] Paragraph (a)(2) requires the lawyer to reasonably consult with the client about the means to be used to accomplish the client's objectives. In some situations — depending on both the importance of the action under consideration and the feasibility of consulting with the client — this duty will require consultation prior to taking action. In other circumstances, such as during a trial when an immediate decision must be made, the exigency of the situation may require the lawyer to act without prior consultation. In such cases the lawyer must nonetheless act reasonably to inform the client of actions the lawyer has taken on the client's behalf. Additionally, paragraph (a)(3) requires that the lawyer keep the client reasonably informed about the status of the matter, such as significant developments affecting the timing or the substance of the representation.

[4] A lawyer's regular communication with clients will minimize the occasions on which a client will need to request information concerning the representation. When a client makes a reasonable request for information, however, paragraph (a)(4) requires prompt compliance with the request, or if a prompt response is not feasible, that the lawyer, or a member of the lawyer's staff, acknowledge receipt of the request and advise the client when a response may be expected. A lawyer should promptly respond to or acknowledge client communications.

Explaining Matters

[5] The client should have sufficient information to participate intelligently in decisions concerning the objectives of the representation and the means by which they are to be pursued, to the extent the client is willing and able to do so. Adequacy of communication depends in part on the kind of advice or assistance that is involved. For example, when there is time to explain a proposal made in a negotiation, the lawyer should review all important provisions with the client before proceeding to an agreement. In litigation a lawyer should explain the general strategy and prospects of success and ordinarily should consult the client on tactics that are likely to result in significant expense or to injure or coerce others. On the other hand, a lawyer ordinarily will not be expected to describe trial or negotiation strategy in detail. The guiding principle is that the lawyer should fulfill reasonable client expectations for information consistent with the duty to act in the client's best interests, and the client's overall requirements as to the character of representation. In certain circumstances, such as when a lawyer asks a client to consent to a representation affected by a conflict of interest, the client must give informed consent, as defined in Rule 1.0(e).

[6] Ordinarily, the information to be provided is that appropriate for a client who is a comprehending and responsible adult. However, fully informing the client according to this standard may be impracticable, for example, where the client is a child or suffers from diminished capacity. See Rule 1.14. When the client is an organization or group, it is often impossible or inappropriate to inform every one of its members about its legal affairs; ordinarily, the lawyer should address communications to the appropriate officials of the organization. See Rule 1.13. Where many routine matters are involved, a system of limited or occasional reporting may be arranged with the client.

Withholding Information

[7] In some circumstances, a lawyer may be justified in delaying transmission of information when the client would be likely to react imprudently to an immediate communication. Thus, a lawyer might withhold a psychiatric diagnosis of a client when the examining psychiatrist indicates that disclosure would harm the client. A lawyer may not withhold information to serve the lawyer's own interest or convenience or the interests or convenience of another person. Rules or court orders governing litigation may provide that information supplied to a lawyer may not be disclosed to the client. Rule 3.4(c) directs compliance with such rules or orders.

ANNOTATIONS
Generally

The Louisiana Supreme Court has held that "[p]roper communication with clients is essential to maintain public confidence in the profession." *See La. State Bar Ass'n v. St. Romain*, 560 So. 2d 820, 824 (La. 1990). Indeed, the duty to communicate is so fundamental that a lawyer cannot delegate this responsibility to lay employees. *Id.* (citing *La. State Bar Ass'n v. Edwins*, 540 So. 2d 294 (La. 1989)). The failure to communicate is one of the most common complaints made about lawyers.[76] Furthermore, in many cases the failure to communicate is the principal reason why clients initially file complaints with the Office of Disciplinary Counsel.

Information that Lawyers Must Communicate to Clients

A lawyer must communicate to all existing and potential clients that the lawyer has been suspended from the practice of law. *See In re Turnage*, 104 So. 3d 397, 398 (La. 2012); *In re Castro*, 737 So. 2d 701 (La. 1999). Moreover, a lawyer must inform the client when the client's case has been dismissed, *see In re Dirks*, 224 So. 3d 346 (La. 2017); *In re Newman*, 83 So. 3d 1018, 1020 (La. 2012); *In re Elbert*, 698 So. 2d 949 (La. 1997); *In re Cade*, 166 So. 3d 243 (La. 2015); or has prescribed before the lawyer filed suit, *see In re Bullock*, 187 So. 3d 986 (La. 2016); *In re Bruscato*, 743 So. 2d 645, 647-48 (La. 1999); *In re Dixon*, 650 So. 2d 740, 741 (La. 1995). In addition, a lawyer must communicate all settlement or plea offers to the client, even if the lawyer personally believes that the offer is undesirable, unless "prior discussions with the client have left it clear that the proposal will be unacceptable." *See* ABA Model Rules of Prof'l Conduct r. 1.4 cmt. 1; *see also In re Conry*, 158 So. 3d 786 (La. 2015); *In re Hollis*, 177 So. 3d 110 (La. 2015); *In re McNeely*, 201 So. 3d 863 (La. 2016); *In re Ruth*, 90 So. 3d 1004, 1013 (La. 2012); *In re Elbert*, 698 So. 2d 949 (La. 1997); *La. State Bar Ass'n v. St. Romain*, 560 So. 2d 820, 824 (La. 1990) (publicly reprimanding a lawyer failing to consult with clients about terms of proposed settlements). Finally, and perhaps obviously, a lawyer must return his client's telephone calls. *See, e.g., In re Armstrong*, 164 So. 3d 817 (La. 2015); *In re Brown-Manning*, 185 So. 3d 728 (La. 2015); *In re Webber*, 2016

---

[76] Disciplinary actions charging violations of Rule 1.4 often include charges that the respondent violated Rule 1.3 (diligence) as well. *See, e.g., In re Bradley*, 917 So. 2d 1068 (La. 2005); *In re Karam*, 852 So. 2d 979 (La. 2003); *In re Phelps*, 827 So. 2d 1140 (La. 2002); *In re Taylor*, 802 So. 2d 1287 (La. 2002).

WL 1178330 (Bankr. W.D. La. Mar. 22, 2016); *Ruth*, 90 So. 3d at 1012, 1014; *In re Williams*, 947 So. 2d 710, 713-14 (La. 2007); *In re Sumpter*, 931 So. 2d 347, 348 (La. 2006); *In re Donnan*, 838 So. 2d 715, 721 (La. 2003).

The duty to keep a client reasonably informed also requires a lawyer to communicate the lawyer's own malpractice to the client. *See In re Bullock*, 187 So. 3d 986 (La. 2016); *Lomont v. Meyer-Bennett*, 172 So. 3d 620 (La. 2015). The North Carolina State Bar Association advises that any "material errors that prejudice the client's rights or interests" or that give rise to a malpractice claim "must always be reported to the client." *See* Formal Ethics Op. 2014-4, N.C. State Bar Assoc., *Disclosing Potential Malpractice to a Client* (Jul. 17, 2015). Minor errors are different: "[I]f the error is easily corrected or negligible and will not materially prejudice the client's rights or interests, the error does not have to be disclosed to the client." *Id.*

> As to what needs to be said, the lawyer should not address whether a legal malpractice claim may exist and should not "provide legal advice about legal malpractice." After all, the lawyer has a potential personal-interest conflict in avoiding liability once the lawyer's client has a viable malpractice claim.

Id.

Communicating with Impaired Clients
The scope of a lawyer's responsibilities and authority when dealing with an impaired client is one of the most vexing issues in professional-responsibility law. Nevertheless, a lawyer should err on the side of providing more rather than less information to a potentially impaired client, unless compelling circumstances suggest otherwise. *See* ABA Model Rules of Prof'l Conduct r. 1.4 cmt.7 (permitting a lawyer to withhold information if providing the information would cause harm to the client). A lawyer representing a potentially impaired client should carefully consider Rule 1.14. *See* La. Rules of Prof'l Conduct r. 1.14 (2004) (client under disability).

Criminal Practice
Defense counsel should keep the client informed regarding the status and progress of the case and promptly respond to reasonable requests for information. *See* ABA Stds. Relating to the Admin. of Crim. Justice–The Def. Function std. 4-3.8. Furthermore, defense counsel must provide the client with all information reasonably necessary for the client to make informed decisions regarding the matter. *Id.* A lawyer who fails to "clearly and unambiguously" communicate the effects and limitations of a guilty plea violates this rule. *See In re Frank*, 942 So. 2d 1050, 1059 (La. 2006); *In re Lafont*, 898 So. 2d 339, 348 (La. 2005). This principle also extends to the appeals process. *See In re Hall*, 69 So. 3d 417, 419-20 (La. 2011) (holding that a lawyer violated Rule 1.4 when the lawyer did not consult with the client about the client's understanding regarding their appeal strategy of a guilty plea entered into by the client).

Disciplinary Sanctions

The failure of a lawyer to communicate with clients is the triggering cause of many complaints to the Office of Disciplinary Counsel. That is, clients often report a lawyer to disciplinary counsel because the lawyer's failure to respond to telephone calls and other reasonable requests for information has resulted in a loss of trust and confidence. Such complaints, because they often are indicative of underlying misconduct, routinely lead to further investigation by disciplinary counsel, and often to formal charges alleging violations of this rule and others. *See, e.g., In re Landry*, 728 So. 2d 833, 834 (La. 1999) (disciplining a lawyer for failure to communicate and other infractions); *In re Bivins*, 724 So. 2d 198 (La. 1998) (same); *In re Broussard*, 26 So. 3d 131, 134 (La. 2010). In *In re Lawrence*, the Louisiana Supreme Court was "particularly disturbed by the testimony of several clients...who testified that they were forced to call respondent from different telephone numbers in order to get him to answer their calls;" the lawyer was subsequently suspended from practice for eighteen months. *In re Lawrence*, 954 So. 2d 113, 120 (La. 2007). The Louisiana Supreme Court has held that in "cases involving multiple instances of neglect, failure to communicate with clients, and failure to cooperate with ODC," disbarment is often warranted. *In re Williams*, 947 So. 2d 710, 714 (La. 2007) (citing *In re Brancato*, 932 So. 2d 651, 659 (La. 2006)); *see also In re Barrio*, 108 So. 3d 742, 746 (La. 2013). *In re Brown*, 189 So. 3d 387 (La. 2016) (lawyer permanently disbarred after multiple instances of receiving settlement funds on behalf of clients and either failing to remit the funds to clients or failing to pay third parties).

The ABA Standards for Imposing Lawyer Sanctions treat violations of Rule 1.4 in a manner similar to violations of Rule 1.3 (diligence). *See* ABA Stds. for Imposing Lawyer Sanctions std. 4.4; *id.* app. 1 (1992) (cross referencing Model Rule 1.4 with Standard 4.4).

RULE 1.5. FEES

(a) A lawyer shall not make an agreement for, charge, or collect an unreasonable fee or an unreasonable amount for expenses. The factors to be considered in determining the reasonableness of a fee include the following:

> (1) the time and labor required, the novelty and difficulty of the questions involved, and the skill requisite to perform the legal service properly;

> (2) the likelihood, if apparent to the client, that the acceptance of the particular employment will preclude other employment by the lawyer;

> (3) the fee customarily charged in the locality for similar legal services;

> (4) the amount involved and the results obtained;

> (5) the time limitations imposed by the client or by the circumstances;

> (6) the nature and length of the professional relationship with the client;

> (7) the experience, reputation, and ability of the lawyer or lawyers performing the services; and

> (8) whether the fee is fixed or contingent.

(b) The scope of the representation and the basis or rate of the fee and expenses for which the client will be responsible shall be communicated to the client, preferably in writing, before or within a reasonable time after commencing the representation, except when the lawyer will charge a regularly represented client on the same basis or rate. Any changes in the basis or rate of the fee or expenses shall also be communicated to the client.

(c) A fee may be contingent on the outcome of the matter for which the service is rendered, except in a matter in which a contingent fee is prohibited by Paragraph (d) or other law. A contingent fee agreement shall be in a writing signed by the client. A copy or duplicate original of the executed agreement shall be given to the client at the time of execution of the agreement. The contingency fee agreement shall state the method by which the fee is to be determined, including the percentage or percentages that shall accrue to the lawyer in the event of settlement, trial or appeal; the litigation and other expenses that are to be deducted from the recovery; and whether such expenses are to be deducted before or after the contingent fee is calculated. The agreement must clearly notify the client of any expenses for which the client will be liable whether or not the client is the prevailing party. Upon conclusion of a contingent fee matter, the lawyer shall provide the client with a written statement stating the outcome of the matter and, if there is a recovery, showing the remittance to the client and the method of its determination.

(d) A lawyer shall not enter into an arrangement for, charge, or collect:

> (1) any fee in a domestic relations matter, the payment or amount of which is contingent upon the securing of a divorce or upon the amount of alimony or support, or property settlement in lieu thereof; or

> (2) a contingent fee for representing a defendant in a criminal case.

(e) A division of fee between lawyers who are not in the same firm may be made only if:

> (1) the client agrees in writing to the representation by all of the lawyers involved, and is advised in writing as to the share of the fee that each lawyer will receive;

> (2) the total fee is reasonable; and

> (3) each lawyer renders meaningful legal services for the client in the matter.

(f) Payment of fees in advance of services shall be subject to the following rules:

> (1) When the client pays the lawyer a fee to retain the lawyer's general availability to the client and the fee is not related to a particular representation, the funds become the property of the lawyer when paid and may be placed in the lawyer's operating account.

(2) When the client pays the lawyer all or part of a fixed fee or of a minimum fee for particular representation with services to be rendered in the future, the funds become the property of the lawyer when paid, subject to the provisions of Rule 1.5(f)(5). Such funds need not be placed in the lawyer's trust account, but may be placed in the lawyer's operating account.

(3) When the client pays the lawyer an advance deposit against fees which are to accrue in the future on an hourly or other agreed basis, the funds remain the property of the client and must be placed in the lawyer's trust account. The lawyer may transfer these funds as fees are earned from the trust account to the operating account, without further authorization from the client for each transfer, but must render a periodic accounting for these funds as is reasonable under the circumstances.

(4) When the client pays the lawyer an advance deposit to be used for costs and expenses, the funds remain the property of the client and must be placed in the lawyer's trust account. The lawyer may expend these funds as costs and expenses accrue, without further authorization from the client for each expenditure, but must render a periodic accounting for these funds as is reasonable under the circumstances.

(5) When the client pays the lawyer a fixed fee, a minimum fee or a fee drawn from an advanced deposit, and a fee dispute arises between the lawyer and the client, either during the course of the representation or at the termination of the representation, the lawyer shall immediately refund to the client the unearned portion of such fee, if any. If the lawyer and the client disagree on the unearned portion of such fee, the lawyer shall immediately refund to the client the amount, if any, that they agree has not been earned, and the lawyer shall deposit into a trust account an amount representing the portion reasonably in dispute. The lawyer shall hold such disputed funds in trust until the dispute is resolved, but the lawyer shall not do so to coerce the client into accepting the lawyer's contentions. As to any fee dispute,

> the lawyer should suggest a means for prompt resolution
> such as mediation or arbitration, including arbitration
> with the Louisiana State Bar Association Fee Dispute
> Program.

BACKGROUND

The Louisiana Supreme Court adopted this rule on January 20, 2004. It became effective on March 1, 2004, and was amended in 2006.

Paragraphs (a), (b) and (d) of this proposed rule are identical to ABA Model Rule of Prof'l Conduct 1.5 (2013). Paragraph (c) contains the words "that are" prior to "to be deducted from the recovery." This addition to the ABA language was intended by the LSBA to be purely semantic and not substantive. Paragraph (c) was amended in 2006 to require the lawyer to give the client a copy of the signed contingent fee agreement. *Advanced Quality Construction, Inc. v. Amtek of Louisiana, Inc. and Aegis Security Insurance Company*, 2016-0359 (La. Ct. App. 1st Cir. Oct. 28, 2016) (billing for secretarial tasks was unreasonable).

Fee Sharing

Paragraph (e), which addresses fee division among lawyers in different firms, varies from ABA Model Rule 1.5(e) in several respects. First, unlike the model rule, paragraph (e)(1) of this proposed rule makes no distinction between fees divided "in proportion to the services performed" and fees divided otherwise. In all cases, the client must agree in writing to the "representation" by all of the lawyers involved.

Second, under paragraph (e)(1), the client must agree "in writing" to the "share of the fee that each lawyer will receive." While the corresponding Model Rule has a similar requirement in Model Rule 1.5(e)(2), the LSBA proposed this language to permit lawyers to inform the client at any time, rather than only at the commencement of the representation as the ABA Model Rule suggests (but does not expressly provide). The LSBA Ethics 2000 Committee made this recommendation to the court after extensive consultation with representatives of the Louisiana Trial Lawyers' Association.

Third, paragraph (e)(3) requires each lawyer to render "meaningful legal services for the client in the matter." The LSBA proposed this departure from the model rule in an effort to curb the abuses attendant to "case brokering" by some lawyers. That is, the rule seeks to protect clients from lawyers who simply "sign up" clients, refer the cases to lawyers in exchange for a share of the fee, and then disappear until it is time to collect that share. As a result of this perceived problem, this rule requires that any lawyer who seeks to share the fee must not only "represent" the client in the matter, but also perform some "meaningful" role. Note that work potentially can be "meaningful" even if it is not time consuming or involves only client-relations activities.

Handling Client Funds and Payments

Paragraph (f), which does not appear in the ABA Model Rule, sets forth detailed guidelines addressing how a lawyer must hold and account for monies received from, or on behalf of, a client during the course of representation. These provisions provide much-needed guidance to Louisiana lawyers handling advance deposits, general retainers, fixed fees and the like. For example, paragraph (f)(5) clarifies how a lawyer must handle disputes arising over a fixed fee, a minimum fee, or a fee drawn from an advanced deposit. When a reasonable dispute arises over one of these types of fees, the lawyer must deposit the disputed portion in a trust account until the dispute is resolved.

COMMENTS TO ABA MODEL RULE 1.5
Reasonableness of Fee and Expenses
[1] Paragraph (a) requires that lawyers charge fees that are reasonable under the circumstances. The factors specified in (1) through (8) are not exclusive. Nor will each factor be relevant in each instance. Paragraph (a) also requires that expenses for which the client will be charged must be reasonable. A lawyer may seek reimbursement for the cost of services performed in-house, such as copying, or for other expenses incurred in-house, such as telephone charges, either by charging a reasonable amount to which the client has agreed in advance or by charging an amount that reasonably reflects the cost incurred by the lawyer.

Basis or Rate of Fee
[2] When the lawyer has regularly represented a client, they ordinarily will have evolved an understanding concerning the basis or rate of the fee and the expenses for which the client will be responsible. In a new client-lawyer relationship, however, an understanding as to fees and expenses must be promptly established. Generally, it is desirable to furnish the client with at least a simple memorandum or copy of the lawyer's customary fee arrangements that states the general nature of the legal services to be provided, the basis, rate or total amount of the fee and whether and to what extent the client will be responsible for any costs, expenses or disbursements in the course of the representation. A written statement concerning the terms of the engagement reduces the possibility of misunderstanding.

[3] Contingent fees, like any other fees, are subject to the reasonableness standard of paragraph (a) of this Rule. In determining whether a particular contingent fee is reasonable, or whether it is reasonable to charge any form of contingent fee, a lawyer must consider the factors that are relevant under the circumstances. Applicable law may impose limitations on contingent fees, such as a ceiling on the percentage allowable, or may require a lawyer to offer clients an alternative basis for the fee. Applicable law also may apply to situations other than a contingent fee, for example, government regulations regarding fees in certain tax matters.

Terms of Payment
[4] A lawyer may require advance payment of a fee, but is obliged to return any unearned portion. See Rule 1.16(d). A lawyer may accept property in payment for services, such as an ownership interest in an enterprise, providing this does not involve acquisition of a proprietary interest in the cause of action or subject matter of the litigation contrary to Rule 1.8(i). However, a fee paid in property instead of money may be subject to the requirements of Rule 1.8(a) because such fees often have the essential qualities of a business transaction with the client.

[5] An agreement may not be made whose terms might induce the lawyer improperly to curtail services for the client or perform them in a way contrary to the client's interest. For example, a lawyer should not enter into an agreement whereby services are to be provided only up to a stated amount when it is foreseeable that more extensive services probably will be required, unless the situation is adequately explained to the client. Otherwise, the client might have to bargain for further assistance in the midst of a proceeding or transaction. However, it is proper to define the extent of services in light of the client's ability to pay. A lawyer should not exploit a fee arrangement based primarily on hourly charges by using wasteful procedures.

Prohibited Contingent Fees

[6] Paragraph (d) prohibits a lawyer from charging a contingent fee in a domestic relations matter when payment is contingent upon the securing of a divorce or upon the amount of alimony or support or property settlement to be obtained. This provision does not preclude a contract for a contingent fee for legal representation in connection with the recovery of post-judgment balances due under support, alimony or other financial orders because such contracts do not implicate the same policy concerns.

Division of Fee

[7] A division of fee is a single billing to a client covering the fee of two or more lawyers who are not in the same firm. A division of fee facilitates association of more than one lawyer in a matter in which neither alone could serve the client as well, and most often is used when the fee is contingent and the division is between a referring lawyer and a trial specialist. Paragraph (e) permits the lawyers to divide a fee either on the basis of the proportion of services they render or if each lawyer assumes responsibility for the representation as a whole. In addition, the client must agree to the arrangement, including the share that each lawyer is to receive, and the agreement must be confirmed in writing. Contingent fee agreements must be in a writing signed by the client and must otherwise comply with paragraph (c) of this Rule. Joint responsibility for the representation entails financial and ethical responsibility for the representation as if the lawyers were associated in a partnership. A lawyer should only refer a matter to a lawyer whom the referring lawyer reasonably believes is competent to handle the matter. See Rule 1.1.

[8] Paragraph (e) does not prohibit or regulate division of fees to be received in the future for work done when lawyers were previously associated in a law firm.

Disputes Over Fees

[9] If a procedure has been established for resolution of fee disputes, such as an arbitration or mediation procedure established by the bar, the lawyer must comply with the procedure when it is mandatory, and, even when it is voluntary, the lawyer should conscientiously consider submitting to it. Law may prescribe a procedure for determining a lawyer's fee, for example, in representation of an executor or administrator, a class or a person entitled to a reasonable fee as part of the measure of damages. The lawyer entitled to such a fee and a lawyer representing another party concerned with the fee should comply with the prescribed procedure.

ANNOTATIONS
Form of Fee Agreements

Although this rule mandates only that contingent fee agreements be set forth in writing, *see* Louisiana Rule 1.5(c), the preferred practice is to memorialize all fee arrangements with new clients in writing before, or within a reasonable time after, commencing the representation, *see* La. Rules of Prof'l Conduct r. 1.5(b) (2004). Courts construe any ambiguity in a fee agreement against the lawyer who drafted the agreement. *See Classic Imports, Inc. v. Singleton*, 765 So. 2d 455, 459 (La. Ct. App. 4th Cir. 2000).

Arbitration Agreements

Most state courts that have considered the enforceability of lawyer-client arbitration clauses have approved them. The issue was an open question in Louisiana, however, until the Louisiana Supreme Court addressed the issue in *Hodges v. Reasonover*, 103 So. 3d 1069 (La. 2012). Noting that an arbitration clause "does not inherently limit or alter either party's substantive rights; it simply provides for an alternative venue for the resolution of disputes," the court held that a "binding arbitration clause between an attorney and client does not violate Rule of Professional Conduct 1.8(h) provided the clause does not limit the attorney's substantive liability, provides for a neutral decision maker, and is otherwise fair and reasonable to the client." *Id.* at 1076. However, the court imposed a number of "minimum" requirements for enforceable arbitration clauses:

> At a minimum, the attorney must disclose the following legal effects of binding arbitration, assuming they are applicable:
>
> - Waiver of the right to a jury trial;
>
> - Waiver of the right to an appeal;
>
> - Waiver of the right to broad discovery under the Louisiana Code of Civil Procedure and/or Federal Rules of Civil Procedure;
>
> - Arbitration may involve substantial upfront costs compared to litigation;

- Explicit disclosure of the nature of claims covered by the arbitration clause, such as fee disputes or malpractice claims;

- The arbitration clause does not impinge upon the client's right to make a disciplinary complaint to the appropriate authorities;

- The client has the opportunity to speak with independent counsel before signing the contract.

Id. at 1077. If a Louisiana lawyer includes these terms in the lawyer's engagement agreement, it will be enforceable. *See id.*

Unreasonable Fees

The factors enumerated in this rule that bear on the reasonableness of fees exist to further three important policies: (1) to ensure that clients make voluntary and informed decisions regarding fee arrangements; (2) to ensure that a lawyer collects fees that are comparable to those collected by a comparable lawyer providing comparable services; and, (3) to prevent an otherwise reasonable fee agreement from becoming unreasonable due to subsequent events. *See* Restatement (Third) of the Law Governing Lawyers § 34 cmt. c (2000). Although an unreasonable fee may lead to discipline, issues regarding the reasonableness of legal fees arise more commonly when a court[77] is called upon to award fees pursuant to law or contract, or to reduce an allegedly excessive fee. *See, e.g., Silwad Two, L.L.C. v. I Zenith, Inc.,* 111 So. 3d 405, 411 (La. Ct. App. 1st Cir. 2012); *Town of Mamou v. Fontenot,* 816 So. 2d 958 (La. Ct. App. 3d Cir. 2002). Courts may inquire into the reasonableness of fees as part of their inherent authority to regulate a lawyer who practices before the court. *See In re Simpson,* 959 So. 2d 836, 841 (La. 2007); *Succession of Bankston,* 844 So. 2d 61, 64 (La. Ct. App. 1st Cir. 2003); *La. Dept. of Transp. & Dev. v. Williamson,* 597 So. 2d 439, 441-42 (La. 1992); *see also Saucier v. Hayes Dairy Prods., Inc.,* 373 So. 2d 102 (La. 1978). Moreover, courts retain this authority even when a fee-award is fixed by statute or contract. *See Health Educ. & Welfare Fed. Credit Union v. Peoples State Bank,* 83 So. 3d 1055 (La. Ct. App. 3rd Cir. 2011); *Rivet v. La. Dept. of Transp. & Dev.,* 680 So. 2d 1154, 1161 (La. 1996); *Warner v. Carimi Law Firm,* 678 So. 2d 561 (La. Ct. App. 5th Cir. 1996); *People's Nat'l Bank of New Iberia v. Smith,* 360 So. 2d 560 (La. Ct. App. 4th Cir. 1978). Courts, however, must temper their reasonableness review "with restraint, especially when the parties have signed a contract which memorializes the terms of their agreed-upon relationship." *See, e.g., In re Interdiction of DeMarco,* 38 So. 3d 417, 427 (La. Ct. App. 1st Cir. 2010); *Gold, Weems, Bruser, Sues & Rundell v. Granger,* 947 So. 2d 835 (La. Ct. App. 3d Cir. 2006); *Drury v. Fawer,* 590 So. 2d 808, 810 (La. Ct. App. 4th Cir. 1991); *Cupp Drug Store, Inc. v. Blue Cross,* 161 So. 3d 860, 870 (La. Ct. App. 2d Cir. 2015) (judgment amended

---

[77] For reported decisions discussing the principles governing a federal court's review of legal fees for reasonableness, *see Louisiana Power & Light Co. v. Kellstrom,* 50 F.3d 319, 324 (5th Cir. 1995); *A C Marine, Inc. v. Axxis Drilling, Inc.,* No. 10-0087, 2011 WL 1595438 at *2 (W.D. La Apr. 25, 2011); *Brown v. Sea Mar Mgmt., LLC,* 288 Fed. Appx. 922 (5th Cir. 2008).

to reasonable fee amount determined by expert testimony of lawyer instead of initial "friendship rate" between plaintiff and longstanding client); *Monster Rentals, LLC v. Coonass Const. of Acadianai, LLC*, 162 So. 3d 1264, 1269-70 (La. Ct. App. 3d Cir. 2015) (because overwhelming amount of work performed by paralegals, court reduced hourly rate from $250.00 to $200.00); *Volentine v. Raeford Farms of Louisiana, LLC*, 201 So. 3d 325, 357 (La. Ct. App. 2d Cir. 2016) (finding no abuse of discretion by trial court despite contention that fee awarded was "abusively low" due to the complex and lengthy nature of the litigation).

In evaluating the reasonableness of a fee, a court may consider the testimony of a lawyer qualified as an expert on legal fees; however, such testimony is not necessarily controlling. *See, e.g., Peiser v. Grand Isle, Inc.*, 224 La. 299, 231, 69 So. 2d 51, 53 (La. 1953); *James, Robinson, Felts & Starnes v. Powell*, 303 So. 2d 229, 231 (La. Ct. App. 2d Cir. 1974).

As to contingent fees, Louisiana courts have reduced large fees when a minimal amount of legal work has resulted in a large recovery. *See, e.g., Thibaut, Thibaut, Garrett & Bacot v. Smith & Loveless, Inc.*, 517 So. 2d 222, 225 (La. Ct. App. 1st Cir. 1987) (remanding for an evidentiary hearing to determine whether a fee of $24,336 was an unreasonable fee for 26 hours of work performed to collect $243,354). Contingent fees can be unreasonable for a number of reasons. First, a contingent fee may be unreasonable due to a lopsided allocation of risk. For example, a lawyer who undertakes a case with a high probability of a large recovery without discussing the availability of alternative fee arrangements with the client might collect a fee that is adjudged to be unreasonable. *See* Restatement (Third) of the Law Governing Lawyers § 35 cmt. c (2000). Second, a contingent fee may be unreasonable if the contingent percentage is unjustifiably large or if an otherwise reasonable percentage is applied to an unreasonable base amount, such as an uncollected judgment or a nondiscounted sum of structured-settlement payments. *Id.* cmts. d-e. However, the reasonableness of a contingent fee "cannot be determined by simply multiplying the hours worked by an hourly rate customary in the legal community." *See Town of Mamou v. Fontenot*, 816 So. 2d 958, 966 (La. Ct. App. 3d Cir. 2002). Such an "overly simplistic" formula would not properly account for the risk undertaken by the lawyer. *See id.; see also Saucier*, 373 So. 2d at 102.

As to hourly fees, it is unreasonable for a lawyer to bill more time to a client than the lawyer in fact spent on that client's matter. Thus, a lawyer would violate Rule 1.5 if the lawyer were to charge a client for phantom hours that were never worked. Rule 1.5 also prohibits a lawyer from double-counting hours. For example, it is unreasonable for a lawyer to bill one client for travel time while simultaneously billing another client for writing a brief on the airplane. Likewise, it is unreasonable for a lawyer to bill one client for work product previously prepared for another client. *See* ABA Comm. on Ethics and Professional Responsibility, Formal Op. 93-379 (1993). To avoid this problem, lawyers should fairly apportion their time between the affected clients. For example, if a lawyer spends an hour traveling to an outlying parish to attend motion hearings for two separate clients, the lawyer should not bill each client for one hour of time. Rather, the lawyer should bill each client for one-half hour.

Fee Sharing and Case Referrals

It is permissible for two lawyers who perform disparate amounts of work on a matter to share a fee. At one time, "referral fees" were strictly prohibited. *See* ABA Model Code of Prof. Resp. DR 2-107(A) (Am. Bar Ass'n 1983) (requiring that division of fees be in proportion to services rendered). However, Rule 1.5(e) permits fee sharing under carefully delineated circumstances. If the participating lawyers do not comply with this rule, then they cannot divide their fee in accordance with their agreement. *See In re Calm C's, Inc.*, 179 F. App'x 911, 913 (5th Cir. 2006) (disallowing division of contingency fee by lawyer not a party to signed contract); *Bertucci v. McIntire*, 693 So. 2d 7, 9 (La. App. 5th Cir. 1997) (dividing fee "in proportion to the services performed").

Although Rule 1.5(e) requires that the fee be in proportion to the services provided, Louisiana courts hesitate to inspect each lawyer's work in a proceeding to assess the validity of a fee division arrangement. *See Murray v. Harang*, 104 So. 3d 694, 698-99 (La. Ct. App. 4th Cir. 2012) (noting "it is not our duty to weigh each lawyer's contribution to the handling of cases"). In *Murray*, the court upheld a 50/50 fee division when both lawyers "contributed to the totality of the work at all stages of litigation and were responsible to their clients, and were both retained throughout the course of the trial." *Id.* at 698. However, "courts have declined to apply the joint venture theory to support an equal division of the fee when the attorneys have not been jointly involved in the representation of the client." *See Robert L. Manard, III, PLC v. Falcon Law Firm, PLC*, 119 So. 3d 1, 7 (La. Ct. App. 4th Cir. 2012) (*citing Dukes v. Matheny*, 878 So. 2d 517, 520 (La. Ct. App. 1st Cir. 2004); *Brown v. Seimers*, 726 So. 2d 1018, 1022 (La. Ct. App. 5th Cir. 1999); *Matter of P & E Boat Rentals, Inc.*, 928 F.2d 662, 665 (5th Cir. 1991)). When lawyers have not been "jointly involved" in a representation, apportionment of the fee is "based on quantum meruit." *Id.* Under a quantum meruit theory, a lawyer "may receive payment only for the services he performed and the responsibilities he assumed." *Id.* (citing *Saucier v. Hayes Dairy Products, Inc.*, 373 So. 2d 102 (La.1978)).

In Scheffler v. Adams & Reese, LLP, 950 So. 2d 641, 653 (La. 2007), the Louisiana Supreme Court held that lawyers serving as co-counsel and sharing fees have no fiduciary relationship vis-a-vis one another:

> [A]s a matter of public policy, based on our authority to regulate the practice of law pursuant to the constitution, no cause of action will exist between co-counsel based on the theory that co-counsel have a fiduciary duty to protect one another's prospective interests in a fee. To allow such an action would be to subject an attorney to potential conflicts of interest in trying to serve two masters and potentially compromise the attorney's paramount duty to serve the best interests of the client.

While an unethical fee-sharing agreement between lawyers may subject them to discipline, it is less clear whether the unethical nature of the agreement will bar its enforcement as between the parties.[78] The United States Court of Appeals for the Seventh Circuit has held that an agreement to divide fees is unenforceable if the agreement violated the applicable professional conduct rules. *See Kaplan v. Pavalon & Gifford*, 12 F.3d 87, 92 (7th Cir. 1993); *see also In re Estate of Katchatag*, 907 P.2d 464-65 (Alaska 1995) (following *Kaplan*); see also *Lemond v. Jamail*, 763 S.W.2d 910, 914 (Tex. App. 1988) (holding that fee-splitting agreement was void because it violated public policy). *But see King v. Housel*, 556 N.E.2d 501, 504-05 (Ohio 1990) (lawyer estopped from claiming that fee-splitting agreement was invalid); *see Grasso v. Galanter*, No 2:12-cv-00738, 2013 WL 5537289, at *3 (D. Nev. Sep. 20, 2013) (same). *See generally* Joseph M. Perillo, *The Law of Lawyers is Different*, 67 Fordham L. Rev. 443, 447-48 (1998) (arguing that under the Restatement of the Law Governing Lawyers, courts have "total discretion" as to whether a lawyer is entitled to compensation despite violation of disciplinary rules).

Some Louisiana courts have permitted lawyers to share fees in an amount in proportion to the services rendered when the lawyer's fee-division agreement did not comport with the Louisiana Rules of Professional Conduct. *In Dukes v. Matheny*, the Louisiana First Circuit Court of Appeals held as follows:

> [Louisiana] courts have declined to apply the joint venture theory to support an equal division of the fee when the attorneys have not been jointly involved in the representation of the client. *See Brown v. Seimers*, 726 So. 2d 1018 (La. Ct. App. 5th Cir. 1999); *see also Matter of P & E Boat Rentals, Inc. v. Martzell, Thomas & Bickford*, 928 F.2d 662, 665 (5th Cir. 1991). Rather, the apportionment of the fee in those types of cases has been based on quantum meruit. Brown, 726 So. 2d at 1023. Such a ruling is in accord with Rule 1.5(e) of the Rules of Professional Conduct . . . .

Dukes v. Matheny, 878 So. 2d 517 (La. Ct. App. 1st Cir. 2004); *see also Chimneywood Homeowners Ass'n, Inc. v. Eagan Ins. Agency, Inc.*, 57 So. 3d 1142, 1152-53 (La. Ct. App. 4th Cir. 2011) (dispersing fee "according to the respective services and contributions of the attorneys for work performed and other relevant factors"); *Bertucci v. McIntire*, 693 So. 2d 7, 9 (La. Ct. App. 5th Cir. 1997) (awarding fees in quantum meruit where division agreement was made in violation of the Rules of Professional Conduct); *see also; Huskinson & Brown, LLP v. Wolf*, 84 P.3d 379, 385 (Cal. 2004) (stating that noncompliance with ethics rules invalidates firms' agreements to divide fees but does not forbid quantum meruit action).[79] However, at least one Louisiana appellate court declined even to consider

---

[78] Louisiana courts have on occasion enforced oral contingent fee agreements that otherwise violated Rule 1.5(c). *See Classic Imports, Inc. v. Singleton*, 765 So. 2d 455, 458-59 (La. Ct. App. 4th Cir. 2000); *Tschirn v. Secor Bank*, 691 So. 2d 1290, 1294 (La. Ct. App. 4th Cir. 1997).

[79] Note that a fee-sharing contract with a nonlawyer made in violation of Louisiana Rule of Professional Conduct 5.4 is null and void. *See "We the People" Paralegal Servs., LLC v.*

the merits of a claim that a lawyer in violation of the Rules may be subject to fee forfeiture. *See Brown v. Seimers*, 726 So. 2d 1018, 1020 (La. Ct. App. 5th Cir. 1999) ("This complaint . . . should be raised with the Bar Association").

A referring lawyer cannot share a legal fee if the lawyer has a conflict of interest that prohibits the lawyer from either performing legal services in connection with the matter. *See* ABA Formal Op. 474 (Apr. 21, 2016) ("Referral Fees and Conflict of Interest"). Because each fee-sharing lawyer in Louisiana must actually represent the client, each lawyer owes the client all of the duties attendant a lawyer-client relationship—including the duty of loyalty.

A referring lawyer who is disbarred or suspended from the practice of law cannot earn a referral fee. *See* R.I. Ethics Advisory Panel Op. 91-71 (Oct. 1991); Ind. St. Bar Op. 9 (1991); Fla. Bar Op. 90-3 (1990). A disbarred lawyer no longer shares "joint representation" of the client and no longer is a "lawyer" for the purposes of fee sharing. *See* La. Rules of Prof'l Conduct r. 5.4 (2004) (stating that a lawyer generally may not share fees with a nonlawyer). However, the lawyer may be permitted to collect in quantum meruit the value of services provided prior to disbarment or suspension from practice. *See Brown v. Seimers*, 726 So. 2d 1018, 1023 (La. Ct. App. 5th Cir. 1999). *But see* N.Y. St. Bar Op. 609 (1990) (implying that no recovery in quantum meruit is permitted when the matter for which a lawyer seeks compensation is the same one that gave rise to discipline).

Finally, a lawyer who receives a to-be-shared fee must place it in trust prior to distribution:

> When one lawyer receives an earned fee that is subject to such an arrangement and both lawyers have an interest in that earned fee, Model Rules 1.15(a) and 1.15(d) require that the receiving lawyer hold the funds in an account separate from the lawyer's own property, appropriately safeguard the funds, promptly notify the other lawyer who holds an interest in the fee of receipt of the funds, promptly deliver to the other lawyer the agreed upon portion of the fee, and, if requested by the other lawyer, provide a full accounting.

ABA Formal Op. 475 at 3 (Dec. 7, 2016).

Fee-Collection

Under the Louisiana Civil Code, contracts generally have the effect of law only as between the parties. *See* La. Civ. Code Ann. art. 1983 (2008). Therefore, if a lawyer is retained by another lawyer to work on a matter, the lawyer generally should look to the retaining lawyer for fee payment. In contrast, if a lawyer is retained by the client to work on a matter,

---

Watley, 766 So. 2d 744 (La. Ct. App. 2d Cir. 2000) (holding that a fee-sharing agreement with a paralegal services firm was null and void, but remanding to allow the firm to state a cause of action for unjust enrichment); *see also In re Watley*, 802 So. 2d 593, 594 n.2 (La. 2001).

the lawyer should look to the client for payment.[80] For these reasons, a lawyer working with another lawyer on a matter should clarify in writing who is responsible for payment.

Responsibility for Expenses

A lawyer is not personally responsible to third persons who supply goods or services to further a client's case if the lawyer's agency is apparent and the client/principal is disclosed. *See Penton v. Healy*, 863 So. 2d 684, 692 (La. Ct. App. 4th Cir. 2003) (finding no evidence that lawyer was a disclosed agent for client). However, a lawyer may become personally liable if the lawyer expressly or impliedly pledges personal responsibility. *See id.*; *see also Weeden Eng'g Corp. v. Hale*, 435 So. 2d 1158, 1160 (La. Ct. App. 3d Cir. 1983).

Unreasonable Expenses

Under paragraph (a) of this rule, courts may inquire into the reasonableness of a lawyer's litigation-related expenses as well as his legal fees. It constitutes sanctionable misconduct to "pad" legitimate expenses, and to charge for "fictitious expenses." *In re Dyer*, 750 So. 2d 942, 948 (La. 1999); *see also In re Mitchell*, 145 So. 3d 305 (La. 2014) (permanently disbarring lawyer for hundreds of unsupported expense reimbursement requests over a period of several years).

Trust Accounting

Paragraph (f) of this rule, unlike the comparable ABA Model Rule, sets forth the following accounting guidelines for fees paid in advance of services.

Type of Funds	Proper Account	Applicable Rules
Fee for lawyer's general availability (unrelated to particular matter)	Operating account	1.5(f)(1)
Fixed or minimum fee for future services on particular matter	Operating account if undisputed, trust account if "reasonably" in dispute	1.5(f)(2); 1.5(f)(5)
Advance deposit for fees, costs or expenses to be incurred in the future	Trust account, but lawyer may transfer funds to operating account as fees are earned or costs are incurred (without further client authorization but with periodic accountings)	1.5(f)(3-4)

---

[80] At least one court has suggested that a lawyer retained by another lawyer already representing a client may establish "some privity of contract" with the client by way of "a stipulation pour autrui." *See Dereyna v. Pennzoil Exploration*, 880 So. 2d 124, 127 (La. Ct. App. 3d Cir. 2004).

| "Reasonably" disputed funds[81] | Trust account | 1.5(f)(2); 1.5(f)(5-6) |

Collecting Fees After Termination

A lawyer who is discharged by a client is generally entitled to recover in quantum meruit for any services provided prior to termination. *See Saucier v. Hayes Dairy Products, Inc.*, 373 So. 2d 102 (La.1979); *see generally* Restatement of Law (Third) Governing Lawyers § 40 (2000). In determining the appropriate quantum meruit amount to be paid to a discharged lawyer, courts consider the following factors:

> (1) the time and labor required, the novelty and difficulty of the questions involved, and the skill requisite to perform the legal service properly;
>
> (2) the likelihood, if apparent to the client, that the acceptance of the particular employment will preclude other employment by the lawyer;
>
> (3) the fee customarily charged in the locality for similar legal services;
>
> (4) the amount involved and the results obtained;
>
> (5) the time limitations imposed by the client or by the circumstances;
>
> (6) the nature and length of the professional relationship with the client;
>
> (7) the experience, reputation, and ability of the lawyer or lawyers performing the services; and
>
> (8) whether the fee is fixed or contingent.

See La. Rules of Prof'l Cond. R. 1.5(a); *Saucier*, 373 So. 2d at 110 (applying similar factors from former disciplinary rule DR 2-106); *Chimneywood Homeowners Association, Inc. v. Eagan Ins. Agency, Inc.*, 57 So. 3d 1142, 1147-48 (La. Ct. App. 4th Cir. 2011) (applying Rule 1.5(a) factors in allocating quantum meruit amount to discharged lawyer); *Mitchell v. Bradford*, 961 So. 2d 1288, 1293 (La. Ct. App. 4th Cir. 2007) (applying Rule 1.5(a) factors in quantum meruit evaluation); *Mie Properties-La, L.L.C. v. Carey*, 213 So. 3d 1274, 1281 (La. Ct. App. 1st Cir. 2017) (applying factors in holding that an "attorney fee award to lessor in the amount of $21,500 was excessive" in a "relatively simple case" when the lease agreement provided "for a 10 percent attorney fee," which equated to "$7,080.36").

A lawyer terminated for cause may suffer a fee reduction as a result of the fault that led to discharge. In *O'Rourke v. Cairns*, the Louisiana Supreme Court held as follows:

> We therefore hold that in cases of discharge with cause of an attorney retained on contingency, the trial court should determine the amount of the fee according to the *Saucier* rule, calculating the highest ethical

---

[81] The term "reasonably" appears in quotes in the table above because the Louisiana Supreme Court has held that a lawyer is required to place only "reasonably" disputed funds into his trust account. Funds that the client disputes without reasonable basis are not required to be placed into trust. *See In re Lucius*, 863 So. 2d 516 (La. 2004).

contingency to which the client contractually agreed in any of the contingency fee contracts executed. The court should then allocate the fee between or among discharged and subsequent counsel based upon the Saucier factors. Thereafter, the court should consider the nature and gravity of the cause which contributed to the dismissal and reduce by a percentage amount the portion discharged counsel otherwise would receive after the Saucier allocation.

O'Rourke v. Cairns, 683 So. 2d 697, 704 (La. 1996); *see also Buras v. Ace Dynasty Transp. Corp.*, 731 So. 2d 1010, 1013 (La. Ct. App. 4th Cir. 1999) ("Considering the nature and gravity of the cause for which [the client] discharged [the lawyer], we do not believe the trial court erred in its reduction of the discharged lawyer's portion of the fee by ten percent."); *see also Gillio v. Hanover American Ins. Co.*, 212 So. 3d 588, 592 (La. Ct. App. 1st Cir. 2017).

Criminal Practice

Whether a fee charged by a criminal defense lawyer is reasonable turns on the factors set forth in Rule 1.5(a). However, a Louisiana criminal defense lawyer may base the lawyer's fee in part on the gravity of the charges lodged against their clients. There is authority suggesting that the seriousness of the charges is a reasonable consideration in structuring a fee arrangement. *See* Standards for Criminal Justice: Defense Function std. 4-3.3(f) (Am. Bar Ass'n 1993); *see also* La. Rules of Prof'l Conduct r. 1.5(a)(4) (2004) (relating to the "amount involved"). Of course, criminal defense lawyers may never charge a fee that is contingent in any respect on the outcome of the prosecution. *See id.* r. 1.5(d)(2). A fee is "contingent" if it is paid by the client for a lawyer-guaranteed result. *See In re Gold*, 734 So. 2d 1210, 1210-11 (La. 1999).

Disciplinary Sanctions

When a lawyer violates Rule 1.5, the following sanctions are generally appropriate: *disbarment*, if the lawyer knowingly violated the rule, intended to obtain a benefit for himself or another, and the lawyer's conduct caused serious or potential injury to a client, the public, or the legal system; *suspension*, if the lawyer knowingly violated the rule, and caused serious or potential injury; *reprimand*, if the lawyer negligently violated the rule, and caused injury or potential injury; and, *admonition*, if the lawyer's conduct was an isolated instance of negligence that caused little or no actual or potential injury. *See* Standards for Imposing Lawyer Sanctions stds. 7.0-7.4 (Am. Bar Ass'n 1992). Reprimand is generally the appropriate sanction in most cases of a violation of a duty owed to the legal profession. *See id.* std. 7.3 cmt. Nevertheless, in Louisiana, the sanction for charging an excessive fee ranges from reprimand to disbarment. *See In re Bailey*, 115 So. 3d 458 (La. 2013); *In re Levingston*, 755 So. 2d 874, 876 n.6 (La. 2000) (citing *In re Juakali*, 699 So. 2d 361 (La. 1997); *In re Little*, No. 95-DB-009, slip op., at 3 (La. 1996); *In re Watkins*, 656 So. 2d 984 (La. 1995); *In re Quaid*, 646 So. 2d 343 (La. 1994); *In re Ford*, 30 So. 3d 742 (La. 2010); *In re Booth*, 6 So. 3d 158, 2008-2353 (La. 2009); *In re Petal*, 972 So. 2d 1138, 2007-1299 (La. 2008). Notably, the Louisiana Supreme Court permanently disbarred a lawyer for multiple violations of Rule 1.5(f)(5), holding that the lawyer's failure to refund unearned fees to 39 clients was "essentially" conversion of the fees to the lawyer's own use. *In re Fleming*, 970 So. 2d 970, 981-982 (La. 2007) (stating that the lawyer "used a law license as pretext to steal money from the citizens of this state"). *See also In re Avery*, 110 So. 3d 563, 570-572 (La. 2013) (permanently disbarring lawyer for, among other offenses, writing personal checks drawn on client trust account and failing to refund unearned fees); *In re Bates*, 33. So. 3d 162 (La. 2010) (permanently disbarring lawyer for accepting more than $51,000 in fees and failing to do any substantial work or refund the funds); *In re Mitchell*, 145 So. 3d 305 (La. 2014) (permanently disbarring lawyer for hundreds of unsupported expense reimbursement requests over a period of several years); *In re Lester*, 31 So. 3d 333 (La. 2010) (disbarring lawyer for multiple violations of Rule 1.5, among several other rules violations); *In re Toaston*, 225 So. 3d 1066 (La. 2017) (holding that "permanent disbarment was appropriate sanction for attorney's numerous instances of misconduct," including several violations of Rule 1.5); and, *In re Gomez*, 29 So. 3d 473 (La. 2010) (disbarring lawyer for failure to refund unearned fees, failure to promptly remit funds to third-party medical provider, and using client funds for unauthorized purposes).

RULE 1.6. CONFIDENTIALITY OF INFORMATION

(a) A lawyer shall not reveal information relating to the representation of a client unless the client gives informed consent, the disclosure is impliedly authorized in order to carry out the representation or the disclosure is permitted by paragraph (b).

(b) A lawyer may reveal information relating to the representation of a client to the extent the lawyer reasonably believes necessary:

> (1) to prevent reasonably certain death or substantial bodily harm;

> (2) to prevent the client from committing a crime or fraud that is reasonably certain to result in substantial injury to the financial interests or property of another and in furtherance of which the client has used or is using the lawyer's services;

> (3) to prevent, mitigate or rectify substantial injury to the financial interests or property of another that is reasonably certain to result or has resulted from the client's commission of a crime or fraud in furtherance of which the client has used the lawyer's services;

> (4) to secure legal advice about the lawyer's compliance with these Rules;

> (5) to establish a claim or defense on behalf of the lawyer in a controversy between the lawyer and the client, to establish a defense to a criminal charge or civil claim against the lawyer based upon conduct in which the client was involved, or to respond to allegations in any proceeding concerning the lawyer's representation of the client;

> (6) to comply with other law or a court order; or

> (7) to detect and resolve conflicts of interest between lawyers in different firms, but only if the revealed information would not compromise the attorney-client privilege or otherwise prejudice the client.

81

(c) A lawyer shall make reasonable efforts to prevent the inadvertent or unauthorized disclosure of, or unauthorized access to, information relating to the representation of a client.

BACKGROUND

The Louisiana Supreme Court adopted this rule on January 20, 2004, and it became effective on March 1, 2004. In 2015, the court amended the rule to permit disclosures to screen conflicts, and to require the exercise of reasonable care to prevent unauthorized disclosures.

This rule is identical to ABA Model Rule of Professional Conduct 1.6 (2003), except for the following: The Louisiana rule does not contain ABA Model Rule paragraph (b)(7) (which allows disclosures "to detect and resolve conflicts of interest arising from the lawyer's change of employment or from changes in the composition or ownership of a firm, but only if the revealed information would not compromise the attorney-client privilege or otherwise prejudice the client").

In 2002, the ABA substantially expanded the grounds for permissive disclosure under Model Rule 1.6. While strongly reaffirming the legal profession's commitment to the core value of confidentiality, the ABA recognized the importance of preserving human life and the integrity of the lawyer's role within the legal system through permitting more disclosures of otherwise confidential information. *See* ABA Ethics 2000 Comm'n Revision Notes to Model Rule 1.6 (2002).

In 2015, the Louisiana Supreme Court adopted a new paragraph, denominated as Louisiana Rule 1.6(b)(7), permitting a lawyer to disclose confidential information to the extent the lawyer "reasonably believes necessary": "(7) to detect and resolve conflicts of interest between lawyers in different firms, but only if the revealed information would not compromise the attorney-client privilege or otherwise prejudice the client." In adopting this amendment, the court made the Louisiana rule similar to the corresponding ABA Model Rule. The ABA adopted similar language because sometimes a lawyer may need to disclose potential conflicts when the lawyer is considering associating with a new firm, or when law firms are considering a merger. *See* ABA Model Rules of Prof'l Conduct r. 1.6(c) cmt. 13. In reality, Louisiana lawyers changing or joining firms have long made these disclosures without this express authorization.

In 2015, the Louisiana Supreme Court adopted a new paragraph, denominated as Rule 1.6(c), that provides as follows: "A lawyer shall make reasonable efforts to prevent the inadvertent or unauthorized disclosure of, or unauthorized access to, information relating to the representation of a client." This is a default rule; a client may demand that a lawyer exercise more—or permit a lawyer to exercise less—than ordinary "reasonable care" of the client's information. In adopting this amendment, the court made the Louisiana rule identical to the corresponding ABA Model Rule.

Disclosures to Prevent Death or Bodily Harm

The ABA expanded the exception for client crimes threatening imminent death or substantial bodily harm in part, to make the Model Rule consistent with Section 66 of the

American Law Institute's Restatement of the Law Governing Lawyers. The Model Rule replaces "imminent" with "reasonably certain," to include a present and substantial threat that a person will suffer such injury at a later date, as in some instances involving toxic torts. *Se* ABA Model Rule 1.6 cmt. 6.

Disclosures of Client Crimes and Frauds

In August 2003, the ABA House of Delegates adopted the paragraphs (b)(2) and (b)(3), provisions it had previously rejected. These provisions permit a lawyer to reveal client confidences to prevent the client from committing a serious crime or fraud that the lawyer unwittingly assisted. The ABA believed that the use of the lawyer's services for such improper ends constitutes a serious abuse of the client-lawyer relationship. Moreover, the ABA believed that the client's entitlement to the protection of the Rule must be balanced against the prevention of the injury that would otherwise be suffered and the interest of the lawyer in being able to prevent the misuse of the lawyer's services.

Disclosures to Secure Legal Advice

In 2002, the ABA adopted paragraph (b)(4) to permit a lawyer to reveal confidential information to secure legal advice regarding his own obligations. In most instances, the ABA presumed disclosing information to secure such advice is impliedly authorized. Nevertheless, in order to clarify that such disclosures are proper even when not impliedly authorized, the ABA revised Model Rule 1.6 to make such disclosures explicitly permissible. *See* ABA Model Rules of Prof'l Conduct r. 1.6(b).

Disclosures to Comply with Law or Court Orders

Prior to 2002, the Model Rules did not address whether a lawyer is permitted or required to disclose information when such disclosure is required by other law or a court order. For this reason, the ABA added paragraph (b)(6) to explicitly permit, but not to require, disclosure in order for a lawyer to comply with law or court orders. *See id.*

Avoiding Inadvertent Disclosures

A mere inadvertent disclosure does not subject a lawyer to discipline under this Rule 1.6(c) if the lawyer has exercised reasonable care to protect client information and data. According to the comment to the corresponding ABA model rule, some factors to consider in evaluating the reasonableness of a lawyer's efforts include:

- The sensitivity and importance of the information disclosed.
- The likelihood of disclosure if more protective measures are not employed.
- The cost and difficulty of employing additional safeguards.
- The extent to which the safeguards "adversely affect the lawyer's ability to represent clients (*e.g.,* by making a device or important piece of software excessively difficult to use)."

See ABA Model Rules of Prof'l Conduct r. 1.6 cmt. 18.

To comply with the obligations imposed by this rule, a lawyer who digitally stores and communicates confidential information generally need not implement über-security measures like encryption or multi-factor authentication. Nor is a lawyer prohibited from using means of communication when the lawyer has a reasonable expectation of privacy, such as when using a public Wi-Fi network for confidential email.

COMMENTS TO ABA MODEL RULE 1.6
Generally

[1] This Rule governs the disclosure by a lawyer of information relating to the representation of a client during the lawyer's representation of the client. See Rule 1.18 for the lawyer's duties with respect to information provided to the lawyer by a prospective client, Rule 1.9(c)(2) for the lawyer's duty not to reveal information relating to the lawyer's prior representation of a former client and Rules 1.8(b) and 1.9(c)(1) for the lawyer's duties with respect to the use of such information to the disadvantage of clients and former clients.

[2] A fundamental principle in the client-lawyer relationship is that, in the absence of the client's informed consent, the lawyer must not reveal information relating to the representation. See Rule 1.0(e) for the definition of informed consent. This contributes to the trust that is the hallmark of the client-lawyer relationship. The client is thereby encouraged to seek legal assistance and to communicate fully and frankly with the lawyer even as to embarrassing or legally damaging subject matter. The lawyer needs this information to represent the client effectively and, if necessary, to advise the client to refrain from wrongful conduct. Almost without exception, clients come to lawyers in order to determine their rights and what is, in the complex of laws and regulations, deemed to be legal and correct. Based upon experience, lawyers know that almost all clients follow the advice given, and the law is upheld.

[3] The principle of client-lawyer confidentiality is given effect by related bodies of law: the attorney-client privilege, the work product doctrine and the rule of confidentiality established in professional ethics. The attorney-client privilege and work product doctrine apply in judicial and other proceedings in which a lawyer may be called as a witness or otherwise required to produce evidence concerning a client. The rule of client-lawyer confidentiality applies in situations other than those where evidence is sought from the lawyer through compulsion of law. The confidentiality rule, for example, applies not only to matters communicated in confidence by the client but also to all information relating to the representation, whatever its source. A lawyer may not disclose such information except as authorized or required by the Rules of Professional Conduct or other law. See also Scope.

[4] Paragraph (a) prohibits a lawyer from revealing information relating to the representation of a client. This prohibition also applies to disclosures by a lawyer that do not in themselves reveal protected information but could reasonably lead to the discovery of such information by a third person. A lawyer's use of a hypothetical to discuss issues relating to the representation is permissible so long as there is no reasonable likelihood that the listener will be able to ascertain the identity of the client or the situation involved.

Authorized Disclosure

[5] Except to the extent that the client's instructions or special circumstances limit that authority, a lawyer is impliedly authorized to make disclosures about a client when

appropriate in carrying out the representation. In some situations, for example, a lawyer may be impliedly authorized to admit a fact that cannot properly be disputed or to make a disclosure that facilitates a satisfactory conclusion to a matter. Lawyers in a firm may, in the course of the firm's practice, disclose to each other information relating to a client of the firm, unless the client has instructed that particular information be confined to specified lawyers.

Disclosure Adverse to Client

[6] Although the public interest is usually best served by a strict rule requiring lawyers to preserve the confidentiality of information relating to the representation of their clients, the confidentiality rule is subject to limited exceptions. Paragraph (b)(1) recognizes the overriding value of life and physical integrity and permits disclosure reasonably necessary to prevent reasonably certain death or substantial bodily harm. Such harm is reasonably certain to occur if it will be suffered imminently or if there is a present and substantial threat that a person will suffer such harm at a later date if the lawyer fails to take action necessary to eliminate the threat. Thus, a lawyer who knows that a client has accidentally discharged toxic waste into a town's water supply may reveal this information to the authorities if there is a present and substantial risk that a person who drinks the water will contract a life-threatening or debilitating disease and the lawyer's disclosure is necessary to eliminate the threat or reduce the number of victims.

[7] Paragraph (b)(2) is a limited exception to the rule of confidentiality that permits the lawyer to reveal information to the extent necessary to enable affected persons or appropriate authorities to prevent the client from committing a crime or fraud, as defined in Rule 1.0(d), that is reasonably certain to result in substantial injury to the financial or property interests of another and in furtherance of which the client has used or is using the lawyer's services. Such a serious abuse of the client-lawyer relationship by the client forfeits the protection of this Rule. The client can, of course, prevent such disclosure by refraining from the wrongful conduct. Although paragraph (b)(2) does not require the lawyer to reveal the client's misconduct, the lawyer may not counsel or assist the client in conduct the lawyer knows is criminal or fraudulent. See Rule 1.2(d). See also Rule 1.16 with respect to the lawyer's obligation or right to withdraw from the representation of the client in such circumstances, and Rule 1.13(c), which permits the lawyer, where the client is an organization, to reveal information relating to the representation in limited circumstances.

[8] Paragraph (b)(3) addresses the situation in which the lawyer does not learn of the client's crime or fraud until after it has been consummated. Although the client no longer has the option of preventing disclosure by refraining from the wrongful conduct, there will be situations in which the loss suffered by the affected person can be prevented, rectified or mitigated. In such situations, the lawyer may disclose information relating to the representation to the extent necessary to enable the affected persons to prevent or mitigate reasonably certain losses or to attempt to recoup their losses. Paragraph (b)(3) does not apply when a person who has committed a crime or fraud thereafter employs a lawyer for representation concerning that offense.

[9] A lawyer's confidentiality obligations do not preclude a lawyer from securing confidential legal advice about the lawyer's personal responsibility to comply with these Rules. In most situations, disclosing information to secure such advice will be impliedly authorized for the lawyer to carry out the representation. Even when the disclosure is not impliedly authorized, paragraph (b)(4) permits such disclosure because of the importance of a lawyer's compliance with the Rules of Professional Conduct.

[10] Where a legal claim or disciplinary charge alleges complicity of the lawyer in a client's conduct or other misconduct of the lawyer involving representation of the client, the lawyer may respond to the extent the lawyer reasonably believes necessary to establish a defense. The same is true with respect to a claim involving the conduct or representation of a former client. Such a charge can arise in a civil, criminal, disciplinary or other proceeding and can be based on a wrong allegedly committed by the lawyer against the client or on a wrong alleged by a third person, for example, a person claiming to have been defrauded by the lawyer and client acting together. The lawyer's right to respond arises when an assertion of such complicity has been made. Paragraph (b)(5) does not require the lawyer to await the commencement of an action or proceeding that charges such complicity, so that the defense may be established by responding directly to a third party who has made such an assertion. The right to defend also applies, of course, where a proceeding has been commenced.

[11] A lawyer entitled to a fee is permitted by paragraph (b)(5) to prove the services rendered in an action to collect it. This aspect of the rule expresses the principle that the beneficiary of a fiduciary relationship may not exploit it to the detriment of the fiduciary.

[12] Other law may require that a lawyer disclose information about a client. Whether such a law supersedes Rule 1.6 is a question of law beyond the scope of these Rules. When disclosure of information relating to the representation appears to be required by other law, the lawyer must discuss the matter with the client to the extent required by Rule 1.4. If, however, the other law supersedes this Rule and requires disclosure, paragraph (b)(6) permits the lawyer to make such disclosures as are necessary to comply with the law.

Detections of Conflicts of Interest

[13] Paragraph (b)(7) recognizes that lawyers in different firms may need to disclose limited information to each other to detect and resolve conflicts of interest, such as when a lawyer is considering an association with another firm, two or more firms are considering a merger, or a lawyer is considering the purchase of a law practice. See Rule 1.17, Comment [7]. Under these circumstances, lawyers and law firms are permitted to disclose limited information, but only once substantive discussions regarding the new relationship have occurred. Any such disclosure should ordinarily include no more than the identity of the persons and entities involved in a matter, a brief summary of the general issues involved, and information about whether the matter has terminated. Even this limited information, however, should be disclosed only to the extent reasonably necessary to detect and resolve conflicts of interest that might arise from the possible new relationship. Moreover, the disclosure of any information is prohibited if it would compromise the attorney-client privilege or otherwise prejudice the client (e.g., the fact that a corporate

client is seeking advice on a corporate takeover that has not been publicly announced; that a person has consulted a lawyer about the possibility of divorce before the person's intentions are known to the person's spouse; or that a person has consulted a lawyer about a criminal investigation that has not led to a public charge). Under those circumstances, paragraph (a) prohibits disclosure unless the client or former client gives informed consent. A lawyer's fiduciary duty to the lawyer's firm may also govern a lawyer's conduct when exploring an association with another firm and is beyond the scope of these Rules.

[14] Any information disclosed pursuant to paragraph (b)(7) may be used or further disclosed only to the extent necessary to detect and resolve conflicts of interest. Paragraph (b)(7) does not restrict the use of information acquired by means independent of any disclosure pursuant to paragraph (b)(7). Paragraph (b)(7) also does not affect the disclosure of information within a law firm when the disclosure is otherwise authorized, see Comment [5], such as when a lawyer in a firm discloses information to another lawyer in the same firm to detect and resolve conflicts of interest that could arise in connection with undertaking a new representation.

[15] A lawyer may be ordered to reveal information relating to the representation of a client by a court or by another tribunal or governmental entity claiming authority pursuant to other law to compel the disclosure. Absent informed consent of the client to do otherwise, the lawyer should assert on behalf of the client all nonfrivolous claims that the order is not authorized by other law or that the information sought is protected against disclosure by the attorney-client privilege or other applicable law. In the event of an adverse ruling, the lawyer must consult with the client about the possibility of appeal to the extent required by Rule 1.4. Unless review is sought, however, paragraph (b)(6) permits the lawyer to comply with the court's order.

[16] Paragraph (b) permits disclosure only to the extent the lawyer reasonably believes the disclosure is necessary to accomplish one of the purposes specified. Where practicable, the lawyer should first seek to persuade the client to take suitable action to obviate the need for disclosure. In any case, a disclosure adverse to the client's interest should be no greater than the lawyer reasonably believes necessary to accomplish the purpose. If the disclosure will be made in connection with a judicial proceeding, the disclosure should be made in a manner that limits access to the information to the tribunal or other persons having a need to know it and appropriate protective orders or other arrangements should be sought by the lawyer to the fullest extent practicable.

[17] Paragraph (b) permits but does not require the disclosure of information relating to a client's representation to accomplish the purposes specified in paragraphs (b)(1) through (b)(6). In exercising the discretion conferred by this Rule, the lawyer may consider such factors as the nature of the lawyer's relationship with the client and with those who might be injured by the client, the lawyer's own involvement in the transaction and factors that may extenuate the conduct in question. A lawyer's decision not to disclose as permitted by paragraph (b) does not violate this Rule. Disclosure may be required, however, by other Rules. Some Rules require disclosure only if such disclosure would be permitted by paragraph (b). See Rules 1.2(d), 4.1(b), 8.1 and 8.3. Rule 3.3, on the other hand, requires

disclosure in some circumstances regardless of whether such disclosure is permitted by this Rule. See Rule 3.3(c).

Acting Competently to Preserve Confidentiality

[18] Paragraph (c) requires a lawyer to act competently to safeguard information relating to the representation of a client against unauthorized access by third parties and against inadvertent or unauthorized disclosure by the lawyer or other persons who are participating in the representation of the client or who are subject to the lawyer's supervision. See Rules 1.1, 5.1 and 5.3. The unauthorized access to, or the inadvertent or unauthorized disclosure of, information relating to the representation of a client does not constitute a violation of paragraph (c) if the lawyer has made reasonable efforts to prevent the access or disclosure. Factors to be considered in determining the reasonableness of the lawyer's efforts include, but are not limited to, the sensitivity of the information, the likelihood of disclosure if additional safeguards are not employed, the cost of employing additional safeguards, the difficulty of implementing the safeguards, and the extent to which the safeguards adversely affect the lawyer's ability to represent clients (e.g., by making a device or important piece of software excessively difficult to use). A client may require the lawyer to implement special security measures not required by this Rule or may give informed consent to forgo security measures that would otherwise be required by this Rule. Whether a lawyer may be required to take additional steps to safeguard a client's information in order to comply with other law, such as state and federal laws that govern data privacy or that impose notification requirements upon the loss of, or unauthorized access to, electronic information, is beyond the scope of these Rules. For a lawyer's duties when sharing information with nonlawyers outside the lawyer's own firm, see Rule 5.3, Comments [3]-[4].

[19] When transmitting a communication that includes information relating to the representation of a client, the lawyer must take reasonable precautions to prevent the information from coming into the hands of unintended recipients. This duty, however, does not require that the lawyer use special security measures if the method of communication affords a reasonable expectation of privacy. Special circumstances, however, may warrant special precautions. Factors to be considered in determining the reasonableness of the lawyer's expectation of confidentiality include the sensitivity of the information and the extent to which the privacy of the communication is protected by law or by a confidentiality agreement. A client may require the lawyer to implement special security measures not required by this Rule or may give informed consent to the use of a means of communication that would otherwise be prohibited by this Rule. Whether a lawyer may be required to take additional steps in order to comply with other law, such as state and federal laws that govern data privacy, is beyond the scope of these Rules.

Former Client

[20] The duty of confidentiality continues after the client-lawyer relationship has terminated. See Rule 1.9(c)(2). See Rule 1.9(c)(1) for the prohibition against using such information to the disadvantage of the former client.

ANNOTATIONS
Scope of Confidentiality Obligation
A lawyer's duty of confidentiality is significantly broader than many lawyers understand. Because this rule prohibits a lawyer from revealing "information relating to representation of a client," it is not limited merely to matters communicated in confidence by the client. *See* ABA Model Rules of Prof'l Conduct r. 1.6 cmt. 5. Thus, this rule prohibits disclosure of confidential information from any source, including from third parties and from documents prepared by third parties. When in doubt, however, the lawyer should seek client consent to disclose the information in question.

A lawyer must preserve the confidences of prospective clients, current clients, and former clients. "This obligation continues even after termination of the attorney-client relationship. This duty of confidentiality is broader than the evidentiary attorney-client privilege and applies not only to matters communicated to the attorney in confidence by the client, but to all information relating to the representation, whatever its source." *State v. Tensley*, 955 So. 2d 227, 242 (La. Ct. App. 2d Cir. 2007).

A lawyer has no duty to keep confidential matters concerning a client that are not related to the representation of the client. Specifically, Rule 1.6 does not disqualify a lawyer from being a witness; and under the rule a lawyer may reveal information unrelated to the representation of a client. *Bernard v. Lott*, 610 So. 2d 1117, 1118 (La. Ct. App. 5th Cir. 1992) (holding that the lawyer was not barred by Rule 1.6 from testifying on matters not related to the representation of the client; namely, the client's consumption of alcohol and drugs and the client's ability to attend parties and date).

When Confidentiality Obligation Attaches
A lawyer's duty of confidentiality attaches even prior to the formal commencement of a lawyer-client relationship. Therefore, a lawyer must maintain the confidentiality of information learned during the initial consultation with a prospective client. *See* La. Rules of Prof'l Conduct r. 1.18 (2004) (addressing duties owed to prospective clients); Restatement (Third) of the Law Governing Lawyers § 59 cmt. c (2000); *id.* at § 15(1)(a) and cmt. c; *see* ABA Comm'n on Ethics and Prof'l Responsibility, Formal Op. 90-358 (1990).

Protecting Confidential Information When Using Digital Means of Communication
Whether it is reasonable for a lawyer to conduct confidential communications using unencrypted email, cordless phones, cellular phones, or wireless messaging is often a source of concern.[82] To address these concerns, on May 22, 2017, the ABA Standing Committee on Ethics and Professional Responsibility issued a new formal opinion on Securing Communication of Protected Client Information. *See* ABA Formal Op. 477R

---

[82] Considering that all persons now have a federally-protected right of privacy when communicating through any type of phone, *see* 18 U.S.C. §§ 2510-2511, an argument may be made that it is almost always reasonable for a lawyer to exchange confidential information through such devices.

(May 22, 2017). In so doing, the committee updated a 1999 opinion on the topic because "the role and risks of technology in the practice of law have evolved" over time.

The regulatory framework governing a lawyer's use of electronic technology for communication is built on reasonableness. A lawyer must be competent by exercising the knowledge, skill, thoroughness, and preparation "reasonably necessary" for the representation. *See* ABA Model Rules of Prof'l Conduct r. 1.1. Further, a lawyer must use "reasonable efforts" to prevent the inadvertent or unauthorized disclosure of client information. *See id.* r. 1.6(c). To comply with these standards, a lawyer must keep "abreast of knowledge of the benefits and risks associated with relevant technology." *See id.* r. 1.1 cmt. 8.

What is "reasonable," of course, changes with the circumstances. Among the factors a lawyer should consider in handling electronic information are the following:

- the sensitivity of the information;

- the likelihood of disclosure if additional safeguards are not employed;

- the cost of employing additional safeguards;

- the difficulty of implementing the safeguards; and,

- the extent to which the safeguards adversely affect the lawyer's ability to represent clients.

See id. r. 1.6 cmt. 18. Given these indeterminate standards, what's a lawyer to do? The opinion offers this advice.

First, a lawyer needs to understand the nature of the threats to security. If the information in question is at high risk for cyber intrusion (such as information relating to trade secrets, mergers, and the like), then "greater effort is warranted" to protect the information.

Second, a lawyer needs to understand how electronic communications are created, where the data is stored, and what "avenues exist to access the information." Only then can the lawyer evaluate each device and access point for vulnerabilities.

Third, a lawyer needs to "understand and use reasonable electronic security measures." This is probably the most practical advice in the opinion. For example, a lawyer should understand how to use "secure internet access methods to communicate, access and store client information (such as through secure Wi-Fi, the use of a Virtual Private Network, or another secure internet portal), using unique complex passwords, changed periodically, implementing firewalls and anti-Malware/AntiSpyware/Antivirus software on all devices upon which client confidential information is transmitted or stored, and applying all necessary security patches and updates to operational and communications software."

Fourth, a lawyer needs to use "different levels of protection" when called for by the circumstances. If information is highly sensitive, "a lawyer should encrypt the transmission," "consider the use of password protection for any attachments," or "consider the use of a well vetted and secure third-party cloud based file storage system to exchange documents normally attached to emails."

Fifth, a lawyer should mark sensitive communications as "privileged and confidential." Such a "clear and conspicuous" label could trigger an inadvertent recipient's obligations under Model Rule 4.4(b) to "promptly notify" the sender of the error.

Sixth, a lawyer should "establish policies and procedures, and periodically train employees, subordinates and others assisting in the delivery of legal services, in the use of reasonably secure methods of electronic communications with clients." A lawyer should also assure that vendors retained by the lawyer protect client information.

In conclusion, the opinion advises that a lawyer should get informed consent from the lawyer's client "as to how to appropriately and safely use technology in their communication." But even without such informed consent, unencrypted email and ordinary cloud-storage facilities (such as Dropbox) are almost always fine. "Special security precautions" are necessary only when "required by an agreement with the client or by law, or when the nature of the information requires a higher degree of security." Which is to say, über-security measures needn't be used often. But, ordinary digital hygiene is required. And unfortunately, practices that are "ordinary" to those with basic technological competence—things like using complex passwords, enabling two-factor authentication, and regularly updating software—are sometimes not ordinarily used by ordinary lawyers. Therein lies the true risk to client data integrity and confidentiality.

Disclosure of Confidential Information

A lawyer is impliedly authorized to reveal confidential information in order to carry out the representation. Indeed, a lawyer routinely discloses confidential information in responding to discovery requests, attempting to negotiate settlements, eliciting testimony from witnesses, or failing to object to evidence offered by opposing counsel, among other circumstances. In so doing, a lawyer sometimes makes tactical decisions to disclose unfavorable information. Such disclosures should not subject the lawyer to discipline if, at the time of the disclosure, the lawyer reasonably believed that making the disclosure would advance the interests of the client. *See* Restatement (Third) of the Law Governing Lawyers § 61 cmt. d (2000); ABA Model Rules of Prof'l Conduct, Preamble and Scope ("[D]isciplinary assessment of a lawyer's conduct will be made on the basis of the facts and circumstances as they existed at the time of the conduct in question.")

The Louisiana Rules of Professional Conduct expressly permit disclosure only of generally-known information relating to former clients. *Compare* La. Rules of Prof'l Conduct r. 1.6(a) (2004) *with* ABA Model Rules of Prof'l Conduct r. 1.9(c)(1) (permitting disclosure of information relating to a former client "when the information has become generally known"). Nevertheless, a lawyer arguably should be permitted to disclose information relating to current clients that has become generally known to the public. *See* Restatement (Third) of the Law Governing Lawyers § 59 (2000) (stating that confidential client information does not include "information that is generally known"). Note, however, that merely because information has become known to one or more third persons does not mean that it has become "generally known" to the public. *Id.* at cmt. d. When information has become "generally known," is often difficult to discern. For example, the recordation of a document in the public records may waive any claim that the recorded information remains confidential, although as a practical matter few people peruse mortgage and conveyance records. *See In re Sellers*, 669 So. 2d 1204, 1206 (La. 1996).

When Disclosure is Required by Other Rules and Laws

This rule permits a lawyer to disclose confidential information when such disclosure is required by other rules or laws. For example, a lawyer may disclose otherwise confidential information that is responsive to lawful discovery requests and subpoenas. Likewise, a lawyer must disclose confidential information when necessary to avoid assisting the client in a crime or fraud or to remedy past client perjury. *See* La. Rules of Prof'l Conduct r. 3.3(a) (2004). Finally, a lawyer must disclose confidential information when required by law or court order. *See* Restatement (Third) of the Law Governing Lawyers § 63 (2000). For example, a prosecutor must disclose exculpatory evidence to a criminal defendant irrespective that such information may otherwise be confidential. *See Brady v. Maryland*, 373 U.S. 83 (1963) (holding that the failure to disclose evidence material to guilt violated the Due Process Clause). A lawyer compelled to disclose confidential information should take reasonably appropriate steps to assert in good faith that the requested information is protected. Moreover, the lawyer should limit the scope of disclosure to that which is required. *See* Restatement (Third) of the Law Governing Lawyers § 63 (2000).

Lawyer's Personal Use of Confidential Information

Under general mandate (agency) principles, a lawyer owes a fiduciary duty of loyalty to the client. As a fiduciary, a lawyer may not personally profit from the use of confidential information in a manner that is detrimental to the client. *See, e.g.*, La. Rules of Prof'l Conduct r. 1.8(b) (2004); *Defcon, Inc. v. Webb*, 687 So. 2d 639, 643 (La. Ct. App. 2d Cir. 1997) (outlining the elements of a claim against a fiduciary for misappropriation of confidential information); *Woodward v. Steed*, 680 So. 2d 1320, 1326 (La. Ct. App. 2d Cir. 1996); *see also Neal v. Daniels*, 47 So. 2d 44, 45 (La. 1950) (agent may not "speculate for his gain in the subject-matter of his employment"); *see generally* Restatement (Third) of the Law Governing Lawyers § 60(2) (2000) ("A lawyer who uses confidential information of a client for the lawyer's pecuniary gain other than in the practice of law must account to the client for any profits made."); Restatement (Second) of Agency § 395 (stating that an agent must not use confidential information "on his own account").

Whether a lawyer may personally profit from the use of confidential information when it does not harm a client is less clear. Under Louisiana Rule of Professional Conduct 1.8(b), a lawyer is prohibited only from using confidential information "to the disadvantage of the client." *See* La. Rules of Prof'l Conduct r. 1.8(b) (2004). But under Louisiana mandate law, a mandatary must account to his or her principal for all profits or advantages obtained in the course of the mandate. *See* La. Civ. Code art. 3004; *id.* at art. 3005 cmt. b ("In the absence of contrary agreement, the mandatary is not entitled to apply to his own use the money or other property of the principal."); *Noe v. Roussel*, 310 So. 2d 806, 818-19 (La. 1975); *Neal*, 47 So. 2d at 44; *Foreman v. Pelican Stores*, 21 So. 2d 64 (La. Ct. App. 2d Cir. 1944); *see also* Restatement (Third) of the Law Governing Lawyers § 60(2) (2000) (requiring a lawyer to account to client for profits made through the use of confidential information). How a Louisiana court would resolve this issue is uncertain.

Applicability to Nonlawyer Support Personnel

Rule 1.6 obviously is not enforceable against a nonlawyer. However, a lawyer may be subject to discipline for disclosures of confidential information by a nonlawyer with whom the lawyer works. Therefore, a lawyer must take reasonable measures to ensure that support personnel protect confidential information. Reasonable measures may include devising policies and practices concerning confidential information, communicating these policies and practices to those with whom the lawyer works, and then enforcing these directives. Whether a lawyer's efforts in this regard are reasonable turns on such factors as "the duties of the agent or other person, the extent to which disclosure would adversely affect the client, the extent of prior training and experience of the person, the existence of other assurances such as adequate supervision by senior employees, and the customs and reputation of independent contractors." Restatement (Third) of the Law Governing Lawyers § 60 cmt. d (2000).

Relationship to Attorney-Client Privilege

Rule 1.6 does not establish an evidentiary privilege against disclosure of confidential information; rather, it establishes a broader ethical duty that is enforced primarily through the lawyer disciplinary system. Thus, a lawyer cannot use this rule as a basis for refusing to divulge confidential information when the lawyer otherwise would be compelled to do so by law or court order. *See* ABA Model Rules of Prof'l Conduct r. 1.6 cmt. 3. Articles 506 through 509 of the Louisiana Code of Evidence address the "lawyer-client" evidentiary privilege. *See* La. Code Evid. arts. 506-509; *see also McGovern v. Moore*, No. 5:13-CV-1353, 2013 WL 5781315 (W.D. La. Oct. 25, 2013) (holding that, where attorney-client privilege does not apply, professional duty of confidentiality under Rule 1.6 cannot be used to suppress evidence).

Disciplinary Sanctions

Absent aggravating or mitigating circumstances, the following sanctions are generally appropriate in cases involving the failure to preserve client confidences: *disbarment*, when the lawyer reveals confidential information with the intent to benefit himself or another, and the disclosure causes injury or potential injury to the client; *suspension*, when the lawyer knowingly reveals confidential information, and the disclosure causes injury or potential injury to the client; *reprimand*, when the lawyer negligently reveals confidential information and the disclosure causes injury or potential injury to the client; and, *admonition*, when the lawyer negligently reveals confidential information, and the disclosure causes little or no actual or potential injury to the client. *See* ABA Stds. for Imposing Lawyer Sanctions stds. 4.21-4.24 (1992).

RULE 1.7. CONFLICT OF INTEREST—CURRENT CLIENTS

(a) Except as provided in paragraph (b), a lawyer shall not represent a client if the representation involves a concurrent conflict of interest. A concurrent conflict of interest exists if:

(1) the representation of one client will be directly adverse to another client; or

(2) there is a significant risk that the representation of one or more clients will be materially limited by the lawyer's responsibilities to another client, a former client or a third person or by a personal interest of the lawyer.

(b) Notwithstanding the existence of a concurrent conflict of interest under paragraph (a), a lawyer may represent a client if:

(1) the lawyer reasonably believes that the lawyer will be able to provide competent and diligent representation to each affected client;

(2) the representation is not prohibited by law;

(3) the representation does not involve the assertion of a claim by one client against another client represented by the lawyer in the same litigation or other proceeding before a tribunal; and

(4) each affected client gives informed consent, confirmed in writing.

BACKGROUND

The Louisiana Supreme Court adopted this rule on January 20, 2004. It became effective on March 1, 2004, and has not been amended since. This rule is identical to ABA Model Rule of Prof'l Conduct 1.7 (2002). The ABA made a number of notable revisions to Model Rule 1.7 in 2002.

Prior to 2002, the relationship between the two paragraphs of former Model Rule 1.7 was not well understood. Lawyers frequently struggled with identifying a direct-adversity conflict under former paragraph (a) when the representation was still problematic because it involved a clear conflict under the "material limitation" standard of former paragraph (b). *See* ABA Ethics 2000 Commission Revision Notes to Model Rule 1.7 (2002). To address this problem, the ABA defined "conflict of interest" to include both direct-adversity conflicts and material-limitation conflicts. *See id.*

Material-Limitation Conflicts

As to material-limitation conflicts, the 2002 revision to Model Rule 1.7 limited the scope of such conflicts to situations in which there is "a significant risk" that the representation will be impaired, rather than to situations in which it "may" be impaired, as was the case prior to the revision. *See id.*

Consentability

The revised model rule makes clear that in certain situations a conflict may not be waived by the client. *See* ABA Model Rules of Prof'l Conduct r. 1.7(b). That is, the representation may not go forward even with the client's consent. Unlike the former Rule, the revised Rule contains a single standard of consentability and informed consent, applicable both to direct-adversity and material-limitation conflicts. This standard is set forth in a separate paragraph, both to reflect the separate steps required in analyzing conflicts (first identify potentially impermissible conflicts, then determine if the representation is permissible with the client's consent), and to highlight the fact that not all conflicts are consentable. *See id.*

Under the former model rule, consentability turned on a determination that the conflict would "not adversely affect the representation." According to the ABA, the difficulty with this standard was that in order to determine that a conflict existed in the first place, the lawyer had to have already determined that the lawyer's duties or interests were likely to "materially limit" the representation. The ABA believed that there is a subtle difference between "material limitation" and "adverse affect on" the representation. As a result, lawyers were understandably confused regarding the circumstances under which consent may be sought. *See id.*

"Informed Consent"

In revised paragraph (b)(4), the ABA substituted "informed consent" of the client for "consent after consultation." The ABA believed that "consultation" did not adequately convey the requirement that the client receive full disclosure of the nature and implications of a lawyer's conflict of interest. The ABA chose the term "informed consent" because it already has a fairly well-accepted meaning in other contexts. That term, which is used throughout the Rules in place of "consent after consultation," is defined in Rule 1.0(e).

COMMENTS TO ABA MODEL RULE 1.7

General Principles

[1] Loyalty and independent judgment are essential elements in the lawyer's relationship to a client. Concurrent conflicts of interest can arise from the lawyer's responsibilities to another client, a former client or a third person or from the lawyer's own interests. For specific Rules regarding certain concurrent conflicts of interest, see Rule 1.8. For former client conflicts of interest, see Rule 1.9. For conflicts of interest involving prospective clients, see Rule 1.18. For definitions of "informed consent" and "confirmed in writing," see Rule 1.0(e) and (b).

[2] Resolution of a conflict of interest problem under this Rule requires the lawyer to: 1) clearly identify the client or clients; 2) determine whether a conflict of interest exists; 3)

95

decide whether the representation may be undertaken despite the existence of a conflict, i.e., whether the conflict is consentable; and 4) if so, consult with the clients affected under paragraph (a) and obtain their informed consent, confirmed in writing. The clients affected under paragraph (a) include both of the clients referred to in paragraph (a)(1) and the one or more clients whose representation might be materially limited under paragraph (a)(2).

[3] A conflict of interest may exist before representation is undertaken, in which event the representation must be declined, unless the lawyer obtains the informed consent of each client under the conditions of paragraph (b). To determine whether a conflict of interest exists, a lawyer should adopt reasonable procedures, appropriate for the size and type of firm and practice, to determine in both litigation and non-litigation matters the persons and issues involved. See also Comment to Rule 5.1. Ignorance caused by a failure to institute such procedures will not excuse a lawyer's violation of this Rule. As to whether a client-lawyer relationship exists or, having once been established, is continuing, see Comment to Rule 1.3 and Scope.

[4] If a conflict arises after representation has been undertaken, the lawyer ordinarily must withdraw from the representation, unless the lawyer has obtained the informed consent of the client under the conditions of paragraph (b). See Rule 1.16. Where more than one client is involved, whether the lawyer may continue to represent any of the clients is determined both by the lawyer's ability to comply with duties owed to the former client and by the lawyer's ability to represent adequately the remaining client or clients, given the lawyer's duties to the former client. See Rule 1.9. See also Comments [5] and [29].

[5] Unforeseeable developments, such as changes in corporate and other organizational affiliations or the addition or realignment of parties in litigation, might create conflicts in the midst of a representation, as when a company sued by the lawyer on behalf of one client is bought by another client represented by the lawyer in an unrelated matter. Depending on the circumstances, the lawyer may have the option to withdraw from one of the representations in order to avoid the conflict. The lawyer must seek court approval where necessary and take steps to minimize harm to the clients. See Rule 1.16. The lawyer must continue to protect the confidences of the client from whose representation the lawyer has withdrawn. See Rule 1.9(c).

Identifying Conflicts of Interest: Directly Adverse

[6] Loyalty to a current client prohibits undertaking representation directly adverse to that client without that client's informed consent. Thus, absent consent, a lawyer may not act as an advocate in one matter against a person the lawyer represents in some other matter, even when the matters are wholly unrelated. The client as to whom the representation is directly adverse is likely to feel betrayed, and the resulting damage to the client-lawyer relationship is likely to impair the lawyer's ability to represent the client effectively. In addition, the client on whose behalf the adverse representation is undertaken reasonably may fear that the lawyer will pursue that client's case less effectively out of deference to the other client, i.e., that the representation may be materially limited by the lawyer's interest in retaining the current client. Similarly, a directly adverse conflict may arise when a

lawyer is required to cross-examine a client who appears as a witness in a lawsuit involving another client, as when the testimony will be damaging to the client who is represented in the lawsuit. On the other hand, simultaneous representation in unrelated matters of clients whose interests are only economically adverse, such as representation of competing economic enterprises in unrelated litigation, does not ordinarily constitute a conflict of interest and thus may not require consent of the respective clients.

[7] Directly adverse conflicts can also arise in transactional matters. For example, if a lawyer is asked to represent the seller of a business in negotiations with a buyer represented by the lawyer, not in the same transaction but in another, unrelated matter, the lawyer could not undertake the representation without the informed consent of each client.

Identifying Conflicts of Interest: Material Limitation
[8] Even where there is no direct adverseness, a conflict of interest exists if there is a significant risk that a lawyer's ability to consider, recommend or carry out an appropriate course of action for the client will be materially limited as a result of the lawyer's other responsibilities or interests. For example, a lawyer asked to represent several individuals seeking to form a joint venture is likely to be materially limited in the lawyer's ability to recommend or advocate all possible positions that each might take because of the lawyer's duty of loyalty to the others. The conflict in effect forecloses alternatives that would otherwise be available to the client. The mere possibility of subsequent harm does not itself require disclosure and consent. The critical questions are the likelihood that a difference in interests will eventuate and, if it does, whether it will materially interfere with the lawyer's independent professional judgment in considering alternatives or foreclose courses of action that reasonably should be pursued on behalf of the client.

Lawyer's Responsibilities to Former Clients and Other Third Persons

[9] In addition to conflicts with other current clients, a lawyer's duties of loyalty and independence may be materially limited by responsibilities to former clients under Rule 1.9 or by the lawyer's responsibilities to other persons, such as fiduciary duties arising from a lawyer's service as a trustee, executor or corporate director.

Personal Interest Conflicts
[10] The lawyer's own interests should not be permitted to have an adverse effect on representation of a client. For example, if the probity of a lawyer's own conduct in a transaction is in serious question, it may be difficult or impossible for the lawyer to give a client detached advice. Similarly, when a lawyer has discussions concerning possible employment with an opponent of the lawyer's client, or with a law firm representing the opponent, such discussions could materially limit the lawyer's representation of the client. In addition, a lawyer may not allow related business interests to affect representation, for example, by referring clients to an enterprise in which the lawyer has an undisclosed financial interest. See Rule 1.8 for specific Rules pertaining to a number of personal interest conflicts, including business transactions with clients. See also Rule 1.10 (personal interest conflicts under Rule 1.7 ordinarily are not imputed to other lawyers in a law firm).

[11] When lawyers representing different clients in the same matter or in substantially related matters are closely related by blood or marriage, there may be a significant risk that client confidences will be revealed and that the lawyer's family relationship will interfere with both loyalty and independent professional judgment. As a result, each client is entitled to know of the existence and implications of the relationship between the lawyers before the lawyer agrees to undertake the representation. Thus, a lawyer related to another lawyer, e.g., as parent, child, sibling or spouse, ordinarily may not represent a client in a matter where that lawyer is representing another party, unless each client gives informed consent. The disqualification arising from a close family relationship is personal and ordinarily is not imputed to members of firms with whom the lawyers are associated. See Rule 1.10.

[12] A lawyer is prohibited from engaging in sexual relationships with a client unless the sexual relationship predates the formation of the client-lawyer relationship. See Rule 1.8(j).

Interest of Person Paying for a Lawyer's Service

[13] A lawyer may be paid from a source other than the client, including a co-client, if the client is informed of that fact and consents and the arrangement does not compromise the lawyer's duty of loyalty or independent judgment to the client. See Rule 1.8(f). If acceptance of the payment from any other source presents a significant risk that the lawyer's representation of the client will be materially limited by the lawyer's own interest in accommodating the person paying the lawyer's fee or by the lawyer's responsibilities to a payer who is also a co-client, then the lawyer must comply with the requirements of paragraph (b) before accepting the representation, including determining whether the conflict is consentable and, if so, that the client has adequate information about the material risks of the representation.

Prohibited Representations

[14] Ordinarily, clients may consent to representation notwithstanding a conflict. However, as indicated in paragraph (b), some conflicts are nonconsentable, meaning that the lawyer involved cannot properly ask for such agreement or provide representation on the basis of the client's consent. When the lawyer is representing more than one client, the question of consentability must be resolved as to each client.

[15] Consentability is typically determined by considering whether the interests of the clients will be adequately protected if the clients are permitted to give their informed consent to representation burdened by a conflict of interest. Thus, under paragraph (b)(1), representation is prohibited if in the circumstances the lawyer cannot reasonably conclude that the lawyer will be able to provide competent and diligent representation. See Rule 1.1 (competence) and Rule 1.3 (diligence).

[16] Paragraph (b)(2) describes conflicts that are nonconsentable because the representation is prohibited by applicable law. For example, in some states substantive law provides that the same lawyer may not represent more than one defendant in a capital case, even with the consent of the clients, and under federal criminal statutes certain representations by a former government lawyer are prohibited, despite the informed

consent of the former client. In addition, decisional law in some states limits the ability of a governmental client, such as a municipality, to consent to a conflict of interest.

[17] Paragraph (b)(3) describes conflicts that are nonconsentable because of the institutional interest in vigorous development of each client's position when the clients are aligned directly against each other in the same litigation or other proceeding before a tribunal. Whether clients are aligned directly against each other within the meaning of this paragraph requires examination of the context of the proceeding. Although this paragraph does not preclude a lawyer's multiple representation of adverse parties to a mediation (because mediation is not a proceeding before a "tribunal" under Rule 1.0(m)), such representation may be precluded by paragraph (b)(1).

Informed Consent

[18] Informed consent requires that each affected client be aware of the relevant circumstances and of the material and reasonably foreseeable ways that the conflict could have adverse effects on the interests of that client. See Rule 1.0(e) (informed consent). The information required depends on the nature of the conflict and the nature of the risks involved. When representation of multiple clients in a single matter is undertaken, the information must include the implications of the common representation, including possible effects on loyalty, confidentiality and the attorney-client privilege and the advantages and risks involved. See Comments [30] and [31] (effect of common representation on confidentiality).

[19] Under some circumstances it may be impossible to make the disclosure necessary to obtain consent. For example, when the lawyer represents different clients in related matters and one of the clients refuses to consent to the disclosure necessary to permit the other client to make an informed decision, the lawyer cannot properly ask the latter to consent. In some cases the alternative to common representation can be that each party may have to obtain separate representation with the possibility of incurring additional costs. These costs, along with the benefits of securing separate representation, are factors that may be considered by the affected client in determining whether common representation is in the client's interests.

Consent Confirmed in Writing

[20] Paragraph (b) requires the lawyer to obtain the informed consent of the client, confirmed in writing. Such a writing may consist of a document executed by the client or one that the lawyer promptly records and transmits to the client following an oral consent. See Rule 1.0(b). *See also* Rule 1.0(n) (writing includes electronic transmission). If it is not feasible to obtain or transmit the writing at the time the client gives informed consent, then the lawyer must obtain or transmit it within a reasonable time thereafter. See Rule 1.0(b). The requirement of a writing does not supplant the need in most cases for the lawyer to talk with the client, to explain the risks and advantages, if any, of representation burdened with a conflict of interest, as well as reasonably available alternatives, and to afford the client a reasonable opportunity to consider the risks and alternatives and to raise questions and concerns. Rather, the writing is required in order to impress upon clients

the seriousness of the decision the client is being asked to make and to avoid disputes or ambiguities that might later occur in the absence of a writing.

Revoking Consent

[21] A client who has given consent to a conflict may revoke the consent and, like any other client, may terminate the lawyer's representation at any time. Whether revoking consent to the client's own representation precludes the lawyer from continuing to represent other clients depends on the circumstances, including the nature of the conflict, whether the client revoked consent because of a material change in circumstances, the reasonable expectations of the other client and whether material detriment to the other clients or the lawyer would result.

Consent to Future Conflict

[22] Whether a lawyer may properly request a client to waive conflicts that might arise in the future is subject to the test of paragraph (b). The effectiveness of such waivers is generally determined by the extent to which the client reasonably understands the material risks that the waiver entails. The more comprehensive the explanation of the types of future representations that might arise and the actual and reasonably foreseeable adverse consequences of those representations, the greater the likelihood that the client will have the requisite understanding. Thus, if the client agrees to consent to a particular type of conflict with which the client is already familiar, then the consent ordinarily will be effective with regard to that type of conflict. If the consent is general and open-ended, then the consent ordinarily will be ineffective, because it is not reasonably likely that the client will have understood the material risks involved. On the other hand, if the client is an experienced user of the legal services involved and is reasonably informed regarding the risk that a conflict may arise, such consent is more likely to be effective, particularly if, e.g., the client is independently represented by other counsel in giving consent and the consent is limited to future conflicts unrelated to the subject of the representation. In any case, advance consent cannot be effective if the circumstances that materialize in the future are such as would make the conflict nonconsentable under paragraph (b).

Conflicts in Litigation

[23] Paragraph (b)(3) prohibits representation of opposing parties in the same litigation, regardless of the clients' consent. On the other hand, simultaneous representation of parties whose interests in litigation may conflict, such as coplaintiffs or codefendants, is governed by paragraph (a)(2). A conflict may exist by reason of substantial discrepancy in the parties' testimony, incompatibility in positions in relation to an opposing party or the fact that there are substantially different possibilities of settlement of the claims or liabilities in question. Such conflicts can arise in criminal cases as well as civil. The potential for conflict of interest in representing multiple defendants in a criminal case is so grave that ordinarily a lawyer should decline to represent more than one codefendant. On the other hand, common representation of persons having similar interests in civil litigation is proper if the requirements of paragraph (b) are met.

[24] Ordinarily a lawyer may take inconsistent legal positions in different tribunals at different times on behalf of different clients. The mere fact that advocating a legal position

100

on behalf of one client might create precedent adverse to the interests of a client represented by the lawyer in an unrelated matter does not create a conflict of interest. A conflict of interest exists, however, if there is a significant risk that a lawyer's action on behalf of one client will materially limit the lawyer's effectiveness in representing another client in a different case; for example, when a decision favoring one client will create a precedent likely to seriously weaken the position taken on behalf of the other client. Factors relevant in determining whether the clients need to be advised of the risk include: where the cases are pending, whether the issue is substantive or procedural, the temporal relationship between the matters, the significance of the issue to the immediate and long-term interests of the clients involved and the clients' reasonable expectations in retaining the lawyer. If there is significant risk of material limitation, then absent informed consent of the affected clients, the lawyer must refuse one of the representations or withdraw from one or both matters.

[25] When a lawyer represents or seeks to represent a class of plaintiffs or defendants in a class-action lawsuit, unnamed members of the class are ordinarily not considered to be clients of the lawyer for purposes of applying paragraph (a)(1) of this Rule. Thus, the lawyer does not typically need to get the consent of such a person before representing a client suing the person in an unrelated matter. Similarly, a lawyer seeking to represent an opponent in a class action does not typically need the consent of an unnamed member of the class whom the lawyer represents in an unrelated matter.

Nonlitigation Conflicts

[26] Conflicts of interest under paragraphs (a)(1) and (a)(2) arise in contexts other than litigation. For a discussion of directly adverse conflicts in transactional matters, see Comment [7]. Relevant factors in determining whether there is significant potential for material limitation include the duration and intimacy of the lawyer's relationship with the client or clients involved, the functions being performed by the lawyer, the likelihood that disagreements will arise and the likely prejudice to the client from the conflict. The question is often one of proximity and degree. See Comment [8].

[27] For example, conflict questions may arise in estate planning and estate administration. A lawyer may be called upon to prepare wills for several family members, such as husband and wife, and, depending upon the circumstances, a conflict of interest may be present. In estate administration the identity of the client may be unclear under the law of a particular jurisdiction. Under one view, the client is the fiduciary; under another view the client is the estate or trust, including its beneficiaries. In order to comply with conflict of interest rules, the lawyer should make clear the lawyer's relationship to the parties involved.

[28] Whether a conflict is consentable depends on the circumstances. For example, a lawyer may not represent multiple parties to a negotiation whose interests are fundamentally antagonistic to each other, but common representation is permissible where the clients are generally aligned in interest even though there is some difference in interest among them. Thus, a lawyer may seek to establish or adjust a relationship between clients on an amicable and mutually advantageous basis; for example, in helping to organize a business in which two or more clients are entrepreneurs, working out the

financial reorganization of an enterprise in which two or more clients have an interest or arranging a property distribution in settlement of an estate. The lawyer seeks to resolve potentially adverse interests by developing the parties' mutual interests. Otherwise, each party might have to obtain separate representation, with the possibility of incurring additional cost, complication or even litigation. Given these and other relevant factors, the clients may prefer that the lawyer act for all of them.

Special Considerations in Common Representation

[29] In considering whether to represent multiple clients in the same matter, a lawyer should be mindful that if the common representation fails because the potentially adverse interests cannot be reconciled, the result can be additional cost, embarrassment and recrimination. Ordinarily, the lawyer will be forced to withdraw from representing all of the clients if the common representation fails. In some situations, the risk of failure is so great that multiple representation is plainly impossible. For example, a lawyer cannot undertake common representation of clients where contentious litigation or negotiations between them are imminent or contemplated. Moreover, because the lawyer is required to be impartial between commonly represented clients, representation of multiple clients is improper when it is unlikely that impartiality can be maintained. Generally, if the relationship between the parties has already assumed antagonism, the possibility that the clients' interests can be adequately served by common representation is not very good. Other relevant factors are whether the lawyer subsequently will represent both parties on a continuing basis and whether the situation involves creating or terminating a relationship between the parties.

[30] A particularly important factor in determining the appropriateness of common representation is the effect on client-lawyer confidentiality and the attorney-client privilege. With regard to the attorney-client privilege, the prevailing rule is that, as between commonly represented clients, the privilege does not attach. Hence, it must be assumed that if litigation eventuates between the clients, the privilege will not protect any such communications, and the clients should be so advised.

[31] As to the duty of confidentiality, continued common representation will almost certainly be inadequate if one client asks the lawyer not to disclose to the other client information relevant to the common representation. This is so because the lawyer has an equal duty of loyalty to each client, and each client has the right to be informed of anything bearing on the representation that might affect that client's interests and the right to expect that the lawyer will use that information to that client's benefit. See Rule 1.4. The lawyer should, at the outset of the common representation and as part of the process of obtaining each client's informed consent, advise each client that information will be shared and that the lawyer will have to withdraw if one client decides that some matter material to the representation should be kept from the other. In limited circumstances, it may be appropriate for the lawyer to proceed with the representation when the clients have agreed, after being properly informed, that the lawyer will keep certain information confidential. For example, the lawyer may reasonably conclude that failure to disclose one client's trade secrets to another client will not adversely affect representation involving a

joint venture between the clients and agree to keep that information confidential with the informed consent of both clients.

[32] When seeking to establish or adjust a relationship between clients, the lawyer should make clear that the lawyer's role is not that of partisanship normally expected in other circumstances and, thus, that the clients may be required to assume greater responsibility for decisions than when each client is separately represented. Any limitations on the scope of the representation made necessary as a result of the common representation should be fully explained to the clients at the outset of the representation. See Rule 1.2(c).

[33] Subject to the above limitations, each client in the common representation has the right to loyal and diligent representation and the protection of Rule 1.9 concerning the obligations to a former client. The client also has the right to discharge the lawyer as stated in Rule 1.16.

Organizational Clients

[34] A lawyer who represents a corporation or other organization does not, by virtue of that representation, necessarily represent any constituent or affiliated organization, such as a parent or subsidiary. See Rule 1.13(a). Thus, the lawyer for an organization is not barred from accepting representation adverse to an affiliate in an unrelated matter, unless the circumstances are such that the affiliate should also be considered a client of the lawyer, there is an understanding between the lawyer and the organizational client that the lawyer will avoid representation adverse to the client's affiliates, or the lawyer's obligations to either the organizational client or the new client are likely to limit materially the lawyer's representation of the other client.

[35] A lawyer for a corporation or other organization who is also a member of its board of directors should determine whether the responsibilities of the two roles may conflict. The lawyer may be called on to advise the corporation in matters involving actions of the directors. Consideration should be given to the frequency with which such situations may arise, the potential intensity of the conflict, the effect of the lawyer's resignation from the board and the possibility of the corporation's obtaining legal advice from another lawyer in such situations. If there is material risk that the dual role will compromise the lawyer's independence of professional judgment, the lawyer should not serve as a director or should cease to act as the corporation's lawyer when conflicts of interest arise. The lawyer should advise the other members of the board that in some circumstances matters discussed at board meetings while the lawyer is present in the capacity of director might not be protected by the attorney-client privilege and that conflict of interest considerations might require the lawyer's recusal as a director or might require the lawyer and the lawyer's firm to decline representation of the corporation in a matter.

ANNOTATIONS
Generally
This rule implements one of the fundamental duties attendant to the lawyer-client relationship–the duty of loyalty. As a loyal fiduciary who must faithfully champion his clients' causes, a lawyer must avoid conflicts between the interests of the lawyer's current clients and those of other persons, including the lawyer himself, his other current clients,

past clients, and third parties. Unidentified or unresolved conflicts may lead to professional discipline, disqualification, fee forfeiture and malpractice liability. *See* Restatement (Third) of the Law Governing Lawyers § 121 cmt. f (2000).

Conflicts Involving a Lawyer's Personal Interest

A lawyer may not represent a client if that representation is materially and adversely affected by the lawyer's financial or other personal interests. *See, e.g.*, Restatement (Third) of the Law Governing Lawyers § 125 (2000). Although there exists no per se prohibition against engaging in sexual relations with clients in Louisiana,[83] such relationships sometimes can present a conflict between the lawyer's personal interest in the relationship and the client's interests. *See* ABA Comm. on Ethics and Professional Responsibility, Formal Op. 92-364 (1992); *see also In re Hammond*, 56 So. 3d 199, 213 (La. 2011) (disciplining lawyer who repeatedly engaged in sexual misconduct with clients for violating rule 1.7); and *In re Fuerst*, 157 So. 3d 569, 577 (La. 2014) (lawyer violated rule 1.7(a)(2) by having sexual relationship with client whose divorce was pending). The Louisiana Supreme Court has disciplined lawyers when personal relationships have interfered with their ability to exercise independent professional judgment and to render candid advice. *See, e.g., In re Bailey*, 115 So. 3d 458 (La. 2013) (finding violation for lawyer appointing wife as succession trustee over client's trust); *In re DeFrancesch*, 877 So. 2d 71 (La. 2004) (sanctioning lawyer for inappropriate sexual relations with client despite the existence of a preexisting relationship); *In re Schambach*, 726 So. 2d 892 (La. 1999); *In re Ashy*, 721 So. 2d 859 (La. 1998); *In re Ryland*, 985 So. 2d 71 (La. 2008).

Conflicts in Litigation

A lawyer typically may not represent a client in litigation if the lawyer will be called upon to cross-examine another (current or former) client as an adverse witness during the course of trial. *See State v. Olivieri*, 74 So. 3d 1191, 1194 (La. Ct. App. 5th Cir. 2011); *State v. Cisco*, 861 So. 2d 118, 129-30 (La. 2003); *see also* ABA Comm. on Ethics and Professional Responsibility, Formal Op. 92-367 (1992).

A lawyer must also be aware of a potential conflict of interest when representing multiple parties in a related matter although only one party is involved in litigation. In *King v. Martin*, No. 10-cv-1774, 2012 WL 4959485, at *4 (W.D. La. Oct. 16, 2012), the court found a conflict of interest between a lawyer representing a seller in a sale of immovable property while simultaneously representing the future purchaser of said property, who was not a party to the suit. The basis of the conflict of interest included the lawyer's previous knowledge of the initial disputed transaction in question; the "competing and conflicting" goals of the litigation between seller and the nonparty future purchaser; the nonparty's payment of legal fees to the lawyer; and the nonparty's veto power over settlements in the litigation. *Id.* at 2-4 (recognizing the existence of a conflict of interest; however, the lawyer's clients had properly waived the conflict of interest pursuant to Rule 1.7(b)).

---

[83] *Compare* La. Rules of Prof'l Conduct r. 1.8(j) (2004) ("Reserved") *with* Model Rules of Prof'l Conduct r. 1.8(j) (2002).

Conflicts in Insurance Defense Practice

Liability insurance policies typically require the insurer to indemnify and to defend the insured for covered claims. Because Louisiana's direct-action statute permits the assertion of claims against liability insurers, *see, e.g.*, La. Rev. Stat. Ann. § 22:1269, a Louisiana lawyer often represents both the insured and the insurer in litigation. As a result, the conflicts issues that arise in Louisiana insurance defense practice are potentially more vexing than those in jurisdictions that do not permit direct actions. Joint representation of the insured and insurer typically does not present a conflict of interest. After all, both the insured and the insurer have a common interest–resolving the claim quickly and inexpensively. However, in at least three instances, the interests of the insured and the insurer may diverge.

First, the interests of the insured and the insurer conflict when the insurer contends that there is no coverage for the claim asserted against the insured. In such a circumstance, the insurer typically provides a defense to the insured, but does so under a "reservation of rights." It is absolutely clear that a lawyer may not represent both the insured and insurer when the insurer denies coverage or reserves its right to deny coverage at a later date. *See, e.g., Emery v. Progressive Cas. Ins. Co.*, 49 So. 3d 17, 20-21 (La. Ct. App. 1st Cir. 2010); *Storm Drilling Co. v. Atlantic Richfield Corp.*, 386 F. Supp. 830, 832 (E.D. La. 1974); *Belanger v. Gabriel Chem., Inc.*, 787 So. 2d 559, 565 (La. Ct. App. 1st Cir. 2001) ("If an insurer chooses to represent the insured but deny coverage, separate counsel must be employed.").

Second, the interests of the insured and the insurer conflict when the claimant offers to settle a claim for an amount at or below policy limits, but the insurer prefers instead to press the matter to trial, potentially exposing the insured to a judgment in excess of policy limits. (As a practical matter, the increased risk to the insurance company of incurring liability for "bad faith" has reduced the occurrence of this conflict.) The lawyer in this situation must report the settlement offer to the insured and then determine whether continued representation of either the insured or the insurance company is appropriate.

Third, the interests of the insured and the insurer conflict when the insurer attempts to interfere with the lawyer's professional judgment in the handling of a matter on behalf of the insured. *See also* La. Rules of Prof'l Conduct r. 1.8(f) (2004) (prohibiting a lawyer from accepting compensation from third party when doing so interferes with the lawyer's professional judgment). For example, if the insurer directs the lawyer to limit the number of depositions taken in a matter and the lawyer believes that complying with that directive will result in incompetent representation of the insured, then the lawyer must consult with the insured and take appropriate action. *See* Restatement (Third) of the Law Governing Lawyers § 134(2)(a) (2000). Depending upon the circumstances, the lawyer facing such a conflict may make arrangements with the insured to pay for the necessary depositions, or withdraw from the representation.

Conflicts in Criminal Defense Practice

Conflicts that arise in criminal litigation present not only disciplinary issues but constitutional ones as well. Every accused individual has a Sixth Amendment right to conflict-free counsel. *See, e.g., Olivieri*, 74 So. 3d at 1193; *State v. Tensley*, 955 So. 2d 227, 245 (La. Ct. App. 2d Cir. 2007); *Wheat v. United States*, 486 U.S. 153 (1988); *Holloway v. Arkansas*, 435 U.S. 475 (1978). Absent the informed consent of all affected clients, a lawyer in a criminal matter may not represent more than one accused person in the same matter. *See* Restatement (Third) of the Law Governing Lawyers § 129 (2000). In 2006, the Louisiana Supreme Court disciplined a criminal defense lawyer for breaching his duty of loyalty to his client by giving legal advice to his client's co-defendant. *In re John*, 924 So. 2d 990, 990 (La. 2006) (the lawyer also violated Rule 1.4(a)(1) for advising the co-defendant without the client's informed consent).

Conflicts in Criminal Prosecution Practice

In many Louisiana jurisdictions, prosecutors are permitted to maintain private practices in addition to their prosecutorial function. The Louisiana Supreme Court has established a bright-line rule as to how such prosecutors must avoid potential conflicts of interest between their governmental clients and their private clients: "[I]n order to comply with the Rules of Professional Conduct, a district attorney must immediately withdraw from the civil representation of a client when there is substantial reason to believe that charges of criminal conduct have been or will be filed by or against the civil client." *In re Caillouet*, 800 So. 2d 367, 370 (La. 2001) (quoting *In re Toups*, 773 So. 2d 709, 716 (La. 2000)) (internal quotation omitted). This rule applies "even if the criminal charges are unrelated to the civil representation." *Id.; see also In re Smith*, 29 So. 3d 1232 (La. 2010) (suspending an Orleans Parish assistant district attorney for one year for representing criminal defendants in that same parish).

Conflicts in Representing Business Organizations

When a lawyer represents a corporation, a limited liability company or other business organization, the lawyer owes the duty of loyalty to the organization rather than to its constituents. *See* La. Rules of Prof'l Conduct r. 1.13(a) (2004); *see Desire Narcotics Rehab. Ctr., Inc. v. White*, 732 So. 2d 144, 146-47 (La. Ct. App. 4th Cir. 1999). Because a lawyer representing an organization owes the organization a duty of loyalty, the lawyer generally must not represent another client if that representation would be adverse to the organization or would materially limit the lawyer's representation of the organization. *See, e.g.*, Restatement (Third) of the Law Governing Lawyers § 131 (2000). From time to time, a lawyer may be called upon to represent a constituent of an organization. For example, a lawyer may be asked to represent an individual director or officer of a corporation or a general partner in a limited partnership. Such a constituent may have interests that materially diverge from or conflict with the interests of the organization. A lawyer for the organization should not represent the interests of such a constituent against the organization unless (1) the lawyer reasonably believes that he or she can competently represent all interested persons, and (2) the lawyer obtains the informed consent, preferably in writing, from all interested persons. Moreover, the lawyer must obtain the organization's informed consent from an appropriate official within the organization other than the constituent whom the lawyer seeks to represent. *See* La. Rules of Prof'l Conduct r. 1.13 (g) (2004) (applying Rule 1.7 to potential conflicts involving representation of an organization's constituents).

Curing Conflicts

Many, but not all, conflicts can be resolved through obtaining the consent of the affected client or clients. As to conflicts that can be resolved through client consent–consentable conflicts–the client's consent must be informed to be effective. "Informed" consent requires that the lawyer consult with each affected client, and in so doing, communicate reasonably adequate information about the material risks of and reasonably available alternatives to the otherwise problematic representation. What information will be reasonably adequate in any given case will vary with the circumstances. However, the lawyer should typically discuss the following with the affected clients: the conflicting interests; the "contingent, optional, and tactical considerations and alternative courses of action that would be foreclosed or made less readily available by the conflict"; any "material reservations" that a disinterested lawyer representing the affected client might reasonably harbor; and, the possibility and consequences of a future withdrawal of consent by the affected clients. *See* Restatement (Third) of the Law Governing Lawyers § 122 cmt. c(i) (2000). Furthermore, the lawyer should discuss the effect of the proposed representation on confidential client information. Finally, the lawyer should make it clear that the affected client is free to decline to consent to the conflict. In *Olivieri*, the court found that a criminal defendant did "not knowingly and intelligently" waive the conflict of interest due to the waiver occurring prior to a discussion of the intricacies of the conflict between the lawyer's representation of both co-defendants. *Olivieri*, 74 So. 3d at 1194. (finding the defendant may not have been informed of his right to obtain a different lawyer).

Some conflicts of interest, however, cannot be resolved through the informed consent of the affected clients. A conflict is consentable only if a reasonable, disinterested lawyer would believe that the representation will not be adversely affected by potentially conflicting interests. If no reasonable lawyer would have such a belief, the conflict is considered to be "nonconsentable." *See* Restatement (Third) of the Law Governing Lawyers § 122(2)(c) (2000). Furthermore, under paragraph (b)(3) of Louisiana Rule of Professional Conduct 1.7, a lawyer may never simultaneously represent opposing parties in litigation. Such conflicting-interest representations are now per se[84] nonconsentable. *See* La. Rules of Prof'l Conduct r. 1.7(b)(3) (2004).

A lawyer sometimes may attempt to cure a potential conflict of interest by dropping a current client like a "hot potato" in order to undertake the representation of another, perhaps more lucrative, client in another matter. *See* Ronald D. Rotunda, Legal Ethics § 8-5 (2000). By doing so, the lawyer hopes to convert a "current" client into a "former" client, whom he may then permissibly sue in an unrelated matter. *See* La. Rules of Prof'l Conduct

---

[84] Prior to the 2004 revision of Rule 1.7, the Louisiana Rules of Professional Conduct classified no subset of direct-adversity conflicts as per se nonconsentable. Rather, the consentability of all direct-adversity conflicts was determined on a case-by-case basis using a rule of reason. *See, e.g., Grant v. Grant*, 734 So. 2d 68 (La. Ct. App. 2d Cir. 1999) ("Rule 1.7 allows a client to consent" to a direct adversity conflict "after consultation").

r. 1.9(a) (2004). However, when the lawyer's primary motivation for dropping the current client is the desire to represent the prospective client, the discharge often will not cure the conflict. *See* Restatement (Third) of the Law Governing Lawyers § 132 cmt. c (2000).

Disciplinary Sanctions

Absent aggravating or mitigating circumstances, the following sanctions are generally appropriate in cases involving conflicts of interest: *disbarment*, when the lawyer without informed consent undertakes representation of a client when he knows that doing so presents a conflict of interest, the lawyer intends to benefit himself or another, and the lawyer causes serious or potentially serious injury to the client; *suspension*, when the lawyer knows of a conflict of interest, does not fully consult with the client about it, and the lawyer causes injury or potential injury to the client; *reprimand*, when the lawyer is negligent in determining whether a conflict exists, and the lawyer causes injury or potential injury to the client; and, *admonition*, when the lawyer engages in an isolated instance of negligence in determining whether the representation may present a conflict of interest, and the lawyer's conduct causes little or no actual or potential injury to the client. *See* ABA Stds. for Imposing Lawyer Sanctions std. 4.3 (1992).

RULE 1.8. CONFLICT OF INTEREST: CURRENT CLIENTS–SPECIFIC RULES

(a) A lawyer shall not enter into a business transaction with a client or knowingly acquire an ownership, possessory, security or other pecuniary interest adverse to a client unless:

> (1) the transaction and terms on which the lawyer acquires the interest are fair and reasonable to the client and are fully disclosed and transmitted in writing in a manner that can be reasonably understood by the client;

> (2) the client is advised in writing of the desirability of seeking and is given a reasonable opportunity to seek the advice of independent legal counsel on the transaction; and

> (3) the client gives informed consent, in a writing signed by the client, to the essential terms of the transaction and the lawyer's role in the transaction, including whether the lawyer is representing the client in the transaction.

(b) A lawyer shall not use information relating to representation of a client to the disadvantage of the client unless the client gives informed consent, except as permitted or required by these Rules.

(c) A lawyer shall not solicit any substantial gift from a client, including a testamentary gift, or prepare on behalf of a client an instrument giving the lawyer or a person related to the lawyer any substantial gift unless the lawyer or other recipient of the gift, is related to the client. For purposes of this paragraph, related persons include a spouse, child, grandchild, parent, or grandparent.

(d) Prior to the conclusion of representation of a client, a lawyer shall not make or negotiate an agreement giving the lawyer literary or media rights to a portrayal or account based in substantial part on information relating to the representation.

(e) A lawyer shall not provide financial assistance to a client in connection with pending or contemplated litigation, except as follows.

> (1) A lawyer may advance court costs and expenses of litigation, the repayment of which may be contingent on

the outcome of the matter, provided that the expenses were reasonably incurred. Court costs and expenses of litigation include, but are not necessarily limited to, filing fees; deposition costs; expert witness fees; transcript costs; witness fees; copy costs; photographic, electronic, or digital evidence production; investigation fees; related travel expenses; litigation related medical expenses; and any other case specific expenses directly related to the representation undertaken, including those set out in Rule 1.8(e)(3).

(2) A lawyer representing an indigent client may pay court costs and expenses of litigation on behalf of the client.

(3) Overhead costs of a lawyer's practice which are those not incurred by the lawyer solely for the purposes of a particular representation, shall not be passed on to a client. Overhead costs include, but are not necessarily limited to, office rent, utility costs, charges for local telephone service, office supplies, fixed asset expenses, and ordinary secretarial and staff services.

With the informed consent of the client, the lawyer may charge as recoverable costs such items as computer legal research charges, long distance telephone expenses, postage charges, copying charges, mileage and outside courier service charges, incurred solely for the purposes of the representation undertaken for that client, provided they are charged at the lawyer's actual, invoiced costs for these expenses.

With client consent and where the lawyer's fee is based upon an hourly rate, a reasonable charge for paralegal services may be chargeable to the client. In all other instances, paralegal services shall be considered an overhead cost of the lawyer.

(4) In addition to costs of court and expenses of litigation, a lawyer may provide financial assistance to a client who is in necessitous circumstances, subject however to the following restrictions.

(i) Upon reasonable inquiry, the lawyer must determine that the client's necessitous circumstances, without minimal financial assistance, would adversely affect the client's ability to initiate and/or maintain the cause for which the lawyer's services were engaged.

(ii) The advance or loan guarantee, or the offer thereof, shall not be used as an inducement by the lawyer, or anyone acting on the lawyer's behalf, to secure employment.

(iii) Neither the lawyer nor anyone acting on the lawyer's behalf may offer to make advances or loan guarantees prior to being hired by a client, and the lawyer shall not publicize nor advertise a willingness to make advances or loan guarantees to clients.

(iv) Financial assistance under this rule may provide but shall not exceed that minimum sum necessary to meet the client's, the client's spouse's, and/or dependents' documented obligations for food, shelter, utilities, insurance, non-litigation related medical care and treatment, transportation expenses, education, or other documented expenses necessary for subsistence.

(5) Any financial assistance provided by a lawyer to a client, whether for court costs, expenses of litigation, or for necessitous circumstances, shall be subject to the following additional restrictions.

(i) Any financial assistance provided directly from the funds of the lawyer to a client shall not bear interest, fees or charges of any nature.

(ii) Financial assistance provided by a lawyer to a client may be made using a lawyer's line of credit or loans obtained from financial institutions in which the lawyer has no ownership, control and/or security interest; provided, however, that this prohibition shall not apply to any federally insured bank, savings and loan association, savings bank, or credit union where the lawyer's ownership, control and/or security interest is less than 15%.

(iii) Where the lawyer uses a line of credit or loans obtained from financial institutions to provide financial assistance to a client, the lawyer shall not pass on to the client interest charges, including any fees or other charges attendant to such loans, in an amount exceeding the actual charge by the third party lender, or ten percentage points above the bank prime loan rate of interest as reported by the Federal Reserve Board on January 15th of each year in which the loan is outstanding, whichever is less.

(iv) A lawyer providing a guarantee or security on a loan made in favor of a client may do so only to the extent that the interest charges, including any fees or other charges attendant to such a loan, do not exceed ten percentage points (10%) above the bank prime loan rate of interest as reported by the Federal Reserve Board on January 15th of each year in which the loan is outstanding. Interest together with other charges attendant to such loans which exceeds this maximum may not be the subject of the lawyer's guarantee or security.

(v) The lawyer shall procure the client's written consent to the terms and conditions under which such financial assistance is made. Nothing in this rule shall require client consent in those matters in which a court has certified a class under applicable state or federal law; provided, however, that the court must have accepted and exercised responsibility for making the determination that interest and fees are owed, and that the amount of interest and fees chargeable to the client is fair and reasonable considering the facts and circumstances presented.

(vi) In every instance where the client has been provided financial assistance by the lawyer, the full text of this rule shall be provided to the client at the time of execution of any settlement documents, approval of any disbursement sheet as provided for in Rule 1.5, or upon submission of a bill for the lawyer's services.

(vii) For purposes of Rule 1.8(e), the term "financial institution" shall include a federally insured financial institution and any of its affiliates, bank, savings and loan, credit union, savings bank, loan or finance company, thrift, and any other business or person that, for a commercial purpose, loans or advances money to attorneys and/or the clients of attorneys for court costs, litigation expenses, or for necessitous circumstances.

(f) A lawyer shall not accept compensation for representing a client from one other than the client unless:

(1) the client gives informed consent, or the compensation is provided by contract with a third person such as an insurance contract or a prepaid legal service plan;

(2) there is no interference with the lawyer's independence or professional judgment or with the client-lawyer relationship; and

(3) information relating to representation of a client is protected as required by Rule 1.6.

(g) A lawyer who represents two or more clients shall not participate in making an aggregate settlement of the claims of or against the clients, or in a criminal case an aggregated agreement as to guilty or nolo contendere pleas, unless each client gives informed consent, in a writing signed by the client, or a court approves a settlement in a certified class action. The lawyer's disclosure shall include the existence and nature of all the claims or pleas involved and of the participation of each person in the settlement.

(h) A lawyer shall not:

> (1) make an agreement prospectively limiting the lawyer's liability to a client for malpractice unless the client is independently represented in making the agreement; or

> (2) settle a claim or potential claim for such liability with an unrepresented client or former client unless that person is advised in writing of the desirability of seeking and is given a reasonable opportunity to seek the advice of independent legal counsel in connection therewith.

(i) A lawyer shall not acquire a proprietary interest in the cause of action or subject matter of litigation the lawyer is conducting for a client, except that the lawyer may:

> (1) acquire a lien authorized by law to secure the lawyer's fee or expenses; and

> (2) contract with a client for a reasonable contingent fee in a civil case.

(j) [Reserved].

(k) A lawyer shall not solicit or obtain a power of attorney or mandate from a client which would authorize the attorney, without first obtaining the client's informed consent to settle, to enter into a binding settlement agreement on the client's behalf or to execute on behalf of the client any settlement or release documents. An attorney may obtain a client's authorization to endorse and negotiate an instrument given in settlement of the client's claim, but only after the client has approved the settlement.

(l) While lawyers are associated in a firm, a prohibition in the foregoing paragraphs (a) through (k) that applies to any one of them shall apply to all of them.

BACKGROUND

The Louisiana Supreme Court adopted this rule on January 20, 2004. It became effective on March 1, 2004, and was amended in 2006 to address financial assistance to clients. The rule contains several significant differences from the corresponding model rule.

Paragraph (a): Business Transactions with Clients

Paragraph (a) is identical to ABA Model Rule of Professional Conduct 1.8(a) (2002).

In 2002, the ABA adopted a provision requiring that a lawyer seeking to do business with a client must advise the client of the desirability of seeking independent counsel. *See* ABA Ethics 2000 Commission Revision Notes to Model Rule 1.8 (2002). The ABA added this provision because it believed that it, and other requirements, were necessary for the protection of clients; moreover, the ABA recognized that some of these requirements were already imposed by common-law decisions providing for the voidability of such transactions.

In addition, the ABA clarified the nature of the consent to be given by the client under this paragraph. Lawyers had reported to the ABA Ethics 2000 Commission that there was considerable confusion regarding its meaning. Several states had specified that the consent refers to the essential terms of the transaction. Case law in some jurisdictions went further and required disclosure regarding the risks of the transaction. For these reasons, the ABA adopted the requirement of informed consent to both the terms of the transaction and the lawyer's role, including whether the lawyer is representing the client in the transaction. *See id.*

Finally, in 2002 the ABA added a signed-writing requirement. It did so because of the perceived risk of overreaching in business transactions between lawyers and clients. *See id.*

Paragraph (b): Use of Information Relating to Representation
Paragraph (b) is identical to Model Rule 1.8(b) (2002).

Paragraph (c): Client-to-Lawyer Gifts
Paragraph (c) is nearly identical to Model Rule 1.8(c) (2002), with one substantive change. The Louisiana Rule excludes language found in the ABA Model Rule that attempts to sweep within the rule an unspecified class of relatives, namely, "other" relatives or individuals "with whom the lawyer or the client maintains a close, familial relationship." The LSBA was concerned that this language was too indeterminate to give lawyers fair notice regarding which relatives are included within its scope.

In 2002, the ABA added a prohibition in the corresponding Model Rule prohibiting a lawyer from soliciting a substantial gift from a client. It adopted this prohibition in order to avoid the danger of overreaching by the lawyer, and because the predecessor Model Rule had been criticized for regulating gifts made by instrument, but not those made in other ways. *See* ABA Ethics 2000 Commission Revision Notes to Model Rule 1.8 (2002).

Paragraph (d): Literary Rights
Paragraph (d) is identical to Model Rule 1.8(d) (2002).

Paragraph (e): Financial Assistance to Clients
Paragraph (e) diverges significantly from Model Rule 1.8(e). Under the Model Rule, a lawyer "shall not provide financial assistance to a client" in connection with litigation other than assisting with court costs and litigation expenses. In 2006, the Louisiana Supreme Court amended Louisiana Rule 1.8(e) to permit certain types of financial assistance unrelated to court costs and litigation expenses, but only under tightly-regulated circumstances. Prior to this revision, Louisiana Rule 1.8(e)–like the corresponding ABA Model Rule–flatly prohibited lawyers from advancing living expenses to clients.

Nevertheless, providing living expenses to clients was a well-established practice in Louisiana. *See In re Maxwell*, 783 So. 2d 1244, 1249 (La. 2001) ("Arguably, a plain reading of Rule 1.8 would indicate that any advance to a client, other than one for court costs and litigation expenses, would constitute a violation of this rule."). This well-established practice stemmed from *La. State Bar Ass'n v. Edwins*, 329 So. 2d 437, 445 (La. 1976), a case in which the Louisiana Supreme Court held that a lawyer may advance "minimal living expenses" to a client to prevent the client from being forced into accepting an unfavorable early settlement. *Id.*

Paragraph (f): Third-Party Payors
Paragraph (f) is identical to Model Rule 1.8(f) (2002), except with the addition of the following language to subsection (i): ". . . or the compensation is provided by contract with a third person such as an insurance contract or a prepaid legal service plan." This is identical to language in the former Louisiana rule, and was intended by the LSBA to relieve lawyers of the burden of securing a client's "informed consent" to payment of fees by a third party when the client has already given consent by contracting for the payment.

Paragraph (g): Aggregate Settlements
Paragraph (g) is identical to Model Rule 1.8(g) (2002), except with the addition of language to address aggregate settlements in "certified class action[s]." The LSBA proposed this addition to relieve class-action lawyers of the obligation of obtaining signed writings from all members of a certified class in order to settle a class-action matter. The LSBA believed that this step is unnecessary to protect clients' interests because the presiding court, in reviewing the settlement, can do so.

In 2002, the ABA added a signed-writing requirement to the corresponding Model Rule. It did so because it believed that aggregate settlements entail settlement offers posing potentially serious conflicts of interest between the clients. *See* ABA Ethics 2000 Commission Revision Notes to Model Rule 1.8 (2002).

Paragraph (h): Agreements Limiting the Lawyer's Liability to the Client
Paragraph (h) is identical to Model Rule 1.8(h) (2002).

As to prospective waivers, the ABA in 2002 deleted language in the former Model Rule allowing such agreements when "permitted by law." It did so because it believed that the phrase had no significant role in addressing these conflicts. Instead, the ABA adopted language permitting such agreements when the client is independently represented. The ABA believed that there may be good reasons to permit a lawyer to limit liability prospectively and that the client is adequately protected when represented by independent counsel. *See* ABA Ethics 2000 Commission Revision Notes to Model Rule 1.8 (2002).

As to retrospective waivers, the ABA added language "or potential claim," to clarify that the Model Rule applies even when the client has not actually asserted a claim, for example, when the lawyer asks the client to sign a release as part of settling a dispute over legal fees. *See id.*

Paragraph (i): Proprietary Interests in Causes of Action
Paragraph (i) is identical to Model Rule 1.8(i) (2002).

In 2002, the ABA substituted the term "authorized by law" for the term "granted by law" found in the former Model Rule. In so doing, the ABA clarified that the exemption applies to all liens authorized by substantive law, including those liens that are contractual in nature. *See* ABA Ethics 2000 Commission Revision Notes to Model Rule 1.8 (2002).

Paragraph (j): Sex with Clients
Paragraph (j) (reserved) differs from the corresponding Model Rule addressing sex with clients. In 2002, the ABA adopted this per se rule following the lead of a number of jurisdictions that have adopted Rules explicitly regulating client-lawyer sexual conduct. Although recognizing that most egregious behavior of lawyers can be addressed through other Rules, the ABA believed that such Rules may not be sufficient. Given the number of complaints of lawyer sexual misconduct that have been filed, the ABA believed that having a specific Rule has the advantage not only of alerting lawyers more effectively to the dangers of sexual relationships with clients, but also of alerting clients that the lawyer may have violated ethical obligations in engaging in such conduct. Furthermore, the ABA adopted a complete, rather than a partial, ban on client-lawyer relationships, except for those pre-dating the formation of the client-lawyer relationship. The ABA believed that partial bans–such as those prohibiting relationships when they involve coercion or incompetence–did not effectively address the problem of conflicts of interest, particularly the difficulty of obtaining an adequately informed consent from the client. *See* ABA Ethics 2000 Revision Notes to Rule 1.8 (2002).

In 2004, the Louisiana Supreme Court, on recommendation of the Ethics 2000 Committee of the Louisiana State Bar Association, declined to adopt paragraph (j). By a 5-5 vote, the Committee recommended no change to the LSBA rules, and thus, did not recommend the adoption of ABA Model Rule 1.8(j).[85]

---

[85] Those members of the LSBA Ethics 2000 Committee who voted against adopting Rule 1.8(j) did so for the following reasons: (1) they felt that the court's existing case law adequately addresses the complex and variable issues associated with "unethical" sexual conduct; (2) they felt that a bright-line rule could serve as a safe harbor sheltering lawyers engaged in sexual conduct that is inappropriate, but that comports with the letter of Rule 1.8(j); and, (3) they felt that there may be situations in which sexual conduct should not be treated as per se sanctionable.

On the other hand, those committee members who voted for adopting ABA Model Rule 1.8(j) did so for the following reasons: (1) they felt that a refusal to adopt Rule 1.8(j) could be misconstrued by the bar and the public as indicating that Louisiana has opted for a more permissive attitude with respect to sexual relations with clients, when that is clearly not the case; (2) they felt that the proposed rule is not inconsistent with existing jurisprudence in Louisiana; and (3) they felt that even if a sexual relationship predates the representation–and thus is not covered by the proposed rule–the lawyer is nonetheless constrained by other rules, including Rule 1.7(b), which the court already has interpreted

No member of the LSBA House of Delegates moved the adoption of ABA Model Rule 1.8(j). Thereafter, the LSBA House of Delegates, without further debate, concurred with the Committee's proposal. For Louisiana case law finding that a lawyer's sexual relationship with a client violated other rules of professional conduct, *see infra*.

Paragraph (k): Powers of Attorney

Paragraph (k) is not contained in Model Rule 1.8. The LSBA recommended that the court retain this provision in order to clarify that a lawyer must have the consent of the client prior to settling a matter, but thereafter, they may obtain a specific mandate from the client to endorse or negotiate an instrument given in settlement of the claim.

Paragraph (l): Imputation of Conflicts of Interest

Paragraph (l) of this rule is identical to Model Rule 1.8(k), with the exception of a reference to Louisiana Rule 1.8(k).

In 2002, the ABA amended the Model Rules to address issues relating to imputation of the prohibitions in Model Rule 1.8 directly in Rule 1.8 (rather than by reference to Rule 1.10). In addition, former Model Rule 1.10 imputed only the prohibition of paragraph (c) (gifts to a lawyer) to another lawyer in a firm, while current Model Rule 1.8 imputes the prohibitions found in all paragraphs–except (j) (sex with clients)–to other members of the conflicted lawyer's firm. *See* ABA Ethics 2000 Commission Revision Notes to Model Rule 1.8 (2002).

COMMENTS TO ABA MODEL RULE 1.8

Business Transactions Between Client and Lawyer

[1] A lawyer's legal skill and training, together with the relationship of trust and confidence between lawyer and client, create the possibility of overreaching when the lawyer participates in a business, property or financial transaction with a client, for example, a loan or sales transaction or a lawyer investment on behalf of a client. The requirements of paragraph (a) must be met even when the transaction is not closely related to the subject matter of the representation, as when a lawyer drafting a will for a client learns that the client needs money for unrelated expenses and offers to make a loan to the client. The Rule applies to lawyers engaged in the sale of goods or services related to the practice of law, for example, the sale of title insurance or investment services to existing clients of the lawyer's legal practice. See Rule 5.7. It also applies to lawyers purchasing property from estates they represent. It does not apply to ordinary fee arrangements between client and lawyer, which are governed by Rule 1.5, although its requirements must be met when the lawyer accepts an interest in the client's business or other nonmonetary property as payment of all or part of a fee. In addition, the Rule does not apply to standard commercial transactions between the lawyer and the client for products or services that the client generally markets to others, for example, banking or brokerage services, medical services, products manufactured or distributed by the client,

---

to prohibit sexual misconduct adversely affecting the client, as was the case in Ashy and Schambach, contrary to the "safe harbor" contention.

and utilities' services. In such transactions, the lawyer has no advantage in dealing with the client, and the restrictions in paragraph (a) are unnecessary and impracticable.

[2] Paragraph (a)(1) requires that the transaction itself be fair to the client and that its essential terms be communicated to the client, in writing, in a manner that can be reasonably understood. Paragraph (a)(2) requires that the client also be advised, in writing, of the desirability of seeking the advice of independent legal counsel. It also requires that the client be given a reasonable opportunity to obtain such advice. Paragraph (a)(3) requires that the lawyer obtain the client's informed consent, in a writing signed by the client, both to the essential terms of the transaction and to the lawyer's role. When necessary, the lawyer should discuss both the material risks of the proposed transaction, including any risk presented by the lawyer's involvement, and the existence of reasonably available alternatives and should explain why the advice of independent legal counsel is desirable. See Rule 1.0(e) (definition of informed consent).

[3] The risk to a client is greatest when the client expects the lawyer to represent the client in the transaction itself or when the lawyer's financial interest otherwise poses a significant risk that the lawyer's representation of the client will be materially limited by the lawyer's financial interest in the transaction. Here the lawyer's role requires that the lawyer must comply, not only with the requirements of paragraph (a), but also with the requirements of Rule 1.7. Under that Rule, the lawyer must disclose the risks associated with the lawyer's dual role as both legal adviser and participant in the transaction, such as the risk that the lawyer will structure the transaction or give legal advice in a way that favors the lawyer's interests at the expense of the client. Moreover, the lawyer must obtain the client's informed consent. In some cases, the lawyer's interest may be such that Rule 1.7 will preclude the lawyer from seeking the client's consent to the transaction.

[4] If the client is independently represented in the transaction, paragraph (a)(2) of this Rule is inapplicable, and the paragraph (a)(1) requirement for full disclosure is satisfied either by a written disclosure by the lawyer involved in the transaction or by the client's independent counsel. The fact that the client was independently represented in the transaction is relevant in determining whether the agreement was fair and reasonable to the client as paragraph (a)(1) further requires.

Use of Information Related to Representation

[5] Use of information relating to the representation to the disadvantage of the client violates the lawyer's duty of loyalty. Paragraph (b) applies when the information is used to benefit either the lawyer or a third person, such as another client or business associate of the lawyer. For example, if a lawyer learns that a client intends to purchase and develop several parcels of land, the lawyer may not use that information to purchase one of the parcels in competition with the client or to recommend that another client make such a purchase. The Rule does not prohibit uses that do not disadvantage the client. For example, a lawyer who learns a government agency's interpretation of trade legislation during the representation of one client may properly use that information to benefit other clients. Paragraph (b) prohibits disadvantageous use of client information unless the client

gives informed consent, except as permitted or required by these Rules. See Rules 1.2(d), 1.6, 1.9(c), 3.3, 4.1(b), 8.1 and 8.3.

Gifts to Lawyers

[6] A lawyer may accept a gift from a client, if the transaction meets general standards of fairness. For example, a simple gift such as a present given at a holiday or as a token of appreciation is permitted. If a client offers the lawyer a more substantial gift, paragraph (c) does not prohibit the lawyer from accepting it, although such a gift may be voidable by the client under the doctrine of undue influence, which treats client gifts as presumptively fraudulent. In any event, due to concerns about overreaching and imposition on clients, a lawyer may not suggest that a substantial gift be made to the lawyer or for the lawyer's benefit, except where the lawyer is related to the client as set forth in paragraph (c).

[7] If effectuation of a substantial gift requires preparing a legal instrument such as a will or conveyance the client should have the detached advice that another lawyer can provide. The sole exception to this Rule is where the client is a relative of the donee.

[8] This Rule does not prohibit a lawyer from seeking to have the lawyer or a partner or associate of the lawyer named as executor of the client's estate or to another potentially lucrative fiduciary position. Nevertheless, such appointments will be subject to the general conflict of interest provision in Rule 1.7 when there is a significant risk that the lawyer's interest in obtaining the appointment will materially limit the lawyer's independent professional judgment in advising the client concerning the choice of an executor or other fiduciary. In obtaining the client's informed consent to the conflict, the lawyer should advise the client concerning the nature and extent of the lawyer's financial interest in the appointment, as well as the availability of alternative candidates for the position.

Literary Rights

[9] An agreement by which a lawyer acquires literary or media rights concerning the conduct of the representation creates a conflict between the interests of the client and the personal interests of the lawyer. Measures suitable in the representation of the client may detract from the publication value of an account of the representation. Paragraph (d) does not prohibit a lawyer representing a client in a transaction concerning literary property from agreeing that the lawyer's fee shall consist of a share in ownership in the property, if the arrangement conforms to Rule 1.5 and paragraphs (a) and (i).

Financial Assistance

[10] Lawyers may not subsidize lawsuits or administrative proceedings brought on behalf of their clients, including making or guaranteeing loans to their clients for living expenses, because to do so would encourage clients to pursue lawsuits that might not otherwise be brought and because such assistance gives lawyers too great a financial stake in the litigation. These dangers do not warrant a prohibition on a lawyer lending a client court costs and litigation expenses, including the expenses of medical examination and the costs of obtaining and presenting evidence, because these advances are virtually indistinguishable from contingent fees and help ensure access to the courts. Similarly, an exception allowing lawyers representing indigent clients to pay court costs and litigation expenses regardless of whether these funds will be repaid is warranted.

Person Paying for a Lawyer's Services

[11] Lawyers are frequently asked to represent a client under circumstances in which a third person will compensate the lawyer, in whole or in part. The third person might be a relative or friend, an indemnitor (such as a liability insurance company) or a co-client (such as a corporation sued along with one or more of its employees). Because third-party payers frequently have interests that differ from those of the client, including interests in minimizing the amount spent on the representation and in learning how the representation is progressing, lawyers are prohibited from accepting or continuing such representations unless the lawyer determines that there will be no interference with the lawyer's independent professional judgment and there is informed consent from the client. See also Rule 5.4(c) (prohibiting interference with a lawyer's professional judgment by one who recommends, employs or pays the lawyer to render legal services for another).

[12] Sometimes, it will be sufficient for the lawyer to obtain the client's informed consent regarding the fact of the payment and the identity of the third-party payer. If, however, the fee arrangement creates a conflict of interest for the lawyer, then the lawyer must comply with Rule. 1.7. The lawyer must also conform to the requirements of Rule 1.6 concerning confidentiality. Under Rule 1.7(a), a conflict of interest exists if there is significant risk that the lawyer's representation of the client will be materially limited by the lawyer's own interest in the fee arrangement or by the lawyer's responsibilities to the third-party payer (for example, when the third-party payer is a co-client). Under Rule 1.7(b), the lawyer may accept or continue the representation with the informed consent of each affected client, unless the conflict is nonconsentable under that paragraph. Under Rule 1.7(b), the informed consent must be confirmed in writing.

Aggregate Settlements

[13] Differences in willingness to make or accept an offer of settlement are among the risks of common representation of multiple clients by a single lawyer. Under Rule 1.7, this is one of the risks that should be discussed before undertaking the representation, as part of the process of obtaining the clients' informed consent. In addition, Rule 1.2(a) protects each client's right to have the final say in deciding whether to accept or reject an offer of settlement and in deciding whether to enter a guilty or nolo contendere plea in a criminal case. The rule stated in this paragraph is a corollary of both these Rules and provides that, before any settlement offer or plea bargain is made or accepted on behalf of multiple clients, the lawyer must inform each of them about all the material terms of the settlement, including what the other clients will receive or pay if the settlement or plea offer is accepted. See also Rule 1.0(e) (definition of informed consent). Lawyers representing a class of plaintiffs or defendants, or those proceeding derivatively, may not have a full client-lawyer relationship with each member of the class; nevertheless, such lawyers must comply with applicable rules regulating notification of class members and other procedural requirements designed to ensure adequate protection of the entire class.

Limiting Liability and Settling Malpractice Claims

[14] Agreements prospectively limiting a lawyer's liability for malpractice are prohibited unless the client is independently represented in making the agreement because they are likely to undermine competent and diligent representation. Also, many clients are unable

to evaluate the desirability of making such an agreement before a dispute has arisen, particularly if they are then represented by the lawyer seeking the agreement. This paragraph does not, however, prohibit a lawyer from entering into an agreement with the client to arbitrate legal malpractice claims, provided such agreements are enforceable and the client is fully informed of the scope and effect of the agreement. Nor does this paragraph limit the ability of lawyers to practice in the form of a limited-liability entity, where permitted by law, provided that each lawyer remains personally liable to the client for his or her own conduct and the firm complies with any conditions required by law, such as provisions requiring client notification or maintenance of adequate liability insurance. Nor does it prohibit an agreement in accordance with Rule 1.2 that defines the scope of the representation, although a definition of scope that makes the obligations of representation illusory will amount to an attempt to limit liability.

[15] Agreements settling a claim or a potential claim for malpractice are not prohibited by this Rule. Nevertheless, in view of the danger that a lawyer will take unfair advantage of an unrepresented client or former client, the lawyer must first advise such a person in writing of the appropriateness of independent representation in connection with such a settlement. In addition, the lawyer must give the client or former client a reasonable opportunity to find and consult independent counsel.

Acquiring Proprietary Interest in Litigation

[16] Paragraph (i) states the traditional general rule that lawyers are prohibited from acquiring a proprietary interest in litigation. Like paragraph (e), the general rule has its basis in common law champerty and maintenance and is designed to avoid giving the lawyer too great an interest in the representation. In addition, when the lawyer acquires an ownership interest in the subject of the representation, it will be more difficult for a client to discharge the lawyer if the client so desires. The Rule is subject to specific exceptions developed in decisional law and continued in these Rules. The exception for certain advances of the costs of litigation is set forth in paragraph (e). In addition, paragraph (i) sets forth exceptions for liens authorized by law to secure the lawyer's fees or expenses and contracts for reasonable contingent fees. The law of each jurisdiction determines which liens are authorized by law. These may include liens granted by statute, liens originating in common law and liens acquired by contract with the client. When a lawyer acquires by contract a security interest in property other than that recovered through the lawyer's efforts in the litigation, such an acquisition is a business or financial transaction with a client and is governed by the requirements of paragraph (a). Contracts for contingent fees in civil cases are governed by Rule 1.5.

Client-Lawyer Sexual Relationships

[17] The relationship between lawyer and client is a fiduciary one in which the lawyer occupies the highest position of trust and confidence. The relationship is almost always unequal; thus, a sexual relationship between lawyer and client can involve unfair exploitation of the lawyer's fiduciary role, in violation of the lawyer's basic ethical obligation not to use the trust of the client to the client's disadvantage. In addition, such a relationship presents a significant danger that, because of the lawyer's emotional involvement, the lawyer will be unable to represent the client without impairment of the

exercise of independent professional judgment. Moreover, a blurred line between the professional and personal relationships may make it difficult to predict to what extent client confidences will be protected by the attorney-client evidentiary privilege, since client confidences are protected by privilege only when they are imparted in the context of the client-lawyer relationship. Because of the significant danger of harm to client interests and because the client's own emotional involvement renders it unlikely that the client could give adequate informed consent, this Rule prohibits the lawyer from having sexual relations with a client regardless of whether the relationship is consensual and regardless of the absence of prejudice to the client.

[18] Sexual relationships that predate the client-lawyer relationship are not prohibited. Issues relating to the exploitation of the fiduciary relationship and client dependency are diminished when the sexual relationship existed prior to the commencement of the client-lawyer relationship. However, before proceeding with the representation in these circumstances, the lawyer should consider whether the lawyer's ability to represent the client will be materially limited by the relationship. See Rule 1.7(a)(2).

[19] When the client is an organization, paragraph (j) of this Rule prohibits a lawyer for the organization (whether inside counsel or outside counsel) from having a sexual relationship with a constituent of the organization who supervises, directs or regularly consults with that lawyer concerning the organization's legal matters.

Imputation of Prohibitions

[20] Under paragraph (k) [Louisiana Rule 1.8(l)], a prohibition on conduct by an individual lawyer in paragraphs (a) through (i) also applies to all lawyers associated in a firm with the personally prohibited lawyer. For example, one lawyer in a firm may not enter into a business transaction with a client of another member of the firm without complying with paragraph (a), even if the first lawyer is not personally involved in the representation of the client. The prohibition set forth in paragraph (j) is personal and is not applied to associated lawyers.

ANNOTATIONS
Business Transactions with Clients

Louisiana Rule 1.8(a) prohibits a lawyer from engaging in any business dealings, either with clients or with others, that are not "fair and reasonable to the client." However, even as to "fair" transactions, the lawyer still must obtain the client's written consent to the transaction after the client has received a written, understandable description of the terms of the deal and has had a reasonable opportunity to seek advice from another lawyer. La. Rules of Prof'l Conduct r. 1.8(a) (2004). The formalities of this rule apply to transactions undertaken to secure the client's payment of the lawyer's fee. *See Breeden v. Cella*, 832 So. 2d 1072, 1079 (La. Ct. App. 4th Cir. 2002) ("[A] collateral mortgage package would clearly be a business transaction . . . and would thus trigger the ethical rule,"). Transactions that should be considered "unfair" under this rule would include those in which a lawyer received a referral kickback from a third-party vendor. The Louisiana Supreme Court has reprimanded a lawyer for improperly entering into business transactions with clients, such as taking out unfair unsecured loans from them regardless of the client's knowledge or consent. *See In re Bradley*, 917 So. 2d 1068, 1078 (La. 2005) (disciplining lawyer for entering into a transaction in which client knowingly pledged collateral for the lawyer's bank loan); *see also In re Yokum*, 85 So. 3d 645, 649, 663 (La. 2012) (sanctioning lawyer who pledged client's funds for personal bank loan unbeknownst to the client); *In re Letellier*, 742 So. 2d 544, 547-48 (La. 1999); *La. State Bar Ass'n. v. Reis*, 513 So. 2d 1173 (La. 1987); *La. State Bar Ass'n. v. Bosworth*, 481 So. 2d 567 (La. 1986).

Ordinary contingent-fee agreements–even in commercial cases–do not necessarily constitute "business transactions with clients" for purposes of Louisiana Rule 1.8(a). However, unusual fee arrangements permitting recovery regardless of results coupled with loan guarantees can implicate this rule. *See In re Curry, Spillers & Theus*, 16 So. 3d 1139 (La. 2009); *see also In re Brown-Mitchell*, 167 So. 3d 545, 556 (La. 2015) (lawyer violated rule 1.8(a) by entering into an agreement with the client to live in half of the client's property and to rent out the remaining portion).

Use of Information Adverse to Client

A lawyer may not use any information relating to the representation of a client (that is, confidential information) to the disadvantage of a client without the client's consent. *See* La. Rules of Prof'l Conduct r. 1.8(b) (2004); *see also In re Maxell*, 44 So. 3d 668 (La. 2010) (disciplining a lawyer who convinced a mentally incapacitated client to endorse checks to the lawyer without performing legal services). As to whether a lawyer may use confidential client information to the lawyer's advantage when the client's interests would be unaffected, *see supra* Annotations to Louisiana Rule of Professional Conduct 1.6.

Gifts from Clients

Louisiana Rule 1.8(c) prohibits a lawyer from preparing an instrument to effect a substantial gift from the client to the lawyer or a close relative of the lawyer–unless the donee is related[86] to the client. According to the Louisiana Supreme Court, "[t]he purpose of the rule is prophylactic" to assure that the client has the opportunity to receive "independent advice." *In re Grevemberg*, 838 So. 2d 1283, 1288 (La. 2003) (disciplining lawyer for writing a will for client naming the lawyer–and alternatively his wife–as executor and residual legatee); *Succession of Parham*, 755 So. 2d 265, 270 (La. Ct. App. 1st Cir. 1999) (holding that a legacy to lawyer that violates Rule 1.8(c) is invalid and unenforceable). Although this rule would seem to allow a lawyer to accept an unsolicited donation from a client that does not require the preparation of a written juridical act, such a transaction would still have to satisfy the requirements of Rule 1.8(a). *See* ABA Model Rules of Prof'l Conduct r. 1.8 cmt. 2. Note that this rule applies even if a lawyer is ignorant about its existence. *See id.* at 1288 ("'[I]gnorance of the Disciplinary Rules which set forth the minimum level of conduct below which no lawyer may fall . . . is no excuse.'") (quoting *La. State Bar Ass'n v. Marinello*, 523 So. 2d 838, 842 (La. 1988)).

---

[86] The Louisiana Supreme Court has interpreted the term "related" to include "those 'related' by blood or marriage," including those related as second cousins. *See Succession of Walters*, 943 So. 2d 1165, 1167 (La. Ct. App. 1st Cir. 2006).

Financial Assistance to Client

Although a lawyer may advance litigation costs and medical expenses to a client, a lawyer's refusal to do so is not "just cause" for denying the lawyer quantum meruit after dismissal by the client. *See Sims v. Selvage*, 499 So. 2d 325, 328 (La. Ct. App. 1st Cir. 1986). A Louisiana lawyer may violate this rule by failing to properly account for overhead and nonlawyer costs, which should not be allocated to fees for legal services of a client without consent. *See e.g., In re Brown*, 42 So. 3d 967 (La. 2010) (finding 1.8(e)(3) violations for lawyer who unsatisfactorily supervised nonlawyer and inadequately billed expenses); *In re Interdiction of DeMarco*, 38 So. 3d 417, 426 (La. Ct. App. 1st Cir. 2010) (finding no violation for lawyer who charged $75 per hour for "nurse-paralegal" with client consent).

Third-Party Payment of Fees

Louisiana Rule 1.8(f) prohibits a lawyer from accepting compensation from a non-client unless the client gives informed consent, the lawyer's professional independence is not compromised, and the lawyer does not disclose confidential client information to the non-client. *See* La. Rules of Prof'l Conduct r. 1.8(f) (2004); *see also id.* r. 5.4(c) ("A lawyer shall not permit a person who recommends, employs, or pays the lawyer to render legal services for another to direct or regulate the exercise of the lawyer's professional judgment in rendering such legal services."). Unlike the comparable ABA Model Rule, Louisiana Rule 1.8(f) specifically allows a lawyer to accept compensation from insurance companies for representing policyholders without the necessity of seeking the insured's consent. Given that policyholders expect the insurer to provide a defense pursuant to the contract of insurance, this modification is sensible.

Aggregate Settlements

The Louisiana Supreme Court has observed that the aggregate-settlement provisions of Rule 1.8(g) exist because "a lawyer might be tempted 'to sacrifice the interests of once client to gain an advantage for the other.'" *In re Hoffman*, 883 So. 2d 425, 432 (La. 2004) (quoting Charles W. Wolfram, *Modern Legal Ethics* 493 (1986)). As a result of this risk, a lawyer seeking to enter into an aggregate settlement must consult with each client "directly," and "fully disclose all details of the proposed settlement including information about each client's claim and share of the proposed settlement." *Id.* at 433. Furthermore, the "requirement of informed consent cannot be avoided by obtaining client consent in advance to a future decision by the attorney or by a majority of the clients about the merits of an aggregate settlement." *Id.*

Prospective Limitations on Lawyer's Liability for Malpractice

Louisiana Rule 1.8(h) prohibits a lawyer from making an agreement prospectively limiting the lawyer's liability to a client for malpractice unless the client is independently represented in making the agreement. The United States Fifth Circuit has held that this provision does not apply to a forum-selection clause in a lawyer-client agreement. Such a clause "is usually not a limitation on malpractice liability." *See Ginter v. Belcher, Prendergast & Laporte*, 536 F.3d 439, 444 (5th Cir. 2008). The same reasoning may apply to lawyer-client arbitration agreements. *See id.* at 443.

Settling Malpractice Claims

Louisiana Rule 1.8(h) prohibits a lawyer from, among other things,[87] attempting to settle a malpractice claim without first advising the client in writing that independent representation is advisable. *See Matter of Selenberg*, 856 F.3d 393, 399 (5th Cir. 2017) (lawyer violated Rule 1.8(h) because the lawyer failed to advise client to seek independent legal counsel before settling malpractice claim). To comply with this rule, the lawyer must make any such settlement offer in writing and must inform the client that independent representation is advisable. *See La. Rules of Prof'l Conduct r. 1.8(h) (2004).*

The Louisiana Office of Disciplinary Counsel routinely charges lawyers with violations of this rule when they attempt to extricate themselves from liability and discipline through a quick settlement with their client. *See, e.g., In re Hanchey*, 148 So. 3d 912, 916-17 (La. 2014) (finding 1.8(h) violation by lawyer who settled with client by improperly writing a $500 check to client from his client trust account; and not advising client to seek independent legal counsel); *Yokum*, 85 So. 3d at 651-53 (finding 1.8(h) violation for lawyer who settled with client by refunding half of the fee without advising client to seek independent representation); *In re Petal*, 972 So. 2d 1138, 1142 (La. 2008); *In re Thompson*, 712 So. 2d 72 (La. 1998); *In re Dunn*, 713 So. 2d 461 (La. 1998). Note, however, that tendering compensation to a client unconditionally and without seeking a release of claims does not run afoul of this rule. *See In re. Leblanc*, 884 So. 2d 552, 557-58 (La. 2004). Moreover, the Louisiana Supreme Court has held that a mere offer to settle a lawyer malpractice claim does not trigger the notice requirements of Rule 1.8(h)(2); *see In re Fazande*, 864 So. 2d 174, 180 (La. 2004) (where "discussions never progressed to the point of a formal offer of settlement . . . or acceptance of any offer . . . the requirement of Rule 1.8(h), that [the lawyer] advise his clients in writing that independent counsel is appropriate, was never triggered"); *see also In re Schiro*, 886 So. 2d 1117, n.5 (La. 2004) (ODC cannot prove violation of Rule 1.8(h) if client does not accept offer to settle).

Proprietary Interests in Subject Matter of Litigation

Louisiana Rule 1.8(i) generally prohibits a lawyer from acquiring an interest in the subject matter of litigation. The Louisiana Supreme Court has not hesitated to discipline Louisiana lawyers who have acquired an interest in property that is the subject matter of litigation. For example, the court suspended a lawyer for nine months for acquiring disputed mineral rights in exchange for legal services. *See La. State Bar Ass'n v. Sanders*, 568 So. 2d 1025, 1029 (La. 1990); *see also Succession of Cloud*, 530 So. 2d 1146 (La. 1988). Nevertheless, 1.8(i) permits a lawyer to acquire a lien to secure payment of fees. For

---

[87] Paragraph (h) of this rule also prohibits prospective agreements limiting a lawyer's malpractice liability. *See La. Rules of Prof'l Conduct r. 1.8(h)(1) (2004).* According to the Louisiana Supreme Court, "[t]he prospective agreement contemplated by this section of the rule refers to an agreement made at the beginning of the representation, such as a hold harmless clause." *See In re Fazande*, 864 So. 2d 174 (La. 2004) (citing ABA/BNA's Lawyer's Manual on Professional Conduct § 51:1104). The court noted that few cases have arisen under this paragraph.

legislation relating to a lawyer's special privilege, *see* La. Rev. Stat. Ann. §§ 9:5001 & 37:218 (2007). Rule 1.8(i) allows a lawyer holding an ownership interest while acting as general counsel for an organization to draft business contracts for the organization as long as the lawyer does not give the impression of representing both parties to the agreement. *See Lighthouse MGA, L.L.C. v. First Premium Ins. Group, Inc.*, 448 F. App'x 512, 516 (5th Cir. 2011).

Settlement Authority

Louisiana Rule 1.8(k) prohibits a lawyer from obtaining a client's prospective consent to settle a claim without further authorization. However, a lawyer may obtain authority from the client to endorse a settlement check on behalf of a client after the client has specifically approved the settlement for which the check was given.

Disciplinary Sanctions

For the disciplinary sanctions that are appropriate for a lawyer's failure to avoid conflicts of interest, *see supra* Annotations to Louisiana Rule 1.7.

RULE 1.9. DUTIES TO FORMER CLIENTS

(a) A lawyer who has formerly represented a client in a matter shall not thereafter represent another person in the same or a substantially related matter in which that person's interests are materially adverse to the interests of the former client unless the former client gives informed consent, confirmed in writing.

(b) A lawyer shall not knowingly represent a person in the same or a substantially related matter in which a firm with which the lawyer formerly was associated had previously represented a client

(1) whose interests are materially adverse to that person; and

(2) about whom the lawyer had acquired information protected by Rules 1.6 and 1.9(c) that is material to the matter; unless the former client gives informed consent, confirmed in writing.

(c) A lawyer who has formerly represented a client in a matter or whose present or former firm has formerly represented a client in a matter shall not thereafter:

(1) use information relating to the representation to the disadvantage of the former client except as these Rules would permit or require with respect to a client, or when the information has become generally known; or

(2) reveal information relating to the representation except as these Rules would permit or require with respect to a client.

BACKGROUND

The Louisiana Supreme Court adopted this rule on January 20, 2004. It became effective on March 1, 2004, and has not been amended since. This rule is identical to ABA Model Rule of Prof'l Conduct 1.9 (2002).

COMMENTS TO ABA MODEL RULE 1.9

Generally

[1] After termination of a client-lawyer relationship, a lawyer has certain continuing duties with respect to confidentiality and conflicts of interest and thus may not represent another client except in conformity with this Rule. Under this Rule, for example, a lawyer could not properly seek to rescind on behalf of a new client a contract drafted on behalf of the former client. So also a lawyer who has prosecuted an accused person could not properly

represent the accused in a subsequent civil action against the government concerning the same transaction. Nor could a lawyer who has represented multiple clients in a matter represent one of the clients against the others in the same or a substantially related matter after a dispute arose among the clients in that matter, unless all affected clients give informed consent. See Comment [9]. Current and former government lawyers must comply with this Rule to the extent required by Rule 1.11.

[2] The scope of a "matter" for purposes of this Rule depends on the facts of a particular situation or transaction. The lawyer's involvement in a matter can also be a question of degree. When a lawyer has been directly involved in a specific transaction, subsequent representation of other clients with materially adverse interests in that transaction clearly is prohibited. On the other hand, a lawyer who recurrently handled a type of problem for a former client is not precluded from later representing another client in a factually distinct problem of that type even though the subsequent representation involves a position adverse to the prior client. Similar considerations can apply to the reassignment of military lawyers between defense and prosecution functions within the same military jurisdictions. The underlying question is whether the lawyer was so involved in the matter that the subsequent representation can be justly regarded as a changing of sides in the matter in question.

[3] Matters are "substantially related" for purposes of this Rule if they involve the same transaction or legal dispute or if there otherwise is a substantial risk that confidential factual information as would normally have been obtained in the prior representation would materially advance the client's position in the subsequent matter. For example, a lawyer who has represented a businessperson and learned extensive private financial information about that person may not then represent that person's spouse in seeking a divorce. Similarly, a lawyer who has previously represented a client in securing environmental permits to build a shopping center would be precluded from representing neighbors seeking to oppose rezoning of the property on the basis of environmental considerations; however, the lawyer would not be precluded, on the grounds of substantial relationship, from defending a tenant of the completed shopping center in resisting eviction for nonpayment of rent. Information that has been disclosed to the public or to other parties adverse to the former client ordinarily will not be disqualifying. Information acquired in a prior representation may have been rendered obsolete by the passage of time, a circumstance that may be relevant in determining whether two representations are substantially related. In the case of an organizational client, general knowledge of the client's policies and practices ordinarily will not preclude a subsequent representation; on the other hand, knowledge of specific facts gained in a prior representation that are relevant to the matter in question ordinarily will preclude such a representation. A former client is not required to reveal the confidential information learned by the lawyer in order to establish a substantial risk that the lawyer has confidential information to use in the subsequent matter. A conclusion about the possession of such information may be based on the nature of the services the lawyer provided the former client and information that would in ordinary practice be learned by a lawyer providing such services.

Lawyers Moving Between Firms

[4] When lawyers have been associated within a firm but then end their association, the question of whether a lawyer should undertake representation is more complicated. There are several competing considerations. First, the client previously represented by the former firm must be reasonably assured that the principle of loyalty to the client is not compromised. Second, the rule should not be so broadly cast as to preclude other persons from having reasonable choice of legal counsel. Third, the rule should not unreasonably hamper lawyers from forming new associations and taking on new clients after having left a previous association. In this connection, it should be recognized that today many lawyers practice in firms, that many lawyers to some degree limit their practice to one field or another, and that many move from one association to another several times in their careers. If the concept of imputation were applied with unqualified rigor, the result would be radical curtailment of the opportunity of lawyers to move from one practice setting to another and of the opportunity of clients to change counsel.

[5] Paragraph (b) operates to disqualify the lawyer only when the lawyer involved has actual knowledge of information protected by Rules 1.6 and 1.9(c). Thus, if a lawyer while with one firm acquired no knowledge or information relating to a particular client of the firm, and that lawyer later joined another firm, neither the lawyer individually nor the second firm is disqualified from representing another client in the same or a related matter even though the interests of the two clients conflict. See Rule 1.10(b) for the restrictions on a firm once a lawyer has terminated association with the firm.

[6] Application of paragraph (b) depends on a situation's particular facts, aided by inferences, deductions or working presumptions that reasonably may be made about the way in which lawyers work together. A lawyer may have general access to files of all clients of a law firm and may regularly participate in discussions of their affairs; it should be inferred that such a lawyer in fact is privy to all information about all the firm's clients. In contrast, another lawyer may have access to the files of only a limited number of clients and participate in discussions of the affairs of no other clients; in the absence of information to the contrary, it should be inferred that such a lawyer in fact is privy to information about the clients actually served but not those of other clients. In such an inquiry, the burden of proof should rest upon the firm whose disqualification is sought.

[7] Independent of the question of disqualification of a firm, a lawyer changing professional association has a continuing duty to preserve confidentiality of information about a client formerly represented. See Rules 1.6 and 1.9(c).

[8] Paragraph (c) provides that information acquired by the lawyer in the course of representing a client may not subsequently be used or revealed by the lawyer to the disadvantage of the client. However, the fact that a lawyer has once served a client does not preclude the lawyer from using generally known information about that client when later representing another client.

[9] The provisions of this Rule are for the protection of former clients and can be waived if the client gives informed consent, which consent must be confirmed in writing under paragraphs (a) and (b). See Rule 1.0(e). With regard to the effectiveness of an advance

waiver, see Comment [22] to Rule 1.7. With regard to disqualification of a firm with which a lawyer is or was formerly associated, see Rule 1.10.

ANNOTATIONS

Suing a Former Client on Behalf of a Current Client

Louisiana Rule 1.7 prohibits a lawyer from taking an adverse position to a current client in any matter. Thus, a lawyer defending a client in a minor redhibition matter could not simultaneously sue that client in an unrelated personal-injury matter. This prohibition exists to ensure that a lawyer remains loyal to the lawyer's current clients.

In contrast, Louisiana Rule 1.9(a) generally permits a lawyer to be adverse to a former client. Thus, a lawyer who has completed the defense of a client in a minor property-related legal matter would be permitted to sue that former client in an unrelated tort action. A lawyer is permitted to sue the lawyer's former clients because the lawyer's duty of loyalty abates to some extent after termination of representation. However, Louisiana Rule of Professional Conduct 1.9[88] does impose a significant limitation on a lawyer's ability to sue his former clients. A lawyer cannot represent "another person"[89] adverse to a former client "in the same or a substantially related[90] matter," unless the former client "gives informed consent, confirmed in writing." La. Rules of Prof'l Conduct r. 1.9(a) (2004).[91]

---

[88] In determining whether former-client conflict requires disqualification, Louisiana courts typically look to the Louisiana Rules of Professional Conduct. *See, e.g., State v. Craddock*, 62 So. 3d 791, 797 (La. Ct. App. 1st Cir. 2011) (citing *Walker v. La. Dep't of Transp. & Dev.*, 817 So. 2d 57, 59-60 (La.2002); *Farrington v. The Law Firm of Sessions, Fishman*, 674 So. 2d 448 (La. Ct. App. 4th Cir. 1996) rev'd judgment by *Farrington v. Law Firm of Sessions, Fishman*, 687 So. 2d 997 (La. 1997)). This is not surprising given that the Louisiana Supreme Court has consistently and repeatedly held that "the ethical rules which regulate attorneys' law practices have been recognized as having the force and effect of substantive law." *See Walker*, 817 So. 2d at 59-60 (citing *Leenerts Farms, Inc. v. Rogers*, 421 So. 2d 216 (La.1982); *Saucier v. Hayes Dairy Prods., Inc.*, 373 So. 2d 102 (La.1979); *Husk v. Blancand*, 99 So. 610 (1924)).

[89] Rule 1.9 does not disqualify a lawyer from representing himself when he has been sued by a former client. According to the Louisiana Supreme Court, "[t]he rule's very wording–represent another person–connotes that the lawyer is representing someone other than the lawyer appearing on his or her own behalf." *See Farrington v. Law Firm of Sessions, Fishman*, 687 So. 2d 997, 1001 (La. 1997).

[90] Likewise, federal caselaw is "categorical in requiring disqualification once a substantial relationship between past and current representations is established." *See In re American Airlines, Inc.*, 972 F.2d 605, 614 (5th Cir. 1992); *see also In re Dresser Indus. Inc.*, 972 F.2d 540, 543 (5th Cir. 1992); *Parker v. Rowan Cos, Inc.*, No. 03-0545, 2003 WL 22852218 (E.D. La. Nov. 25, 2003).

[91] Although the standards set forth in the substantial-relationship test of Rule 1.9(a) are straightforward, some courts have analyzed former-client conflicts by applying

Additionally, a lawyer may not intervene on behalf of a current client against a former client "in the same proceeding in which the lawyer initially represented the former client." *See Dhaliwal v. Dhaliwal*, 184 So. 3d 773, 782-83 (La. Ct. App. 2d Cir. 2015).

This rule exists both to enforce the lawyer's residual duty of loyalty to the former client,[92] and to protect the former client's confidential information from misuse. *See* La. Rules of Prof'l Conduct r. 1.9(a) (2004); *In re Abadie Inter Vivos Trust*, 791 So. 2d 181, 185 (La. Ct. App. 4th Cir. 2001) ("Rule 1.9 of the Rules of Professional Conduct seeks to protect each client from the use or misuse of that client's confidential information by a lawyer and to assure the lawyer's loyalty to each client."); *In re American Airlines, Inc.*, 972 F.2d 605, 618-19 (5th Cir. 1992); *Parker v. Rowan Cos., Inc.*, Civ. A. No. 03-0545, 2003 WL 22852218 (E.D. La. Nov. 25, 2003) ("There are two underlying concerns of the substantial relationship test: 'the duty to preserve confidences and the duty of loyalty to the former client.'"); *see also* Restatement (Third) of the Law Governing Lawyers § 132 (2000).

Whether two matters are "substantially related" turns on all of the relevant facts and circumstances. In resolving the issue, courts often consider the similarity of the pertinent legal and factual issues presented, the lapse of time, the overlap of parties, and the overlap of witnesses and documents. *See generally* Charles Wolfram, *Former Client Conflicts*, 10

"irrebuttable presumptions." *See, e.g., Parker v. Rowan Cos., Inc.*, Civ. A. No. 03-0545, 2003 WL 22852218 (E.D. La. Nov. 25, 2003). The court in *Parker*, following United States Fifth Circuit precedent, characterized the former-client conflict analysis as follows:

> Two irrebuttable presumptions apply under the substantial relationship test in this circuit: First, once it is established that the previous matters are substantially related to the present case, "the court will irrebuttably presume that relevant confidential information was disclosed during the former period of representation." . . . Second, there is an irrebuttable presumption that "confidences obtained by an individual lawyer will be shared with the other members of his firm."

Id. at *5 (citations omitted). *But see Kennedy v. Mindprint*, 587 F.3d 296, 304 n. 7 (5th Cir. 2009) ("It is unclear whether a rebuttable presumption replaces the *American Airlines* irrebuttable presumption, or whether no presumption remains. We do not reach this question . . ."). While this approach is not necessarily erroneous, it is needlessly complicated because it adds nothing to the substantial-relationship standard set forth in the test of Rule 1.9(a).

[92] Because this rule safeguards the client's interest in loyalty–and not just the client's interest in confidentiality–this rule is implicated even in the absence of proof that the lawyer used or communicated his former client's confidential information. *See Parker v. Rowan Cos., Inc.*, Civ. A. No. 03-0545, 2003 WL 22852218 (E.D. La. Nov. 25, 2003) (disqualification movant "need not prove communication of confidential information or its use").

Geo. J. Legal Ethics 677 (1997). The Louisiana Supreme Court has defined the meaning of the term "substantially related" as follows: "In our view, two matters are 'substantially related' when they are so interrelated both in fact and substance that a reasonable person would not be able to disassociate the two." *See Walker v. La. Dep't of Transp. & Development*, 817 So. 2d 57, 62 (La. 2002); *see also Parker*, 2003 WL 22852218, at *10 (E.D. La. 2003) ("[T]he substantial relationship test requires common subject matters, issues and causes of action, but it does not require the same factual scenarios in both cases."); *Koch v. Koch Indus., Inc.*, 798 F. Supp. 1525, 1536 (D. Kan.1992) ("substantially related" means that the cases "involve the same client and the matters or transactions in question are relatively interconnected"), *rev'd on other grounds, Koch v. Koch Indus., Inc.*, 203 F.3d 1202 (10th Cir. 2000); *Trust Corp. v. Piper Aircraft Corp.*, 701 F.2d 85, 87 (9th Cir. 1983) ("substantially related" means that "the factual contexts of the two representations are similar or related").

In *Parker v. Rowan Cos., Inc.*, United States District Judge Vance of the Eastern District of Louisiana observed that cases addressing the substantial-relationship issue "fall along a continuum, from those in which the linkage is clear to those in which the connection is nebulous and superficial." *Parker*, 2003 WL 22852218, at *5. On one end of the spectrum are cases in which former clients have sought–unsuccessfully–to disqualify a former lawyer on the basis of "superficial" resemblances between past and present matter. On the other end of the spectrum are cases in which former clients have identified "specific issues" common to the former and present matters, and have described in "detail the extent of the attorney's involvement" in both cases. *See id.* at *6-*7. In *Parker*, Judge Vance found more than "superficial similarities," and disqualified a lawyer from suing his former client because both the present and former matters: involved Jones Act and unseaworthiness claims; alleged damages for pain and suffering, lost future wages, and emotional distress; involved the same corporate representative, the same rig, and the same crew members; presented safety training issues; and, raised issues relating to subsequent remedial measures. *See id.* at *9-*10. Moreover, the fact that the former client "viewed [the former lawyer] as a part of its team of defense lawyers, regularly communicating and sharing information with it on matters [it] considered important to its defense of maritime personal injury cases, such as case law developments" provided "additional insight" into the context of the former attorney-client relationship, although it was not in and of itself dispositive. *See id.* at *10.

Confidential Information

Although a lawyer's duty of loyalty diminishes precipitously upon termination of representation, the independent duty to preserve the confidentiality of information relating to the representation does not. *See* La. Rules of Prof'l Conduct r. 1.6(a) (2004). A corollary of this continuing confidentiality obligation set forth in Louisiana Rule 1.9(c), is that a lawyer may not use confidential information to the disadvantage of a former client, unless that information has become generally known. Thus, even when a lawyer is permitted to sue a former client in an unrelated matter, the lawyer still cannot use confidential information in the course of that otherwise permissible adverse representation.

Use of Confidential Information of Former Client by a Lawyer

Both the ABA Model Rules of Professional Conduct and the corresponding Louisiana Rules broadly prohibit a lawyer from *revealing* former-client confidences. A lawyer may do so rarely and then only when a specific exception in the rule governing existing-client confidentiality applies.

The rules, however, permit more liberal *use* of former-client confidences. Model Rule 1.9(c)(1) and Louisiana Rule 1.9(c)(1) permit a lawyer to use confidential information if it does no harm to a former client. Moreover, the rules permit use of such information to the disadvantage of a former client "when the information has become generally known." *See* ABA Formal Op. No. 479 (Dec. 15, 2017).

But confusion exists as to just when information is "generally known." Some lawyers believe, incorrectly, that information is "generally known" when it is a matter of public record or when it is publicly accessible. On the contrary, "the fact that the information may have been discussed in open court, or may be available in court records, in public libraries, or in other public repositories does not, standing alone, mean that the information is generally known for Model Rule 1.9(c)(1)." Indeed, "[i]nformation that is publicly available is not necessarily generally known." *See id.* at 5.

Formal Opinion 479 attempts to clear up this confusion and to craft a "workable definition" of the generally-known standard. To this end, the opinion defines two circumstances under which information is "generally known."

First, information is "generally known" when it is "widely recognized by members of the public in the relevant geographic area." *Id.* Such wide recognition—or "public notoriety"—can result from "publicity through traditional media sources, such as newspapers, magazines, radio, or television; through publication on internet web sites; or through social media." *Id.*

Second, information is "generally known" when it is "widely recognized in the former client's industry, profession, or trade." Such recognition can exist if the information "is announced, discussed, or identified in what reasonable members of the industry, profession, or trade would consider a leading print or online publication or other resource in the particular field. Information may be widely recognized within a former client's industry, profession, or trade without being widely recognized by the public." *Id.*

General Knowledge of a Former Client's Policies

Conflict-of-interest charges by former clients are particularly nettlesome when the lawyer has done a substantial amount of work on numerous matters for a former client. A recent ABA ethics opinion addressing the duties of former in-house lawyer notes that a lawyer's "general knowledge of the strategies, policies, or personnel" of the former client is "not sufficient by itself to establish a substantial relationship between the current matter" and past matters. *See* ABA Comm. on Ethics and Prof'l Responsibility, Formal Op. 99-415

(1999). Moreover, the mere "appearance of impropriety"[93] does not render the former lawyer's representation improper absent substantial relationship or the use of confidential information. *See In re American Airlines*, 972 F.2d 605, 619 (5th Cir. 1992) ("[T]he 'appearance of impropriety' has no relevance to our probe of ethical restraints."); *Parker v. Rowan Cos. Inc.*, No. Civ. A 03-0545, 2003 WL 22852218 (E.D. La. Nov. 25, 2003) (same).

Disqualification

A violation of Rule 1.9 typically disqualifies the lawyer–and his firm[94]–from representing a party adverse to his former client. Indeed, the Louisiana Supreme Court has held that "[t]he customary remedy for an alleged conflict of interest is disqualification of the attorney or firm with the conflict." *See Walker*, 817 So. 2d at 60 (citing *Corbello v. Iowa Production Co.*, 787 So. 2d 596 (La. Ct. App. 3d Cir. 2001)); *see generally* Restatement (Third) of the Law Governing Lawyers § 6 (2000) ("For a lawyer's breach of a duty owed to the lawyer's client, judicial remedies include . . . disqualifying a lawyer from representation.").

The "burden of proving disqualification of an attorney or other officer of the court rests on the party making the challenge."[95] *See State v. Craddock*, 62 So. 3d at 797 (La. Ct. App. 1st Cir. 2011) (citing *Walker*, 817 So. 2d at 60); *see also Duncan v. Merrill Lynch, Pierce, Fenner & Smith, Inc.*, 646 F.2d 1020, 1028 (5th Cir. 1981) (overruled on other grounds by *Gibbs v. Paluk*, 742 F.2d 181, 186 (5th Cir. 1986); *Gibbs* court acknowledged that it created a conflict in the rulings of the circuit courts); *Sumpter v. Hungerford*, No. 12-717, 7 (E.D. La. May 20, 2013) (quoting *Parker*, 2003 WL 22852218, at *5) ("The party who seeks to disqualify his former lawyer bears the burden of proving that the present and former representations are substantially related."). To carry this burden, the movant must "'delineate with specificity the subject matters, issues and causes of action presented in the former representation' so that the district court can determine if the substantial relationship test has been met." *Parker*, 2003 WL 22852218, at *5 (E.D. La. 2003) (quoting *Duncan*, 646 F.2d at 1029). The party seeking to disqualify his opponent's lawyer under

---

[93] This term is a relic of Canon 9 of the 1969 ABA Model Code of Professional Responsibility. *See* Model Code of Prof'l Responsibility Canon 9 (1969) ("A lawyer should avoid even the appearance of professional impropriety."); Warren L. Mengis, *Developments in the Law 1986-1987–Professional Responsibility*, 48 La. L. Rev. 437, 439 (1987) ("The old Canon 9 'appearance of impropriety' has now been suppressed."). The ABA later clarified that a lawyer should not be sanctioned or disqualified under such an "undefined," "question-begging" standard. *See* ABA Comm. on Ethics and Prof'l Responsibility, Formal Op. 342 (1975).

[94] *See* La. Rules of Prof'l Conduct r. 1.10 (2004).

[95] Because the movant bears the burden of proof, "the right of an attorney freely to practice his profession must, in the public interest, give way in cases of doubt." *See Doe v. A Corp.*, 709 F.2d 1043, 1047 (5th Cir. 1983) (quoting *Chugach Elec. Ass'n v. U.S. Dist. Ct.*, 370 F.2d 441, 444 (9th Cir. 1966)).

Rule 1.9 may be entitled to an *in-camera* hearing in order to protect confidential information. *See Keith v. Keith*, 140 So. 3d 1202 (La. Ct. App. 2d Cir. 2014).

The policies underlying this "customary remedy" are significant: "[d]isqualification, where appropriate, ensures that the case is well presented in court, that confidential information of present or former clients is not misused, and that a client's substantial interest in a lawyer's loyalty is protected." *See* Restatement (Third) of the Law Governing Lawyers § 6 cmt. i (2000). However, in evaluating whether disqualification is appropriate, courts must not ignore the significant associated costs:

> The costs imposed on a client deprived of a lawyer's services by disqualification can be substantial. At a minimum, the client is forced to incur the cost of finding a new lawyer not burdened by conflict in whom the client has confidence and educating that lawyer about the facts and issues. The costs of delay in the proceeding are borne by that client in part, but also by the tribunal and society. Disqualification is often the most effective sanction for a conflict of interest and will likely continue to be vigorously applied where necessary to protect the integrity of a proceeding or an important interest of the moving party. In applying it, however, tribunals should be vigilant to prevent its use as a tactic by which one party may impose unwarranted delay, costs, and other burdens on another. *Id.*

When disqualification is appropriate, it must be sought expeditiously. Louisiana courts have held that the former client must object to the representation timely or else lose the right to seek disqualification later. *See, e.g., Barre v. St. Martin*, 636 So. 2d 1061, 1063-1064 (La. Ct. App. 5th Cir. 1994) (reasoning that failure to object timely tacitly waives a party's right to object to his former lawyer's adverse position); *Brasseaux v. Girouard*, 214 So. 2d 401, 409 (La. Ct. App. 3d Cir. 1968) (reasoning that allowing a tardy objection in this context would allow disqualification to be used as a "purely dilatory or obstructive tactic").

Disciplinary Sanctions

For the disciplinary sanctions that are appropriate for a lawyer's failure to avoid conflicts of interest, *see supra* Annotations to Louisiana Rule 1.7; *In re Cudzik*, 738 So. 2d 1054, 1058-59 (La. 1999) (applying standard 4.3 to Rule 1.9 violation); *see also In re Barrios*, 929 So. 2d 63 (La. 2006) (suspending lawyer for two years for violation of 1.9 among other violations).

RULE 1.10. IMPUTATION OF CONFLICTS OF INTEREST: GENERAL RULE

(a) While lawyers are associated in a firm, none of them shall knowingly represent a client when any one of them practicing alone would be prohibited from doing so by Rules 1.7 or 1.9, unless the prohibition is based on a personal interest of the prohibited lawyer and does not present a significant risk of materially limiting the representation of the client by the remaining lawyers in the firm.

(b) When a lawyer has terminated an association with a firm, the firm is not prohibited from thereafter representing a person with interests materially adverse to those of a client represented by the formerly associated lawyer and not currently represented by the firm, unless:

(1) the matter is the same or substantially related to that in which the formerly associated lawyer represented the client; and

(2) any lawyer remaining in the firm has information protected by Rules 1.6 and 1.9(c) that is material to the matter.

(c) A disqualification prescribed by this rule may be waived by the affected client under the conditions stated in Rule 1.7.

(d) The disqualification of lawyers associated in a firm with former or current government lawyers is governed by Rule 1.11.

BACKGROUND

The Louisiana Supreme Court adopted this rule on January 20, 2004. It became effective on March 1, 2004, and has not been amended since.

Louisiana Rule 1.10 differs from ABA Model Rule of Professional Conduct 1.10 (2009) in one significant respect. The ABA Model Rule does not impute former-client conflicts arising under Model Rule 1.9(a) and Model Rule 1.9(b) to other members of the disqualified lawyer's firm if: (a) the disqualified lawyer represented the former client at another firm, (b) the new firm screens the disqualified lawyer from the matter, (c) the new firm provides notice to the affected former client, and (d) the new firm periodically certifies to the former client its compliance with the Model Rules and screening procedures. *See* ABA Model Rules of Prof'l Conduct r. 1.10 (2009).

Paragraph (a): Nonimputation of Personal Interest Conflicts

In 2002, the ABA included a reference in Model Rule 1.10(a) to exclude "personal interest" conflicts from the scope of imputation. The ABA included this reference to eliminate imputation in the case of conflicts involving a lawyer's own personal interest, at least when the usual concerns justifying imputation are not present. The exception applies only when the prohibited lawyer does not personally represent the client in the matter and no other circumstances suggest that the conflict of the prohibited lawyer is likely to influence the others' work. This was a substantive change in the Rule, but the ABA believed that Rule 1.10 provides clients with all the protection they need, given that the exception applies only when there is no significant risk that the personal-interest conflict will affect others in the lawyer's firm. *See* ABA Ethics 2000 Revision Notes to R. 1.10 (2002).

Paragraph (d): Former Government Lawyers

In 2002, the ABA included paragraph (d) to clarify that Rule 1.11 is intended to be the exclusive Model Rule governing the imputation of conflicts of interests of a current or former government lawyer. *See id.*

COMMENTS TO ABA MODEL RULE 1.10
Definition of "Firm"

[1] For purposes of the Rules of Professional Conduct, the term "firm" denotes lawyers in a law partnership, professional corporation, sole proprietorship or other association authorized to practice law; or lawyers employed in a legal services organization or the legal department of a corporation or other organization. *See* Rule 1.0(c). Whether two or more lawyers constitute a firm within this definition can depend upon the specific facts. *See* Rule 1.10, Comments [2] – [4].

Principles of Imputed Disqualification

[2] The rule of imputed disqualification stated in paragraph (a) gives effect to the principle of loyalty to the client as it applies to lawyers who practice in a law firm. Such situations can be considered from the premise that a firm of lawyers is essentially one lawyer for purposes of the rules governing loyalty to the client, or from the premise that each lawyer is vicariously bound by the obligation of loyalty owed by each lawyer with whom the lawyer is associated. Paragraph (a)(1) operates only among the lawyers currently associated in a firm. When a lawyer moves from one firm to another, the situation is governed by Rules 1.9(b) and 1.10(a)(2) and 1.10 (b).

[3] The rule in paragraph (a) does not prohibit representation whether neither questions regarding client loyalty nor protection of confidential information are presented. Where one lawyer in a firm could not effectively represent a given client because of strong political beliefs, for example, but that lawyer will do no work on the case and the personal beliefs of the lawyer will not materially limit the representation by others in the firm, the firm should not be disqualified. On the other hand, if an opposing party in a case were owned by a lawyer in the law firm, and others in the firm would be materially limited in pursuing the matter because of loyalty to that lawyer, the personal disqualification of the lawyer would be imputed to all others in the firm.

[4] The rule in paragraph (a) also does not prohibit representation by others in the law firm where the person prohibited from involvement in a matter is a nonlawyer, such as a paralegal or legal secretary. Nor does paragraph (a) prohibit representation if the lawyer is prohibited from acting because of events before the person became a lawyer, for example,

work that the person did as a law student. Such persons, however, ordinarily must be screened from any personal participation in the matter to avoid communication to others in the firm of confidential information that both the nonlawyers and the firm have a legal duty to protect. See Rules 1.0(k) and 5.3.

[5] Rule 1.10(b) operates to permit a law firm, under certain circumstances, to represent a person with interests directly adverse to those of a client represented by a lawyer who formerly was associated with the firm. The Rule applies regardless of when the formerly associated lawyer represented the client. However, the law firm may not represent a person with interests adverse to those of a present client of the firm, which would violate Rule 1.7. Moreover, the firm may not represent the person where the matter is the same or substantially related to that in which the formerly associated lawyer represented the client and any other lawyer currently in the firm has material information protected by Rules 1.6 and 1.9(c).

[6] Rule 1.10(c) removes imputation with the informed consent of the affected client or former client under the conditions stated in Rule 1.7. The conditions stated in Rule 1.7 require the lawyer to determine that the representation is not prohibited by Rule 1.7(b) and that each affected client or former client has given informed consent to the representation, confirmed in writing. In some cases, the risk may be so severe that the conflict may not be cured by client consent. For a discussion of the effectiveness of client waivers of conflicts that might arise in the future, see Rule 1.7, Comment [22]. For a definition of informed consent, see Rule 1.0(e).

[7] Rule 1.10(a)(2) similarly removes the imputation otherwise required by Rule 1.10(a), but unlike section (c), it does so without requiring that there be informed consent by the former client. Instead, it requires that the procedures laid out in sections (a)(2)(i)-(iii) be followed. A description of effective screening mechanisms appears in Rule 1.0(k). Lawyers should be aware, however, that, even where screening mechanisms have been adopted, tribunals may consider additional factors in ruling upon motions to disqualify a lawyer from pending litigation.

[8] Paragraph (a)(2)(i) does not prohibit the screened lawyer from receiving a salary or partnership share established by prior independent agreement, but that lawyer may not receive compensation directly related to the matter in which the lawyer is disqualified.

[9] The notice required by paragraph (a)(2)(ii) generally should include a description of the screened lawyer's prior representation and be given as soon as practicable after the need for screening becomes apparent. It also should include a statement by the screened lawyer and the firm that the client's material confidential information has not been disclosed or used in violation of the Rules. The notice is intended to enable the former client to evaluate and comment upon the effectiveness of the screening procedures.

[10] The certifications required by paragraph (a)(2)(iii) give the former client assurance that the client's material confidential information has not been disclosed or used inappropriately, either prior to timely implementation of a screen or thereafter. If compliance cannot be certified, the certificate must describe the failure to comply.

[11] Where a lawyer has joined a private firm after having represented the government, imputation is governed under Rule 1.11(b) and (c), not this Rule. Under Rule 1.11(d), where a lawyer represents the government after having served clients in private practice, nongovernmental employment or in another government agency, former client conflicts are not imputed to government lawyers associated with the individually disqualified lawyer.

[12] Where a lawyer is prohibited from engaging in certain transactions under Rule 1.8, paragraph (k) of that Rule, and not this Rule, determines whether that prohibition also applies to other lawyers associated in a firm with the personally prohibited lawyer.

ANNOTATIONS

Generally

Louisiana Rule 1.10(a) sets forth a simple rule: if one lawyer in the firm has a nonpersonal conflict of interest, the rest of the lawyers in the firm do as well. Thus, if Partner A is currently handling a matter that is directly adverse to a prospective client of Partner Z, then Partner Z may not undertake the representation of that prospective client. Not all conflicts are imputed to other members of a disqualified lawyer's firm.

Defining "Firm"

Rule 1.10 imputes disqualification to all members of the disqualified lawyer's "firm." Rule 1.0(c) uses the term "firm" to denote "a lawyer or lawyers in a law partnership, professional corporation, sole proprietorship or other association authorized to practice law; or lawyers employed in a legal services organization or the legal department of a corporation or other organization." *See* La. Rules of Prof'l Conduct r. 1.0(c) (2004). While the term "firm" has an obvious meaning in the context of traditional law partnerships and law corporations, its meaning in looser associations is less clear. For example, the Restatement suggests that lawyers who "share office facilities without reasonable adequate measures to protect confidential client information" may be considered "affiliated lawyers" for purposes of imputation of conflicts of interest. *See* Restatement (Third) of the Law Governing Lawyers § 123(3) (2000).

Indigent defender boards in Louisiana generally are "treated . . . as the equivalent of private law firms." *State v. Garcia*, 108 So. 3d 1, 38 (La. 2012), *cert. denied*, 133 S. Ct. 2863 (U.S. 2013); *State v. Connolly*, 930 So. 2d 951, 955 n.1 (La. 2006); *State v. McNeal*, 594 So. 2d 876 (La. 1992); *State v. Wells*, 191 So. 3d 1127, 1144 (La. Ct. App. 4th Cir. 2016) (citing *State v. Garcia*, 108 So. 3d 1, 28 (La. 2012). However, whether conflicts are imputed among independent contractors engaged by an indigent defender board is a question of fact that turns on all of the relevant facts and circumstances. *See Garcia*, 108 So. 3d at 1.

Interfirm Mobility and Imputed Conflicts

When a new lawyer ("New Lawyer") joins a firm ("New Firm"), and New Lawyer, while at another firm ("Old Firm"), personally represented a client ("Former Client"), that client–Former Client–is the lawyer's "former client." Rule 1.9(a) prohibits the lawyer from undertaking a representation for a new client ("New Client") that is adverse to Former Client in a substantially-related matter, and Louisiana Rule 1.10(a) imputes this conflict to everyone at New Firm. *See* La. Rules of Prof'l Conduct r. 1.9(a) (2004); *id.* R. 1.10(a).[96] However, if New Lawyer did not personally represent another client of Old Firm (i.e., that client was represented by another lawyer at Old Firm), that client is not considered to be New Lawyer's "former client," and there would be no conflict under Rule 1.9(a). Whether New Lawyer (or any other lawyer at New Firm) can represent New Client against the client of Old Firm turns on whether New Lawyer acquired confidential information that is "material to the matter" while at Old Firm. *See id.* R. 1.9(b). If New Lawyer neither represented the client at Old Firm nor acquired confidential information (sometimes called "water-cooler knowledge") while at Old Firm, New Firm can be adverse to that client. *See Willis v. TRC Companies, Inc.*, 2006 WL 2803058 at *6 (W.D. La. Sep. 28, 2006); *Kennedy v. Mindprint*, 08-20398 (5th Cir. Oct. 30, 2009).

When a lawyer ("Departing Lawyer") leaves a firm ("Abandoned Firm") and takes clients ("Departed Clients"), Abandoned Firm may sue Departed Clients in unrelated matters. Furthermore, Abandoned Firm may sue Departed Clients in substantially-related matters as long as no lawyers remaining at Abandoned Firm have confidential information that is "material to the matter." *See id.* R. 1.10(b).

The ABA has issued a formal opinion suggesting that a lawyer may reveal otherwise confidential information to evaluate conflicts associated with interfirm mobility. *See* ABA Formal Opinion 09-455 (Oct. 8, 2009). According to the ABA:

> When a lawyer moves between law firms, both the moving lawyer and the prospective new firm have a duty to detect and resolve conflicts of interest. Although Rule 1.6(a) generally protects conflicts information . . . disclosure of conflicts information during the process of lawyers moving between firms is ordinarily permissible, subject to limitations. Any disclosure of conflicts information should be no greater than reasonably necessary to accomplish the purpose of detecting and resolving conflicts and must not compromise the attorney-client privilege or otherwise prejudice a client or former client . . . .

Id.

"Of Counsel" Lawyers

A lawyer who is associated with a law firm in an "Of Counsel" capacity is treated like any other lawyer associated with the firm for purposes of imputation of conflicts of interest. In *In re Fuerst*, 157 So. 3d 569, 577 (La. 2014), the court stated that "[a] lawyer who is 'Of Counsel' to a law firm is considered to be a member of the firm for purposes of analyzing imputed disqualification questions." Therefore, a lawyer who is loosely associated with a firm in an "of counsel" capacity is treated no differently from any other firm lawyer.

---

[96] In contrast to the Louisiana Rule, ABA Model R. 1.10(a)(2) (2009) permits New Firm to use screening to avoid imputation of New Lawyer's conflict to other members of New Firm.

Screening to Remove Imputation of Conflicts?

Some jurisdictions, the Restatement and ABA Model Rule 1.10(a)(2), permit a law firm to avoid imputation of a conflict of interest by screening a disqualified lawyer from the other lawyers in the firm. *See* Restatement (Third) of the Law Governing Lawyers § 124 (2000). However, the Louisiana Rules of Professional Conduct do not offer screening as a means of avoiding or removing imputation. (Although Louisiana does permit screening in the context of successive government and private employment. *See* Louisiana R. 1.11.) Likewise, federal district courts in Louisiana, and the Fifth Circuit, have refused to allow the use of "Chinese Walls" or "Screens" to avoid imputed disqualification. *See, e.g., Green v. Admin. of Tulane Educational Fund*, No. Civ.A. 97-1869, 1998 WL 61041 (E.D. La. Feb. 13, 1998). Although one Louisiana appellate court has suggested that a "cone of silence" constructed around a disqualified lawyer may resolve a conflict, *see Petrovich v. Petrovich*, 556 So. 2d 281, 282 (La. Ct. App. 4th Cir. 1990), cert. denied, 559 So. 2d 1377 (La. 1990), this opinion is inconsistent with the express language of the Louisiana Rules of Professional Conduct.

Disciplinary Sanctions

For the disciplinary sanctions that are appropriate for a lawyer's failure to avoid conflicts of interest, *see supra* Annotations to Louisiana Rule 1.7.

RULE 1.11. SPECIAL CONFLICTS OF INTEREST FOR FORMER AND CURRENT GOVERNMENT OFFICERS AND EMPLOYEES

(a) Except as law may otherwise expressly permit, a lawyer who has formerly served as a public officer or employee of the government:

> (1) is subject to Rule 1.9(c); and

> (2) shall not otherwise represent a client in connection with a matter in which the lawyer participated personally and substantially as a public officer or employee, unless the appropriate government agency gives its informed consent, confirmed in writing, to the representation.

(b) When a lawyer is disqualified from representation under paragraph (a), no lawyer in a firm with which that lawyer is associated may knowingly undertake or continue representation in such a matter unless:

> (1) the disqualified lawyer is timely screened from any participation in the matter and is apportioned no part of the fee therefrom; and

> (2) written notice is promptly given to the appropriate government agency to enable it to ascertain compliance with the provisions of this rule.

(c) Except as law may otherwise expressly permit, a lawyer having information that the lawyer knows is confidential government information about a person acquired when the lawyer was a public officer or employee, may not represent a private client whose interests are adverse to that person in a matter in which the information could be used to the material disadvantage of that person. As used in this Rule, the term "confidential government information" means information that has been obtained under governmental authority and which, at the time this Rule is applied, the government is prohibited by law from disclosing to the public or has a legal privilege not to disclose and which is not otherwise available to the public. A firm with which that lawyer is associated may undertake or continue representation in the matter only if the disqualified lawyer is timely screened from any participation in the matter and is apportioned no part of the fee therefrom.

(d) Except as law may otherwise expressly permit, a lawyer currently serving as a public officer or employee:

(1) is subject to Rules 1.7 and 1.9; and

(2) shall not:

(i) participate in a matter in which the lawyer participated personally and substantially while in private practice or nongovernmental employment, unless the appropriate government agency gives its informed consent, confirmed in writing; or

(ii) negotiate for private employment with any person who is involved as a party or as lawyer for a party in a matter in which the lawyer is participating personally and substantially, except that a lawyer serving as a law clerk to a judge, other adjudicative officer or arbitrator may negotiate for private employment as permitted by Rule 1.12(b) and subject to the conditions stated in Rule 1.12(b).

(e) As used in this Rule, the term "matter" includes:

(1) any judicial or other proceeding, application, request for a ruling or other determination, contract, claim, controversy, investigation, charge, accusation, arrest or other particular matter involving a specific party or parties; and

(2) any other matter covered by the conflict of interest rules of the appropriate government agency.

BACKGROUND

The Louisiana Supreme Court adopted this rule on January 20, 2004. It became effective on March 1, 2004, and has not been amended since. This rule is identical to ABA Model Rule of Prof'l Conduct 1.11 (2013).

Caption

In 2002, the ABA changed the caption to the corresponding Model Rule to clarify that the Rule applies not only to a lawyer moving from government service to private practice (and vice versa), but also to a lawyer moving from one government agency to another.

Paragraph (a)

In 2002, the ABA amended Model Rule 1.11 to clarify that a lawyer who formerly served as a public officer or government employee is subject only to Rule 1.11 and not to Rule 1.9. Prior to this revision, there was disagreement as to whether an individual lawyer who has served as a government official or employee was subject to Rule 1.9 regarding obligations to former clients or whether their obligations under Rule 1.11(a) were exclusive. The ABA decided that representation adverse to a former government client is better determined under Rule 1.11(a), which also addresses representation in connection with any other matter in which the lawyer previously participated personally and substantially as a public officer or employee. In order not to inhibit transfer of employment to and from the government, the ABA believed that disqualification resulting from representation adverse to the former government client should be limited to particular matters in which the lawyer participated personally and substantially. This is also the standard for determining disqualification resulting from prior participation as a public officer or employee. The ABA addressed the meaning of the term "matter" in new Comment 10. *See* ABA Ethics 2000 Commission Revision Notes to Model Rule 1.11 (2013).

In paragraph (a)(1), the ABA further clarified that a former government lawyer is subject to Rule 1.9(c) regarding the confidentiality of information relating to the former representation of a government client. *See id.*

Paragraph (b): Imputation of Conflicts

In paragraph (b), the ABA clarified that conflicts arising under paragraph (a)–including former client conflicts–are not imputed to a different associated lawyer when the disqualified lawyer is properly screened. In so doing, the ABA intended no change in the basic rule of imputation for situations governed under former Rule 1.11(a). Rather, the ABA intended the change for situations that previously might have been governed by Rule 1.9 rather than 1.11(a). Although former client conflicts under Rule 1.9 are imputed to an associated lawyer under Rule 1.10, this paragraph states clearly that when the conflict arises from the individually disqualified lawyer's service as a public officer or employee of the government, the conflict is governed by paragraphs (a) and (b) of this Rule, and is not imputed if the lawyer is screened and the appropriate government agency is notified of the representation. The ABA believed that this result is necessary in order to continue to encourage lawyers to work in the public sector without fear that their service will unduly burden their future careers in the private sector. *See id.*

In addition, the ABA in 2002 added a scienter prerequisite to paragraph (b). This revision was intended to conform this Rule to Rule 1.10, in which an associated lawyer is not subject to discipline unless the lawyer "knows" of the disqualification of the lawyer's colleague. *See id.*

Paragraph (d): Relationship to Rules 1.9 and 1.10

The ABA intended paragraph (d) to clarify that an individual lawyer may not undertake representation adverse to former clients when doing so would violate Rule 1.9, even when the representation was not in the same matter but rather was in a substantially related matter in which it is likely that the lawyer received confidential client information. *See*

ABA Ethics 2000 Commission Revision Notes to Model Rule 1.11. However, under the Model Rules, such conflicts are not imputed to a lawyer associated in a government agency, even when formal screening mechanisms are not instituted. The lack of imputation applied to disqualifications under former Model Rule 1.11(c), but not necessarily to disqualifications of a current government lawyer under Rule 1.9, in which Rule 1.10 otherwise would apply. Screening is not required for public agencies because it may not be practical in some situations. Nevertheless, Comment 2 states the expectation that such a lawyer will in fact be screened where it is practical to do so.

Paragraph (d)(1): Relationship to Rule 1.7

The ABA decided to address in Rule 1.11 not only the imputation of former-client conflicts, but also the imputation of current conflicts of interest under Rule 1.7. As with former-client conflicts, the ABA decided that these conflicts should not be imputed to a lawyer associated in a government agency, even when formal screening mechanisms are not instituted. Screening is not required in the disciplinary context because it may not be practical in some situations. Nevertheless, as with Rule 1.9 conflicts, Comment 2 states the expectation that such a lawyer should in fact be screened where it is practicable to do so. *See id.*

COMMENTS TO ABA MODEL RULE 1.11

Generally

[1] A lawyer who has served or is currently serving as a public officer or employee is personally subject to the Rules of Professional Conduct, including the prohibition against concurrent conflicts of interest stated in Rule 1.7. In addition, such a lawyer may be subject to statutes and government regulations regarding conflict of interest. Such statutes and regulations may circumscribe the extent to which the government agency may give consent under this Rule. See Rule 1.0(e) for the definition of informed consent.

[2] Paragraphs (a)(1), (a)(2) and (d)(1) restate the obligations of an individual lawyer who has served or is currently serving as an officer or employee of the government toward a former government or private client. Rule 1.10 is not applicable to the conflicts of interest addressed by this Rule. Rather, paragraph (b) sets forth a special imputation rule for former government lawyers that provides for screening and notice. Because of the special problems raised by imputation within a government agency, paragraph (d) does not impute the conflicts of a lawyer currently serving as an officer or employee of the government to other associated government officers or employees, although ordinarily it will be prudent to screen such lawyers.

[3] Paragraphs (a)(2) and (d)(2) apply regardless of whether a lawyer is adverse to a former client and are thus designed not only to protect the former client, but also to prevent a lawyer from exploiting public office for the advantage of another client. For example, a lawyer who has pursued a claim on behalf of the government may not pursue the same claim on behalf of a later private client after the lawyer has left government service, except when authorized to do so by the government agency under paragraph (a). Similarly, a lawyer who has pursued a claim on behalf of a private client may not pursue the claim on behalf of the government, except when authorized to do so by paragraph (d). As

with paragraphs (a)(1) and (d)(1), Rule 1.10 is not applicable to the conflicts of interest addressed by these paragraphs.

[4] This Rule represents a balancing of interests. On the one hand, where the successive clients are a government agency and another client, public or private, the risk exists that power or discretion vested in that agency might be used for the special benefit of the other client. A lawyer should not be in a position where benefit to the other client might affect performance of the lawyer's professional functions on behalf of the government. Also, unfair advantage could accrue to the other client by reason of access to confidential government information about the client's adversary obtainable only through the lawyer's government service. On the other hand, the rules governing lawyers presently or formerly employed by a government agency should not be so restrictive as to inhibit transfer of employment to and from the government. The government has a legitimate need to attract qualified lawyers as well as to maintain high ethical standards. Thus a former government lawyer is disqualified only from particular matters in which the lawyer participated personally and substantially. The provisions for screening and waiver in paragraph (b) are necessary to prevent the disqualification rule from imposing too severe a deterrent against entering public service. The limitation of disqualification in paragraphs (a)(2) and (d)(2) to matters involving a specific party or parties, rather than extending disqualification to all substantive issues on which the lawyer worked, serves a similar function.

[5] When a lawyer has been employed by one government agency and then moves to a second government agency, it may be appropriate to treat that second agency as another client for purposes of this Rule, as when a lawyer is employed by a city and subsequently is employed by a federal agency. However, because the conflict of interest is governed by paragraph (d), the latter agency is not required to screen the lawyer as paragraph (b) requires a law firm to do. The question of whether two government agencies should be regarded as the same or different clients for conflict of interest purposes is beyond the scope of these Rules. See Rule 1.13 Comment [9].

[6] Paragraphs (b) and (c) contemplate a screening arrangement. See Rule 1.0(k) (requirements for screening procedures). These paragraphs do not prohibit a lawyer from receiving a salary or partnership share established by prior independent agreement, but that lawyer may not receive compensation directly relating the lawyer's compensation to the fee in the matter in which the lawyer is disqualified.

[7] Notice, including a description of the screened lawyer's prior representation and of the screening procedures employed, generally should be given as soon as practicable after the need for screening becomes apparent.

[8] Paragraph (c) operates only when the lawyer in question has knowledge of the information, which means actual knowledge; it does not operate with respect to information that merely could be imputed to the lawyer.

[9] Paragraphs (a) and (d) do not prohibit a lawyer from jointly representing a private party and a government agency when doing so is permitted by Rule 1.7 and is not otherwise prohibited by law.

[10] For purposes of paragraph (e) of this Rule, a "matter" may continue in another form. In determining whether two particular matters are the same, the lawyer should consider the extent to which the matters involve the same basic facts, the same or related parties, and the time elapsed.

ANNOTATIONS
Generally
Louisiana Rule 1.11(a) prohibits a former government lawyer from handling the same matter in private practice that the lawyer handled while in government service–absent prior consent of the agency. *See State v. Craddock*, 62 So. 3d 791, 797 (La. Ct. App. 1st Cir. 2011); *Walker v. La. Dep't of Transp. & Dev.*, 817 So. 2d 57 (La. 2002); *see also Louisiana v. Sparkman*, 443 So. 2d 700 (La. Ct. App. 4th Cir. 1983) (holding that a former district attorney who participated in a matter and later served as defense counsel in the same should have been disqualified from representing accused). This conflict–sometimes known as a "revolving-door"conflict–is also imputed to the lawyer's new firm. Unlike the imputation provided for in Rule 1.10, which cannot be cured by screening, Rule 1.11 permits a different lawyer in the disqualified lawyer's new firm to handle such a matter with appropriate screening and agency notification.

Louisiana Rule 1.11(b) prohibits a former government lawyer from being adverse to a person about whom the lawyer acquired confidential, potentially damaging information. Although this conflict is imputed to the lawyer's new firm, it too can be cured through nonconsensual screening.

Relationship to Rules 1.9 and 1.10
Louisiana Rule 1.11, like Rules 1.9 and 1.10, addresses conflicts of interest (and imputation of such conflicts) that arise when a lawyer handles a matter adverse to a former client. However, when the former client is a government agency, the scope of conduct that constitutes a "conflict of interest" is significantly narrower. *See, e.g., Babineaux v. Foster*, No. Civ. A 04-1679, 2005 WL 711604, at *3 (E.D. La. Mar. 21, 2005) (holding that subsections (a) and (b) of Rule 1.9 do not apply to a former government lawyer). Indeed, Rule 1.11 gives a former government lawyer and the lawyer's new firm more latitude to be adverse to a former agency than Rules 1.9 and 1.10 give a private lawyer and the lawyer's new firm to be adverse to former clients. However, such latitude has its boundaries. *Compare State v. Clausen*, 104 So. 3d 410, 412 (La. 2012) (holding client's current law firm be disqualified due to the firm's hiring of and failure to timely screen an assistant district attorney who participated in interviews of client while at the district attorney's office) *with Craddock*, 62 So. 3d at 798 (2011) (finding no disqualification for defense lawyer representing client when lawyer worked at district attorney's office at time of client's arrest but had no involvement or knowledge of client's case).

First, a lawyer is disqualified only if the lawyer participated "personally and substantially" in the relevant matter. La. Rules of Prof'l Conduct r. 1.11(a) (2004); *see also Clausen*, 104 So. 3d 410, 412 (law firm disqualified because of failure to provide prompt, written notice of firm's possible conflict of interest to district attorney's office in criminal case where lawyer in firm had previously worked on substantially related matter); Restatement

(Third) of the Law Governing Lawyers § 133(1) (2000). Performing merely perfunctory or insubstantial administrative tasks will not result in disqualification. *See e.g.*, *Craddock*, 62 So. 3d at 798; *see generally* ABA Comm. on Ethics and Professional Responsibility, Formal Op. 342 (1975) ("Substantial responsibility envisages a much closer and more direct relationship than that of a mere perfunctory approval or disapproval of the matter in question."); *see also Banineaux*, 2005 WL 711604 at *5 ("Personal and substantial involvement can be created through decision, disapproval, recommendation, the rendering of advice, investigation, or otherwise.") (quoting *United States v. Clark*, 333 F. Supp. 2d 789, 794 (E.D. Wis. 2004)).

Second, although the partners of a private lawyer are forbidden from being adverse to their partner's former client in the same or a substantially-related matter, the partners of a former government lawyer may undertake matters adverse to the government agency with appropriate screening. *See generally* ABA Comm. on Ethics and Professional Responsibility, Formal Op. 97-409 (1997). This rule is designed to ensure that a former government lawyer does not abuse the information gleaned through public service, and, on an institutional level, to ensure that governmental agencies maintain the ability to attract competent lawyers.

Screening a Disqualified Lawyer

To adequately screen a disqualified former government lawyer from a matter being handled by the lawyer's new partner, the lawyer should refrain from discussing the matter and from sharing fees relating to the matter. In addition, the new firm should ensure that all files and documents related to the matter are segregated from other firm files and that the disqualified lawyer has no access to them. Finally, the firm should notify all lawyers and support staff, preferably in writing, of the existence of the screen. *See* La. Rules of Prof'l Conduct r. 1.0(k) (2004) (defining "screened").

Other Laws Governing Former Government Lawyers

In addition to the provisions of this rule, other laws affect a former government lawyer's ability to be adverse to the lawyer's former agency. *See* Ethics in Government Act of 1978, 18 U.S.C. § 207(b) (prohibiting former federal officials from representing parties in dealings with former agency for a period of one year); Louisiana Code of Governmental Ethics, La. Rev. Stat. Ann. § 42:1121(C) (prohibiting certain state officials from representing parties in dealings with former agency for a period of two years). The Louisiana Supreme Court has held that section 42:1121(C) of the Code of Governmental Ethics does not violate the Louisiana Constitution. *See Midboe v. Comm'n on Ethics for Pub. Emps.'*, 646 So. 2d 351, 359-60 (La. 1994), *rev'd on other grounds by Transit Mgmt of Se. Louisiana, Inc. v. Com'n on Ethics for Pub. Emps.'*, 703 So. 2d 576 (La. 1997).

Private Lawyers Moving Into Public Service

A lawyer who has passed through the revolving door into government service likewise must not handle matters that the lawyer participated in "personally and substantially" while in private practice. La. Rules of Prof'l Conduct r. 1.11(d)(2) (2004); *see In re Smith*, 29 So. 3d 1232, 1236 (La. 2010) (suspending lawyer for violating Rule 1.11(d) among others through the lawyer's continued representation of criminal defendant once hired and while serving as assistant district attorney in same parish). These conflicts–unlike those arising in the context of a former government lawyer in private practice–are not imputed to different lawyers in the agency. *Id.* However, the agency should still screen the lawyer from any involvement in the matter. *See* ABA Comm. on Ethics and Professional Responsibility, Formal Op. 342 (1975).

Disciplinary Sanctions

For the disciplinary sanctions that are appropriate for a lawyer's failure to avoid conflicts of interest, *see supra* Annotations to Louisiana Rule 1.7

Rule 1.12. Former Judge, Arbitrator, Mediator or Other Third-Party Neutral

(a) Except as stated in paragraph (d), a lawyer shall not represent anyone in connection with a matter in which the lawyer participated personally and substantially as a judge or other adjudicative officer or law clerk to such a person or as an arbitrator, mediator or other third-party neutral, unless all parties to the proceeding give informed consent, confirmed in writing.

(b) A lawyer shall not negotiate for employment with any person who is involved as a party or as lawyer for a party in a matter in which the lawyer is participating personally and substantially as a judge or other adjudicative officer or as an arbitrator, mediator or other third-party neutral. A lawyer serving as a law clerk to a judge or other adjudicative officer may negotiate for employment with a party or lawyer involved in a matter in which the clerk is participating personally and substantially, but only after the lawyer has notified the judge, or other adjudicative officer.

(c) If a lawyer is disqualified by paragraph (a), no lawyer in a firm with which that lawyer is associated may knowingly undertake or continue representation in the matter unless:

> (1) the disqualified lawyer is timely screened from any participation in the matter and is apportioned no part of the fee therefrom; and

> (2) written notice is promptly given to the parties and any appropriate tribunal to enable them to ascertain compliance with the provisions of this rule.

(d) An arbitrator selected as a partisan of a party in a multi-member arbitration panel is not prohibited from subsequently representing that party.

Background

The Louisiana Supreme Court adopted this rule on January 20, 2004. It became effective on March 1, 2004, and has not been amended since. This rule is identical to ABA Model Rule of Prof'l Conduct 1.12 (2013).

Paragraph (c): Nonconsensual Screening of Other Third-Party Neutrals

Under the former Model Rule, the individual disqualification of a former judge or arbitrator was not imputed to an associated lawyer in a law firm if the conditions in (c)(1) and (2) were satisfied. The ABA determined that mediators and other third-party neutrals should be treated in the same manner because (1) there is typically less confidential information obtained in these proceedings than when the lawyer represents clients in a client-lawyer relationship, and (2) although the third-party neutral usually owes a duty of confidentiality to the parties, it is not the same duty of confidentiality owed under Rule 1.6. The ABA Ethics 2000 Commission also heard testimony that third-party neutrals do not share information with other lawyers in the firm in the same manner as lawyers representing clients. Finally, the ABA was concerned that failure to permit screening might inhibit the extent to which lawyers serve as third-party neutrals, particularly in voluntary, court-based alternative dispute resolution programs. *See* ABA Ethics 2000 Commission Revision Notes to Model Rule 1.12 (2002).

COMMENTS TO ABA MODEL RULE 1.12

[1] This Rule generally parallels Rule 1.11. The term "personally and substantially" signifies that a judge who was a member of a multimember court, and thereafter left judicial office to practice law, is not prohibited from representing a client in a matter pending in the court, but in which the former judge did not participate. So also the fact that a former judge exercised administrative responsibility in a court does not prevent the former judge from acting as a lawyer in a matter where the judge had previously exercised remote or incidental administrative responsibility that did not affect the merits. Compare the Comment to Rule 1.11. The term "adjudicative officer" includes such officials as judges pro tempore, referees, special masters, hearing officers and other parajudicial officers, and also lawyers who serve as part-time judges. Compliance Canons A(2), B(2) and C of the Model Code of Judicial Conduct provide that a part-time judge, judge pro tempore or retired judge recalled to active service, may not "act as a lawyer in any proceeding in which he served as a judge or in any other proceeding related thereto." Although phrased differently from this Rule, those Rules correspond in meaning.

[2] Like former judges, lawyers who have served as arbitrators, mediators or other third-party neutrals may be asked to represent a client in a matter in which the lawyer participated personally and substantially. This Rule forbids such representation unless all of the parties to the proceedings give their informed consent, confirmed in writing. See Rule 1.0(e) and (b). Other law or codes of ethics governing third-party neutrals may impose more stringent standards of personal or imputed disqualification. See Rule 2.4.

[3] Although lawyers who serve as third-party neutrals do not have information concerning the parties that is protected under Rule 1.6, they typically owe the parties an obligation of confidentiality under law or codes of ethics governing third-party neutrals. Thus, paragraph (c) provides that conflicts of the personally disqualified lawyer will be imputed to other lawyers in a law firm unless the conditions of this paragraph are met.

[4] Requirements for screening procedures are stated in Rule 1.0(k). Paragraph (c)(1) does not prohibit the screened lawyer from receiving a salary or partnership share established

by prior independent agreement, but that lawyer may not receive compensation directly related to the matter in which the lawyer is disqualified.

[5] Notice, including a description of the screened lawyer's prior representation and of the screening procedures employed, generally should be given as soon as practicable after the need for screening becomes apparent.

ANNOTATIONS
Generally
Louisiana Rule 1.12(a) generally prohibits a former judge, arbitrator, law clerk or third-party neutral from acting as a lawyer in connection with a matter in which the person participated "personally and substantially" as an adjudicative officer or law clerk. However, this conflict can be cured through securing the consent of "all parties to the proceeding."

It is permissible for a former judicial law clerk to join a law firm with cases pending before the former clerk's judge. *Dussouy v. Dussouy*, 220 So. 3d 197 (La. Ct. App. 4th Cir. 2017) (holding that recusal not required when presiding judge's former law clerk joined a law firm representing a party in a suit pending before the judge). Said the court:

> We find no legal basis in Rule of Professional Conduct 1.12 for the recusal of Judge D'Souza based on the alleged failure of [the former law clerk or her new firm] to notify [their opponents] in writing that Judge D'Souza's law clerk was hired by [the new firm]. Rule 1.12 requires only that the [former clerk's new] law firm withdraw from representing [a party before the judge], which it did in this matter.

Id. at 200.

Louisiana Rule 1.12(b) prohibits a current judge or arbitrator from negotiating employment with a lawyer who is "personally and substantially" involved in a pending proceeding. This conflict is nonconsentable. In contrast, a current law clerk may negotiate employment with a lawyer involved in a proceeding before the judge or arbitrator after the law clerk has so notified the judge or arbitrator.

Disciplinary Sanctions
For the disciplinary sanctions that are appropriate for a lawyer's failure to avoid conflicts of interest, see *supra* Annotations to Louisiana Rule 1.7.

RULE 1.13. ORGANIZATION AS CLIENT

(a) A lawyer employed or retained by an organization represents the organization acting through its duly authorized constituents.

(b) If a lawyer for an organization knows that an officer, employee or other person associated with the organization is engaged in action, intends to act or refuses to act in a matter related to the representation that is a violation of a legal obligation to the organization, or a violation of law that reasonably might be imputed to the organization, and that is likely to result in substantial injury to the organization, then the lawyer shall proceed as is reasonably necessary in the best interest of the organization. Unless the lawyer reasonably believes that it is not necessary in the best interest of the organization to do so, the lawyer shall refer the matter to higher authority in the organization, including, if warranted by the circumstances to the highest authority that can act on behalf of the organization as determined by applicable law.

(c) Except as provided in paragraph (d), if

(1) despite the lawyer's efforts in accordance with paragraph (b) the highest authority that can act on behalf of the organization insists upon or fails to address in a timely and appropriate manner an action, or a refusal to act, that is clearly a violation of law, and

(2) the lawyer reasonably believes that the violation is reasonably certain to result in substantial injury to the organization, then the lawyer may reveal information relating to the representation whether or not Rule 1.6 permits such disclosure, but only if and to the extent the lawyer reasonably believes necessary to prevent substantial injury to the organization.

(d) Paragraph (c) shall not apply with respect to information relating to a lawyer's representation of an organization to investigate an alleged violation of law, or to defend the organization or an officer, employee or other constituent associated with the organization against a claim arising out of an alleged violation of law.

154

(e) A lawyer who reasonably believes that he or she has been discharged because of the lawyer's actions taken pursuant to paragraphs (b) or (c), or who withdraws under circumstances that require or permit the lawyer to take action under either of those paragraphs, shall proceed as the lawyer reasonably believes necessary to assure that the organization's highest authority is informed of the lawyer's discharge or withdrawal.

(f) In dealing with an organization's directors, officers, employees, members, shareholders or other constituents, a lawyer shall explain the identity of the client when the lawyer knows or reasonably should know that the organization's interests are adverse to those of the constituents with whom the lawyer is dealing.

(g) A lawyer representing an organization may also represent any of its directors, officers, employees, members, shareholders or other constituents, subject to the provisions of Rule 1.7. If the organization's consent to the dual representation is required by Rule 1.7, the consent shall be given by an appropriate official of the organization other than the individual who is to be represented, or by the shareholders.

BACKGROUND

The Louisiana Supreme Court adopted this rule on January 20, 2004. It became effective on March 1, 2004, and has not been amended since. This rule is identical to ABA Model Rule of Prof'l Conduct 1.13 (2003).

COMMENTS TO ABA MODEL RULE 1.13

The Entity as the Client

[1] An organizational client is a legal entity, but it cannot act except through its officers, directors, employees, shareholders and other constituents. Officers, directors, employees and shareholders are the constituents of the corporate organizational client. The duties defined in this Comment apply equally to unincorporated associations. "Other constituents" as used in this Comment means the positions equivalent to officers, directors, employees and shareholders held by persons acting for organizational clients that are not corporations.

[2] When one of the constituents of an organizational client communicates with the organization's lawyer in that person's organizational capacity, the communication is protected by Rule 1.6. Thus, by way of example, if an organizational client requests its lawyer to investigate allegations of wrongdoing, interviews made in the course of that investigation between the lawyer and the client's employees or other constituents are covered by Rule 1.6. This does not mean, however, that constituents of an organizational client are the clients of the lawyer. The lawyer may not disclose to such constituents

information relating to the representation except for disclosures explicitly or impliedly authorized by the organizational client in order to carry out the representation or as otherwise permitted by Rule 1.6.

[3] When constituents of the organization make decisions for it, the decisions ordinarily must be accepted by the lawyer even if their utility or prudence is doubtful. Decisions concerning policy and operations, including ones entailing serious risk, are not as such in the lawyer's province. Paragraph (b) makes clear, however, that when the lawyer knows that the organization is likely to be substantially injured by action of an officer or other constituent that violates a legal obligation to the organization or is in violation of law that might be imputed to the organization, the lawyer must proceed as is reasonably necessary in the best interest of the organization. As defined in Rule 1.0(f), knowledge can be inferred from circumstances, and a lawyer cannot ignore the obvious.

[4] In determining how to proceed under paragraph (b), the lawyer should give due consideration to the seriousness of the violation and its consequences, the responsibility in the organization and the apparent motivation of the person involved, the policies of the organization concerning such matters, and any other relevant considerations. Ordinarily, referral to a higher authority would be necessary. In some circumstances, however, it may be appropriate for the lawyer to ask the constituent to reconsider the matter; for example, if the circumstances involve a constituent's innocent misunderstanding of law and subsequent acceptance of the lawyer's advice, the lawyer may reasonably conclude that the best interest of the organization does not require that the matter be referred to higher authority. If a constituent persists in conduct contrary to the lawyer's advice, it will be necessary for the lawyer to take steps to have the matter reviewed by a higher authority in the organization. If the matter is of sufficient seriousness and importance or urgency to the organization, referral to higher authority in the organization may be necessary even if the lawyer has not communicated with the constituent. Any measures taken should, to the extent practicable, minimize the risk of revealing information relating to the representation to persons outside the organization. Even in circumstances where a lawyer is not obligated by Rule 1.13 to proceed, a lawyer may bring to the attention of an organizational client, including its highest authority, matters that the lawyer reasonably believes to be of sufficient importance to warrant doing so in the best interest of the organization.

[5] Paragraph (b) also makes clear that when it is reasonably necessary to enable the organization to address the matter in a timely and appropriate manner, the lawyer must refer the matter to higher authority, including, if warranted by the circumstances, the highest authority that can act on behalf of the organization under applicable law. The organization's highest authority to whom a matter may be referred ordinarily will be the board of directors or similar governing body. However, applicable law may prescribe that under certain conditions the highest authority reposes elsewhere, for example, in the independent directors of a corporation.

Relation to Other Rules

[6] The authority and responsibility provided in this Rule are concurrent with the authority and responsibility provided in other Rules. In particular, this Rule does not limit or expand the lawyer's responsibility under Rules 1.8, 1.16, 3.3 or 4.1. Paragraph (c) of this Rule supplements Rule 1.6(b) by providing an additional basis upon which the lawyer may reveal information relating to the representation, but does not modify, restrict, or limit the provisions of Rule 1.6(b)(1) – (6). Under paragraph (c) the lawyer may reveal such information only when the organization's highest authority insists upon or fails to address threatened or ongoing action that is clearly a violation of law, and then only to the extent the lawyer reasonably believes necessary to prevent reasonably certain substantial injury to the organization. It is not necessary that the lawyer's services be used in furtherance of the violation, but it is required that the matter be related to the lawyer's representation of the organization. If the lawyer's services are being used by an organization to further a crime or fraud by the organization, Rules 1.6(b)(2) and 1.6(b)(3) may permit the lawyer to disclose confidential information. In such circumstances Rule 1.2(d) may also be applicable, in which event, withdrawal from the representation under Rule 1.16(a)(1) may be required.

[7] Paragraph (d) makes clear that the authority of a lawyer to disclose information relating to a representation in circumstances described in paragraph (c) does not apply with respect to information relating to a lawyer's engagement by an organization to investigate an alleged violation of law or to defend the organization or an officer, employee or other person associated with the organization against a claim arising out of an alleged violation of law. This is necessary in order to enable organizational clients to enjoy the full benefits of legal counsel in conducting an investigation or defending against a claim.

[8] A lawyer who reasonably believes that he or she has been discharged because of the lawyer's actions taken pursuant to paragraph (b) or (c), or who withdraws in circumstances that require or permit the lawyer to take action under either of these paragraphs, must proceed as the lawyer reasonably believes necessary to assure that the organization's highest authority is informed of the lawyer's discharge or withdrawal.

Government Agency

[9] The duty defined in this Rule applies to governmental organizations. Defining precisely the identity of the client and prescribing the resulting obligations of such lawyers may be more difficult in the government context and is a matter beyond the scope of these Rules. See Scope [18]. Although in some circumstances the client may be a specific agency, it may also be a branch of government, such as the executive branch, or the government as a whole. For example, if the action or failure to act involves the head of a bureau, either the department of which the bureau is a part or the relevant branch of government may be the client for purposes of this Rule. Moreover, in a matter involving the conduct of government officials, a government lawyer may have authority under applicable law to question such conduct more extensively than that of a lawyer for a private organization in similar circumstances. Thus, when the client is a governmental organization, a different balance may be appropriate between maintaining confidentiality and assuring that the wrongful act is prevented or rectified, for public business is involved. In addition, duties of

lawyers employed by the government or lawyers in military service may be defined by statutes and regulation. This Rule does not limit that authority. See Scope.

Clarifying the Lawyer's Role

[10] There are times when the organization's interest may be or become adverse to those of one or more of its constituents. In such circumstances the lawyer should advise any constituent, whose interest the lawyer finds adverse to that of the organization of the conflict or potential conflict of interest, that the lawyer cannot represent such constituent, and that such person may wish to obtain independent representation. Care must be taken to assure that the individual understands that, when there is such adversity of interest, the lawyer for the organization cannot provide legal representation for that constituent individual, and that discussions between the lawyer for the organization and the individual may not be privileged.

[11] Whether such a warning should be given by the lawyer for the organization to any constituent individual may turn on the facts of each case.

Dual Representation

[12] Paragraph (g) recognizes that a lawyer for an organization may also represent a principal officer or major shareholder.

Derivative Actions

[13] Under generally prevailing law, the shareholders or members of a corporation may bring suit to compel the directors to perform their legal obligations in the supervision of the organization. Members of unincorporated associations have essentially the same right. Such an action may be brought nominally by the organization, but usually is, in fact, a legal controversy over management of the organization.

[14] The question can arise whether counsel for the organization may defend such an action. The proposition that the organization is the lawyer's client does not alone resolve the issue. Most derivative actions are a normal incident of an organization's affairs, to be defended by the organization's lawyer like any other suit. However, if the claim involves serious charges of wrongdoing by those in control of the organization, a conflict may arise between the lawyer's duty to the organization and the lawyer's relationship with the board. In those circumstances, Rule 1.7 governs who should represent the directors and the organization.

ANNOTATIONS

Generally

Paragraph (a) sets forth the fundamental principle that serves as the starting point for the analysis of any conflict-of-interest–or other ethical issue–facing a lawyer representing a juridical person or one of its constituents. The overarching principle set forth in this paragraph is that a lawyer "retained by an organization" represents the organization and not its employees, officers, directors or other constituents. However, because a juridical person functions only through its human agents, issues often arise regarding the lawyer's role vis-à-vis the organization and its constituents. *See also* Restatement (Third) of the Law Governing Lawyers § 96 (2000) (Representing an Organization as Client).

Dealing with Unlawful Conduct of Organizational Constituents

Paragraphs (b), (c) and (d) address the lawyer's obligations when the lawyer learns that an organizational constituent is acting in an unlawful manner that will likely cause substantial harm to the organizational client. Paragraph (b) counsels, consistent with the core principles set forth in paragraph (a), that the lawyer in this situation must act to protect the interests of the organization rather than those of its constituents.

Avoiding Role Confusion in Dealing with Organizational Constituents

Paragraph (f) recognizes that organizational constituents are sometimes, perhaps often, confused regarding the role of the lawyer in a matter. For example, a lawyer representing a corporation in a criminal or administrative environmental matter very well may have a conflict of interest in also representing employees who may have engaged in a potentially unlawful toxic waste discharge. In such a case, the lawyer must carefully identify the client and ensure that there is no confusion regarding the lawyer's role in the matter. *See* La. Rules of Prof'l Conduct r. 1.13(f) (2004) (relating to a lawyer's duties to organizational constituents); *see also id.* r. 4.3 (relating to a lawyer's duties to unrepresented persons).

Multiple Representation of Organization and Constituents

Paragraph (g) acknowledges, however, that there are circumstances under which a lawyer can represent both the organization and its constituents. Indeed, such joint representation is appropriate if there is no conflict of interest. Moreover, such joint representation is appropriate, even in the face of a conflict, if each affected party gives informed consent. The lawyer must obtain the consent of the organization either from its equity participants, or from a duly authorized, independent constituent–not from the party to be represented.

Partnerships and Partnerships In Commendam

Louisiana partnerships and partnerships in commendam (limited partnerships) are, and have long been, distinct legal entities rather than mere aggregations of individuals. A lawyer representing a partnership represents that entity and not its constituents. As a result, the limited partnership in such a representation is the "client" to whom the lawyer owes the duties of competence, loyalty, and confidentiality, among others. *See generally* ABA Comm. on Ethics and Professional Responsibility, Formal Op. 91-361 (1991) (Representation of Partnership); Restatement (Third) of the Law Governing Lawyers § 96 cmt. c (2000).

Derivative Actions

Shareholders (or other equity participants) of an organization typically commence a derivative action when one or more members of management have violated their duty of care or loyalty to the organization through malfeasance or nonfeasance. Such an action belongs not to the shareholder but to the organization. *See, e.g., Noe v. Roussel*, 310 So. 2d 806 (La. 1975). Many near-frivolous derivative actions are "a normal incident of an organization's affairs, to be defended by the organization's lawyer like any other suit." ABA Model R. 1.13 cmt. 14. In such cases, conflicts are unlikely to arise when the organization's lawyer defends a director charged with such wrongdoing. In contrast, cases presenting serious and nonfrivolous charges of insider misconduct are significantly more likely to give rise to conflicting interests.

In *Robinson v. Snell's Limbs and Braces of New Orleans, Inc.*, 538 So. 2d 1045 (La. Ct. App. 4th Cir. 1989), the Louisiana Fourth Circuit Court of Appeal found no conflict of interest in a lawyer representing both a corporation's officers and the nominal corporate defendant because the organizational interests were represented solely by the plaintiff-shareholders. *Id.* at 1047-49. Assuming that the lawyer's representation of both the corporation and its constituents was not adversely affected by the lawyer's duties to the other, the court's conclusion is unassailable. *See* Restatement (Third) of the Law Governing Lawyers § 131 (2000).

Disciplinary Sanctions

For the disciplinary sanctions that are appropriate for a lawyer's failure to avoid conflicts of interest, see *supra* Annotations to Louisiana Rule 1.7.

RULE 1.14. CLIENT WITH DIMINISHED CAPACITY

(a) When a client's capacity to make adequately considered decisions in connection with a representation is diminished, whether because of minority, mental impairment or for some other reason, the lawyer shall, as far as reasonably possible, maintain a normal client-lawyer relationship with the client.

(b) When the lawyer reasonably believes that the client has diminished capacity, is at risk of substantial physical, financial or other harm unless action is taken and cannot adequately act in the client's own interest, the lawyer may take reasonably necessary protective action, including consulting with individuals or entities that have the ability to take action to protect the client and, in appropriate cases, seeking the appointment of a fiduciary, including a guardian, curator or tutor, to protect the client's interests.

(c) Information relating to the representation of a client with diminished capacity is protected by Rule 1.6. When taking protective action pursuant to paragraph (b), the lawyer is impliedly authorized under Rule 1.6(a) to reveal information about the client, but only to the extent reasonably necessary to protect the client's interests.

BACKGROUND

The Louisiana Supreme Court adopted this rule on January 20, 2004. It became effective on March 1, 2004, and has not been amended since.

This rule is identical in substance to ABA Model Rule of Prof'l Conduct 1.14 (2002). The only difference between this rule and the corresponding model rule is the deletion of the terms "guardian ad litem, conservator or guardian," and the insertion of analogous Louisiana terms.

Paragraph (b): Protective Measures

In 2002, the ABA amended Model Rule 1.14 to provide guidance to lawyers regarding the "protective action" that a lawyer may take short of seeking a guardian. The revision permits a lawyer to "take reasonably necessary protective action, including consulting with individuals or entities that have the ability to take action to protect the client, and, in appropriate cases, seeking the appointment of a guardian ad litem, conservator or guardian." The ABA believed that the modified provision offers the lawyer flexibility when a client faces substantial risk of harm or when emergency legal assistance is required as described in Comments [9] and [10]. *See* ABA Ethics 2000 Commission Revision Notes to Model Rule 1.14 (2002).

Paragraph (c): Limitation on Permissible "Protective Action"

The ABA adopted paragraph (c) to specify the means by which "protective action" should be limited to avoid client harm. This paragraph explicitly recognizes the relationship of Rule 1.14(b) to Rule 1.6, and states that Rule 1.6 allows disclosure of information under Rule 1.14(b) only as "reasonably necessary to protect the client's interests." *See id.*

COMMENTS TO ABA MODEL RULE 1.14

Generally

[1] The normal client-lawyer relationship is based on the assumption that the client, when properly advised and assisted, is capable of making decisions about important matters. When the client is a minor or suffers from a diminished mental capacity, however, maintaining the ordinary client-lawyer relationship may not be possible in all respects. In particular, a severely incapacitated person may have no power to make legally binding decisions. Nevertheless, a client with diminished capacity often has the ability to understand, deliberate upon, and reach conclusions about matters affecting the client's own well-being. For example, children as young as five or six years of age, and certainly those of ten or twelve, are regarded as having opinions that are entitled to weight in legal proceedings concerning their custody. So also, it is recognized that some persons of advanced age can be quite capable of handling routine financial matters while needing special legal protection concerning major transactions.

[2] The fact that a client suffers a disability does not diminish the lawyer's obligation to treat the client with attention and respect. Even if the person has a legal representative, the lawyer should as far as possible accord the represented person the status of client, particularly in maintaining communication.

[3] The client may wish to have family members or other persons participate in discussions with the lawyer. When necessary to assist in the representation, the presence of such persons generally does not affect the applicability of the attorney-client evidentiary privilege. Nevertheless, the lawyer must keep the client's interests foremost and, except for protective action authorized under paragraph (b), must to look to the client, and not family members, to make decisions on the client's behalf.

[4] If a legal representative has already been appointed for the client, the lawyer should ordinarily look to the representative for decisions on behalf of the client. In matters involving a minor, whether the lawyer should look to the parents as natural guardians may depend on the type of proceeding or matter in which the lawyer is representing the minor. If the lawyer represents the guardian as distinct from the ward, and is aware that the guardian is acting adversely to the ward's interest, the lawyer may have an obligation to prevent or rectify the guardian's misconduct. See Rule 1.2(d).

Taking Protective Action

[5] If a lawyer reasonably believes that a client is at risk of substantial physical, financial or other harm unless action is taken, and that a normal client-lawyer relationship cannot be maintained as provided in paragraph (a) because the client lacks sufficient capacity to communicate or to make adequately considered decisions in connection with the representation, then paragraph (b) permits the lawyer to take protective measures deemed

necessary. Such measures could include: consulting with family members, using a reconsideration period to permit clarification or improvement of circumstances, using voluntary surrogate decisionmaking tools such as durable powers of attorney or consulting with support groups, professional services, adult-protective agencies or other individuals or entities that have the ability to protect the client. In taking any protective action, the lawyer should be guided by such factors as the wishes and values of the client to the extent known, the client's best interests and the goals of intruding into the client's decisionmaking autonomy to the least extent feasible, maximizing client capacities and respecting the client's family and social connections.

[6] In determining the extent of the client's diminished capacity, the lawyer should consider and balance such factors as: the client's ability to articulate reasoning leading to a decision, variability of state of mind and ability to appreciate consequences of a decision; the substantive fairness of a decision; and the consistency of a decision with the known long-term commitments and values of the client. In appropriate circumstances, the lawyer may seek guidance from an appropriate diagnostician.

[7] If a legal representative has not been appointed, the lawyer should consider whether appointment of a guardian ad litem, conservator or guardian is necessary to protect the client's interests. Thus, if a client with diminished capacity has substantial property that should be sold for the client's benefit, effective completion of the transaction may require appointment of a legal representative. In addition, rules of procedure in litigation sometimes provide that minors or persons with diminished capacity must be represented by a guardian or next friend if they do not have a general guardian. In many circumstances, however, appointment of a legal representative may be more expensive or traumatic for the client than circumstances in fact require. Evaluation of such circumstances is a matter entrusted to the professional judgment of the lawyer. In considering alternatives, however, the lawyer should be aware of any law that requires the lawyer to advocate the least restrictive action on behalf of the client.

Disclosure of the Client's Condition
[8] Disclosure of the client's diminished capacity could adversely affect the client's interests. For example, raising the question of diminished capacity could, in some circumstances, lead to proceedings for involuntary commitment. Information relating to the representation is protected by Rule 1.6. Therefore, unless authorized to do so, the lawyer may not disclose such information. When taking protective action pursuant to paragraph (b), the lawyer is impliedly authorized to make the necessary disclosures, even when the client directs the lawyer to the contrary. Nevertheless, given the risks of disclosure, paragraph (c) limits what the lawyer may disclose in consulting with other individuals or entities or seeking the appointment of a legal representative. At the very least, the lawyer should determine whether it is likely that the person or entity consulted with will act adversely to the client's interests before discussing matters related to the client. The lawyer's position in such cases is an unavoidably difficult one.

Emergency Legal Assistance

[9] In an emergency where the health, safety or a financial interest of a person with seriously diminished capacity is threatened with imminent and irreparable harm, a lawyer may take legal action on behalf of such a person even though the person is unable to establish a client-lawyer relationship or to make or express considered judgments about the matter, when the person or another acting in good faith on that person's behalf has consulted with the lawyer. Even in such an emergency, however, the lawyer should not act unless the lawyer reasonably believes that the person has no other lawyer, agent or other representative available. The lawyer should take legal action on behalf of the person only to the extent reasonably necessary to maintain the status quo or otherwise avoid imminent and irreparable harm. A lawyer who undertakes to represent a person in such an exigent situation has the same duties under these Rules as the lawyer would with respect to a client.

[10] A lawyer who acts on behalf of a person with seriously diminished capacity in an emergency should keep the confidences of the person as if dealing with a client, disclosing them only to the extent necessary to accomplish the intended protective action. The lawyer should disclose to any tribunal involved and to any other counsel involved the nature of his or her relationship with the person. The lawyer should take steps to regularize the relationship or implement other protective solutions as soon as possible. Normally, a lawyer would not seek compensation for such emergency actions taken.

ANNOTATIONS

Generally

Dealing with an incapacitated, or potentially incapacitated, client presents difficult, and sometimes intractable, issues. Paragraph (a) of this rule directs the lawyer to maintain a normal lawyer-client relationship with the client if at all possible. Thus, even if a client appears to be moderately or intermittently impaired, the lawyer must communicate and consult with the client just as the lawyer would with any other client.

However, if the lawyer reasonably believes that the impairment has substantially affected the client's ability consistently to make reasoned decisions regarding the matter, the lawyer should consider seeking the appointment of a curator, tutor, or other legal representative. In deciding whether this or similar action is appropriate, the lawyer generally should pursue the "least restrictive action" necessitated by the circumstances. ABA Comm. on Ethics and Professional Responsibility, Formal Op. 96-404 (1996). Once a curator or tutor has qualified for office and has received appropriate letters from the court, the lawyer generally should seek direction from that fiduciary rather than from the incapacitated client. Nevertheless, vis-à-vis the fiduciary and the incapacitated person, the "client" remains the incapacitated person for purposes of determining whose best interest should be protected.

Representing Minors

A lawyer representing a minor is entitled to learn through discovery the location of the lawyer's client, even though the client is in foster care. *See In re Genusa*, 381 So. 2d 504, 506 (La. 1980). Moreover, a lawyer representing a child who "has no legal representative to whom the attorney may look in making decisions... may be forced to make them himself." *Id.* at 505. In so doing, the lawyer should "consider all the circumstances," and act in the best interests of the client. *Id.*

Disciplinary Sanctions

The Louisiana Supreme Court imposed disbarment where a lawyer's violation of Rule 1.14 was "egregious" because he "intentionally used his legal skills" to take advantage of an "obviously vulnerable victim." *In re Letellier,* 742 So. 2d 544 (La. 1999); *In re Cofield,* 937 So. 2d 330, 343 (La. 2006) (lawyer breached his fiduciary obligations as a trustee for a mentally-disabled client, engaged in questionable transactions with the client, and attempted to thwart attempts by the client's family to remove the lawyer as trustee) (citing *In re Letellier,* 742 So. 2d 544 (La. 1999)); *see also In re Maxwell,* 44 So. 2d 668, 675 (La. 2010) (permanently disbarring lawyer for misconduct towards incapacitated client); Maunsel W. Hickey et al., *Incapacity of Clients or Family Members,* 1 La. Prac. Est. Plan. § 4:149 (2015-2016 ed.)

RULE 1.15. SAFEKEEPING PROPERTY

(a) A lawyer shall hold property of clients or third persons that is in a lawyer's possession in connection with a representation separate from the lawyer's own property. Except as provided in (g) and the IOLTA Rules below, funds shall be kept in one or more separate interest-bearing client trust accounts maintained in a bank or savings and loan association: 1) authorized by federal or state law to do business in Louisiana, the deposits of which are insured by an agency of the federal government; 2) in the state where the lawyer's primary office is situated, if not within Louisiana; or 3) elsewhere with the consent of the client or third person. No earnings on a client trust account may be made available to or utilized by a lawyer or law firm. Other property shall be identified as such and appropriately safeguarded. Complete records of such account funds and other property shall be kept by the lawyer and shall be preserved for a period of five years after termination of the representation.

(b) A lawyer may deposit the lawyer's own funds in a client trust account for the sole purpose of paying bank service charges on that account or obtaining a waiver of those charges, but only in an amount necessary for that purpose.

(c) A lawyer shall deposit into a client trust account legal fees and expenses that have been paid in advance, to be withdrawn by the lawyer only as fees are earned or expenses incurred. The lawyer shall deposit legal fees and expenses into the client trust account consistent with Rule 1.5(f).

(d) Upon receiving funds or other property in which a client or third person has an interest, a lawyer shall promptly notify the client or third person. For purposes of this rule, the third person's interest shall be one of which the lawyer has actual knowledge, and shall be limited to a statutory lien or privilege, a final judgment addressing disposition of those funds or property, or a written agreement by the client or the lawyer on behalf of the client guaranteeing payment out of those funds or property. Except as stated in this rule or otherwise permitted by law or by agreement with the client, a lawyer shall promptly deliver to the client or third person any funds or other property that the client or third person is entitled to receive and, upon request by the client or third person, shall promptly render a full accounting regarding such property.

(e) When in the course of representation a lawyer is in possession of property in which two or more persons (one of whom may be the lawyer) claim interests, the property shall be kept separate by the lawyer until the dispute is resolved. The lawyer shall promptly distribute all portions of the property as to which the interests are not in dispute.

(f) Every check, draft, electronic transfer, or other withdrawal instrument or authorization from a client trust account shall be personally signed by a lawyer or, in the case of electronic, telephone, or wire transfer, from a client trust account, directed by a lawyer or, in the case of a law firm, one or more lawyers authorized by the law firm. A lawyer shall not use any debit card or automated teller machine card to withdraw funds from a client trust account. On client trust accounts, cash withdrawals and checks made payable to "Cash" are prohibited. A lawyer shall subject all client trust accounts to a reconciliation process at least quarterly, and shall maintain records of the reconciliation as mandated by this rule.

(g) A lawyer shall create and maintain an "IOLTA Account," which is a pooled interest-bearing client trust account for funds of clients or third persons which are nominal in amount or to be held for such a short period of time that the funds would not be expected to earn income for the client or third person in excess of the costs incurred to secure such income.

> (1) IOLTA Accounts shall be of a type approved and authorized by the Louisiana Bar Foundation and maintained only in "eligible" financial institutions, as approved and certified by the Louisiana Bar Foundation. The Louisiana Bar Foundation shall establish regulations, subject to approval by the Supreme Court of Louisiana, governing the determination that a financial institution is eligible to hold IOLTA Accounts and shall at least annually publish a list of LBF-approved/certified eligible financial institutions. Participation in the IOLTA program is voluntary for financial institutions.

IOLTA Accounts shall be established at a bank or savings and loan association authorized by federal or state law to do business in Louisiana, the deposits of which are insured by an agency of the federal government or at an open-end investment company registered with the Securities and Exchange Commission authorized by federal or state law to do business in Louisiana which shall be invested solely in or fully collateralized by U.S. Government Securities with total assets of at least $250,000,000 and in order for a financial institution to be approved and certified by the Louisiana Bar Foundation as eligible, shall comply with the following provisions:

(A) No earnings from such an account shall be made available to a lawyer or law firm.

(B) Such account shall include all funds of clients or third persons which are nominal in amount or to be held for such a short period of time the funds would not be expected to earn income for the client or third person in excess of the costs incurred to secure such income.

(C) Funds in each interest-bearing client trust account shall be subject to withdrawal upon request and without delay, except as permitted by law.

(2) To be approved and certified by the Louisiana Bar Foundation as eligible, financial institutions shall maintain IOLTA Accounts which pay an interest rate comparable to the highest interest rate or dividend generally available from the institution to its non-IOLTA customers when IOLTA Accounts meet or exceed the same minimum balance or other eligibility qualifications, if any. In determining the highest interest rate or dividend generally available from the institution to its non-IOLTA accounts, eligible institutions may consider factors, in addition to the IOLTA Account balance, customarily considered by the institution when setting interest rates or dividends for its customers, provided that such factors do not discriminate between IOLTA

Accounts and accounts of non-IOLTA customers, and that these factors do not include that the account is an IOLTA Account. The eligible institution shall calculate interest and dividends in accordance with its standard practice for non-IOLTA customers, but the eligible institution may elect to pay a higher interest or dividend rate on IOLTA Accounts.

(3) To be approved and certified by the Louisiana Bar Foundation as eligible, a financial institution may achieve rate comparability required in (g)(2) by:

> (A) Establishing the IOLTA Account as: (1) an interest-bearing checking account; (2) a money market deposit account with or tied to checking; (3) a sweep account which is a money market fund or daily (overnight) financial institution repurchase agreement invested solely in or fully collateralized by U.S. Government Securities; or (4) an open-end money market fund solely invested in or fully collateralized by U.S. Government Securities. A daily financial institution repurchase agreement may be established only with an eligible institution that is "well-capitalized" or "adequately capitalized" as those terms are defined by applicable federal statutes and regulations. An open-end money market fund must be invested solely in U.S. Government Securities or repurchase agreements fully collateralized by U.S. Government Securities, must hold itself out as a "money-market fund" as that term is defined by federal statutes and regulations under the Investment Company Act of 1940, and, at the time of the investment, must have total assets of at least $250,000,000. "U.S. Government Securities" refers to U.S. Treasury obligations and obligations issued or guaranteed as to principal and interest by the United States or any agency or instrumentality thereof.

(B) Paying the comparable rate on the IOLTA checking account in lieu of establishing the IOLTA Account as the higher rate product; or

(C) Paying a "benchmark" amount of qualifying funds equal to 60% of the Federal Fund Target Rate as of the first business day of the quarter or other IOLTA remitting period; no fees may be deducted from this amount which is deemed already to be net of "allowable reasonable fees."

(4) Lawyers or law firms depositing the funds of clients or third persons in an IOLTA Account shall direct the depository institution:

(A) To remit interest or dividends, net of any allowable reasonable fees on the average monthly balance in the account, or as otherwise computed in accordance with an eligible institution's standard accounting practice, at least quarterly, to the Louisiana Bar Foundation, Inc.;

(B) to transmit with each remittance to the Foundation, a statement, on a form approved by the LBF, showing the name of the lawyer or law firm for whom the remittance is sent and for each account: the rate of interest or dividend applied; the amount of interest or dividends earned; the types of fees deducted, if any; and the average account balance for each account for each month of the period in which the report is made; and

(C) to transmit to the depositing lawyer or law firm a report in accordance with normal procedures for reporting to its depositors.

(5) "Allowable reasonable fees" for IOLTA Accounts are: per check charges; per deposit charges; a fee in lieu of minimum balance; sweep fees and a reasonable IOLTA Account administrative fee. All other fees are the responsibility of, and may be charged to, the lawyer or law firm maintaining the IOLTA Account. Fees or service charges that are not "allowable reasonable fees" include, but are not limited to: the cost of check printing; deposit

stamps; NSF charges; collection charges; wire transfers; and fees for cash management. Fees or charges in excess of the earnings accrued on the account for any month or quarter shall not be taken from earnings accrued on other IOLTA Accounts or from the principal of the account. Eligible financial institutions may elect to waive any or all fees on IOLTA Accounts.

(6) A lawyer is not required independently to determine whether an interest rate is comparable to the highest rate or dividend generally available and shall be in presumptive compliance with Rule 1.15(g) by maintaining a client trust account of the type approved and authorized by the Louisiana Bar Foundation at an "eligible" financial institution.

(7) "Unidentified Funds" are funds on deposit in an IOLTA account for at least one year that after reasonable due diligence cannot be documented as belonging to a client, a third person, or the lawyer or law firm.

(h) A lawyer who learns of Unidentified Funds in an IOLTA account must remit the funds to the Louisiana Bar Foundation. No charge of misconduct shall attend to a lawyer's exercise of reasonable judgment under this paragraph (h). A lawyer who either remits funds in error or later ascertains the ownership of remitted funds may make a claim to the Louisiana Bar Foundation, which after verification of the claim will return the funds to the lawyer.

BACKGROUND

In 2010, the Louisiana Supreme Court amended this rule to prohibit "cash" and ATM withdrawals from a lawyer's trust account. In March 2016, the court amended it to address a lawyer's duties with regard to "unidentified funds" in a trust account.

For additional provisions governing Interest on Lawyers' Trust Accounts, see Louisiana Supreme Court IOLTA Rules.

Paragraph (a) is identical to ABA Model Rule of Professional Conduct 1.15(a), with the additional requirement that the lawyer's trust account must be maintained in "a bank or similar institution." This requirement assures that lawyers do not attempt to set up trust accounts using shoe boxes at their offices.

Paragraph (b) is identical to Model Rule 1.15(b).

Paragraph (c) is identical to Model Rule 1.15(c), with the addition of the last sentence: "The lawyer shall deposit legal fees and expenses into the client trust account consistent with Rule 1.5(f)." This sentence simply directs lawyers to the provisions of Rule 1.5(f), which outlines in detail how lawyers are to handle payments of different types of legal fees, expenses, general retainers and advance deposits.

Paragraph (d) is identical to Model Rule 1.15(d), with the addition of the second sentence, which begins with the language "[f]or purposes of this rule . . . ." This sentence serves to clarify and limit when a lawyer must recognize a nonclient's interest in funds that the lawyer holds on behalf of a client. Only when the lawyer holding the funds knows that such a third party has an identifiable and proprietary interest in the specific funds held by the lawyer must the lawyer respect the interest.

Paragraph (e) is identical to Model Rule 1.15(e).

Paragraph (f) contains provisions necessary to implement Louisiana's Interest on Lawyers' Trust Accounts ("IOLTA") program. It also includes the following language not found in the Model Rules: "A lawyer shall not use any debit card or automated teller machine card to withdraw funds from a client trust account. On client trust accounts, cash withdrawals and checks made payable to "Cash" are prohibited." On January 13, 2015, the Louisiana Supreme Court adopted a Louisiana State Bar Association recommendation to amend Rule 1.15(f) to require periodic reconciliations of client trust accounts.

Paragraphs (g)(7) and (h) require a lawyer who learns of "Unidentified Funds in an IOLTA account" to "remit the funds to the Louisiana Bar Foundation." *See* Order Amending Louisiana Rule of Professional Conduct 1.15 (signed and effective March 23, 2016). The rule defines "Unidentified Funds" as: "[F]unds on deposit in an IOLTA account for at least one year that after reasonable due diligence cannot be documented as belonging to a client, a third person, or the lawyer or law firm."

COMMENTS TO ABA MODEL RULE 1.15

[1] A lawyer should hold property of others with the care required of a professional fiduciary. Securities should be kept in a safe deposit box, except when some other form of safekeeping is warranted by special circumstances. All property that is the property of clients or third persons, including prospective clients, must be kept separate from the lawyer's business and personal property and, if monies, in one or more trust accounts. Separate trust accounts may be warranted when administering estate monies or acting in similar fiduciary capacities. A lawyer should maintain on a current basis books and records in accordance with generally accepted accounting practice and comply with any recordkeeping rules established by law or court order. *See, e.g.,* Model Rules for Client Trust Account Records.

[2] While normally it is impermissible to commingle the lawyer's own funds with client funds, paragraph (b) provides that it is permissible when necessary to pay bank service charges on that account. Accurate records must be kept regarding which part of the funds are the lawyer's.

[3] Lawyers often receive funds from which the lawyer's fee will be paid. The lawyer is not required to remit to the client funds that the lawyer reasonably believes represent fees owed. However, a lawyer may not hold funds to coerce a client into accepting the lawyer's contention. The disputed portion of the funds must be kept in a trust account and the lawyer should suggest means for prompt resolution of the dispute, such as arbitration. The undisputed portion of the funds shall be promptly distributed.

[4] Paragraph (e) also recognizes that third parties may have lawful claims against specific funds or other property in a lawyer's custody, such as a client's creditor who has a lien on funds recovered in a personal injury action. A lawyer may have a duty under applicable law to protect such third-party claims against wrongful interference by the client. In such cases, when the third-party claim is not frivolous under applicable law, the lawyer must refuse to surrender the property to the client until the claims are resolved. A lawyer should not unilaterally assume to arbitrate a dispute between the client and the third party, but, when there are substantial grounds for dispute as to the person entitled to the funds, the lawyer may file an action to have a court resolve the dispute.

[5] The obligations of a lawyer under this Rule are independent of those arising from activity other than rendering legal services. For example, a lawyer who serves only as an escrow agent is governed by the applicable law relating to fiduciaries even though the lawyer does not render legal services in the transaction and is not governed by this Rule.

[6] A lawyers' fund for client protection provides a means through the collective efforts of the bar to reimburse persons who have lost money or property as a result of dishonest conduct of a lawyer. Where such a fund has been established, a lawyer must participate where it is mandatory, and, even when it is voluntary, the lawyer should participate.

ANNOTATIONS
Generally

This rule requires a lawyer to segregate property belonging to others, to maintain separate accounting records for such property, and to preserve all records for at least five years after termination of the representation to which they relate. *See* Restatement (Third) of the Law Governing Lawyers § 44 (2000). Although Rule 1.15 covers all types of client and third-party property, its most common application is to funds received by a lawyer. Thus, the rule forbids a lawyer from commingling personal funds with those of clients and third parties. A lawyer typically avoids commingling by establishing a trust account. Any such account must be established at a bank (or similar institution) in the state in which the lawyer practices, unless the lawyer and the client agree otherwise.

Furthermore, Rule 1.15 requires a lawyer to notify the relevant client or third party[97] as soon as the lawyer receives funds or property belonging to them. Thereafter, the lawyer

---

[97] Whether a lawyer's failure to remit payroll taxes withheld from employees' paychecks constitutes conversion or otherwise violates this rule is uncertain. *See In re Wittenbrink*, 849 So. 2d 18 (La. 2003) (finding the rule not violated because "under the unique facts of this case, respondent did not convert an identifiable sum of money to a third person").

must promptly deliver and account for such property. *See* Restatement (Third) of the Law Governing Lawyers § 45 (2000). Failure to do so constitutes conversion and violates this rule.

Commingling Funds

Commingling of funds, whether inadvertent or intentional, is one of the most common infractions prosecuted by the Louisiana Office of Disciplinary Counsel. *See, e.g., In re Wilson*, 90 So. 3d 1018, 1022 (La. 2012); *In re Dobbins*, 805 So. 2d 133, 136 (La. 2002) ("Commingling and conversion are among the most serious professional breaches an attorney can commit."); *In re Floyd*, 742 So. 2d 868 (La. 1999); *In re Horne*, 721 So. 2d 846 (La. 1998). Commingling charges are often joined with allegations of conversion of client funds. *See, e.g., In re Avery*, 110 So. 3d 563, 571 (La. 2013); *In re Aubrey*, 928 So. 2d 524 (La. 2006); *In re Bradley*, 917 So. 2d 1068 (La. 2005); *Dobbins*, 805 So. 2d at 133; *In re Aime*, 653 So. 2d 1173 (La. 1995); *In re Bourg*, 644 So. 2d 371 (La. 1994).

Lawyers often do not realize the breadth of this rule's prohibition against commingling. Commingling funds even for an instant violates this rule. *See e.g., In re Wilson*, 90 So. 3d 1018, 1023 (La. 2012) (suspending lawyer for improper use of accounts, creating potential harm, despite no actual harm); *In re Mayeux*, 762 So. 2d 1072 (La. 2000) (disciplining lawyer for commingling client funds even though funds never in actual danger of loss). For example, if a plaintiff's lawyer receives a settlement check from an insurance company, deposits the check into the lawyer's personal checking account and then immediately disburses the client's share of the proceeds, the lawyer has violated Rule 1.15. Likewise, if a lawyer retains earned fees in a client trust account for an inordinate period of time, the lawyer has violated Rule 1.15. *See In re Caskey*, 866 So. 2d 226 (La. 2004). Furthermore, commingling is a strict-liability offense–it is irrelevant that the lawyer's commingling was done innocently or that no harm befell the lawyer's client. *See In re Wilson*, 90 So. 3d at 1023; *In re Mayeux*, 762 So. 2d at 1072; *In re Dumas*, 187 So. 3d 428 (La. 2016) (lawyer suspended for two years for grossly mishandling trust account and comingling and converting client funds).

A lawyer who employs others to handle client funds must put into place reasonable measures to ensure that employees–and partners[98]–do not engage in conversion or commingling. The negligent failure of a lawyer to create reasonable safeguards may subject the lawyer to discipline. *See, e.g., In re Bailey*, 115 So. 3d 458, 465 (La. 2013); *In re Caver*, 632 So. 2d 1157 (La. 1994); *La. State Bar Ass'n. v. Keys*, 567 So. 2d 588 (La. 1990).

The obligation to segregate funds applies not only to client funds, but also to funds belonging to third parties. *See, e.g., In re Yonter*, 930 So. 2d 956, 959-960 (La. 2006); *see also* Restatement (Third) of the Law Governing Lawyers § 44(1) (2000). For further example, a lawyer who receives funds from a settlement of a personal injury claim must segregate any portion that is designated for third-party medical service providers. *See, e.g., In re Robinson*, 129 So. 3d 513 (La. 2013); *In re Cooper*, 90 So. 3d 1023, 1027 (La. 2012); *In re*

---

[98] *See In re Leitz*, 728 So. 2d 835, 836 (La. 1999) (lawyer "stipulated that he failed to properly supervise [his partner] and the law firm's trust account").

Scheurich, 871 So. 2d 1104, 1107 (La. 2004); *In re Lewis*, 728 So. 2d 846 (La. 1999); *In re Pinkston*, 728 So. 2d 381 (La. 1998); *In re Constantino*, 714 So. 2d 690 (La. 1998).

Location of Trust Account
Under this rule, the lawyer must keep all client funds in a bank or similar institution in the state in which the lawyer's office is located. However, the lawyer and client can agree that client funds will be kept elsewhere. A lawyer who, without such consent, keeps client funds elsewhere and later relies on a "black box" defense (i.e., that the lawyer kept the client's funds secretly but securely in a safe or unregulated depository) is presumed to have embezzled such funds. *See La. State Bar Ass'n v. Krasnoff*, 515 So. 2d 780, 783 (La. 1987). As a result of this presumption of embezzlement, a lawyer seeking to exonerate himself or herself bears both the burden of going forward with evidence and the burden of persuasion. *Id.*

Reconciling the Trust Account
While it is clear that the Rule 1.5(f) requires quarterly trust account reconciliations, it is less clear *who* must perform these reconciliations. By its terms, however, Rule 1.5(f) does not require a lawyer to personally perform the reconciliation—the lawyer passively must "subject all client trust accounts to a reconciliation process." It is not realistic to expect every Louisiana lawyer to perform a personal quarterly reconciliation. Instead, lawyers rely on nonlawyer assistants.

Of course, a lawyer must adequately supervise these assistants. *See* La. Rules of Prof'l Conduct r. 5.3 (2004); *In re Wahlder*, 728 So. 2d 837 (La. 1999) (holding that a lawyer has ultimate responsibility for actions of nonlawyer staff); *In re Serret*, 35 So. 3d 256, 259 (La. 2011) (disciplining lawyer for failure to recognize and prevent secretary's embezzlement); *In re Geiger*, 27 So. 3d 280 (La. 2010) (disciplining lawyer for not adequately supervising his non-lawyer employee who had access to and may have misappropriated funds from client trust accounts); *In re McClanahan*, 26 So. 3d 756 (La. 2010) (disbarring lawyer for, among other things, instructing a non-lawyer assistant to cash a check issued from a client's trust account instead of the operating account); *see also* Restatement (Third) of the Law Governing Lawyers § 11(4)(a) (2000). Adequate supervision might include the following measures, among others:

- Assuring that a lawyer reviews the nonlawyer's reconciliation report each month.
- Registering for an email or text message alert to be sent to a lawyer whenever funds are disbursed from trust.
- Assuring that a lawyer receives and reviews the firm's trust account bank statement each month.
- Assuring that nonlawyer personnel cannot draw checks from trust without a lawyer's signature. *See* Rule 1.15(f).
- Assuring that nonlawyer personnel cannot electronically withdraw or disburse funds from trust without a lawyer's express approval. *See id.*

Return of Client Property
On request, a lawyer must permit a client or a former client to inspect and copy any documents possessed by the lawyer that relate to the representation, unless substantial

grounds exist for the lawyer to refuse. *See* Restatement (Third) of the Law Governing Lawyers § 46(1) (2000). Furthermore, upon request, a lawyer must deliver to the client all original files that relate to the client's matter–regardless of whether the client has paid all outstanding invoices for fees and costs. *See* La. Rules of Prof'l Conduct r. 1.16(d) (2004); *see also* Restatement (Third) of the Law Governing Lawyers § 46(3) (2000). The lawyer, of course, is free to copy such files before releasing them to the client. Note that under the Louisiana Civil Code, the prescriptive period for an action by a client for the return of papers relating to a lawsuit is three years. La. Civ. Code Ann. art. 3496 (2007). Prescription runs from the rendition of a final judgment in the lawsuit or the termination of the attorney-client relationship. *Id.*

Predecessor Lawyer with Interest in Settlement Funds

A lawyer who receives funds in which a predecessor lawyer has an interest must "promptly notify" that lawyer if he "knows" of the predecessor's interest, and the "interest" is perfected through a statutory lien or privilege, a final judgment, or a written agreement guaranteeing payment out of the disputed funds. *See* La. Rules of Prof'l Conduct r. 1.15(d) (2004). A predecessor lawyer may acquire a protectable "interest" in the proceeds of a lawsuit from a contingency fee contract, with his former client. Such an interest operates as a privilege on funds eventually obtained in the lawsuit.[99] Recordation under Louisiana Revised Statutes § 37:218A is not necessary for enforcement of a contingency contract as between the lawyer and the client. However, to be effective against third parties, the contract must be recorded. *See Breeden v. Crumes*, 102 So. 3d 133, 136 (La. Ct. App. 4th Cir. 2012); *Hall v. St. Paul Fire and Marine Ins. Co.*, 868 So. 2d 910 (La. Ct. App. 5th Cir. 2004) (citing *Hawthorne v. National Union Fire Insurance Company*, 562 So. 2d 473 (La. Ct. App. 3d Cir. 1990)); *Ruiz v. Williams*, 425 So. 2d 929 (La. Ct. App. 4th Cir. 1983).

Interest on Lawyers' Trust Accounts Program

Participation in the IOLTA program is mandatory for all lawyers and law firms in Louisiana.[100] If a client demands the interest earned on client funds, the lawyer must, if reasonably feasible, comply with the client's request. Interestingly, however, the IOLTA rules expressly state that a lawyer is not required to inform the client about the disposition of the interest earned on the client's funds. *See* La. S. Ct. IOLTA Rules 1-3 (Dec. 13, 1990).

IOLTA Rules

> (1) The IOLTA program shall be a mandatory program requiring participation by lawyers and law firms, whether proprietorships, partnerships, limited liability companies or professional corporations.

---

[99] The predecessor lawyer, however, has no present ownership interest in the lawsuit. *See Saucier v. Hayes Dairy Prods., Inc.*, 373 So. 2d 102, 117 (La.1979).

[100] The United States Supreme Court has held that IOLTA programs do not run afoul of the Just Compensation Clause of Fifth Amendment to the United States Constitution. *See Brown v. Legal Foundation of Wash.*, 538 U.S. 216 (2003).

(2) The following principles shall apply to funds of clients or third persons which are held by lawyers and law firms:

(a) No earnings on the IOLTA Accounts may be made available to or utilized by a lawyer or law firm.

(b) Upon the request of, or with the informed consent of a client or third person, a lawyer may deposit funds of the client or third person into a non-IOLTA, interest-bearing client trust account and earnings may be made available to the client or third person, respectively, whenever possible upon deposited funds which are not nominal in amount or are to be held for a period of time long enough that the funds would be expected to earn income for the client or third person in excess of the costs incurred to secure such income; however, traditional lawyer-client relationships do not compel lawyers either to invest such funds or to advise clients or third persons to make their funds productive.

(c) Funds of clients or third-persons which are nominal in amount or to be held for such a short period of time that the funds would not be expected to earn income for the client or third person in excess of the costs incurred to secure such income shall be retained in an IOLTA Account at an eligible financial institution as outlined above in section (g), with the interest or dividend (net of allowable reasonable fees) made payable to the Louisiana Bar Foundation, Inc., said payments to be made at least quarterly.

(d) In determining whether the funds of a client or third person can earn income in excess of costs, a lawyer or law firm shall consider the following factors:

(1) The amount of the funds to be deposited;

(2) The expected duration of the deposit, including the likelihood of delay in the matter for which the funds are held;

(3) The rates of interest or yield at financial institutions where the funds are to be deposited;

(4) The cost of establishing and administering non-IOLTA accounts for the benefit of the client or third person including service charges, the costs of the lawyer's services, and the costs of preparing any tax

reports required for income accruing to the benefit of the client or third person;

(5) The capability of financial institutions, lawyers or law firms to calculate and pay income to individual clients or third persons;

(6) Any other circumstances that affect the ability of the funds of the client or third person to earn a positive return for the client or third person. The determination of whether funds to be invested could be utilized to provide a positive net return to the client or third person rests in the sound judgment of each lawyer or law firm. The lawyer or law firm shall review its IOLTA Account at reasonable intervals to determine whether changed circumstances require further action with respect to the funds of any client or third person.

(e) Although notification of a lawyer's participation in the IOLTA Program is not required to be given to clients or third persons whose funds are held in IOLTA Accounts, many lawyers may want to notify their clients or third persons of their participation in the program in some fashion. The Rules do not prohibit a lawyer from advising all clients or third persons of the lawyer's advancing the administration of justice in Louisiana beyond the lawyer's individual abilities in conjunction with other public-spirited members of the profession. The placement of funds of clients or third persons in an IOLTA Account is within the sole discretion of the lawyer in the exercise of the lawyer's independent professional judgment; notice to the client or third person is for informational purposes only.

(3) The Louisiana Bar Foundation shall hold the entire beneficial interest in the interest or dividend income derived from client trust accounts in the IOLTA program. Interest or dividend earned by the program will be paid to the Louisiana Bar Foundation, Inc. to be used solely for the following purposes:

(a) to provide legal services to the indigent and to the mentally disabled;

(b) to provide law-related educational programs for the public;

(c) to study and support improvements to the administration of justice; and

(d) for such other programs for the benefit of the public and the legal system of the state as are specifically approved from time to time by the Supreme Court of Louisiana.

(4) The Louisiana Bar Foundation shall prepare an annual report to the Supreme Court of Louisiana that summarizes IOLTA income, grants, operating expenses and any other problems arising out of administration of the IOLTA program. In addition, the Louisiana Bar Foundation shall also prepare an annual report to the Supreme Court of Louisiana that summarizes all other Foundation income, grants, operating expenses and activities, as well as any other problems which arise out of the Foundation's implementation of its corporate purposes. The Supreme Court of Louisiana shall review, study and analyze such reports and shall make recommendations to the Foundation with respect thereto.

American Bar Association Model Rule on Financial Record Keeping

Although not mandatory, the following ABA Model Rule on Financial Recordkeeping provides useful guidance to lawyers and law firms "particularly those new to the practice of law." *See* ABA Model Rule on Fin. Recordkeeping preface (1993).

(A) A lawyer who practices in this jurisdiction shall maintain current financial records as provided in this rule, and shall retain the following records for a period of [five years] after termination of the representation:

(1) receipt and disbursement journals containing a record of deposits to and withdrawals from bank accounts which concern or affect the lawyer's practice of law, specifically identifying the date, source, and description of each item deposited, as well as the date, payee and purpose of each disbursement;

(2) ledger records for all trust accounts required by [Rule 1.15 of the Model Rules of Professional Conduct], showing, for each separate trust client or beneficiary, the source of all funds deposited, the names of all persons for whom the funds are or were held, the amount of such funds, the descriptions and amounts of charges or withdrawals, and the names of all persons to whom such funds were disbursed;

(3) copies of retainer and compensation agreements with clients [as required by Rule 1.5 of the Model Rules of Professional Conduct];

(4) copies of accountings to clients or third persons showing the disbursement of funds to them or on their behalf;

(5) copies of bills for legal fees and expenses rendered to clients;

(6) copies of records showing disbursements on behalf of clients;

(7) checkbook registers or check stubs, bank statements, records of deposit, and prenumbered canceled checks or their equivalent;

(8) copies of [monthly] trial balances and [quarterly] reconciliations of the lawyer's trust accounts; and

(9) copies of those portions of clients' files that are reasonably necessary for a complete understanding of the financial transactions pertaining to them.

(B) With respect to trust accounts required by [Rule 1.15 of the Model Rules of Professional Conduct]:

(1) only a lawyer admitted to practice law in this jurisdiction shall be an authorized signatory on the account;

(2) receipts shall be deposited intact and records of deposit should be sufficiently detailed to identify each item; and

(3) withdrawals shall be made only by check payable to a named payee and not to cash, or by authorized bank transfer.

(C) Records required by this rule may be maintained by electronic, photographic, computer or other media provided that they otherwise comply with this rule and provided further that printed copies can be produced. These records shall be located at the lawyer's principal office in the jurisdiction or in a readily accessible location.

(D) Upon dissolution of any partnership of lawyers or of any legal professional corporation, the partners or shareholders shall make appropriate arrangements for the maintenance of the records specified in Paragraph A of this rule.

(E) Upon the sale of a law practice, the seller shall make appropriate arrangements for the maintenance of the records specified in Paragraph A of this rule.

Disciplinary Sanctions

Absent aggravating or mitigating circumstances, the following sanctions are generally appropriate in cases involving a lawyer's failure to preserve client property: *disbarment*, when the lawyer knowingly converts client property and causes injury or potential injury to the client;[101] *suspension*, when the lawyer knows or should know that he is dealing improperly with client property and causes injury or potential injury to a client;[102] *reprimand*, when the lawyer is negligent in dealing with client property and causes injury or potential injury to a client; and, *admonition*, when the lawyer is negligent in dealing with client property and causes little or no actual or potential injury to a client.

---

[101] The Louisiana Supreme Court has held, "[a]n attorney's misuse of a client's funds represents the 'gravest form of professional misconduct' and disbarment is warranted." *In re Boohaker*, 927 So. 2d 268, 270 (La. 2006) (citing *La. State Bar Ass'n v. Selenberg*, 270 So. 2d 848 (La. 1972).

[102] *See, e.g., In re Duplechain*, 131 So. 3d 843 (La. 2014) (suspending lawyer for three years for using client's funds to pay business operating expenses, including employee salaries).

The Louisiana Supreme Court has consistently held that the baseline sanction for negligent mismanagement of a trust account is a fully-deferred suspension. In *In re Alex*, 205 So. 3d 895 (La. 2016), the court stated as follows:

> In its report, the board cited cases in which we have imposed fully deferred suspensions for trust account mismanagement when there was little or no actual harm. We agree that respondent's misconduct is similar to those cases, in that she mismanaged her trust account, creating the potential for harm to clients and third parties. However, itis significant that unlike the attorneys in those cases, respondent has a disciplinary history for similar misconduct. Accordingly, we find a fully deferred suspension is not appropriate. Rather, considering all the factors of this case, we will adopt the board's recommendation and suspend respondent from the practice of law for one year and one day, with all but thirty days deferred . . . .

Id. at 900-01.[103] Other Louisiana Supreme Court cases are in accord. *See In re Monroe*, 121 So. 3d 1199 (La. 2013) (public reprimand for lawyer who misused and commingled trust account by keeping earned fees and personal funds in trust account); *In re Fowler*, 122 So. 3d (La. 2013) (public reprimand for errors in trust accounting and failure to supervise nonlawyers); *In re Bloom*, 103 So. 3d 357 (La. 2012) (year-and-a-day suspension, fully deferred, for negligent conversion of client funds); *In re Spears*, 72 So. 3d 819 (La. 2011) (same); *In re Coleman*, 66 So. 3d 430 (La. 2011) (same); *In re Milton*, 48 So. 3d 277 (La. 2010) (same).

---

[103] In so doing, the court cited the following cases: *In re Spears*, 72 So. 3d 819 (La. 2011) (fully deferred one year and one day suspension, subject to a two-year period of supervised probation, imposed upon an attorney who failed to maintain the financial records of his trust account, which resulted in a negligent commingling and conversion of funds); *In re Cicardo*, 877 So. 2d 980 (La. 2004) (fully deferred one year suspension, subject to a two-year period of probation with conditions, imposed upon an attorney who mishandled his client trust account by keeping personal funds in the account, which he occasionally borrowed to fund his operating account, but caused no actual harm to his clients or to third parties); *In re Crooks*, 762 So. 2d 1077 (La. 2000) (fully deferred one year and one day suspension, subject to a two-year period of probation with conditions, imposed upon an attorney for the unintentional conversion of three clients' funds stemming from negligent mismanagement of his trust account and failure to supervise his non-lawyer assistants).

RULE 1.16. DECLINING OR TERMINATING REPRESENTATION

(a) Except as stated in paragraph (c), a lawyer shall not represent a client or, where representation has commenced, shall withdraw from the representation of a client if:

> (1) the representation will result in violation of the rules of professional conduct or other law;

> (2) the lawyer's physical or mental condition materially impairs the lawyer's ability to represent the client; or

> (3) the lawyer is discharged.

(b) Except as stated in paragraph (c), a lawyer may withdraw from representing a client if:

> (1) withdrawal can be accomplished without material adverse effect on the interests of the client;

> (2) the client persists in a course of action involving the lawyer's services that the lawyer reasonably believes is criminal or fraudulent;

> (3) the client has used the lawyer's services to perpetrate a crime or fraud;

> (4) the client insists upon taking action that the lawyer considers repugnant or with which the lawyer has a fundamental disagreement;

> (5) the client fails substantially to fulfill an obligation to the lawyer regarding the lawyer's services and has been given reasonable warning that the lawyer will withdraw unless the obligation is fulfilled;

> (6) the representation will result in an unreasonable financial burden on the lawyer or has been rendered unreasonably difficult by the client; or

> (7) other good cause for withdrawal exists.

(c) A lawyer must comply with applicable law requiring notice to or permission of a tribunal when terminating a representation. When ordered to do so by a tribunal, a lawyer shall continue representation notwithstanding good cause for terminating the representation.

(d) Upon termination of representation, a lawyer shall take steps to the extent reasonably practicable to protect a client's interests, such as giving reasonable notice to the client, allowing time for employment of other counsel, surrendering papers and property to which the client is entitled and refunding any advance payment of fee or expense that has not been earned or incurred. Upon written request by the client, the lawyer shall promptly release to the client or the client's new lawyer the entire file relating to the matter. The lawyer may retain a copy of the file but shall not condition release over issues relating to the expense of copying the file or for any other reason. The responsibility for the cost of copying shall be determined in an appropriate proceeding.

BACKGROUND

The Louisiana Supreme Court adopted this rule on January 20, 2004. It became effective on March 1, 2004, and has not been amended since.

Paragraphs (a) through (c) are identical to ABA Model Rule of Professional Conduct 1.16(a-c) (2002).

Paragraph (d) is identical to the model rule, with the additional language set forth in the last three sentences (beginning with: "Upon written request . . . ."). This language, initially adopted by the Louisiana Supreme Court in 2001, clarifies that client files belong to clients, and that lawyers must promptly and unconditionally return any client files upon request.

COMMENTS TO ABA MODEL RULE 1.16

GENERALLY

[1] A lawyer should not accept representation in a matter unless it can be performed competently, promptly, without improper conflict of interest and to completion. Ordinarily, a representation in a matter is completed when the agreed-upon assistance has been concluded. See Rules 1.2(c) and 6.5. See also Rule 1.3, Comment [4].

Mandatory Withdrawal

[2] A lawyer ordinarily must decline or withdraw from representation if the client demands that the lawyer engage in conduct that is illegal or violates the Rules of Professional Conduct or other law. The lawyer is not obliged to decline or withdraw simply because the client suggests such a course of conduct; a client may make such a suggestion in the hope that a lawyer will not be constrained by a professional obligation.

[3] When a lawyer has been appointed to represent a client, withdrawal ordinarily requires approval of the appointing authority. See also Rule 6.2. Similarly, court approval or notice to the court is often required by applicable law before a lawyer withdraws from pending litigation. Difficulty may be encountered if withdrawal is based on the client's demand that the lawyer engage in unprofessional conduct. The court may request an explanation for the

withdrawal, while the lawyer may be bound to keep confidential the facts that would constitute such an explanation. The lawyer's statement that professional considerations require termination of the representation ordinarily should be accepted as sufficient. Lawyers should be mindful of their obligations to both clients and the court under Rules 1.6 and 3.3.

Discharge

[4] A client has a right to discharge a lawyer at any time, with or without cause, subject to liability for payment for the lawyer's services. Where future dispute about the withdrawal may be anticipated, it may be advisable to prepare a written statement reciting the circumstances.

[5] Whether a client can discharge appointed counsel may depend on applicable law. A client seeking to do so should be given a full explanation of the consequences. These consequences may include a decision by the appointing authority that appointment of successor counsel is unjustified, thus requiring self-representation by the client.

[6] If the client has severely diminished capacity, the client may lack the legal capacity to discharge the lawyer, and in any event the discharge may be seriously adverse to the client's interests. The lawyer should make special effort to help the client consider the consequences and may take reasonably necessary protective action as provided in Rule 1.14.

Optional Withdrawal

[7] A lawyer may withdraw from representation in some circumstances. The lawyer has the option to withdraw if it can be accomplished without material adverse effect on the client's interests. Withdrawal is also justified if the client persists in a course of action that the lawyer reasonably believes is criminal or fraudulent, for a lawyer is not required to be associated with such conduct even if the lawyer does not further it. Withdrawal is also permitted if the lawyer's services were misused in the past even if that would materially prejudice the client. The lawyer may also withdraw where the client insists on taking action that the lawyer considers repugnant or with which the lawyer has a fundamental disagreement.

[8] A lawyer may withdraw if the client refuses to abide by the terms of an agreement relating to the representation, such as an agreement concerning fees or court costs or an agreement limiting the objectives of the representation.

Assisting the Client upon Withdrawal

[9] Even if the lawyer has been unfairly discharged by the client, a lawyer must take all reasonable steps to mitigate the consequences to the client. The lawyer may retain papers as security for a fee only to the extent permitted by law. See Rule 1.15.

ANNOTATIONS
Generally

This rule is organized as follows: paragraph (a) addresses those circumstances under which a lawyer must terminate representation; paragraph (b) addresses when a lawyer may terminate representation; paragraph (c) addresses when a lawyer must not terminate representation, namely when a tribunal orders the lawyer to continue the representation; and, paragraph (d) addresses a lawyer's obligations upon termination of the representation.

Under paragraph (a), a lawyer must decline (or terminate) representation if the representation will result in a violation of the ethics rules or the law, if the lawyer's representation is or would be impaired by a physical or mental condition, or if the client discharges the lawyer. Nevertheless, the lawyer must continue the representation if so ordered by a tribunal.

Under paragraph (b), a lawyer may withdraw from representation at any time if the lawyer can do so without material adverse effect on the interests of the client. Furthermore, a lawyer may withdraw, even when doing so would adversely affect the client, if any of the following circumstances exist: the client persists in using the lawyer's services, or has used the lawyer's services in the past, in connection with a crime or fraud; the client insists on pursuing a repugnant or imprudent objective; the client has persistently refused to pay the lawyer's fees or costs; the representation has become an unreasonable financial burden to the lawyer; the client has made the representation unreasonably difficult; or "other good cause for withdrawal exists." Notwithstanding a basis for permissive withdrawal, the lawyer must continue to represent the client if so ordered by a tribunal.

Under paragraph (c), a lawyer must continue to represent a client when ordered to do so by a tribunal, even though grounds exist for either mandatory or permissive withdrawal. A trial court's decision to grant or deny a motion to withdraw is a matter left to the court's sound discretion. *See WSF, Inc. v. Carter*, 803 So. 2d 445, 448 (La. Ct. App. 2d Cir. 2001); *see also Hill v. Tanner*, No. 12-369, 2012 WL 4059898 at *6 (E.D. La. July 5, 2012) (denying lawyer's request to withdraw after disclosure of client's criminal activity pursuant to Rule 3.3(b)). Note that a lawyer who withdraws with permission of the tribunal under Rule 1.16(c) must also comply with Uniform Rule for Louisiana Courts Rule 9.13. *See Berwick v. Berwick*, 2015 La. App. Unpub. LEXIS 501, *10 (La. Ct. App. 3rd Cir. 2015); *see also Jackson v. Fedex Corporated Servs.*, 165 So. 3d 206, 208 (La. Ct. App. 4th Cir. 2015) (holding that rule 9.13 of the Uniform Rules of Louisiana Courts and the Louisiana Rules of Professional Conduct require, a lawyer to notify client of withdrawal and the status of the case in writing.).

Under paragraph (d), once a lawyer has decided to withdraw from an ongoing representation, the lawyer must take whatever steps are necessary to protect the client's interests. For example, the lawyer must give the client reasonable notice and opportunity to hire substitute counsel. *See In re Gaharan*, 6 So. 3d 745, 748-49 (La. 2009) (suspending lawyer for failure to inform client and court of the lawyer's withdrawal from client's bankruptcy proceeding); *see also Blank v. Equisol, L.L.C.*, 2015 La. App. Unpub. LEXIS 305, *8 (La. Ct. App. 1st Cir. June 18, 2015) (finding that lawyer's motion to withdraw filed ten months before the trial date was "more than sufficient for [client] to hire new counsel"). Also, a discharged lawyer with a fee lien may not hold a client's settlement proceeds hostage to further the lawyer's self-interest. In *In re Williams-Bensaadat*, No.

2015-B-1535 (La. Nov. 6, 2015), the court suspended a lawyer for refusing to endorse a settlement check in an effort to force a resolution of her fee claim.

Obligation to Return Client File

The lawyer must surrender to the client all papers and property to which the client is entitled, and refund any fees that have been paid but not yet earned. *See, e.g., Edwin K. Hunter, APC v. Blazier,* 203 So. 3d 515, 518 (La. Ct. App. 3 Cir. 2016) (finding that a file is the client's property, and the client's interests in it supersedes the lawyer's interests); *In re McNeely,* 98 So. 3d 275, 279 (La. 2012) (suspending lawyer for failure to properly withdraw from representation and failure to return client's file and unearned fee); *In re Guste,* 185 So. 3d 740 (La. 2016) (suspending lawyer for failing to return client's file and refund unearned fees after several other similar disciplinary matters); *In re Bolton,* 820 So. 2d 548, 554 (La. 2002) (suspending lawyer for failing to timely return an original will to client); *In re Wharton,* 964 So. 2d 311, 315-316 (La. 2007) (disbarring a lawyer for failure to return unearned fees and failure to return a client's file subsequent to a three-year suspension for similar misconduct); *In re Hyman,* 958 So. 2d 646 (La. 2007) (disciplining lawyer for failing to return three clients' files upon termination of representation); *In re Salinas,* 202 So. 3d 163, 164 (La. 2016) (suspending lawyer for failure to return client's file upon request, among other reasons); *In re Renfroe,* 800 So. 2d 371, 373 (La. 2001) (disciplining lawyer under this paragraph for failing to return unearned portion of fee at termination); *In re Turnage,* 790 So. 2d 620 (La. 2001) (finding violation of Rule 1.16 (d) where lawyer failed to comply with client's requests for file). The lawyer may not hold the file "hostage" and demand payment of outstanding costs related to the matter or to copying the file before turning over the file.

As to what constitutes "the file," an ABA formal opinion from the ABA Standing Committee on Lawyers' Professional Responsibility has clarified what files, papers, and property must be surrendered to the lawyer's client. *See* ABA Formal Op. 471 at 3 (Jul. 1, 2015). Most jurisdictions, and the Restatement of Law (Third) Governing Lawyers, require a lawyer to surrender the "entire file" of the client—namely, all documents "possessed by the lawyer relating to the representation, unless substantial grounds exist to refuse." *See id.* at 3; Restatement of the Law (Third) the Law Governing Lawyers § 46 (2000). The entire-file approach "assumes that the client has an expansive general right to materials related to the representation and retains that right when the representation ends." *See* ABA Formal Op. 471 at 3.

Notwithstanding this broad principle, a lawyer need not produce every scrap of paper and every bit of electronic information in the lawyer's possession relating to a client's matter. Among other materials, a lawyer typically need not surrendering the following:

- materials that would violate a duty of nondisclosure to another person;
- materials containing a lawyer's assessment of the client;
- materials containing information which if released could endanger the health, safety, or welfare of the client or others; and,
- documents reflecting only internal firm communications and assignments.

See Formal Op. 471 at 3. "Internal" firm documents prepared for administrative purposes could include documents relating to matters such as:

- conflicts checks and potential conflicts of interest;
- the client's creditworthiness;
- firm personnel or staffing matters; and,
- ethics consultations within the firm or with outside experts.

Id. at 4-6. Such documents are not subject to surrender because they are "generated for internal use primarily for the lawyer's own purpose in working on the [client's] matters." *id.* Note, however, that surrendering these types of documents may be necessitated by compelling circumstances, such as to avoid causing harm to the client in on-going litigation. *Id.* at 6.

Note under Civil Code article 3496, "[a]n action by a client against an attorney for the return of papers delivered to him for purposes of a law suit is subject to a liberative prescription of three years. This prescription commences to run from the rendition of a final judgment in the law suit or the termination of the attorney-client relationship." *See* La. Civ. Code art. 3496.

Disclosing Confidential Information in a Motion to Withdraw

A lawyer who seeks to withdraw from the representation of a client involved in litigation typically must seek permission of the presiding tribunal to do so. Indeed, Louisiana Rule 1.16, governing withdrawal and termination of representation, provides that "a lawyer must comply with applicable law requiring notice to or permission of a tribunal when terminating a representation." *See* La. Rules of Prof'l Cond. R. 1.16(c). To obtain such permission, a lawyer sometimes must disclose the reasons why the court should permit withdrawal notwithstanding the ongoing litigation. Such a disclosure can involve confidential information, such as that the client has violated the law, that the client has failed to pay the lawyer's invoices, or that the lawyer would have a conflict of interest in continuing the representation. Rule 1.6(b) permits such disclosures to the extent "reasonably necessary" to comply with law or to respond to "allegations" concerning the lawyer's representation of the client. *See id.* R. 1.6(b)(5-6). However, there are limits as to what a lawyer can and cannot disclose in attempting to withdraw. To balance the client's interest in confidentiality with the tribunal's interest in making an informed decision on a motion to withdraw, an ABA formal opinion[104] advises a lawyer seeking to withdraw as counsel of record to do the following:

1. First, the lawyer should submit a motion to withdraw that discloses no client information other than, perhaps, a reference to the need to withdraw for "professional considerations." In addition, the lawyer may disclose the procedural

---

[104] *See* ABA Std'g Comm. on Ethics & Prof'l Resp., Formal Op. 476 (Dec. 19, 2016) ("Confidentiality Issues when Moving to Withdraw for Nonpayment of Fees in Civil Litigation").

steps taken prior to filing the motion, such as providing notice to the client. The lawyer may also update the court on the procedural status of the litigation. *Id*. at 9.

2. If the court insists on additional information, the lawyer should then "seek[] to persuade the court to rule on the motion without requiring the disclosure of confidential client information," and assert "all non-frivolous claims of confidentiality and privilege." *Id*.

3. If the court *still* insists on receiving additional information before ruling on the motion to withdraw, then the lawyer should, pursuant to Rule 1.6(b)(5), provide "only such information as is reasonably necessary to satisfy the needs of the court and preferably by whatever restricted means of submission, such as in camera review under seal, or such other procedures designated to minimize disclosure as the court determines is appropriate." *Id*.

4. Finally, if the court "expressly orders" the lawyer to make full, public disclosure of the otherwise confidential information, then Rule 1.6(b)(6) would permit the disclosure to allow the lawyer "to comply with a court order." *Id*.

Mandatory Withdrawal to Avoid Violation of Rules or Law

Paragraph (a) requires a lawyer to withdraw from a representation when continued representation "will result in violation of the rules of professional conduct or other law." La. Rules of Prof'l Conduct r. 1.16(a)(1) (2004). To avoid violating Rule 1.16(a), a lawyer should withdraw from an engagement once a lawyer is ineligible to practice. *See In re Thomas*, 115 So. 3d 466, 472 (La. 2013) (finding lawyer's continued representation while ineligible to practice law violated Rules 1.16(a) and 1.16(d)); *In re Polk*, 174 So. 3d 1131, 1135 (La. 2015) (imposing discipline for practicing law while ineligible). Note that a lawyer may have addition obligations upon learning that a client has used the lawyer's services to violate the law.

Mandatory Withdrawal Upon Discharge by Client

A lawyer must withdraw from representing a client once the client has instructed the lawyer to do so. *See, e.g., In re Cooper*; 23 So. 3d 886 (La. 2009); *In re White*, 706 So. 2d 964 (La. 1998); *American Gen. Inv. Corp. v. St. Elmo Lands*, 391 So. 2d 570, 573 (La. Ct. App. 4th Cir. 1980); *In re Gilbert*, 185 So. 3d 734 (La. 2016). A lawyer designated in a will as the lawyer for the executor must withdraw if directed to do so by the executor. Although Louisiana Revised Statutes section 9:2448 provides that such an attorney may be discharged only for "just cause," Louisiana jurisprudence holds that a client's right to discharge an attorney at any time nonetheless controls. *See Succession of Wallace*, 574 So. 2d 348, 355 (La. 1991) (recognizing that Rule 1.16(a)(3) gives "the client the absolute right to fire a lawyer in whom he has lost faith or confidence" and prevails over section 9:2448(b)(2) to preserve the court's power and responsibility to define and regulate the practice of law).

Disciplinary Sanctions

Absent aggravating or mitigating circumstances, the following sanctions are generally appropriate in cases involving a lawyer's duty to withdraw properly from representation: *disbarment*, when the lawyer knowingly engages in conduct that is a violation of a duty owed to the profession with the intent to obtain a benefit for the lawyer or another, and causes serious or potentially serious injury to a client, the public, or the legal system; *suspension*, when the lawyer knowingly engages in conduct that is a violation of a duty owed to the profession, and causes injury or potential injury to a client, the public, or the legal system; *reprimand*, when the lawyer negligently engages in conduct that is a violation of a duty owed to the profession, and causes injury or potential injury to a client, the public, or the legal system; and, *admonition*, when the lawyer engages in an isolated instance of negligence that is a violation of a duty owed to the profession, and causes little or no actual or potential injury to a client, the public, or the legal system. *See* ABA Stds. for Imposing Lawyer Sanctions stds. 7.1-7.4 (1992).

RULE 1.17. SALE OF LAW PRACTICE

A lawyer or a law firm may sell or purchase a law practice, or an area of law practice, including good will, if the following conditions are satisfied:

(a) The selling lawyer has not been disbarred or permanently resigned from the practice of law in lieu of discipline, and permanently ceases to engage in the practice of law, or has disappeared or died;

(b) The entire law practice, or area of law practice, is sold to another lawyer admitted and currently eligible to practice in this jurisdiction;

(c) At least ninety (90) days in advance of the sale, actual notice, either by in-person consultation confirmed in writing, or by U.S. mail, is given to each of the clients of the law practice being sold, indicating:

> (1) the proposed sale of the law practice;

> (2) the identity and background of the lawyer or law firm that proposes to acquire the law practice, including principal office address, number of years in practice in Louisiana, and disclosure of any prior formal discipline for professional misconduct, as well as the status of any disciplinary proceeding currently pending in which the lawyer or law firm is a named respondent;

> (3) the client's right to choose and retain other counsel and/or take possession of the client's files(s); and

> (4) the fact that the client's consent to the transfer of the client's file(s) will be presumed if the client does not take any action or does not otherwise object within ninety (90) days of the notice.

(d) In addition to the advance notice to each client described above, at least thirty (30) days in advance of the sale, an announcement or notice of the sale of the law practice, including the proposed date of the sale, the name of the selling lawyer, the name(s) of the purchasing lawyer(s) or law firm(s), and the address and telephone number where any person entitled to do so may object to the proposed sale and/or take possession of a client file, shall also be published: (1) in the Louisiana Bar Journal; and (2) once a week for at least two (2) consecutive weeks in a newspaper of general circulation in the city or town (or parish if located outside a city or town) in which the principal office of the law practice is located. The announcement or notice required by this Rule does not fall within the scope of Rules 7.1 through 7.10 of these Rules.

(e) The fees or costs charged clients shall not be increased by reason of the sale.

(f)

(1) A lawyer or law firm that proposes to acquire a law practice may be provided, initially, with only enough information regarding the matters involved reasonably necessary to enable the lawyer or law firm to determine whether any conflicts of interest exist. If there is reason to believe that the identity of a client or the fact of representation itself constitutes confidential information under the circumstances, such information shall not be provided to the purchasing lawyer or law firm without first advising the client of the identity of the purchasing lawyer or law firm and obtaining the client's informed consent in writing to the proposed disclosure.

If the purchasing lawyer or law firm determines that a conflict of interest exists prior to reviewing the information, or determines during the course of review that a conflict of interest exists, the lawyer or law firm shall not review or continue to review the information unless the conflict has been disclosed to and the informed written consent of the client has been obtained.

(2) A lawyer or law firm that proposes to acquire a law practice shall maintain the confidentiality of and shall not use any client information received in connection with the proposed sale in the same manner and to the same extent as if the clients of the law practice were already the clients of that acquiring lawyer or law firm.

(g) Consistent with Rule 1.16(c) of these Rules, before responsibility for a matter in litigation can be sold as part of a law practice, any necessary notice to and permission of a tribunal shall be given/obtained.

(h) Notwithstanding any sale, the client shall retain unfettered discretion to terminate the selling or purchasing lawyer or law firm at any time, and upon termination, the selling or purchasing lawyer in possession shall return such client's file(s) in accordance with Rule 1.16(d) of these Rules.

BACKGROUND

The Louisiana Supreme Court adopted this rule on June 21, 2016. It became effective on July 1, 2016. *See* Order Enacting Rule 1.17 of the Rules of Professional Conduct and Amending Rule 5.4(a)(4) of the Rules of Professional Conduct (signed June 21, 2016 and effective July 1, 2016).

This rule differs from ABA Model Rule 1.17 in several respects. First, the Model Rule permits any lawyer to sell a practice. The Louisiana Rule, however, prohibits a lawyer who has been disbarred or who has permanently resigned in lieu of discipline from selling a practice.

Second, the Model Rule requires only "written notice" to the seller's clients. The Louisiana Rule requires that such notice be given either through an in-person consultation (later confirmed in writing) or through United States mail. Moreover, the Louisiana Rule requires publication of the transfer in a local newspaper and in the LSBA Bar Journal. In addition, the notice must provide the seller's clients with more detailed information about the buyer, including the buyer's disciplinary history and years in practice.

Third, the Model Rule does not address related confidentiality and conflicts issues associated with a sale of a law practice. The Louisiana Rule, however, requires that a potential buyer receive only limited information about the seller's clients to evaluate whether conflicts of interest would exist. It further requires that the potential buyer safeguard the confidentiality of any information received.

Finally, the Model Rule does not provide that "the client shall retain unfettered discretion to terminate the selling or purchasing lawyer or law firm at any time." Although the Louisiana Rule expressly so provides, this principle is no doubt true under the Model Rule as well.

COMMENTS TO ABA MODEL RULE 1.17
Generally

[1] The practice of law is a profession, not merely a business. Clients are not commodities that can be purchased and sold at will. Pursuant to this Rule, when a lawyer or an entire firm ceases to practice, or ceases to practice in an area of law, and other lawyers or firms take over the representation, the selling lawyer or firm may obtain compensation for the reasonable value of the practice as may withdrawing partners of law firms. See Rules 5.4 and 5.6.

Termination of Practice by the Seller

[2] The requirement that all of the private practice, or all of an area of practice, be sold is satisfied if the seller in good faith makes the entire practice, or the area of practice, available for sale to the purchasers. The fact that a number of the seller's clients decide not to be represented by the purchasers but take their matters elsewhere, therefore, does not result in a violation. Return to private practice as a result of an unanticipated change in circumstances does not necessarily result in a violation. For example, a lawyer who has sold the practice to accept an appointment to judicial office does not violate the requirement that the sale be attendant to cessation of practice if the lawyer later resumes private practice upon being defeated in a contested or a retention election for the office or resigns from a judiciary position.

[3] The requirement that the seller cease to engage in the private practice of law does not prohibit employment as a lawyer on the staff of a public agency or a legal services entity that provides legal services to the poor, or as in-house counsel to a business.

[4] The Rule permits a sale of an entire practice attendant upon retirement from the private practice of law within the jurisdiction. Its provisions, therefore, accommodate the lawyer who sells the practice on the occasion of moving to another state. Some states are so large that a move from one locale therein to another is tantamount to leaving the jurisdiction in which the lawyer has engaged in the practice of law. To also accommodate lawyers so situated, states may permit the sale of the practice when the lawyer leaves the geographical area rather than the jurisdiction. The alternative desired should be indicated by selecting one of the two provided for in Rule 1.17(a).

[5] This Rule also permits a lawyer or law firm to sell an area of practice. If an area of practice is sold and the lawyer remains in the active practice of law, the lawyer must cease accepting any matters in the area of practice that has been sold, either as counsel or co-counsel or by assuming joint responsibility for a matter in connection with the division of a fee with another lawyer as would otherwise be permitted by Rule 1.5(e). For example, a lawyer with a substantial number of estate planning matters and a substantial number of probate administration cases may sell the estate planning portion of the practice but remain in the practice of law by concentrating on probate administration; however, that practitioner may not thereafter accept any estate planning matters. Although a lawyer who leaves a jurisdiction or geographical area typically would sell the entire practice, this Rule permits the lawyer to limit the sale to one or more areas of the practice, thereby preserving the lawyer's right to continue practice in the areas of the practice that were not sold.

Sale of Entire Practice or Entire Area of Practice

[6] The Rule requires that the seller's entire practice, or an entire area of practice, be sold. The prohibition against sale of less than an entire practice area protects those clients whose matters are less lucrative and who might find it difficult to secure other counsel if a sale could be limited to substantial fee-generating matters. The purchasers are required to undertake all client matters in the practice or practice area, subject to client consent. This requirement is satisfied, however, even if a purchaser is unable to undertake a particular client matter because of a conflict of interest.

193

Client Confidences, Consent and Notice

[7] Negotiations between seller and prospective purchaser prior to disclosure of information relating to a specific representation of an identifiable client no more violate the confidentiality provisions of Model Rule 1.6 than do preliminary discussions concerning the possible association of another lawyer or mergers between firms, with respect to which client consent is not required. *See* Rule 1.6 (b)(7). Providing the purchaser access to client-specific information relating to the representation and to the file, however, requires client consent. The Rule provides that before such information can be disclosed by the seller to the purchaser the client must be given actual written notice of the contemplated sale, including the identity of the purchaser, and must be told that the decision to consent or make other arrangements must be made within 90 days. If nothing is heard from the client within that time, consent to the sale is presumed.

[8] A lawyer or law firm ceasing to practice cannot be required to remain in practice because some clients cannot be given actual notice of the proposed purchase. Since these clients cannot themselves consent to the purchase or direct any other disposition of their files, the Rule requires an order from a court having jurisdiction authorizing their transfer or other disposition. The court can be expected to determine whether reasonable efforts to locate the client have been exhausted, and whether the absent client's legitimate interests will be served by authorizing the transfer of the file so that the purchaser may continue the representation. Preservation of client confidences requires that the petition for a court order be considered in camera. (A procedure by which such an order can be obtained needs to be established in jurisdictions in which it presently does not exist).

[9] All elements of client autonomy, including the client's absolute right to discharge a lawyer and transfer the representation to another, survive the sale of the practice or area of practice.

Fee Arrangements Between Client and Purchaser

[10] The sale may not be financed by increases in fees charged the clients of the practice. Existing arrangements between the seller and the client as to fees and the scope of the work must be honored by the purchaser.

Other Applicable Ethical Standards

[11] Lawyers participating in the sale of a law practice or a practice area are subject to the ethical standards applicable to involving another lawyer in the representation of a client. These include, for example, the seller's obligation to exercise competence in identifying a purchaser qualified to assume the practice and the purchaser's obligation to undertake the representation competently (see Rule 1.1); the obligation to avoid disqualifying conflicts, and to secure the client's informed consent for those conflicts that can be agreed to (see Rule 1.7 regarding conflicts and Rule 1.0(e) for the definition of informed consent); and the obligation to protect information relating to the representation (see Rules 1.6 and 1.9).

[12] If approval of the substitution of the purchasing lawyer for the selling lawyer is required by the rules of any tribunal in which a matter is pending, such approval must be obtained before the matter can be included in the sale (see Rule 1.16).

Applicability of the Rule

[13] This Rule applies to the sale of a law practice of a deceased, disabled or disappeared lawyer. Thus, the seller may be represented by a non-lawyer representative not subject to these Rules. Since, however, no lawyer may participate in a sale of a law practice which does not conform to the requirements of this Rule, the representatives of the seller as well as the purchasing lawyer can be expected to see to it that they are met.

[14] Admission to or retirement from a law partnership or professional association, retirement plans and similar arrangements, and a sale of tangible assets of a law practice, do not constitute a sale or purchase governed by this Rule.

[15] This Rule does not apply to the transfers of legal representation between lawyers when such transfers are unrelated to the sale of a practice or an area of practice.

RULE 1.18. DUTIES TO PROSPECTIVE CLIENT

(a) A person who consults with a lawyer about the possibility of forming a client-lawyer relationship with respect to a matter is a prospective client.

(b) Even when no client-lawyer relationship ensues, a lawyer who has learned information from a prospective client shall not use or reveal information learned in the consultation, except as Rule 1.9 would permit with respect to information of a former client.

(c) A lawyer subject to paragraph (b) shall not represent a client with interests materially adverse to those of a prospective client in the same or a substantially related matter if the lawyer received information from the prospective client that could be significantly harmful to that person in the matter, except as provided in paragraph (d). If a lawyer is disqualified from representation under this paragraph, no lawyer in a firm with which that lawyer is associated may knowingly undertake or continue representation in such a matter, except as provided in paragraph (d).

(d) When the lawyer has received disqualifying information as defined in paragraph (c), representation is permissible if:

(1) both the affected client and the prospective client have given informed consent, confirmed in writing, or:

(2) the lawyer who received the information took reasonable measures to avoid exposure to more disqualifying information than was reasonably necessary to determine whether to represent the prospective client; and

(i) the disqualified lawyer is timely screened from any participation in the matter and is apportioned no part of the fee therefrom; and

(ii) written notice is promptly given to the prospective client.

BACKGROUND

The Louisiana Supreme Court adopted this rule on January 20, 2004. It became effective on March 1, 2004. The court amended this rule in 2015 to implement 2012 revisions to the corresponding ABA model rule. The ABA amended the model rule to more narrowly define a prospective client as someone who "consults with" a lawyer rather than someone who merely "discusses" the possibility of forming a lawyer-client relationship. The Louisiana rule is now identical to ABA Model Rule of Professional Conduct 1.18 (2013).

Paragraph (b): Duty of Confidentiality Owed to Prospective Client

Paragraph (b) clarifies the lawyer's duty to treat all communications with a prospective client as confidential. The ABA adopted this provision because it believed that this obligation was well-settled matter under the law of attorney-client privilege, although it was omitted from Model Rules 1.6 and 1.9. *See* ABA Ethics 2000 Revision Notes to Model Rule 1.18 (2002).

Paragraph (c): Later Representations Adverse to Prospective Client

Paragraph (c) extends the application of Rule 1.9 to prohibit representation adverse to the prospective client in the same or a substantially related matter. Unlike Rule 1.9, however, this Rule does so only if the lawyer received information from the prospective client that could be "significantly harmful" to that person in the later representation. *See id.*

Paragraph (d): Representation Permitted with Client Consent

In paragraph (d), the ABA made clear that the prohibition imposed by this Rule can be waived with the informed consent, confirmed in writing, of both the former prospective client and the client on whose behalf the lawyer later plans to take action adverse to the former prospective client. The expression of this requirement parallels Rules 1.7 and 1.9. *See id.*

Paragraph (d): Screening of Disqualified Lawyer

In the event that "significantly harmful" information is revealed, paragraph (d) provides that the lawyer who received the information may be screened from any involvement in the subsequent matter but others in the law firm may represent the adverse party. *See id.*

COMMENTS TO ABA MODEL RULE 1.18

[1] Prospective clients, like clients, may disclose information to a lawyer, place documents or other property in the lawyer's custody, or rely on the lawyer's advice. A lawyer's consultations with a prospective client usually are limited in time and depth and leave both the prospective client and the lawyer free (and sometimes required) to proceed no further. Hence, prospective clients should receive some but not all of the protection afforded clients.

[2] A person becomes a prospective client by consulting with a lawyer about the possibility of forming a client-lawyer relationship with respect to a matter. Whether communications, including written, oral, or electronic communications, constitute a consultation depends on the circumstances. For example, a consultation is likely to have occurred if a lawyer, either in person or through the lawyer's advertising in any medium, specifically requests or invites the submission of information about a potential representation without clear and reasonably understandable warnings and cautionary statements that limit the lawyer's obligations, and a person provides information in response. See also Comment [4]. In contrast, a consultation does not occur if a person provides information to a lawyer in response to advertising that merely describes the lawyer's education, experience, areas of

practice, and contact information, or provides legal information of general interest. Such a person communicates information unilaterally to a lawyer, without any reasonable expectation that the lawyer is willing to discuss the possibility of forming a client-lawyer relationship, and is thus not a "prospective client." Moreover, a person who communicates with a lawyer for the purpose of disqualifying the lawyer is not a "prospective client."

[3] It is often necessary for a prospective client to reveal information to the lawyer during an initial consultation prior to the decision about formation of a client-lawyer relationship. The lawyer often must learn such information to determine whether there is a conflict of interest with an existing client and whether the matter is one that the lawyer is willing to undertake. Paragraph (b) prohibits the lawyer from using or revealing that information, except as permitted by Rule 1.9, even if the client or lawyer decides not to proceed with the representation. The duty exists regardless of how brief the initial conference may be.

[4] In order to avoid acquiring disqualifying information from a prospective client, a lawyer considering whether or not to undertake a new matter should limit the initial consultation to only such information as reasonably appears necessary for that purpose. Where the information indicates that a conflict of interest or other reason for non-representation exists, the lawyer should so inform the prospective client or decline the representation. If the prospective client wishes to retain the lawyer, and if consent is possible under Rule 1.7, then consent from all affected present or former clients must be obtained before accepting the representation.

[5] A lawyer may condition a consultation with a prospective client on the person's informed consent that no information disclosed during the consultation will prohibit the lawyer from representing a different client in the matter. See Rule 1.0(e) for the definition of informed consent. If the agreement expressly so provides, the prospective client may also consent to the lawyer's subsequent use of information received from the prospective client.

[6] Even in the absence of an agreement, under paragraph (c), the lawyer is not prohibited from representing a client with interests adverse to those of the prospective client in the same or a substantially related matter unless the lawyer has received from the prospective client information that could be significantly harmful if used in the matter.

[7] Under paragraph (c), the prohibition in this Rule is imputed to other lawyers as provided in Rule 1.10, but, under paragraph (d)(1), imputation may be avoided if the lawyer obtains the informed consent, confirmed in writing, of both the prospective and affected clients. In the alternative, imputation may be avoided if the conditions of paragraph (d)(2) are met and all disqualified lawyers are timely screened and written notice is promptly given to the prospective client. See Rule 1.0(k) (requirements for screening procedures). Paragraph (d)(2)(i) does not prohibit the screened lawyer from receiving a salary or partnership share established by prior independent agreement, but that lawyer may not receive compensation directly related to the matter in which the lawyer is disqualified.

[8] Notice, including a general description of the subject matter about which the lawyer was consulted, and of the screening procedures employed, generally should be given as soon as practicable after the need for screening becomes apparent.

[9] For the duty of competence of a lawyer who gives assistance on the merits of a matter to a prospective client, see Rule 1.1. For a lawyer's duties when a prospective client entrusts valuables or papers to the lawyer's care, see Rule 1.15.

ANNOTATIONS

No significant reported Louisiana decisions have discussed, applied or interpreted this rule.

Article 2. Counselor

RULE 2.1. ADVISOR

In representing a client, a lawyer shall exercise independent professional judgment and render candid advice. In rendering advice, a lawyer may refer not only to law but to other considerations such as moral, economic, social and political factors, that may be relevant to the client's situation.

BACKGROUND

The Louisiana Supreme Court adopted this rule on January 20, 2004. It became effective on March 1, 2004, and has not been amended since. This rule is identical to ABA Model Rule of Professional Conduct 2.1 (2002).

COMMENTS TO ABA MODEL RULE 2.1

Scope of Advice

[1] A client is entitled to straightforward advice expressing the lawyer's honest assessment. Legal advice often involves unpleasant facts and alternatives that a client may be disinclined to confront. In presenting advice, a lawyer endeavors to sustain the client's morale and may put advice in as acceptable a form as honesty permits. However, a lawyer should not be deterred from giving candid advice by the prospect that the advice will be unpalatable to the client.

[2] Advice couched in narrow legal terms may be of little value to a client, especially where practical considerations, such as cost or effects on other people, are predominant. Purely technical legal advice, therefore, can sometimes be inadequate. It is proper for a lawyer to refer to relevant moral and ethical considerations in giving advice. Although a lawyer is not a moral advisor as such, moral and ethical considerations impinge upon most legal questions and may decisively influence how the law will be applied.

[3] A client may expressly or impliedly ask the lawyer for purely technical advice. When such a request is made by a client experienced in legal matters, the lawyer may accept it at face value. When such a request is made by a client inexperienced in legal matters, however, the lawyer's responsibility as advisor may include indicating that more may be involved than strictly legal considerations.

[4] Matters that go beyond strictly legal questions may also be in the domain of another profession. Family matters can involve problems within the professional competence of psychiatry, clinical psychology or social work; business matters can involve problems within the competence of the accounting profession or of financial specialists. Where consultation with a professional in another field is itself something a competent lawyer would recommend, the lawyer should make such a recommendation. At the same time, a lawyer's advice at its best often consists of recommending a course of action in the face of conflicting recommendations of experts.

OFFERING ADVICE

[5] In general, a lawyer is not expected to give advice until asked by the client. However, when a lawyer knows that a client proposes a course of action that is likely to result in substantial adverse legal consequences to the client, the lawyer's duty to the client under Rule 1.4 may require that the lawyer offer advice if the client's course of action is related to the representation. Similarly, when a matter is likely to involve litigation, it may be necessary under Rule 1.4 to inform the client of forms of dispute resolution that might constitute reasonable alternatives to litigation. A lawyer ordinarily has no duty to initiate investigation of a client's affairs or to give advice that the client has indicated is unwanted, but a lawyer may initiate advice to a client when doing so appears to be in the client's interest.

ANNOTATIONS

Generally

Rule 2.1 is the first of three rules addressing a lawyer's duties when serving as a "counselor." When acting as a counselor or advisor, a lawyer "provides a client with an informed understanding of the client's legal rights and obligations and explains their practical implications." *See* ABA Model Rules of Prof'l Conduct Preamb. ¶ 2 (Am. Bar Ass'n 2002).

Under Rule 2.1, a lawyer must exercise "independent professional judgment" and render "candid advice" to the client. In rendering candid advice, the lawyer may refer not only to the law and facts directly relevant to the client's matter, but also to any other pertinent considerations, including "moral, economic, social and political factors." La. Rules of Prof'l Conduct r. 2.1 (2004).

Candid Advice

In rendering candid advice, the lawyer must give the client an honest opinion regarding the merits of the client's matter. The lawyer should not simply tell the client what the client wants to hear. For example, if the lawyer believes that the client's claim, although not frivolous, is unlikely to succeed, then the lawyer must tell the client so.

Sexual Relationships with Clients

This rule's requirement that a lawyer exercise "independent professional judgment" is a corollary of the conflicts-of-interest rules mandating that a lawyer not compromise the loyalty owed to all clients. The Louisiana Supreme Court has disciplined lawyers who have violated this rule, among others, by compromising their "independent professional judgment" and emotional detachment through becoming involved in inappropriate personal or sexual relationships with their clients. In two disciplinary proceedings, *In re Ashy*, 721 So. 2d 859 (La. 1998), and *In re Schambach*, 726 So. 2d 892 (La. 1999), the court acknowledged that the current Louisiana Rules of Professional Conduct include no provisions specifically prohibiting Louisiana lawyers from engaging in sexual relations with their clients. Nevertheless, in each case, the court concluded that the particular sexual relationship in issue substantially interfered with the lawyer's professional responsibilities.[105] *See also In re DeFrancesch*, 877 So. 2d 71 (La. 2004) (sanctioning lawyer for inappropriate sexual relations with client despite the existence of a preexisting relationship); *In re Ryland*, 985 So. 2d 71, 73-74 (La. 2009) (suspending a lawyer 90 days for engaging in a consensual sexual relationship with the client while representing the client in a divorce proceeding despite the absence of actual harm).

In *Ashy*, the court found that the respondent attempted to engage in a sexual relationship with his client "in exchange for certain efforts he would exert on her behalf as her lawyer." *Ashy*, 721 So. 2d at 864. In a thorough and exhaustive review of the case law and commentary on the issue of client sexual relations, the court held that the respondent's conduct violated several rules set forth in the Louisiana Rules of Professional Conduct. First, the court held that the respondent violated Rule 1.7 because his representation was materially limited and adversely affected by his own interest in engaging in a sexual relationship with his client. *Id.* at 867. Second, the court found that the respondent's conduct violated Rule 2.1 because he failed to exercise "independent professional judgment" on behalf of his client. *Id.* at 867. Finally, the court found that the respondent's conduct violated Rule 8.4 because his actions violated the Rules of Professional Conduct, involved dishonesty and misrepresentation, and reflected that he was unworthy of the confidence reposed in him by his client. *Id.* at 867-68. As a result of these violations, the court suspended the respondent from the practice of law for a period of two years. *Id.* at 868.

In *Schambach*, the respondent engaged in a mutual and consensual sexual relationship with his client. *Schambach*, 726 So. 2d at 894. Furthermore, the respondent borrowed a substantial sum of money from his client, and then had failed to pay it back until "the eve of the [disciplinary] committee hearing." *Id.* at 894. As in *Ashy*, the court held that the "respondent violated the Rules of Professional Conduct by allowing his personal relationship with [his client] to interfere with his professional responsibilities toward her." *Id.* at 896. For this reason, the court suspended the respondent from the practice of law for a period of three years. *Id.*; *see also In re Touchet*, 753 So. 2d 820, 823 (La. 2000) ("By attempting to sexually exploit his clients, respondent unquestionably violated his professional duty to protect their interests."); *In re Withers*, 747 So. 2d 514 (La. 1999) (suspending a lawyer for six months for, among other things, becoming involved in a "highly improper relationship" with her client). *See generally* ABA Comm'n on Ethics and Prof'l Responsibility, Formal Op. 92-364 (1992).

Disciplinary Sanctions

Absent aggravating or mitigating circumstances, the following sanctions are generally appropriate in cases involving violations of Rule 2.1: *disbarment*, when the lawyer knowingly engages in conduct that is a violation of a duty owed to the profession with the intent to obtain a benefit for the lawyer or another, and causes serious or potentially

---

[105] Even sexual relationships between lawyers and clients that are not coercive can result in discipline as a result of the "potential to create a conflict of interest." *In re Gore*, 752 So. 2d 853, 856 (La. 2000).

serious injury to a client, the public, or the legal system; *suspension*, when the lawyer knowingly engages in conduct that is a violation of a duty owed as a professional, and causes injury or potential injury to a client, the public, or the legal system; *reprimand*, when the lawyer negligently engages in conduct that is a violation of a duty owed as a professional, and causes injury or potential injury to a client, the public, or the legal system; and, *admonition*, when the lawyer engages in an isolated instance of negligence that is a violation of a duty owed as a professional, and causes little or no actual or potential injury to a client, the public or the legal system. *See* ABA Stds. for Imposing Lawyer Sanctions stds. 7.0-7.4 (1992).

RULE 2.2. INTERMEDIARY [DELETED]

ANNOTATIONS

Former Louisiana Rule of Professional Conduct Rule 2.2–as well as former ABA Model Rule 2.2–addressed a lawyer's obligations when functioning as an "Intermediary." In 2002, the ABA deleted Model Rule 2.2 on recommendation of the ABA Ethics 2000 Commission. The Commission believed that neither the concept of "intermediation" (as distinct from either "representation" or "mediation") nor the relationship between Rules 2.2 and 1.7 had been well understood by practicing lawyers. For this reason, the Commission recommended that the ABA delete the rule entirely and address the issues associated with intermediation in Comment to Rule 1.7. *See* ABA Model Rules of Prof'l Conduct r. 1.7 cmts. 26-29. When the Louisiana Supreme Court adopted the revised Model Rules in January 2004, it followed the lead of the ABA and deleted this rule from the Louisiana Rules of Professional Conduct.

RULE 2.3. EVALUATION FOR USE BY THIRD PERSONS

(a) A lawyer may provide an evaluation of a matter affecting a client for the use of someone other than the client if the lawyer reasonably believes that making the evaluation is compatible with other aspects of the lawyer's relationship with the client.

(b) When the lawyer knows or reasonably should know that the evaluation is likely to affect the client's interests materially and adversely, the lawyer shall not provide the evaluation unless the client gives informed consent.

(c) Except as disclosure is authorized in connection with a report of an evaluation, information relating to the evaluation is otherwise protected by Rule 1.6.

BACKGROUND

The Louisiana Supreme Court adopted this rule on January 20, 2004. It became effective on March 1, 2004, and has not been amended since. This rule is identical to ABA Model Rule of Professional Conduct 2.3 (2002).

In 2002, the ABA restructured the text of the corresponding Model Rule to clarify its application in two situations. First, when the evaluation poses no significant risk to the client, paragraph (a) requires only that the lawyer conclude that providing the evaluation is compatible with other aspects of the client-lawyer relationship. Second, when there is a significant risk of material and adverse effect on the client's interests, paragraph (b) provides that the lawyer may not proceed without obtaining the client's informed consent. *See* ABA Ethics 2000 Commission Revision Notes to Model Rule 2.3 (2002).

COMMENTS TO ABA MODEL RULE 2.3
Definition

[1] An evaluation may be performed at the client's direction or when impliedly authorized in order to carry out the representation. See Rule 1.2. Such an evaluation may be for the primary purpose of establishing information for the benefit of third parties; for example, an opinion concerning the title of property rendered at the behest of a vendor for the information of a prospective purchaser, or at the behest of a borrower for the information of a prospective lender. In some situations, the evaluation may be required by a government agency; for example, an opinion concerning the legality of the securities registered for sale under the securities laws. In other instances, the evaluation may be required by a third person, such as a purchaser of a business.

[2] A legal evaluation should be distinguished from an investigation of a person with whom the lawyer does not have a client-lawyer relationship. For example, a lawyer retained by a purchaser to analyze a vendor's title to property does not have a client-lawyer relationship with the vendor. So also, an investigation into a person's affairs by a government lawyer, or by special counsel employed by the government, is not an evaluation as that term is used in

this Rule. The question is whether the lawyer is retained by the person whose affairs are being examined. When the lawyer is retained by that person, the general rules concerning loyalty to client and preservation of confidences apply, which is not the case if the lawyer is retained by someone else. For this reason, it is essential to identify the person by whom the lawyer is retained. This should be made clear not only to the person under examination, but also to others to whom the results are to be made available.

Duties Owed to Third Person and Client

[3] When the evaluation is intended for the information or use of a third person, a legal duty to that person may or may not arise. That legal question is beyond the scope of this Rule. However, since such an evaluation involves a departure from the normal client-lawyer relationship, careful analysis of the situation is required. The lawyer must be satisfied as a matter of professional judgment that making the evaluation is compatible with other functions undertaken in behalf of the client. For example, if the lawyer is acting as advocate in defending the client against charges of fraud, it would normally be incompatible with that responsibility for the lawyer to perform an evaluation for others concerning the same or a related transaction. Assuming no such impediment is apparent, however, the lawyer should advise the client of the implications of the evaluation, particularly the lawyer's responsibilities to third persons and the duty to disseminate the findings.

Access to and Disclosure of Information

[4] The quality of an evaluation depends on the freedom and extent of the investigation upon which it is based. Ordinarily a lawyer should have whatever latitude of investigation seems necessary as a matter of professional judgment. Under some circumstances, however, the terms of the evaluation may be limited. For example, certain issues or sources may be categorically excluded, or the scope of search may be limited by time constraints or the noncooperation of persons having relevant information. Any such limitations that are material to the evaluation should be described in the report. If after a lawyer has commenced an evaluation, the client refuses to comply with the terms upon which it was understood the evaluation was to have been made, the lawyer's obligations are determined by law, having reference to the terms of the client's agreement and the surrounding circumstances. In no circumstances is the lawyer permitted to knowingly make a false statement of material fact or law in providing an evaluation under this Rule. See Rule 4.1.

Obtaining Client's Informed Consent

[5] Information relating to an evaluation is protected by Rule 1.6. In many situations, providing an evaluation to a third party poses no significant risk to the client; thus, the lawyer may be impliedly authorized to disclose information to carry out the representation. See Rule 1.6(a). Where, however, it is reasonably likely that providing the evaluation will affect the client's interests materially and adversely, the lawyer must first obtain the client's consent after the client has been adequately informed concerning the important possible effects on the client's interests. See Rules 1.6(a) and 1.0(e).

Financial Auditors' Requests for Information

[6] When a question concerning the legal situation of a client arises at the instance of the client's financial auditor and the question is referred to the lawyer, the lawyer's response may be made in accordance with procedures recognized in the legal profession. Such a procedure is set forth in the American Bar Association Statement of Policy Regarding Lawyers' Responses to Auditors' Requests for Information, adopted in 1975.

ANNOTATIONS
Generally

This rule addresses a lawyer's duties to a client in the context of preparing an evaluation for use by a nonclient. Other rules address the lawyer's duties to third persons in connection with such an evaluation. *See* La. Rules of Prof'l Conduct r. 4.1 (2004) (Truthfulness in Statements to Others).

Paragraph (a) permits a lawyer to prepare an evaluation of a matter that will be used by a nonclient if the lawyer reasonably believes that the evaluation will be compatible with the lawyer's relationship with the client and the client gives informed consent.

Paragraph (b) permits the lawyer to make disclosures in connection with the evaluation. Otherwise, all other information relating to the representation is protected by Rule 1.6.

Ensuring "Compatibility" with Lawyer's Obligations to the Client

Among other things, a lawyer must remain loyal to a client even when preparing an evaluation that will be relied upon by a third party. Therefore, when it appears reasonably likely that the lawyer's evaluation or opinion may be adverse to the client's interests, the lawyer should first obtain the client's consent to releasing the evaluation. The consent of the client should be obtained only after the lawyer has fully informed the client concerning the "possible effects on the client's interests." *See* Restatement (Third) of the Law Governing Lawyers § 95(2) (2000).

Tort Liability to Nonclients

The extent of a lawyer's possible tort liability to third parties is beyond the scope of these annotations. However, lawyers preparing evaluations for use by nonclients should be cautioned that they may be liable for injuries caused to such persons by their failure to exercise reasonable competence and diligence in preparing such evaluations. *See* Restatement (Third) of the Law Governing Lawyers § 51(2) (2000); *id.* § 48; *id.* § 52. Lawyers may be liable not only for their negligence in preparing such evaluations, but also for making false statements of material fact or law, for making other statements prohibited by law, or for failing to make a disclosure required by law. *See* Restatement (Third) of the Law Governing Lawyers § 95(3) (2000); *id.* § 157; *see also* La. Rules of Prof'l Conduct r. 4.1 (2004) (Truthfulness in Statements to Others).

Disciplinary Sanctions

Absent aggravating or mitigating circumstances, the following sanctions are generally appropriate in cases involving a violation of Rule 2.3: *disbarment*, when the lawyer knowingly engages in conduct that is a violation of a duty owed to the profession with the intent to obtain a benefit for the lawyer or another, and causes serious or potentially serious injury to a client, the public, or the legal system; *suspension*, when the lawyer knowingly engages in conduct that is a violation of a duty owed to the profession, and causes injury or potential injury to a client, the public, or the legal system; *reprimand*, when the lawyer negligently engages in conduct that is a violation of a duty owed to the profession, and causes injury or potential injury to a client, the public, or the legal system; and, *admonition*, when the lawyer engages in an isolated instance of negligence that is a violation of a duty owed to the profession, and causes little or no actual or potential injury to a client, the public, or the legal system. *See* ABA Stds. for Imposing Lawyer Sanctions std. 7.0 (1992) (Violations of Duties Owed as a Professional).

RULE 2.4. LAWYER SERVING AS THIRD-PARTY NEUTRAL

(a) A lawyer serves as a third-party neutral when the lawyer assists two or more persons who are not clients of the lawyer to reach a resolution of a dispute or other matter that has arisen between them. Service as a third-party neutral may include service as an arbitrator, a mediator or in such other capacity as will enable the lawyer to assist the parties to resolve the matter.

(b) A lawyer serving as a third-party neutral shall inform unrepresented parties that the lawyer is not representing them. When the lawyer knows or reasonably should know that a party does not understand the lawyer's role in the matter, the lawyer shall explain the difference between the lawyer's role as a third-party neutral and a lawyer's role as one who represents a client.

BACKGROUND

The Louisiana Supreme Court adopted this rule on January 20, 2004. It became effective on March 1, 2004, and has not been amended since. This rule is identical to ABA Model Rule of Professional Conduct 2.4 (2002).

The ABA Ethics 2000 Commission recognized that lawyers and nonlawyers alike are increasingly serving as third-party neutrals in mediation, arbitration and other ADR procedures. Unlike nonlawyers who serve in this capacity, lawyers may experience unique ethical problems arising from confusion about the nature of the lawyer's role. For this reason, the Commission recommended, and the ABA adopted, Model Rule 2.4 in an effort to promote ADR parties' understanding of the lawyer-neutral's role. *See* ABA Ethics 2000 Commission Revision Notes to Model Rule 2.4 (2002).

To this end, paragraph (b) requires the lawyer serving as a third-party neutral to inform unrepresented parties in all cases that the lawyer does not represent them. The potential for confusion is sufficiently great to mandate this requirement in all cases involving unrepresented parties. Consistent with the standard of Rule 4.3, paragraph (b) requires the lawyer to explain the differences in a lawyer's role as a third-party neutral and the role of a lawyer representing a party in situations where the lawyer knows or reasonably should know that the unrepresented party does not understand the lawyer's role as a third-party neutral. *See* ABA Ethics 2000 Commission Revision Notes to Model Rule 2.4 (2002).

COMMENTS TO ABA MODEL RULE 2.4

[1] Alternative dispute resolution has become a substantial part of the civil justice system. Aside from representing clients in dispute-resolution processes, lawyers often serve as third-party neutrals. A third-party neutral is a person, such as a mediator, arbitrator, conciliator or evaluator, who assists the parties, represented or unrepresented, in the resolution of a dispute or in the arrangement of a transaction. Whether a third-party

neutral serves primarily as a facilitator, evaluator or decisionmaker depends on the particular process that is either selected by the parties or mandated by a court.

[2] The role of a third-party neutral is not unique to lawyers, although, in some court-connected contexts, only lawyers are allowed to serve in this role or to handle certain types of cases. In performing this role, the lawyer may be subject to court rules or other law that apply either to third-party neutrals generally or to lawyers serving as third-party neutrals. Lawyer-neutrals may also be subject to various codes of ethics, such as the Code of Ethics for Arbitration in Commercial Disputes prepared by a joint committee of the American Bar Association and the American Arbitration Association or the Model Standards of Conduct for Mediators jointly prepared by the American Bar Association, the American Arbitration Association and the Society of Professionals in Dispute Resolution.

[3] Unlike nonlawyers who serve as third-party neutrals, lawyers serving in this role may experience unique problems as a result of differences between the role of a third-party neutral and a lawyer's service as a client representative. The potential for confusion is significant when the parties are unrepresented in the process. Thus, paragraph (b) requires a lawyer-neutral to inform unrepresented parties that the lawyer is not representing them. For some parties, particularly parties who frequently use dispute-resolution processes, this information will be sufficient. For others, particularly those who are using the process for the first time, more information will be required. Where appropriate, the lawyer should inform unrepresented parties of the important differences between the lawyer's role as third-party neutral and a lawyer's role as a client representative, including the inapplicability of the attorney-client evidentiary privilege. The extent of disclosure required under this paragraph will depend on the particular parties involved and the subject matter of the proceeding, as well as the particular features of the dispute-resolution process selected.

[4] A lawyer who serves as a third-party neutral subsequently may be asked to serve as a lawyer representing a client in the same matter. The conflicts of interest that arise for both the individual lawyer and the lawyer's law firm are addressed in Rule 1.12.

[5] Lawyers who represent clients in alternative dispute-resolution processes are governed by the Rules of Professional Conduct. When the dispute-resolution process takes place before a tribunal, as in binding arbitration (see Rule 1.0(m)), the lawyer's duty of candor is governed by Rule 3.3. Otherwise, the lawyer's duty of candor toward both the third-party neutral and other parties is governed by Rule 4.1.

ANNOTATIONS
No significant reported Louisiana decisions have discussed, applied or interpreted this rule.

Article 3. Advocate

RULE 3.1. MERITORIOUS CLAIMS AND CONTENTIONS

A lawyer shall not bring or defend a proceeding, or assert or controvert an issue therein, unless there is a basis in law and fact for doing so that is not frivolous, which includes a good faith argument for an extension, modification or reversal of existing law. A lawyer for the defendant in a criminal proceeding, or the respondent in a proceeding that could result in incarceration, may nevertheless so defend the proceeding as to require that every element of the case be established.

BACKGROUND

The Louisiana Supreme Court adopted this rule on January 20, 2004. It became effective on March 1, 2004, and has not been amended since. This rule is identical to ABA Model Rule of Professional Conduct 3.1 (2002).

COMMENTS TO ABA MODEL RULE 3.1

[1] The advocate has a duty to use legal procedure for the fullest benefit of the client's cause, but also a duty not to abuse legal procedure. The law, both procedural and substantive, establishes the limits within which an advocate may proceed. However, the law is not always clear and never is static. Accordingly, in determining the proper scope of advocacy, account must be taken of the law's ambiguities and potential for change.

[2] The filing of an action or defense or similar action taken for a client is not frivolous merely because the facts have not first been fully substantiated or because the lawyer expects to develop vital evidence only by discovery. What is required of lawyers, however, is that they inform themselves about the facts of their clients' cases and the applicable law and determine that they can make good faith arguments in support of their clients' positions. Such action is not frivolous even though the lawyer believes that the client's position ultimately will not prevail. The action is frivolous, however, if the lawyer is unable either to make a good faith argument on the merits of the action taken or to support the action taken by a good faith argument for an extension, modification or reversal of existing law.

[3] The lawyer's obligations under this Rule are subordinate to federal or state constitutional law that entitles a defendant in a criminal matter to the assistance of counsel in presenting a claim or contention that otherwise would be prohibited by this Rule.

ANNOTATIONS

Generally

A lawyer owes duties not only to the lawyer's clients (such as competence, diligence, loyalty and confidentiality), but also to the legal system. Rule 3.1 sets forth the first of several duties owed by lawyer-advocates to the system of justice.

A lawyer who files frivolous lawsuits, or otherwise makes nonmeritorious claims or contentions, is typically sanctioned judicially rather than through disciplinary proceedings. *See* La. Code Civ. Proc. Ann. art. 863 (2007); Fed. R. Civ. P. 11; *Chesire v. Air Methods Corp.*, No. 3:15-0933, 2016 WL 6471235, at *1, 6-8 (W.D. La. Nov. 1, 2016) (imposing sanction for improperly threatening to expose confidential information to gain leverage in settlement talks). However, some Louisiana lawyers have been disciplined for filing wholly meritless lawsuits. *See, e.g., In re Harvin*, 117 So. 3d 907, 913 (La. 2013) (suspending lawyer for 30 days for causing unnecessary litigation when the lawyer filed notice of lis pendens for client who had no claim to the property in question). *In re Cook*, 932 So. 2d 669, 676 (La. 2006) (disciplining lawyer for filing "repetitive and unwarranted pleadings" and making "frivolous and harassing claims for discovery"); *In re Zohdy*, 892 So. 2d 1277 (La. 2005) (suspending lawyer for six months for, among other offenses, unjustifiably obstructing a class action lawsuit); *In re Stratton*, 869 So. 2d 794 (La. 2004) (suspending lawyer for three years for filing frivolous lawsuit "designed to harass" former secretary); *In re Hackett*, 701 So. 2d 920 (La. 1997) (reprimanding lawyer for filing meritless motion to dissolve temporary restraining order); *In re Caulfield*, 683 So. 2d 714 (La. 1996) (disbarring a lawyer for staging fake automobile accident to defraud rental car company); *In re Forman*, 634 So. 2d 330 (La. 1994) (suspending a lawyer for six months for filing frivolous fee-collection lawsuit); *In re Williams-Bensaadat*, 181 So. 3d 684, 691-92 (La. 2015) (suspending lawyer for instituting a lawsuit against a former client instead of endorsing a settlement check and resolving fee dispute through concursus proceeding). A lawyer can also be disciplined for vexatious litigation conduct. *See, e.g., In re DuBarry*, 814 So. 2d 1273 (La. 2002); *see also In re Lester*, 133 So. 3d 1248 (La. 2014) (disbarring lawyer for engaging in "frivolous and vexatious litigation," among other rule violations).

It is often difficult to determine whether a lawyer's conduct warrants the imposition of sanctions pursuant to this and related standards. *See e.g., In re Mincilier*, 74 So. 3d 687, 692 (La. 2011) (finding no violation for lawyer facing 3.1 charge for filing a pleading contrary to a court's order); *In re Cucci*, 85 So. 3d 62 (La. 2012) (noting the ODC alleged a 3.1 violation but the hearing committee saw lawyer's filing as "creative, if novel" argument). Most modern authorities hold lawyers to an objective rather than to a purely subjective standard of behavior. Thus, a lawyer with a "pure heart, but empty head," should not avoid an appropriate sanction merely because the lawyer acted without ill will. *See* Restatement (Third) of the Law Governing Lawyers § 110 cmt. d (2000) ("A frivolous position is one that a lawyer of ordinary competence would recognize as so lacking in merit that there is no substantial possibility that the tribunal would accept it."); *see also* Fed. R. Civ. P. 11.

For a rule addressing frivolous conduct in discovery proceedings, see La. Rules of Prof'l Conduct r. 3.4(d) (2004).

Related Authority: Louisiana Code of Civil Procedure Article 863

Under Louisiana Code of Civil Procedure article 863, the signature of a lawyer on a pleading filed in a civil case, "shall constitute a certification by him that he has read the pleading, and that to the best of his knowledge, information, and belief formed after reasonable inquiry, he certifies all of the following: (1) The pleading is not being presented for any improper purpose, such as to harass, cause unnecessary delay, or needlessly increase the cost of litigation; (2) Each claim, defense, or other legal assertion in the pleading is warranted by existing law or by a nonfrivilous argument for the extension, modification, or reversal of existing law; (3) Each allegation or other factual assertion in the pleading has evidentiary support or, for a specifically identified allegation or factual assertion, is likely to have evidentiary support after a reasonable opportunity for further investigation or discovery; (4) Each denial in the pleading of a factual assertion is warranted by the evidence or, for a specifically identified denial, is reasonably based on law of information or belief." La. Code Civ. Proc. Ann. art. 863(A-B) (2010). A violation of this rule can subject the lawyer to "an appropriate sanction which may include an order to pay to the other party the amount of the reasonable expenses incurred because of the filing of the pleading, including a reasonable attorney fees." *Id.* art. 863(D). However, a lawyer is entitled to a hearing prior to the imposition of such a sanction. *Id.* art. 863(E). Furthermore, article 863 provides a safe harbor for lawyers who file questionable lawsuits on or near a prescription date: "A sanction authorized in Paragraph D shall not be imposed with respect to an original petition which is filed within sixty days of an applicable prescriptive date and then voluntarily dismissed within ninety days after its filing or on the date of a hearing on the pleading, whichever is earlier." *Id.* art. 863(F). Finally, if a sanction is imposed, the court must "describe the conduct determined to constitute a violation of the provisions of this Article and explain the basis for the sanction imposed." *Id.* art 863(G).

Disciplinary Sanctions

Absent aggravating or mitigating circumstances, the following sanctions are generally appropriate in cases involving a lawyer's abuse of the legal process: *disbarment*, when the lawyer knowingly violates a court rule with the intent to obtain a benefit for the lawyer or another, and causes serious injury or potentially serious injury to a party, or causes serious or potentially serious interference with a legal proceeding; *suspension*, when the lawyer knows that he is violating a court rule, and there is injury or potential injury to a client or a party, or interference or potential interference with a legal proceeding; *reprimand*, when the lawyer negligently fails to comply with a court rule, and causes injury or potential injury to a client or other party, or causes interference or potential interference with a court proceeding; *admonition*, when the lawyer engages in an isolated instance of negligence in complying with a court rule, and causes little or no actual or potential injury to a party, or causes little or no actual or potential interference with a legal proceeding. *See* ABA Stds. for Imposing Lawyer Sanctions std. 6.2 (1992) (Abuse of Legal Process); *id.* stds. 6.21-6.24.

RULE 3.2. EXPEDITING LITIGATION

A lawyer shall make reasonable efforts to expedite litigation consistent with the interests of the client.

BACKGROUND

The Louisiana Supreme Court adopted this rule on January 20, 2004. It became effective on March 1, 2004, and has not been amended since. This rule is identical to ABA Model Rule of Professional Conduct 3.2 (2002).

COMMENT TO ABA MODEL RULE 3.2

[1] Dilatory practices bring the administration of justice into disrepute. Although there will be occasions when a lawyer may properly seek a postponement for personal reasons, it is not proper for a lawyer to routinely fail to expedite litigation solely for the convenience of the advocates. Nor will a failure to expedite be reasonable if done for the purpose of frustrating an opposing party's attempt to obtain rightful redress or repose. It is not a justification that similar conduct is often tolerated by the bench and bar. The question is whether a competent lawyer acting in good faith would regard the course of action as having some substantial purpose other than delay. Realizing financial or other benefit from otherwise improper delay in litigation is not a legitimate interest of the client.

ANNOTATIONS

Generally

The obligation imposed by this rule is straightforward: a lawyer shall not unreasonably delay litigation. This obligation is simply a specific application of a lawyer's more general duty to act with "reasonable diligence and promptness in representing a client." *See* La. Rules of Prof'l Conduct r. 1.3 (2004). A lawyer charged with violating Rule 1.3 (Diligence) is often charged with violating Rule 3.2 as well. *See, e.g., In re Nelson,* 146 So. 3d 176 (La. 2014); *In re Jones-Joseph,* 181 So. 3d 651, 652 (La. 2015); *In re Southall,* 165 So. 3d 894, 897 (La. 2015); *In re Hawkins,* 90 So. 3d 377 (La. 2012); *In re Schnyder,* 918 So. 2d 455 (La. 2006); *In re Schiro,* 886 So. 2d 1117 (La. 2004); *In re Beauchamp,* 821 So. 2d 1281 (La. 2002); *In re Harris,* 818 So. 2d 741 (La. 2002); *In re Collinsworth,* 795 So. 2d 312 (La. 2001); *In re Schnyder,* 918 So. 2d 455 (La. 2006); *In re Sims,* 994 So. 2d (La. 2008); *In re Jones-Joseph,* 181 So. 3d 651 (La. 2015). Thus, a lawyer who fails to comply with court-imposed deadlines and to otherwise advance the progress of a case is subject to discipline. *See In re White,* 699 So. 2d 375 (La. 1997).

When Delay is in the Client's Interest

Whether a lawyer can delay the progress of a matter when delay is a client goal is a more difficult issue. On the one hand, Rule 3.2 suggests that a lawyer shall expedite litigation only to the extent that doing so is "consistent with the interests of the client." La. Rules of Prof'l Conduct r. 3.2 (2004). On the other hand, the comment to Model Rule 3.2 suggests that a lawyer should not delay litigation merely to realize a "financial or other benefit" for the client. ABA Model Rules of Prof'l Conduct r. 3.2 cmt. Nevertheless, a lawyer should not run afoul of this rule by undertaking a nonfrivolous action that has a substantial purpose other than merely causing delay.

Disciplinary Sanctions

Absent aggravating or mitigating circumstances, the following sanctions are generally appropriate in cases involving a lawyer's abuse of the legal process: *disbarment*, when the lawyer knowingly violates a court rule with the intent to obtain a benefit for the lawyer or another, and causes serious injury or potentially serious injury to a party, or causes serious or potentially serious interference with a legal proceeding; *suspension*, when the lawyer knows that he is violating a court rule, and there is injury or potential injury to a client or a party, or interference or potential interference with a legal proceeding; *reprimand*, when the lawyer negligently fails to comply with a court rule, and causes injury or potential injury to a client or other party, or causes interference or potential interference with a court proceeding; and, *admonition*, when the lawyer engages in an isolated instance of negligence in complying with a court rule, and causes little or no actual or potential injury to a party, or causes little or no actual or potential interference with a legal proceeding. *See* ABA Stds. for Imposing Lawyer Sanctions std. 6.2 (1986) (Abuse of Legal Process); *id.* stds. 6.21-6.24.

RULE 3.3. CANDOR TOWARD THE TRIBUNAL

(a) A lawyer shall not knowingly:

(1) make a false statement of fact or law to a tribunal or fail to correct a false statement of material fact or law previously made to the tribunal by the lawyer;

(2) fail to disclose to the tribunal legal authority in the controlling jurisdiction known to the lawyer to be directly adverse to the position of the client and not disclosed by opposing counsel; or

(3) offer evidence that the lawyer knows to be false. If a lawyer, the lawyer's client, or a witness called by the lawyer, has offered material evidence and the lawyer comes to know of its falsity, the lawyer shall take reasonable remedial measures including, if necessary, disclosure to the tribunal. A lawyer may refuse to offer evidence, other than the testimony of a defendant in a criminal matter, that the lawyer reasonably believes is false.

(b) A lawyer who represents a client in an adjudicative proceeding and who knows that a person intends to engage, is engaging or has engaged in criminal or fraudulent conduct related to the proceeding shall take reasonable remedial measures, including, if necessary, disclosure to the tribunal.

(c) The duties stated in paragraphs (a) and (b) continue to the conclusion of the proceeding, and apply even if compliance requires disclosure of information otherwise protected by Rule 1.6.

(d) In an ex parte proceeding, a lawyer shall inform the tribunal of all material facts known to the lawyer that will enable the tribunal to make an informed decision, whether or not the facts are adverse.

BACKGROUND

The Louisiana Supreme Court adopted this rule on January 20, 2004. It became effective on March 1, 2004, and has not been amended since. This rule is identical to ABA Model Rule of Prof'l Conduct 3.3 (2002).

In 2002, the ABA reorganized the corresponding model rule to clarify a lawyer's obligation of candor to the tribunal with respect to testimony given and actions taken by the client and other witnesses. In some particulars, the ABA strengthened lawyers' obligations to the tribunal. For example, the Rule now makes clear that the lawyer must not allow the introduction of false evidence and must take remedial steps where the lawyer comes to know that material evidence offered by the client or a witness called by the lawyer is false—regardless of the client's wishes. As under the former Rule, the lawyer's obligations to the tribunal may require the lawyer to reveal information otherwise protected by Rule 1.6. The lawyer's obligation in the former Rule to avoid assisting client crime or fraud was replaced by a broader obligation to ensure the integrity of the adjudicative process. The lawyer must take remedial measures whenever the lawyer comes to know that any person is engaging or has engaged in criminal or fraudulent conduct related to the proceeding, such as jury tampering or document destruction. *See* ABA Ethics 2000 Commission Revision Notes to Model Rule 3.3 (2002).

In one case, however, the ABA strengthened the lawyer's obligation to the client, namely, when the lawyer represents the defendant in a criminal proceeding. In such a case, a lawyer does not have the same discretion regarding the client's own testimony as do lawyers representing clients in civil proceedings. While a criminal defense lawyer is subject to the general rule prohibiting the offering of testimony the lawyer knows to be false, the lawyer may not refuse to allow a defendant to testify in the defendant's defense if the lawyer only reasonably believes the testimony will be false. The commentary also provides that where a court insists that a criminal defendant be permitted to testify in his defense, the lawyer commits no ethical violation in allowing the client to do so even if the lawyer knows the client intends to lie. *See id.*

Paragraph (a) (1): False Statements to Tribunal

In 2002, the ABA deleted the term "material" of the former Model Rule 3.3(a)(1) that previously qualified the lawyer's duty not to knowingly make false statements of fact or law to a tribunal, and brought this duty into conformity with the duty not to offer false evidence set forth in paragraph (a)(3). In addition, the ABA added a new phrase to address the lawyer's duty to correct a false statement of material fact or law previously made to the tribunal to parallel the duty to take remedial measures in paragraph (a)(3). *See id.*

Paragraph (a)(2): Duty to Disclose Client Crime or Fraud

In 2002 the ABA deleted paragraph (a)(2) of the former Model Rule which prohibited a lawyer from knowingly failing to disclose to the tribunal material facts when necessary to avoid assisting client crime or fraud. Instead, the ABA chose to address a lawyer's duty to disclose crime or fraud in connection with a proceeding before a tribunal more comprehensively in paragraph (b). (Note also that lawyers have disclosure obligations under paragraphs (a)(1) and (a)(3), when they come to know of the falsity of statements previously made to the tribunal or evidence previously offered. The general duty to avoid assisting client crime or fraud is addressed in Rules 1.2(d) and 4.1.) *See id.*

Paragraph (a)(3): Remedial Measures

In 2002, the ABA amplified a lawyer's duty to take remedial measures in connection with material evidence the lawyer comes to know is false and gave the lawyer discretion to refuse to offer evidence that the lawyer reasonably believes is false. It also extended a lawyer's remedial obligations to situations in which the lawyer's client or a witness called by the lawyer has offered material evidence that the lawyer subsequently comes to know is false. Required remedial measures may, if necessary, include disclosure to the tribunal.

Paragraph (b): Duty to Preserve Integrity of Adjudicative Process

In 2002, the ABA adopted paragraph (b) addressing the lawyer's obligation to take reasonable remedial measures, including disclosure if necessary, when the lawyer comes to know that a person is engaging or has engaged in any sort of criminal or fraudulent conduct related to the proceeding. This new provision incorporated the substance of former Model Rule 3.3 paragraph (a)(2), as well as two provisions of the ABA Model Code of Professional Responsibility. *See* ABA Model Code of Prof'l Responsibility DR 7-102(B)(2) (1969) ("A lawyer who receives information clearly establishing that a person other than the client has perpetrated a fraud upon a tribunal shall promptly reveal the fraud to the tribunal"); *id*. DR 7-108(G) ("A lawyer shall reveal promptly to the court improper conduct by a venireperson or juror, or by another toward a venireperson or juror or a member of the venireperson's or juror's family, of which the lawyer has knowledge").

Paragraph (c): Duration of Duties in Paragraphs (a) and (b)

In 2002, the ABA did not change the scope and duration of the lawyer's duty of candor to the tribunal but extended it to paragraph (b).

COMMENTS TO ABA MODEL RULE 3.3

Generally

[1] This Rule governs the conduct of a lawyer who is representing a client in the proceedings of a tribunal. See Rule 1.0(m) for the definition of "tribunal." It also applies when the lawyer is representing a client in an ancillary proceeding conducted pursuant to the tribunal's adjudicative authority, such as a deposition. Thus, for example, paragraph (a)(3) requires a lawyer to take reasonable remedial measures if the lawyer comes to know that a client who is testifying in a deposition has offered evidence that is false.

[2] This Rule sets forth the special duties of lawyers as officers of the court to avoid conduct that undermines the integrity of the adjudicative process. A lawyer acting as an advocate in an adjudicative proceeding has an obligation to present the client's case with persuasive force. Performance of that duty while maintaining confidences of the client, however, is qualified by the advocate's duty of candor to the tribunal. Consequently, although a lawyer in an adversary proceeding is not required to present an impartial exposition of the law or to vouch for the evidence submitted in a cause, the lawyer must not allow the tribunal to be misled by false statements of law or fact or evidence that the lawyer knows to be false.

Representations by a Lawyer

[3] An advocate is responsible for pleadings and other documents prepared for litigation, but is usually not required to have personal knowledge of matters asserted therein, for

litigation documents ordinarily present assertions by the client, or by someone on the client's behalf, and not assertions by the lawyer. Compare Rule 3.1. However, an assertion purporting to be on the lawyer's own knowledge, as in an affidavit by the lawyer or in a statement in open court, may properly be made only when the lawyer knows the assertion is true or believes it to be true on the basis of a reasonably diligent inquiry. There are circumstances where failure to make a disclosure is the equivalent of an affirmative misrepresentation. The obligation prescribed in Rule 1.2(d) not to counsel a client to commit or assist the client in committing a fraud applies in litigation. Regarding compliance with Rule 1.2(d), see the Comment to that Rule. See also the Comment to Rule 8.4(b).

Legal Argument

[4] Legal argument based on a knowingly false representation of law constitutes dishonesty toward the tribunal. A lawyer is not required to make a disinterested exposition of the law, but must recognize the existence of pertinent legal authorities. Furthermore, as stated in paragraph (a)(2), an advocate has a duty to disclose directly adverse authority in the controlling jurisdiction that has not been disclosed by the opposing party. The underlying concept is that legal argument is a discussion seeking to determine the legal premises properly applicable to the case.

Offering Evidence

[5] Paragraph (a)(3) requires that the lawyer refuse to offer evidence that the lawyer knows to be false, regardless of the client's wishes. This duty is premised on the lawyer's obligation as an officer of the court to prevent the trier of fact from being misled by false evidence. A lawyer does not violate this Rule if the lawyer offers the evidence for the purpose of establishing its falsity.

[6] If a lawyer knows that the client intends to testify falsely or wants the lawyer to introduce false evidence, the lawyer should seek to persuade the client that the evidence should not be offered. If the persuasion is ineffective and the lawyer continues to represent the client, the lawyer must refuse to offer the false evidence. If only a portion of a witness's testimony will be false, the lawyer may call the witness to testify but may not elicit or otherwise permit the witness to present the testimony that the lawyer knows is false.

[7] The duties stated in paragraphs (a) and (b) apply to all lawyers, including defense counsel in criminal cases. In some jurisdictions, however, courts have required counsel to present the accused as a witness or to give a narrative statement if the accused so desires, even if counsel knows that the testimony or statement will be false. The obligation of the advocate under the Rules of Professional Conduct is subordinate to such requirements. See also Comment [9].

[8] The prohibition against offering false evidence only applies if the lawyer knows that the evidence is false. A lawyer's reasonable belief that evidence is false does not preclude its presentation to the trier of fact. A lawyer's knowledge that evidence is false, however, can be inferred from the circumstances. See Rule 1.0(f). Thus, although a lawyer should resolve doubts about the veracity of testimony or other evidence in favor of the client, the lawyer cannot ignore an obvious falsehood.

[9] Although paragraph (a)(3) only prohibits a lawyer from offering evidence the lawyer knows to be false, it permits the lawyer to refuse to offer testimony or other proof that the lawyer reasonably believes is false. Offering such proof may reflect adversely on the lawyer's ability to discriminate in the quality of evidence and thus impair the lawyer's effectiveness as an advocate. Because of the special protections historically provided criminal defendants, however, this Rule does not permit a lawyer to refuse to offer the testimony of such a client where the lawyer reasonably believes but does not know that the testimony will be false. Unless the lawyer knows the testimony will be false, the lawyer must honor the client's decision to testify. See also Comment [7].

Remedial Measures

[10] Having offered material evidence in the belief that it was true, a lawyer may subsequently come to know that the evidence is false. Or, a lawyer may be surprised when the lawyer's client, or another witness called by the lawyer, offers testimony the lawyer knows to be false, either during the lawyer's direct examination or in response to cross-examination by the opposing lawyer. In such situations or if the lawyer knows of the falsity of testimony elicited from the client during a deposition, the lawyer must take reasonable remedial measures. In such situations, the advocate's proper course is to remonstrate with the client confidentially, advise the client of the lawyer's duty of candor to the tribunal and seek the client's cooperation with respect to the withdrawal or correction of the false statements or evidence. If that fails, the advocate must take further remedial action. If withdrawal from the representation is not permitted or will not undo the effect of the false evidence, the advocate must make such disclosure to the tribunal as is reasonably necessary to remedy the situation, even if doing so requires the lawyer to reveal information that otherwise would be protected by Rule 1.6. It is for the tribunal then to determine what should be done—making a statement about the matter to the trier of fact, ordering a mistrial or perhaps nothing.

[11] The disclosure of a client's false testimony can result in grave consequences to the client, including not only a sense of betrayal but also loss of the case and perhaps a prosecution for perjury. But the alternative is that the lawyer cooperate in deceiving the court, thereby subverting the truth-finding process which the adversary system is designed to implement. See Rule 1.2(d). Furthermore, unless it is clearly understood that the lawyer will act upon the duty to disclose the existence of false evidence, the client can simply reject the lawyer's advice to reveal the false evidence and insist that the lawyer keep silent. Thus the client could in effect coerce the lawyer into being a party to fraud on the court.

Preserving Integrity of Adjudicative Process

[12] Lawyers have a special obligation to protect a tribunal against criminal or fraudulent conduct that undermines the integrity of the adjudicative process, such as bribing, intimidating or otherwise unlawfully communicating with a witness, juror, court official or other participant in the proceeding, unlawfully destroying or concealing documents or other evidence or failing to disclose information to the tribunal when required by law to do so. Thus, paragraph (b) requires a lawyer to take reasonable remedial measures, including disclosure if necessary, whenever the lawyer knows that a person, including the lawyer's

client, intends to engage, is engaging or has engaged in criminal or fraudulent conduct related to the proceeding.

Duration of Obligation

[13] A practical time limit on the obligation to rectify false evidence or false statements of law and fact has to be established. The conclusion of the proceeding is a reasonably definite point for the termination of the obligation. A proceeding has concluded within the meaning of this Rule when a final judgment in the proceeding has been affirmed on appeal or the time for review has passed.

Ex Parte Proceedings

[14] Ordinarily, an advocate has the limited responsibility of presenting one side of the matters that a tribunal should consider in reaching a decision; the conflicting position is expected to be presented by the opposing party. However, in any ex parte proceeding, such as an application for a temporary restraining order, there is no balance of presentation by opposing advocates. The object of an ex parte proceeding is nevertheless to yield a substantially just result. The judge has an affirmative responsibility to accord the absent party just consideration. The lawyer for the represented party has the correlative duty to make disclosures of material facts known to the lawyer and that the lawyer reasonably believes are necessary to an informed decision.

Withdrawal

[15] Normally, a lawyer's compliance with the duty of candor imposed by this Rule does not require that the lawyer withdraw from the representation of a client whose interests will be or have been adversely affected by the lawyer's disclosure. The lawyer may, however, be required by Rule 1.16(a) to seek permission of the tribunal to withdraw if the lawyer's compliance with this Rule's duty of candor results in such an extreme deterioration of the client-lawyer relationship that the lawyer can no longer competently represent the client. Also see Rule 1.16(b) for the circumstances in which a lawyer will be permitted to seek a tribunal's permission to withdraw. In connection with a request for permission to withdraw that is premised on a client's misconduct, a lawyer may reveal information relating to the representation only to the extent reasonably necessary to comply with this Rule or as otherwise permitted by Rule 1.6.

ANNOTATIONS
Generally

A lawyer's duty of candor to the tribunal is sometimes difficult to reconcile with responsibilities to clients. This rule is intended to provide guidance to a lawyer facing such conflicts. On balance, this rule resolves most of these conflicts in favor of the lawyer's duties to the tribunal and the justice system.

This rule applies only in matters pending before a "tribunal."[106] Thus, while it applies to matters pending before arbitrators, it does not necessarily apply in matters before

---

[106] The Rules define "tribunal" as "a court, an arbitrator in a binding arbitration proceeding or a legislative body, administrative agency or other body acting in an adjudicative capacity...." *See* La. Rules of Prof'l Conduct r. 1.0(m) (2004).

nonjudicial mediators or in nonadjudicative proceedings. *See In re Jones*, 106 So. 3d 1019, 1026 (La. 2013) (finding no 3.3 violation for a lawyer's filing false documents in the public conveyance records outside of a court). As to the candor obligations of lawyers appearing before mediators, see La. Rules of Prof'l Conduct r. 4.1 (2004) (Truthfulness in Statements to Others). As to the disclosure obligations of a lawyer representing a client in a nonadjudicative proceeding, see La. Rules of Prof'l Conduct r. 3.9 (2004) (Advocate in Nonadjudicative Proceedings); *see also* ABA Comm. on Ethics and Professional Responsibility, Formal Op. 93-375 (1993).

False Statements of Fact or Law

As to intentional false statements, paragraph (a)(1) prohibits a lawyer from "knowingly" making false statements of fact or law–whether material or immaterial–to the tribunal.[107] La. Rules of Prof'l Conduct r. 3.3(a)(1) (2004). *See In re Lightfoot*, 85 So. 3d 56, 61-62 (La. 2012) (disciplining lawyer for using a known fictitious name for client in bankruptcy pleading to avoid negative press attention for the client); *see also* Restatement (Third) of the Law Governing Lawyers § 111(1) (2000). Lawyers have been disciplined under this rule for, among other conduct, misrepresenting the status of other proceedings in motions to continue, *see In re Bailey*, 848 So. 2d 530, 537 (La. 2003), as well as for filing an affidavit containing false information, *see, e.g., In re Aldige*, 133 So. 3d 663 (La. 2014). This obligation terminates at the conclusion of the "proceeding." *See* La. Rules of Prof'l Conduct r. 3.3(c) (2004); *In re Hall*, 181 So. 3d 643 (La. Sept. 15, 2015) (finding lawyer's denial in a pretrial conference that the client was not using drugs was dishonest when he later provided masking shampoo to her prior to hair-follicle drug test).

As to inadvertent false statements, however, the rule requires the lawyer to correct only "material" falsities that the lawyer has "previously made to the tribunal." La. Rules of Prof'l Conduct r. 3.3(a)(1) (2004). Whether a fact is "material" is sometimes a difficult issue. No Louisiana case defines the term "material" for purposes of the Louisiana Rules of Professional Conduct. However, the Louisiana Supreme Court has held in another context that a "material fact" is one whose "existence or nonexistence" is "essential" to the resolution of a matter. *See Benoit v. St. Charles Gaming Co., Inc.*, 2017 WL 5178888 (La. Ct. App. 3d Cir. Nov. 8, 2017); *Smith v. Our Lady of the Lake Hosp., Inc.*, 639 So. 2d 730, 751 (La. 1994), *superseded on other grounds by* La. Code Civ. Proc. Ann. art 966 (2007). Likewise, in the context of securities law, a fact is "material" if it is one which an average, prudent person would consider important in making a decision. *See, e.g., Simpson v. Se. Inv. Trust*, 697 F.2d 1257, 1258 (5th Cir. 1983) (holding that the standard for materiality with regard to misstatements is whether an average, prudent investor would consider the truth important in making investment decision); *see also Dennis v. General Imaging*, 918

---

[107] For a case imposing discipline under this rule for false statements by a lawyer in his capacity as a litigant rather than as a lawyer, see *In re Soileau*, 737 So. 2d 23, 27 (La. 1999). *See In re Richmond*, 996 So. 2d 282 (La. 2008) (disciplining a lawyer who was also a state representative for falsely representing his domicile on notarized Notice of Candidacy Form).

F.2d 496, 505 (5th Cir. 1990) (same). Therefore, by analogy, a fact should be considered to be "material" for purposes of this rule if an ordinary judge would consider the fact "important" in the context asserted.

Adverse Authority

Paragraph (a)(2) requires a lawyer to disclose to the court or opposing counsel known legal authority "in the controlling jurisdiction" that is directly adverse[108] to a client's position. *Id.* r. 3.3(a)(2); *see also* Restatement (Third) of the Law Governing Lawyers § 111(2) (2000). The standard that lawyers should use for determining whether a potentially adverse authority must be disclosed is not whether it is precisely on point and dispositive of the relevant issue. Rather, the test is as follows: "Is the decision which opposing counsel has overlooked one which the court should clearly consider in deciding the case? Would a reasonable judge properly feel that a lawyer who advanced, as the law, a proposition adverse to the undisclosed decision was lacking in candor and fairness to him?" *See* ABA Comm. on Prof'l Ethics and Grievances, Formal Op. 280 (1949). This disclosure obligation terminates at the conclusion of the "proceeding." *Id.* R. 3.3(c).

Offering False Evidence

Paragraph (a)(3) addresses a lawyer's obligations to the tribunal with regard to false documentary or testimonial evidence. As to evidence that the lawyer "knows" is false, paragraph (a)(3) prohibits the lawyer from offering it into evidence. Furthermore, a lawyer who has inadvertently done so must "take reasonable remedial measures." *Id.* R. 3.3(a)(3); *see also* Restatement (Third) of the Law Governing Lawyers § 120 (2000). What remedial measures are "reasonable" in any given case turns on the circumstances. Clearly the lawyer must attempt to convince the client or other person who has offered the false testimony or document to correct the error. *See* ABA Model Rules of Prof'l Conduct r. 3.3 cmts. 5-11. In addition, the lawyer may consider withdrawing from the representation. *Id.* cmt. 10. However, withdrawal alone typically will not satisfy the lawyer's obligations under this rule, unless the withdrawal is "noisy"–that is, unless the lawyer discloses the false evidence to the tribunal at the time of withdrawal. *Id.* Finally, although some lawyers believe that they can comply with this rule through permitting their client (or other witness) to testify falsely in narrative form (that is, without questioning by the lawyer), the ABA has soundly rejected that approach. *See* ABA Comm. on Ethics and Professional Responsibility, Formal Op. 87-353 (1987); ABA Stds. Relating to the Admin. of Crim. Justice–The Def. Function std. 4–7.5(a) (1992).

Although perhaps obvious, this rule applies in the context of civil pretrial discovery. *See In re Marshall*, 753 So. 2d 166, 167-68 (La. 2000) (disbarring lawyer for, among other things, advising clients to testify falsely in depositions). Therefore, this rule requires a lawyer to take reasonable "remedial measures" to correct the record when the lawyer learns that a client or another witness has testified falsely during a civil deposition or has otherwise

---

[108] The failure to cite cases overruling precedent cited in a brief may violate this rule. *See State v. Harris*, 911 So. 2d 361, 364 n.1 (La. Ct. App. 2d Cir. 2005) (admonishing lawyer "to avoid citing jurisprudence that announces obsolete or abrogated legal theories").

furnished untruthful discovery responses. *See, e.g., Jones v. Clinton*, 36 F. Supp. 2d 1118, 1130 n.15 (E.D. Ark. 1999); *Zatzkis v. Zatzkis*, 632 So. 2d 302, 304-05 (La. Ct. App. 4th Cir. 1993) (finding that lawyer failed to reveal false nature of backdated document offered into evidence); *see also La. State Bar Ass'n v. White*, 539 So. 2d 1216, 1219 (La. 1989). The lawyer may not simply withdraw from further representation in the matter. *See, e.g.,* ABA Comm. on Ethics and Professional Responsibility, Formal Op. 93-376 (1993).

A lawyer's obligation to take "reasonable remedial measures" terminates at "the conclusion of the proceeding," and requires disclosure of information "otherwise protected by Rule 1.6." *See* La. Rules of Prof'l Conduct r. 3.3(c) (2004).

Disclosure Obligations in Adjudicated Proceedings

Paragraph (b) requires a lawyer in an adjudicative proceeding to "take remedial measures, including, if necessary disclosure to tribunal" when the lawyer knows of criminal or fraudulent activity involving the client. *Id.* R. 3.3(b). A lawyer's compliance with this rule does not violate a client's right to effective counsel. *See Hill v. Tanner*, No. 12-369, 2012 WL 4059899 at *6 (E. D. La. July 5, 2012) (noting defense lawyer's ethical obligation to disclose to the court that client engaged in witness tampering).

Paragraph (d) requires a lawyer in an ex parte proceeding to "inform the tribunal of all material facts known to the lawyer" bearing on the issue before the tribunal in order to enable it to make an "informed decision." *Id.* r. 3.3(d). This rule applies broadly to all material facts–not just those that are "adverse" to the lawyer's client. *Id.*; *see also* Restatement (Third) of the Law Governing Lawyers § 112 (2000).

Disciplinary Sanctions

Absent aggravating or mitigating circumstances, the following sanctions are generally appropriate in cases involving conduct that is prejudicial to the administration of justice or that involves dishonesty, fraud, deceit, or misrepresentation to a court: *disbarment*, when a lawyer, with intent to deceive the court, makes a false statement, submits a false document, or improperly withholds material information, and causes serious or potentially serious injury to a party, or causes a significant or potentially significant adverse effect on the legal proceeding; *suspension*, when a lawyer knows that false statements or documents are being submitted to the court or that material information is improperly being withheld, and takes no remedial action, and causes injury or potential injury to a party or to the legal proceeding, or causes an adverse or potentially adverse effect on the legal proceeding; *reprimand*, when a lawyer is negligent either in determining whether statements or documents are false or in taking remedial action when material information is being withheld, and causes injury or potential injury to a party to the legal proceeding, or causes an adverse or potentially adverse effect on the legal proceeding; and, *admonition*, when a lawyer engages in an isolated instance of neglect in determining whether submitted statements or documents are false or in failing to disclose material information upon learning of its falsity, and causes little or no actual or potential injury to a party, or causes little or no adverse or potentially adverse effect on the legal proceeding. *See* ABA Stds. for Imposing Lawyer Sanctions stds. 6.11-6.14 (1992) (False Statements, Fraud, and Misrepresentation); *id.* std. 6.1. The Louisiana Supreme Court has not hesitated to impose the sanction of permanent disbarment for perjury. *See In re Norris*, 939 So. 2d 1221 (La. 2006).

RULE 3.4. FAIRNESS TO OPPOSING PARTY AND COUNSEL

A lawyer shall not:

(a) unlawfully obstruct another party's access to evidence or unlawfully alter, destroy or conceal a document or other material having potential evidentiary value. A lawyer shall not counsel or assist another person to do any such act;

(b) falsify evidence, counsel or assist a witness to testify falsely, or offer an inducement to a witness that is prohibited by law;

(c) knowingly disobey an obligation under the rules of a tribunal, except for an open refusal based on an assertion that no valid obligation exists;

(d) in pretrial procedure, make a frivolous discovery request or fail to make reasonably diligent effort to comply with a legally proper discovery request by an opposing party;

(e) in trial, allude to any matter that the lawyer does not reasonably believe is relevant or that will not be supported by admissible evidence, assert personal knowledge of facts in issue except when testifying as a witness, or state a personal opinion as to the justness of a cause, the credibility of a witness, the culpability of a civil litigant or the guilt or innocence of an accused; or

(f) request a person other than a client to refrain from voluntarily giving relevant information to another party unless:

> (1) the person is a relative or an employee or other agent of a client, and

> (2) the lawyer reasonably believes that the person's interests will not be adversely affected by refraining from giving such information.

BACKGROUND

The Louisiana Supreme Court adopted this rule on January 20, 2004. It became effective on March 1, 2004, and has not been amended since. This rule is identical to ABA Model Rule of Professional Conduct 3.4 (2002).

COMMENTS TO ABA MODEL RULE 3.4

[1] The procedure of the adversary system contemplates that the evidence in a case is to be marshalled competitively by the contending parties. Fair competition in the adversary

system is secured by prohibitions against destruction or concealment of evidence, improperly influencing witnesses, obstructive tactics in discovery procedure, and the like.

[2] Documents and other items of evidence are often essential to establish a claim or defense. Subject to evidentiary privileges, the right of an opposing party, including the government, to obtain evidence through discovery or subpoena is an important procedural right. The exercise of that right can be frustrated if relevant material is altered, concealed or destroyed. Applicable law in many jurisdictions makes it an offense to destroy material for purpose of impairing its availability in a pending proceeding or one whose commencement can be foreseen. Falsifying evidence is also generally a criminal offense. Paragraph (a) applies to evidentiary material generally, including computerized information. Applicable law may permit a lawyer to take temporary possession of physical evidence of client crimes for the purpose of conducting a limited examination that will not alter or destroy material characteristics of the evidence. In such a case, applicable law may require the lawyer to turn the evidence over to the police or other prosecuting authority, depending on the circumstances.

[3] With regard to paragraph (b), it is not improper to pay a witness's expenses or to compensate an expert witness on terms permitted by law. The common law rule in most jurisdictions is that it is improper to pay an occurrence witness any fee for testifying and that it is improper to pay an expert witness a contingent fee.

[4] Paragraph (f) permits a lawyer to advise employees of a client to refrain from giving information to another party, for the employees may identify their interests with those of the client. See also Rule 4.2.

ANNOTATIONS
Destroying and Falsifying Evidence or Testimony
A lawyer may not take part in unlawfully altering, destroying or concealing documentary or other evidence that is potentially relevant to a matter. *See* La. Rules of Prof'l Conduct r. 3.4(a) (2004); *see also* Restatement (Third) of the Law Governing Lawyers § 118 (2000).

In *Reynolds v. Bordelon*, No. 2014-2362 (La. Jun. 30, 2015), the Louisiana Supreme Court held that Louisiana does not recognize a cause of action for negligent destruction of evidence. Other remedies exist, however. As to parties to litigation, negligent spoliation can be redressed through the imposition of discovery sanctions and through an adverse evidentiary presumption. As to nonparties to litigation, those who fear destruction can enter into contracts to preserve evidence or seek court orders to preserve evidence. *Id.*

Social Media
Given the potential harm social media can cause to people's lives and cases, is it appropriate for a lawyer to advise a client to take down an embarrassing or case-imperiling post? An ethics opinion from the New York County Lawyers' Association reached this conclusion:

> An attorney may advise clients to keep their social media privacy settings turned on or maximized and may advise clients as to what should or should not be posted on public and/or private pages,

consistent with the principles stated above. Provided that there is no violation of the rules or substantive law pertaining to the preservation and/or spoliation of evidence, an attorney may offer advice as to what may be kept on "private" social media pages, and what may be "taken down" or removed.

See NYCLA Ethics Op. No. 745 (Jul. 2, 2013); *see also* Op. No. 14-1, Professional Ethics of the Florida Bar (Jun. 25, 2015, approved Oct. 16, 2015); N.C. Formal Ethics Opinion 5 (July 25, 2014). This is good advice. Rule 1.1, which requires a lawyer to be competent, suggests that a lawyer not only can, but should, advise his client about the possible case-related consequences of social-media postings. A client needs to know that the other side may be watching.

Rule 4.1 and Rule 3.3 would prohibit a lawyer from advising a client to post false images or information on a social media site for purposes of manufacturing favorable evidence (for example, by encouraging a personal injury client to post a sad picture of herself in a wheelchair when she was neither sad nor wheelchair-bound).

Note that. Rule 3.4(a) prohibits a lawyer from counseling a person, including a client (1) to engage in spoliation[109] of evidence, (2) to "unlawfully obstruct another party's access to evidence," or (3) to "unlawfully alter, destroy or conceal a document or other material having potential evidentiary value." A picture of a personal injury plaintiff jumping on a trampoline *is* a document "having potential evidentiary value" in a case in which the plaintiff claims that she cannot walk. Therefore, a lawyer clearly could not advise the plaintiff to destroy all extant copies of the photograph. But advising a client to remove a photo from Facebook is not advice "to destroy" or "to conceal" it. Such advice is equivalent to advising a client to remove—but not to destroy—an embarrassing picture posted on a billboard. In short, advising a client to take down a Facebook photo and to preserve it for production in the course of discovery[110] should not run afoul of the rules.

---

[109] Under Louisiana law, the term "spoliation of evidence" refers to "an intentional destruction of evidence for purpose of depriving opposing parties of its use." *Pham v. Contico International, Inc.,* 759 So. 2d 880, 882 (La. Ct. App. 5th Cir. 2000) (*citing Hooker v. Super Products Corp.,* 751 So. 2d 889 (La. Ct. App. 5th Cir. 1999); *Kammerer v. Sewerage and Water Board of New Orleans,* 633 So. 2d 1357 (La. Ct. App. 4th Cir. 1994)). The *Pham* court noted that "the tort of spoliation of evidence has its roots in the evidentiary doctrine of 'adverse presumption,' which allows a jury instruction for the presumption that the destroyed evidence contained information detrimental to the party who destroyed the evidence unless such destruction is adequately explained." *Id.* (*citing Randolph v. General Motors Corp.,* 646 So. 2d 1019 (La. Ct. App. 1st Cir. 1994)).

[110] In contrast, a lawyer who advises a client to take down and destroy digital photographs from a social media site would violate Rule 3.4 and face the risk of severe sanctions. *See* Debra Cassens Weiss, *Lawyer Agrees to Five-Year Suspension for Advising Client to Clean Up His Facebook Photos,* ABA Journal On-Line, Aug. 7, 2013

Witness Preparation

Likewise, a lawyer may not assist a witness in testifying falsely. *See id.* § 120(1)(a). Nevertheless, it is permissible for a lawyer to "interview a witness for the purpose of preparing the witness to testify." *Id.* § 116(1); *see also State v. Morgan*, 472 So. 2d 934 (La. Ct. App. 1st Cir. 1985). The line between permissible witness preparation and impermissible witness "education" is sometimes difficult to draw.

Obstructing Access to Evidence or Testimony

A lawyer may not take part in unlawfully obstructing another party's access to documentary or other evidence that is potentially relevant to a matter. *See* La. Rules of Prof'l Conduct r. 3.4(a) (2004); Restatement (Third) of the Law Governing Lawyers § 118(2) (2000) (stating that lawyer cannot obstruct access to evidence in violation of court order or obstruction of justice statute). Likewise, a lawyer may not request that a person other than a client refrain from talking with an opponent or an opponent's lawyer unless: (1) that person is a relative, employee or other agent of the client, and (2) the lawyer reasonably believes that the person's interests will not thereby be adversely affected. *See* La. Rules of Prof'l Conduct r. 3.4(f) (2004); *see also* Restatement (Third) of the Law Governing Lawyers § 116 (2000). *In re Hall*, 184 So. 3d 1279, (La. 2016) (defendant violated Rule 3.4(b) by giving detox shampoo to client before hair-follicle drug test).

Payment of Witnesses

Paragraph (b) prohibits lawyers from offering "an inducement to a witness that is prohibited by law." Given this language, a lawyer must "look outside the rule to ascertain which inducements are prohibited by law and therefore unethical." *See* ABA/BNA Lawyers' Manual on Professional Cond. § 61:718 (2007). Louisiana law expressly prohibits only one type of "inducement"—a bribe. "Bribery" is the "giving or offering to give, directly or indirectly, anything of apparent present or prospective value" to any "[w]itness, or person about to be called as a witness, upon a trial or other proceeding" if the payment is made "with the intent to influence his conduct . . . ." *See* La. Rev. Stat. § 14:118(A)(1)(d); *see also* 18 U.S.C.A. § 201.

Louisiana decisional law contains no per se prohibition against payments to fact witnesses. The few reported decisions that address the issue reflect judicial disapproval only when the payment is made with improper motive. For example, the Louisiana Supreme Court disbarred a lawyer for paying a bribe to a witness with the intent to influence the witness's testimony. *See In re Hingle*, 717 So. 2d 636 (La. 1998). Likewise, the Louisiana Supreme Court disbarred a lawyer who made a payment to a witness for the purpose of inducing him "to provide false and misleading information." *See La. State Bar Assoc. v. Thierry*, 573 So. 2d 1099, 1103 (La. 1991). The Louisiana Supreme Court suspended a lawyer, in part, because he made a payment to a fact witness whose cooperation was contingent on the payment. *See In re Bruno*, 956 So. 2d 577, 578-79 (La. 2007).

(http://www.abajournal.com/news/article/lawyer_agrees_to_five-year_suspension_for_advising_client_to_clean_up_his_f).

Although no reported Louisiana decision addresses whether it is appropriate to pay a fact witness for the witness's lost income and expenses attendant to trial or deposition preparation, the preponderance of persuasive authority suggests that a lawyer should not be subjected to discipline for making such a payment. For example, the Restatement of the Law Governing Lawyers permits a lawyer to pay the "reasonable expenses of the witness incurred and the reasonable value of the witness's time spent in providing evidence." *See* Restatement (Third) of the Law Governing Lawyers § 117(1) (2000). Comment "b" to this section clarifies that it encompasses time and expenses "incurred in preparation for and giving testimony, such as lost wages caused by the witness's absence from employment." *Id.* cmt. b (emphasis added). Likewise, the American Bar Association Committee on Ethics and Professional Responsibility has opined, as have most state bar associations that have considered the issue, that Rule 3.4(b) permits lawyers to pay fact witnesses for the income actually lost and expenses actually incurred to prepare for trial testimony. *See* ABA Comm. on Ethics and Professional Responsibility, Formal Op. 96-402 (1996). According to the committee:

> there is no reason to draw a distinction between (a) compensating a witness for time spent in actually attending a deposition or a trial and (b) compensating the witness for time spent in pretrial interviews with the lawyer in preparation for testifying, so long as the lawyer makes it clear to the witness that the payment is not being made for the substance (or efficacy) of the witness's testimony or as an inducement to "tell the truth." The Committee is further of the view that the witness may also be compensated for time spent in reviewing and researching records that are germane to his or her testimony, provided, of course, that such compensation is not barred by local law.

Id.; *see also* W.V. Legal Ethics Op. 2017-01 (May 22, 2017) ("[C]ompensating a fact witness for time spent preparing for testimony and being interviewed is permissible under the Rules of Professional Conduct. This is only allowed if the compensation is reasonable and not based upon the outcome of the litigation. The agreement to pay compensation should be in writing and disclosed to the opposing side.").

In summary, the Louisiana Rules of Professional Conduct, relevant statutory law, case law, and persuasive authority all indicate that a lawyer should *not* be subjected to discipline for paying a fact witness if:

1. the payment is not motivated by an improper purpose, such as to obtain "inside information," to obtain false testimony or to influence the content of the witness's testimony;
2. the amount paid merely compensates the witness for the reasonable value of the time and expenses actually incurred by the witness; and,
3. the amount of the payment is not contingent on the witness's testimony.

As to expert witnesses, a lawyer can lawfully pay a reasonable, noncontingent witness fee. *See* Restatement (Third) of the Law Governing Lawyers § 117(1) (2000).

Complying with Orders of the Tribunal

Paragraph (c) prohibits a lawyer from knowingly disobeying an obligation under the rules or rulings of a tribunal, unless the lawyer does so openly and because the lawyer contends that no "valid obligation exists." *See* La. Rules of Prof'l Conduct r. 3.4(c) (2004); *see also* Restatement (Third) of the Law Governing Lawyers § 105 (2000). For example, a lawyer may be found to have violated this rule Also, a lawyer can violate this rule by failing to cooperate with ODC requests. *See In re Bark*, 72 So. 3d 853, 856 (La. 2011) (disciplining lawyer for failure to appear for sworn statement and to provide financial records for trust accounts after promising to do so under oath pursuant to ODC investigation). Nor may a lawyer advise a client to disobey such an obligation.

Pretrial and Trial Conduct

As an analogue to Rule 3.1 (which prohibits lawyers from making frivolous claims and contentions), paragraph (d) of this rule prohibits lawyers from making "a frivolous discovery request," or from failing "to make [a] reasonably diligent effort to comply with a legally proper discovery request." La. Rules of Prof'l Conduct r. 3.4(d) (2004); Restatement (Third) of the Law Governing Lawyers § 110(3) (2000). During trial, a lawyer may not "allude to any matter" that is irrelevant or will not be supported by the evidence. *See* La. Rules of Prof'l Conduct r. 3.4(e) (2004); *see also State v. Brisibi*, No. 2011 KA 1517, 2012 WL 1012305, at *1-2 (La. Ct. App. 1st Cir. Mar. 23, 2012) (finding that prosecuting lawyer who improperly referred to voicemails not admitted into evidence during cross-examination violated 3.4). Furthermore, during trial a lawyer must not inject himself or herself personally into the merits of the case by asserting personal knowledge of facts, or by stating an opinion regarding various aspects of the case, unless the lawyer is a witness. *See* La. Rules of Prof'l Conduct r. 3.4(e) (2004); *see also* Restatement (Third) of the Law Governing Lawyers § 107 (2000). For example, it is improper for a prosecutor to state at trial that he "expected" a witness "to tell the truth." *See State v. Floyd*, 544 So. 2d 616, 619 (La. Ct. App. 3d Cir. 1989).

Disciplinary Sanctions

Absent aggravating or mitigating circumstances, the following sanctions are generally appropriate in cases involving a lawyer's abuse of the legal process: *disbarment*, when the lawyer knowingly violates a court rule with the intent to obtain a benefit for the lawyer or another, or when the lawyer intentionally tampers with a witness, and causes serious or potentially serious injury to a party, or causes significant or potentially significant interference with the outcome of the legal proceeding; *suspension*, when the lawyer knows that he is violating a court rule, and there is injury or potential injury to a client or a party, or interference or potential interference with a legal proceeding; *reprimand*, when the lawyer negligently fails to comply with a court rule, and causes injury or potential injury to a client or other party, or causes interference or potential interference with a court proceeding; and, *admonition*, when the lawyer engages in an isolated instance of negligence in complying with a court rule, and causes little or no actual or potential injury to a party, or causes little or no actual or potential interference with a legal proceeding. *See* ABA Stds. for Imposing Lawyer Sanctions std. 6.2 (1992) (Abuse of Legal Process); *id.* stds. 6.21-6.24; *id.* std. 6.31 (Intentional Witness Tampering).

231

RULE 3.5. IMPARTIALITY AND DECORUM OF THE TRIBUNAL

A lawyer shall not:

(a) seek to influence a judge, juror, prospective juror or other official by means prohibited by law;

(b) communicate ex parte with such a person during the proceeding unless authorized to do so by law or court order;

(c) communicate with a juror or prospective juror after discharge of the jury if:

> (1) the communication is prohibited by law or court order;

> (2) the juror has made known to the lawyer a desire not to communicate; or

> (3) the communication involves misrepresentation, coercion, duress or harassment; or

(d) engage in conduct intended to disrupt a tribunal.

BACKGROUND

The Louisiana Supreme Court adopted this rule on January 20, 2004. It became effective on March 1, 2004, and has not been amended since. This rule is identical to ABA Model Rule of Professional Conduct 3.5 (2002).

Paragraph (b): Contact During the Proceeding

In 2002, the ABA modified the corresponding Model Rule to address communications "during the proceeding" and to address post-proceeding communication with jurors in a new paragraph (c). In addition, the ABA added the reference to "court order" to alert lawyers as to the availability of judicial relief in the rare situation in which an ex parte communication is needed. *See* ABA Ethics 2000 Commission Revision Notes to Model Rule 3.5 (2002).

Paragraph (c): Contact with Jurors After the Proceeding

In 2002, the ABA adopted this paragraph on recommendation of the ABA Ethics 2000 Commission. It did so because the Commission noted that former Rule 3.5(b) was held to be unconstitutionally overbroad when applied to post-verdict communications with jurors. *See Rapp v. Disciplinary Bd.*, 916 F. Supp. 1525, 1534-38 (D. Hawaii 1996). The Commission proposed the addition of a new paragraph (c) to permit such communications unless prohibited by law or court order or unless the lawyer knows that the juror does not wish to be contacted. Also prohibited by this rule are communications involving misrepresentation, duress, coercion or harassment. In the view of the Ethics 2000 Commission, the newly-revised Model Rule permits more post-verdict communication with jurors than the prior Rule, but affords greater juror protection than did ABA Model Code of Professional Responsibility DR 7-108(D), which stated, "After discharge of the jury from further consideration of a case with which the lawyer was connected, the lawyer shall not ask questions of or make comments to a member of that jury that are calculated merely to harass or embarrass the juror or to influence his actions in future jury service." *See* ABA Ethics 2000 Commission Revision Notes to Model Rule 3.5 (2002).

COMMENTS TO ABA MODEL RULE 3.5

[1] Many forms of improper influence upon a tribunal are proscribed by criminal law. Others are specified in the ABA Model Code of Judicial Conduct, with which an advocate should be familiar. A lawyer is required to avoid contributing to a violation of such provisions.

[2] During a proceeding a lawyer may not communicate ex parte with persons serving in an official capacity in the proceeding, such as judges, masters or jurors, unless authorized to do so by law or court order.

[3] A lawyer may on occasion want to communicate with a juror or prospective juror after the jury has been discharged. The lawyer may do so unless the communication is prohibited by law or a court order but must respect the desire of the juror not to talk with the lawyer. The lawyer may not engage in improper conduct during the communication.

[4] The advocate's function is to present evidence and argument so that the cause may be decided according to law. Refraining from abusive or obstreperous conduct is a corollary of the advocate's right to speak on behalf of litigants. A lawyer may stand firm against abuse by a judge but should avoid reciprocation; the judge's default is no justification for similar dereliction by an advocate. An advocate can present the cause, protect the record for subsequent review and preserve professional integrity by patient firmness no less effectively than by belligerence or theatrics.

[5] The duty to refrain from disruptive conduct applies to any proceeding of a tribunal, including a deposition. See Rule 1.0(m).

ANNOTATIONS
Improperly Influencing a Judge

Paragraph (a) prohibits a lawyer from seeking to influence a judge "by means prohibited by law." *See* La. Rules of Prof'l Conduct r. 3.5(a) (2004); *see also* Restatement (Third) of the Law Governing Lawyers § 113(1) (2000). Thus, a lawyer may not provide a gift or loan to a judge in an effort to affect the outcome of matters that are or may come before the judge. *See* Restatement (Third) of the Law Governing Lawyers § 113(2) (2000). Indeed, Louisiana judges are prohibited from accepting from lawyers or others, "any gifts or favors which might reasonably appear as designed to affect the judgment of the judge or influence the judge's official conduct." La. Code of Judicial Conduct Canon 6(B)(1). Nevertheless, a lawyer can permissibly provide a judge a gift or favor that constitutes nothing more than ordinary social hospitality. La. Code of Judicial Conduct Canon 6(B)(2)(d). Finally, a lawyer should not "state or imply an ability . . . to influence a judicial officer," other than by "legally proper procedures." Restatement (Third) of the Law Governing Lawyers § 113(2) (2000).

Louisiana trial and appellate judges in Louisiana are, of course, elected in general elections. As a result, persons seeking election or reelection to judicial office must run and finance campaigns. A judge or judicial candidate is prohibited from soliciting or accepting campaign contributions directly from any person, including a lawyer. *See* La. Code of Judicial Conduct Canon 7(D)(1). As a result, lawyers are prohibited from giving a campaign contribution directly to a judge or judicial candidate. *See Louisiana State Bar Ass' n v. Harrington*, 585 So. 2d 514, 521-522 (La. 1990) (holding that "means prohibited by law" includes any attempt by a lawyer to induce a violation of the Code of Judicial Conduct); La. Rules of Prof'l Conduct r. 8.4(f) (2004) (making it professional misconduct to assist judge in violating rules of judicial conduct). However, a judge or judicial candidate is permitted to establish a campaign committee to solicit and accept campaign contributions from lawyers. *See* La. Code of Judicial Conduct Canon 7(D)(3) ("Such committees are not prohibited from soliciting or accepting campaign contributions or public support from lawyers."). Therefore, lawyers are free to contribute campaign contributions to judicial campaign committees.

This rule also forbids lawyers from using social media or third parties to influence judges. *In re McCool*, 172 So. 3d 1058 (La. 2015). In *In re McCool*, a lawyer started an online petition to attempt to influence judges in pending proceedings. *McCool*, 172 So. 3d at 1072. The petition included inflammatory, false, and misleading statements, encouraged readers to contact the court, and provided the judges' contact information. *Id.* at 1069-70. The court rejected the lawyer's First Amendment defense and disbarred her for violating Rule 3.5(a)-(b). *Id.* at 1076-78, 1083-84.

Improperly Influencing a Juror or Potential Juror

Paragraph (a) prohibits a lawyer from seeking to influence a juror or prospective juror "by means prohibited by law." La. Rules of Prof'l Conduct r. 3.5(a) (2004); *see also* Restatement (Third) of the Law Governing Lawyers § 115 (2000). In addition, paragraph (b) prohibits a lawyer from communicating ex parte with a juror or a judge during a trial about any matter.

However, the extent to which a lawyer can contact prospective jurors in anticipation of trial, or former jurors after verdict, is less clear. Paragraph (c) broadens the scope of permissible contact with jurors after discharge. Moreover, neither the Louisiana Code of Civil Procedure nor the Louisiana Code of Criminal Procedure prohibits communications with prospective or former jurors. *See Jones v. Swift Transp. Co. Inc.*, 464 F. App'x. 252, 254 (5th Cir. 2012) (finding no 3.5(c) violation when a lawyer communicated with a discharged jury foreperson about verdict when the district court directed the jury foreperson to the lawyer). However, any attempt to prejudice or influence a prospective juror about a future case, or any effort to harass a former juror about a past case would violate this rule and, perhaps, others (including Rule 8.4(d)). Note also that several Louisiana state and federal courts have, by local rule, restricted the extent to which lawyers can communicate with past or prospective jurors. *See* E.D. La. Civ. R. 47.5(B)-(C); M.D. La. Civ. R. 47(e); W.D.

La. Civ. R. 47.5(B)-(C); La. 31st Jud. Dist. Ct. R. XXII, §§ 2-4." Running afoul of any such a local rule would violate Louisiana Rule of Professional Conduct 3.4(c) ("A lawyer shall not . . . knowingly disobey an obligation under the rules of a tribunal . . . ."). In short, the best practice is for lawyers to avoid all contact with prospective jurors without prior court authorization, *see* Restatement (Third) of the Law Governing Lawyers § 115(1) (2000) (prohibiting a lawyer from communicating with prospective juror "except as allowed by law"), and to approach former jurors cautiously. *Id.* § 115(3)(a) (prohibiting lawyer from communicating with former juror if doing so constitutes harassment).

Ex Parte Communications with Judges and Jurors During a Proceeding

Paragraph (b) prohibits a lawyer from communicating ex parte with a judge, juror or prospective juror "except as permitted by law." *See* La. Rules of Prof'l Conduct r. 3.5(b) (2004); *see* Restatement (Third) of the Law Governing Lawyers § 113(1) (2000). This paragraph prohibits lawyers from making any statements to the jury venire outside of the presence of the judge and opposing counsel. *See Louisiana v. Washington*, 626 So. 2d 841, 842-43 (La. Ct. App. 2d Cir. 1993).

This rule applies to lawyers who are not even counsel of record in the matter pending before the contacted judge or juror. *See La. State Bar Ass'n v. Harrington*, 585 So. 2d 514, 522 (La. 1990) ("[A] lawyer need not represent a party to a case to be subject to the Rule 3.5(b) proscription . . . ." (internal quotation omitted)).

A 3.5(b) violation may also occur when a lawyer communicates with a judge ex parte through an agent. *See In re Beck*, 109 So. 3d 897, 906 (La. 2013). In *In re Beck*, the Louisiana Supreme Court found a 3.5(b) violation when a lawyer requested an explanation for a ruling regarding the lawyer's case through the judge's golfing partner and did not discourage the agent from further ex parte communications involving the case. *Id.* ; *see also In re McCool*, 172 So. 3d 1058, 1069-70 (La. 2015) (finding that a lawyer encouraged *ex parte* communications by posting judges' contact information online and inviting readers to contact the judges about a particular case).

A lawyer may communicate ex parte with a judge or the judge's staff about "routine and customary" administrative matters. For example, a lawyer may communicate with a judge or court personnel for the purpose of "scheduling a hearing" or to tend to "similar" matters. *See* Restatement (Third) of the Law Governing Lawyers § 113 cmt. c. (2000); Ronald D. Rotunda & John S. Dzienkowski, Legal Ethics—The Lawyer's Deskbook on Prof'l Resp. § 3.5-3 (2016-2017 ed.) ("As one can imagine, courts and parties need to communicate about scheduling and other administrative matters. However, ex parte communications that address the merits of a matter undermine the public confidence in the judiciary."). Canon 3A(6) of the Louisiana Code of Judicial Conduct similarly permits ex parte communications between a judge and a lawyer "for scheduling, administrative purposes or emergencies that do not deal with substantive matters or issues on the merits, provided the judge reasonably believes that no party will gain a procedural or tactical advantage as a result of the ex parte communication." *See* La. Code of Jud. Cond. Canon 3A(6).

Disruptive Conduct

Paragraph (d) prohibits a lawyer from engaging in conduct intended to disrupt a tribunal. *See* La. Rules of Prof'l Conduct r. 3.5(d) (2004). This rule prohibits lawyers from cursing or otherwise expressing disrespect for the court, opposing counsel or the judicial process. *See In re Ruth*, 90 So. 3d 1004, 1012-1015 (La. 2012) (finding 3.5(d) violation for lawyer's delay and subsequent failure to appear for new trial date); *In re Collins*, 941 So. 2d 19 (La. 2006) (accepting consent discipline for lawyer who made an "obscene gesture" in response to an adverse ruling); *In re Bilbe*, 841 So. 2d 729, 739 (La. 2003) ("Respondent's conduct during that hearing was grossly inappropriate and would not have been tolerated by any judge in any courtroom."). In addition to violating this rule, such conduct is unprofessional. *See In re Mclanahan*, 26 So. 3d 756, 765 (La. 2010) (lawyer agreed that failure to appear for trial due to the lawyer's substance abuse constituted a 3.5 violation); *In re Mire*, 197 So. 3d 656, 657-58 (La. 2016) (holding that lawyer violated Rule 3.5 by filing unfounded motions to recuse the judge, repeated appeals in her client's bankruptcy case, and repeated accusations in a writ application that the judiciary is incompetent and corrupt).

Disciplinary Sanctions

Absent aggravating or mitigating circumstances, the following sanctions are generally appropriate in cases involving a lawyer's attempt to influence a judge, juror, prospective juror or other official by means prohibited by law: *disbarment*, when a lawyer intentionally tampers with a witness, or makes an improper ex parte communication with a judge or juror or other person in the legal system with intent to affect the outcome of the proceeding, and causes significant or potentially significant interference with the outcome of the legal proceeding; *suspension*, when a lawyer engages in communication with an individual in the legal system when the lawyer knows that such communication is improper, and causes injury or potential injury to a party or causes interference or potential interference with the outcome of the legal proceeding; *reprimand*, when a lawyer is negligent in determining whether it is proper to engage in communication with an individual in the legal system, and causes injury or potential injury to a party or interference with or potential interference with the outcome of a legal proceeding; and, *admonition*, when a lawyer engages in an isolated instance of negligence in improperly communicating with an individual in the legal system, and causes little or no actual or potential injury to a party, or causes little or no actual or potential interference with the outcome of the legal proceeding. *See* ABA Standards for Imposing Lawyer Sanctions stds. 6.3-6.34 (1992) (Improper Communications with Individuals in the Legal System).

In the matter of *In re O'Dwyer*, 221 So. 3d 1 (La. 2017), the Louisiana Supreme Court permanently disbarred a lawyer for repeated unethical and unprofessional misconduct, including, using improper language directed to the federal court and others, filing groundless pleadings and sanction requests, failing to keep his clients informed, and engaging in the unauthorized practice of law.

RULE 3.6. TRIAL PUBLICITY

(a) A lawyer who is participating or has participated in the investigation or litigation of a matter shall not make an extrajudicial statement that the lawyer knows or reasonably should know will be disseminated by means of public communication and will have a substantial likelihood of materially prejudicing an adjudicative proceeding in the matter.

(b) Notwithstanding paragraph (a), a lawyer may state:

(1) the claim, offense or defense involved and, except when prohibited by law, the identity of the persons involved;

(2) information contained in a public record;

(3) that an investigation of a matter is in progress;

(4) the scheduling or result of any step in litigation;

(5) a request for assistance in obtaining evidence and information necessary thereto;

(6) a warning of danger concerning the behavior of a person involved, when there is reason to believe that there exists the likelihood of substantial harm to an individual or to the public interest; and

(7) in a criminal case, in addition to subparagraphs (1) through (6):

(i) the identity, residence, occupation and family status of the accused;

(ii) if the accused has not been apprehended, information necessary to aid in apprehension of that person;

(iii) the fact, time and place of arrest; and

(iv) the identity of investigating and arresting officers or agencies and the length of the investigation.

(c) Notwithstanding paragraph (a), a lawyer may make a statement that a reasonable lawyer would believe is required to protect a client from the substantial undue prejudicial effect of recent publicity not initiated by the lawyer or the lawyer's client. A statement made pursuant to this paragraph shall be limited to such information as is necessary to mitigate the recent adverse publicity.

(d) No lawyer associated in a firm or government agency with a lawyer subject to paragraph (a) shall make a statement prohibited by paragraph (a).

BACKGROUND

The Louisiana Supreme Court adopted this rule on January 20, 2004. It became effective on March 1, 2004, and has not been amended since. This rule is identical to ABA Model Rule of Professional Conduct 3.6 (2002).

Paragraph (a): Clarification of Objective Standard

In 2002, the ABA modified paragraph (a) of the corresponding Model Rule to require that a lawyer's assessment of the likelihood that a statement will be disseminated by means of public communication be judged from the perspective of a reasonable "lawyer" rather than a reasonable "person." Whether a statement about legal proceedings will be publicly disseminated is an issue that may be viewed differently by lawyers and nonlawyers. The ABA believed that a lawyer should only be subject to professional discipline when the lawyer's judgment is unreasonably inconsistent with those of the lawyer's professional peers. *See* ABA Ethics 2000 Commission Revision Notes to Model Rule 3.6 (2002).

COMMENTS TO ABA MODEL RULE 3.6

[1] It is difficult to strike a balance between protecting the right to a fair trial and safeguarding the right of free expression. Preserving the right to a fair trial necessarily entails some curtailment of the information that may be disseminated about a party prior to trial, particularly where trial by jury is involved. If there were no such limits, the result would be the practical nullification of the protective effect of the rules of forensic decorum and the exclusionary rules of evidence. On the other hand, there are vital social interests served by the free dissemination of information about events having legal consequences and about legal proceedings themselves. The public has a right to know about threats to its safety and measures aimed at assuring its security. It also has a legitimate interest in the conduct of judicial proceedings, particularly in matters of general public concern. Furthermore, the subject matter of legal proceedings is often of direct significance in debate and deliberation over questions of public policy.

[2] Special rules of confidentiality may validly govern proceedings in juvenile, domestic relations and mental disability proceedings, and perhaps other types of litigation. Rule 3.4(c) requires compliance with such rules.

[3] The Rule sets forth a basic general prohibition against a lawyer's making statements that the lawyer knows or should know will have a substantial likelihood of materially prejudicing an adjudicative proceeding. Recognizing that the public value of informed commentary is great and the likelihood of prejudice to a proceeding by the commentary of a lawyer who is not involved in the proceeding is small, the rule applies only to lawyers

who are, or who have been involved in the investigation or litigation of a case, and their associates.

[4] Paragraph (b) identifies specific matters about which a lawyer's statements would not ordinarily be considered to present a substantial likelihood of material prejudice, and should not in any event be considered prohibited by the general prohibition of paragraph (a). Paragraph (b) is not intended to be an exhaustive listing of the subjects upon which a lawyer may make a statement, but statements on other matters may be subject to paragraph (a).

[5] There are, on the other hand, certain subjects that are more likely than not to have a material prejudicial effect on a proceeding, particularly when they refer to a civil matter triable to a jury, a criminal matter, or any other proceeding that could result in incarceration. These subjects relate to:

> (1) the character, credibility, reputation or criminal record of a party, suspect in a criminal investigation or witness, or the identity of a witness, or the expected testimony of a party or witness;

> (2) in a criminal case or proceeding that could result in incarceration, the possibility of a plea of guilty to the offense or the existence or contents of any confession, admission, or statement given by a defendant or suspect or that person's refusal or failure to make a statement;

> (3) the performance or results of any examination or test or the refusal or failure of a person to submit to an examination or test, or the identity or nature of physical evidence expected to be presented;

> (4) any opinion as to the guilt or innocence of a defendant or suspect in a criminal case or proceeding that could result in incarceration;

> (5) information that the lawyer knows or reasonably should know is likely to be inadmissible as evidence in a trial and that would, if disclosed, create a substantial risk of prejudicing an impartial trial; or

> (6) the fact that a defendant has been charged with a crime, unless there is included therein a statement explaining that the charge is merely an accusation and that the defendant is presumed innocent until and unless proven guilty.

[6] Another relevant factor in determining prejudice is the nature of the proceeding involved. Criminal jury trials will be most sensitive to extrajudicial speech. Civil trials may be less sensitive. Non-jury hearings and arbitration proceedings may be even less affected. The Rule will still place limitations on prejudicial comments in these cases, but the likelihood of prejudice may be different depending on the type of proceeding.

[7] Finally, extrajudicial statements that might otherwise raise a question under this Rule may be permissible when they are made in response to statements made publicly by another party, another party's lawyer, or third persons, where a reasonable lawyer would believe a public response is required in order to avoid prejudice to the lawyer's client. When prejudicial statements have been publicly made by others, responsive statements

may have the salutary effect of lessening any resulting adverse impact on the adjudicative proceeding. Such responsive statements should be limited to contain only such information as is necessary to mitigate undue prejudice created by the statements made by others.

[8] See Rule 3.8(f) for additional duties of prosecutors in connection with extrajudicial statements about criminal proceedings.

ANNOTATIONS
Generally

This rule prohibits a lawyer from making a public statement regarding a matter when he knows or reasonably should know that his statement will have a "substantial likelihood of materially prejudicing an adjudicative proceeding." La. Rules of Prof'l Conduct r. 3.6(a) (2004); *see also* Restatement (Third) of the Law Governing Lawyers § 109 (2000). Whether a lawyer's statement is substantially likely to have such an effect turns on all of the circumstances including, but not limited to, the following: whether the matter is a civil or criminal proceeding; whether the finder of fact is a jury or a judge; whether the statement consists of information that was already public; and, whether the statement was made at or near the time of trial.

Disciplinary Sanctions

Absent aggravating or mitigating circumstances, the following sanctions are generally appropriate in cases involving a lawyer's abuse of the legal process: *disbarment*, when the lawyer knowingly violates a court rule with the intent to obtain a benefit for the lawyer or another, and causes serious injury or potentially serious injury to a party, or causes serious or potentially serious interference with a legal proceeding; *suspension*, when the lawyer knows that he is violating a court rule, and there is injury or potential injury to a client or a party, or interference or potential interference with a legal proceeding; *reprimand*, when the lawyer negligently fails to comply with a court rule, and causes injury or potential injury to a client or other party, or causes interference or potential interference with a court proceeding; *admonition*, when the lawyer engages in an isolated instance of negligence in complying with a court rule, and causes little or no actual or potential injury to a party, or causes little or no actual or potential interference with a legal proceeding. *See* ABA Stds. for Imposing Lawyer Sanctions std. 6.2 (1992) (Abuse of Legal Process); *id.* stds. 6.21-6.24.

RULE 3.7. LAWYER AS WITNESS

(a) A lawyer shall not act as advocate at a trial in which the lawyer is likely to be a necessary witness unless:

(1) the testimony relates to an uncontested issue;

(2) the testimony relates to the nature and value of legal services rendered in the case; or

(3) disqualification of the lawyer would work substantial hardship on the client.

(b) A lawyer may act as advocate in a trial in which another lawyer in the lawyer's firm is likely to be called as a witness unless precluded from doing so by Rule 1.7 or Rule 1.9.

BACKGROUND

The Louisiana Supreme Court adopted this rule on January 20, 2004. It became effective on March 1, 2004, and has not been amended since. This rule is identical to ABA Model Rule of Professional Conduct 3.7 (2002).

COMMENTS TO ABA MODEL RULE 3.7

Generally

[1] Combining the roles of advocate and witness can prejudice the tribunal and the opposing party and can also involve a conflict of interest between the lawyer and client.

Advocate-Witness Rule

[2] The tribunal has proper objection when the trier of fact may be confused or misled by a lawyer serving as both advocate and witness. The opposing party has proper objection where the combination of roles may prejudice that party's rights in the litigation. A witness is required to testify on the basis of personal knowledge, while an advocate is expected to explain and comment on evidence given by others. It may not be clear whether a statement by an advocate-witness should be taken as proof or as an analysis of the proof.

[3] To protect the tribunal, paragraph (a) prohibits a lawyer from simultaneously serving as advocate and necessary witness except in those circumstances specified in paragraphs (a)(1) through (a)(3). Paragraph (a)(1) recognizes that if the testimony will be uncontested, the ambiguities in the dual role are purely theoretical. Paragraph (a)(2) recognizes that where the testimony concerns the extent and value of legal services rendered in the action in which the testimony is offered, permitting the lawyers to testify avoids the need for a second trial with new counsel to resolve that issue. Moreover, in such a situation the judge has firsthand knowledge of the matter in issue; hence, there is less dependence on the adversary process to test the credibility of the testimony.

[4] Apart from these two exceptions, paragraph (a)(3) recognizes that a balancing is required between the interests of the client and those of the tribunal and the opposing

party. Whether the tribunal is likely to be misled or the opposing party is likely to suffer prejudice depends on the nature of the case, the importance and probable tenor of the lawyer's testimony, and the probability that the lawyer's testimony will conflict with that of other witnesses. Even if there is risk of such prejudice, in determining whether the lawyer should be disqualified, due regard must be given to the effect of disqualification on the lawyer's client. It is relevant that one or both parties could reasonably foresee that the lawyer would probably be a witness. The conflict of interest principles stated in Rules 1.7, 1.9 and 1.10 have no application to this aspect of the problem.

[5] Because the tribunal is not likely to be misled when a lawyer acts as advocate in a trial in which another lawyer in the lawyer's firm will testify as a necessary witness, paragraph (b) permits the lawyer to do so except in situations involving a conflict of interest.

Conflict of Interest

[6] In determining if it is permissible to act as advocate in a trial in which the lawyer will be a necessary witness, the lawyer must also consider that the dual role may give rise to a conflict of interest that will require compliance with Rules 1.7 or 1.9. For example, if there is likely to be substantial conflict between the testimony of the client and that of the lawyer the representation involves a conflict of interest that requires compliance with Rule 1.7. This would be true even though the lawyer might not be prohibited by paragraph (a) from simultaneously serving as advocate and witness because the lawyer's disqualification would work a substantial hardship on the client. Similarly, a lawyer who might be permitted to simultaneously serve as an advocate and a witness by paragraph (a)(3) might be precluded from doing so by Rule 1.9. The problem can arise whether the lawyer is called as a witness on behalf of the client or is called by the opposing party. Determining whether or not such a conflict exists is primarily the responsibility of the lawyer involved. If there is a conflict of interest, the lawyer must secure the client's informed consent, confirmed in writing. In some cases, the lawyer will be precluded from seeking the client's consent. See Rule 1.7. See Rule 1.0(b) for the definition of "confirmed in writing" and Rule 1.0(e) for the definition of "informed consent."

[7] Paragraph (b) provides that a lawyer is not disqualified from serving as an advocate because a lawyer with whom the lawyer is associated in a firm is precluded from doing so by paragraph (a). If, however, the testifying lawyer would also be disqualified by Rule 1.7 or Rule 1.9 from representing the client in the matter, other lawyers in the firm will be precluded from representing the client by Rule 1.10 unless the client gives informed consent under the conditions stated in Rule 1.7.

ANNOTATIONS
Generally

Paragraph (a) prohibits a lawyer from acting as an advocate at trial when the lawyer is likely to be a "necessary witness." La. Rules of Prof'l Conduct r. 3.7(a) (2004). Courts typically consider a lawyer to be a "necessary" witness if the lawyer's testimony is "relevant, material, and unobtainable elsewhere." *See* ABA Annotated Model Rules of Prof'l Conduct 384-85 (5th ed. 2003); *see also* Restatement (Third) of the Law Governing Lawyers § 108 cmt. (2000) (stating that a tribunal should not permit party to call opposing

242

trial lawyer as witness when testimony would be "merely cumulative of evidence readily available by less intrusive means"). Note that the Restatement does not use "necessity" as the touchstone for disqualification. Rather, the Restatement would call for an advocate-lawyer's disqualification if the lawyer's testimony was "material to establishing a claim or defense of the client," and the client has not consented to the lawyer's failure to testify. Restatement (Third) of the Law Governing Lawyers § 108(1)(b) (2000).

The rule set forth in paragraph (a) is a rule of professional conduct–not a rule of witness competence. Therefore, it does not bear on whether a lawyer-advocate is competent to serve as a trial witness, but rather, on whether a trial witness is permitted to serve as an advocate. As the Louisiana First Circuit Court of Appeals has held, "[t]here is nothing in the Rules of Professional Conduct or the Louisiana Code of Evidence providing that an attorney is not a competent witness in a trial in which he represents a party to the litigation." *See Jordan v. Intercontinental Bulktank Corp.*, 621 So. 2d 1141, 1148-49 (La. Ct. App. 1st Cir. 1993).

Finally, paragraph (a) only prohibits a lawyer from acting as an advocate at trial. The advocate-lawyer still may handle pretrial matters without being disqualified. *See* ABA Annotated Model Rules of Professional Conduct 387-88 (5th ed. 2003); *see also State v. Marinello*, 49 So. 3d 488, 506-07 (La. Ct. App. 3rd Cir. 2010) (describing lawyer's involvement in criminal grand jury proceedings as a pretrial matter); *In re Phenylpropanolamine Products Liability Litigation, Fuller v. Whitehall-Robbins Healthcare*, No. MDL 1407, 2006 WL 2473484 (W.D. Wash. Aug. 28, 2006) (holding that Rule 3.7 "relates to testimony at trial, not at the summary judgment stage"); *see also,* LSBA Public Opinion 05-RPCC-007 (2005). ("[T]he lawyer-witness is not barred from representing the client prior to trial, but he may do so only with the client's informed consent and only so long as it appears his testimony would not be prejudicial to his client.") (citing ABA Informal Ethics Opinion 89-1529 (1989)). Under these circumstances, the lawyer's dual role presents no risk of confusion and prejudice at trial. *See* ABA Model Rules of Prof'l Conduct r. 3.7 cmt. 2 (2004). *But see Adcock v. Ewing*, 57 So. 3d 434, 441 (La. Ct. App. 2nd Cir. 2011) (holding that Rule 3.7 is applicable to summary judgment proceedings) (citing *Franklin Credit Mgmt. Corp. v. Gray*, 2 So. 3d 598 (La. Ct. App. 4th Cir. 2009)).

Exceptions

Paragraphs (a)(1) through (a)(3) set forth three exceptions to the general rule that a lawyer may not serve as both advocate and witness. First, a lawyer may testify on an uncontested issue. La. Rules of Prof'l Conduct r. 3.7(a)(1) (2004). Second, a lawyer may testify about the nature and value of the legal services that the lawyer has provided, for example, when a claimant seeks an award of attorneys' fees. *Id.* r. 3.7(a)(2); *see also Adcock*, 57 So. 3d at 440-41 (holding that a lawyer's affidavit submitted for summary judgment describing a clerical error in regards to the filing of a court document related to the "nature of ... legal services") (quoting Rule 3.7(a)(2)). Third, a lawyer may testify if disqualification would work substantial hardship on the lawyer's client. La. Rules of Prof'l Conduct r. 3.7(a)(3); *see, e.g., Nicholas v. Nicholas*, 923 So. 2d 690, 695 (La. Ct. App. 1st Cir. 2005) (holding that it would have caused substantial hardship on a client to prevent lawyer from testifying on her behalf when she fell ill on the date of the hearing). Louisiana courts note 3.7(a)(3) exceptions are rare and occur only in "extraordinary circumstances." *See Franklin Credit Mgmt. Corp. v. Gray*, 2 So. 3d 598, 605 (La. Ct. App. 4th Cir. 2009) (citing *Nicholas* as an "extraordinary circumstance"). The factors that courts have considered in evaluating whether disqualification would cause hardship on the client include, but are not limited to, the following: the time and money invested by the client in the lawyer; the timing of the filing of the motion to disqualify; and whether the necessity of calling the lawyer as a witness was foreseeable. *See* ABA Annotated Model Rules of Professional Conduct at 388-89 (5th ed. 2003). The trial judge is vested with much discretion regarding the application of this hardship exception. *See Exnicios v. Saunders*, 448 So. 2d 751, 752 (La. Ct. App. 4th Cir. 1984).

This rule does not disqualify a lawyer from representing himself pro se in a matter in which the lawyer is a litigant. In *Farrington v. Law Firm of Sessions, Fishman*, 687 So. 2d 997 (La. 1997), the Louisiana Supreme Court squarely held that "Rule 3.7 does not apply to the situation where the lawyer is representing himself." *See also Jackson v. Adcock*, 2004 U.S. Dist. LEXIS 14222 (E.D. La. Jul. 22, 2004).

Disqualification is Nonwaivable

Because the problems arising from a lawyer serving as advocate and witness can prejudice not only the "opposing party," *see* ABA Model Rules of Prof'l Conduct r. 3.7 cmt. 1, but also the system of justice by causing jury confusion, the mandate of this rule is generally not waivable by the client. *See, e.g., Freeman v. Vicchiarelli*, 827 F. Supp. 300 (D.N.J. 1993). Note, however, that the Restatement would permit an advocate-lawyer to testify with the consent of both the lawyer's client and the "opposing parties who would be adversely affected by the lawyer's testimony." Restatement (Third) of the Law Governing Lawyers § 108(2)(c) (2000).

No Imputation

Paragraph (b) provides that a lawyer may act as an advocate in a trial even though a partner or associate from the lawyer's firm is likely to be called as a witness. La. Rules of Prof'l Conduct r. 3.7(b) (2004). Because the disqualification imposed by this rule is not imputed to a lawyers' firm, a litigator at a firm, for example, may freely call as a trial witness the transactional partner who drafted a contract that is the subject of litigation. However, if the advocate-lawyer's partner will testify in a manner adverse to the client, this may give rise to a conflict of interest under Rules 1.7 and 1.9. For example, a potentially disqualifying Rule 1.7 conflict would exist if the advocate-lawyer's representation of the client was materially limited by friendship with the witness-lawyer. *See* La. Rules of Prof'l Conduct r. 1.7(b) (2004).

Disciplinary Sanctions

This rule is typically invoked in the context of motions to disqualify lawyers rather than in the context of disciplinary proceedings. However, a lawyer who violates this rule certainly is subject to discipline. For the disciplinary sanctions that are appropriate for lawyers' failure to avoid conflicts of interest, *see supra* Annotations to Louisiana Rule of Professional Conduct 1.7.

RULE 3.8. SPECIAL RESPONSIBILITIES OF A PROSECUTOR

The prosecutor in a criminal case shall:

(a) refrain from prosecuting a charge that the prosecutor knows is not supported by probable cause;

(b) make reasonable efforts to assure that the accused has been advised of the right to, and the procedure for obtaining, counsel and has been given reasonable opportunity to obtain counsel;

(c) not seek to obtain from an unrepresented accused a waiver of important pretrial rights, such as the right to preliminary hearing;

(d) make timely disclosure to the defense of all evidence or information known to the prosecutor that the prosecutor knows, or reasonably should know, either tends to negate the guilt of the accused or mitigates the offense, and, in connection with sentencing, disclose to the defense and to the tribunal all unprivileged mitigating information known to the prosecutor, except when the prosecutor is relieved of this responsibility by a protective order of the tribunal;

(e) not subpoena a lawyer in a grand jury or other criminal proceeding to present evidence about a past or present client unless the prosecutor reasonably believes:

(1) the information sought is not protected from disclosure by any applicable privilege;

(2) the evidence sought is essential to the successful completion of an ongoing investigation or prosecution; and

(3) there is no other feasible alternative to obtain the information;

(f) except for statements that are necessary to inform the public of the nature and extent of the prosecutor's action and that serve a legitimate law enforcement purpose, refrain from making extrajudicial comments that have a substantial likelihood of heightening public condemnation of the accused and exercise reasonable care to prevent investigators, law enforcement personnel, employees or other persons assisting or

245

associated with the prosecutor in a criminal case from making an extrajudicial statement that the prosecutor would be prohibited from making under Rule 3.6 or this Rule.

BACKGROUND

The Louisiana Supreme Court adopted this rule on January 20, 2004. It became effective on March 1, 2004. Louisiana Rule 3.8 differs from ABA Model Rule of Professional Conduct 3.8 (2009) in two significant respects:

First, paragraph (d) of the Louisiana Rule, which was amended effective April 12, 2006, requires disclosure of evidence known to the prosecutor that the prosecutor "knows, or reasonably should know" is exculpatory or mitigating. The Louisiana Rule imposes a significantly greater obligation on prosecutors, given that it requires disclosure not only of evidence that the prosecutor "knows" to be exculpatory, but also disclosure of evidence that the prosecutor "reasonably should know" is exculpatory.

Second, the Model Rule, as revised by the ABA in 2009, contains two paragraphs not included in Louisiana Rule 3.8. These paragraphs impose obligations on a prosecutor with regard to wrongfully convicted defendants. Model Rule paragraph 3.8(g) requires a prosecutor who "knows of new, credible and material evidence creating a reasonable likelihood that a convicted defendant did not commit an offense of which the defendant was convicted" to "(1) promptly disclose that evidence to an appropriate court or authority, and (2) if the conviction was obtained in the prosecutor's jurisdiction, to promptly disclose that evidence to the defendant unless a court authorizes delay, and undertake further investigation, or make reasonable efforts to cause an investigation, to determine whether the defendant was convicted of an offense that the defendant did not commit." *See* ABA Model Rules of Prof'l Conduct r. 3.8(g). Similarly, Model Rule paragraph 3.8(h) requires a prosecutor who "knows of clear and convincing evidence establishing that a defendant in the prosecutor's jurisdiction was convicted of an offense that the defendant did not commit" to "seek to remedy the conviction." *See* ABA Model Rules of Prof'l Conduct r. 3.8(h).

COMMENTS TO ABA MODEL RULE 3.8

[1] A prosecutor has the responsibility of a minister of justice and not simply that of an advocate. This responsibility carries with it specific obligations to see that the defendant is accorded procedural justice, that guilt is decided upon the basis of sufficient evidence, and that special precautions are taken to prevent and to rectify the conviction of innocent persons. The extent of mandated remedial action is a matter of debate and varies in different jurisdictions. Many jurisdictions have adopted the ABA Standards of Criminal Justice Relating to the Prosecution Function, which are the product of prolonged and careful deliberation by lawyers experienced in both criminal prosecution and defense. Competent representation of the sovereignty may require a prosecutor to undertake some procedural and remedial measures as a matter of obligation. Applicable law may require other measures by the prosecutor and knowing disregard of those obligations or a systematic abuse of prosecutorial discretion could constitute a violation of Rule 8.4.

[2] In some jurisdictions, a defendant may waive a preliminary hearing and thereby lose a valuable opportunity to challenge probable cause. Accordingly, prosecutors should not seek to obtain waivers of preliminary hearings or other important pretrial rights from unrepresented accused persons. Paragraph (c) does not apply, however, to an accused appearing pro se with the approval of the tribunal. Nor does it forbid the lawful questioning of an uncharged suspect who has knowingly waived the rights to counsel and silence.

[3] The exception in paragraph (d) recognizes that a prosecutor may seek an appropriate protective order from the tribunal if disclosure of information to the defense could result in substantial harm to an individual or to the public interest.

[4] Paragraph (e) is intended to limit the issuance of lawyer subpoenas in grand jury and other criminal proceedings to those situations in which there is a genuine need to intrude into the client-lawyer relationship.

[5] Paragraph (f) supplements Rule 3.6, which prohibits extrajudicial statements that have a substantial likelihood of prejudicing an adjudicatory proceeding. In the context of a criminal prosecution, a prosecutor's extrajudicial statement can create the additional problem of increasing public condemnation of the accused. Although the announcement of an indictment, for example, will necessarily have severe consequences for the accused, a prosecutor can, and should, avoid comments which have no legitimate law enforcement purpose and have a substantial likelihood of increasing public opprobrium of the accused. Nothing in this Comment is intended to restrict the statements which a prosecutor may make which comply with Rule 3.6(b) or 3.6(c).

[6] Like other lawyers, prosecutors are subject to Rules 5.1 and 5.3, which relate to responsibilities regarding lawyers and nonlawyers who work for or are associated with the lawyer's office. Paragraph (f) reminds the prosecutor of the importance of these obligations in connection with the unique dangers of improper extrajudicial statements in a criminal case. In addition, paragraph (f) requires a prosecutor to exercise reasonable care to prevent persons assisting or associated with the prosecutor from making improper extrajudicial statements, even when such persons are not under the direct supervision of the prosecutor. Ordinarily, the reasonable care standard will be satisfied if the prosecutor issues the appropriate cautions to law- enforcement personnel and other relevant individuals.

[7] When a prosecutor knows of new, credible and material evidence creating a reasonable likelihood that a person outside the prosecutor's jurisdiction was convicted of a crime that the person did not commit, paragraph (g) requires prompt disclosure to the court or other appropriate authority, such as the chief prosecutor of the jurisdiction where the conviction occurred. If the conviction was obtained in the prosecutor's jurisdiction, paragraph (g) requires the prosecutor to examine the evidence and undertake further investigation to determine whether the defendant is in fact innocent or make reasonable efforts to cause another appropriate authority to undertake the necessary investigation, and to promptly disclose the evidence to the court and, absent court-authorized delay, to the defendant. Consistent with the objectives of Rules 4.2 and 4.3, disclosure to a represented defendant

must be made through the defendant's counsel, and, in the case of an unrepresented defendant, would ordinarily be accompanied by a request to a court for the appointment of counsel to assist the defendant in taking such legal measures as may be appropriate.

[8] Under paragraph (h), once the prosecutor knows of clear and convincing evidence that the defendant was convicted of an offense that the defendant did not commit, the prosecutor must seek to remedy the conviction. Necessary steps may include disclosure of the evidence to the defendant, requesting that the court appoint counsel for an unrepresented indigent defendant and, where appropriate, notifying the court that the prosecutor has knowledge that the defendant did not commit the offense of which the defendant was convicted.

[9] A prosecutor's independent judgment, made in good faith, that the new evidence is not of such nature as to trigger the obligations of sections (g) and (h), though subsequently determined to have been erroneous, does not constitute a violation of this Rule.

ANNOTATIONS
Generally
Unlike other litigating lawyers, prosecutors are not merely advocates and officers of the courts, but also administrators of justice who have a duty to "seek justice, [and] not merely to convict." See ABA Stds. Relating to the Admin. of Crim. Justice–The Prosec. Function std. 3–1.2 (3d ed. 1992). For other standards addressing the special responsibilities of prosecutors, see ABA Standards on Prosecutorial Investigations (2008); National Dist. Attorneys' Assoc. Prosec. Stds. (2d ed. 1991).

The Charging Decision
Paragraph (a) of this rule prohibits a prosecutor from accepting and prosecuting charges that the prosecutor "knows" are not supported by "probable cause." La. Rules of Prof'l Conduct r. 3.8(a) (2004). Prosecutors have an enormous amount of discretion in making charging decisions. In exercising discretion in determining whether to charge an accused with a crime, a prosecutor may properly consider the following factors, among others: reasonable doubt that the accused is guilty; the extent of harm caused by the offense; the disproportion of the authorized punishment in relation to the offense or offender; the motives of the complainant; the reluctance of the victim or witnesses to testify; the cooperation of the accused in identifying other wrongdoers; and the likelihood of prosecution by another jurisdiction. See ABA Stds. Relating to the Admin. of Crim. Justice–The Prosec. Function std. 3–3.9(b) (3d ed. 1992). The charging decision should not turn to any extent on the "personal or political advantages or disadvantages which might be involved" or on the prosecutor's "desire to enhance his or her record of conviction." Id. std. 3–3.9(d) (3d ed. 1992). Furthermore, a prosecutor should not "bring or seek charges greater in number or degree than can reasonably be supported with evidence at trial or than are necessary to fairly reflect the gravity of the offense." Id. std. 3–3.9(f).

General Pretrial Responsibilities
Paragraph (b) of the rule requires a prosecutor to make reasonable efforts to ensure that the accused is represented by counsel. La. Rules of Prof'l Conduct r. 3.8(b) (2004).

Paragraph (c) prohibits a prosecutor from requesting that an accused person waive important pretrial rights such as the right to a preliminary hearing. *Id.* 3.8(c); *see also* ABA Stds. Relating to the Admin. of Crim. Justice–The Prosec. Function std. 3–3.10(c) (3d ed. 1992). Furthermore, the ABA Standards Relating to the Administration of Criminal Justice further admonish prosecutors against communicating with an accused "unless a waiver of counsel has been entered, except for the purpose of aiding in obtaining counsel or in arranging for the pretrial release of the accused." *Id.* std. 3–3.10(a). As to preliminary hearings, a prosecutor "should not seek to delay a preliminary hearing" if the accused is in custody, nor should he or she seek a continuance of such a hearing "solely for the purpose of mooting the preliminary hearing by securing an indictment." *Id.* stds. 3–3.10(d-e).

Disclosure of Exculpatory *Brady* Material

Paragraph (d) of the rule requires a prosecutor to disclose promptly all information that the prosecutor knows, or should know, is exculpatory or mitigating. *See* La. Rules of Prof'l Conduct r. 3.8(d) (2004); ABA Stds. Relating to the Admin. of Crim. Justice–The Prosec. Function std. 3–3.11 (3d ed. 1992); *see also Brady v. Maryland*, 373 U.S. 83 (1963); *State v. Carter*, 939 So. 2d 600, 603 n.2 (La. Ct. App. 2nd Cir. 2006) (commending assistant district attorney for compliance with Rule 3.8(d) by acknowledging the record indicated an absence of a valid waiver of defendant's privilege against self-incrimination). In addition, a prosecutor has a constitutional duty—although perhaps not an ethical one[111]—to review all files under the prosecutor's control and under the control of relevant law enforcement officers to search for exculpatory information. *See Kyles v. Whitley*, 514 U.S. 419, 437 (1995) (holding that a prosecutor has duty to learn of any favorable evidence known to others acting on state's behalf); *State v. Marshall*, 660 So. 2d 819, 826 (La. 1995) (holding that prosecutor has a duty to learn of any favorable evidence known to anyone acting on state's behalf, including police officers); *see also State v. Oliver*, 682 So. 2d 301, 311 (La. Ct. App. 4th Cir. 1996).

On July 8, 2009, the ABA Standing Committee on Ethics and Professional Responsibility issued Formal Opinion 09-454 entitled Prosecutor's Duty to Disclose Evidence and Information Favorable to the Defense. This opinion comprehensively discusses a prosecutor's duties under Model Rule 3.8.

A number of criminal convictions have been reversed in Louisiana over the years as a result of the failure of prosecutors to disclose exculpatory *Brady* information. However, disciplinary actions against prosecutors are rare. *See generally* Kathleen "Cookie" Ridolfi, Tiffany M. Joslyn & Todd H. Fries, *Material Indifference: How Courts are Impeding Fair Disclosure in Criminal Cases* (N.A.C.D.L. 2014).

What constitutes "exculpatory" evidence is often a matter of confusion. However, the term "exculpatory evidence" includes evidence that may reasonably be used to impeach any

---

[111] The ABA has opined that "Rule 3.8(d) does not establish a duty to undertake an investigation in search of exculpatory evidence." ABA Formal Op. 09-454 at 5 (Jul. 8, 2009); *id.* at 6 (the rule "does not require prosecutors to conduct searches or investigations for favorable evidence that may possibly exist but of which they are unaware").

witness whom the state may call at trial, including the following: evidence relating to any plea bargains or promises made to such witnesses, *see In re Jordan*, 913 So. 2d 775, 781 (La. 2005) (holding that a witness' statement to police that it was dark and she did not have her glasses when she witnessed the crime was exculpatory evidence that the prosecutor had a duty to disclose); *State v. Lindsey*, 621 So. 2d 618, 628 (La. Ct. App. 2d Cir. 1993); *State v. Williams*, 338 So. 2d 672, 677 (La. 1976); evidence relating to any prior criminal record of arrests or convictions of such witnesses, *see State v. Whitlock*, 454 So. 2d 871, 873 (La. Ct. App. 4th Cir. 1984); evidence relating to any witness statements that are inconsistent with statements made by that or other witnesses at any time, *see State v. Hunter*, 648 So. 2d 1025, 1034 (La. Ct. App. 4th Cir. 1994) (witness' prior inconsistent statement on a material issue is exculpatory).

Furthermore, "exculpatory" evidence includes evidence that any eyewitness who participated in an identification procedure identified a person other than the accused as the perpetrator of the charged crime, *see State v. Falkins*, 356 So. 2d 415, 417 (La. 1978), or failed to identify the accused as a participant in the charged crime, *see State v. Curtis*, 384 So. 2d 396, 398 (La. 1980); *State v. Landry*, 384 So. 2d 786, 788 (La. 1980). Finally, the term "exculpatory evidence" should also include any evidence establishing that the witness hesitated or was in any way equivocal in his or her identification of accused as a participant in the charged crime.

It was once uncertain in Louisiana whether a prosecutor's "ethical" obligation under Rule 3.8(d) was broader than a prosecutor's parallel "Due Process" obligation under the Constitution. Rule 3.8(d) "requires the disclosure of evidence or information favorable to the defense without regard to the anticipated impact of the evidence or information on a trial's outcome." *See* ABA Formal Op. 09-454 (Jul. 8, 2009). That is, the rule arguably could require disclosure of even "immaterial" exculpatory evidence. *See id. (citing e.g., Cone v. Bell*, 556 U.S. 449, 470 n. 15 (2009)); *see also Schultz v. Comm'n for Lawyer Discipline of the State Bar of Tx.*, SBOT Case No. D0121247202 (Dec. 17, 2015).

On October 18, 2017, the Louisiana Supreme Court resolved this unsettled question. In an opinion written by Justice Crichton, the court determined that a prosecutor's "ethical" and "constitutional" duties "are coextensive." *See In re Seastrunk*, No. 2017-B-0178, 2017 WL 4681906 (La. Oct. 18, 2017). In so doing, the court reasoned that "under conflicting standards, prosecutors would face uncertainty as to how to proceed, as they could find themselves in compliance with the standard enumerated in *Brady*, but in potential violation of the obligation set forth in Rule 3.8(d)." *Id*. at 18. Furthermore, a broader obligation under Rule 3.8(d) would invite "the use of an ethical rule as a tactical weapon in criminal litigation." *Id*. As a result, the court dismissed the formal charges against Mr. Seastrunk.

The court's decision in *Seastrunk* was correct. Expanding Louisiana Rule 3.8(d) beyond the limits of *Brady* would have been bad policy. Although a minority of states[112] impose a

---

[112] *See In re Larsen*, No. 20140535, 2016 WL 3369545 (Utah 2016); *In re Disciplinary Action Against Feland*, 820 N.W.2d 672 (N.D. 2012); ABA Formal Op. 09-454 (2009).

broader "ethical" obligation to disclose exculpatory information, doing so in Louisiana would have subjected prosecutors to unwarranted discipline. Among other problems, untethering Rule 3.8(d) from *Brady* and the Louisiana Rules of Criminal Procedure[113] would have exposed prosecutors to discipline for simply complying with federal constitutional law and state statutory law. Disconnecting Rule 3.8(d) and *Brady* would have transformed routine discovery disputes into disciplinary actions. Imposing discipline on a prosecutor for failing to turn over information that is absolutely inconsequential would have been pointless and unfair. For that reason, the *Seastrunk* opinion correctly brings Louisiana into line with a majority of states.[114]

Evidence is "material" when "there is a reasonable probability that, had the evidence been disclosed, the result of the proceeding would have been different." *Turner v. United States*, 137 S. Ct. 1885, 1893 (2017) (citations omitted). "A 'reasonable probability' of a different result" is one in which the suppressed evidence "'undermines confidence in the outcome of the trial.'" *Id.*

Applicability of Louisiana Rules of Professional Conduct to Federal Prosecutors

In the wake of the McDade Amendment of 1998, "[a]n attorney for the Government shall be subject to State laws and rules, and local Federal court rules, governing attorneys in each State where such attorney engages in that attorney's duties, to the same extent and in the same manner as other attorneys in that State." *See* 28 U.S.C. § 530B(a) (1998).

Disciplinary Sanctions

Absent aggravating or mitigating circumstances, the following sanctions are generally appropriate in cases involving public officials who engage in conduct that is prejudicial to the administration of justice or who state or imply an ability to influence improperly a government agency or official: *disbarment*, when a lawyer in an official position misuses that position with the intent to obtain a significant benefit for himself or another, or with the intent to cause serious or potential injury to a party or to the integrity of the legal process; *suspension*, when such a lawyer knowingly fails to follow proper procedures or rules, and causes injury or potential injury to a party or to the integrity of the legal process; *reprimand*, when such a lawyer negligently fails to follow proper procedures or rules, and causes injury or potential injury to a party or to the integrity of the legal process; and, *admonition*, when such a lawyer engages in an isolated instance of negligence in not following proper procedures or rules, and causes little or no actual or potential injury to a party or to the integrity of the legal process. ABA Stds. for Imposing Lawyer Sanctions std. 5.2 (1992)(Failure to Maintain the Public Trust); *id.* stds. 5.21-5.24.

---

[113] La. Code Crim. P. art. 723(B) (requiring disclosure of "any evidence constitutionally required to be disclosed pursuant to *Brady v. Maryland*, 373 U.S. 83 (1963) and its progeny.").

[114] *See State ex rel. Okla. Bar Ass'n v. Ward*, 353 P.3d 509 (Okla. 2015); *Disciplinary Counsel v. Kellogg-Martin*, 923 N.E.2d 125 (Ohio 2010); *United States v. Weiss*, No. 05-CR-179-B, 2006 WL 1752373 (D. Colo. June 21, 2006); *In re Attorney C*, 47 P.3d 1167 (Colo. 2002).

RULE 3.9. ADVOCATE IN NONADJUDICATIVE PROCEEDINGS

A lawyer representing a client before a legislative body or administrative agency in a non-adjudicative proceeding shall disclose that the appearance is in a representative capacity and shall conform to the provisions of Rule 3.3(a) through (c), 3.4(a) through (c), and 3.5.

BACKGROUND

The Louisiana Supreme Court adopted this rule on January 20, 2004. It became effective on March 1, 2004, and has not been amended since. This rule is identical to ABA Model Rule of Professional Conduct 3.9 (2002).

In 2002, the ABA amended the text of the corresponding Model Rule to replace the former reference to "legislative or administrative tribunal" with "legislative body or administrative agency." The ABA defined the term "tribunal" in Rule 1.0(m) to denote courts and other agencies when those agencies are acting in an adjudicative capacity. The ABA believed that this change was necessary to clarify that Rule 3.9 applies only when the lawyer is representing a client in a nonadjudicative proceeding of a legislative body or administrative agency. *See* ABA Ethics 2000 Commission Revision Notes to Model Rule 3.9 (2002).

COMMENTS TO ABA MODEL RULE 3.9

[1] In representation before bodies such as legislatures, municipal councils, and executive and administrative agencies acting in a rulemaking or policy-making capacity, lawyers present facts, formulate issues, and advance arguments in the matters under consideration. The decision-making body, like a court, should be able to rely on the integrity of the submissions made to it. A lawyer appearing before such a body must deal with it honestly and in conformity with applicable rules of procedure. See Rules 3.3(a) through (c), 3.4(a) through (c) and 3.5.

[2] Lawyers have no exclusive right to appear before nonadjudicative bodies, as they do before a court. The requirements of this Rule therefore may subject lawyers to regulations inapplicable to advocates who are not lawyers. However, legislatures and administrative agencies have a right to expect lawyers to deal with them as they deal with courts.

[3] This Rule only applies when a lawyer represents a client in connection with an official hearing or meeting of a governmental agency or a legislative body to which the lawyer or the lawyer's client is presenting evidence or argument. It does not apply to representation of a client in a negotiation or other bilateral transaction with a governmental agency or in connection with an application for a license or other privilege or the client's compliance with generally applicable reporting requirements, such as the filing of income-tax returns. Nor does it apply to the representation of a client in connection with an investigation or examination of the client's affairs conducted by government investigators or examiners. Representation in such matters is governed by Rules 4.1 through 4.4.

ANNOTATIONS

Generally

This rule requires a lawyer to disclose to a legislative body or administrative agency whether he appears on behalf of himself or on behalf of a client. La. Rules of Prof'l Conduct r. 3.9 (2004); *see also* Restatement (Third) of the Law Governing Lawyers § 104(1) (2000) (requiring a lawyer to "disclose that the appearance is in a representative capacity and not misrepresent the capacity in which the lawyer appears"). Furthermore, a lawyer appearing before such a tribunal in a nonadjudicative proceeding must comply with Louisiana Rules 3.3(a-c) (Candor Toward the Tribunal), 3.4(a-c) (Fairness to Opposing Party and Counsel), and 3.5 (Impartiality and Decorum of the Tribunal). *Id.* Note, however, that since this rule does not contain any cross reference to 3.1 and 3.2, among others, lawyers arguably "enjoy somewhat greater latitude in nonadjudicative administrative proceedings." ABA Annotated Model Rules of Prof'l Conduct at 407 (5th ed. 2003).

Disciplinary Sanctions

Absent aggravating or mitigating circumstances, the following sanctions are generally appropriate in cases involving a lawyer's abuse of the legal process: *disbarment*, when the lawyer knowingly violates a court rule with the intent to obtain a benefit for the lawyer or another, and causes serious injury or potentially serious injury to a party, or causes serious or potentially serious interference with a legal proceeding; *suspension*, when the lawyer knows that he is violating a court rule, and there is injury or potential injury to a client or a party, or interference or potential interference with a legal proceeding; *reprimand*, when the lawyer negligently fails to comply with a court rule, and causes injury or potential injury to a client or other party, or causes interference or potential interference with a court proceeding; and, *admonition*, when the lawyer engages in an isolated instance of negligence in complying with a court rule, and causes little or no actual or potential injury to a party, or causes little or no actual or potential interference with a legal proceeding. *See* ABA Stds. for Imposing Lawyer Sanctions std. 6.2 (1992) (Abuse of Legal Process); *id.* stds. 6.21-6.24.

Article 4. Transactions with Persons Other than Clients

RULE 4.1. TRUTHFULNESS IN STATEMENTS TO OTHERS

In the course of representing a client a lawyer shall not knowingly:

(a) make a false statement of material fact or law to a third person; or

(b) fail to disclose a material fact when disclosure is necessary to avoid assisting a criminal or fraudulent act by a client, unless disclosure is prohibited by Rule 1.6.

BACKGROUND

The Louisiana Supreme Court adopted this rule on January 20, 2004. It became effective on March 1, 2004, and has not been amended since. This rule is identical to ABA Model Rule of Professional Conduct 4.1 (2002).

COMMENTS TO ABA MODEL RULE 4.1

Misrepresentation

[1] A lawyer is required to be truthful when dealing with others on a client's behalf, but generally has no affirmative duty to inform an opposing party of relevant facts. A misrepresentation can occur if the lawyer incorporates or affirms a statement of another person that the lawyer knows is false. Misrepresentations can also occur by partially true but misleading statements or omissions that are the equivalent of affirmative false statements. For dishonest conduct that does not amount to a false statement or for misrepresentations by a lawyer other than in the course of representing a client, see Rule 8.4.

Statements of Fact

[2] This Rule refers to statements of fact. Whether a particular statement should be regarded as one of fact can depend on the circumstances. Under generally accepted conventions in negotiation, certain types of statements ordinarily are not taken as statements of material fact. Estimates of price or value placed on the subject of a transaction and a party's intentions as to an acceptable settlement of a claim are ordinarily in this category, and so is the existence of an undisclosed principal except where nondisclosure of the principal would constitute fraud. Lawyers should be mindful of their obligations under applicable law to avoid criminal and tortious misrepresentation.

Crime or Fraud by Client

[3] Under Rule 1.2(d), a lawyer is prohibited from counseling or assisting a client in conduct that the lawyer knows is criminal or fraudulent. Paragraph (b) states a specific application of the principle set forth in Rule 1.2(d) and addresses the situation where a client's crime or fraud takes the form of a lie or misrepresentation. Ordinarily, a lawyer can avoid assisting a client's crime or fraud by withdrawing from the representation. Sometimes it may be necessary for the lawyer to give notice of the fact of withdrawal and

to disaffirm an opinion, document, affirmation or the like. In extreme cases, substantive law may require a lawyer to disclose information relating to the representation to avoid being deemed to have assisted the client's crime or fraud. If the lawyer can avoid assisting a client's crime or fraud only by disclosing this information, then under paragraph (b) the lawyer is required to do so, unless the disclosure is prohibited by Rule 1.6.

ANNOTATIONS
Generally

This rule prohibits a lawyer from knowingly making a false statement of material fact or law to a third person. La. Rules of Prof'l Conduct r. 4.1(a) (2004); *see also* Restatement (Third) of the Law Governing Lawyers § 98(1) (2000). Louisiana lawyers have been disciplined under this rule for, among other things, backdating documents, *see In re Sealed Appellant*, 194 F.3d 666 (5th Cir. 1999), forging affidavits, *In re Stephens*, 645 So. 2d 1133 (La. 1994); *La. State Bar Ass'n v. Boutall*, 597 So. 2d 444 (La. 1992), misrepresenting that a deceased client is still alive, *In re Warner*, 851 So. 2d 1029, 1036 (La. 2003); lying about the existence of liens, *see also La. State Bar Ass'n v. Harrington*, 585 So. 2d 514 (La. 1990); and failing to disclose disbarment to a client while continuing representation, *see In re Turnage*, 104 So. 3d 397, 398-400 (La. 2012). A lawyer was also disciplined for three years for, among other things, requesting that his client come to his office to sign some "paperwork." *In re Meisner*, 11 So. 3d 1096, 1101-12 (La. 2009). Among the papers was a new retainer agreement which, once signed by the client, would be used to represent to a federal court that the lawyer was hired the day before he was to appear at the call docket setting, thereby setting up an excuse as to why he failed to appear and why his "new" client's case should be reinstated. *Id* at 1101. The client was unaware of his lawyer's scheme at the time he signed this "paperwork", and his case was ultimately dismissed. *Id.*

Lying During Investigations

This rule prohibits lawyers (and their nonlawyer assistants and investigators) from lying about material facts to opponents and third persons during investigations. In a 2009 advisory opinion, the Philadelphia Bar Association opined that lying about a lawyer's true identity to befriend a witness or opponent on Facebook could violate this rule. *See* Phil. Bar Assoc. Opinion 2009-02 (Mar. 2009).

"Material" Fact or Law

Paragraph (a) of this rule prohibits a lawyer from knowingly making a false statement of "material fact or law" to a third person. La. Rules of Prof'l Conduct r. 4.1(a) (2004). Whether a fact is "material" is sometimes a difficult issue. No Louisiana case defines the term "material" for purposes of the Louisiana Rules of Professional Conduct. However, the Louisiana Supreme Court has held in another context that a "material fact" is one whose "existence or nonexistence" is "essential" to the outcome of a matter. *See Smith v. Our Lady of the Lake Hosp., Inc.*, 639 So. 2d 730, 751 (La. 1994) *superseded on other grounds by* La. Code Civ. Proc. Ann. art. 966 (2007). Likewise, in the context of securities law, a fact is "material" if it is one which an average, prudent person would consider important in making a decision. *See, e.g., Simpson v. Se. Inv. Trust*, 697 F.2d 1257, 1258 (5th Cir. 1983) (holding that the test of materiality for securities law is "whether a reasonable man would attach importance to the fact misrepresented in determining his course of action" (quoting *Huddleston v. Herman & MacLean*, 640 F.2d 534, 543 (5th Cir. 1981)); *see also Dennis v. Gen. Imaging, Inc.*, 918 F.2d 496, 505 (5th Cir. 1990) (same). Therefore, by analogy, a fact should be considered to be "material" for purposes of this rule if an ordinary person would consider the fact "important" in the context asserted.

"Third Persons"

Paragraph (a) of this rule prohibits a lawyer from knowingly making a false statement of material fact or law to a "third person." La. Rules of Prof'l Conduct r. 4.1(a) (2004). This rule covers not only statements made to adverse counsel and adverse parties, *see, e.g.*, ABA Comm. on Ethics and Prof'l Responsibility, Formal Op. 95-397 (1995), but also to clients and other persons. *See In re Hackett*, 42 So. 3d 972,973-78 (La. 2010) (disbarring lawyer for telling client that proceeds from settlement were seized by a bank when in fact lawyer retained client's award). Of course, it does not cover statements made to tribunals, whether adjudicative or nonadjudicative, given that such statements are covered by Louisiana Rules 3.3 and 3.9; *Hoffman v. 21st Century N. Am. Ins. Co.*, 2014-2279 (La. 2015) (lawyer who negotiates a discount with a medical provider and then attempts to recover the undiscounted full "cost" from the defendant might run afoul of Rule 4.1).

Truthfulness in Negotiation

Lawyers often engage in "posturing" and "puffery" in the context of negotiations. That is, they sometimes attempt to exaggerate the value of their case or strength of their defenses in an effort to convince an opposing party to settle an ongoing matter. The ABA Committee on Ethics and Prof'l Responsibility has opined that some degree of "posturing" and "puffery" between opposing counsel is an accepted convention in negotiation. *See* ABA Comm. on Ethics and Prof'l Responsibility, Formal Op. 93-370 (1993). Likewise, comment 2 to Model Rule 4.1(b) notes that "[u]nder generally accepted conventions in negotiation, certain types of statements ordinarily are not taken as statements of material fact. Estimates of price or value placed on the subject of a transaction and a party's intentions as to an acceptable settlement of a claim are in this category . . . ." ABA Model Rules of Prof'l Conduct r. 4.1 cmt. 2. Nevertheless, the line between acceptable "puffery" and unethical misrepresentation is sometimes a difficult one to draw. For a classic essay discussing this problem, *see* Alvin Rubin, *A Causerie on Lawyer's Ethics in Negotiation*, 35 La. L. Rev. 577 (1975); *see also* Geoffrey C. Hazard, Jr., *The Lawyer's Obligation to be Trustworthy When Dealing With Opposing Parties*, 33 S.C.L. Rev. 181 (1981).

A lawyer would violate Rule 4.1 if the lawyer negotiated a discount with a treating physician and thereafter attempted to recover the undiscounted "cost" from the defendant *See Hoffman v. 21st Century N. Am. Ins. Co.*, No. 2014-C-2279 (La. Oct. 2, 2015) (2015 WL 5776131). In *Hoffman*, the court held as follows:

> We adopt a bright-line rule that such attorney-negotiated discounts do
> not fall within the ambit of the collateral source rule because to do
> otherwise would invite a variety of evidentiary and ethical dilemmas
> for counsel. For example, an evidentiary hearing inquiring into the
> details of the attorney-client relationship to uncover a "diminution in

patrimony" resulting from the attorney negotiated medical discount might intrude upon the privilege surrounding the employment contract and communications as to fee arrangements. *See* La. Code Evid. Art. 506(B)(1). Additionally, a lawyer who negotiates a discount with a medical provider and then attempts to recover the undiscounted full "cost" from the defendant might run afoul of Rule 4.1 of the Rules of Professional Conduct, entitled "Truthfulness in Statements to Others," which provides in Subsection (a) that a lawyer in the course of representing a client shall not knowingly make a false statement of material fact to a third person.

Id.. Although the plaintiff's lawyer in *Hoffman* did nothing unethical, the court's opinion makes it clear that a lawyer cannot, for example, claim during settlement negotiations to have incurred $1,000 in medical expenses when, in fact, the client's (discounted) medical expenses actually totaled $250. Thus, a plaintiff's lawyer is prohibited from collecting a back-door discount after claiming prediscounted amounts as special damages.

Duty to Disclose Material Fact

Paragraph (b) of this rule affirmatively requires a lawyer to disclose a material fact when disclosure is "necessary to avoid assisting a criminal or fraudulent act by a client." La. Rules of Prof'l Conduct r. 4.1(b) (2004). Similarly, Louisiana Rule 1.2(c) prohibits a lawyer from assisting a client in criminal or fraudulent conduct. La. Rules of Prof'l Conduct r. 1.2(c) (2004). Applying Rule 4.1, the Louisiana Supreme Court has disciplined a lawyer who remained silent at a real estate closing at which his client defrauded a third person. *See In re Sellers*, 669 So. 2d 1204, 1206 (La. 1996). Thus, the *Sellers* decision suggests that a lawyer may have a duty to blow the whistle on a client who has used the lawyer's services to commit a crime or a fraud.

However, the issue is far from settled. Paragraph (b) prohibits a lawyer from disclosing any material fact that constitutes "confidential information" protected by Rule 1.6. La. Rules of Prof'l Conduct r. 4.1(b) (2004); *id.* r. 1.6. The American Bar Association added this restriction to Model Rule 4.1 during the House of Delegates floor debate in 1983. Given that Louisiana Rule 1.6(a) broadly defines as confidential all "information relating to the representation of a client," and given that Rule 1.6(b) recognizes only limited exceptions to the rule of confidentiality, much information that Louisiana Rule 4.1(b) would seem to require the lawyer to disclose, Louisiana Rule 1.6 prohibits the lawyer from revealing. *See, e.g.*, ABA Comm. on Ethics and Prof'l Responsibility, Formal Op. 93-375 (1993). The lawyer in such a predicament should quietly withdraw from the representation. *See* La. Rules of Prof'l Conduct r. 1.16(a)(1) (2004); *see also* Ronald D. Rotunda, *The Notice of Withdrawal and the New Model Rules of Professional Conduct: Blowing the Whistle and Waving the Red Flag*, 63 Or. L. Rev. 455 (1984).

Note that other authorities suggest that a lawyer would be obligated to blow the whistle on a client notwithstanding the "unless-disclosure-is-prohibited" clause in Model Rule (and Louisiana Rule) 4.1(b). Professor Wolfram has argued that a lawyer must disclose otherwise confidential information if required by "other law." *See* Charles W. Wolfram,

Modern Legal Ethics § 13.5.8, at 724 (1986). Likewise, the Restatement provides that a lawyer communicating with a third party on behalf of a client may not "fail to make a disclosure required by law." *See* Restatement (Third) of the Law Governing Lawyers § 98(3) (2000). Therefore, as to a lawyer's obligations under Rule 4.1, Rule 1.2(c), and other law, "one can say with confidence . . . only that active misrepresentation is prohibited, while passive misrepresentation [through nondisclosure] is problematical." Wolfram, *supra*, § 13.5.8, at 722-23.

Disciplinary Sanctions

Absent aggravating or mitigating circumstances, the following sanctions are generally appropriate in cases involving conduct that involves dishonesty, fraud or deceit: *disbarment*, when a lawyer, with intent to deceive the court, makes a false statement, submits a false document, or improperly withholds material information, and causes serious or potentially serious injury to a party, or causes a significant or potentially significant adverse effect on the legal proceeding (*see generally*, *In re Engolio*, 7 So. 3d 1162 (La. 2009) (permanently disbarring lawyer for, among many other rules violations, forging a judge's signature on a judgment of divorce, and then falsely representing to his client that it was real)); *suspension*, when a lawyer knows that false statements or documents are being submitted to the court or that material information is improperly being withheld, and takes no remedial action, and causes injury or potential injury to a party or to the legal proceeding, or causes an adverse or potentially adverse effect on the legal proceeding (*see In re Stanford*, 48 So. 3d 224, 232 (La. 2010) (suspension as baseline sanction for lawyer having witness sign confidentiality agreement in criminal proceeding to dissuade witness from appearing in court)); *reprimand*, when a lawyer is negligent either in determining whether statements or documents are false or in taking remedial action when material information is being withheld, and causes injury or potential injury to a party to the legal proceeding, or causes an adverse or potentially adverse effect on the legal proceeding; and, *admonition*, when a lawyer engages in an isolated instance of neglect in determining whether submitted statements or documents are false or in failing to disclose material information upon learning of its falsity, and causes little or no actual or potential injury to a party, or causes little or no adverse or potentially adverse effect on the legal proceeding. *See* ABA Stds. for Imposing Lawyer Sanctions stds. 6.11-6.14 (1992) (False Statements, Fraud, and Misrepresentation); *id.* std. 6.1.

RULE 4.2. COMMUNICATION WITH PERSON REPRESENTED BY COUNSEL

Unless the lawyer has the consent of the other lawyer or is authorized to do so by law or a court order, a lawyer in representing a client shall not communicate about the subject of the representation with:

(a) a person the lawyer knows to be represented by another lawyer in the matter; or

(b) a person the lawyer knows is presently a director, officer, employee, member, shareholder or other constituent of a represented organization and

> (1) who supervises, directs or regularly consults with the organization's lawyer concerning the matter;

> (2) who has the authority to obligate the organization with respect to the matter; or

> (3) whose act or omission in connection with the matter may be imputed to the organization for purposes of civil or criminal liability.

BACKGROUND

The Louisiana Supreme Court adopted this rule on January 20, 2004. It became effective on March 1, 2004. The Louisiana Supreme Court amended this rule effective September 30, 2011 to clarify that a lawyer may communicate with persons identified in either paragraph (a) or (b) if authorized to do so by law, by court order or by the lawyer representing the person in question.

Paragraph (a) of this rule is substantially similar in substance to ABA Model Rule of Professional Conduct 4.2 (2002). The ABA in 2002 added a reference in the corresponding model rule to "court order." Although a communication with a represented person pursuant to a court order will ordinarily fall within the "authorized by law" exception, the specific reference to a court order was intended to alert lawyers to the availability of judicial relief in the rare situations in which it is needed. These situations are described generally in Comment [6]. *See also* ABA Ethics 2000 Commission Revision Notes to Model Rule 4.2 (2002).

Paragraph (b) does not appear in the text of ABA Model Rule 4.2. However, this paragraph contains language that is identical in substance to language set forth in Comment 7 to Model Rule 4.2. The LSBA recommended adoption of this paragraph to provide much-needed guidance to Louisiana lawyers regarding which constituents of a represented organization may be contacted directly without having to go through the organization's lawyer.

COMMENTS TO ABA MODEL RULE 4.2

[1] This Rule contributes to the proper functioning of the legal system by protecting a person who has chosen to be represented by a lawyer in a matter against possible overreaching by other lawyers who are participating in the matter, interference by those lawyers with the client-lawyer relationship and the uncounselled disclosure of information relating to the representation.

[2] This Rule applies to communications with any person who is represented by counsel concerning the matter to which the communication relates.

[3] The Rule applies even though the represented person initiates or consents to the communication. A lawyer must immediately terminate communication with a person if, after commencing communication, the lawyer learns that the person is one with whom communication is not permitted by this Rule.

[4] This Rule does not prohibit communication with a represented person, or an employee or agent of such a person, concerning matters outside the representation. For example, the existence of a controversy between a government agency and a private party, or between two organizations, does not prohibit a lawyer for either from communicating with nonlawyer representatives of the other regarding a separate matter. Nor does this Rule preclude communication with a represented person who is seeking advice from a lawyer who is not otherwise representing a client in the matter. A lawyer may not make a communication prohibited by this Rule through the acts of another. See Rule 8.4(a). Parties to a matter may communicate directly with each other, and a lawyer is not prohibited from advising a client concerning a communication that the client is legally entitled to make. Also, a lawyer having independent justification or legal authorization for communicating with a represented person is permitted to do so.

[5] Communications authorized by law may include communications by a lawyer on behalf of a client who is exercising a constitutional or other legal right to communicate with the government. Communications authorized by law may also include investigative activities of lawyers representing governmental entities, directly or through investigative agents, prior to the commencement of criminal or civil enforcement proceedings. When communicating with the accused in a criminal matter, a government lawyer must comply with this Rule in addition to honoring the constitutional rights of the accused. The fact that a communication does not violate a state or federal constitutional right is insufficient to establish that the communication is permissible under this Rule.

[6] A lawyer who is uncertain whether a communication with a represented person is permissible may seek a court order. A lawyer may also seek a court order in exceptional circumstances to authorize a communication that would otherwise be prohibited by this Rule, for example, where communication with a person represented by counsel is necessary to avoid reasonably certain injury.

[7] In the case of a represented organization, this Rule prohibits communications with a constituent of the organization who supervises, directs or regularly consults with the organization's lawyer concerning the matter or has authority to obligate the organization

with respect to the matter or whose act or omission in connection with the matter may be imputed to the organization for purposes of civil or criminal liability. Consent of the organization's lawyer is not required for communication with a former constituent. If a constituent of the organization is represented in the matter by his or her own counsel, the consent by that counsel to a communication will be sufficient for purposes of this Rule. Compare Rule 3.4(f). In communicating with a current or former constituent of an organization, a lawyer must not use methods of obtaining evidence that violate the legal rights of the organization. See Rule 4.4.

[8] The prohibition on communications with a represented person only applies in circumstances where the lawyer knows that the person is in fact represented in the matter to be discussed. This means that the lawyer has actual knowledge of the fact of the representation; but such actual knowledge may be inferred from the circumstances. See Rule 1.0(f). Thus, the lawyer cannot evade the requirement of obtaining the consent of counsel by closing eyes to the obvious.

[9] In the event the person with whom the lawyer communicates is not known to be represented by counsel in the matter, the lawyer's communications are subject to Rule 4.3.

ANNOTATIONS
Generally
This "anti-contact" rule prohibits lawyers from communicating with represented persons without authority either from the law, the court or the represented person's lawyer. *See generally* Restatement (Third) of the Law Governing Lawyers §§ 99-102 (2000). It exists to protect third parties and to safeguard the attorney-client relationship from unexpected and unwarranted intrusions. *See, e.g.,* ABA Comm. on Ethics and Prof'l Responsibility, Formal Op. 95-396 (1995); *see also In re Blanche*, 44 So. 3d 263, 267-70 (La. 2010) (disciplining lawyer for adversely affecting a former client's current representation by preparing and sending an amended bankruptcy plan to the former client without consent from the former client's current lawyer); *In re Frank*, No. Misc. 06-04, 2006 WL 1133871 (W.D. La. April 25, 2006) (stating that a lawyer "cannot evade the requirement of obtaining the consent of counsel by closing his eyes to the obvious," where the lawyer communicated with his clients' criminal co-defendants and claimed ignorance to whether the co-defendants were represented by counsel). More particularly, Rule 4.2 protects against the disclosure of privileged communications, and "liability-creating" statements. *See State v. Gilliam*, 748 So. 2d 622, 638 (La. Ct. App. 4th Cir. 1999); *see also Jenkins v. Wal-Mart Stores, Inc.*, 956 F. Supp. 695, 696 (W.D. La. 1997).

Contact Between Opposing Parties
Comment 4 to Model Rule 4.2 states that "parties to a matter may communicate directly with each other . . . ." ABA Model Rules of Prof'l Conduct r. 4.2 cmt. 4 (2002); *see also* ABA Comm. on Ethics and Prof'l Responsibility, Formal Op. 92-362 (1992). Nevertheless, a lawyer may not orchestrate a communication between a client and a represented person in an effort to circumvent this rule. *See, e.g.,* La. Rules of Prof'l Conduct r. 8.4 (2004); *see also* Restatement (Third) of the Law Governing Lawyers § 99(2) (2000) (permitting a lawyer to assist client in an "otherwise proper communication . . . with a represented non-client,"

unless the lawyer thereby seeks to deceive or overreach the nonclient); ABA Formal Op. 11-461 (Aug. 4, 2011). ("Parties to a legal matter have the right to communicate directly with each other. A lawyer may advise a client of that right and may assist the client regarding the substance of any proposed communication. The lawyer's assistance need not be prompted by a request from the client. Such assistance may not, however, result in overreaching by the lawyer."). ABA Formal Op. 11-461 suggests the following would constitute circumvention of the rule and overreaching:

> Prime examples of overreaching include assisting the client in securing from the represented person an enforceable obligation, disclosure of confidential information, or admissions against interest without the opportunity to seek the advice of counsel. To prevent such overreaching, a lawyer must, at a minimum, advise her client to encourage the other party to consult with counsel before entering into obligations, making admissions or disclosing confidential information.

ABA Formal. Op. 11-461 at 5.

Contact with Constituents and Former Constituents of Business Organizations

The extent to which a lawyer may contact current and former employees of a represented organization is a recurring issue that is addressed in paragraph (b). Prior to the adoption of this paragraph, many lawyers struggled with the issue of contacting current[115] employees of a corporate adversary because Louisiana courts had not articulated a bright-line rule. *See, e.g., Jenkins v. Wal-Mart Stores, Inc.*, 956 F. Supp. 695 (W.D. La. 1997); *In re Shell Oil Refinery*, 143 F.R.D. 105 (E.D. La. 1992); *see also* ABA Model Rules of Prof'l Conduct r. 4.2 cmt. 4 (2002); Restatement (Third) of the Law Governing Lawyers § 100(2) (2000).

In no event, however, may a lawyer seek to communicate with an employee or former employee who is independently represented by counsel. *See* La. Rules of Prof'l Conduct r. 4.2(a) (2004). Furthermore, in no event may a lawyer seek to obtain from any present or former organizational constituent "information that the lawyer reasonably should know the non-client may not reveal without violating a duty of confidentiality" to the organization. *See* Restatement (Third) of the Law Governing Lawyers § 102 (2000).

---

[115] As to former employees, the controlling law has always been clear. A lawyer generally may conduct ex parte interviews with unrepresented former employees of a represented business organization provided that the lawyer does not discuss matters protected by attorney-client privilege. *See Buford v. Cargill, Inc.*, No. 05-0283, 2009 WL 2381328, at *16 (W.D. La. Jul. 30, 2009); *see also Schmidt v. Gregorio*, 705 So. 2d 742 (La. Ct. App. 2d Cir. 1993) (employees are not "parties" represented by organization's lawyer); *Jenkins v. Wal-Mart Stores, Inc.*, 956 F. Supp. 695, 697 (W.D. La. 1997); ABA Comm. on Ethics and Prof'l Responsibility, Formal Op. 91-359 (1991).

Contact with Officials and Employees of Governmental Entities

This rule permits a lawyer to contact a person represented by counsel if the lawyer is authorized to do so by law. La. Rules of Prof'l Conduct r. 4.2 (2004). Comment 5 to Model Rule 4.2 states: "Communications authorized by law may include communications by a lawyer on behalf of a client who is exercising a constitutional or other legal right to communicate with the government."[116] ABA Model Rules of Prof'l Conduct r. 4.2 cmt. 5 (2002). Although the Louisiana Supreme Court has not spoken on the issue, some courts have held that Model Rule 4.2 does not apply in the context of communications with government officials. *See Camden v. Maryland*, 910 F. Supp. 1115, 1118 (D. Md. 1996); Cal. R. Prof. Cond. 7-103. The inapplicability of Rule 4.2 in this context stems from the First Amendment right to petition the government for redress of grievances. *See* U.S. Const. amend. I. *See* ABA Comm. on Ethics and Prof'l Responsibility, Formal Op. 97-408 (1997).

Note that the Restatement of Law Governing Lawyers does not give blanket approval for all communications with all officials of governmental entities. Rather, the Restatement distinguishes contacts in connection with routine litigation from those in connection with matters raising "an issue of general policy." Restatement (Third) of the Law Governing Lawyers § 101(2) (2000). As to policy-related issues, the anti-contact rule "does not apply to communications with the agency or the officer in the officer's official capacity." *Id.* § 101 (2000). As to routine, "specific-claim litigation" not involving broad public policy issues, ex parte contact is permissible so long as it does not create an opportunity for substantially unfair advantage against the governmental party. *Id.* cmt.

Remedy: Exclusion of Statements

Louisiana courts have excluded from evidence statements made by represented persons in violation of this rule. For example, in *State v. Gilliam*, 748 So. 2d 622 (La. Ct. App. 4th Cir. 1999), the Louisiana Fourth Circuit held that "where there is an improper communication discovered or considered before it is used at trial, and a violation of the ethical rule is found, it should be held inadmissible." *See id.* (citing *Jenkins v. Wal-Mart Stores, Inc.*, 956 F. Supp. 695 (W.D. La. 1997); *In re Shell Oil Refinery*, 144 F.R.D. 73 (E.D. La. 1992)).

Disciplinary Sanctions

Absent aggravating or mitigating circumstances, the following sanctions are generally appropriate in cases involving a lawyer's attempt to influence a judge, juror, prospective juror or other official by means prohibited by law: *disbarment*, when a lawyer improperly communicates with someone in the legal system with intent to affect the outcome of the

---

[116] The ABA Ethics 2000 Commission considered concerns aired by prosecutors about the effect of Rule 4.2 on their ability to carry out their investigative responsibilities. However, the Commission decided against recommending adoption of special rules governing communications with represented persons by government lawyers engaged in law enforcement. The Commission concluded that Rule 4.2 strikes the proper balance between effective law enforcement and the need to protect the client-lawyer relationships that are essential to the proper functioning of the justice system. *See* ABA Ethics 2000 Commission Revision Notes to Model R. 4.2 (2002).

proceeding, and causes significant or potentially significant interference with the outcome of the legal proceeding; *suspension*, when a lawyer engages in communication with an individual in the legal system when the lawyer knows that such communication is improper, and causes injury or potential injury to a party or causes interference or potential interference with the outcome of the legal proceeding; *reprimand*, when a lawyer is negligent in determining whether it is proper to engage in communication with an individual in the legal system, and causes injury or potential injury to a party or interference with or potential interference with the outcome of a legal proceeding; and, *admonition*, when a lawyer engages in an isolated instance of negligence in improperly communicating with an individual in the legal system, and causes little or no actual or potential injury to a party, or causes little or no actual or potential interference with the outcome of the legal proceeding. *See* ABA Stds. for Imposing Lawyer Sanctions std. 6.3 (1992) (Improper Communications with Individuals in the Legal System); *id.* stds. 6.31-6.34.

RULE 4.3. DEALING WITH UNREPRESENTED PERSON

> In dealing on behalf of a client with a person who is not
> represented by counsel, a lawyer shall not state or imply that the
> lawyer is disinterested. When the lawyer knows or reasonably
> should know that the unrepresented person misunderstands the
> lawyer's role in a matter, the lawyer shall make reasonable
> efforts to correct the misunderstanding. The lawyer shall not
> give legal advice to an unrepresented person, other than the
> advice to secure counsel, if the lawyer knows or reasonably
> should know that the interests of such a person are or have a
> reasonable possibility of being in conflict with the interests of
> the client.

BACKGROUND

The Louisiana Supreme Court adopted this rule on January 20, 2004. It became effective
on March 1, 2004, and has not been amended since. This rule is identical to ABA Model
Rule of Professional Conduct 4.3 (2002).

Giving Legal Advice to Unrepresented Persons

In 2002, the ABA added to the corresponding model rule a prohibition against giving legal
advice to unrepresented persons. Under former ABA Model Code of Professional
Responsibility, DR 7-104(A)(2), a lawyer was prohibited from giving advice to an
unrepresented person, other than the advice to secure counsel. The Commission
recommended reinstating the substance of this provision after considering reports that it
was not uncommon for lawyers to provide legal advice in negotiations between lawyers
and unrepresented parties.

The reason for the initial decision to delete the Model Code prohibition from text was the
difficulty of determining what constitutes impermissible advice-giving. The Commission
recommended that language be included in the Comments to address the application of
the textual prohibition in some common situations. Although the line may be difficult to
draw, it is important to discourage lawyers from overreaching in their negotiations with
unrepresented persons. *See* ABA Ethics 2000 Commission Revision Notes to Model R. 4.3
(2002).

COMMENTS TO ABA MODEL RULE 4.3

[1] An unrepresented person, particularly one not experienced in dealing with legal
matters, might assume that a lawyer is disinterested in loyalties or is a disinterested
authority on the law even when the lawyer represents a client. In order to avoid a
misunderstanding, a lawyer will typically need to identify the lawyer's client and, where
necessary, explain that the client has interests opposed to those of the unrepresented
person. For misunderstandings that sometimes arise when a lawyer for an organization
deals with an unrepresented constituent, see Rule 1.13(f).

[2] The Rule distinguishes between situations involving unrepresented persons whose interests may be adverse to those of the lawyer's client and those in which the person's interests are not in conflict with the client's. In the former situation, the possibility that the lawyer will compromise the unrepresented person's interests is so great that the Rule prohibits the giving of any advice, apart from the advice to obtain counsel. Whether a lawyer is giving impermissible advice may depend on the experience and sophistication of the unrepresented person, as well as the setting in which the behavior and comments occur. This Rule does not prohibit a lawyer from negotiating the terms of a transaction or settling a dispute with an unrepresented person. So long as the lawyer has explained that the lawyer represents an adverse party and is not representing the person, the lawyer may inform the person of the terms on which the lawyer's client will enter into an agreement or settle a matter, prepare documents that require the person's signature and explain the lawyer's own view of the meaning of the document or the lawyer's view of the underlying legal obligations.

ANNOTATIONS
Generally

This rule requires a lawyer to be forthright about his or her role in a matter when dealing with unrepresented lay persons. More particularly, it requires a lawyer to explain his role to the third person if a third party is laboring under a misunderstanding. La. Rules of Prof'l Conduct r. 4.3 (2004). In explaining his or her role, the lawyer must be truthful and must not misrepresent where his or her loyalties lie. *See, e.g.*, La. Rules of Prof'l Conduct r. 4.1(a) (2004) (stating that a lawyer shall not "make a false statement of material fact . . . to a third person"); *see also* Restatement (Third) of the Law Governing Lawyers § 103 (2000) (prohibiting a lawyer from "mislead[ing] the non-client . . . concerning the identity and interests of the person the lawyer represents"); ABA Model Rules of Prof'l Conduct r. 4.3 (stating that a lawyer "shall not state or imply that the lawyer is disinterested").

A lawyer who interacts with a potentially adverse third party must do so with care. A lawyer violated Rule 4.3 when the lawyer prepared an assignment of rights form for the lawyer's client to present to an unrepresented person. *See In re Guilbeau*, 35 So. 3d 207, 214 (La. 2010). The lawyer failed to disclose a potential conflict of interest between the client and the unrepresented party prior to the third party's receipt of the assignment document. *Id.* The Louisiana Supreme Court noted in *Guilbeau*, 35 So. 3d at 214, that Rule 4.3 imposes three requirements upon a lawyer who deals with an unrepresented person:

> Thus, Rule 4.3 has three components which come into play whenever a lawyer is dealing on a client's behalf with a person [who] is not represented by an attorney: first, the lawyer may not imply disinterestedness; second, the lawyer must clear up any misunderstanding about his or her role; and third, the lawyer may not give legal advice if the unrepresented person's interests may be adverse.

Giving Legal Advice

This rule prohibits a lawyer from giving "legal advice" to an adverse unrepresented person, "other than the advice to secure counsel." La. Rules of Prof'l Conduct r. 4.3 (2004). The Louisiana Fourth Circuit Court of Appeal has held that "[T]he term 'advice', in the legal context, contemplates something of more substance" than a suggestion that the unrepresented person "have her son call the bank." *First Nat'l Bank of St. Bernard v. Assavedo*, 764 So. 2d 162, 164 (La. Ct. App. 4th Cir. 2000).

Unrepresented Employees of Business Organizations

A lawyer retained by a business organization represents the organization distinct from its constituents. La. Rules of Prof'l Conduct r. 1.13(a) (2004). It is common for the organization's employees to be confused about whether the lawyer represents them or the organization, or both. Louisiana Rule 1.13(f) provides that a lawyer representing an organization must "explain the identity of the client," only when the interests of the organization and the client diverge. *See id.* r. 1.13(f). In contrast, Louisiana Rule 4.3 imposes an affirmative obligation upon the lawyer to explain to the unrepresented person the lawyer's role in the matter if there is a reasonable likelihood of a misunderstanding. *Id.* r. 4.3.

Disciplinary Sanctions

Absent aggravating or mitigating circumstances, the following sanctions are generally appropriate in cases involving a lawyer's attempt to influence a judge, juror, prospective juror or other official by means prohibited by law: *disbarment*, when a lawyer improperly communicates with someone in the legal system with intent to affect the outcome of the proceeding, and causes significant or potentially significant interference with the outcome of the legal proceeding; *suspension*, when a lawyer engages in communication with an individual in the legal system when the lawyer knows that such communication is improper, and causes injury or potential injury to a party or causes interference or potential interference with the outcome of the legal proceeding; *reprimand*, when a lawyer is negligent in determining whether it is proper to engage in communication with an individual in the legal system, and causes injury or potential injury to a party or interference with or potential interference with the outcome of a legal proceeding; and, *admonition*, when a lawyer engages in an isolated instance of negligence in improperly communicating with an individual in the legal system, and causes little or no actual or potential injury to a party, or causes little or no actual or potential interference with the outcome of the legal proceeding. *See* ABA Stds. for Imposing Lawyer Sanctions std. 6.3 (1992) (Improper Communications with Individuals in the Legal System); *id.* stds. 6.31-6.34.

RULE 4.4. RESPECT FOR RIGHTS OF THIRD PERSONS

(a) In representing a client, a lawyer shall not use means that have no substantial purpose other than to embarrass, delay, or burden a third person, or use methods of obtaining evidence that violate the legal rights of such a person.

(b) A lawyer who receives a writing or electronically stored information that, on its face, appears to be subject to the attorney-client privilege or otherwise confidential, under circumstances where it is clear that the writing or electronically stored information was not intended for the receiving lawyer, shall refrain from examining or reading the writing or electronically stored information, promptly notify the sending lawyer, and return the writing or delete the electronically stored information.

BACKGROUND

The Louisiana Supreme Court adopted this rule on January 20, 2004. It amended the rule in 2012 to include "electronically stored information."

Paragraph (a) of this rule is identical to ABA Model Rule of Professional Conduct 4.4(a) (2002).

Paragraph (b) of this rule departs significantly from ABA Model Rule 4.4(b). In contrast to the model rule–which requires only that the lawyer who receives an inadvertently-sent document notify the sender of that fact–this rule requires a lawyer not only to notify the sender of receipt, but also to refrain from examining the writing or electronically stored information and to return it to the sender or delete the electronically stored information. *See* ABA Model Rules of Prof'l Conduct r. 4.4(b).[117] A 2012 amendment to the model rule

---

[117] In 2002, the ABA Ethics 2000 Commission noted that numerous inquiries have been directed to ethics committees regarding the proper course of conduct for a lawyer who receives a fax or other document from opposing counsel that was not intended for the receiving lawyer. ABA Standing Committee on Ethics and Professional Responsibility Formal Opinion 92-368 advised that the receiving lawyer is obligated to refrain from examining the materials, to notify the sending lawyer and to abide by that lawyer's instructions. The Commission noted, however, that Opinion 92-368 had been criticized, in part because there is no provision of the Model Rules directly on point. The Commission decided that this Rule should require only that the lawyer notify the sender when the lawyer knows or reasonably should know that material was inadvertently sent, thus permitting the sending lawyer to take whatever steps might be necessary or available to protect the interests of the sending lawyer's client. *See* ABA Ethics 2000 Commission Revision Notes to Model Rule 4.4(b) (2002). The Louisiana Supreme Court, on

also inserted the term "electronically stored information" in addition to "document," although this change is likely not substantive given that the term "document" should already include "electronically stored information."

COMMENTS TO ABA MODEL RULE 4.4

[1] Responsibility to a client requires a lawyer to subordinate the interests of others to those of the client, but that responsibility does not imply that a lawyer may disregard the rights of third persons. It is impractical to catalogue all such rights, but they include legal restrictions on methods of obtaining evidence from third persons and unwarranted intrusions into privileged relationships, such as the client-lawyer relationship.

[2] Paragraph (b) recognizes that lawyers sometimes receive a document or electronically stored information that was mistakenly sent or produced by opposing parties or their lawyers. A document or electronically stored information is inadvertently sent when it is accidentally transmitted, such as when an email or letter is misaddressed or a document or electronically stored information is accidentally included with information that was intentionally transmitted. If a lawyer knows or reasonably should know that such a document or electronically stored information was sent inadvertently, then this Rule requires the lawyer to promptly notify the sender in order to permit that person to take protective measures. Whether the lawyer is required to take additional steps, such as returning the document or electronically stored information, is a matter of law beyond the scope of these Rules, as is the question of whether the privileged status of a document or electronically stored information has been waived. Similarly, this Rule does not address the legal duties of a lawyer who receives a document or electronically stored information that the lawyer knows or reasonably should know may have been inappropriately obtained by the sending person. For purposes of this Rule, "document or electronically stored information" includes, in addition to paper documents, email and other forms of electronically stored information, including embedded data (commonly referred to as "metadata"), that is subject to being read or put into readable form. Metadata in electronic documents creates an obligation under this Rule only if the receiving lawyer knows or reasonably should know that the metadata was inadvertently sent to the receiving lawyer.

[3] Some lawyers may choose to return a document or delete electronically stored information unread, for example, when the lawyer learns before receiving the document that it was inadvertently sent. Where a lawyer is not required by applicable law to do so, the decision to voluntarily return such a document is a matter of professional judgment ordinarily reserved to the lawyer. See Rules 1.2 and 1.4.

ANNOTATIONS
Generally
This rule prohibits a lawyer from engaging in conduct intended purely to harass third persons. *See* La. Rules of Prof'l Conduct r. 4.4(a) (2004); Restatement (Third) of the Law Governing Lawyers § 106 (2000) (prohibiting a lawyer from using "means that have no

recommendation of the LSBA Ethics 2000 Committee, took a different approach in paragraph (b) of this rule.

substantial purpose other than to embarrass, delay, or burden a third person or use methods of obtaining evidence that are prohibited by law"). Courts have used this rule to sanction lawyers for conduct arising both out of litigation and out of nonlitigation matters. *See In re Cook*, 932 So. 2d 669 (La. 2006) (suspending a lawyer for three years for "tirelessly" pursuing a motion to recuse the judge in her clients' case, thereby causing the defendants to accrue extra expenses); *see also In re Humphrey*, 15 So. 3d 960 (La. 2009) (disbarring lawyer for, among other things, misrepresenting her client's (also the lawyer's sister) marital residence to obtain a temporary restraining order against her client's husband, thereby causing the husband to be evicted from his office without cause, and severely damaging his business). ABA Annotated Model Rules of Prof'l Conduct at 437-42 (5th ed. 2003). At least one court has applied Rule 4.4 to a lawyer's internet postings. *See Marceaux v. Lafayette City–Parish Consol. Gov't*, 731 F.3d 488 (5th Cir. 2013). Furthermore, courts have sanctioned lawyers under this rule for conduct directed at opposing counsel, ABA Annotated Model Rules of Prof'l Conduct at 437, and witnesses, *id.* at 438*; see also In re Wells*, 36 So. 3d 198, 205-08 (La. 2010) (lawyer's filing of vindictive personal suit against opposing lawyer violated Rule 4.4). Note that a lawyer does not violate this rule if the lawyer has any "substantial purpose other than to embarrass, delay, or burden" the third person who is the target of the lawyer's actions. La. Rules of Prof'l Conduct r. 4.4(a) (2004). *See In re Mincilier*, 74 So. 3d 687, 693 (La. 2011) (lawyer did not violate Rule 4.4 by repeatedly asserting RICO claims despite previous dismissals because he was mainly motivated by the best interest of the client).

Misdirected Communications

Paragraph (b) of this rule mandates the return or deleting of misdirected communications. Although a lawyer must comply with the letter and spirit of this rule by returning the original and deleting all electronic copies of the communication, it is not impermissible for the lawyer to thereafter file an appropriate pleading or motion in an effort to recover the document under any controlling principles of substantive, evidentiary or procedural law.

Disciplinary Sanctions

Absent aggravating or mitigating circumstances, the following sanctions are generally appropriate in cases involving a lawyer's abuse of the legal process: *disbarment*, when the lawyer knowingly violates a court rule with the intent to obtain a benefit for the lawyer or another, and causes serious injury or potentially serious injury to a party, or causes serious or potentially serious interference with a legal proceeding; *suspension*, when the lawyer knows that he is violating a court rule, and there is injury or potential injury to a client or a party, or interference or potential interference with a legal proceeding; *reprimand*, when the lawyer negligently fails to comply with a court rule, and causes injury or potential injury to a client or other party, or causes interference or potential interference with a court proceeding; and, *admonition*, when the lawyer engages in an isolated instance of negligence in complying with a court rule, and causes little or no actual or potential injury to a party, or causes little or no actual or potential interference with a legal proceeding. *See* ABA Stds. for Imposing Lawyer Sanctions std. 6.2 (1992) (Abuse of Legal Process); *id.* stds. 6.21-6.24.

Article 5. Law Firms and Associations

RULE 5.1. RESPONSIBILITIES OF PARTNERS, MANAGERS, AND SUPERVISORY LAWYERS

(a) A partner in a law firm, and a lawyer who individually or together with other lawyers possesses comparable managerial authority in a law firm, shall make reasonable efforts to ensure that the firm has in effect measures giving reasonable assurance that all lawyers in the firm conform to the Rules of Professional Conduct.

(b) A lawyer having direct supervisory authority over another lawyer shall make reasonable efforts to ensure that the other lawyer conforms to the Rules of Professional Conduct.

(c) A lawyer shall be responsible for another lawyer's violation of the Rules of Professional Conduct if:

(1) the lawyer orders or, with knowledge of the specific conduct, ratifies the conduct involved; or

(2) the lawyer is a partner or has comparable managerial authority in the law firm in which the other lawyer practices, or has direct supervisory authority over the other lawyer, and knows of the conduct at a time when its consequences can be avoided or mitigated but fails to take reasonable remedial action.

BACKGROUND

The Louisiana Supreme Court adopted this rule on January 20, 2004. It became effective on March 1, 2004, and has not been amended since. This rule is identical to ABA Model Rule of Professional Conduct 5.1 (2002).

In 2002, the ABA revised the corresponding model rule to clarify that it applies to managing lawyers in corporate and government legal departments and legal services organizations, as well as to partners in private law firms. The ABA intended no change in substance. *See* ABA Ethics 2000 Commission Revision Notes to Model Rule 5.1 (2002).

COMMENTS TO ABA MODEL RULE 5.1

[1] Paragraph (a) applies to lawyers who have managerial authority over the professional work of a firm. See Rule 1.0(c). This includes members of a partnership, the shareholders in a law firm organized as a professional corporation, and members of other associations authorized to practice law; lawyers having comparable managerial authority in a legal services organization or a law department of an enterprise or government agency; and

271

lawyers who have intermediate managerial responsibilities in a firm. Paragraph (b) applies to lawyers who have supervisory authority over the work of other lawyers in a firm.

[2] Paragraph (a) requires lawyers with managerial authority within a firm to make reasonable efforts to establish internal policies and procedures designed to provide reasonable assurance that all lawyers in the firm will conform to the Rules of Professional Conduct. Such policies and procedures include those designed to detect and resolve conflicts of interest, identify dates by which actions must be taken in pending matters, account for client funds and property and ensure that inexperienced lawyers are properly supervised.

[3] Other measures that may be required to fulfill the responsibility prescribed in paragraph (a) can depend on the firm's structure and the nature of its practice. In a small firm of experienced lawyers, informal supervision and periodic review of compliance with the required systems ordinarily will suffice. In a large firm, or in practice situations in which difficult ethical problems frequently arise, more elaborate measures may be necessary. Some firms, for example, have a procedure whereby junior lawyers can make confidential referral of ethical problems directly to a designated senior partner or special committee. See Rule 5.2. Firms, whether large or small, may also rely on continuing legal education in professional ethics. In any event, the ethical atmosphere of a firm can influence the conduct of all its members and the partners may not assume that all lawyers associated with the firm will inevitably conform to the Rules.

[4] Paragraph (c) expresses a general principle of personal responsibility for acts of another. See also Rule 8.4(a).

[5] Paragraph (c)(2) defines the duty of a partner or other lawyer having comparable managerial authority in a law firm, as well as a lawyer who has direct supervisory authority over performance of specific legal work by another lawyer. Whether a lawyer has supervisory authority in particular circumstances is a question of fact. Partners and lawyers with comparable authority have at least indirect responsibility for all work being done by the firm, while a partner or manager in charge of a particular matter ordinarily also has supervisory responsibility for the work of other firm lawyers engaged in the matter. Appropriate remedial action by a partner or managing lawyer would depend on the immediacy of that lawyer's involvement and the seriousness of the misconduct. A supervisor is required to intervene to prevent avoidable consequences of misconduct if the supervisor knows that the misconduct occurred. Thus, if a supervising lawyer knows that a subordinate misrepresented a matter to an opposing party in negotiation, the supervisor as well as the subordinate has a duty to correct the resulting misapprehension.

[6] Professional misconduct by a lawyer under supervision could reveal a violation of paragraph (b) on the part of the supervisory lawyer even though it does not entail a violation of paragraph (c) because there was no direction, ratification or knowledge of the violation.

[7] Apart from this Rule and Rule 8.4(a), a lawyer does not have disciplinary liability for the conduct of a partner, associate or subordinate. Whether a lawyer may be liable civilly

or criminally for another lawyer's conduct is a question of law beyond the scope of these Rules.

[8] The duties imposed by this Rule on managing and supervising lawyers do not alter the personal duty of each lawyer in a firm to abide by the Rules of Professional Conduct. See Rule 5.2(a).

ANNOTATIONS

Ensuring Compliance with the Rules of Professional Conduct

Paragraph (a) provides that a partner in a law firm must make reasonable efforts to ensure that other lawyers in the firm conform their conduct to the Louisiana Rules of Professional Conduct. La. Rules of Prof'l Conduct r. 5.1(a) (2004); *see In re Trahant*, 108 So. 3d 67, 75 (La. 2012) (disciplining lawyer for relinquishing legal responsibilities to employees resulting in fraudulent real estate transactions); *In re Tolchinsky*, 740 So. 2d 109 (La. 1999) (disbarring lawyer for failure to supervise subordinate lawyer and for subsequent failure to report that lawyer's egregious ethical violations); *see also* Restatement (Third) of the Law Governing Lawyers § 11(1) (2000). Similarly, paragraph (b) provides that a lawyer with "direct supervisory" authority over another lawyer must undertake such efforts. La. Rules of Prof'l Conduct r. 5.1(b) (2004); *see, e.g., In re Comish*, 889 So. 2d 236 (La. 2004) (disciplining lawyer for failure to supervise disbarred lawyer he hired as his legal assistant); *In re Wilkinson*, 805 So. 2d 142, 146-47 (La. 2002) (disciplining lawyer for failure to supervise new admittee's handling of succession matter). This paragraph requires lawyers who are not "partners," for example senior associates, to ensure that the lawyers whom they supervise comply with the rules. *See* La. Rules of Prof'l Conduct r. 5.1(b) (2004); *see also* Restatement (Third) of the Law Governing Lawyers § 11(2) (2000).

What measures are "reasonable" under the circumstances turns on a number of factors, including, the size of the firm, the firm's management structure, and the nature of the firm's practice. *See* ABA Model Rules of Prof'l Conduct r. 5.1 cmt. 3 (2002). To comply with this rule, a partner or supervisory lawyer should consider establishing a committee to address and to resolve "ethical" issues. Moreover, the firm should implement policies to ensure that all of its lawyers: (1) have successfully completed a legal-ethics class in law school; (2) comply with mandatory continuing legal education requirements; (3) present complex ethics issues to firm management for resolution; (4) have knowledge of the availability of extra-firm resources, including the LSBA Ethics Advisory Service Committee, for issues relating to legal ethics; (5) have access to an adequate library of ethics-related materials; and, (6) are handling all matters competently and diligently, and are not perilously overburdened with work.

Supervisory Responsibility

Paragraph (c) sets forth the standards for holding a supervisory lawyer responsible for another lawyer's violation of the rules of conduct. *See In re Jones*, 894 So. 2d 338 (La. 2005) (noting lawyer's Rule 5.1(c) violation due to lawyer's partner's noncompliance with Rule 1.8(a)); Under these standards, no lawyer is "vicariously" responsible for another's unethical conduct–at least for purposes of professional discipline. Rather, a lawyer is subject to discipline only for the lawyer's own culpable conduct in dealing with or supervising a lawyer who violates the rules.

However, a lawyer may be vicariously liable for the harms caused by a partner under other law. *See* Restatement (Third) of the Law Governing Lawyers § 58 (2000) (addressing vicarious civil liability of partners and principals of law firms). For example, a lawyer is responsible for another lawyer's violation if the lawyer "orders" or "ratifies" the unethical conduct of another lawyer. La. Rules of Prof'l Conduct r. 5.1(c)(1) (2004); *see also id.* r. 8.4(a) (providing that it constitutes "professional misconduct for a lawyer to violate this Rules of Professional Conduct, knowingly assist or induce another to do so, or do so through the acts of another"); Restatement (Third) of the Law Governing Lawyers § 11(3)(a) (2000). This paragraph imposes responsibility irrespective of whether there is a supervisor-subordinate relationship between the lawyers. In addition, a lawyer is responsible for a subordinate lawyer's violation if the lawyer learns that the subordinate lawyer has violated the rules of professional conduct, but then does nothing to avoid or mitigate the consequences of that unethical conduct. La. Rules of Prof'l Conduct r. 5.1(c)(2) (2004); *see also* Restatement (Third) of the Law Governing Lawyers § 11(3)(b) (2000).

Disciplinary Sanctions

Absent aggravating or mitigating circumstances, the following sanctions are generally appropriate in cases involving violations of Rule 5.1: *disbarment*, when the lawyer knowingly engages in conduct that is a violation of a duty owed to the profession with the intent to obtain a benefit for the lawyer or another, and causes serious or potentially serious injury to a client, the public, or the legal system; *suspension*, when the lawyer knowingly engages in conduct that is a violation of a duty owed to the profession, and causes injury or potential injury to a client, the public, or the legal system; *reprimand*, when the lawyer negligently engages in conduct that is a violation of a duty owed to the profession, and causes injury or potential injury to a client, the public, or the legal system; and, *admonition*, when the lawyer engages in an isolated instance of negligence that is a violation of a duty owed to the profession, and causes little or no actual or potential injury to a client, the public or the legal system. *See* ABA Stds. for Imposing Lawyer Sanctions stds. 7.0-7.4 (1992). *See In re McBride*, 167 So. 3d 619 (La. 2015) (court imposed public reprimand for failure to make reasonable efforts to ensure that other lawyers in his law firm conformed their conduct to the Rules of Professional Conduct, in violation of Rule 5.1(a) of the Rules of Professional Conduct).

RULE 5.2. RESPONSIBILITIES OF A SUBORDINATE LAWYER

(a) A lawyer is bound by the Rules of Professional Conduct notwithstanding that the lawyer acted at the direction of another person.

(b) A subordinate lawyer does not violate the Rules of Professional Conduct if that lawyer acts in accordance with a supervisory lawyer's reasonable resolution of an arguable question of professional duty.

BACKGROUND
The Louisiana Supreme Court adopted this rule on January 20, 2004. It became effective on March 1, 2004, and has not been amended since. This rule is identical to ABA Model Rule of Professional Conduct 5.2 (2002).

COMMENTS TO ABA MODEL RULE 5.2
[1] Although a lawyer is not relieved of responsibility for a violation by the fact that the lawyer acted at the direction of a supervisor, that fact may be relevant in determining whether a lawyer had the knowledge required to render conduct a violation of the Rules. For example, if a subordinate filed a frivolous pleading at the direction of a supervisor, the subordinate would not be guilty of a professional violation unless the subordinate knew of the document's frivolous character.

[2] When lawyers in a supervisor-subordinate relationship encounter a matter involving professional judgment as to ethical duty, the supervisor may assume responsibility for making the judgment. Otherwise a consistent course of action or position could not be taken. If the question can reasonably be answered only one way, the duty of both lawyers is clear and they are equally responsible for fulfilling it. However, if the question is reasonably arguable, someone has to decide upon the course of action. That authority ordinarily reposes in the supervisor, and a subordinate may be guided accordingly. For example, if a question arises whether the interests of two clients conflict under Rule 1.7, the supervisor's reasonable resolution of the question should protect the subordinate professionally if the resolution is subsequently challenged.

ANNOTATIONS
Generally
A lawyer working at the direction of another lawyer or nonlawyer is not excused from responsibility for violating these rules merely because the subordinate lawyer dutifully followed instructions. Thus, there is generally no "Nuremberg Defense" for junior lawyers who are merely carrying out the orders of a superior. *See* La. Rules of Prof'l Conduct r. 5.2(a) (2004); *see also* Restatement (Third) of the Law Governing Lawyers § 12(1) (2000). Moreover, as to the appropriate sanction for a disciplinary violation, it is not a "mitigating factor" that the client "made the lawyer do it." *See* ABA Stds. for Imposing Lawyer Sanctions std. 9.4(b) (1986). Note, however, that a young lawyer's "inexperience in the

practice of law" may be a factor mitigating the sanction imposed under certain circumstances. *See id.* std. 9.32(f).

Limited Safe Harbor

Paragraph (b) provides a safe harbor for a subordinate lawyer who follows the directives of a supervisory lawyer. The channel to this safe harbor, however, is narrow and shallow. Only when a subordinate lawyer follows the "reasonable" advice of a supervisor on an "arguable question of professional duty," is the lawyer's conduct excused. La. Rules of Prof'l Conduct r. 5.2(b) (2004); *see also* Restatement (Third) of the Law Governing Lawyers § 12(2) (2000); ABA Comm. on Ethics and Prof'l Responsibility, Formal Op. 347 (1981). In practice, this safe harbor is rarely used because "reasonable" resolutions of "arguable questions" are rarely prosecuted by the Office of Disciplinary Counsel.

Disciplinary Sanctions

Absent aggravating or mitigating circumstances, the following sanctions are generally appropriate in cases involving violations of Rule 5.2: *disbarment*, when the lawyer knowingly engages in conduct that is a violation of a duty owed to the profession with the intent to obtain a benefit for the lawyer or another, and causes serious or potentially serious injury to a client, the public, or the legal system; *suspension*, when the lawyer knowingly engages in conduct that is a violation of a duty owed to the profession, and causes injury or potential injury to a client, the public, or the legal system; *reprimand*, when the lawyer negligently engages in conduct that is a violation of a duty owed to the profession, and causes injury or potential injury to a client, the public, or the legal system; and, *admonition*, when the lawyer engages in an isolated instance of negligence that is a violation of a duty owed to the profession, and causes little or no actual or potential injury to a client, the public or the legal system. *See* ABA Stds. for Imposing Lawyer Sanctions stds. 7.0-7.4 (1992).

RULE 5.3. RESPONSIBILITIES REGARDING NONLAWYER ASSISTANTS

With respect to a nonlawyer employed or retained by or associated with a lawyer:

(a) a partner, and a lawyer who individually or together with other lawyers possesses comparable managerial authority in a law firm shall make reasonable efforts to ensure that the firm has in effect measures giving reasonable assurance that the person's conduct is compatible with the professional obligations of the lawyer;

(b) a lawyer having direct supervisory authority over the nonlawyer shall make reasonable efforts to ensure that the person's conduct is compatible with the professional obligations of the lawyer; and

(c) a lawyer shall be responsible for conduct of such a person that would be a violation of the Rules of Professional Conduct if engaged in by a lawyer if:

  (1) the lawyer orders or, with the knowledge of the specific conduct, ratifies the conduct involved; or

  (2) the lawyer is a partner or has comparable managerial authority in the law firm in which the person is employed, or has direct supervisory authority over the person, and knows of the conduct at a time when its consequences can be avoided or mitigated but fails to take reasonable remedial action.

BACKGROUND

The Louisiana Supreme Court adopted this rule on January 20, 2004. It became effective on March 1, 2004, and has not been amended since. This rule is identical to ABA Model Rule of Professional Conduct 5.3 (2002), except the title of the rule. In 2012, the ABA changed the title of the model rule to "Responsibilities Regarding Nonlawyer Assistance" from "Responsibilities Regarding Nonlawyer Assistants."

In 2002, the ABA revised the corresponding model rule to clarify that it applies to managing lawyers in corporate and government legal departments and legal services organizations, as well as to partners in private law firms. The ABA intended no change in substance. *See* ABA Ethics 2000 Commission Revision Notes to Model Rule 5.3 (2002).

COMMENTS TO ABA MODEL RULE 5.3

[1] Paragraph (a) requires lawyers with managerial authority within a law firm to make reasonable efforts to ensure that the firm has in effect measures giving reasonable

assurance that nonlawyers in the firm and nonlawyers outside the firm who work on firm matters act in a way compatible with the professional obligations of the lawyer. See Comment [6] to Rule 1.1 (retaining lawyers outside the firm) and Comment [1] to Rule 5.1 (responsibilities with respect to lawyers within a firm). Paragraph (b) applies to lawyers who have supervisory authority over such nonlawyers within or outside the firm. Paragraph (c) specifies the circumstances in which a lawyer is responsible for the conduct of such nonlawyers within or outside the firm that would be a violation of the Rules of Professional Conduct if engaged in by a lawyer.

Nonlawyers Within the Firm

[2] Lawyers generally employ assistants in their practice, including secretaries, investigators, law student interns, and paraprofessionals. Such assistants, whether employees or independent contractors, act for the lawyer in rendition of the lawyer's professional services. A lawyer must give such assistants appropriate instruction and supervision concerning the ethical aspects of their employment, particularly regarding the obligation not to disclose information relating to representation of the client, and should be responsible for their work product. The measures employed in supervising nonlawyers should take account of the fact that they do not have legal training and are not subject to professional discipline.

Nonlawyers Outside the Firm

[3] A lawyer may use nonlawyers outside the firm to assist the lawyer in rendering legal services to the client. Examples include the retention of an investigative or paraprofessional service, hiring a document management company to create and maintain a database for complex litigation, sending client documents to a third party for printing or scanning, and using an Internet-based service to store client information. When using such services outside the firm, a lawyer must make reasonable efforts to ensure that the services are provided in a manner that is compatible with the lawyer's professional obligations. The extent of this obligation will depend upon the circumstances, including the education, experience and reputation of the nonlawyer; the nature of the services involved; the terms of any arrangements concerning the protection of client information; and the legal and ethical environments of the jurisdictions in which the services will be performed, particularly with regard to confidentiality. See also Rules 1.1 (competence), 1.2 (allocation of authority), 1.4 (communication with client), 1.6 (confidentiality), 5.4(a) (professional independence of the lawyer), and 5.5(a) (unauthorized practice of law). When retaining or directing a nonlawyer outside the firm, a lawyer should communicate directions appropriate under the circumstances to give reasonable assurance that the nonlawyer's conduct is compatible with the professional obligations of the lawyer.

[4] Where the client directs the selection of a particular nonlawyer service provider outside the firm, the lawyer ordinarily should agree with the client concerning the allocation of responsibility for monitoring as between the client and the lawyer. See Rule 1.2. When making such an allocation in a matter pending before a tribunal, lawyers and parties may have additional obligations that are a matter of law beyond the scope of these Rules.

ANNOTATIONS
Generally

A lawyer's obligation to supervise nonlawyer assistants is very similar to a lawyer's responsibility to supervise subordinate lawyers. First, the lawyer must exercise reasonable care in overseeing the work of nonlawyers. Thus, a partner must ensure that the firm has in place reasonable measures to ensure that nonlawyers conduct themselves in a manner consistent with these rules–although as a technical matter these rules do not apply to nonlawyers. *See* La. Rules of Prof'l Conduct r. 5.3(a) (2004); *In re Bailey*, 115 So. 3d 458, 465 (La. 2013) (disbarring lawyer for failure to ensure lawyer's nonlawyer wife, who lawyer appointed as trustee of client's trust, followed proper accounting and adequate preservation of client's trust among other violations stemming from appointment of wife as trustee). *In re Wahlder*, 728 So. 2d 837 (La. 1999) (holding that a lawyer has ultimate responsibility for actions of nonlawyer staff); *see also* Restatement (Third) of the Law Governing Lawyers § 11(4)(a)(i) (2000). Likewise, a supervisory lawyer must ensure that the conduct of nonlawyers whom he or she supervises conforms to these rules. *See* La. Rules of Prof'l Conduct r. 5.3(b) (2004); *see also* Restatement (Third) of the Law Governing Lawyers § 11(4)(a)(ii) (2000); *In re Serret*, 35 So. 3d 256, 259 (La. 2011) (disciplining lawyer for failure to recognize and prevent secretary's embezzlement); *In re Shortess*, 950 So. 2d 570 (La. 2007) (disciplining lawyer for not adequately supervising a non-lawyer assistant in preparing pleadings); *In re Brown*, 813 So. 2d 325 (La. 2002) (disciplining lawyer for failure to supervise paralegal who was functioning like a lawyer); *In re Wilkinson*, 805 So. 2d 142 (La. 2002) (disciplining a lawyer for failure to supervise nonlawyer's handling of succession matters); *see also La. State Bar Ass'n v. Keys*, 567 So. 2d 588 (La. 1990); *La. State Bar Ass'n v. Edwins*, 540 So. 2d 294, 299 (La. 1989). To comply with this rule, a partner or supervisory lawyer should inform all nonlawyer assistants in writing about the fundamental duties owed by lawyers to their clients, particularly the duties of confidentiality, loyalty, competence, and diligence. Furthermore, a lawyer should supervise with particular care all staff members entrusted with the handling of client or third-party[118] funds.

Second, a lawyer is subject to discipline if he or she "orders" or knowingly "ratifies" conduct by a nonlawyer that would be unethical if that person were a lawyer. La. Rules of Prof'l Conduct r. 5.3(c)(1) (2004); *id.* r. 8.4(a); *see also* Restatement (Third) of the Law Governing Lawyers § 11(4)(b)(i) (2000). Furthermore, a lawyer is subject to discipline if the lawyer learns of such conduct by a nonlawyer after the fact, but then fails to attempt to

---

[118] In *In re Cline*, 756 So. 2d 284 (La. 2000), the Louisiana Supreme Court suspended a lawyer for six months for his failure to assure that his (nonlawyer) client properly obtained her prior lawyer's endorsement on settlement checks; *see also In re Geiger*, 27 So. 3d 280 (La. 2010) (disciplining lawyer for not adequately supervising his non-lawyer employee who had access to and may have misappropriated funds from client trust accounts); *In re McClanahan* (26 So. 3d 756 (La. 2010) (disbarring lawyer for, among other things, instructing a non-lawyer assistant to cash a check issued from a client's trust account instead of the operating account).

avoid or mitigate the consequences of that nonlawyer's conduct. La. Rules of Prof'l Conduct r. 5.3(c)(2) (2004); *see also* Restatement (Third) of the Law Governing Lawyers § 11(4)(b)(ii) (2000).

Vicarious Disqualification for Conflict of Nonlawyer Assistant

A lawyer is potentially subject to disqualification if the lawyer's paralegal possesses information that would be disqualifying if the paralegal were a lawyer. The Louisiana Third Circuit held:

> [B]ecause [the respondent's lawyer] is responsible for the conduct of her employees and because her paralegal has a direct conflict of interest in this case, this conflict disqualifies her from representing respondent.

T.S.L. v. G.L., 976 So. 2d 793 (La. Ct. App. 3d Cir. 2008).

Using Investigators

A lawyer who knowingly uses an investigator or other third party to engage in conduct that the rules would forbid the lawyer from engaging in faces the risk of discipline. It is not uncommon for a lawyer to hire an investigator to surreptitiously gather evidence. However, the lawyer must not dispatch the investigator to engage in conduct that would otherwise be unethical for a lawyer. This could occur if the lawyer engages an investigator knowing that the investigator will (1) make a false statement of material fact to a third person, or (2) contact a represented person.

The Kentucky Supreme Court publicly reprimanded a lawyer who, while representing a client in a wrongful termination case, used an investigation firm to interview directly the client's former employer. *See Bracher v. Kentucky Bar Ass'n*, 290 S.W. 3d 648 (Ky. 2009). In that case, the Kentucky lawyer hired Documented Reference Check, a company that contacted the client's former employer to see what the company had to say about the client. The Kentucky Supreme Court found that in so doing, the lawyer violated Kentucky Rule of Professional Conduct 4.2.

Much the same result could occur in Louisiana. Louisiana Rule 4.1(a) prohibits a lawyer from "knowingly" making "a false statement of material fact or law to a third person." Louisiana Rule 4.2(a) prohibits a lawyer from communicating "about the subject of the representation with . . . a person the lawyer knows to be represented by another lawyer in the matter, unless the lawyer has the consent of the other lawyer or is authorized to do so by law or a court order." Louisiana Rule 8.4(a) prohibits a lawyer from violating or attempting to violate the rules through the acts of another." *See also* La. Rules of Prof'l Conduct r. 5.3.

Job Titles for Nonlawyers

If a Louisiana lawyer employs and reasonably supervises a nonlawyer with a job title such as "office manager," "chief technology officer," or "chief operating officer," the lawyer does not violate these rules so long as the nonlawyer is not impairing the lawyer's "professional" judgment in the handling of client matters. Moreover, a lawyer's use of such job titles does not suggest that a nonlawyer has control over the lawyer's "professional judgment." Such innocuous titles suggest only subordinate responsibility for administrative aspects of the lawyer's business operations and are not "false or misleading." *See* Op. No. 642 (Revised), The Professional Ethics Committee for the State Bar of Tx. (Sep. 2015) (opining that "certain titles for non-lawyer employees of a law firm that include the terms "officer," "principal," or "director" are permissible under the Texas Disciplinary Rules because the titles could not reasonably be understood to indicate authority to exercise control over the law practice of firm lawyers.").

Disciplinary Sanctions

Absent aggravating or mitigating circumstances, the following sanctions are generally appropriate in cases involving violations of Rule 5.3: *disbarment*, when the lawyer knowingly engages in conduct that is a violation of a duty owed to the profession with the intent to obtain a benefit for the lawyer or another, and causes serious or potentially serious injury to a client, the public, or the legal system; *suspension*, when the lawyer knowingly engages in conduct that is a violation of a duty owed to the profession, and causes injury or potential injury to a client, the public, or the legal system; *reprimand*, when the lawyer negligently engages in conduct that is a violation of a duty owed to the profession, and causes injury or potential injury to a client, the public, or the legal system; and, *admonition*, when the lawyer engages in an isolated instance of negligence that is a violation of a duty owed to the profession, and causes little or no actual or potential injury to a client, the public or the legal system. *See* ABA Stds. for Imposing Lawyer Sanctions stds. 7.0-7.4 (1992).

RULE 5.4. PROFESSIONAL INDEPENDENCE OF A LAWYER

(a) A lawyer or law firm shall not share legal fees with a nonlawyer, except that:

> (1) an agreement by a lawyer with the lawyer's firm, partner, or associate may provide for the payment of money, over a reasonable period of time after the lawyer's death, to the lawyer's estate or to one or more specified persons;

> (2) a lawyer who undertakes to complete unfinished legal business of a deceased lawyer may pay to the estate of the deceased lawyer that proportion of the total compensation which fairly represents the services rendered by the deceased lawyer;

> (3) a lawyer or law firm may include nonlawyer employees in a compensation or retirement plan, even though the plan is based in whole or in part on a profit-sharing arrangement;

> (4) a lawyer who purchases the practice of a deceased, disabled, or disappeared lawyer may, pursuant to the provisions of Rule 1.17, pay to the estate or other representative of that lawyer the agreed upon purchase price; and

> (5) a lawyer may share legal fees as otherwise provided in Rule 7.2(c)(13).

(b) A lawyer shall not form a partnership with a nonlawyer if any of the activities of the partnership consist of the practice of law.

(c) A lawyer shall not permit a person who recommends, employs, or pays the lawyer to render legal services for another to direct or regulate the lawyer's professional judgment in rendering such legal services.

(d) A lawyer shall not practice with or in the form of a professional corporation or association authorized to practice law for profit, if:

(1) a nonlawyer owns any interest therein, except that a fiduciary representative of the estate of a lawyer may hold the stock or interest of the lawyer for a reasonable time during administration;

(2) a nonlawyer is a corporate director or officer thereof or occupies the position of similar responsibility in any form of association other than a corporation; or

(3) a nonlawyer has the right to direct or control the professional judgment of a lawyer.

BACKGROUND

The Louisiana Supreme Court adopted this rule on January 20, 2004. It became effective on March 1, 2004. The Louisiana Supreme Court amended this rule effective September 30, 2011, to change the cross-referenced rule to 7.2(c)(13). Most recently, the Louisiana Supreme Court amended this rule in 2016 to accommodate the sale of a law practice.

This rule differs from ABA Model Rule of Professional Conduct 5.4 (2002) because it provides that "a lawyer may share court-awarded legal fees with a nonprofit organization that employed, retained or recommended employment of the lawyer in the matter." *Compare* ABA Model Rules of Prof'l Conduct r. 5.4(a)(4) (2002) *with* La. Rules of Prof'l Conduct r. 5.4(a)(4) (2004) ("Reserved"). The ABA included this language in the corresponding Model Rule largely because such fee-sharing arrangements were upheld in Formal Opinion 93-374 of the ABA Standing Committee on Ethics and Professional Responsibility. The ABA adopted this rule because some state ethics committees, while agreeing with the policy underlying the ABA Opinion, found violations of state versions of Model Rule 5.4 because the text of the Rule appeared to prohibit such fee-sharing. In adopting this paragraph, the ABA agreed with its Standing Committee on Ethics that the threat to independent professional judgment was less than in circumstances involving for-profit organizations. *See* ABA Ethics 2000 Commission Revision Notes to Model Rule 5.4 (2002).

For these same reasons, the LSBA recommended adoption of ABA Model Rule 5.4(a)(4). The Louisiana Supreme Court, however, declined to adopt this paragraph. The court's decision should have little effect on local bar association lawyer-referral services because Louisiana Rule of Professional Conduct 7.2 permits Louisiana lawyers to pay the "usual, reasonable and customary charges of a lawyer referral service operated by the Louisiana State Bar Association, any local bar association, or any other not-for-profit organization," provided that the lawyer referral service: (1) refers all persons who request legal services to a participating lawyer; (2) prohibits lawyers from increasing their fee to a client to compensate for the referral service charges; and, (3) fairly and equitably distributes referral cases among the participating lawyers, within their area of practice, by random allotment or by rotation. La. Rules of Prof'l Conduct r. 7.2(b) (2004); *see* also ABA Model Rules of Prof'l Conduct r. 7.2(b)(2) (2002).

COMMENTS TO ABA MODEL RULE 5.4

[1] The provisions of this Rule express traditional limitations on sharing fees. These limitations are to protect the lawyer's professional independence of judgment. Where someone other than the client pays the lawyer's fee or salary, or recommends employment of the lawyer, that arrangement does not modify the lawyer's obligation to the client. As stated in paragraph (c), such arrangements should not interfere with the lawyer's professional judgment.

[2] This Rule also expresses traditional limitations on permitting a third party to direct or regulate the lawyer's professional judgment in rendering legal services to another. See also Rule 1.8(f) (lawyer may accept compensation from a third party as long as there is no interference with the lawyer's independent professional judgment and the client gives informed consent).

ANNOTATIONS

Fee Sharing and Business Associations with Nonlawyers

This rule exists to ensure that the independent judgment a lawyer exercises as a loyal professional is not affected by relationships with nonlawyers. *See, e.g.,* ABA Comm. on Ethics and Prof'l Responsibility, Formal Op. 87-355 (1987). To this end, paragraph (a) prohibits a lawyer from sharing fees with nonlawyers except under limited circumstances. *See* La. Rules of Prof'l Conduct r. 5.4(a) (2004); *see also* Restatement (Third) of the Law Governing Lawyers § 10(3) (2000). For example, this rule prohibits a lawyer from sharing with a paralegal firm 40% of the legal fees earned in a personal injury matter. *See In re Watley,* 802 So. 2d 593 (La. 2001); *see also In re Garrett,* 12 So. 3d 332 (La. 2009); *In re Jackson,* 1 So. 3d 454 (La. 2009);.[119] Likewise, in the matter of *In re Guirard & Pittinger,* 11 So. 3d 1017, 1026 (La. 2009), the Louisiana Supreme Court imposed the sanction of disbarment because nonlawyers:

> were paid by a commission method of compensation based upon the gross attorney's fees of a particular file and not the firm's net profits. The record also indicate[d] that the firm's office manager and at least one secretary of the firm were paid commissions on the firm's gross legal fees collected on various cases.

Paragraph (b) prohibits a lawyer from forming a business association with nonlawyers[120] for purposes of practicing law. *See* La. Rules of Prof'l Conduct r. 5.4(b) (2004); *see also*

---

[119] Note also that a fee-sharing contract made in violation of Rule 5.4 is null and void. *See In re Watley,* 802 So. 2d 593, 594 n.2 (La. 2001); *"We the People" Paralegal Servs., LLC v. Watley,* 766 So. 2d 744 (La. Ct. App. 2d Cir. 2000).

[120] Similarly, paragraph (d) prohibits a lawyer from entering into a for-profit business enterprise related to the practice of law with nonlawyers if any nonlawyer is an owner, director, or officer of the enterprise or otherwise has the right to "direct or control the professional judgment of a lawyer." La. Rules of Prof'l Conduct r. 5.4(d) (2004); *see also* Restatement (Third) of the Law Governing Lawyers § 10(2) (2000); *id.* § 10(1) ("[A] non-

Restatement (Third) of the Law Governing Lawyers § 10(2) (2000). Lawyers are, of course, free to enter into business associations with nonlawyers for purposes other than practicing law. As to what constitutes the "unauthorized practice of law" in Louisiana, *see infra* Annotations to Louisiana Rule 5.5.

Independent Professional Judgment and Nonlawyer Payers and Employers

Paragraph (c) of this rule admonishes a lawyer to ensure that a person who "recommends, employs, or pays" the lawyer does not "direct or regulate the lawyer's professional judgment" in rendering legal services on behalf of a client. La. Rules of Prof'l Conduct r. 5.4(c) (2004). This paragraph, in conjunction with Rule 1.8(f) (which prohibits lawyers from accepting compensation from a nonclient when doing so would interfere with the lawyer's independent judgment), prohibits a lawyer from, for example, relegating to an insurance company adjuster the task of deciding how the lawyer is to defend an insured under a liability insurance policy. Rule 5.4(c) also prevents a lawyer from reducing a criminal defendant's bond at the direction of a bail bonding company without defendant's consent. *See In re Fazande*, 23 So. 3d 247, 252 (La. 2009).

Fee Sharing with Unlicensed Lawyers

Rule 5.4 prohibits the sharing of legal fees with unlicensed lawyers. For example, a lawyer who has resigned from the practice of law is not a "lawyer" eligible to share legal fees under this rule and Rule 1.5(e). *See Phillips v. Rowe*, 499 So. 2d 208 (La. Ct. App. 2d Cir. 1986).

Fee Sharing with Lawyer in Another Jurisdiction Even Though Nonlawyer May Own Part of Firm There

ABA Formal Opinion 464 (Aug. 19, 2013), considered whether a lawyer in, for example, Louisiana, could share legal fees with a lawyer in, for example, the District of Columbia even though the District allows a nonlawyer to own a law firm. The obvious concern is that such fee sharing would, through a roundabout way, be fee sharing with a nonlawyer in violation of Model Rule 5.4(a) (which is substantively identical—at least on this issue— to Louisiana Rule 5.4(a)). The ABA committee, however, was unfazed:

> In summary, a division of a legal fee by a lawyer or law firm in a Model Rules jurisdiction with a lawyer or law firm in another jurisdiction that permits the sharing of legal fees with nonlawyers does not violate Model Rule 5.4(a) simply because a nonlawyer could ultimately receive some portion of the fee under the applicable law of the other jurisdiction.

Id. The committee reached this sensible conclusion because of (1) the low risk of a nonlawyer in one jurisdiction actually influencing the professional judgment of a lawyer in another; (2) the inability of the lawyer in the more restrictive jurisdiction to understand and police the bookkeeping practices of a distant firm; and (3) the impairment of client interests in retaining competent counsel in both jurisdictions. Significantly, however, the

---

lawyer may not be empowered to or actually exercise the right to direct or control the professional activities of a lawyer in the firm.")

committee noted that "[l]awyers must continue to comply with the requirement of Model Rule 5.4(c) to maintain professional independence." *Id.*

It is unclear whether Louisiana would follow suit. Unfortunately, Louisiana has been ultra-restrictive with regard to nonlawyers working with lawyers.

Sharing Office Space with Nonlawyers

Technological improvements have allowed lawyers to practice in nontraditional settings. From homes to beaches to shared office suites, lawyers can get more and more work done without secretaries, dictaphones and law libraries. As to shared office suites, choices in Louisiana are ever increasing (Regus Virtual Office and LaunchPad are just two examples).

What ethical issues arise when lawyers take advantage of shared office space? The Louisiana State Bar Association Rules of Professional Conduct Committee addressed these issues in a public advisory opinion entitled "Sharing Office Space with Non-Lawyers." LSBA Public Op. 08-RPCC-017 (2008). The take away from the opinion is this: a lawyer may share office space with nonlawyers, but must (1) assure confidentiality and professional independence, and (2) avoid assisting in the unauthorized practice of law, avoid improper business transactions with clients and avoid solicitation and paid referrals.

As to confidentiality, a lawyer must avoid disclosure of confidential information at "leak points" such as shared printers, copiers and fax machines. A lawyer should avoid using shared paper file storage areas (they should probably avoid paper file storage). A lawyer should use great care employing, and then must adequately train, any support staff as to handling confidential information. *See* Louisiana Rule 5.3.

As to professional independence, a lawyer who exchanges legal services for "free" office space must avoid providing "free" legal services to clients of the landlord/lessor, and must not allow the landlord/lessor to offer "included" legal services to other tenants. Also, the lawyer must not take client- or case-related instructions from the lawyer's landlord/lessor. This conduct also could be construed as assisting the unauthorized practice of law.

As to solicitation and paid referrals, a lawyer must not offer services in-person to other tenants. Moreover, a lawyer must not "kick back" some portion of fees received from clients referred by the landlord/lessor or co-tenants in the space.

Finally, as to engaging in business transactions with clients, a lawyer must be mindful that there are particular hoops through which the lawyer must jump if the lawyer decides to engage in business transactions with any co-tenants or with the landlord/lessor who are also the lawyer's clients. *See* Louisiana Rule 1.8(a). The term "business transactions" could include loans, service exchanges or partnerships, among other transactions.

Assuming the lawyer is mindful of these issues, office sharing with nonlawyers is permissible.

Disciplinary Sanctions

In cases involving violations of Rule 5.4(a), 5.4(b) and 5.4(d), absent aggravating or mitigating circumstances, the following sanctions are generally appropriate: *disbarment*, when the lawyer knowingly engages in conduct that is a violation of a duty owed to the profession with the intent to obtain a benefit for the lawyer or another, and causes serious or potentially serious injury to a client, the public, or the legal system; *suspension*, when the lawyer knowingly engages in conduct that is a violation of a duty owed to the profession, and causes injury or potential injury to a client, the public, or the legal system; *reprimand*, when the lawyer negligently engages in conduct that is a violation of a duty owed to the profession, and causes injury or potential injury to a client, the public, or the legal system; and, *admonition*, when the lawyer engages in an isolated instance of negligence that is a violation of a duty owed to the profession, and causes little or no actual or potential injury to a client, the public or the legal system. *See* ABA Stds. for Imposing Lawyer Sanctions stds. 7.0-7.4 (1986).

In cases involving violations of 5.4(c), absent aggravating or mitigating circumstances, the following sanctions are generally appropriate: *disbarment*, when the lawyer without informed consent undertakes representation of a client when he knows that doing so presents a conflict of interest, the lawyer intends to benefit himself or another, and the lawyer causes serious or potentially serious injury to the client; *suspension*, when the lawyer knows of a conflict of interest, does not fully consult with the client about it, and the lawyer causes injury or potential injury to the client; *reprimand*, when the lawyer is negligent in determining whether a conflict exists, and the lawyer causes injury or potential injury to the client; and, *admonition*, when the lawyer engages in an isolated instance of negligence in determining whether the representation may present a conflict of interest, and the lawyer's conduct causes little or no actual or potential injury to the client. *See* ABA Stds. for Imposing Lawyer Sanctions std. 4.3 (1992).

RULE 5.5. UNAUTHORIZED PRACTICE OF LAW; MULTIJURISDICTIONAL PRACTICE OF LAW

(a) A lawyer shall not practice law [in a jurisdiction] in violation of the regulation of the legal profession in that jurisdiction, or assist another in doing so.

(b) A lawyer who is not admitted to practice in this jurisdiction shall not:

(1) except as authorized by these Rules or other law, establish an office or other systematic and continuous presence in this jurisdiction for the practice of law; or

(2) hold out to the public or otherwise represent that the lawyer is admitted to practice law in this jurisdiction.

(c) A lawyer admitted in another United States jurisdiction, and not disbarred or suspended from practice in any jurisdiction, may provide legal services on a temporary basis in this jurisdiction that:

(1) are undertaken in association with a lawyer who is admitted to practice in this jurisdiction and who actively participates in the matter;

(2) are in or reasonably related to a pending or potential proceeding before a tribunal in this or another jurisdiction, if the lawyer, or a person the lawyer is assisting, is authorized by law or order to appear in such proceeding or reasonably expects to be so authorized;

(3) are in or reasonably related to a pending or potential arbitration, mediation, or other alternative dispute resolution proceeding in this or another jurisdiction, if the services arise out of or are reasonably related to the lawyer's practice in a jurisdiction in which the lawyer is admitted to practice and are not services for which the forum requires pro hac vice admission; or

(4) are not within paragraphs (c)(2) or (c)(3) and arise out of or are reasonably related to the lawyer's practice in a jurisdiction in which the lawyer is admitted to practice.

(d) A lawyer admitted in another United States jurisdiction, and not disbarred or suspended from practice in any jurisdiction, may provide legal services in this jurisdiction that:

>   (1) are provided to the lawyer's employer or its organizational affiliates and are not services for which the forum requires pro hac vice admission and that are provided by an attorney who has received a limited license to practice law pursuant to La. S. Ct. Rule XVII, § 14; or

(2) are services that the lawyer is authorized to provide by federal law or other law of this jurisdiction.

(e)(1) A lawyer shall not:

>   (i) employ, contract with as a consultant, engage as an independent contractor, or otherwise join in any other capacity, in connection with the practice of law, any person the attorney knows or reasonably should know is a disbarred attorney, during the period of disbarment, or any person the attorney knows or reasonably should know is an attorney who has permanently resigned from the practice of law in lieu of discipline; or

>   (ii) employ, contract with as a consultant, engage as an independent contractor, or otherwise join in any other capacity, in connection with the practice of law, any person the attorney knows or reasonably should know is a suspended attorney, or an attorney who has been transferred to disability inactive status, during the period of suspension or transfer, unless first preceded by the submission of a fully executed employment registration statement to the Office of Disciplinary Counsel, on a registration form provided by the Louisiana Attorney Disciplinary Board, and approved by the Louisiana Supreme Court.

(e)(2) The registration form provided for in Section (e)(1) shall include:

>   (i) the identity and bar roll number of the suspended or transferred attorney sought to be hired;

(ii) the identity and bar roll number of the attorney having direct supervisory responsibility over the suspended attorney, or the attorney transferred to disability inactive status, throughout the duration of employment or association;

(iii) a list of all duties and activities to be assigned to the suspended attorney, or the attorney transferred to disability inactive status, during the period of employment or association;

(iv) the terms of employment of the suspended attorney, or the attorney transferred to disability inactive status, including method of compensation;

(v) a statement by the employing attorney that includes a consent to random compliance audits, to be conducted by the Office of Disciplinary Counsel, at any time during the employment or association of the suspended attorney or the attorney transferred to disability inactive status; and

(vi) a statement by the employing attorney certifying that the order giving rise to the suspension or transfer of the proposed employee has been provided for review and consideration in advance of employment by the suspended attorney, or the attorney transferred to disability inactive status.

(e)(3) For purposes of this Rule, the practice of law shall include the following activities:

(i) holding oneself out as an attorney or lawyer authorized to practice law;

(ii) rendering legal consultation or advice to a client;

(iii) appearing on behalf of a client in any hearing or proceeding, or before any judicial officer, arbitrator, mediator, court, public agency, referee, magistrate, commissioner, hearing officer, or governmental body operating in an adjudicative capacity, including submission of pleadings, except as may otherwise be permitted by law;

(iv) appearing as a representative of the client at a deposition or other discovery matter;

(v) negotiating or transacting any matter for or on behalf of a client with third parties;

(vi) otherwise engaging in activities defined by law or Supreme Court decision as constituting the practice of law.

(e)(4) In addition, a suspended lawyer, or a lawyer transferred to disability inactive status, shall not receive, disburse or otherwise handle client funds.

(e)(5) Upon termination of the suspended attorney, or the attorney transferred to disability inactive status, the employing attorney having direct supervisory authority shall promptly serve upon the Office of Disciplinary Counsel written notice of the termination.

BACKGROUND

The Louisiana Supreme Court promulgated a major revision to this rule which became effective on April 1, 2005. This rule contains significant differences from ABA Model Rule 5.5, as discussed below.

Multijurisdictional Practice Provisions

In August 2002, the ABA adopted the sweeping changes to Model Rule 5.5 proposed by its Commission on Multijurisdictional Practice. Among other changes, the ABA in 2002 amended the title of Model Rule 5.5 to "Unauthorized Practice of Law; Multijurisdictional Practice of Law."

The ABA adopted Model Rule 5.5(a) to provide that a lawyer may not practice law in a jurisdiction, or assist another in doing so, in violation of the regulations of the legal profession in that jurisdiction.

The ABA adopted Model Rule 5.5(b) to prohibit a lawyer from establishing an office or other systematic and continuous presence in a jurisdiction, unless permitted to do so by law, or by another provision of Rule 5.5. It also amended 5.5(b) to prohibit a lawyer from representing that he is admitted to practice law in a jurisdiction in which the lawyer is not admitted.

The ABA adopted Model Rule 5.5(c) to permit a lawyer in good standing to practice law on a temporary basis in another jurisdiction when the lawyer's services are performed in active association with a lawyer admitted to practice law in the jurisdiction, when his services are ancillary to pending or prospective litigation or administrative agency proceedings in a state where the lawyer is admitted or expects to be admitted pro hac vice or is otherwise authorized to appear, when his services are performed in an alternative dispute resolution ("ADR") setting, such as arbitration or mediation, and when his services involve non-litigation work that arise out of or are reasonably related to the lawyer's practice in a jurisdiction in which the lawyer is admitted to practice.

Finally, it adopted Rule 5.5(d) to identify multijurisdictional practice standards relating to (i) legal services by a lawyer who is an employee of a client, and (ii) legal services that the lawyer is authorized by federal or other law or rule to render in a jurisdiction in which the lawyer is not licensed to practice law. *See* ABA Multijurisdictional Practice Committee, Client Representation in the 21st Century, Final Report (adopted August 12, 2002); *see also* ABA Ethics 20/20 Revisions in 2012 (tweaking language to clarify that "legal services" may be provided in a jurisdiction either "through an office or other systematic and continuous presence").

The Louisiana Supreme Court did not adopt the revised version of Model Rule 5.5 in January 2004 because it chose to await a final report and recommendations from the LSBA Multijurisdictional Practice Committee. That committee concluded its work later in 2004 and recommended the verbatim adoption of ABA Model Rule 5.5. The court concurred, and effective April 1, 2005, the multijurisdictional practice provisions of this Rule are virtually identical to the ABA counterparts.[121] Note that unlike the model rule, however, the Louisiana Rule requires an in-house lawyer seeking to practice in this state to obtain "a limited license to practice law" pursuant to Louisiana Supreme Court Rule XVII, § 14. *See* La. Rules of Prof'l Conduct r. 5.5(d)(1) (2005). For the text of this in-house lawyer admission rule, *see infra* on page 302.

Dealing with Disbarred and Suspended Lawyers

Paragraph (e) of this rule is not found in the Model Rules. The Louisiana Supreme Court adopted the substance of these provisions in 2002 to preclude disbarred and suspended lawyers from skirting court-imposed disciplinary sanctions by participating in the practice of law in a purportedly paraprofessional capacity.

ABA MODEL RULE 5.5

(a) A lawyer shall not practice law in a jurisdiction in violation of the regulation of the legal profession in that jurisdiction, or assist another in doing so.

(b) A lawyer who is not admitted to practice in this jurisdiction shall not:

> (1) except as authorized by these Rules or other law, establish an office or other systematic and continuous presence in this jurisdiction for the practice of law; or

> (2) hold out to the public or otherwise represent that the lawyer is admitted to practice law in this jurisdiction.

(c) A lawyer admitted in another United States jurisdiction, and not disbarred or suspended from practice in any jurisdiction, may provide legal services on a temporary basis in this jurisdiction that:

---

[121] Note that there appears to be a typographical error in Louisiana Rule 5.5(a) in that the Louisiana Rule deletes the ABA language "in a jurisdiction" that is bracketed in the black-letter text above.

(1) are undertaken in association with a lawyer who is admitted to practice in this jurisdiction and who actively participates in the matter;

(2) are in or reasonably related to a pending or potential proceeding before a tribunal in this or another jurisdiction, if the lawyer, or a person the lawyer is assisting, is authorized by law or order to appear in such proceeding or reasonably expects to be so authorized;

(3) are in or reasonably related to a pending or potential arbitration, mediation, or other alternative dispute resolution proceeding in this or another jurisdiction, if the services arise out of or are reasonably related to the lawyer's practice in a jurisdiction in which the lawyer is admitted to practice and are not services for which the forum requires pro hac vice admission; or

(4) are not within paragraphs (c)(2) or (c)(3) and arise out of or are reasonably related to the lawyer's practice in a jurisdiction in which the lawyer is admitted to practice.

(d) A lawyer admitted in another United States jurisdiction or in a foreign jurisdiction, and not disbarred or suspended from practice in any jurisdiction, or the equivalent thereof, or a person otherwise lawfully practicing as an in-house counsel under the laws of a foreign jurisdiction may provide legal services through an office or other systematic and continuous presence in this jurisdiction that:

(1) are provided to the lawyer's employer or its organizational affiliates, are not services for which the forum requires pro hac vice admission; and when performed by a foreign lawyer and requires advice on the law of this or another jurisdiction or of the United States, such advice shall be based upon the advice of a lawyer who is duly licensed and authorized by the jurisdiction to provide such advice; or

(2) are services that the lawyer is authorized by federal or other law or rule to provide in this jurisdiction.

(e) For purposes of paragraph (d):

(1) the foreign lawyer must be a member in good standing of a recognized legal profession in a foreign jurisdiction, the members of which are admitted to practice as lawyers or counselors at law or the equivalent, and are subject to effective regulation and discipline by a duly constituted professional body or a public authority; or

(2) the person otherwise lawfully practicing as an in-house counsel under the laws of a foreign jurisdiction must be authorized to practice under this rule by, in the exercise of its discretion, [the highest court of this jurisdiction].

COMMENTS TO ABA MODEL RULE 5.5

[1] A lawyer may practice law only in a jurisdiction in which the lawyer is authorized to practice. A lawyer may be admitted to practice law in a jurisdiction on a regular basis or may be authorized by court rule or order or by law to practice for a limited purpose or on a

restricted basis. Paragraph (a) applies to unauthorized practice of law by a lawyer, whether through the lawyer's direct action or by the lawyer assisting another person. For example, a lawyer may not assist a person in practicing law in violation of the rules governing professional conduct in that person's jurisdiction.

[2] The definition of the practice of law is established by law and varies from one jurisdiction to another. Whatever the definition, limiting the practice of law to members of the bar protects the public against rendition of legal services by unqualified persons. This Rule does not prohibit a lawyer from employing the services of paraprofessionals and delegating functions to them, so long as the lawyer supervises the delegated work and retains responsibility for their work. See Rule 5.3.

[3] A lawyer may provide professional advice and instruction to nonlawyers whose employment requires knowledge of the law; for example, claims adjusters, employees of financial or commercial institutions, social workers, accountants and persons employed in government agencies. Lawyers also may assist independent nonlawyers, such as paraprofessionals, who are authorized by the law of a jurisdiction to provide particular law-related services. In addition, a lawyer may counsel nonlawyers who wish to proceed pro se.

[4] Other than as authorized by law or this Rule, a lawyer who is not admitted to practice generally in this jurisdiction violates paragraph (b)(1) if the lawyer establishes an office or other systematic and continuous presence in this jurisdiction for the practice of law. Presence may be systematic and continuous even if the lawyer is not physically present here. Such a lawyer must not hold out to the public or otherwise represent that the lawyer is admitted to practice law in this jurisdiction. See also Rules 7.1(a) and 7.5(b).

[5] There are occasions in which a lawyer admitted to practice in another United States jurisdiction, and not disbarred or suspended from practice in any jurisdiction, may provide legal services on a temporary basis in this jurisdiction under circumstances that do not create an unreasonable risk to the interests of their clients, the public or the courts. Paragraph (c) identifies four such circumstances. The fact that conduct is not so identified does not imply that the conduct is or is not authorized. With the exception of paragraphs (d)(1) and (d)(2), this Rule does not authorize a U.S. or foreign lawyer to establish an office or other systematic and continuous presence in this jurisdiction without being admitted to practice generally here.

[6] There is no single test to determine whether a lawyer's services are provided on a "temporary basis" in this jurisdiction, and may therefore be permissible under paragraph (c). Services may be "temporary" even though the lawyer provides services in this jurisdiction on a recurring basis, or for an extended period of time, as when the lawyer is representing a client in a single lengthy negotiation or litigation.

[7] Paragraphs (c) and (d) apply to lawyers who are admitted to practice law in any United States jurisdiction, which includes the District of Columbia and any state, territory or commonwealth of the United States. Paragraph (d) also applies to lawyers admitted in a foreign jurisdiction. The word "admitted" in paragraph (c), (d) and (e) contemplates that

the lawyer is authorized to practice in the jurisdiction in which the lawyer is admitted and excludes a lawyer who while technically admitted is not authorized to practice, because, for example, the lawyer is on inactive status.

[8] Paragraph (c)(1) recognizes that the interests of clients and the public are protected if a lawyer admitted only in another jurisdiction associates with a lawyer licensed to practice in this jurisdiction. For this paragraph to apply, however, the lawyer admitted to practice in this jurisdiction must actively participate in and share responsibility for the representation of the client.

[9] Lawyers not admitted to practice generally in a jurisdiction may be authorized by law or order of a tribunal or an administrative agency to appear before the tribunal or agency. This authority may be granted pursuant to formal rules governing admission pro hac vice or pursuant to informal practice of the tribunal or agency. Under paragraph (c)(2), a lawyer does not violate this Rule when the lawyer appears before a tribunal or agency pursuant to such authority. To the extent that a court rule or other law of this jurisdiction requires a lawyer who is not admitted to practice in this jurisdiction to obtain admission pro hac vice before appearing before a tribunal or administrative agency, this Rule requires the lawyer to obtain that authority.

[10] Paragraph (c)(2) also provides that a lawyer rendering services in this jurisdiction on a temporary basis does not violate this Rule when the lawyer engages in conduct in anticipation of a proceeding or hearing in a jurisdiction in which the lawyer is authorized to practice law or in which the lawyer reasonably expects to be admitted pro hac vice. Examples of such conduct include meetings with the client, interviews of potential witnesses, and the review of documents. Similarly, a lawyer admitted only in another jurisdiction may engage in conduct temporarily in this jurisdiction in connection with pending litigation in another jurisdiction in which the lawyer is or reasonably expects to be authorized to appear, including taking depositions in this jurisdiction.

[11] When a lawyer has been or reasonably expects to be admitted to appear before a court or administrative agency, paragraph (c)(2) also permits conduct by lawyers who are associated with that lawyer in the matter, but who do not expect to appear before the court or administrative agency. For example, subordinate lawyers may conduct research, review documents, and attend meetings with witnesses in support of the lawyer responsible for the litigation.

[12] Paragraph (c)(3) permits a lawyer admitted to practice law in another jurisdiction to perform services on a temporary basis in this jurisdiction if those services are in or reasonably related to a pending or potential arbitration, mediation, or other alternative dispute resolution proceeding in this or another jurisdiction, if the services arise out of or are reasonably related to the lawyer's practice in a jurisdiction in which the lawyer is admitted to practice. The lawyer, however, must obtain admission pro hac vice in the case of a court-annexed arbitration or mediation or otherwise if court rules or law so require.

[13] Paragraph (c)(4) permits a lawyer admitted in another jurisdiction to provide certain legal services on a temporary basis in this jurisdiction that arise out of or are reasonably

related to the lawyer's practice in a jurisdiction in which the lawyer is admitted but are not within paragraphs (c)(2) or (c)(3). These services include both legal services and services that nonlawyers may perform but that are considered the practice of law when performed by lawyers.

[14] Paragraphs (c)(3) and (c)(4) require that the services arise out of or be reasonably related to the lawyer's practice in a jurisdiction in which the lawyer is admitted. A variety of factors evidence such a relationship. The lawyer's client may have been previously represented by the lawyer, or may be resident in or have substantial contacts with the jurisdiction in which the lawyer is admitted. The matter, although involving other jurisdictions, may have a significant connection with that jurisdiction. In other cases, significant aspects of the lawyer's work might be conducted in that jurisdiction or a significant aspect of the matter may involve the law of that jurisdiction. The necessary relationship might arise when the client's activities or the legal issues involve multiple jurisdictions, such as when the officers of a multinational corporation survey potential business sites and seek the services of their lawyer in assessing the relative merits of each. In addition, the services may draw on the lawyer's recognized expertise developed through the regular practice of law on behalf of clients in matters involving a particular body of federal, nationally-uniform, foreign, or international law. Lawyers desiring to provide pro bono legal services on a temporary basis in a jurisdiction that has been affected by a major disaster, but in which they are not otherwise authorized to practice law, as well as lawyers from the affected jurisdiction who seek to practice law temporarily in another jurisdiction, but in which they are not otherwise authorized to practice law, should consult the [*Model Court Rule on Provision of Legal Services Following Determination of Major Disaster*].

[15] Paragraph (d) identifies two circumstances in which a lawyer who is admitted to practice in another United States or a foreign jurisdiction, and is not disbarred or suspended from practice in any jurisdiction, or the equivalent thereof, may establish an office or other systematic and continuous presence in this jurisdiction for the practice of law. Pursuant to paragraph (c) of this Rule, a lawyer admitted in any U.S. jurisdiction may also provide legal services in this jurisdiction on a temporary basis. *See also Model Rule on Temporary Practice by Foreign Lawyers.* Except as provided in paragraphs (d)(1) and (d)(2), a lawyer who is admitted to practice law in another United States or foreign jurisdiction and who establishes an office or other systematic or continuous presence in this jurisdiction must become admitted to practice law generally in this jurisdiction.

[16] Paragraph (d)(1) applies to a U.S. or foreign lawyer who is employed by a client to provide legal services to the client or its organizational affiliates, i.e., entities that control, are controlled by, or are under common control with the employer. This paragraph does not authorize the provision of personal legal services to the employer's officers or employees. The paragraph applies to in-house corporate lawyers, government lawyers and others who are employed to render legal services to the employer. The lawyer's ability to represent the employer outside the jurisdiction in which the lawyer is licensed generally serves the interests of the employer and does not create an unreasonable risk to the client and others because the employer is well situated to assess the lawyer's qualifications and

the quality of the lawyer's work. To further decrease any risk to the client, when advising on the domestic law of a United States jurisdiction or on the law of the United States, the foreign lawyer authorized to practice under paragraph (d)(1) of this Rule needs to base that advice on the advice of a lawyer licensed and authorized by the jurisdiction to provide it.

[17] If an employed lawyer establishes an office or other systematic presence in this jurisdiction for the purpose of rendering legal services to the employer, the lawyer may be subject to registration or other requirements, including assessments for client protection funds and mandatory continuing legal education. See Model Rule for Registration of In-House Counsel.

[18] Paragraph (d)(2) recognizes that a U.S. or foreign lawyer may provide legal services in a jurisdiction in which the lawyer is not licensed when authorized to do so by federal or other law, which includes statute, court rule, executive regulation or judicial precedent. See, e.g., Model Rule on Practice Pending Admission.

[19] A lawyer who practices law in this jurisdiction pursuant to paragraphs (c) or (d) or otherwise is subject to the disciplinary authority of this jurisdiction. *See* Rule 8.5(a).

[20] In some circumstances, a lawyer who practices law in this jurisdiction pursuant to paragraphs (c) or (d) may have to inform the client that the lawyer is not licensed to practice law in this jurisdiction. For example, that may be required when the representation occurs primarily in this jurisdiction and requires knowledge of the law of this jurisdiction. *See* Rule 1.4(b).

[21] Paragraphs (c) and (d) do not authorize communications advertising legal services in this jurisdiction by lawyers who are admitted to practice in other jurisdictions. Whether and how lawyers may communicate the availability of their services in this jurisdiction is governed by Rules 7.1 to 7.5.

ANNOTATIONS
Generally
A Louisiana lawyer must not practice in a jurisdiction where doing so would violate that jurisdiction's statutes and rules governing the practice of law. *See* La. Rules of Prof'l Conduct r. 5.5(a) (2004); *see also id.* r. 8.5 ("A lawyer admitted to practice in this jurisdiction is subject to the disciplinary authority of this jurisdiction" although engaged in practice elsewhere.). Thus, for example, a Louisiana lawyer is subject to discipline in this state if he engages in the unauthorized practice of law in Texas.[122]

---

[122] The Louisiana Supreme Court in *In re Cortigene*, 144 So. 3d 915, 920 (La. 2014), addressed the *res nova* question of whether it could discipline a lawyer who is not admitted to the Louisiana bar. The court determined that its "plenary power to define and regulate the practice of law . . . is broad enough to encompass persons not admitted to the bar who attempt to practice law in this state." *Id.* After deciding that the appropriate sanction for a Louisiana lawyer would have been a three-year suspension, the court enjoined the out-of-state lawyer "from seeking full admission to the Louisiana bar or seeking admission to

Defining "The Practice of Law"

What constitutes the "practice of law" is often a difficult question to answer. For the ABA's attempt to address this issue, *see* ABA Model Definition of "The Practice of Law." In essence, the ABA concluded that "the practice of law is the application of legal principles and judgment to the circumstances or objectives of another person or entity." *Id.*

Disbarred and Suspended Lawyers

This rule prohibits a disbarred or suspended Louisiana lawyer from practicing law while under an order of disbarment or suspension. *See, e.g., In re Nalls*, 145 So. 3d 1011, 1018 (La. 2014) (disbarring lawyer for continuing to practice law after order of suspension came into effect); *In re Jones*, 99 So. 3d 20, 24 (La. 2012); *In re Turnage*, 104 So. 3d 397, 400 (La. 2012) (disbarring Louisiana lawyer permanently for practicing law in Mississippi after previous disbarment); *In re Jefferson*, 789 So. 2d 569, 572 (La. 2001); *In re Jones*, 747 So. 2d 1081, 1084-85 (La. 1999); *In re Withers*, 747 So. 2d 514, 516 (La. 1999); *In re Moeller*, 111 So. 3d 325, 328-29 (La. 2013); *In re Quaid*, 740 So. 2d 104, 107 (La. 1999); *In re Lindsay*, 976 So. 2d 1261, 1264 (La. 2008); *In re Matthews*, 30 So. 3d 737, 740 (La. 2010); *In re Petal*, 30 So. 3d 728 (La. 2010); *In re Vaaston*, 2017-0702 (La. 09/06/17); *In re Bates*, 33 So. 3d 162, 175 (La. 2010); *In re Harper*, 205 So. 3d 901, 905 (La. 2016); *In re O'Dwyer*, 221 So. 3d 1, 19 (La. 2017); *In re Hebert*, 214 So. 3d 836, 840-41 (La. 2017); *In re Gilbert*, NO. 2017–B–0524, 2017 WL 4227487, at **7 (La. Sept. 22, 2017); *In re Purser*, NO. 2017–B–1170, 2017 WL 4479619, at **17 (La. Oct. 9, 2017). Moreover, this rule strictly regulates the extent to which, and conditions under which, licensed lawyers can employ suspended and disbarred lawyers. *See In re Sharp*, 106 So. 3d 105 (La. 2013). The Louisiana Supreme Court has also used Rule 5.5 to enforce compliance with a lawyer's obligation to pay bar dues, disciplinary assessments and to comply with MCLE requirements. *See, e.g., In re Thomas*, 115 So. 3d 466, 472 (La. 2013) (disciplining lawyer for unauthorized practice of law while ineligible due to failure to pay bar dues and disciplinary assessment); *In re Toaston*, 225 So. 3d 1066, 1085 (La. 2017); *In re Johnson*, 217 So. 3d 323, 326 (La. 2017).

Assisting Nonlawyers in the Unauthorized Practice of Law

In addition, this rule prohibits a lawyer from assisting a person who is not a licensed lawyer in the unauthorized practice of law. La. Rules of Prof'l Conduct r. 5.5(e) (2004); *see also* Restatement (Third) of the Law Governing Lawyers § 4 (2000); *Sharp*, 106 So. 3d at 105 (disciplining lawyer for employing disbarred lawyer as paralegal); *In re Guirard & Pittinger*, 11 So. 3d 1017, 1030 (La. 2009) (disbarment imposed because "[r]espondents delegated the handling of their clients' cases to their nonlawyer staff."); *In re Goff*, 837 So. 2d 1201, 1202 (La. 2003) (disciplining lawyer for assisting "paralegals with their own clientele" in the unauthorized practice of law); *In re Brown*, 813 So. 2d 325, 328-29 (La. 2002) (lawyer disciplined for assisting "paralegal" functioning like a lawyer in settling cases). Although a lawyer may be assisted by nonlawyers in the practice of law, a lawyer may not delegate to

practice in Louisiana on any temporary or limited basis" for a period of three years. *Id.* at 921.

paralegals or legal secretaries tasks that call for the exercise of professional judgment by a licensed lawyer. *See La. State Bar Ass'n v. Edwins*, 540 So. 2d 294, 300 (La. 1989). Unfortunately, it is notoriously difficult to determine when the performance of a particular task by a nonlawyer constitutes the unauthorized "practice of law." *See In re Elkins*, 700 So. 2d 211, 212 (La. 1997) (concluding that it was permissible for a suspended lawyer acting as a paralegal to contact the district attorney's office for the purpose of gathering information for his employer)); *see also In re Unauthorized Practice of Law Rules Proposed by S.C. Bar*, 422 S.E.2d 123, 124 (S.C. 1992).

Disciplinary Sanctions

Absent aggravating or mitigating circumstances, the following sanctions are generally appropriate in cases involving violations of Rule 5.5: *disbarment*, when the lawyer knowingly engages in conduct that is a violation of a duty owed to the profession with the intent to obtain a benefit for the lawyer or another, and causes serious or potentially serious injury to a client, the public, or the legal system; *suspension*, when the lawyer knowingly engages in conduct that is a violation of a duty owed to the profession, and causes injury or potential injury to a client, the public, or the legal system; *reprimand*, when the lawyer negligently engages in conduct that is a violation of a duty owed to the profession, and causes injury or potential injury to a client, the public, or the legal system; and, *admonition*, when the lawyer engages in an isolated instance of negligence that is a violation of a duty owed to the profession, and causes little or no actual or potential injury to a client, the public or the legal system. *See* ABA Stds. for Imposing Lawyer Sanctions stds. 7.0-7.4 (1992). The Louisiana Supreme Court has held that its "prior decisions in *Sledge, Brown*, and *Edwins* establish that the baseline sanction for the facilitation of the unauthorized practice of law by a nonlawyer is disbarment." *See In re Guirard & Pittinger*, 11 So. 3d 1017, 1030 (La. 2009); *see also In re Moeller*, 111 So. 3d 325, 328-29 (La. 2013) (suspending lawyer for repeatedly practicing law while ineligible and noting typical sanctions in prior Louisiana case law for the unauthorized practice of law).

RELATED AUTHORITIES
Louisiana Revised Statutes § 37:212 ("Practice of Law" Defined)

A. The practice of law means and includes:

(1) In a representative capacity, the appearance as an advocate, or the drawing of papers, pleadings or documents, or the performance of any act in connection with pending or prospective proceedings before any court of record in this state; or

(2) For a consideration, reward, or pecuniary benefit, present or anticipated, direct or indirect;

(a) The advising or counseling of another as to secular law;

(b) In behalf of another, the drawing or procuring, or the assisting in the drawing or procuring of a paper, document, or instrument affecting or relating to secular rights;

(c) The doing of any act, in behalf of another, tending to obtain or secure for the other the prevention or the redress of a wrong or the enforcement or establishment of a right; or

(d) Certifying or giving opinions, or rendering a title opinion as a basis of any title insurance report or title insurance policy as provided in R.S. 22:512(17), as it relates to title to immovable property or any interest therein or as to the rank or priority or validity of a lien, privilege or mortgage as well as the preparation of acts of sale, mortgages, credit sales or any acts or other documents passing titles to or encumbering immovable property.

B. Nothing in this Section prohibits any person from attending to and caring for his own business, claims, or demands; or from preparing abstracts of title; or from insuring titles to property, movable or immovable, or an interest therein, or a privilege and encumbrance thereon, but every title insurance contract relating to immovable property must be based upon the certification or opinion of a licensed Louisiana attorney authorized to engage in the practice of law. Nothing in this Section prohibits any person from performing, as a notary public, any act necessary or incidental to the exercise of the powers and functions of the office of notary public, as those powers are delineated in Louisiana Revised Statutes of 1950, Title 35, Section 1, et seq.

C. Nothing in this Section shall prohibit any partnership, corporation, or other legal entity from asserting or defending any claim, not exceeding five thousand dollars, on its own behalf in the courts of limited jurisdiction or on its own behalf through a duly authorized partner, shareholder, officer, employee, or duly authorized agent or representative. No partnership, corporation, or other entity may assert any claim on behalf of another entity or any claim assigned to it.

D. Nothing in Article V, Section 24, of the Constitution of Louisiana or this Section shall prohibit justices or judges from performing all acts necessary or incumbent to the authorized exercise of duties as judge advocates or legal officers.

Louisiana Revised Statutes § 37:213 (Persons, professional associations, professional corporations, and limited liability companies entitled to practice law; penalty for unlawful practice)

A. No natural person, who has not first been duly and regularly licensed and admitted to practice law by the supreme court of this state, no corporation or voluntary association except a professional law corporation organized pursuant to Chapter 8 of Title 12 of the Revised Statutes, and no partnership or limited liability company except one formed for the practice of law and composed of such natural persons, corporations, voluntary associations, or limited liability companies, all of whom are duly and regularly licensed and admitted to the practice of law, shall:

(1) Practice law.

(2) Furnish attorneys or counsel or an attorney and counsel to render legal services.

(3) Hold himself or itself out to the public as being entitled to practice law.

(4) Render or furnish legal services or advice.

(5) Assume to be an attorney at law or counselor at law.

(6) Assume, use, or advertise the title of lawyer, attorney, counselor, advocate or equivalent terms in any language, or any phrase containing any of these titles, in such manner as to convey the impression that he is a practitioner of law.

(7) In any manner advertise that he, either alone or together with any other person, has, owns, conducts, or maintains an office of any kind for the practice of law.

B. This Section does not prevent any corporation or voluntary association formed for benevolent or charitable purposes and recognized by law, from furnishing an attorney at law to give free assistance to persons without means.

C. Any natural person who violates any provision of this Section shall be fined not more than one thousand dollars or imprisoned for not more than two years, or both.

D. Any partnership, corporation or voluntary association which violates this Section shall be fined not more than five thousand dollars. Every officer, trustee, director, agent, or employee of a corporation or voluntary association who, directly or indirectly, engages in any act violating any provision of this Section or assists the corporation or voluntary association in the performance of any such violation is subject to the penalties prescribed in this Section for violations by a natural person.

Louisiana Revised Statutes § 37:214 (Visiting Attorneys of Other States; Reciprocity)

Except as provided in this Section, no person licensed or qualified to practice as an attorney at law or as an attorney and counselor at law in any other state and temporarily present in this state shall practice law in this state, unless he has been first duly licensed to practice law by the supreme court of this state or unless he acts in association with some attorney duly licensed to practice law by the supreme court of this state.

Nothing in this Chapter prevents the practice of law in this state by a visiting attorney from a state which, either by statute or by some rule of practice accorded specific recognition by the highest court of that state, has adopted a rule of reciprocity that permits an attorney duly licensed and qualified to practice law in this state to appear alone as an attorney in all courts of record in the other state, without being required to be admitted to practice in such other state, and without being required to associate with himself some attorney admitted to practice in the other state.

Whoever violates any provision of this Section shall be fined not more than one thousand dollars or imprisoned for not more than two years, or both.

Louisiana Revised Statutes § 37:215 (Procedure by Visiting Attorney for Recognition in Louisiana Courts Under Reciprocity Rule)

Whenever any visiting attorney desires to exercise the privilege of appearing alone as counsel of record in any case in any court of record in this state, under the provisions of the second paragraph of R.S. 37:214, he shall, before filing the first pleading or other appearance on behalf of his client in the cause, produce evidence satisfactory to the court before which he wishes to appear, or to the presiding judge if there be two or more judges of the court, to the effect that the state in which he is then licensed and qualified to practice law has in force a statute or rule of practice of the character specified in R.S. 37:214. Upon the judge being satisfied of this, he shall enter an order authorizing the appearance of the visiting attorney before his court in the case. This order shall specifically refer to the appropriate statutory provision or to the requisite judicial recognition of the appropriate rule of practice of the other state in question.

Louisiana Revised Statutes § 37:216 (Filing of Pleadings by Visiting Attorney Under Reciprocity Rule

No clerk of any court of record in this state shall file any pleading, brief, or other appearance signed on behalf of any party or litigant solely by a visiting attorney, unless it or some prior pleading, brief, or appearance filed in the cause by the visiting attorney is accompanied by an order of court of the character specified in R.S. 37:215. If any such pleading, brief, or other appearance is inadvertently filed without a compliance with the provisions of R.S. 37:215, it may be ordered stricken from the record ex parte on motion of any party at interest, or by the court of its own motion.

Supreme Court Rule XVII § 14: Limited Admission for In-House Counsel (Effective April 1, 2005)

(A) A lawyer admitted and authorized to practice law in another state or territory of the United States may receive a limited license to practice law in this state when the lawyer is employed in Louisiana as a lawyer exclusively for: a corporation, its subsidiaries or affiliates; an association; and/or a business which consists of activities other than the practice of law or the provision of legal services, if the lawyer:

> (1) Has filed an application for a limited license pursuant to this Rule with the Committee on Bar Admissions of the Supreme Court of Louisiana containing the following:

>> (a) A written application in the form prescribed by the Committee;

>> (b) A sworn statement that either:

>>> (i) no complaints with any disciplinary authority are pending in any jurisdiction and that no charges of professional misconduct are pending against the applicant in any jurisdiction; or

>>> (ii) if any such complaints or charges are pending, full details of the complaints or charges, and the current status of same;

>> (c) Information which indicates that the applicant meets the requirements of subparts (A), (B), (C), and (D) of Rule XVII, Section 3;

>> (d) An affidavit from an officer, director or general counsel of the applicant's employer in this state attesting the fact that the applicant is employed as a lawyer exclusively for the employer, that the applicant is an

individual of good moral character, and that the nature of the employment conforms to the requirements of this Rule;

(e) The National Conference of Bar Examiners Character Report.

(i) If the applicant has completed an NCBE character report within three years of the application for limited licensure, the prior report may be submitted in lieu of a new report.

(ii) In the event a prior NCBE report is submitted, the applicant shall also append to the prior report the NCBE Supplemental Character Report.

(f) The non-refundable prescribed application fee set by the Supreme Court of Louisiana;

(2) Otherwise meets the character and fitness requirements of this Rule and the Committee on Bar Admissions of the Supreme Court of Louisiana; and

(3) Receives the recommendation and approval of the Committee on Bar Admissions of the Supreme Court of Louisiana.

(B) The application, affidavits, and other materials, including the report of character and fitness, shall be reviewed by the Committee on Bar Admissions of the Supreme Court of Louisiana. The Louisiana Supreme Court, in its discretion, may issue the limited license to practice law in the State of Louisiana based on the recommendations and approval of the Committee on Bar Admissions.

(C) Licensure pursuant to the Rule is not a matter of right and shall be granted only in those cases where the public interest, considering the character, background and employment of the applicant, is furthered by issuing a license. In the event the Committee does not recommend the limited licensure of an applicant, the applicant may then appeal in accordance with Rule XVII, Section 9.

(D) The license issued pursuant to this Rule only authorizes the lawyer to practice exclusively for the employer filing the affidavit required by subpart (A)(1)(d) of this rule. Nothing in this rule or in this subpart shall be deemed to allow court appearances by any lawyer who has been issued a limited license pursuant to this rule. Any such appearance, or contemplated appearance, by a lawyer who has been issued a limited license pursuant to this rule shall be governed by rules and procedures applicable to *pro hac vice* admission.

(E) A limited license issued pursuant to this Rule shall be valid for four years from the date of issuance. The license is automatically terminated if the lawyer is admitted to the practice of law pursuant to any other provisions of Rule XVII. The license is automatically suspended if the lawyer's employment by the employer filing the affidavit required by subpart (A)(1)(d) of this rule is terminated. If a lawyer's employment is terminated but the lawyer is immediately thereafter employed by an employer filing the affidavit required by subpart (A)(1)(d) of this rule, the limited license shall be reinstated for the remainder of the period of four years from the date the license originally was issued.

(F) A limited license issued pursuant to this Rule may be renewed for a successive four year period by filing the written application required by the Committee. The application shall be filed at least ninety days prior to the expiration of the current license. For good cause shown, the Court may permit the late filing of an application. The application shall include at least the following:

(1) The licensee's sworn statement that no complaints with any disciplinary authority are pending and that no charges of professional misconduct are pending against the licensee in any jurisdiction. Alternatively, if any such complaints or charges are pending or any disciplinary action has been taken against the licensee in any jurisdiction, full details of the complaint and charges, the current status of the complaint or charges, and the disposition thereof, if not currently pending, shall be set forth;

(2) An affidavit from an officer, director or general counsel of the licensee's employer in this state attesting the fact that the licensee remains employed as a lawyer exclusively for the employer and that the nature of the employment continues to conform to the requirements of this Rule;

(3) An affidavit from the licensee setting forth any changes in information from that provided in his or her immediately preceding application pursuant to this Rule or attesting that there are no such changes;

(4) The NCBE Supplemental Character Report;

(5) The application for renewal shall be accompanied by the non-refundable fee approved by the Court.

(G) A lawyer admitted pursuant to this Rule is required to pay the annual Disciplinary Assessment required of attorneys admitted to practice three years or more pursuant to La. S. Ct. Rule XIX, Section 8; and Louisiana State Bar Association annual dues pursuant to Article V of the Articles of Incorporation of the Louisiana State Bar Association during the period of the limited license.

(H) A lawyer admitted pursuant to this rule shall be subject to the Louisiana Rules of Professional Conduct and to the disciplinary authority of the courts and the Louisiana Attorney Disciplinary Board.

(I) A lawyer admitted pursuant to this rule shall comply with the annual registration requirements contained in Louisiana Supreme Court Rule XIX, §8.

(J) A lawyer admitted pursuant to this Rule is required to meet the continuing legal education requirements specified in La. S. Ct. Rule XXX.

RULE 5.6. RESTRICTIONS ON RIGHT TO PRACTICE

A lawyer shall not participate in offering or making:

(a) a partnership, shareholders, operating, employment, or other similar type of agreement that restricts the rights of a lawyer to practice after termination of the relationship, except an agreement concerning benefits upon retirement; or

(b) an agreement in which a restriction on the lawyer's right to practice is part of the settlement of a client controversy.

BACKGROUND

The Louisiana Supreme Court adopted this rule on January 20, 2004. It became effective on March 1, 2004, and has not been amended since. This rule is identical to the ABA Model Rule of Professional Conduct 5.6 (2002).

In 2002, the ABA amended paragraph (b) of the corresponding Model Rule to clarify that it applies to settlements not only between purely private parties, but also between a private party and the government. *See* ABA Ethics 2000 Commission Revision Notes to Model Rule 5.6 (2002) (citing ABA Formal Ethics Op. 394).

COMMENTS TO ABA MODEL RULE 5.6

[1] An agreement restricting the right of lawyers to practice after leaving a firm not only limits their professional autonomy but also limits the freedom of clients to choose a lawyer. Paragraph (a) prohibits such agreements except for restrictions incident to provisions concerning retirement benefits for service with the firm.

[2] Paragraph (b) prohibits a lawyer from agreeing not to represent other persons in connection with settling a claim on behalf of a client.

[3] This Rule does not apply to prohibit restrictions that may be included in the terms of the sale of a law practice pursuant to Rule 1.17.

ANNOTATIONS

Law Firms and Restrictive Covenants

Paragraph (a) generally prohibits lawyers associated in a firm from entering into a post-termination noncompete agreement or other restrictive covenant–other than one incident to a lawyer's retirement from law practice. La. Rules of Prof'l Conduct r. 5.6(a) (2004); *see also* Restatement (Third) of the Law Governing Lawyers § 13(1) (2000). The purpose of this rule is "to ensure the client's freedom to select counsel of his or her choice." *See Minge v. Weeks*, 629 So. 2d 545, 547 (La. Ct. App. 4th Cir. 1993); *see also Regional Urology, L.L.C. v. Price*, 966 So. 2d 1087, 1095 (La. Ct. App. 2nd Cir. 2007) (Brown, C.J., dissenting) (noting that the rule is a matter of public policy, which facilitates a client's trust in the client's lawyer).

This rule also prohibits a firm from doing indirectly what it may not do directly. For example, it prohibits firms from imposing unreasonable financial disincentives on a departing lawyer that are intended to curtail that lawyer's ability either to compete with the firm in the future, or to continue representing existing clients after termination. *See Minge v. Weeks*, 629 So. 2d 545 (La. Ct. App. 4th Cir. 1993) (holding that a firm may not require a departing lawyer to either leave clients with firm, or else pay 80% of any fee obtained through post-termination representation). Note that Rule 5.6 does not prohibit lawyers associated in a firm from agreeing that none will practice law "on the side"—that is, that none will practice other than for the benefit of the firm. Nevertheless, a firm may contractually require a departing lawyer to reimburse the firm for advances and expenses previously incurred by the firm on matters taken by the departing lawyer. *See Warner v. Carimi Law Firm*, 678 So. 2d 561 (La. Ct. App. 5th Cir. 1996).

Settlement Agreements Attempting to Restrict Practice

Paragraph (b) prohibits a lawyer from participating in any settlement negotiation or agreement in which a settlement term would restrict the right of any lawyer to practice law on behalf of any client. La. Rules of Prof'l Conduct r. 5.6(b) (2004); *see also* Restatement (Third) of the Law Governing Lawyers § 13(2) (2000) ("[A] lawyer may not offer or enter into an agreement in settling a client claim restricting the right of the lawyer to practice law, including the right to represent or take particular action on behalf of other clients."); ABA Comm. on Ethics and Prof'l Responsibility, Formal Op. 94-381 (1994). This rule exists not only to ensure that the public has access to capable lawyers, but also to avoid conflicts between a lawyer's present clients and his personal interest in obtaining future clients. *See, e.g.*, ABA Comm. on Ethics and Prof'l Responsibility, Formal Op. 93-371 (1993). Note that this rule does not prohibit lawyers from entering into agreements restricting their right to use or reveal information relating to a particular matter. *See* ABA, Annotated Model Rules Prof'l Conduct at 497 (5th ed. 2003). Furthermore, it does not prohibit a lawyer from agreeing to a restriction on the lawyer's right to practice law as part of the resolution of a disciplinary proceeding. *See* ABA Comm. on Ethics and Prof'l Responsibility, Formal Op. 95-394 (1995).

Disciplinary Sanctions

Absent aggravating or mitigating circumstances, the following sanctions are generally appropriate in cases involving violations of Rule 5.6: *disbarment*, when the lawyer knowingly engages in conduct that is a violation of a duty owed to the profession with the intent to obtain a benefit for the lawyer or another, and causes serious or potentially serious injury to a client, the public, or the legal system; *suspension*, when the lawyer knowingly engages in conduct that is a violation of a duty owed to the profession, and causes injury or potential injury to a client, the public, or the legal system; *reprimand*, when the lawyer negligently engages in conduct that is a violation of a duty owed to the profession, and causes injury or potential injury to a client, the public, or the legal system; and, *admonition*, when the lawyer engages in an isolated instance of negligence that is a violation of a duty owed to the profession, and causes little or no actual or potential injury to a client, the public or the legal system. *See* ABA Stds. for Imposing Lawyer Sanctions stds. 7.0-7.4 (1992).

RULE 5.7. RESPONSIBILITIES REGARDING LAW-RELATED SERVICES [RESERVED]

BACKGROUND

The Louisiana Supreme Court has not adopted ABA Model Rule 5.7 (2002). In 2004, the LSBA recommended against adoption of this rule because it was concerned that adoption might lead Louisiana lawyers to believe that they were not subject to discipline under the Louisiana Rules of Professional Conduct for engaging in misconduct unrelated to the practice of law. On the contrary, Louisiana Rule of Professional Conduct 8.4 makes it clear that Louisiana lawyers are in fact subject to discipline for committing unlawful acts wholly unrelated to the practice of law. Thus, Louisiana lawyers can be disciplined under the Louisiana Rules of Professional Conduct irrespective whether they engage in "misconduct" while providing law-related services or while providing other services.

ABA MODEL RULE 5.7

(a) A lawyer shall be subject to the Rules of Professional Conduct with respect to the provision of law-related services, as defined in paragraph (b), if the law-related services are provided:

> (1) by the lawyer in circumstances that are not distinct from the lawyer's provision of legal services to clients; or

> (2) in other circumstances by an entity controlled by the lawyer individually or with others if the lawyer fails to take reasonable measures to assure that a person obtaining the law-related services knows that the services are not legal services and that the protections of the client-lawyer relationship do not exist.

(b) The term "law-related services" denotes services that might reasonably be performed in conjunction with and in substance are related to the provision of legal services, and that are not prohibited as unauthorized practice of law when provided by a nonlawyer.

COMMENTS TO ABA MODEL RULE 5.7

[1] When a lawyer performs law-related services or controls an organization that does so, there exists the potential for ethical problems. Principal among these is the possibility that the person for whom the law-related services are performed fails to understand that the services may not carry with them the protections normally afforded as part of the client-lawyer relationship. The recipient of the law-related services may expect, for example, that the protection of client confidences, prohibitions against representation of persons with conflicting interests, and obligations of a lawyer to maintain professional independence apply to the provision of law-related services when that may not be the case.

[2] Rule 5.7 applies to the provision of law-related services by a lawyer even when the lawyer does not provide any legal services to the person for whom the law-related services are performed and whether the law-related services are performed through a law firm or a separate entity. The Rule identifies the circumstances in which all of the Rules of Professional Conduct apply to the provision of law-related services. Even when those circumstances do not exist, however, the conduct of a lawyer involved in the provision of

law-related services is subject to those Rules that apply generally to lawyer conduct, regardless of whether the conduct involves the provision of legal services. See, e.g., Rule 8.4.

[3] When law-related services are provided by a lawyer under circumstances that are not distinct from the lawyer's provision of legal services to clients, the lawyer in providing the law-related services must adhere to the requirements of the Rules of Professional Conduct as provided in paragraph (a)(1). Even when the law-related and legal services are provided in circumstances that are distinct from each other, for example through separate entities or different support staff within the law firm, the Rules of Professional Conduct apply to the lawyer as provided in paragraph (a)(2) unless the lawyer takes reasonable measures to assure that the recipient of the law-related services knows that the services are not legal services and that the protections of the client-lawyer relationship do not apply.

[4] Law-related services also may be provided through an entity that is distinct from that through which the lawyer provides legal services. If the lawyer individually or with others has control of such an entity's operations, the Rule requires the lawyer to take reasonable measures to assure that each person using the services of the entity knows that the services provided by the entity are not legal services and that the Rules of Professional Conduct that relate to the client-lawyer relationship do not apply. A lawyer's control of an entity extends to the ability to direct its operation. Whether a lawyer has such control will depend upon the circumstances of the particular case.

[5] When a client-lawyer relationship exists with a person who is referred by a lawyer to a separate law-related service entity controlled by the lawyer, individually or with others, the lawyer must comply with Rule 1.8(a).

[6] In taking the reasonable measures referred to in paragraph (a)(2) to assure that a person using law-related services understands the practical effect or significance of the inapplicability of the Rules of Professional Conduct, the lawyer should communicate to the person receiving the law-related services, in a manner sufficient to assure that the person understands the significance of the fact, that the relationship of the person to the business entity will not be a client-lawyer relationship. The communication should be made before entering into an agreement for provision of or providing law-related services, and preferably should be in writing.

[7] The burden is upon the lawyer to show that the lawyer has taken reasonable measures under the circumstances to communicate the desired understanding. For instance, a sophisticated user of law-related services, such as a publicly held corporation, may require a lesser explanation than someone unaccustomed to making distinctions between legal services and law-related services, such as an individual seeking tax advice from a lawyer-accountant or investigative services in connection with a lawsuit.

[8] Regardless of the sophistication of potential recipients of law-related services, a lawyer should take special care to keep separate the provision of law-related and legal services in order to minimize the risk that the recipient will assume that the law-related services are legal services. The risk of such confusion is especially acute when the lawyer renders both

types of services with respect to the same matter. Under some circumstances the legal and law-related services may be so closely entwined that they cannot be distinguished from each other, and the requirement of disclosure and consultation imposed by paragraph (a)(2) of the Rule cannot be met. In such a case a lawyer will be responsible for assuring that both the lawyer's conduct and, to the extent required by Rule 5.3, that of nonlawyer employees in the distinct entity that the lawyer controls complies in all respects with the Rules of Professional Conduct.

[9] A broad range of economic and other interests of clients may be served by lawyers' engaging in the delivery of law-related services. Examples of law-related services include providing title insurance, financial planning, accounting, trust services, real estate counseling, legislative lobbying, economic analysis, social work, psychological counseling, tax preparation, and patent, medical or environmental consulting.

[10] When a lawyer is obliged to accord the recipients of such services the protections of those Rules that apply to the client-lawyer relationship, the lawyer must take special care to heed the proscriptions of the Rules addressing conflict of interest (Rules 1.7 through 1.11, especially Rules 1.7(a)(2) and 1.8(a), (b) and (f)), and to scrupulously adhere to the requirements of Rule 1.6 relating to disclosure of confidential information. The promotion of the law-related services must also in all respects comply with Rules 7.1 through 7.3, dealing with advertising and solicitation. In that regard, lawyers should take special care to identify the obligations that may be imposed as a result of a jurisdiction's decisional law.

[11] When the full protections of all of the Rules of Professional Conduct do not apply to the provision of law-related services, principles of law external to the Rules, for example, the law of principal and agent, govern the legal duties owed to those receiving the services. Those other legal principles may establish a different degree of protection for the recipient with respect to confidentiality of information, conflicts of interest and permissible business relationships with clients. See also Rule 8.4 (Misconduct).

Article 6. Public Service

RULE 6.1. VOLUNTARY PRO BONO PUBLICO SERVICE

Every lawyer should aspire to provide legal services to those unable to pay. A lawyer should aspire to render at least (50) hours of pro bono publico legal services per year. In fulfilling this aspirational goal, the lawyer should:

(a) provide a substantial majority of the (50) hours of legal services without fee or expectation of fee to:

(1) persons of limited means or

(2) charitable, religious, civic, community, governmental and educational organizations in matters that are designed primarily to address the needs of persons of limited means; and

(b) provide any additional services through:

(1) delivery of legal services at no fee or substantially reduced fee to individuals, groups or organizations seeking to secure or protect civil rights, civil liberties or public rights, or charitable, religious, civic, community, governmental and educational organizations in matters in furtherance of their organizational purposes, where the payment of standard legal fees would significantly deplete the organization's economic resources or would be otherwise inappropriate;

(2) delivery of legal services at a substantially reduced fee to persons of limited means; or

(3) participation in activities for improving the law, legal system or the legal profession.

BACKGROUND

The Louisiana Supreme Court adopted this rule on January 20, 2004. It became effective on March 1, 2004, and has not been amended since.

This rule is identical in substance to ABA Model Rule of Professional Conduct 6.1 (2002),[123] except for the omission of the final sentence of the Model Rule. That sentence

---

[123] The corresponding Model Rule characterizes the lawyer's "obligation" under this rule as a "professional responsibility" to provide legal services to those who are unable to pay. Model Rules of Prof'l Conduct r. 6.1 (2002). In contrast, this rule emphasizes that the

provides as follows: "In addition, a lawyer should voluntarily contribute financial support to organizations that provide legal services to persons of limited means." *See* ABA Model Rules of Prof'l Conduct r. 6.1. The court deleted this language on recommendation of the LSBA House of Delegates, which believed that lawyers should be permitted to make their own decisions regarding the types of charitable organizations to which to contribute.

COMMENTS TO ABA MODEL RULE 6.1

[1] Every lawyer, regardless of professional prominence or professional work load, has a responsibility to provide legal services to those unable to pay, and personal involvement in the problems of the disadvantaged can be one of the most rewarding experiences in the life of a lawyer. The American Bar Association urges all lawyers to provide a minimum of 50 hours of pro bono services annually. States, however, may decide to choose a higher or lower number of hours of annual service (which may be expressed as a percentage of a lawyer's professional time) depending upon local needs and local conditions. It is recognized that in some years a lawyer may render greater or fewer hours than the annual standard specified, but during the course of his or her legal career, each lawyer should render on average per year, the number of hours set forth in this Rule. Services can be performed in civil matters or in criminal or quasi-criminal matters for which there is no government obligation to provide funds for legal representation, such as post-conviction death penalty appeal cases.

[2] Paragraphs (a)(1) and (2) recognize the critical need for legal services that exists among persons of limited means by providing that a substantial majority of the legal services rendered annually to the disadvantaged be furnished without fee or expectation of fee. Legal services under these paragraphs consist of a full range of activities, including individual and class representation, the provision of legal advice, legislative lobbying, administrative rule making and the provision of free training or mentoring to those who represent persons of limited means. The variety of these activities should facilitate participation by government lawyers, even when restrictions exist on their engaging in the outside practice of law.

[3] Persons eligible for legal services under paragraphs (a)(1) and (2) are those who qualify for participation in programs funded by the Legal Services Corporation and those whose incomes and financial resources are slightly above the guidelines utilized by such programs but nevertheless, cannot afford counsel. Legal services can be rendered to individuals or to organizations such as homeless shelters, battered women's centers and food pantries that serve those of limited means. The term "governmental organizations" includes, but is not limited to, public protection programs and sections of governmental or public sector agencies.

"obligation" imposed is more of an "aspirational goal" than it is a "professional responsibility." *See* La. Rules of Prof'l Conduct r. 6.1 (2004). Notwithstanding this semantic difference, neither the Model Rule nor the Louisiana Rule imposes an obligation enforceable through the disciplinary process (or otherwise).

[4] Because service must be provided without fee or expectation of fee, the intent of the lawyer to render free legal services is essential for the work performed to fall within the meaning of paragraphs (a)(1) and (2). Accordingly, services rendered cannot be considered pro bono if an anticipated fee is uncollected, but the award of statutory attorneys' fees in a case originally accepted as pro bono would not disqualify such services from inclusion under this section. Lawyers who do receive fees in such cases are encouraged to contribute an appropriate portion of such fees to organizations or projects that benefit persons of limited means.

[5] While it is possible for a lawyer to fulfill the annual responsibility to perform pro bono services exclusively through activities described in paragraphs (a)(1) and (2), to the extent that any hours of service remained unfulfilled, the remaining commitment can be met in a variety of ways as set forth in paragraph (b). Constitutional, statutory or regulatory restrictions may prohibit or impede government and public sector lawyers and judges from performing the pro bono services outlined in paragraphs (a)(1) and (2). Accordingly, where those restrictions apply, government and public sector lawyers and judges may fulfill their pro bono responsibility by performing services outlined in paragraph (b).

[6] Paragraph (b)(1) includes the provision of certain types of legal services to those whose incomes and financial resources place them above limited means. It also permits the pro bono lawyer to accept a substantially reduced fee for services. Examples of the types of issues that may be addressed under this paragraph include First Amendment claims, Title VII claims and environmental protection claims. Additionally, a wide range of organizations may be represented, including social service, medical research, cultural and religious groups.

[7] Paragraph (b)(2) covers instances in which lawyers agree to and receive a modest fee for furnishing legal services to persons of limited means. Participation in judicare programs and acceptance of court appointments in which the fee is substantially below a lawyer's usual rate are encouraged under this section.

[8] Paragraph (b)(3) recognizes the value of lawyers engaging in activities that improve the law, the legal system or the legal profession. Serving on bar association committees, serving on boards of pro bono or legal services programs, taking part in Law Day activities, acting as a continuing legal education instructor, a mediator or an arbitrator and engaging in legislative lobbying to improve the law, the legal system or the profession are a few examples of the many activities that fall within this paragraph.

[9] Because the provision of pro bono services is a professional responsibility, it is the individual ethical commitment of each lawyer. Nevertheless, there may be times when it is not feasible for a lawyer to engage in pro bono services. At such times a lawyer may discharge the pro bono responsibility by providing financial support to organizations providing free legal services to persons of limited means. Such financial support should be reasonably equivalent to the value of the hours of service that would have otherwise been provided. In addition, at times it may be more feasible to satisfy the pro bono responsibility collectively, as by a firm's aggregate pro bono activities.

[10] Because the efforts of individual lawyers are not enough to meet the need for free legal services that exists among persons of limited means, the government and the profession have instituted additional programs to provide those services. Every lawyer should financially support such programs, in addition to either providing direct pro bono services or making financial contributions when pro bono service is not feasible.

[11] Law firms should act reasonably to enable and encourage all lawyers in the firm to provide the pro bono legal services called for by this Rule.

[12] The responsibility set forth in this Rule is not intended to be enforced through disciplinary process.

ANNOTATIONS
Generally

Whether the rules of professional conduct should impose a mandatory requirement or hortatory "responsibility" to engage in pro bono work has long been a controversial issue.[124] In 2004, the Louisiana Supreme Court was concerned that the adoption of this rule would adversely affect those employed to represent a single private client or a governmental entity, and who are prohibited by the terms of their employment from representing other clients. As a result of this concern, the court considered whether such lawyers (and others) should be permitted to discharge their responsibilities under this rule by donating money to pro bono service organizations. Notwithstanding these concerns, the court adopted the corresponding ABA Model Rule with only a minimal revision. *See, e.g., State v. Singleton*, 216 So. 3d 985 (La. Ct. App. 4th Cir. 2016) (noting that lawyers have a professional obligation to serve and represent indigent clients unless the appointment is unreasonable and oppressive). To encourage pro bono legal services, the Louisiana Supreme Court in 2015 adopted a rule granting CLE credit to lawyers providing uncompensated pro bono legal representation to indigent clients.[125]

---

[124] In 1987, the Louisiana Supreme Court adopted an earlier version of this rule despite that the Louisiana Task Force to Evaluate the American Bar Association's Model Rules of Professional Conduct and the LSBA House of Delegates recommended that this rule "be deleted in its entirety [because it] . . . is aspirational in nature and the matters set forth therein do not rise to the dignity of ethical obligations." *See* Report and Recommendation of the Task Force to Evaluate the American Bar Association's Model Rules of Prof'l Conduct, at 21 (Nov. 23, 1985); *cf.* Letter, Chief Justice John A. Dixon to John C. Combe, Jr., at 2 (Jun. 2, 1986) ("The entire Rule 6 of the ABA Model Rules should be included in the LSBA Rules.").

[125] To be eligible, the matter must have been assigned to the lawyer by a court, a bar association, or a legal services or pro bono organization that has as its primary purpose the furnishing of pro bono legal services, and must also file a statement with the Louisiana Committee on Mandatory Continuing Legal Education (CLE). A lawyer providing such pro bono legal representation shall receive one (1) hour of CLE credit for each five (5) hours of pro bono representation, up to a maximum of three (3) hours of CLE credit for

Disciplinary Sanctions

None. This rule is purely aspirational. As Comment 12 to Model Rule 6.1 notes, "[t]he responsibility set forth in this Rule is not intended to be enforced through disciplinary process." *See* ABA Model Rules of Prof'l Conduct r. 6.1 cmt. 12 (2002).

each calendar year. *See* La. Rules for Continuing Legal Educ. Rule 3 Regulation 3.21 (2015).

RULE 6.2. ACCEPTING APPOINTMENTS

A lawyer shall not seek to avoid appointment by a tribunal to represent a person except for good cause, such as:

(a) representing the client is likely to result in violation of the Rules of Professional Conduct or other law;

(b) representing the client is likely to result in an unreasonable financial burden on the lawyer; or

(c) the client or the cause is so repugnant to the lawyer as to be likely to impair the client-lawyer relationship or the lawyer's ability to represent the client.

BACKGROUND

The Louisiana Supreme Court adopted this rule on January 20, 2004. It became effective on March 1, 2004, and has not been amended since. This rule is identical to ABA Model Rule of Professional Conduct 6.2 (2002).

COMMENTS TO ABA MODEL RULE 6.2

Generally

[1] A lawyer ordinarily is not obliged to accept a client whose character or cause the lawyer regards as repugnant. The lawyer's freedom to select clients is, however, qualified. All lawyers have a responsibility to assist in providing pro bono publico service. See Rule 6.1. An individual lawyer fulfills this responsibility by accepting a fair share of unpopular matters or indigent or unpopular clients. A lawyer may also be subject to appointment by a court to serve unpopular clients or persons unable to afford legal services.

Appointed Counsel

[2] For good cause a lawyer may seek to decline an appointment to represent a person who cannot afford to retain counsel or whose cause is unpopular. Good cause exists if the lawyer could not handle the matter competently, see Rule 1.1, or if undertaking the representation would result in an improper conflict of interest, for example, when the client or the cause is so repugnant to the lawyer as to be likely to impair the client-lawyer relationship or the lawyer's ability to represent the client. A lawyer may also seek to decline an appointment if acceptance would be unreasonably burdensome, for example, when it would impose a financial sacrifice so great as to be unjust.

[3] An appointed lawyer has the same obligations to the client as retained counsel, including the obligations of loyalty and confidentiality, and is subject to the same limitations on the client-lawyer relationship, such as the obligation to refrain from assisting the client in violation of the Rules.

ANNOTATIONS
Generally

This rule prohibits Louisiana lawyers from attempting to avoid being appointed by courts to represent indigent persons unless compelling reasons exist. *See* La. Rules of Prof'l Conduct r. 6.2 (2004). Such compelling reasons include the following: when the representation will result in a violation of the law, when the representation places an unreasonable financial burden on the lawyer, or when the client-lawyer relationship is impaired because the client or the client's cause is "repugnant" to the lawyer. *Id.*; *see, e.g., State v. Singleton*, 216 So. 3d 985 (La. Ct. App. 4th Cir. 2016) (holding that a lawyer serving as head of the public defender's office had good cause to avoid appointment in the lawyer's personal capacity for prisoner's post-conviction relief proceeding as the lawyer has extensive duties as head of an office facing increasing caseloads amid a shrinking budget).

In addition to violating this rule, unjustified attempts to avoid appointment are often futile, particularly when the appointment has been made by a determined judge. For more than a century, Louisiana courts have exercised their inherent judicial authority to appoint lawyers to represent indigent defendants. *See, e.g., State v. Simmons*, 43 La. Ann. 991, 994-95, 10 So. 382 (1891) (denying appointed lawyer's request to have his fees paid by the parish). The Louisiana Supreme Court has held that:

> [t]he professional obligations assumed by attorneys in this State require that a reasonable amount of time and effort be devoted to promoting the cause of justice, including the defense of indigent accused without compensation. The high purpose and traditions of the legal profession require that this burden be shouldered by its members. So long as the burden is not oppressive and is fairly shared among the members of the bar to which they belong there is no cause for complaint.

State v. Clifton, 172 So. 2d 657, 667 (La. 1965); *see State v. Wigley*, 624 So. 2d 425, 428 (La. 1993); *State v. Campbell*, 324 So. 2d 395 (La. 1975); *see also Hurtado v. United States*, 410 U.S. 578, 588-89 (1973) (holding that the Fifth Amendment does not require the government pay for the performance of a public duty it is already owed); *State in Interest of Johnson,* 475 So. 2d 340, 342 (La. 1985) (asserting Louisiana courts' inherent authority to appoint a lawyer "to represent an indigent, with or without compensation, as an obligation burdening his privileges to practice and to serve as an officer of the court"); *State v. Doucet*, 352 So. 2d 222, 222 (La. 1977) (holding that an uncompensated lawyer's rights under the Fifth and Fourteenth Amendments were not violated by appointment); *State v. Bryant*, 324 So. 2d 389, 389 (La. 1975) (holding that uncompensated lawyers representing indigents are not "deprived of property without due process and equal protection" or "forced into involuntary servitude").

Note, however, that although Louisiana courts may appoint lawyers to represent indigent clients without fee, a court-appointed lawyer is entitled to be reimbursed for reasonable case-related out-of-pocket expenses and overhead costs. *State v. Wigley*, 624 So. 2d 425,

429 (La.1993); *State v. Citizen*, 898 So. 2d 325 (La. 2005); *see also State v. Jeff*, 761 So. 2d 574 (La. Ct. App. 1st Cir. 1999); La. Rev. Stat. Ann. § 15:304 (addressing responsibility for paying costs of criminal prosecutions). The legislature, to satisfy its constitutional mandate to "provide for a uniform system for securing and compensating qualified counsel for indigents," (*see* La. Const. art. 1, § 13) implemented statewide standards and guidelines for indigent defense through the Louisiana Public Defender Act of 2007. *See* La. R.S. 15:141-184, amended by La. R.S. 15:146, 162, 167 (2016).; *State v. Reeves*, 11 So. 3d 1031, 1042-43 (La. 2009)

Disciplinary Sanctions

Absent aggravating or mitigating circumstances, the following sanctions are generally appropriate in cases involving violations of Rule 6.2: *disbarment*, when the lawyer knowingly engages in conduct that is a violation of a duty owed to the profession with the intent to obtain a benefit for the lawyer or another, and causes serious or potentially serious injury to a client, the public, or the legal system; *suspension*, when the lawyer knowingly engages in conduct that is a violation of a duty owed to the profession, and causes injury or potential injury to a client, the public, or the legal system; *reprimand*, when the lawyer negligently engages in conduct that is a violation of a duty owed to the profession, and causes injury or potential injury to a client, the public, or the legal system; and, *admonition*, when the lawyer engages in an isolated instance of negligence that is a violation of a duty owed to the profession, and causes little or no actual or potential injury to a client, the public or the legal system. *See* ABA Stds. for Imposing Lawyer Sanctions stds. 7.0-7.4 (1992).

RULE 6.3. MEMBERSHIP IN LEGAL SERVICES ORGANIZATION

A lawyer may serve as a director, officer or member of a legal services organization, apart from the law firm in which the lawyer practices, notwithstanding that the organization serves persons having interests adverse to a client of the lawyer. The lawyer shall not knowingly participate in a decision or action of the organization:

(a) if participating in the decision or action would be incompatible with the lawyer's obligations to a client under Rule 1.7; or

(b) where the decision or action could have a material adverse effect on the representation of a client of the organization whose interests are adverse to a client of the lawyer.

BACKGROUND

The Louisiana Supreme Court adopted this rule on January 20, 2004. It became effective on March 1, 2004, and has not been amended since. This rule is identical to ABA Model Rule of Professional Conduct 6.3 (2002).

COMMENTS TO ABA MODEL RULE 6.3

[1] Lawyers should be encouraged to support and participate in legal service organizations. A lawyer who is an officer or a member of such an organization does not thereby have a client-lawyer relationship with persons served by the organization. However, there is potential conflict between the interests of such persons and the interests of the lawyer's clients. If the possibility of such conflict disqualified a lawyer from serving on the board of a legal services organization, the profession's involvement in such organizations would be severely curtailed.

[2] It may be necessary in appropriate cases to reassure a client of the organization that the representation will not be affected by conflicting loyalties of a member of the board. Established, written policies in this respect can enhance the credibility of such assurances.

ANNOTATIONS

Generally

This rule addresses the potential conflicts of interest faced by a lawyer who serves in a legal-services organization in a nonlawyer capacity. Under this rule, a lawyer serving as a director, officer or member of such an organization is not necessarily conflicted out of representations that happen to be adverse to persons served by the organization. La. Rules of Prof'l Conduct r. 6.3 (2004). This is so because a lawyer serving an organization in a nonlawyer capacity "does not thereby have a client-lawyer relationship" with the persons it serves. *See* ABA Model Rules of Prof'l Conduct r. 6.3 cmt. 1. Nevertheless, if the lawyer's personal participation in a matter on behalf of the organization would be materially adverse to a client, the lawyer should refrain from participating. *See* La. Rules of Prof'l Conduct r. 6.3(a) (2004). Moreover, if the lawyer's personal participation in a matter could have an adverse effect on a client of the organization, and the interests of that client are adverse to those of one of the lawyer's private clients, the lawyer should refrain from participating. *Id.* r. 6.3(b).

Disciplinary Sanctions

For the disciplinary sanctions that are appropriate for a lawyer's failure to avoid conflicts of interest, *see supra* Annotations to Louisiana Rule 1.7.

RULE 6.4. LAW REFORM ACTIVITIES AFFECTING CLIENT INTERESTS

A lawyer may serve as a director, officer or member of an organization involved in reform of the law or its administration notwithstanding that the reform may affect the interests of a client of the lawyer. When the lawyer knows that the interests of a client may be materially benefitted by a decision in which the lawyer participates, the lawyer shall disclose that fact but need not identify the client.

BACKGROUND

The Louisiana Supreme Court adopted this rule on January 20, 2004. It became effective on March 1, 2004, and has not been amended since. This rule is identical to ABA Model Rule of Professional Conduct 6.4 (2002).

COMMENT TO ABA MODEL RULE 6.4

[1] Lawyers involved in organizations seeking law reform generally do not have a client-lawyer relationship with the organization. Otherwise, it might follow that a lawyer could not be involved in a bar association law reform program that might indirectly affect a client. See also Rule 1.2(b). For example, a lawyer specializing in antitrust litigation might be regarded as disqualified from participating in drafting revisions of rules governing that subject. In determining the nature and scope of participation in such activities, a lawyer should be mindful of obligations to clients under other Rules, particularly Rule 1.7. A lawyer is professionally obligated to protect the integrity of the program by making an appropriate disclosure within the organization when the lawyer knows a private client might be materially benefitted.

ANNOTATIONS

Generally

This rule permits lawyers to engage in law-reform activities–for example, Louisiana State Bar Association or Louisiana State Law Institute activities–that may affect the interests of one or more clients. Thus, there is no conflict of interest or other breach of the duty of loyalty for a lawyer to advocate law reform of which his client may disapprove.

Furthermore, the second sentence of the rule requires a lawyer who serves a law-reform organization to be forthright about the lawyer's loyalties when participating in organizational activities. Thus, when a lawyer participating in the decision-making process of the organization "knows" that a particular decision "may" materially benefit a client, the lawyer must "disclose that fact," but need not identify the client. La. Rules of Prof'l Conduct r. 6.4(2004). Hence, this rule furthers similar interests to those addressed by Rule 3.9.

Disciplinary Sanctions

Absent aggravating or mitigating circumstances, the following sanctions are generally appropriate in cases involving lawyers who engage in conduct that violates the public trust: *disbarment*, when the lawyer knowingly misuses a position with the intent to obtain a significant benefit or advantage for the lawyer or another, or with the intent to cause serious or potentially serious injury to a party or to the integrity of the legal process; *suspension*, when the lawyer knowingly fails to follow proper procedures or rules, and causes injury or potential injury to a party or to the integrity of the legal process; *reprimand*, when the lawyer negligently fails to follow proper procedures or rules, and causes injury or potential injury to a party or to the integrity of the legal process; and, *admonition*, when the lawyer engages in an isolated instance of negligence in not following proper procedures or rules, and causes little or no actual or potential injury to a party or to the integrity of the legal process. *See* ABA Stds. for Imposing Lawyer Sanctions stds. 5.2-5.24 (1992).

RULE 6.5. NONPROFIT AND COURT-ANNEXED LIMITED LEGAL SERVICES PROGRAMS

(a) A lawyer who, under the auspices of a program sponsored by a nonprofit organization or court, provides short-term limited legal services to a client without expectation by either the lawyer or the client that the lawyer will provide continuing representation in the matter:

(1) is subject to Rules 1.7 and 1.9(a) only if the lawyer knows that the representation of the client involves a conflict of interest; and

(2) is subject to Rule 1.10 only if the lawyer knows that another lawyer associated with the lawyer in a law firm is disqualified by Rule 1.7 or 1.9(a) with respect to the matter.

(b) Except as provided in paragraph (a)(2), Rule 1.10 is inapplicable to a representation governed by this Rule.

BACKGROUND

The Louisiana Supreme Court adopted this rule on January 20, 2004. It became effective on March 1, 2004, and has not been amended since. This rule is identical to ABA Model Rule of Professional Conduct 6.5 (2002).

The ABA adopted Model Rule 6.5 in 2002 in response to the ABA Ethics 2000 Commission's concern that a strict application of the conflict-of-interest rules could deter lawyers from serving as volunteers in programs in which clients are provided short-term limited legal services under the auspices of a nonprofit organization or a court-annexed program. *See* ABA Ethics 2000 Commission Revision Notes to Model Rule 6.5 (2002). Paradigmatic programs would include legal-advice hotlines and pro se clinics providing short-term limited legal assistance to persons of limited means. *See id.*

Paragraph (a) limits Rule 6.5 to situations in which lawyers provide clients short-term limited legal services under the auspices of a program sponsored by a nonprofit organization or court. The ABA Ethics 2000 Commission believed that the proposed relaxation of the conflict rules does not pose a significant risk to clients when the lawyer is working in a program sponsored by a nonprofit organization or a court and will eliminate an impediment to lawyer participation in such programs. *See id.*

Paragraph (a)(1) provides that the lawyer is subject to the requirements of Rules 1.7 and 1.9(a) only if the lawyer knows that the representation involves a conflict of interest. *See id.* This provision was intended to make it unnecessary for the lawyer to do a comprehensive conflicts check in a practice setting in which it normally is not feasible to do so. In cases in which the lawyer knows of a conflict of interest, however, compliance with Rules 1.7 and 1.9(a) is required. *See id.*

Paragraph (a)(2) provides that a lawyer participating in a short-term legal services program must comply with Rule 1.10 if the lawyer knows that a lawyer with whom he is associated in a firm would be disqualified from handling the matter by Rule 1.7 or Rule 1.9(a). *See id.* By otherwise exempting a representation governed by this Rule from Rule 1.10, however, paragraph (b) was intended to protect lawyers associated with the participating lawyer from vicarious disqualification. As explained in Comment 4 to the Model Rule, a lawyer's participation in a short-term limited legal services program will not preclude the lawyer's firm from undertaking or continuing the representation of a client with interests adverse to a client being represented under the program's auspices. Nor will the personal disqualification of a lawyer participating in the program be imputed to other lawyers participating in the program. Given the limited nature of the representation provided in nonprofit short-term limited legal services programs, the ABA Ethics 2000 Commission believed that the protections afforded clients by Rule 1.10 are unnecessary except in the circumstances specified in paragraph (a)(2). *See id.*

COMMENTS TO ABA MODEL RULE 6.5

[1] Legal services organizations, courts and various nonprofit organizations have established programs through which lawyers provide short-term limited legal services — such as advice or the completion of legal forms – that will assist persons to address their legal problems without further representation by a lawyer. In these programs, such as legal-advice hotlines, advice-only clinics or pro se counseling programs, a client-lawyer relationship is established, but there is no expectation that the lawyer's representation of the client will continue beyond the limited consultation. Such programs are normally operated under circumstances in which it is not feasible for a lawyer to systematically screen for conflicts of interest as is generally required before undertaking a representation. See, e.g., Rules 1.7, 1.9 and 1.10.

[2] A lawyer who provides short-term limited legal services pursuant to this Rule must secure the client's informed consent to the limited scope of the representation. See Rule 1.2(c). If a short-term limited representation would not be reasonable under the circumstances, the lawyer may offer advice to the client but must also advise the client of the need for further assistance of counsel. Except as provided in this Rule, the Rules of Professional Conduct, including Rules 1.6 and 1.9(c), are applicable to the limited representation.

[3] Because a lawyer who is representing a client in the circumstances addressed by this Rule ordinarily is not able to check systematically for conflicts of interest, paragraph (a) requires compliance with Rules 1.7 or 1.9(a) only if the lawyer knows that the representation presents a conflict of interest for the lawyer, and with Rule 1.10 only if the lawyer knows that another lawyer in the lawyer's firm is disqualified by Rules 1.7 or 1.9(a) in the matter.

[4] Because the limited nature of the services significantly reduces the risk of conflicts of interest with other matters being handled by the lawyer's firm, paragraph (b) provides that

Rule 1.10 is inapplicable to a representation governed by this Rule except as provided by paragraph (a)(2). Paragraph (a)(2) requires the participating lawyer to comply with Rule 1.10 when the lawyer knows that the lawyer's firm is disqualified by Rules 1.7 or 1.9(a). By virtue of paragraph (b), however, a lawyer's participation in a short-term limited legal services program will not preclude the lawyer's firm from undertaking or continuing the representation of a client with interests adverse to a client being represented under the program's auspices. Nor will the personal disqualification of a lawyer participating in the program be imputed to other lawyers participating in the program.

[5] If, after commencing a short-term limited representation in accordance with this Rule, a lawyer undertakes to represent the client in the matter on an ongoing basis, Rules 1.7, 1.9(a) and 1.10 become applicable.

ANNOTATIONS

No significant reported Louisiana decisions have discussed, applied or interpreted this rule.

Article 7. Information About Legal Services

RULE 7.1. GENERAL

(a) Permissible Forms of Advertising. Subject to all the requirements set forth in these Rules, including the filing requirements of Rule 7.7, a lawyer may advertise services through public media, including but not limited to: print media, such as a telephone directory, legal directory, newspaper or other periodical; outdoor advertising, such as billboards and other signs; radio, television, and computer-accessed communications; recorded messages the public may access by dialing a telephone number; and written communication in accordance with Rule 7.4.

(b) Advertisements Not Disseminated in Louisiana. These Rules shall not apply to any advertisement broadcast or disseminated in another jurisdiction in which the advertising lawyer is admitted if such advertisement complies with the Rules governing lawyer advertising in that jurisdiction and is not intended for broadcast or dissemination within the state of Louisiana.

(c) Communications for Non-Profit Organizations. Publications, educational materials, websites and other communications by lawyers on behalf of non-profit organizations that are not motivated by pecuniary gain are not advertisements or unsolicited written communications within the meaning of these Rules.

BACKGROUND

The Louisiana Supreme Court adopted this rule on June 26, 2008. It became effective October 1, 2009.

The LSBA has stated that "[a]ll inquiries regarding the new lawyer advertising rules (whether for lawyer advertising within LSBA publications or for lawyer advertising in outside media outlets) should be directed to Richard P. Lemmler, Jr., Ethics Counsel, Louisiana State Bar Association, 601 St. Charles Avenue, New Orleans, LA 70130; toll free: 1-800-421-LSBA (5722), ext. 144; direct dial: (504) 619-0144; fax: (504) 598-6753. The LSBA website for lawyer advertising is: http://www.lsba.org/Members/LawyerAdvertising.aspx.

COMMENTS TO ABA MODEL RULE 7.1

[1] This Rule governs all communications about a lawyer's services, including advertising permitted by Rule 7.2. Whatever means are used to make known a lawyer's services, statements about them must be truthful.

[2] Truthful statements that are misleading are also prohibited by this Rule. A truthful statement is misleading if it omits a fact necessary to make the lawyer's communication considered as a whole not materially misleading. A truthful statement is also misleading if there is a substantial likelihood that it will lead a reasonable person to formulate a specific conclusion about the lawyer or the lawyer's services for which there is no reasonable factual foundation.

[3] An advertisement that truthfully reports a lawyer's achievements on behalf of clients or former clients may be misleading if presented so as to lead a reasonable person to form an unjustified expectation that the same results could be obtained for other clients in similar matters without reference to the specific factual and legal circumstances of each client's case. Similarly, an unsubstantiated comparison of the lawyer's services or fees with the services or fees of other lawyers may be misleading if presented with such specificity as would lead a reasonable person to conclude that the comparison can be substantiated. The inclusion of an appropriate disclaimer or qualifying language may preclude a finding that a statement is likely to create unjustified expectations or otherwise mislead the public.

[4] See also Rule 8.4(e) for the prohibition against stating or implying an ability to influence improperly a government agency or official or to achieve results by means that violate the Rules of Professional Conduct or other law.

ANNOTATIONS

LSBA Resources

The Louisiana State Bar Association has assembled materials relating to lawyer advertising here: LSBA Resources on Lawyer Advertising. Among other resources, the LSBA has created a "Handbook on Lawyer Advertising and Solicitation" to help Louisiana lawyers understand the new advertising provisions that became effective on October 1, 2009. The handbook includes, among other things:

1. An overview of applicable regulations broken down by the type of advertisement/communication to which they apply.
2. A reproduction of the actual Louisiana Rules of Professional Conduct that deal with lawyer advertising and solicitation.
3. Answers to frequently asked questions about lawyer advertising regulations.
4. A Quick Reference Checklist for lawyer advertisers.
5. Examples of exempt and non-exempt, compliant and non-compliant print advertisements and unsolicited written communications.

The handbook is available at: https://www.lsba.org/Members/lawyeradvertising.aspx.

ABA Aspirational Goals

In 1988, the ABA adopted aspirational goals to provide nonbinding guidance to lawyers who advertise. *See* ABA Aspirational Goals on Lawyer Advertising (1988). The ABA noted that these aspirational goals were "not intended to establish mandatory requirements which might form the basis for disciplinary enforcement." Rather, the goals were "intended to provide suggested objectives which all lawyers who engage in advertising their services should be encouraged to achieve in order that lawyer advertising may be more effective and reflect the professionalism of the legal community." *See id.*

Federal Litigation

Note that several of the advertising rules that became effective on October 1, 2009 were the subject of First Amendment litigation in the United States District Court for the Eastern District of Louisiana and the United States Fifth Circuit Court of Appeals. *See, e.g., Public Citizen, Inc. v. La. Atty. Disciplinary Bd.*, 642 F. Supp. 2d 539 (E.D. La. 2009); *aff'd, Public Citizen, Inc. v. La. Atty. Disciplinary Bd.*, 632 F.3d 212 (5th Cir. 2011) ("The court affirmed the district court, finding that Rules 7.2(c)(1)(E), 7.2(c)(1)(I), and 7.2(c)(1)(L) did not regulate attorneys' commercial speech in a way that violated the First Amendment. In reversing the district court, the court found that Rules 7.2(c)(1)(D), 7.2(c)(1)(J), and 7.2(c)(10) did violate the First Amendment."). In that litigation, the United States Fifth Circuit Court of Appeals declared several provisions in Louisiana Rules 7.5, 7.6 and 7.7 to be unconstitutional and unenforceable. Please see the sections containing those rules for additional details.

RULE 7.2. COMMUNICATIONS CONCERNING A LAWYER'S SERVICES

The following shall apply to any communication conveying information about a lawyer, a lawyer's services or a law firm's services:

(a) *Required Content of Advertisements and Unsolicited Written Communications.*

> (1) *Name of Lawyer.* All advertisements and unsolicited written communications pursuant to these Rules shall include the name of at least one lawyer responsible for their content.

> (2) *Location of Practice.* All advertisements and unsolicited written communications provided for under these Rules shall disclose, by city or town, one or more bona fide office location(s) of the lawyer or lawyers who will actually perform the services advertised. If the office location is outside a city or town, the parish where the office is located must be disclosed. For the purposes of this Rule, a bona fide office is defined as a physical location maintained by the lawyer or law firm where the lawyer or law firm reasonably expects to furnish legal services in a substantial way on a regular and continuing basis, and which physical location shall have at least one lawyer who is regularly and routinely present in that physical location. In the absence of a bona fide office, the lawyer shall disclose the city or town of the primary registration statement address as it appears on the lawyer's annual registration statement. If an advertisement or unsolicited written communication lists a telephone number in connection with a specified geographic area other than an area containing a bona fide office or the lawyer's primary registration statement address, appropriate qualifying language must appear in the advertisement.

> (3) The following items may be used without including the content required by subdivisions (a)(l) and (a)(2) of this Rule 7.2:

(A) *Sponsorships.* A brief announcement in any public media that identifies a lawyer or law firm as a contributor to a specified charity or as a sponsor of a public service announcement or a specified charitable, community, or public interest program, activity, or event, provided that the announcement contains no information about the lawyer or the law firm other than permissible content of advertisements listed in Rule 7.2(b) and the fact of the sponsorship or contribution, in keeping with Rule 7.8(b);

(B) *Gift/Promotional Items.* Items, such as coffee mugs, pens, pencils, apparel, and the like, that identity a lawyer or law firm and are used/disseminated by a lawyer or law firm not in violation of these Rules, including but not limited to Rule 7.2(c)(13) and Rule 7.4; and

(C) *Office Sign(s) for Bona Fide Office Location(s).* A sign, placard, lettering, mural, engraving, carving or other alphanumeric display conveying information about a lawyer, a lawyer's services or a law firm's services that is permanently affixed, hanging, erected or otherwise attached to the physical structure of the building containing a bona fide office location for a lawyer or law firm, or to the property on which that bona fide office location sits.

(b) *Permissible Content of Advertisements and Unsolicited Written Communications.* If the content of an advertisement in any public media or unsolicited written communication is limited to the following information, the advertisement or unsolicited written communication is exempt from the filing and review requirement and, if true, shall be presumed not to be misleading or deceptive.

(1) *Lawyers and Law Firms.* A lawyer or law firm may include the following information in advertisements and unsolicited written communications:

(A) subject to the requirements of this Rule and Rule 7.10, the name of the lawyer or law firm, a listing of lawyers associated with the firm, office locations and parking arrangements, disability accommodations, telephone numbers, Web site addresses, and electronic mail addresses, office and telephone service hours, and a designation such as "attorney", "lawyer" or "law firm";

(B) date of admission to the Louisiana State Bar Association and any other bars, current membership or positions held in the Louisiana State Bar Association, its sections or committees, former membership or positions held in the Louisiana State Bar Association, its sections or committees, together with dates of membership, former positions of employment held in the legal profession, together with dates the positions were held, years of experience practicing law, number of lawyers in the advertising law firm, and a listing of federal courts and jurisdictions other than Louisiana where the lawyer is licensed to practice;

(C) technical and professional licenses granted by the State or other recognized licensing authorities and educational degrees received, including dates and institutions;

(D) military service, including branch and dates of service;

(E) foreign language ability;

(F) fields of law in which the lawyer practices, including official certification logos, subject to the requirements of subdivision (c)(5) of this Rule;

(G) prepaid or group legal service plans in which the lawyer participates;

(H) fee for initial consultation and fee schedule, subject to the requirements of subdivisions (c)(6) and (c)(7) of this Rule;

(I) common salutatory language such as "best wishes," "good luck," "happy holidays," or "pleased to announce";

(J) punctuation marks and common typographical marks; and

(K) a photograph or image of the lawyer or lawyers who are members of or employed by the firm against a plain background.

(2) *Public Service Announcements.* A lawyer or law firm may be listed as a sponsor of a public service announcement or charitable, civic, or community program or event as long as the information about the lawyer or law firm is limited to the permissible content set forth in subdivision (b)(1) of this Rule.

(c) Prohibitions and General Rules Governing Content of Advertisements and Unsolicited Written Communications.

(1) *Statements About Legal Services.* A lawyer shall not make or permit to be made a false, misleading or deceptive communication about the lawyer, the lawyer's services or the law firm's services. A communication violates this Rule if it:

(A) contains a material misrepresentation of fact or law;

(B) is false, misleading or deceptive;

(C) fails to disclose material information necessary to prevent the information supplied from being false, misleading or deceptive;

[(D) contains a reference or testimonial to past successes or results obtained, except as allowed in the Rule regulating information about a lawyer's services provided upon request][126];

---

[126] Enforcement of Rule 7.2(c)(1)(D) was suspended by Louisiana Supreme Court order dated April 27, 2011. *See* Louisiana Supreme Court Order of April 27, 2011.

> *Pursuant to Louisiana Supreme Court order*
> *dated April 27, 2011, the enforcement of Rule*
> *7.2(c)(1)(D) was suspended.*

(E) promises results;

(F) states or implies that the lawyer can achieve results by means that violate the Rules of Professional Conduct or other laws;

(G) compares the lawyer's services with other lawyers' services, unless the comparison can be factually substantiated;

(H) contains a paid testimonial or endorsement, unless the fact of payment is disclosed;

(I) includes (i) a portrayal of a client by a non-client without disclaimer of such, as required by Rule 7.2(c)(10); (ii) the depiction of any events or scenes, other than still pictures, photographs or other static images, that are not actual or authentic without disclaimer of such, as required by Rule 7.2(c)(10); or (iii) a still picture, photograph or other static image that, due to alteration or the context of its use, is false, misleading or deceptive;

(J) includes the portrayal of a lawyer by a non-lawyer,[127] the portrayal of a law firm as a fictionalized entity, the use of a fictitious name to refer to lawyers not associated together in a law firm, or otherwise implies that lawyers are associated in a law firm if that is not the case;

(K) resembles a legal pleading, notice, contract or other legal document;

---

[127] Enforcement of the entirety of Rule 7.2(c)(1)(J) was suspended by the Louisiana Supreme Court on April 27, 2011. *See* Louisiana Supreme Court Order of April 27, 2011. Two days later, however, the court resumed enforcement of this paragraph, except for the portion prohibiting "the portrayal of a judge or jury." *See* Louisiana Supreme Court Order of April 29, 2011. The rule text set forth above (and the version of the rules posted on-line by the Louisiana Supreme Court) deletes that language from the paragraph.

(L) utilizes a nickname, moniker, motto or trade name that states or implies an ability to obtain results in a matter; or

(M) fails to comply with Rule 1.8(e)(4)(iii).

(2) *Prohibited Visual and Verbal Portrayals and Illustrations.* A lawyer shall not include in any advertisement or unsolicited written communication any visual or verbal descriptions, depictions, illustrations (including photographs) or portrayals of persons, things, or events that are false, misleading or deceptive.

(3) *Advertising Areas of Practice.* A lawyer or law firm shall not state or imply in advertisements or unsolicited written communications that the lawyer or law firm currently practices in an area of practice when that is not the case.

(4) *Stating or Implying Louisiana State Bar Association Approval.* A lawyer or law firm shall not make any statement that directly or impliedly indicates that the communication has received any kind of approval from The Louisiana State Bar Association.

(5) *Communication of Fields of Practice.* A lawyer may communicate the fact that the lawyer does or does not practice in particular fields of law. A lawyer may state that the lawyer is a "specialist," practices a "specialty," or "specializes in" particular fields, but such communications are subject to the "false and misleading" standard applied in Rule 7.2(c)(1) to communications concerning a lawyer's services. A lawyer shall not state or imply that the lawyer is "certified," or "board certified" except as follows:

(A) *Lawyers Certified by the Louisiana Board of Legal Specialization.* A lawyer who complies with the Plan of Legal Specialization, as determined by the Louisiana Board of Legal Specialization, may inform the public and other lawyers of the lawyer's certified area(s) of legal practice. Such communications should identify the Louisiana Board of Legal Specialization as the certifying organization and may state that the lawyer is "certified" or "board certified in (area of certification)."

(B) *Lawyers Certified by Organizations Other Than the Louisiana Board of Legal Specialization or Another State*

Bar. A lawyer certified by an organization other than the Louisiana Board of Legal Specialization or another state bar may inform the public and other lawyers of the lawyer's certified area(s) of legal practice by stating that the lawyer is "certified" or "board certified in (area of certification)" if:

> (i) the lawyer complies with Section 6.2 of the Plan of Legal Specialization for the Louisiana Board of Legal Specialization; and,

> (ii) the lawyer includes the full name of the organization in all communications pertaining to such certification. A lawyer who has been certified by an organization that is accredited by the American Bar Association is not subject to Section 6.2 of the Plan of Legal Specialization.

(C) *Certification by Other State Bars.* A lawyer certified by another state bar may inform the public and other lawyers of the lawyer's certified area(s) of legal practice and may state in communications to the public that the lawyer is "certified" or "board certified in (area of certification)" if:

> (i) the state bar program grants certification on the basis of standards reasonably comparable to the standards of the Plan of Legal Specialization, as determined by the Louisiana Board of Legal Specialization; and,

> (ii) the lawyer includes the name of the state bar in all communications pertaining to such certification.

(6) *Disclosure of Liability For Expenses Other Than Fees.* Every advertisement and unsolicited written communication that contains information about the lawyer's fee, including those that indicate no fee will be charged in the absence of a recovery, shall disclose whether the client will be liable for any costs and/or expenses in addition to the fee.

(7) *Period for Which Advertised Fee Must be Honored.* A lawyer who advertises a specific fee or range of fees for a particular

service shall honor the advertised fee or range of fees for at least ninety days from the date last advertised unless the advertisement specifies a shorter period; provided that, for advertisements in the yellow pages of telephone directories or other media not published more frequently than annually, the advertised fee or range of fees shall be honored for no less than one year following publication.

(8) *Firm Name.* A lawyer shall not advertise services under a name that violates the provisions of Rule 7.10.

(9) *Language of Required Statements.* Any words or statements required by these Rules to appear in an advertisement or unsolicited written communication must appear in the same language in which the advertisement or unsolicited written communication appears. If more than one language is used in an advertisement or unsolicited written communication, any words or statements required by these Rules must appear in each language used in the advertisement or unsolicited written communication.

(10) *Appearance of Required Statements, Disclosures and Disclaimers.* Any words or statements required by these Rules to appear in an advertisement or unsolicited written communication must be clearly legible if written or intelligible if spoken aloud.

All disclosures and disclaimers required by these Rules shall be clear, conspicuous, and clearly associated with the item requiring disclosure or disclaimer. Written disclosures and disclaimers shall be clearly legible and, if televised or displayed electronically, shall be displayed for a sufficient time to enable the viewer to easily see and read the disclosure or disclaimer. Spoken disclosures and disclaimers shall be plainly audible and clearly intelligible.[128]

(11) *Payment by Non-Advertising Lawyer.* No lawyer shall, directly or indirectly, pay all or a part of the cost of an advertisement by a lawyer not in the same firm.

---

[128] As deleted and replaced by Louisiana Supreme Court order of April 27, 2011. *See* Louisiana Supreme Court Order of April 27, 2011.

(12) *Referrals to Another Lawyer*. If the case or matter will be, or is likely to be, referred to another lawyer or law firm, the communication shall include a statement so advising the prospective client.

(13) *Payment for Recommendations; Lawyer Referral Service Fees*. A lawyer shall not give anything of value to a person for recommending the lawyer's services, except that a lawyer may pay the reasonable cost of advertising or written or recorded communication permitted by these Rules, and may pay the usual charges of a lawyer referral service or other legal service organization only as follows:

> (A) A lawyer may pay the usual, reasonable and customary charges of a lawyer referral service operated by the Louisiana State Bar Association, any local bar association, or any other not-for-profit organization, provided the lawyer referral service:
>
> > (i) refers all persons who request legal services to a participating lawyer;
> >
> > (ii) prohibits lawyers from increasing their fee to a client to compensate for the referral service charges; and
> >
> > (iii) fairly and equitably distributes referral cases among the participating lawyers, within their area of practice, by random allotment or by rotation.
>
> [(B) There is no paragraph 7.2(13)(B) in the rule adopted by the Louisiana Supreme Court.]

BACKGROUND

The Louisiana Supreme Court adopted this rule on June 26, 2008. It was amended on June 4, 2009 and became effective October 1, 2009. In the wake of the Fifth Circuit's 2011 declaration that some of Louisiana's lawyer advertising rules were unconstitutional, the Louisiana Supreme Court amended this rule on June 22, 2011.

Louisiana Rule of Professional Conduct 7.2(13)(A)(i)-(iii) (2009) is nearly identical to the prior version of this rule, which was adopted on January 20, 2004, and became effective March 1, 2004. *See also* ABA Model Rule of Prof'l Conduct 7.2 (2002).

The current version of Rule 7.2 sets forth rules for required content, permissible content, and prohibited content of advertisements and unsolicited written communications. *See* La. Rules of Prof'l Conduct r 7.2(a)-(c) (2009).

In 2016, the Louisiana Supreme Court amended paragraph 7.2(c)(5) of this rule to permit a lawyer to use the words "specialize" and "expert" to describe areas of practice. The court's amendment is sensible and brings Louisiana's professional conduct standards into line with the ABA Model Rules. Model Rule 7.4 permits a lawyer to state that the lawyer "specializes" in an area of practice–provided that the lawyer does not "state or imply that the lawyer is certified as a specialist in a particular field of law" without formal certification, and provided that the statement is not false or misleading. *See* ABA Model Rules of Prof'l Conduct r. 7.4;j *see id.* cmt. 1 ("A lawyer is generally permitted to state that the lawyer is a 'specialist,' practices a 'specialty,' or 'specializes in' particular fields," provided that the statement is not false or misleading). Most lawyers who state that they "specialize" in a practice area don't intend to suggest that the Louisiana Board of Legal Specialization, or any other organization, has formally certified them as an "expert" or a "specialist" in a field of practice. On the contrary, most simply use the term "specialize" in its nontechnical sense: "to concentrate one's efforts in a special activity, field, or practice." See Merriam-Webster Dictionary (def. "specialized"). As a result of the 2016 amendment, the Louisiana Rules now expressly permit such innocuous statements.

ABA MODEL RULE 7.2

(a) Subject to the requirements of Rules 7.1 and 7.3, a lawyer may advertise services through written, recorded or electronic communication, including public media.

(b) A lawyer shall not give anything of value to a person for recommending the lawyer's services except that a lawyer may

> (1) pay the reasonable costs of advertisements or communications permitted by this Rule;

> (2) pay the usual charges of a legal service plan or a not-for-profit or qualified lawyer referral service. A qualified lawyer referral service is a lawyer referral service that has been approved by an appropriate regulatory authority;

> (3) pay for a law practice in accordance with Rule 1.17; and

> (4) refer clients to another lawyer or a nonlawyer professional pursuant to an agreement not otherwise prohibited under these Rules that provides for the other person to refer clients or customers to the lawyer, if

>> (i) the reciprocal referral agreement is not exclusive, and

>> (ii) the client is informed of the existence and nature of the agreement.

(c) Any communication made pursuant to this rule shall include the name and office address of at least one lawyer or law firm responsible for its content.

COMMENTS TO ABA MODEL RULE 7.2
Generally

[1] To assist the public in learning about and obtaining legal services, lawyers should be allowed to make known their services not only through reputation but also through organized information campaigns in the form of advertising. Advertising involves an active quest for clients, contrary to the tradition that a lawyer should not seek clientele. However,

the public's need to know about legal services can be fulfilled in part through advertising. This need is particularly acute in the case of persons of moderate means who have not made extensive use of legal services. The interest in expanding public information about legal services ought to prevail over considerations of tradition. Nevertheless, advertising by lawyers entails the risk of practices that are misleading or overreaching.

[2] This Rule permits public dissemination of information concerning a lawyer's name or firm name, address, email address, website, and telephone number; the kinds of services the lawyer will undertake; the basis on which the lawyer's fees are determined, including prices for specific services and payment and credit arrangements; a lawyer's foreign language ability; names of references and, with their consent, names of clients regularly represented; and other information that might invite the attention of those seeking legal assistance.

[3] Questions of effectiveness and taste in advertising are matters of speculation and subjective judgment. Some jurisdictions have had extensive prohibitions against television and other forms of advertising, against advertising going beyond specified facts about a lawyer, or against "undignified" advertising. Television, the Internet, and other forms of electronic communication are now among the most powerful media for getting information to the public, particularly persons of low and moderate income; prohibiting television, Internet, and other forms of electronic advertising, therefore, would impede the flow of information about legal services to many sectors of the public. Limiting the information that may be advertised has a similar effect and assumes that the bar can accurately forecast the kind of information that the public would regard as relevant. But see Rule 7.3(a) for the prohibition against a solicitation through a real-time electronic exchange initiated by the lawyer.

[4] Neither this Rule nor Rule 7.3 prohibits communications authorized by law, such as notice to members of a class in class action litigation.

Paying Others to Recommend a Lawyer

[5] Except as permitted under paragraphs (b)(1)-(b)(4), lawyers are not permitted to pay others for recommending the lawyer's services or for channeling professional work in a manner that violates Rule 7.3. A communication contains a recommendation if it endorses or vouches for a lawyer's credentials, abilities, competence, character, or other professional qualities. Paragraph (b)(1), however, allows a lawyer to pay for advertising and communications permitted by this Rule, including the costs of print directory listings, on-line directory listings, newspaper ads, television and radio airtime, domain-name registrations, sponsorship fees, Internet-based advertisements, and group advertising. A lawyer may compensate employees, agents and vendors who are engaged to provide marketing or client development services, such as publicists, public-relations personnel, business-development staff and website designers. Moreover, a lawyer may pay others for generating client leads, such as Internet-based client leads, as long as the lead generator does not recommend the lawyer, any payment to the lead generator is consistent with Rules 1.5(e) (division of fees) and 5.4 (professional independence of the lawyer), and the lead generator's communications are consistent with Rule 7.1 (communications

concerning a lawyer's services). To comply with Rule 7.1, a lawyer must not pay a lead generator that states, implies, or creates a reasonable impression that it is recommending the lawyer, is making the referral without payment from the lawyer, or has analyzed a person's legal problems when determining which lawyer should receive the referral. See also Rule 5.3 (duties of lawyers and law firms with respect to the conduct of nonlawyers); Rule 8.4(a) (duty to avoid violating the Rules through the acts of another).

[6] A lawyer may pay the usual charges of a legal service plan or a not-for-profit or qualified lawyer referral service. A legal service plan is a prepaid or group legal service plan or a similar delivery system that assists prospective clients to secure legal representation. A lawyer referral service, on the other hand, is any organization that holds itself out to the public as a lawyer referral service. Such referral services are understood by laypersons to be consumer-oriented organizations that provide unbiased referrals to lawyers with appropriate experience in the subject matter of the representation and afford other client protections, such as complaint procedures or malpractice insurance requirements. Consequently, this Rule only permits a lawyer to pay the usual charges of a not-for-profit or qualified lawyer referral service. A qualified lawyer referral service is one that is approved by an appropriate regulatory authority as affording adequate protections for prospective clients. See, e.g., the American Bar Association's Model Supreme Court Rules Governing Lawyer Referral Services and Model Lawyer Referral and Information Service Quality Assurance Act (requiring that organizations that are identified as lawyer referral services (i) permit the participation of all lawyers who are licensed and eligible to practice in the jurisdiction and who meet reasonable objective eligibility requirements as may be established by the referral service for the protection of prospective clients; (ii) require each participating lawyer to carry reasonably adequate malpractice insurance; (iii) act reasonably to assess client satisfaction and address client complaints; and (iv) do not refer prospective clients to lawyers who own, operate or are employed by the referral service.)

[7] A lawyer who accepts assignments or referrals from a legal service plan or referrals from a lawyer referral service must act reasonably to assure that the activities of the plan or service are compatible with the lawyer's professional obligations. See Rule 5.3. Legal service plans and lawyer referral services may communicate with prospective clients, but such communication must be in conformity with these Rules. Thus, advertising must not be false or misleading, as would be the case if the communications of a group advertising program or a group legal services plan would mislead prospective clients to think that it was a lawyer referral service sponsored by a state agency or bar association. Nor could the lawyer allow in-person, telephonic, or real-time contacts that would violate Rule 7.3.

[8] A lawyer also may agree to refer clients to another lawyer or a nonlawyer professional, in return for the undertaking of that person to refer clients or customers to the lawyer. Such reciprocal referral arrangements must not interfere with the lawyer's professional judgment as to making referrals or as to providing substantive legal services. See Rules 2.1 and 5.4(c). Except as provided in Rule 1.5(e), a lawyer who receives referrals from a lawyer or nonlawyer professional must not pay anything solely for the referral, but the lawyer does not violate paragraph (b) of this Rule by agreeing to refer clients to the other lawyer

or nonlawyer professional, so long as the reciprocal referral agreement is not exclusive and the client is informed of the referral agreement. Conflicts of interest created by such arrangements are governed by Rule 1.7. Reciprocal referral agreements should not be of indefinite duration and should be reviewed periodically to determine whether they comply with these Rules. This Rule does not restrict referrals or divisions of revenues or net income among lawyers within firms comprised of multiple entities.

ANNOTATIONS
Advertising
Rule 7.1(a), like Model Rule 7.2(a), expressly authorizes lawyer advertising. *See* La. Rules of Prof'l Conduct r. 7.1(a) (2009). Furthermore, the United States Supreme Court has held repeatedly that lawyers have a First Amendment right to engage in truthful, nonmisleading commercial speech–including advertising. *See Zauderer v. Office of Disciplinary Counsel*, 471 U.S. 626 (1985); *In re R.M.J.*, 455 U.S. 191, 199 (1982); *Bates v. State Bar of Ariz.*, 433 U.S. 350, 374 (1977); *see also Central Hudson Gas & Elec. Corp. v. Public Serv. Comm'n*, 447 U.S. 557, 563 (1980).

No Payments for Recommending Lawyer's Services
Paragraph 7.2(c)(13) of this rule prohibits a lawyer from paying any third person for recommending the lawyer's services. *See* La. Rules of Prof'l Conduct r. 7.2(c)(13) (2009). In so doing, it prohibits, among other things, a lawyer from paying a "runner" to "hustle" cases from prospective clients. *See, e.g., In re Coney*, 891 So. 2d 858 (La. 2005) (disbarring lawyer for paying "runners" to solicit personal injury cases); *In re Kirchberg*, 856 So. 2d 1162 (La. 2003) (disbarring lawyer permanently for criminal convictions and payments to runners); *In re Sledge*, 859 So. 2d 671, 673-74 (La. 2003) (disbarring lawyer for paying nonlawyers $50 to $100 for case referrals); *In re Lockhart*, 795 So. 2d 309 (La. 2001); *In re Grand*, 778 So. 2d 580 (La. 2001); *see also In re Cuccia*, 752 So. 2d 796 (La. 1999); *In re Tolchinsky*, 740 So. 2d 109 (La. 1999); *In re Brass*, 696 So. 2d 967 (La. 1997). The rule does permit a lawyer to pay the costs associated with permissible advertising or other communications. *See* La. Rules of Prof'l Conduct r. 7.2(13) (2009).

AVVO ADVISOR INVOLVES IMPERMISSIBLE PAYMENTS
Avvo Advisor is a service that connects prospective clients with Louisiana lawyers—for a fee. How does it work? A prospective client visits the website https://www.avvo.com/advisor, selects the legal services needed, pays Avvo a fixed fee, and Avvo arranges for an "experienced Louisiana lawyer" to return the prospective client's call within minutes.

From the lawyer's standpoint, participating is easy. The lawyer simply clicks the "Join Today" button and agrees to provide certain legal services for a fixed fee. For example, the flat fee for a "15-minute Family advice session" is $39.00; filing for an "uncontested divorce" is $995.00; and creating a "last will and testament" is $295.00. Avvo boasts:

> With more than 8 million visits to Avvo each month, we can connect you with clients who have already paid for limited-scope legal services. There's no chasing leads.

> You choose from dozens of legal services and control your availability. Clients only buy what you want to sell, when you want to sell it.
>
> Avvo handles the billing up front, so you can focus on getting the client the help they need. No sending invoices.

After the lawyer provides the services, Avvo sends the lawyer "100% of the client's payment." The lawyer then "[a]s a completely separate transaction," pays a "per-service marketing fee." The amount of that marketing fee "depends on the service, and ranges from a $10 marketing fee for a $39 service, to $40 marketing fee for a $149 service, up to a $400 marketing fee for a $2995 service. *See* Attorney FAQ for Avvo Legal Services.

"Is it ethical?," you ask. According to Avvo, "yes, it is." Avvo says that it is not getting paid for lawyer referrals: "Avvo is not referring people to a particular lawyer. Potential clients choose which attorney they would like to work with from all available, participating attorneys." Furthermore, Avvo says that it is not sharing in legal fees: "Fee splits are not inherently unethical. They only become a problem if the split creates a situation that may compromise a lawyer's professional independence of judgment. We believe that Avvo Legal Services fees, if deducted like credit card fees, would involve the sort of technical fee split that would not create such a potential for compromise." *See id.*

The problem is that Avvo is wrong. As several ethics opinions have correctly concluded: "The referral service described in the request violates Rule 5.4 as impermissible fee sharing, [and] violates Rule 7.2 as paying for a recommendation of services beyond the reasonable costs of advertising" among other problems. *See* Utah Ethics Advisory Opinion Committee, Op. No. 17-05 at 4-5 (Sep. 27, 2017); *see also* S.C. Ethics Op. 16-06 (2016); Pa. Ethics Op. 2016-200 (2016); Ohio Ethics Op. 2016-3 (2016); N.Y. State Bar Ethics Op. 1132, (2017); N.J. Ethics Op. 732 (2017). Considering these unfavorable ethics opinions, Louisiana lawyers should avoid participating in Avvo Advisor. Louisiana Rule 5.4(a) provides that a "lawyer or law firm shall not share legal fees with a nonlawyer," except under unusual circumstances. Similarly, Louisiana Rule 7.2(c)(13) provides that a "lawyer shall not give anything of value to a person for recommending the lawyer's services, except that a lawyer may pay the reasonable cost of advertising or written or recorded communication permitted by these Rules, and may pay the usual charges of a lawyer referral service . . . ." Both rules are squarely implicated by Avvo's questionable business model.

Payments for "Lead Generation"

In August 2012, the ABA amended the comments to the corresponding model rule to expressly provide that:

> a lawyer may pay others for generating client leads, such as Internet-based client leads, as long as the lead generator does not recommend the lawyer, any payment to the lead generator is consistent with Rules 1.5(e) (division of fees) and 5.4 (professional independence of the lawyer), and the lead generator's communications are consistent with

Rule 7.1 (communications concerning a lawyer's services). To comply with Rule 7.1, a lawyer must not pay a lead generator that states, implies, or creates a reasonable impression that it is recommending the lawyer, is making the referral without payment from the lawyer, or has analyzed a person's legal problems when determining which lawyer should receive the referral. See also Rule 5.3 (duties of lawyers and law firms with respect to the conduct of nonlawyers); Rule 8.4(a) (duty to avoid violating the Rules through the acts of another).

It is uncertain, however, whether Louisiana would allow this practice. Some other states have not. *See, e.g., Zelotes v. Rousseau*, No. 09-0412, Connecticut Statewide Grievance Committee (Feb. 8, 2010).

Disciplinary Sanctions

Absent aggravating or mitigating circumstances, the following sanctions are generally appropriate in cases involving violations of Rule 7.2: *disbarment*, when the lawyer knowingly engages in conduct that is a violation of a duty owed to the profession with the intent to obtain a benefit for the lawyer or another, and causes serious or potentially serious injury to a client, the public, or the legal system; *suspension*, when the lawyer knowingly engages in conduct that is a violation of a duty owed to the profession, and causes injury or potential injury to a client, the public, or the legal system; *reprimand*, when the lawyer negligently engages in conduct that is a violation of a duty owed to the profession, and causes injury or potential injury to a client, the public, or the legal system; and, *admonition*, when the lawyer engages in an isolated instance of negligence that is a violation of a duty owed to the profession, and causes little or no actual or potential injury to a client, the public or the legal system. *See* ABA Stds. for Imposing Lawyer Sanctions stds. 7.0-7.4 (1986).

However, not all technical violations of this rule subject a lawyer to discipline. In the matter of *In re Loughlin*, 148 So. 3d 176 (La. 2014), the Louisiana Supreme Court found that the lawyer's use of the term "specializing" on his website caused no harm to the public and, therefore, did not rise to the level of sanctionable misconduct.

RULE 7.3. [RESERVED]

ANNOTATIONS

This rule number is "reserved." ABA Model Rule of Professional Conduct 7.3 addresses direct contact with prospective clients. *See* ABA Model Rules of Prof'l Cond. Rule 7.3. The Louisiana rules address this topic in Louisiana Rule of Professional Conduct 7.4.

RULE 7.4. DIRECT CONTACT WITH PROSPECTIVE CLIENTS

(a) *Solicitation.* Except as provided in subdivision (b) of this Rule, a lawyer shall not solicit professional employment from a prospective client with whom the lawyer has no family or prior lawyer-client relationship, in person, by person to person verbal telephone contact, through others acting at the lawyer's request or on the lawyer's behalf or otherwise, when a significant motive for the lawyer's doing so is the lawyer's pecuniary gain. A lawyer shall not permit employees or agents of the lawyer to solicit on the lawyer's behalf. A lawyer shall not enter into an agreement for, charge, or collect a fee for professional employment obtained in violation of this Rule. The term "solicit" includes contact in person, by telephone, telegraph, or facsimile, or by other communication directed to a specific recipient and includes (i) any written form of communication directed to a specific recipient and not meeting the requirements of subdivision (b) of this Rule, and (ii) any electronic mail communication directed to a specific recipient and not meeting the requirements of subdivision (c) of Rule 7.6. For the purposes of this Rule 7.4, the phrase "prior lawyer-client relationship" shall not include relationships in which the client was an unnamed member of a class action.

(b) *Written Communication Sent on an Unsolicited Basis.*

> (1) A lawyer shall not send, or knowingly permit to be sent, on the lawyer's behalf or on behalf of the lawyer's firm or partner, an associate, or any other lawyer affiliated with the lawyer or the lawyer's firm, an unsolicited written communication directly or indirectly to a prospective client for the purpose of obtaining professional employment if:
>
> > (A) the written communication concerns an action for personal injury or wrongful death or otherwise relates to an accident or disaster involving the person to whom the communication is addressed or a relative of that person, unless the accident or disaster occurred more than thirty days prior to the mailing of the communication;

(B) it has been made known to the lawyer that the person does not want to receive such communications from the lawyer;

(C) the communication involves coercion, duress, fraud, overreaching, harassment, intimidation, or undue influence;

(D) the communication contains a false, misleading or deceptive statement or claim or is improper under subdivision (c)(1) of Rule 7.2; or

(E) the lawyer knows or reasonably should know that the physical, emotional, or mental state of the person makes it unlikely that the person would exercise reasonable judgment in employing a lawyer.

(2) Unsolicited written communications to prospective clients for the purpose of obtaining professional employment are subject to the following requirements:

(A) Unsolicited written communications to a prospective client are subject to the requirements of Rule 7.2.

(B) In instances where there is no family or prior lawyer-client relationship, a lawyer shall not initiate any form of targeted solicitation, whether a written or recorded communication, of a person or persons known to need legal services of a particular kind provided by the lawyer in a particular matter for the purpose of obtaining professional employment unless such communication complies with the requirements set forth below and is not otherwise in violation of these Rules:

(i) Such communication shall state clearly the name of at least one member in good standing of the Association responsible for its content.

(ii) The top of each page of such written communication and the lower left comer of the face of the envelope in which the written communication is enclosed shall be plainly marked "ADVERTISEMENT" in print size at least as large as the largest print used in the written communication. If the written communication is in the form of a self-mailing brochure or pamphlet, the "ADVERTISEMENT" mark shall appear above the address panel of the brochure or pamphlet and on the inside of the brochure or pamphlet. Written communications solicited by clients or prospective clients, or written communications sent only to other lawyers need not contain the "ADVERTISEMENT" mark.

(C) Unsolicited written communications mailed to prospective clients shall not resemble a legal pleading, notice, contract or other legal document and shall not be sent by registered mail, certified mail or other forms of restricted delivery.

(D) If a lawyer other than the lawyer whose name or signature appears on the communication will actually handle the case or matter, any unsolicited written communication concerning a specific matter shall include a statement so advising the client.

(E) Any unsolicited written communication prompted by a specific occurrence involving or affecting the intended recipient of the communication or a family member of that person shall disclose how the lawyer obtained the information prompting the communication.

(F) An unsolicited written communication seeking employment by a specific prospective client in a specific matter shall not reveal on the envelope, or on the outside of a self-mailing brochure or pamphlet, the nature of the client's legal problem.

BACKGROUND

The Louisiana Supreme Court adopted this rule on June 26, 2008. It became effective October 1, 2009. In the wake of the Fifth Circuit's 2011 declaration that some of Louisiana's lawyer advertising rules were unconstitutional, the Louisiana Supreme Court amended this rule on June 22, 2011. Louisiana Rule 7.4 is based on ABA Model Rule of Professional Conduct 7.3 (2002). However, Louisiana Rule 7.4 differs significantly from the corresponding ABA model rule, ABA Model Rule 7.3.

1. First, ABA Model Rule 7.3(a)(1) specifically permits a lawyer to solicit legal business from another lawyer. *See* ABA Model Rules of Prof'l Conduct r. 7.3(a)(1) (2002).

2. Second, paragraph (b) of this rule–which relates only to written communications sent on an unsolicited basis and not to in-person communications–is similar to Model Rule 7.3(c), with several additional requirements. The Louisiana Rule requires that a targeted communication identify at least one Louisiana lawyer responsible for its content (7.4(b)(2)(b)(i)); the Louisiana Rule requires that a written communication not resemble a legal document and not be sent via restricted delivery (7.4(b)(2)(C)). The Louisiana Rule sets forth detailed specifications relating to the required notice that the communication is an "advertisement" (7.4(b)(2)(B)(ii)). The Louisiana Rule imposes a 30-day waiting period for written communications relating to personal-injury matters (7.4(b)(1)(A)). And finally, the Louisiana Rule requires that a lawyer disclose how the lawyer "obtained the information prompting the communication" if it was made in a response to a "specific occurrence involving or affecting the intended recipient." La. Rules of Prof'l Conduct r. 7.4(b)(2)(E) (2009).

3. Third, Louisiana Rule 7.4(b)(1)(C) additionally prohibits a Louisiana lawyer from engaging in solicitations involving "fraud, overreaching, intimidation or undue influence." La. Rules of Prof'l Conduct 7.4(b)(1)(C) (2009).

4. Fourth, Model Rule 7.3(d) contains a paragraph not found in the Louisiana Rules. Namely, Model Rule 7.3(d) permits a lawyer to participate with a prepaid or group legal service plan operated by an organization not owned or directed by the lawyer even though that plan may solicit clients not known to need legal services for a particular matter. *See* ABA Model Rules of Prof'l Conduct r. 7.3(d) (2002); *Allison v. La. State Bar Ass'n*, 362 So. 2d 489 (La. 1978).

ABA MODEL RULE 7.3: SOLICITATION OF CLIENTS (2012)

(a) A lawyer shall not by in-person, live telephone or real-time electronic contact solicit professional employment when a significant motive for the lawyer's doing so is the lawyer's pecuniary gain, unless the person contacted:

    (1) is a lawyer; or

    (2) has a family, close personal, or prior professional relationship with the lawyer.

(b) A lawyer shall not solicit professional employment by written, recorded or electronic communication or by in-person, telephone or real-time electronic contact even when not otherwise prohibited by paragraph (a), if:

(1) the target of the solicitation has made known to the lawyer a desire not to be solicited by the lawyer; or

(2) the solicitation involves coercion, duress or harassment.

(c) Every written, recorded or electronic communication from a lawyer soliciting professional employment from anyone known to be in need of legal services in a particular matter shall include the words "Advertising Material" on the outside envelope, if any, and at the beginning and ending of any recorded or electronic communication, unless the recipient of the communication is a person specified in paragraphs (a)(1) or (a)(2).

(d) Notwithstanding the prohibitions in paragraph (a), a lawyer may participate with a prepaid or group legal service plan operated by an organization not owned or directed by the lawyer that uses in-person or telephone contact to solicit memberships or subscriptions for the plan from persons who are not known to need legal services in a particular matter covered by the plan.

Comments to ABA Model Rule 7.3

[1] A solicitation is a targeted communication initiated by the lawyer that is directed to a specific person and that offers to provide, or can reasonably be understood as offering to provide, legal services. In contrast, a lawyer's communication typically does not constitute a solicitation if it is directed to the general public, such as through a billboard, an Internet banner advertisement, a website or a television commercial, or if it is in response to a request for information or is automatically generated in response to Internet searches.

[2] There is a potential for abuse when a solicitation involves direct in-person, live telephone or real-time electronic contact by a lawyer with someone known to need legal services. These forms of contact subject a person to the private importuning of the trained advocate in a direct interpersonal encounter. The person, who may already feel overwhelmed by the circumstances giving rise to the need for legal services, may find it difficult fully to evaluate all available alternatives with reasoned judgment and appropriate self-interest in the face of the lawyer's presence and insistence upon being retained immediately. The situation is fraught with the possibility of undue influence, intimidation, and over-reaching.

[3] This potential for abuse inherent in direct in-person, live telephone or real-time electronic solicitation justifies its prohibition, particularly since lawyers have alternative means of conveying necessary information to those who may be in need of legal services. In particular, communications can be mailed or transmitted by email or other electronic means that do not involve real-time contact and do not violate other laws governing solicitations. These forms of communications and solicitations make it possible for the public to be informed about the need for legal services, and about the qualifications of available lawyers and law firms, without subjecting the public to direct in-person, telephone or real-time electronic persuasion that may overwhelm a person's judgment.

[4] The use of general advertising and written, recorded or electronic communications to transmit information from lawyer to the public, rather than direct in-person, live telephone or real-time electronic contact, will help to assure that the information flows cleanly as well as freely. The contents of advertisements and communications permitted under Rule 7.2 can be permanently recorded so that they cannot be disputed and may be shared with others who know the lawyer. This potential for informal review is itself likely to help guard against statements and claims that might constitute false and misleading communications, in violation of Rule 7.1. The contents of direct in-person, live telephone or real-time electronic contact can be disputed and may not be subject to third-party scrutiny. Consequently, they are much more likely to approach (and occasionally cross) the dividing line between accurate representations and those that are false and misleading.

[5] There is far less likelihood that a lawyer would engage in abusive practices against a, former client, or a person with whom the lawyer has close personal or family relationship, or in situations in which the lawyer is motivated by considerations other than the lawyer's pecuniary gain. Nor is there a serious potential for abuse when the person contacted is a lawyer. Consequently, the general prohibition in Rule 7.3(a) and the requirements of Rule 7.3(c) are not applicable in those situations. Also, paragraph (a) is not intended to prohibit a lawyer from participating in constitutionally protected activities of public or charitable legal- service organizations or bona fide political, social, civic, fraternal, employee or trade organizations whose purposes include providing or recommending legal services to their members or beneficiaries.

[6] But even permitted forms of solicitation can be abused. Thus, any solicitation which contains information which is false or misleading within the meaning of Rule 7.1, which involves coercion, duress or harassment within the meaning of Rule 7.3(b)(2), or which involves contact with someone who has made known to the lawyer a desire not to be solicited by the lawyer within the meaning of Rule 7.3(b)(1) is prohibited. Moreover, if after sending a letter or other communication as permitted by Rule 7.2 the lawyer receives no response, any further effort to communicate with the recipient of the communication may violate the provisions of Rule 7.3(b).

[7] This Rule is not intended to prohibit a lawyer from contacting representatives of organizations or groups that may be interested in establishing a group or prepaid legal plan for their members, insureds, beneficiaries or other third parties for the purpose of informing such entities of the availability of and details concerning the plan or arrangement which the lawyer or lawyer's firm is willing to offer. This form of communication is not directed to people who are seeking legal services for themselves. Rather, it is usually addressed to an individual acting in a fiduciary capacity seeking a supplier of legal services for others who may, if they choose, become prospective clients of the lawyer. Under these circumstances, the activity which the lawyer undertakes in communicating with such representatives and the type of information transmitted to the individual are functionally similar to and serve the same purpose as advertising permitted under Rule 7.2.

[8] The requirement in Rule 7.3(c) that certain communications be marked "Advertising Material" does not apply to communications sent in response to requests of potential clients or their spokespersons or sponsors. General announcements by lawyers, including changes in personnel or office location, do not constitute communications soliciting professional employment from a client known to be in need of legal services within the meaning of this Rule.

[9] Paragraph (d) of this Rule permits a lawyer to participate with an organization which uses personal contact to solicit members for its group or prepaid legal service plan, provided that the personal contact is not undertaken by any lawyer who would be a provider of legal services through the plan. The organization must not be owned by or directed (whether as manager or otherwise) by any lawyer or law firm that participates in the plan. For example, paragraph (d) would not permit a lawyer to create an organization controlled directly or indirectly by the lawyer and use the organization for the in-person or telephone solicitation of legal employment of the lawyer through memberships in the plan or otherwise. The communication permitted by these organizations also must not be directed to a person known to need legal services in a particular matter, but is to be designed to inform potential plan members generally of another means of affordable legal services. Lawyers who participate in a legal service plan must reasonably assure that the plan sponsors are in compliance with Rules 7.1, 7.2 and 7.3(b). See 8.4(a).

ANNOTATIONS
In-Person Solicitation

Paragraph (a) of this rule prohibits a lawyer from soliciting employment from an unrelated, new client either in person or by telephone when "a significant motive" for doing so is pecuniary gain. La. Rules of Prof'l Conduct r. 7.4(a) (2009); *see also Ohralik v. Ohio State Bar Ass'n*, 436 U.S. 447, 449 (1978); *In re Jones*, 952 So. 2d 673 (La. 2007) (disbarring lawyer for, among other things, soliciting at a funeral home where parents of a man killed by police were making funeral arrangements). The rule prohibits such in-person or telephone solicitation whether or not the lawyer knows that the person needs legal services. Although a lawyer may call prospective clients for purposes other than to "solicit professional employment," the line between a call that is merely informational and one that constitutes impermissible solicitation is sometimes difficult to draw. *See In re D'Amico*, 668 So. 2d 730, 733 (La. 1996). The Louisiana Supreme Court has "consistently found solicitation to be a very serious professional violation." *E.g., In re Broome*, 815 So. 2d 1, 5 (La. 2002) (citing *In re D'Amico*, 688 So. 2d 730 (La. 1996); *La. State Bar Ass'n v. St. Romain*, 560 So. 2d 820 (La. 1990)); *In re Goff*, 837 So. 2d 1201, 1206 (La. 2003) ("Unquestionably, engaging in runner-based solicitation is one of the most serious professional violations a lawyer may commit."). Given the seriousness of client solicitation, the court has not hesitated to disbar lawyers for egregious violations of this rule. *See, e.g., In re Sledge*, 859 So. 2d 671 (La. 2003); *In re Cuccia*, 752 So. 2d 796 (La. 1999).

This rule does not prohibit noncoercive in-person or telephonic solicitation that is driven by nonpecuniary motives. Thus, for example, this rule does not prohibit, and the United

States Constitution protects, solicitation to pursue social, political or ideological goals. *See, e.g., In re Primus*, 436 U.S. 412, 426-31 (1978).

Written Targeted Solicitation

Paragraph (b) of this rule sets forth detailed prerequisites for written communications sent on an unsolicited basis. *See* La. Rules of Prof'l Conduct r. 7.4(b) (2009); *see also Shapero v. Ky. Bar Ass'n*, 486 U.S. 466 (1988); *In re Schmidt*, 976 So. 2d 1267 (La. 2008). As to all written targeted communications, the communication must state the name of at least one Louisiana lawyer responsible for the communication. La. Rules of Prof'l Conduct r. 7.4(b)(2)(B)(i) (2009). The lawyer also (1) must ensure that the writing does not resemble a legal document and is not sent via restricted delivery (7.4(b)(2)(C) (2009)), (2) must mark the term "advertisement" on the writing in specified places (7.4(b)(2)(B)(ii) (2009)), (3) must refrain from sending the writing until 30 days after any personal-injury or "accident" which the writing concerns (7.4(b)(1)(A) (2009)) and, (4) must "disclose how the lawyer obtained the information prompting the communication," if the targeted communication was "prompted by a specific occurrence involving or affecting the intended recipient" (7.4(b)(2)(E) (2009).

Unwanted and Impermissible Solicitation

Paragraph (b)(1)(B) prohibits a lawyer from any otherwise permissible solicitation if the prospective client has told the lawyer that he or she is not interested in being solicited. La. Rules of Prof'l Conduct r. 7.4(b)(1)(B) (2009). Furthermore, paragraph (b)(1)(C) prohibits any solicitation involving "coercion, duress, harassment, fraud, overreaching, intimidation or undue influence." *Id.* r. 7.4(b)(1)(C).

Federal Law Regarding Solicitation After Air Crash

Note that 49 U.S.C. §1136(g)(2) prohibits a lawyer from engaging in certain unsolicited communications after an air crash: In the event of an accident involving an air carrier providing interstate or foreign air transportation and in the event of an accident involving a foreign air carrier that occurs within the United States, no unsolicited communication concerning a potential action for personal injury or wrongful death may be made by a lawyer (including any associate, agent, employee, or other representative of a lawyer) or any potential party to the litigation to an individual injured in the accident, or to a relative of an individual involved in the accident, before the 45th day following the date of the accident.

Disciplinary Sanctions

Absent aggravating or mitigating circumstances, the following sanctions are generally appropriate in cases involving violations of Rule 7.4: *disbarment*, when the lawyer knowingly engages in conduct that is a violation of a duty owed to the profession with the intent to obtain a benefit for the lawyer or another, and causes serious or potentially serious injury to a client, the public, or the legal system; *suspension*, when the lawyer knowingly engages in conduct that is a violation of a duty owed to the profession, and causes injury or potential injury to a client, the public, or the legal system; *reprimand*, when the lawyer negligently engages in conduct that is a violation of a duty owed to the profession, and causes injury or potential injury to a client, the public, or the legal system;

and, *admonition*, when the lawyer engages in an isolated instance of negligence that is a violation of a duty owed to the profession, and causes little or no actual or potential injury to a client, the public or the legal system. *See* ABA Stds. for Imposing Lawyer Sanctions stds. 7.0-7.4 (1992).

RULE 7.5. ADVERTISEMENTS IN THE ELECTRONIC MEDIA OTHER THAN COMPUTER-ACCESSED COMMUNICATIONS

(a) *Generally.* With the exception of computer-based advertisements (which are subject to the special requirements set forth in Rule 7.6), all advertisements in the electronic media, including but not limited to television and radio, are subject to the requirements of Rule 7.2.

(b) *Appearance on Television or Radio.* Advertisements on the electronic media such as television and radio shall conform to the requirements of this Rule.

(1) *Prohibited Content.* Television and radio advertisements shall not contain:

(A) any feature, including, but not limited to, background sounds, that is false, misleading or deceptive; or

(B) lawyers who are not members of the advertising law firm speaking on behalf of the advertising lawyer or law firm.

(2) *Permissible Content.* Television and radio advertisements may contain:

(A) images that otherwise conform to the requirements of these Rules;

(B) a lawyer who is a member of the advertising firm personally appearing to speak regarding the legal services the lawyer or law firm is available to perform, the fees to be charged for such services, and the background and experience of the lawyer or law firm; or

[(C) a non-lawyer spokesperson speaking on behalf of the lawyer or law firm, as long as that spokesperson shall provide a spoken and written disclosure, as required by Rule 7.2(c)(10), identifying the spokesperson as a spokesperson, disclosing that the spokesperson is not a lawyer and disclosing that the spokesperson is being paid to be a spokesperson, if paid.]

353

> *Pursuant to Louisiana Supreme Court order dated*
> *September 22, 2009, enforcement of Rule*
> *7.5(b)(2)(C) was suspended.*

BACKGROUND

The Louisiana Supreme Court adopted this rule on June 26, 2008. It was amended June 4, 2009 and became effective October 1, 2009. Pursuant to an order dated September 22, 2009, the court suspended enforcement of Rule 7.5(b)(2)(C) in the wake of an opinion from the United States Court of Appeals for the Fifth Circuit holding that portions of Rule 7.5 were unconstitutional. *See Public Citizen, Inc. v. Louisiana Attorney Disciplinary Bd.*, 642 F. Supp. 539 (E.D. La. 2009), *aff'd in part, rev'd in part*, 632 F.3d 212 (5th Cir. 2011).

RULE 7.6. COMPUTER-ACCESSED COMMUNICATION

(a) *Definition.* For purposes of these Rules, "computer-accessed communications" are defined as information regarding a lawyer's or law firm's services that is read, viewed, or heard directly through the use of a computer. Computer-accessed communications include, but are not limited to, Internet presences such as home pages or World Wide Web sites, unsolicited electronic mail communications, and information concerning a lawyer's or law firm's services that appears on World Wide Web search engine screens and elsewhere.

(b) *Internet Presence.* All World Wide Web sites and home pages accessed via the Internet that are controlled, sponsored, or authorized by a lawyer or law firm and that contain information concerning the lawyer's or law firm's services:

> (1) shall disclose all jurisdictions in which the lawyer or members of the law firm are licensed to practice law;

> (2) shall disclose one or more bona fide office location(s) of the lawyer or law firm or, in the absence of a bona fide office, the city or town of the lawyer's primary registration statement address, in accordance with subdivision (a)(2) of Rule 7.2; and

> (3) are considered to be information provided upon request and, therefore, are otherwise governed by the requirements of Rule 7.9.

(c) *Electronic Mail Communications.* A lawyer shall not send, or knowingly permit to be sent, on the lawyer's behalf or on behalf of the lawyer's firm or partner, an associate, or any other lawyer affiliated with the lawyer or the lawyer's firm, an unsolicited electronic mail communication directly or indirectly to a prospective client for the purpose of obtaining professional employment unless:

> (1) the requirements of subdivisions (b)(1), (b)(2)(A), (b)(2)(B)(i), (b)(2)(C), (b)(2)(D), (b)(2)(E) and (b)(2)(F) of Rule 7.4 are met;

> (2) the communication discloses one or more bona fide office location(s) of the lawyer or lawyers who will

actually perform the services advertised or, in the absence of a bona fide office, the city or town of the lawyer's primary registration statement address, in accordance with subdivision (a)(2) of Rule 7.2; and

(3) the subject line of the communication states "LEGAL ADVERTISEMENT". This is not required for electronic mail communications sent only to other lawyers.

[(d) Advertisements. All computer-accessed communications concerning a lawyer's or law firm's services, other than those subject to subdivisions (b) and (c) of this Rule, are subject to the requirements of Rule 7.2 when a significant motive for the lawyer's doing so is the lawyer's pecuniary gain.]

Pursuant to order dated September 22, 2009, the Louisiana Supreme Court suspended enforcement of Rule 7.6(d).

BACKGROUND

The Louisiana Supreme Court adopted this rule on June 26, 2008. It was amended on June 4, 2009, and became effective on October 1, 2009. The Louisiana Attorney Disciplinary Board was enjoined from enforcing Rule 7.6(d) by a United States District Court judgment dated August 19, 2009 in *Pub. Citizen, Inc. v. La. Att'y Disciplinary Bd.*, 642 F. Supp. 2d 539 (E.D. La. 2009), *aff'd in part and rev'd in part, Public Citizen, Inc. v. La. Att'y Disciplinary Bd.*, 632 F.3d 212 (5th Cir. 2011). Thereafter, in an order dated September 22, 2009, the Louisiana Supreme Court suspended enforcement of Rule 7.6(d). *See* Louisiana Supreme Court Order of Sept. 22, 2009. In the wake of the Fifth Circuit's 2011 declaration that some of Louisiana's lawyer advertising rules were unconstitutional, the Louisiana Supreme Court amended this rule on June 22, 2011.

RULE 7.7. EVALUATION OF ADVERTISEMENTS

(a) *Louisiana State Bar Association Rules of Professional Conduct Committee.* With respect to said Committee, it shall be the task of the Committee, or any subcommittee designated by the Rules of Professional Conduct Committee (hereinafter collectively referred to as "the Committee"): 1) to evaluate all advertisements filed with the Committee for compliance with the Rules governing lawyer advertising and solicitation and to provide written advisory opinions concerning compliance with those Rules to the respective filing lawyers; 2) to develop a handbook on lawyer advertising for the guidance of and dissemination to the members of the Louisiana State Bar Association; and 3) to recommend, from time to time, such amendments to the Rules of Professional Conduct as the Committee may deem advisable.

(1) *Recusal of Members.* Members of the Committee shall recuse themselves from consideration of any advertisement proposed or used by themselves or by other lawyers in their firms.

(2) *Meetings.* The Committee shall meet as often as is necessary to fulfill its duty to provide prompt opinions regarding submitted advertisements' compliance with the lawyer advertising and solicitation rules.

(3) *Procedural Rules.* The Committee may adopt such procedural rules for its activities as may be required to enable the Committee to fulfill its functions.

(4) *Reports to the Court.* Within six months following the conclusion of the first year of the Committee's evaluation of advertisements in accordance with these Rules, and annually thereafter, the Committee shall submit to the Supreme Court of Louisiana a report detailing the year's activities of the Committee. The report shall include such information as the Court may require.

(b) *Advance Written Advisory Opinion.* Subject to the exemptions stated in Rule 7.8, any lawyer who advertises services through any public media or through unsolicited written communications sent in compliance with Rule 7.4 or

7.6(c) may obtain a written advisory opinion concerning the compliance of a contemplated advertisement or unsolicited written communication in advance of disseminating the advertisement or communication by submitting to the Committee the material and fee specified in subdivision (d) of this Rule at least thirty days prior to such dissemination. If the Committee finds that the advertisement or unsolicited written communication complies with these Rules, the lawyer's voluntary submission in compliance with this subdivision shall be deemed to satisfy the regular filing requirement set forth below in subdivision (c) of this Rule.

(c) *Regular Filing.* Subject to the exemptions stated in Rule 7.8, any lawyer who advertises services through any public media[129] or through unsolicited written communications sent in compliance with Rule 7.4 or 7.6(c) shall file a copy of each such advertisement or unsolicited written communication with the Committee for evaluation of compliance with these Rules. The copy shall be filed either prior to or concurrently with the lawyer's first dissemination of the advertisement or unsolicited written communication and shall be accompanied by the information and fee specified in subdivision (d) of this Rule. If the lawyer has opted to submit an advertisement or unsolicited written communication in advance of dissemination, in

---

[129] The Louisiana Attorney Disciplinary Board was enjoined from enforcing Rule 7.7(c) "as it pertains to filing requirements for internet advertising" by a United States District Court judgment of August 19, 2009. *See Public Citizen, Inc. v. La. Att'y. Disciplinary Bd.,* 642 F. Supp. 2d 539 (E.D. La. 2009), *aff'd in part and rev'd in part, Public Citizen, Inc. v. La. Att'y. Disciplinary Bd.,* 632 F.3d 212 (5th Cir. 2011). Thereafter, the Louisiana Supreme Court issued an order on September 22, 2009, suspending enforcement of Louisiana Rule of Professional Conduct 7.7 as it pertains to *filing requirements* (not all other requirements) for internet advertising. *See* Louisiana Supreme Court Order of September 22, 2009 (emphasis added). The "internet advertising" this order exempts from the filing requirement includes only advertisements by a lawyer on a third-party internet site (such as, banner advertisements, "click-throughs," "pop-ups," and the like). The order does not affect: (1) "unsolicited electronic mail communications directly or indirectly to a prospective client for the purpose of obtaining professional employment," which are still regulated by Rule 7.6(c); or (2) "internet presences" that are "controlled, sponsored, or authorized by a lawyer or law firm and that contain information concerning the lawyer's or law firm's services" (that is, a lawyer's own website), which are still regulated by Rules 7.2, 7.6(b), 7.8(g), and 7.9 (no filing requirement as per Rule 7.8(g)).

compliance with subdivision (b) of this Rule, and the advertisement or unsolicited written communication is then found to be in compliance with the Rules, that voluntary advance submission shall be deemed to satisfy the regular filing requirement set forth above.

> *The Louisiana Supreme Court issued an order on September 22, 2009, suspending enforcement of Rule 7.7 as it pertains to filing requirements for internet advertising.*

(d) *Contents of Filing.* A filing with the Committee as permitted by subdivision (b) or as required by subdivision (c) shall consist of:

(1) a copy of the advertisement or communication in the form or forms in which it is to be disseminated and is readily-capable of duplication by the Committee (e.g., videotapes, audiotapes, print media, photographs of outdoor advertising, etc.);

(2) a typewritten transcript of the advertisement or communication, if any portion of the advertisement or communication is on videotape, audiotape; electronic/digital media or otherwise not embodied in written/printed form;

(3) a printed copy of all text used in the advertisement;

(4) an accurate English translation, if the advertisement appears or is audible in a language other than English;

(5) a sample envelope in which the written communication will be enclosed, if the communication is to be mailed;

(6) a statement listing all media in which the advertisement or communication will appear, the anticipated frequency of use of the advertisement or communication in each medium in which it will appear, and the anticipated time period during which the advertisement or communication will be used; and

(7) fees paid to the Louisiana State Bar Association, in an amount set by the Supreme Court of Louisiana: (A) for submissions filed prior to or concurrently with the lawyer's first dissemination of the advertisement or

unsolicited written communication, as provided in subdivisions (b) and (c); or (B) for submissions not filed until after the lawyer's first dissemination of the advertisement or unsolicited written communication.

(e) *Evaluation of Advertisements.* The Committee shall evaluate all advertisements and unsolicited written communications filed with it pursuant to this Rule for compliance with the applicable rules on lawyer advertising and solicitation. The Committee shall complete its evaluation within thirty days following receipt of a filing unless the Committee determines that there is reasonable doubt that the advertisement or unsolicited written communication is in compliance with the Rules and that further examination is warranted but cannot be completed within the thirty-day period, and so advises the filing lawyer in writing within the thirty-day period. In the latter event, the Committee shall complete its review as promptly as the circumstances reasonably allow. If the Committee does not send any communication in writing to the filing lawyer within thirty days following receipt of the filing, the advertisement or unsolicited written communication will be deemed approved.

(f) *Additional Information.* If the Committee requests additional information, the filing lawyer shall comply promptly with the request. Failure to comply with such requests may result in a finding of non-compliance for insufficient information.

(g) *Notice of Noncompliance; Effect of Continued Use of Advertisement.* When the Committee determines that an advertisement or unsolicited written communication is not in compliance with the applicable Rules, the Committee shall advise the lawyer in writing that dissemination or continued dissemination of the advertisement or unsolicited written communication may result in professional discipline. The Committee shall report to the Office of Disciplinary Counsel a finding under subsections (c) or (f) of this Rule that the advertisement or unsolicited written communication is not in compliance, unless, within ten days of notice from the Committee, the filing lawyer certifies in writing that the advertisement or unsolicited written communication has not and will not be disseminated.

(h) *Committee Determination Not Binding; Evidence.* A finding by the Committee of either compliance or noncompliance shall not be binding in a disciplinary proceeding, but may be offered as evidence.

(i) *Change of Circumstances; Re-filing Requirement.* If a change of circumstances occurring subsequent to the Committee's evaluation of an advertisement or unsolicited written communication raises a substantial possibility that the advertisement or communication has become false, misleading or deceptive as a result of the change in circumstances, the lawyer shall promptly re-file the advertisement or a modified advertisement with the Committee along with an explanation of the change in circumstances and an additional fee as set by the Court.

(j) *Maintaining Copies of Advertisements.* A copy or recording of an advertisement or written or recorded communication shall be submitted to the Committee in accordance with the requirements of Rule 7.7, and the lawyer shall retain a copy or recording for five years after its last dissemination along with a record of when and where it was used. If identical unsolicited written communications are sent to two or more prospective clients, the lawyer may comply with this requirement by filing a copy of one of the identical unsolicited written communications and retaining for five years a single copy together with a list of the names and addresses of all persons to whom the unsolicited written communication was sent.

BACKGROUND

The Louisiana Supreme Court adopted this rule on June 26, 2008. It became effective October 1, 2009. The court issued an order on September 22, 2009, suspending enforcement of this rule as it pertains to *filing requirements* (not other requirements) for internet advertising. *See* Louisiana Supreme Court Order of September 22, 2009 (emphasis added). The "internet advertising" this order exempts from the filing requirement includes only advertisements by a lawyer on a third-party internet site (such as, banner advertisements, "click-throughs," "pop-ups," and the like). The order does not affect: (1) "unsolicited electronic mail communications directly or indirectly to a prospective client for the purpose of obtaining professional employment," which are still regulated by Rule 7.6(c); or (2) "internet presences" that are "controlled, sponsored, or authorized by a lawyer or law firm and that contain information concerning the lawyer's or law firm's services" (that is, a lawyer's own website), which are still regulated by Rules 7.2, 7.6(b), 7.8(g), and 7.9 (no filing requirement as per Rule 7.8(g)).

RULE 7.8. EXEMPTIONS FROM THE FILING AND REVIEW REQUIREMENT

The following are exempt from the filing and review requirements of Rule 7.7:

(a) any advertisement or unsolicited written communication that contains only content that is permissible under Rule 7.2(b).

(b) a brief announcement in any public media that identifies a lawyer or law firm as a contributor to a specified charity or as a sponsor of a public service announcement or a specified charitable, community, or public interest program, activity, or event, provided that the announcement contains no information about the lawyer or law firm other than permissible content of advertisements listed in Rule 7.2(b) and the fact of the sponsorship or contribution. In determining whether an announcement is a public service announcement for purposes of this Rule and the Rule setting forth permissible content of advertisements, the following are criteria that may be considered:

> (1) whether the content of the announcement appears to serve the particular interests of the lawyer or law firm as much as or more than the interests of the public;

> (2) whether the announcement contains information concerning the lawyer's or law firm's area(s) of practice, legal background, or experience;

> (3) whether the announcement contains the address or telephone number of the lawyer or law firm;

> (4) whether the announcement concerns a legal subject;

> (5) whether the announcement contains legal advice; and

> (6) whether the lawyer or law firm paid to have the announcement published.

(c) A listing or entry in a law list or bar publication.

(d) A communication mailed only to existing clients, former clients, or other lawyers.

(e) Any written communications requested by a prospective client.

(f) Professional announcement cards stating new or changed associations, new offices, and similar changes relating to a lawyer or law firm, and that are mailed only to other lawyers, relatives, close personal friends, and existing or former clients.

(g) Computer-accessed communications as described in subdivision (b) of Rule 7.6.

(h) *Gift/Promotional Items.* Items, such as coffee mugs, pens, pencils, apparel, and the like, that identify a lawyer or law firm and are used/disseminated by a lawyer or law firm not in violation of these Rules, including but not limited to Rule 7.2(c)(13) and Rule 7.4; and

(i) *Office Sign(s) for Bona Fide Office Location(s).* A sign, placard, lettering, mural, engraving, carving or other alphanumeric display conveying information about a lawyer, a lawyer's services or a law firm's services that is permanently affixed, hanging, erected or otherwise attached to the physical structure of the building containing a bona fide office location for a lawyer or law firm, or to the property on which that bona fide office location sits.

BACKGROUND

The Louisiana Supreme Court adopted this rule on June 26, 2008. It became effective October 1, 2009. The court added paragraphs (h) and (i) effective June 22, 2011.

RULE 7.9. INFORMATION ABOUT A LAWYER'S SERVICES PROVIDED UPON REQUEST

(a) *Generally.* Information provided about a lawyer's or law firm's services upon request shall comply with the requirements of Rule 7.2 unless otherwise provided in this Rule 7.9.

(b) *Request for Information by Potential Client.* Whenever a potential client shall request information regarding a lawyer or law firm for the purpose of making a decision regarding employment of the lawyer or law firm:

> (1) The lawyer or law firm may furnish such factual information regarding the lawyer or law firm deemed valuable to assist the client.

> (2) The lawyer or law firm may furnish an engagement letter to the potential client; however, if the information furnished to the potential client includes a contingency fee contract, the top of each page of the contract shall be marked "SAMPLE" in print size at least as large as the largest print used in the contract and the words "DO NOT SIGN" shall appear on the client signature line.

> (3) Notwithstanding the provisions of subdivision (c)(1)(D) of Rule 7.2, information provided to a potential client in response to a potential client's request may contain factually verifiable statements concerning past results obtained by the lawyer or law firm, if, either alone or in the context in which they appear, such statements are not otherwise false, misleading or deceptive.

(c) *Disclosure of Intent to Refer Matter to Another Lawyer or Law Firm.* A statement and any information furnished to a prospective client, as authorized by subdivision (b) of this Rule, that a lawyer or law firm will represent a client in a particular type of matter, without appropriate qualification, shall be presumed to be misleading if the lawyer reasonably believes that a lawyer or law firm not associated with the originally-retained lawyer or law firm will be associated or act as primary counsel in representing the client. In determining whether the statement is misleading in this respect, the history of prior conduct by the lawyer in similar matters may be considered.

BACKGROUND

The Louisiana Supreme Court adopted this rule on June 26, 2008. It became effective October 1, 2009.

RULE 7.10. FIRM NAMES AND LETTERHEAD

(a) *False, Misleading, or Deceptive.* A lawyer or law firm shall not use a firm name, logo, letterhead, professional designation, trade name or service mark that violates the provisions of these Rules.

(b) *Trade Names.* A lawyer or law firm shall not practice under a trade name that implies a connection with a government agency, public or charitable services organization or other professional association, that implies that the firm is something other than a private law firm, or that is otherwise in violation of subdivision (c)(1) of Rule 7.2.

(c) *Advertising Under Trade Name.* A lawyer shall not advertise under a trade or fictitious name, except that a lawyer who actually practices under a trade name as authorized by subdivision (b) may use that name in advertisements. A lawyer who advertises under a trade or fictitious name shall be in violation of this Rule unless the same name is the law firm name that appears on the lawyer's letterhead, business cards, office sign, and fee contracts, and appears with the lawyer's signature on pleadings and other legal documents.

(d) *Law Firm with Offices in More Than One Jurisdiction.* A law firm with offices in more than one jurisdiction may use the same name in each jurisdiction, but identification of the lawyers in an office of the firm shall indicate the jurisdictional limitations on those not licensed to practice in any jurisdiction where an office is located.

(e) *Name of Public Officer or Former Member in Firm Name.* The name of a lawyer holding a public office or formerly associated with a firm shall not be used in the name of a law firm, on its letterhead, or in any communications on its behalf, during any substantial period in which the lawyer is not actively and regularly practicing with the firm.

(f) *Partnerships and Organizational Business Entities.* Lawyers may state or imply that they practice in a partnership or other organizational business entity only when that is the fact.

(g) *Deceased or Retired Members of Law Firm.* If otherwise lawful and permitted under these Rules, a law firm may use as, or continue to include in, its name, the name or names of one or more deceased or retired members of the law firm, or of a predecessor firm in a continuing line of succession.

BACKGROUND

The Louisiana Supreme Court adopted this rule on June 26, 2008. It became effective on October 1, 2009. This rule is based on ABA Model Rule of Professional Conduct 7.5. However, there are several differences between this rule and Model Rule 7.5.

1. First, Louisiana Rule 7.10(a) itemizes more types of professional designations that must conform with the Rules than does Model Rule 7.5. *Compare* La. Rules of Prof'l Conduct r. 7.10(a) (2009) ("firm name, logo, letterhead, professional designation, trade name or trademark") *with* ABA Model Rules of Prof'l Conduct r. 7.5(a) ("firm name, letterhead or other professional designation").

2. Second, Louisiana Rule 7.10, unlike the corresponding Model Rule 7.5, prohibits a lawyer from using a trade name that implies a connection not only to a government agency, public services organization or charity, but also to any "other professional association." La. Rules of Prof'l Conduct r. 7.10(a) (2009).

3. Third, Louisiana Rule 7.10(c), unlike the corresponding Model Rule, prohibits a lawyer from using a "trade or fictitious name" unless the lawyer also uses that name on all other documents such as letterheads, fee contracts, and pleadings. *See id.*

4. Fourth, paragraph (e) of the Louisiana Rule, unlike Model Rule 7.5, prohibits a firm from using the name of a "formerly associated" lawyer "during any substantial period in which the lawyer is not actively and regularly practicing with the firm," unless the lawyer has died or retired. *See* Louisiana Rule 7.10(g) (permitting a firm to use the name of a deceased or retired former firm member). La. Rules of Prof'l Conduct r. 7.10(g) (2009); *see also* ABA Comm. on Ethics and Prof'l Responsibility, Informal Op. 85-1511 (1985) (interpreting ABA rules to reach the same result).

ABA MODEL RULE 7.5

(a) A lawyer shall not use a firm name, letterhead or other professional designation that violates Rule 7.1. A trade name may be used by a lawyer in private practice if it does not imply a connection with a government agency or with a public or charitable legal services organization and is not otherwise in violation of Rule 7.1.

(b) A law firm with offices in more than one jurisdiction may use the same name or other professional designation in each jurisdiction, but identification of the lawyers in an office of the firm shall indicate the jurisdictional limitations on those not licensed to practice in the jurisdiction where the office is located.

(c) The name of a lawyer holding a public office shall not be used in the name of a law firm, or in communications on its behalf, during any substantial period in which the lawyer is not actively and regularly practicing with the firm.

(d) Lawyers may state or imply that they practice in a partnership or other organization only when that is the fact.

Comments to ABA Model Rule 7.5

[1] A firm may be designated by the names of all or some of its members, by the names of deceased members where there has been a continuing succession in the firm's identity or by a trade name such as the "ABC Legal Clinic." A lawyer or law firm may also be designated by a distinctive website address or comparable professional designation. Although the United States Supreme Court has held that legislation may prohibit the use of trade names in professional practice, use of such names in law practice is acceptable so long as it is not misleading. If a private firm uses a trade name that includes a geographical name such as "Springfield Legal Clinic," an express disclaimer that it is a public legal aid agency may be required to avoid a misleading implication. It may be observed that any firm name including the name of a deceased partner is, strictly speaking, a trade name. The use of such names to designate law firms has proven a useful means of identification. However, it is misleading to use the name of a lawyer not associated with the firm or a predecessor of the firm, or the name of a nonlawyer.

[2] With regard to paragraph (d), lawyers sharing office facilities, but who are not in fact associated with each other in a law firm, may not denominate themselves as, for example, "Smith and Jones," for that title suggests that they are practicing law together in a firm.

ANNOTATIONS
Firm Names

Lawyers may not use a firm name, logo, letterhead or other professional designation that violates these rules. *See* La. Rules of Prof'l Conduct r. 7.10(a) (2009). Most obviously, this rule requires that any professional designation must not be "false, misleading, or deceptive." *Id.* r. 7.10(a). Furthermore, a firm may not use a name that implies a connection with a governmental, public, charitable, or professional organization. *Id.* r. 7.10(a). Finally, a lawyer who uses a trade name must not attempt to use it selectively; rather, the lawyer must use it on all business cards, office signs, pleadings and the like. *Id.*

Identifying an Association with Other Lawyers

A lawyer may not falsely imply an association with another lawyer or organization. La. Rules of Prof'l Conduct r. 7.10(f) (2009). Thus, for example, a lawyer practicing alone may not name his firm "Smith & Associates." Furthermore, a lawyer merely sharing office space with another must not share letterhead that implies the existence of a partnership.

A lawyer who is not a partner or an associate of a law firm may be designated "of counsel," "special counsel," "senior attorney," or "senior counsel," under appropriate circumstances. Such a designation is appropriate when the lawyer so designated is, for example, a part-time lawyer, a retired partner who remains available for consultation with practicing members of the firm, or a tenured lawyer below the rank of partner. *See* ABA Comm. on

Ethics and Prof'l Responsibility, Formal Op. 90-357 (1990); *see also* ABA Comm. on Ethics and Prof'l Responsibility, Informal Op. 84-1506 (1984).

Formerly Associated Lawyers

This rule prohibits a firm from using a name that suggests a continuing association between the firm and any formerly-associated lawyer who is not actively and regularly practicing with the firm. La. Rules of Prof'l Conduct r. 7.10(e) (2009). Under this rule, it is irrelevant whether the lawyer in question became "formerly associated" because the lawyer changed firms or because he or she assumed public office. However, if a lawyer becomes "formerly associated" through retirement or death, the firm may continue to use the lawyer's name thereafter. *See id.* r. 7.10(g).

Multistate Firms

A firm with an office in another state may use the names of out-of-state lawyers in the firm name. However, any identification of the lawyers in an office–in firm letterhead or otherwise–must note the jurisdictional limitations on those not licensed to practice where the office is located. La. Rules of Prof'l Conduct r. 7.10(d) (2009); *see also Singer Hutner Levine Seeman & Stuart v. La. State Bar Ass'n*, 378 So. 2d 423, 426 (La. 1979).

Disciplinary Sanctions

Absent aggravating or mitigating circumstances, the following sanctions are generally appropriate in cases involving violations of Rule 7.10: *disbarment*, when the lawyer knowingly engages in conduct that is a violation of a duty owed to the profession with the intent to obtain a benefit for the lawyer or another, and causes serious or potentially serious injury to a client, the public, or the legal system; *suspension*, when the lawyer knowingly engages in conduct that is a violation of a duty owed to the profession, and causes injury or potential injury to a client, the public, or the legal system; *reprimand*, when the lawyer negligently engages in conduct that is a violation of a duty owed to the profession, and causes injury or potential injury to a client, the public, or the legal system; and, *admonition*, when the lawyer engages in an isolated instance of negligence that is a violation of a duty owed to the profession, and causes little or no actual or potential injury to a client, the public, or the legal system. *See* ABA Stds. for Imposing Lawyer Sanctions stds. 7.0-7.4 (1986).

Article 8. Maintaining the Integrity of the Profession

RULE 8.1. BAR ADMISSION AND DISCIPLINARY MATTERS

An applicant for admission to the bar, or a lawyer in connection with a bar admission application or in connection with a disciplinary matter, shall not:

(a) Knowingly make a false statement of material fact;

(b) Fail to disclose a fact necessary to correct a misapprehension known by the person to have arisen in the matter, or knowingly fail to respond to a lawful demand for information from an admissions or disciplinary authority, except that this rule does not require disclosure of information otherwise protected by Rule 1.6; or

(c) Fail to cooperate with the Office of Disciplinary Counsel in its investigation of any matter before it except for an openly expressed claim of a constitutional privilege.

BACKGROUND

The Louisiana Supreme Court adopted this rule on January 20, 2004. It became effective on March 1, 2004, and has not been amended since.

Paragraphs (a) and (b) are identical to ABA Model Rule of Professional Conduct 8.1 (2002).[130] Paragraph (c) is not contained in the Model Rules but has long been a part of the Louisiana Rules of Professional Conduct. In 1985, the Louisiana Task Force on Adoption of the Model Rules recommended adoption of this paragraph "in order to facilitate the Committee on Professional Responsibility in its investigation and, most importantly, to expedite those investigations to the extent possible." Report and Recommendation of the Task Force to Evaluate the American Bar Association's Model Rules of Professional Conduct, at 23-24 (Nov. 23, 1985).

COMMENTS TO ABA MODEL RULE 8.1

[1] The duty imposed by this Rule extends to persons seeking admission to the bar as well as to lawyers. Hence, if a person makes a material false statement in connection with an application for admission, it may be the basis for subsequent disciplinary action if the person is admitted, and in any event may be relevant in a subsequent admission application. The duty imposed by this Rule applies to a lawyer's own admission or discipline as well as that of others. Thus, it is a separate professional offense for a lawyer to

---

[130] The ABA made no changes to the corresponding Model Rule in 2002.

knowingly make a misrepresentation or omission in connection with a disciplinary investigation of the lawyer's own conduct. Paragraph (b) of this Rule also requires correction of any prior misstatement in the matter that the applicant or lawyer may have made and affirmative clarification of any misunderstanding on the part of the admissions or disciplinary authority of which the person involved becomes aware.

[2] This Rule is subject to the provisions of the Fifth Amendment of the United States Constitution and corresponding provisions of state constitutions. A person relying on such a provision in response to a question, however, should do so openly and not use the right of nondisclosure as a justification for failure to comply with this Rule.

[3] A lawyer representing an applicant for admission to the bar, or representing a lawyer who is the subject of a disciplinary inquiry or proceeding, is governed by the rules applicable to the client-lawyer relationship, including Rule 1.6 and, in some cases, Rule 3.3.

ANNOTATIONS
Generally
This rule imposes a duty of candor in bar admissions and disciplinary matters similar to that imposed by Rule 3.3(a) in matters pending before tribunals. However, the duty of candor imposed by this rule is broader than the duty imposed by Rule 3.3 because it applies not only to licensed lawyers, but also to nonlawyers who eventually become licensed. La. Rules of Prof'l Conduct r. 8.1 (2004).

False Statements
Paragraph (a) prohibits a lawyer or bar applicant from making any false statement of material fact in connection with a bar application[131] or disciplinary matter. La. Rules of Prof'l Conduct r. 8.1(a) (2004); *see also In re Ford* 30 So. 3d 742, 745 (La. 2010) (finding 8.1(a) violation for lawyer who lied to ODC about conversation with client, which never took place); *In re Banks*, 18 So. 3d 57 (La. 2009) (lawyer stole a $7 pair of shoes from Walmart, subsequently did not contest the fact that he committed theft, but then insisted during disciplinary proceedings that he was simply exchanging the shoes). Nonlawyers who make false or misleading statements in seeking admission to the Louisiana bar would be subject to discipline under this rule after admission. ABA Model Rules of Prof'l Conduct r. 8.1 cmt. 1.

The Louisiana Supreme Court has struggled with bar applications submitted by law graduates who omitted criminal history information on their law school applications. For example, in *In re Committee on Bar Admissions CFN-52*, No. 2014-DA-2452 (Dec. 8, 2015), the court admitted an applicant who failed to "disclose three arrests on his law school application." *Id.* The court's decision in this regard is consistent with other recent orders

---

[131] In addition to complying with this rule by supplying truthful information to the Committee on Bar Admissions, applicants for admission to the bar must pass the bar examination and have "good moral character and fitness" to obtain admission to practice. *See, e.g., In re Thomas*, 761 So. 2d 531 (La. 2000) (conditionally admitting applicant who had defaulted on student loans).

admitting bar applicants.[132] What is particularly interesting about this order, however, is the concurring opinion.

The concurrence, written by Associate Justice Weimer, notes the problem: "Annually, it seems this court is confronted with this issue: an applicant is less than candid on an application, but the indiscretions omitted from the application would probably not adversely impact admission. *Id*. As a result of such lack of candor, applicants' lives are "cast into limbo" while the court undertakes a costly and protracted character and fitness evaluation. *Id*. Justice Weimer's advice? Avoid the problem in the first place:

> Practical advice to law school applicants and bar applicants is this: only you can place yourself in a situation which calls into question your ability to be candid and truthful; do not place yourself in that situation. Demonstrating that something in your past you do not relish disclosing to a law school or to the Committee on Bar Admissions is no longer indicative of your character and that you do possess the requisite character and fitness to practice law may be possible. However, if you are not candid in your applications, then not only must you overcome whatever you did not want to disclose in the first place, but you must also overcome the suspicion that your lack of candor casts upon anything you might say in support of your character. As Albert Einstein observed: "Whoever is careless with the truth in small matters cannot be trusted in important affairs." Youthful indiscretion and human frailty are more easily explained than a lack of candor.

---

[132] *See, e.g., In re Committee on Bar Admissions, CFN-295378*, No. 2015-BA-1938 (admitting applicant who omitted criminal-history information on Loyola law school application); *In re Confidential Party, CFN-618845*, No. 2015-BA-0975 (Jun. 25, 2015) (admitting applicant who omitted criminal-history information on application to Tulane University Law School); *In re Confidential Party, CFN-1913*, No. 13-OB-2575 (Oct. 15, 2014) (admitting applicant who omitted criminal-history information on application to Southern University Law Center and the National Conference of Bar Examiners); *In re Confidential Party, CFN-1317*, No. 2014-BA-2264 (May 5, 2015) (admitting applicant who omitted criminal-history information on application to Southern University Law Center); *In re Confidential Party, CFN-746*, No. 2015-BA-0906 (Jun. 19, 2015) (admitting applicant who omitted criminal-history information on application to Southern University Law Center); *In re Confidential Party, CFN-1248*, No. 2014-BA-2277 (May 5, 2015) (admitting applicant who omitted criminal-history information on application to Southern University Law Center); *In re Confidential Party, CFN-2792*, No. 13-OB-2152 (Oct. 15, 2014) (admitting applicant who omitted criminal-history information on application to South Texas College of Law and the Texas Committee on Bar Admissions); *In re Rusten May*, No. 12-OB-1031 (Oct. 23, 2012) (admitting applicant who omitted criminal-history information on application to Loyola University New Orleans College of Law).

Id.

Affirmative Duty to Disclose

Paragraph (b) requires a lawyer to disclose information when necessary either (1) to "correct a misapprehension" known to exist in connection with a bar admissions or disciplinary matter, or (2) to respond to a lawful request from an admissions or disciplinary authority. La. Rules of Prof'l Conduct r. 8.1(b) (2004). Thus, a lawyer or bar applicant who unwittingly makes a false statement is bound to correct it if he or she later becomes aware of its falsity. However, a lawyer's duty to disclose under this rule is subordinate to the lawyer's confidentiality obligation to clients. *Id.* Therefore, a lawyer has no duty to disclose if doing so would result in the disclosure of information that is confidential under Rule 1.6. *Id.*

Duty to Cooperate with Office of Disciplinary Counsel

Paragraph (c) requires a lawyer to cooperate with the Office of Disciplinary Counsel in any investigation, unless the lawyer openly pleads the Fifth Amendment. La. Rules of Prof'l Conduct r. 8.1(c) (2004); *see also* Model R. of Prof'l Conduct r. 8.1 cmt. 2 (stating that the rule is "subject to the provisions of the Fifth Amendment"). Louisiana lawyers who ignore subpoenas from the Office of Disciplinary Counsel or otherwise fail to cooperate in disciplinary investigations have been severely sanctioned by the Louisiana Supreme Court. *See, e.g., In re LaMartina*, 2017 WL 6031791 (Dec. 6, 2017); *In re Fahrenholtz*, 215 So. 3d 204 (La. 2017); *In re Murphy*, 224 So. 3d 947 (La. 2017); *In re Ford*, 141 So. 3d 800 (La. 2014); *In re Barrios*, 108 So. 3d 742, 746 (La. 2013); *In re Dunn*, 98 So. 3d 289, 295 (La. 2012); *In re Cooper*, 23 So. 3d 886 (La. 2009); *In re Hatfield*, 2 So. 3d 425 (La. 2009). Additionally, if a lawyer does not answer the formal charges filed against him by the ODC, the factual allegations of the charges will be deemed admitted. *In re Lester*, 133 So. 3d 1248, 1253 (La. 2014); *see also In re Richard*, 188 So. 3d 1035, 1038 (La. 2016) (lawyer suspended for one year and one day for failing to cooperate with Office of Disciplinary Counsel); *In re Brown-Mitchell*, 167 So. 3d 545 (La. 2015) (lawyer disbarred for conversion of client funds by failing to remit fees totaling $1,500 to client, then failing to respond to ODC); *In re Armstrong*, 164 So. 3d 817 (La. 2015) (lawyer disbarred for converting client funds and then failing to cooperate with ODC); *In re Brown-Manning*, 185 So. 3d 728 (La. 2016) (lawyer suspended for one year and one day for failing to expunge client's arrest record and then failing to cooperate with ODC in its investigation).

The Self-incrimination Clause of the Fifth Amendment, as incorporated in the Fourteenth Amendment, extends to disciplinary proceedings. *Spevack v. Klein*, 385 U.S. 511 (1967). However, there must be a reasonable basis for the assertion of the privilege. As the United States Supreme Court explained in *Hoffman v. United States*, 341 U.S. 479, 486 (1951), "[t]he witness is not exonerated from answering merely because he declares that in so doing he would incriminate himself—his say-so does not of itself establish the hazard of incrimination." Rather, the protection of the Fifth Amendment must be confined to instances where the witness has reasonable cause to apprehend danger from a direct answer. *Id.* Although a lawyer can assert the protections of the Fifth Amendment when appropriate, the assertion must be "reasonable under the facts." The Louisiana Supreme

Court has found such an assertion to be an unreasonable "failure to cooperate" when the respondent was not reasonably in jeopardy because of a previous guilty plea. *See In re Holliday*, 15 So. 3d 82 (La. 2009).

Disciplinary Sanctions

Depending on the nature of the violation of this rule, the applicable standard for determining an appropriate sanction is governed by either ABA Standard for Imposing Lawyer Sanctions standard 7.0 (violations of duties owed to the profession), or standard 5.1 (failure to maintain personal integrity). *See* ABA Stds. for Imposing Lawyer Sanctions stds. 7.0-7.4 (1986); *id.* stds. 5.1-5.14.

In most cases of misconduct in connection with the bar admissions or disciplinary process, the following sanctions are generally appropriate (absent aggravating or mitigating circumstances): *disbarment*, when the lawyer knowingly engages in conduct that is a violation of a duty owed to the profession with the intent to obtain a benefit for the lawyer or another, and causes serious or potentially serious injury to a client, the public, or the legal system; *suspension*, when the lawyer knowingly engages in conduct that is a violation of a duty owed to the profession, and causes injury or potential injury to a client, the public, or the legal system; *reprimand*, when the lawyer negligently engages in conduct that is a violation of a duty owed to the profession, and causes injury or potential injury to a client, the public, or the legal system; and, *admonition*, when the lawyer engages in an isolated instance of negligence that is a violation of a duty owed to the profession, and causes little or no actual or potential injury to a client, the public or the legal system. *See* ABA Stds. for Imposing Lawyer Sanctions stds. 7.0-7.4 (1986).

However, in cases involving misconduct in connection with the bar admissions or disciplinary process involving dishonesty, deceit, misrepresentation or similar conduct that calls into questions the lawyer's fundamental fitness to practice law, the following sanctions are generally appropriate (absent aggravating or mitigating circumstances): *disbarment*, when the lawyer engages in intentional conduct involving dishonesty, fraud, deceit, or misrepresentation that seriously adversely reflects on the lawyer's fitness to practice; *suspension*, when the lawyer knowingly engages in criminal conduct that seriously adversely reflects on the lawyer's fitness to practice; *reprimand*, when the lawyer knowingly engages in any other conduct that involves dishonesty, fraud, deceit, or misrepresentation and that adversely reflects on the lawyer's fitness to practice law; and, *admonition*, when the lawyer engages in any other conduct that reflects adversely on the lawyer's fitness to practice law. *See* ABA Stds. for Imposing Lawyer Sanctions stds. 5.1-5.14 (1992).

RULE 8.2. JUDICIAL AND LEGAL OFFICIALS

(a) A lawyer shall not make a statement that the lawyer knows to be false or with reckless disregard as to its truth or falsity concerning the qualifications or integrity of a judge, adjudicatory officer or public legal officer, or of a candidate for election or appointment to judicial or legal office.

(b) A lawyer who is a candidate for judicial office shall comply with the applicable provisions of the Code of Judicial Conduct.

BACKGROUND

The Louisiana Supreme Court adopted this rule on January 20, 2004. It became effective on March 1, 2004, and has not been amended since. This rule is identical to the ABA Model Rule of Professional Conduct 8.2 (2002).

COMMENTS TO ABA MODEL RULE 8.2

[1] Assessments by lawyers are relied on in evaluating the professional or personal fitness of persons being considered for election or appointment to judicial office and to public legal offices, such as attorney general, prosecuting attorney and public defender. Expressing honest and candid opinions on such matters contributes to improving the administration of justice. Conversely, false statements by a lawyer can unfairly undermine public confidence in the administration of justice.

[2] When a lawyer seeks judicial office, the lawyer should be bound by applicable limitations on political activity.

[3] To maintain the fair and independent administration of justice, lawyers are encouraged to continue traditional efforts to defend judges and courts unjustly criticized.

ANNOTATIONS
Generally

A lawyer must refrain from knowingly or recklessly making a false statement[133] about the integrity of a judge, adjudicatory officer, public legal officer or candidate for judicial or legal office. La. Rules of Prof'l Conduct r. 8.2(a) (2004); Restatement (Third) of the Law Governing Lawyers § 114 (2000); *In re Cooper*, 32 So. 3d 221 (La. 2010); *In re Larvadain*, 664 So. 3d 395 (La. 1995); *Fox v. LAM*, 632 So. 3d 877 (La. Ct. App. 2d Cir. 1994); *In re Moity*, 2008 WL 104209 (W.D. La. 2008). A lawyer also violates this rule if the lawyer knowingly or recklessly files an affidavit in the public record on behalf of another person that refers to the integrity of a judge, adjudicatory officer, public legal officer or candidate for judicial or legal office. *See In re Wells*, 36 So. 3d 198, 203-206 (La. 2010) (disciplining lawyer who filed an affidavit from a felon that stated the district attorney conspired in a

---

[133] The Louisiana Supreme Court has suggested in dicta that reckless but true statements about a judge are not prohibited by this rule. *See In re Simon*, 913 So. 3d 816, 824 n.7 (La. 2005).

murder-for-hire scheme). The mere fact that a lawyer subjectively believes statements about a judge or judicial candidate are true will not exonerate the lawyer. *In re Mire*, 197 So. 3d 656 (La. 2016); *In re Lee*, 977 So. 2d 852 (La. 2008); *In re Simon*, 913 So. 2d 816, 824 (La. 2005); *see La. State Bar Ass'n v. Karst*, 428 So. 2d 406 (La. 1983); *In re Simon*, 913 So. 2d 816, 824 (La. 2005); *In re Lee*, 977 So. 2d 852 (La. 2008). Indeed, a lawyer violates this rule if the lawyer has exhibited "reckless disregard" for the truth irrespective of any subjective belief that he was not speaking falsely. *See* La. Rules of Prof'l Conduct r. 8.2(a) (2004). This is so because the Louisiana Supreme Court has "adopted an objective standard, rather than a subjective standard, in analyzing whether a statement is . . . a violation of the rule." *In re Simon*, 913 So. 2d 816, 824 (La. 2005); *In re Mire*, 197 So. 3d 656 (La 2016). False statements about the judiciary are arguably protected by the First Amendment if made neither knowingly nor recklessly. *See Garrison v. Louisiana*, 379 U.S. 64 (1964), *overruled on other grounds by Curtis Pub. Co. v. Butts*, 388 U.S. 130 (1967). Therefore, the constitutionality of the Louisiana Supreme Court's decisions in *Simon* and *Mire* remains an open issue. *See generally* David L. Hudson, Jr., *How Far Can Crticism of Judges Go Under Ethics Rules*, ABA Journal, Dec. 1, 2016 (http://www.abajournal.com/magazine/article/criticism_judges_ethics_rules)

This rule is directed primarily to statements of fact made to the public at large that would undermine public confidence in the administration of justice. *See United States v. Brown*, 72 F.3d 25, 29 (5th Cir. 1995); *In re Palmisano*, 70 F.3d 483 (7th Cir. 1995). However, this rule should not stand as an obstacle to a nonfrivolous challenge to a judge's partiality, if there is a need for recusal in an appropriate proceeding. *See id.*

Finally, this rule does not prohibit a lawyer from expressing a personal opinion regarding a judge. Comment 1 to Model Rule 8.2 states that "[e]xpressing honest and candid opinions on such matters, contributes to improving the administration of justice." *See* Model Rules of Prof. Conduct R. 8.2 cmt. 1 (2002); *see also State Bar of Tex. v. Semaan*, 508 S.W.2d 429, 432 (Tex. Civ. App. 1974). Of course, the distinction between a statement of personal opinion and a statement of fact is often evanescent.

Disciplinary Sanctions

Absent aggravating or mitigating circumstances, the following sanctions are generally appropriate in cases involving conduct that is prejudicial to the administration of justice: *disbarment*, when a lawyer, with intent to deceive the court, makes a false statement, submits a false document, or improperly withholds material information, and causes serious or potentially serious injury to a party, or causes a significant or potentially significant adverse effect on the legal proceeding; *suspension*, when a lawyer knows that false statements or documents are being submitted to the court or that material information is improperly being withheld, and takes no remedial action, and causes injury or potential injury to a party or to the legal proceeding, or causes an adverse or potentially adverse effect on the legal proceeding; *reprimand*, when a lawyer is negligent either in determining whether statements or documents are false or in taking remedial action when material information is being withheld, and causes injury or potential injury to a party to the legal proceeding, or causes an adverse or potentially adverse effect on the legal proceeding; and, *admonition*, when a lawyer engages in an isolated instance of neglect in determining whether submitted statements or documents are false or in failing to disclose material information upon learning of its falsity, and causes little or no actual or potential injury to a party, or causes little or no adverse or potentially adverse effect on the legal proceeding. *See* ABA Stds. for Imposing Lawyer Sanctions stds. 6.1-6.14 (1992) (False Statements, Fraud, and Misrepresentation); *id.* std. 6.1.

RULE 8.3. REPORTING PROFESSIONAL MISCONDUCT

(a) A lawyer who knows that another lawyer has committed a violation of the Rules of Professional Conduct that raises a question as to the lawyer's honesty, trustworthiness or fitness as a lawyer in other respects, shall inform the Office of Disciplinary Counsel.

(b) A lawyer who knows that a judge has committed a violation of the applicable rules of judicial conduct that raises a question as to the judge's honesty, trustworthiness or fitness for office shall inform the Judiciary Commission. Complaints concerning the conduct of federal judges shall be filed with the appropriate federal authorities in accordance with federal laws and rules governing federal judicial conduct and disability.

(c) This rule does not require the disclosure of information otherwise protected by Rule 1.6 or information gained by a lawyer or judge while participating in an approved lawyers assistance program or while serving as a member of the Ethics Advisory Service Committee.

BACKGROUND

The Louisiana Supreme Court adopted this rule on January 20, 2004. It became effective on March 1, 2004. The court amended the rule shortly thereafter, on May 12, 2004, to address in paragraph (b) reporting of wrongdoing by federal judges. This rule differs from ABA Model Rule of Professional Conduct 8.3 (2002) in some minor and in some major respects.

As to the minor differences, paragraphs (a) and (b) designate the "Office of Disciplinary Counsel" and the "Judiciary Commission" as the appropriate professional authorities to whom lawyers must report violations of the relevant standards of professional conduct. Paragraph (b) directs lawyers to report the wrongdoing of federal judges to federal authorities rather than to the Louisiana Judiciary Commission. Finally, paragraph (c) identifies the "Ethics Advisory Service Committee" in addition to the "approved lawyers assistance program" mentioned in Model Rule 8.3(c).

As to the major differences, this rule contains more expansive reporting obligations than are found in Model Rule 8.3(a-b). As to reporting lawyer misconduct, paragraph (a) requires the reporting of misconduct that raises a "question" as to another lawyer's "honesty, trustworthiness or fitness as a lawyer in other respects . . . ." La. Rules of Prof'l Conduct r. 8.3(a) (2004). In contrast, Model Rule 8.3 requires reporting only if the misconduct in question raises a "substantial question . . . ." ABA Model Rules of Prof'l Conduct r. 8.3(a) (2002) (emphasis added).[134]

As to judicial misconduct, paragraph (b) requires the reporting of misconduct that raises a "question" as to a judge's "honesty, trustworthiness or fitness for office . . . ." La. Rules of Prof'l Conduct r. 8.3(b) (2004). In contrast, Model Rule 8.3(b) requires reporting only if the misconduct in question raises a "substantial question as to the judge's fitness for office . . . ." ABA Model Rules of Prof'l Conduct r. 8.3(b) (2002) (emphasis added).[135]

COMMENTS TO ABA MODEL RULE 8.3

[1] Self-regulation of the legal profession requires that members of the profession initiate disciplinary investigation when they know of a violation of the Rules of Professional Conduct. Lawyers have a similar obligation with respect to judicial misconduct. An apparently isolated violation may indicate a pattern of misconduct that only a disciplinary investigation can uncover. Reporting a violation is especially important where the victim is unlikely to discover the offense.

[2] A report about misconduct is not required where it would involve violation of Rule 1.6. However, a lawyer should encourage a client to consent to disclosure where prosecution would not substantially prejudice the client's interests.

[3] If a lawyer were obliged to report every violation of the Rules, the failure to report any violation would itself be a professional offense. Such a requirement existed in many jurisdictions but proved to be unenforceable. This Rule limits the reporting obligation to

---

[134] The former Louisiana rule on reporting lawyer misconduct, in effect from 1987 through February 29, 2004, had an even broader reporting obligation than is contained in the current rule. The former rule required a lawyer to report "unprivileged knowledge or evidence" of any ethical violation by a lawyer–no matter how trivial. *Compare* Model Rules of Prof'l Conduct r. 8.3(a) (2002) *with* La. Rules of Prof'l Conduct r. 8.3(a) (1987). In 1985, the Task Force concluded that it was inappropriate to put a lawyer "in the position of making a subjective judgment" regarding the significance of a violation. *See* Report and Recommendation of the Task Force to Evaluate the American Bar Association's Model Rules of Prof'l Conduct, at 24 (Nov. 23, 1985). The Task Force concluded that it was "preferable to put the burden on every lawyer to report all violations, regardless of their nature or kind, whether or not they raised a substantial question as to honesty, trustworthiness or fitness." *Id.* at 24-25.

In 2002, a divided LSBA Ethics 2000 Committee recommended that the provisions of the former rule be retained. However, the LSBA House of Delegates thereafter rejected the Committee's recommendation and suggested that the court adopt ABA Model Rule 8.3 verbatim. In January 2004, the court opted for middle ground and enacted the present rule.

[135] The former Louisiana rule on reporting judicial misconduct, in effect from 1987 through February 29, 2004, had a significantly narrower reporting obligation than is contained in the present rule. The former rule did not require lawyers affirmatively to report judicial misconduct, but merely to "reveal fully such knowledge or evidence upon proper request of a tribunal or other authority empowered to investigate or act upon the conduct of lawyers or judges." La. Rules of Prof'l Conduct r. 8.3 (a) (1987).

those offenses that a self-regulating profession must vigorously endeavor to prevent. A measure of judgment is, therefore, required in complying with the provisions of this Rule. The term "substantial" refers to the seriousness of the possible offense and not the quantum of evidence of which the lawyer is aware. A report should be made to the bar disciplinary agency unless some other agency, such as a peer review agency, is more appropriate in the circumstances. Similar considerations apply to the reporting of judicial misconduct.

[4] The duty to report professional misconduct does not apply to a lawyer retained to represent a lawyer whose professional conduct is in question. Such a situation is governed by the Rules applicable to the client-lawyer relationship.

[5] Information about a lawyer's or judge's misconduct or fitness may be received by a lawyer in the course of that lawyer's participation in an approved lawyers or judges assistance program. In that circumstance, providing for an exception to the reporting requirements of paragraphs (a) and (b) of this Rule encourages lawyers and judges to seek treatment through such a program. Conversely, without such an exception, lawyers and judges may hesitate to seek assistance from these programs, which may then result in additional harm to their professional careers and additional injury to the welfare of clients and the public. These Rules do not otherwise address the confidentiality of information received by a lawyer or judge participating in an approved lawyers assistance program; such an obligation, however, may be imposed by the rules of the program or other law.

ANNOTATIONS
Reporting Lawyer Misconduct
A lawyer must immediately report to the Office of Disciplinary Counsel any violation of the Rules of Professional Conduct that raises a question as to another lawyer's honesty, trustworthiness or fitness as a lawyer in other respects–unless doing so would divulge confidential information. *See* La. Rules of Prof'l Conduct r. 8.3(a) (2004); *id.* r. 8.3(c); *In re Tolchinsky*, 740 So. 2d 109 (La. 1999) (failure to report unauthorized practice of law by another lawyer). This reporting obligation is "triggered when, under the circumstances, a reasonable lawyer[136] would have 'a firm opinion that the conduct in question more likely than not occurred.'"[137] *See In re Riehlmann*, 891 So. 2d 1239, 1244 (La. 2005) (quoting *Attorney U v. Mississippi Bar*, 678 So. 2d 963 (Miss. 1996); Restatement (Third) of the Law Governing Lawyers § 5 cmt. 1 (2000)). For a general discussion of a lawyer's reporting obligations, particularly in the context of litigation, see ABA Comm. on Ethics and Prof'l Responsibility, Formal Op. 94-383 (1994).

---

[136] Arguably, the Louisiana Supreme Court in *Riehlmann* erroneously created an objective reporting trigger despite that the plain language of Louisiana Rule 8.3 requires subjective knowledge.

[137] Note that the *Riehlmann* opinion applied the pre-2004 revision version of Rule 8.3. Under the new rule, mere knowledge of a rule violation does not trigger a reporting obligation unless that violation *also* raises a question as to the lawyer's honesty, trustworthiness or fitness as a lawyer. *See* La. Rules of Prof'l Conduct r. 8.3(a) (2004).

No Duty to Self Report

This rule does not require a lawyer to report the lawyer's own violation of the Rules of Professional Conduct. First, the text of the rule refers explicitly to the obligation to report a violation by "another lawyer." *See* La. Rules of Prof'l Conduct r. 8.3(a) (2004) (emphasis added). In contrast, the 1987 version of this rule imposed the reporting obligation as to any "violation of this code" without reference to the violation being committed by "another" lawyer. *See* La. Rules of Prof'l Conduct r. 8.3(a) (1987). Second, the ABA Standing Committee on Ethics and Professional Responsibility has opined that a lawyer is not obliged to report his or her own misconduct. *See* ABA Comm. on Ethics and Prof'l Responsibility, Informal Op. 1279 (1973). Finally, the Fifth Amendment privilege against self-incrimination should protect lawyers from having to self-report certain types of serious misconduct to the Office of Disciplinary Counsel. *See* ABA Model Rules of Prof'l Conduct r. 8.1 cmt. 2; *see also* La. Rules of Prof'l Conduct r. 8.1(c) (2004) (permitting lawyers to refrain from cooperating with ODC investigation upon "openly expressed claim of a constitutional privilege").

Disciplinary Sanctions

Absent aggravating or mitigating circumstances, the following sanctions are generally appropriate in cases involving violations of Rule 8.3: *disbarment*, when the lawyer knowingly engages in conduct that is a violation of a duty owed to the profession with the intent to obtain a benefit for the lawyer or another, and causes serious or potentially serious injury to a client, the public, or the legal system; *suspension*, when the lawyer knowingly engages in conduct that is a violation of a duty owed to the profession, and causes injury or potential injury to a client, the public, or the legal system; *reprimand*, when the lawyer negligently engages in conduct that is a violation of a duty owed to the profession, and causes injury or potential injury to a client, the public, or the legal system; and, *admonition*, when the lawyer engages in an isolated instance of negligence that is a violation of a duty owed to the profession, and causes little or no actual or potential injury to a client, the public or the legal system. *See* ABA Stds. for Imposing Lawyer Sanctions stds. 7.0-7.4 (1992).

RULE 8.4. MISCONDUCT

It is professional misconduct for a lawyer to:

(a) Violate or attempt to violate the Rules of Professional Conduct, knowingly assist or induce another to do so, or do so through the acts of another;

(b) Commit a criminal act especially one that reflects adversely on the lawyer's honesty, trustworthiness or fitness as a lawyer in other respects;

(c) Engage in conduct involving dishonesty, fraud, deceit or misrepresentation;

(d) Engage in conduct that is prejudicial to the administration of justice;

(e) State or imply an ability to influence improperly a judge, judicial officer, governmental agency or official or to achieve results by means that violate the Rules of Professional Conduct or other law;

(f) Knowingly assist a judge or judicial officer in conduct that is a violation of applicable Rules of Judicial Conduct or other law; or

(g) Threaten to present criminal or disciplinary charges solely to obtain an advantage in a civil matter.

BACKGROUND

The Louisiana Supreme Court adopted this rule on January 20, 2004. It became effective on March 1, 2004, and has not been amended since. This rule is identical to ABA Model Rule of Professional Conduct 8.4 (2002) with three substantive differences.

First, Model Rule 8.4(b) brands a criminal act as "misconduct" only if the crime "reflects adversely on the lawyer's honesty, trustworthiness or fitness as a lawyer in other respects." *See* ABA Model Rules of Prof'l Conduct r. 8.4(b). In contrast, Louisiana Rule 8.4(b) (2002) casts a wider net by branding as "misconduct" any criminal act by a lawyer–irrespective of whether it casts doubt on the lawyer's honesty, trustworthiness or fitness to practice. The rule has this effect as a result of the inclusion of the language "especially one that" between "criminal act" and "that reflects."[138]

---

[138] This language was retained from the 1987 version of this rule. However, it is unclear whether the Louisiana Supreme Court or the Task Force intended the result in 1987, given that the Task Force's commentary fails even to mention this significant difference in

Second, paragraph (g) is not found in the Model Rules. This paragraph prohibits Louisiana lawyers from threatening to present criminal or disciplinary charges "solely to obtain an advantage in a civil matter." Although no similar provision exists in Model Rule 8.4 (*see* ABA Comm. on Ethics and Prof'l Responsibility, Formal Op. 92-363 (1992)), the ABA has issued a formal ethics opinion condemning the practice. *See* ABA Comm. on Ethics and Prof'l Responsibility, Formal Op. 94-383 (1994).

Third, on August 8, 2016, the ABA House of Delegates amended Model Rule 8.4 to include a broad anti-discrimination and anti-harassment provision. The amendment, which was sponsored by several ABA groups, added this new paragraph (g) to the black-letter of Model Rule 8.4:

> It is professional misconduct for a lawyer to: . . . (g) engage in conduct that the lawyer knows or reasonably should know is harassment or discrimination on the basis of race, sex, religion, national origin, ethnicity, disability, age, sexual orientation, gender identity, marital status or socioeconomic status in conduct related to the practice of law. This paragraph does not limit the ability of a lawyer to accept, decline, or withdraw from a representation in accordance with Rule 1.16. This paragraph does not preclude legitimate advice or advocacy consistent with these rules.

See ABA Revised Resolution 109 (adopted Aug. 8, 2016). Furthermore, the comment to the model rule broadly defines "harassment" to include any "derogatory or demeaning verbal conduct" by a lawyer relating to a person's "race, sex, religion, national origin, ethnicity, disability, age, sexual orientation, gender identity, marital status or socioeconomic status." Even words that are not "harmful" meet the definition of "harassment" if they are "derogatory or demeaning" and relate to a designated category of person. Moreover, the rule subjects to discipline not only a lawyer who slings a "derogatory or demeaning comment" directly at another person, but also a lawyer who makes an abstract comment about general types or categories of people. Indeed, in revising comment 4, the ABA expressly deleted language that would have limited the definition of "harassment" to include only derogatory or demeaning conduct directed "towards a person who is, or is perceived to be, a member of one of the groups."

COMMENTS TO ABA MODEL RULE 8.4

[1] Lawyers are subject to discipline when they violate or attempt to violate the Rules of Professional Conduct, knowingly assist or induce another to do so or do so through the acts of another, as when they request or instruct an agent to do so on the lawyer's behalf. Paragraph (a), however, does not prohibit a lawyer from advising a client concerning action the client is legally entitled to take.

---

language. *See* Report and Recommendation of the Task Force to Evaluate the American Bar Association's Model Rules of Prof'l Conduct at 25 (Nov. 23, 1985). Anecdotally, however, some Task Force members recall this language being proposed to the court to broaden the scope of criminal conduct that could result in discipline.

[2] Many kinds of illegal conduct reflect adversely on fitness to practice law, such as offenses involving fraud and the offense of willful failure to file an income tax return. However, some kinds of offenses carry no such implication. Traditionally, the distinction was drawn in terms of offenses involving "moral turpitude." That concept can be construed to include offenses concerning some matters of personal morality, such as adultery and comparable offenses, that have no specific connection to fitness for the practice of law. Although a lawyer is personally answerable to the entire criminal law, a lawyer should be professionally answerable only for offenses that indicate lack of those characteristics relevant to law practice. Offenses involving violence, dishonesty, breach of trust, or serious interference with the administration of justice are in that category. A pattern of repeated offenses, even ones of minor significance when considered separately, can indicate indifference to legal obligation.

[3] Discrimination and harassment by lawyers in violation of paragraph (g) undermines confidence in the legal profession and the legal system. Such discrimination includes harmful verbal or physical conduct that manifests bias or prejudice towards others. Harassment includes sexual harassment and derogatory or demeaning verbal or physical conduct. Sexual harassment includes unwelcome sexual advances, requests for sexual favors, and other unwelcome verbal or physical conduct of a sexual nature. The substantive law of antidiscrimination and anti-harassment statutes and case law may guide application of paragraph (g).

[4] Conduct related to the practice of law includes representing clients; interacting with witnesses, coworkers, court personnel, lawyers and others while engaged in the practice of law; operating or managing a law firm or law practice; and participating in bar association, business or social activities in connection with the practice of law. Lawyers may engage in conduct undertaken to promote diversity and inclusion without violating this rule by, for example, implementing initiatives aimed at recruiting, hiring, retaining and advancing diverse employees or sponsoring diverse law student organizations.

[5] A trial judge's finding that peremptory challenges were exercised on a discriminatory basis does not alone establish a violation of paragraph (g). A lawyer does not violate paragraph (g) by limiting the scope or subject matter of the lawyer's practice or by limiting the lawyer's practice to members of underserved populations in accordance with these Rules and other law. A lawyer may charge and collect reasonable fees and expenses for a representation. Rule 1.5(a). Lawyers also should be mindful of their professional obligations under Rule 6.1 to provide legal services to those who are unable to pay, and their obligation under Rule 6.2 not to avoid appointments from a tribunal except for good cause. See Rule 6.2(a), (b) and (c). A lawyer's representation of a client does not constitute an endorsement by the lawyer of the client's views or activities. See Rule 1.2(b).

[6] A lawyer may refuse to comply with an obligation imposed by law upon a good faith belief that no valid obligation exists. The provisions of Rule 1.2(d) concerning a good faith challenge to the validity, scope, meaning or application of the law apply to challenges of legal regulation of the practice of law.

[7] Lawyers holding public office assume legal responsibilities going beyond those of other citizens. A lawyer's abuse of public office can suggest an inability to fulfill the professional role of lawyers. The same is true of abuse of positions of private trust such as trustee, executor, administrator, guardian, agent and officer, director or manager of a corporation or other organization.

ANNOTATIONS
Generally

This Rule broadly defines professional "misconduct." The significance of conduct being so classified is perhaps obvious: conduct classified as "misconduct" can form the basis for professional discipline. Most fundamentally, a lawyer engages in "misconduct" if the lawyer violates the Louisiana Rules of Professional Conduct. La. Rules of Prof'l Conduct r. 8.4(a) (2004); *see also* Restatement (Third) of the Law Governing Lawyers § 5(1) (2000). Moreover, a lawyer engages in misconduct if the lawyer "attempts" to violate the Louisiana Rules but does not complete the violation. La. Rules of Prof'l Conduct r. 8.4(a) (2004). Finally, it is professional misconduct not only for a lawyer to personally violate the rules, but also to "assist or induce another to do so, or do so through the acts of another." *Id.*; *In re Guirard*, 11 So. 3d 1017, 1026 (La. 2009) (finding 8.4(b) violation for lawyers assisting their case managers and investigators in the unauthorized practice of law); *In re Brown*, 813 So. 2d 325, 327 (La. 2002) (disbarring lawyer for, among other things, assisting another lawyer in the unauthorized practice of law); *see also* Restatement (Third) of the Law Governing Lawyers § 5(2) (2000).

It constitutes "misconduct" for a lawyer to violate "any other rule of this jurisdiction regarding professional conduct of lawyers." *See* La. Sup. Ct. R. XIX § 9(a). Applying this principle, the Louisiana Supreme Court in *In re Raspanti*, 8 So. 3d 526, 535 (La. 2009), held that a lawyer's violation of the immunity provisions of Rule XIX (through filing a defamation suit against a complainant) subjected the lawyer to discipline. However, the court has held that a lawyer's violation of the confidentiality provisions of Rule XIX § 16 does not subject a lawyer to discipline because a lawyer participating in the disciplinary process has a First Amendment right to reveal the substance of such proceedings. *See In re Warner and Rando*, 21 So. 3d 218 (La. 2009).

Although lawyers are often mistaken on this point, the term "misconduct" clearly does not include conduct that may have the "appearance of impropriety." Indeed, that term appears neither in the Louisiana Rules of Professional Conduct, nor in the ABA Model Rules of Professional Conduct. On the contrary, the ABA has repeatedly stated that a lawyer should not be sanctioned or disqualified under such an "undefined," "question-begging" standard. *See* ABA Comm. on Ethics and Prof'l Responsibility, Formal Op. 342 (1975).

Criminal Acts

A lawyer engages in "misconduct" and is thus subject to discipline under this rule if he or she engages in any "criminal act." La. Rules of Prof'l Conduct r. 8.4(b) (2004). The Louisiana Supreme Court routinely has disbarred lawyers convicted of serious crimes. *See, e.g., In re Fahrenholtz*, 215 So. 3d 204 (La. 2017) (disbarring lawyer for conviction of illegal possession of stolen things); *In re Broussard*, 219 So. 3d 290 (La. 2017) (disbarring lawyer for conviction of making false claims to IRS); *In re Shaw*, 141 So. 3d 795 (La. 2014) (permanently disbarring lawyer for conviction of theft by fraud); *In re Richard*, 50 So. 3d 1284, 1290 (La. 2010) (disbarring lawyer for conviction of criminal mischief relating to a violent altercation in addition to other violations); *In re Meece*, 6 So. 3d 751 (La. 2009) (imposing permanent disbarment for armed bank robbery); *In re Norris*, 939 So. 2d 1221 (La. 2006) (imposing permanent disbarment on lawyer who had been convicted of four counts of perjury); *In re O'Keefe*, 877 So. 2d 79 (La. 2004) (ordering permanent disbarment in connection with federal fraud and conspiracy convictions); *In re Lynch*, 840 So. 2d 508 (La. 2003) (imposing discipline for child pornography and obstruction of justice convictions); *In re Kirchberg*, 856 So. 2d 1162 (La. 2003) (ordering permanent disbarment for federal fraud conviction); *In re Nevitte*, 827 So. 2d 1135 (La. 2002) (imposing discipline for conspiracy to commit fraud); *In re Sentenn*, 730 So. 2d 868 (La. 1999) (imposing discipline for federal fraud and conspiracy convictions); *In re Mmahat*, 736 So. 2d 1285 (La. 1999) (imposing discipline for federal fraud convictions); *In re Pardue*, 731 So. 2d 224 (La. 1999) (imposing discipline for federal tax crimes); *In re Naccari*, 705 So. 2d 734 (La. 1997); *In re Mitchell*, 679 So. 2d 385 (La. 1996) (imposing discipline for drug-distribution convictions); *In re James D. Mecca*, No. 15-DB-001 (LADB HC No. 6, Oct. 19, 2015) (recommending suspension for accepting marijuana as fee for legal services). Moreover, a lawyer is subject to discipline under this rule even if the criminal act does not result in conviction. *See, e.g., In re Williams*, 85 So. 3d 583, 591-92 (La. 2012) (disbarring lawyer for homicide despite not being convicted of any crime related to the homicide because the ODC met its burden of proving that lawyer did not act in self-defense); *In re Estiverne*, 741 So. 2d 649, 652-54 (La. 1999) (suspending lawyer for assault with a handgun that did not result in conviction). Finally, a lawyer may be sanctioned for criminal conduct that is wholly unrelated to the practice of law. *See In re James*, 108 So. 3d 747 (La. 2013) (suspending lawyer for 2 DWI convictions); *In re Blanche*, 90 So. 3d 1034, 1039 (La. 2012) (suspending lawyer for three alcohol and drug related criminal offenses); *In re Cook*, 33 So. 3d 155 160-61 (La. 2010) (suspending lawyer for failing to pay income taxes over a period of two years); *In re Brown*, 674 So. 2d 243, 246 (La. 1996) (ordering disbarment for negligent homicide conviction) (citing *La. State Bar Ass'n v. Frank*, 472 So. 2d 1 (La. 1985)); *La. State Bar Ass'n v. Bensabat*, 378 So. 2d 380, 382 (La. 1979) (ordering disbarment for cocaine distribution conviction); *In re George William Jarman*, No. 2015-B-2105 (La. Nov. 18, 2015) (lawyer suspended indefinitely after conviction on federal child-pornography related conspiracy charges); *see also* ABA Comm. on Ethics and Prof'l Responsibility, Formal Op. 336 (1974).

Dishonesty, Fraud, Deceit or Misrepresentation

Professional "misconduct" includes conduct "involving dishonesty, fraud, deceit or misrepresentation," even if the conduct is not criminal in nature. *See* La. Rules of Prof'l Conduct r. 8.4(c) (2004). Conversion of client funds is a classic act of "dishonesty" for which the Louisiana Supreme Court has disciplined lawyers under this paragraph. *See, e.g., In re Miller*, 139 So. 3d 993 (La. 2014); *In re Bailey*, 115 So. 3d 458, 465 (La. 2013); *In re Alleman*, 982 So. 2d 814 (La. 2008); *In re Boone*, 766 So. 2d 533 (La. 2000); *In re Ferrand*, 731 So. 2d 874 (La. 1999). For example, a lawyer engages in misconduct by improperly backdating stock certificates in the course of representing a client. *See In re Sealed Appellant*, 194 F.3d 666, 672 (5th Cir. 1999). A lawyer also engages in misconduct by misappropriating funds or property belonging to the lawyer's law firm, or by engaging in improper billing practices. *See, e.g., In re Wallace*, 2017 WL 4227483 (La. Sep. 22, 2017) (one-year suspension for falsely inflating timesheets); *In re Abdalla*, 2017 WL 4736903 (disbarment for converting $39,085.86 from law firm); *In re Sharp*, 16 So. 3d 343 (La. 2009). Note that a violation of Rule 8.4(c) often entails a violation of one or more additional rules of conduct, for example, Rules 3.3 and 4.1. *See, e.g., In re Hackett*, 42 So. 3d 972, 978 (La. 2010); *In re McKee*, 976 So. 2d 152 (La. 2008); *see also In re Calahan*, 930 So. 2d 916 (La. 2006) (disbarring lawyer for violations of rules 3.3, 4.1 and 8.4(c), among other rules violations).

Conduct Prejudicial to the Administration of Justice

Professional "misconduct" includes conduct that is "prejudicial to the administration of justice." La. Rules of Prof'l Conduct r. 8.4(d) (2004). In one case, the court considered such conduct to have occurred when an assistant district attorney threatened criminal prosecution to a person to collect a personal debt. *See In re Ruffin*, 54 So. 3d 645, 646-648 (La. 2011). Also, a lawyer who, for example, improperly acts as a "witness" to the signature of an absent person engages in such prejudicial misconduct. *See In re Wahlder*, 728 So. 2d 837, 839 (La. 1999); *see also In re Warner*, 851 So. 2d 1029 (La. 2003) (suspending lawyer for directing client to sign her deceased father's name on release and settlement check). A lawyer who pointed a gun at another lawyer during a deposition engaged in conduct prejudicial to the administration of justice. *See In re Estiverne*, 741 So. 2d 649 (La. 1999) (suspending lawyer for a year and a day). An appointed IDB lawyer who failed to disclose to the court that he had accepted a private fee for representing a purportedly indigent defendant committed prejudicial conduct. *See In re Barstow*, 817 So. 2d 1123, 1129 (La. 2002). Further, a lawyer handling a personal injury case who approached the presiding judge ex parte to inquire about making a $5,000 campaign contribution engaged in conduct prejudicial to the administration of justice. *See In re Bolton*, 820 So. 2d 548 (La. 2002). A criminal defense lawyer who failed to provide information necessary to complete a client's pre-sentence report (which could have resulted in the client's receiving a significantly longer prison sentence) violated Rule 8.4(d) (2004). *In re Martin*, 982 So. 2d 765, 769 (La. 2008). A lawyer who filed five nearly identical lawsuits in the same court on the same date to get a judge of his choosing engaged in conduct prejudicial to the administration of justice. *See In re Eddington*, 166 So. 3d 239 (La. 2015). A lawyer who filed frivolous judicial complaints and lawsuits against a judge engaged in conduct prejudicial to the administration of justice. *See In re Nugent*, 2017 WL 6015022 (La. Dec. 5, 2017). A lawyer who retained co-counsel solely to force the recusal of impeached federal district judge G. Thomas Porteous, Jr., engaged in conduct prejudicial to the administration of justice. *See In re Joseph Nicolas Mole*, No. 15-30647 (May 4, 2016). Finally, a lawyer who offered a witness in a criminal case $300 if the witness would execute an affidavit requesting dismissal of the burglary charges then pending against the lawyer's client violated Rule 8.4. *See In re Pryor*, No. 2015-B-0243 (La. Sep. 1, 2015).

AGREEMENT TO REFRAIN FROM REPORTING LAWYER TO ODC

An agreement with anyone to refrain from reporting a lawyer to the Office of Disciplinary Counsel would likely constitute conduct prejudicial to justice. *Cf. In re Laura Lee Robinson*, IL Atty. Registration and Disciplinary Comm. No. 2016PR00126 (Aug. 15, 2017). While Louisiana has no rule expressly on point, it is certain that the Office of Disciplinary Counsel would consider such an agreement to violate Rule 8.4(d).[139]

UNCIVIL AND UNDIGNIFIED CONDUCT

The Louisiana Supreme Court has noted that while Rule 8.4(d) typically applies to "litigation-related misconduct," it is broader in scope. *See In re Downing*, 930 So. 2d 897, 904 n.5 (La. 2006). The rule also "reaches conduct that is uncivil, undignified, or unprofessional, regardless of whether it is directly connected to a legal proceeding." *Id.* For example, a lawyer received a thirty-day suspension for disrupting a court proceeding by "using vulgarities in the courtroom." *See In re Sanford*, 214 So. 3d 841 (La. 2017). Although not a Louisiana case, a North Carolina "activist" lawyer purporting to represent an "occupy movement" engaged in conduct "prejudicial to the administration of justice" by exclaiming to a magistrate, "what the fu** is going on around here." *See N.C. State Bar v. Foster*, No. COA17-443 (N.C. Dec. 19, 2017).

FAILURE TO PAY LITIGATION-RELATED EXPENSES AS "CONDUCT PREJUDICIAL TO THE ADMINISTRATION OF JUSTICE"

The Office of Disciplinary Counsel traditionally does not allow itself to be used as a collection agent for the vendors and creditors of lawyers. In so doing, the office has relied upon the Louisiana Supreme Court's 2003 decision in *In re Bilbe*, 841 So. 2d 729 (La. 2003). In that case, the hearing committee opined that "the failure to pay an invoice of a court reporter does not constitute action that is prejudicial to the administration of justice even though Respondent has no justification for not paying the invoice." Otherwise, the disciplinary counsel "would become a collection agency for creditors of attorneys." *Id.* at 736.

On January 9, 2017, however, the Louisiana Supreme Court reinstated a disciplinary investigation that was closed by ODC arising out of a lawyer's failure to pay unspecified litigation expenses:

> Based on our review of the record, we find the disciplinary board was arbitrary and capricious in dismissing the complaint. This court's opinion in *In re Bilbe*, 02-1740 (La. 2/7/03), 841 So. 2d 729, is limited to the unique facts presented and does not stand for the blanket proposition that an attorney's failure to pay litigation-related expenses can never constitute conduct prejudicial to the administration of justice.

---

[139] Note also that another lawyer could not participate in the making of such a nondisclosure agreement in the context or a settlement (or otherwise). Louisiana lawyers have an obligation to report serious misconduct by other lawyers to the Office of Disciplinary Counsel. *See* La. Rules of Prof'l Conduct r. 8.3(a).

See In re Appeal of Decision of the Disciplinary Board, 208 So. 3d 370 (La. 2017). As a result, the court remanded the matter to ODC "to conduct further investigation and to institute formal charges, if appropriate." *Id*. In the wake of this decision, the failure of a lawyer to pay litigation-related expenses alone may constitute a disciplinary offense.

Threatening to Press Criminal Charges for Tactical Advantage

A lawyer engages in professional misconduct if the lawyer threatens to press criminal or disciplinary charges "solely to obtain an advantage in a civil matter." La. Rules of Prof'l Conduct r. 8.4(g) (2004); *see Ruffin*, 54 So. 3d at 648; *In re Exnicios*, 218 So. 3d 94 (La. 2017) (six-month deferred suspension for threatening "to bring a disciplinary complaint against an attorney in an effort to gain an advantage in a civil case"). In addition to being professional misconduct, such threats may constitute extortion under the Louisiana Criminal Code depending, of course, on the context. *See* La. Rev. Stat. Ann. § 14:66(2) (stating that a "threat to accuse" a person "of any crime" can be "sufficient to constitute extortion"). On the propriety of threatening to file a disciplinary complaint against another lawyer in order to gain an advantage in a civil matter, see ABA Comm. on Ethics and Prof'l Responsibility, Formal Op. 94-383 (1994).

"SOLELY"

While there is no case law on this specific issue in Louisiana, the California State Bar's Ethics Committee stated that the "rule [against threatening administrative charges solely to gain an advantage in a civil matter] seems to suggest that where an administrative claim is brought *even with a scintilla of justification*, there will be no violation of [the Rules of Professional Conduct]." *See* State Bar of Cal. Comm. on Prof'l Responsibility and Conduct Formal Op. 73 (1983). The Committee opined that "where there is a dual motive on the part of counsel in presenting charges, one motive being legitimate and the other not, the benefit of the doubt *must be given* to the attorney such that there can be no violation" of the rule. *See id*. (emphasis added). The California committee found that this result was warranted for at least three different reasons. First, the Committee looked to the plain language of the rule with reference to the word "solely." *See id*. Second, the Committee stated that "when there is more than one subjective motivating factor for a decision to present administrative or disciplinary charges it becomes virtually impossible to balance an improper motive against a proper one." *See id*. Furthermore, the Committee reasoned, "[t]he fact that an attorney may have an ulterior purpose of dubious legitimacy should not negate the weight and legitimacy of a coexisting proper objective." *See id*. The third and most important reason stated by the Committee was that:

> [I]n most instances, there is a public policy recognizing the filing of administrative complaints against government-regulated persons and entities. The filing of such complaints tends to insure that the regulated party operates within the bounds of the law...In addition, the client may have a constitutional right to petition the government for redress of grievances through quasi-judicial channels...The qualification of the second clause by the word "solely" is therefore justified on the basis that there is little public benefit gained when a party threatens prosecution. That is, a narrower prohibition is needed where a lawyer presents charges, than

where the lawyer threatens to do so. Rather than conferring a public benefit, the attorney threatening charges is in most instances likely to be seeking a private benefit to his client in the civil matter.

State Bar of Cal. Comm. on Prof's Responsibility and Conduct Formal Op. 73 (1983).[140]

The Ethics Committee of the New York State Bar addressed the extent to which, and under what circumstances, a lawyer may threaten a third party with administrative penalties or criminal prosecution in order to recover a civil claim against a stock broker who had converted the funds of a client.[141] After examining the purpose underlying the rule, the prevention of the subversion of both the criminal and civil processes, the Committee stated that:

> DR 7-105(A) is intended to preserve the integrity of both the system of civil liability and the criminal justice system by making sure that a lawyer's actual or threatened invocation of the criminal justice system is not motivated *solely* by the effect such invocation is likely to have on a client's interests in a civil matter. When, however, a lawyer's motive to prosecute is genuine—that is, actuated by a sincere interest in and respect for the purposes of the criminal justice system—DR 7-105(A) would be *inapplicable, even if such prosecution resulted in a benefit to a client's interest in a civil matter.*

N.Y. State Bar Ethics Comm. Op. 772 (2003). The Committee further discussed the issue of the client's intent in bringing the complaint, stating that: "[t]he 'solely' requirement makes the propriety of filing such a complaint contingent upon the client's intent. As long as one purpose of the client in filing such a complaint with a Prosecutor is to have the Broker prosecuted, convicted, or punished, then such a complaint would not offend the letter or spirit of DR 7-105(A)." *See id.* Therefore, the Committee concluded that "as long as the client's motivation includes that purpose, DR 7-105(A) would not be violated even if the filing of such a complaint resulted in the Broker returning the client's funds and even if the

---

[140]Finally, the Committee concluded that "although on the surface the word 'solely' may appear to give an attorney a license to use marginally justifiable administrative or disciplinary proceedings as a subterfuge for exerting leverage in a civil matter, this fear is allayed by" other Rules of Professional Conduct, namely the one "which prohibits an attorney from taking steps for the purpose of harassing or maliciously injuring any person." *See id.*

[141] Note that Opinion 772 dismissed the notion of discipline for the threat of *administrative penalties* because the New York Rule covers only the threat of *criminal* charges. NY DR 7-105(A) states: "A lawyer shall not present, participate in presenting, or threaten to present criminal charges solely to obtain an advantage in a civil matter."

client also intended that result, because the lawyer would not have filed such a complaint 'solely' to obtain the return of the client's funds." *See id.* [142]

Discrimination and Harassment

In 2016, the ABA amended Model Rule 8.4 to include a broad anti-discrimination and anti-harassment provision, and three revised comments. The amendment added a new paragraph (g) to the black-letter of Rule 8.4: "It is professional misconduct for a lawyer

---

[142] *See also* Conn. Informal Op. 19 (1998) ("Such an examination [of a lawyer's motivation] is very fact specific"); Conn. Informal Op. 50 (1999) ("[T]here is no *per se* prohibition against simultaneously pursuing a criminal complaint and a civil action against the same party unless the attorney's sole reason for filing a criminal complaint is to seek an advantage in the civil action...Thus, it appears that if the attorney has at least one other reason to counsel or bring a criminal prosecution while a civil action is pending or intended, he or she may enjoy the advantage in a civil action without violating the rule"); *Somers v. Statewide Grievance Committee,* 245 Conn. 277, 292 (1998) (Connecticut Supreme Court looked for the lawyer's motive and intention in filing the criminal complaint in examining whether gaining an advantage in the civil action was the lawyer's "sole" reason.); Fla. Bar Op.3 (19 89) ("The motivation and intent of the attorney involved obviously will be a major factor in determining whether his or her actions are ethically improper. The Committee believes that such determinations necessarily must be made on a case-by-case basis"); Supreme Court of Texas Prof'l Ethics Comm., Tex. Eth. Op. 589 (2009), 2009 WL 4073666 (Sept. 2009) ("Under Rule 4.04, it does not matter whether the lawyer is reporting the possibly illegal activity on his own initiative or at the direction of or in concert with his client. Determining if such reporting is permissible under the Rule turns on whether the only substantial purpose for reporting is to embarrass, delay or burden a third person and whether the report is being made solely to gain an advantage in a civil matter. Moreover, under Rule 8.04(a)(1), the lawyer is prohibited from seeking to circumvent the requirements of Rule 4.04 by causing the lawyer's client to make a report that would violate Rule 4.04 if the report was made directly by the lawyer."). Mich. State Bar. Comm. on Prof'l & Judicial Ethics Informal Op. RI-78 (1991) (good-faith assertion of possible criminal prosecution to opposing party in civil suit permissible); *Ruberton v. Gabage,* 280 N.J. Super. 125, 654 A.2d 1002 (App. Div. 1995); *In re Conduct of McCurdy,* 297 Or. 217, 681 P.2d 131 (1984); W.Va. Off. Disc. Csl. Op. 01 (2000) (good-faith threat of criminal prosecution permissible); *In re Finkelstein,* 901 F.2d 1560 (11th Cir. 1990) (The Eleventh Circuit Court of Appeals ruled that threats relating to bad publicity made in order to induce a civil settlement, while "lawyerlike" and "offensive," are not prohibited by existing professional ethics codes.); *Committee on Legal Ethics of the West Virginia State Bar v. Printz,* 416 S.E.2d 720, 727 (1992) (The West Virginia Supreme Court of Appeals has ruled that DR 7-105(A) "has proven to be unworkable" and is an inappropriate basis for professional discipline as "[t]he rules of legal ethics should not prohibit lawyers from engaging in otherwise legitimate negotiations."); Alaska Bar Ass'n Ethics Comm. Op. 2 (1997) (threat of criminal prosecution made in related civil action not unethical where lawyer has well-founded belief that such prosecution is warranted by the facts and law).

to: . . . (g) engage in conduct that the lawyer knows or reasonably should know is harassment or discrimination on the basis of race, sex, religion, national origin, ethnicity, disability, age, sexual orientation, gender identity, marital status or socioeconomic status in conduct related to the practice of law." *See* ABA Revised Resolution 109 (adopted Aug. 8, 2016).

On November 27, 2017, the LSBA Rules of Professional Conduct Committee reported that it would make "no recommendation" regarding the adoption of a rule prohibiting discrimination and harassment in conduct related to the practice of law. Although the LSBA committee's chairperson noted that "it is difficult to summarize the rationale of the lengthy debate in its entirety, the primary arguments made by those opposing the rule" were as follows:

- Existing rules permit ODC to prosecute much of the conduct that would be covered by the proposed rule, "thus making it unnecessary."

- The proposed rule contains ambiguous terms that could engender litigation and create uncertainty.

- The proposed rule may be unconstitutional.

Disciplinary Sanctions

The sanctions appropriate for a violation of paragraph (a) of this rule are those applicable to the underlying rule that the lawyer has violated, attempted to violate or assisted another in violating. *See* ABA Stds. for Imposing Lawyer Sanctions appx. 1 (1986).

The sanctions appropriate for a violation of paragraph (b) are as follows (absent aggravating or mitigating circumstances): *disbarment*, when the lawyer either (a) engages in serious criminal conduct, a necessary element of which includes intentional interference with the administration of justice, false swearing, misrepresentation, fraud, extortion, misappropriation, or theft; or the sale, distribution or importation of controlled substances; or the intentional killing of another; or an attempt or conspiracy or solicitation of another to commit any of these offenses; or (b) engages in intentional conduct involving dishonesty, fraud, deceit, or misrepresentation that seriously adversely reflects on the lawyer's fitness to practice; *suspension*, when the lawyer knowingly engages in other types of criminal conduct that seriously adversely reflects on the lawyer's fitness to practice; *reprimand*, when the lawyer knowingly engages in any other conduct that involves dishonesty, fraud, deceit, or misrepresentation and that adversely reflects on the lawyer's fitness to practice law; and, *admonition*, when the lawyer engages in any other conduct that reflects adversely on his or her fitness to practice law. *See id.* stds. 5.1-5.14.

The sanctions appropriate for a violation of paragraph (c) turn on the person to whom the lawyer directs the fraud, deceit or misrepresentation. If the lawyer directs such conduct toward anyone other than a client, the appropriate sanctions are the same as those which are appropriate for a violation of paragraph (b) of this rule. *See id.*; *see also In re McKee*, 976 So. 2d at 154 (permanently disbarring lawyer for, among other things, entering into a contract to purchase a home; writing a personal check at the closing instead of using certified funds; and, to prove sufficiency of funds, producing documentation purporting to show she had obtained a $529,000 default judgment for a client when, in fact, that judgment had been set aside). If the lawyer directs such conduct toward a client, however, the appropriate sanctions are as follows (absent aggravating or mitigating circumstances): *disbarment*, when the lawyer knowingly deceives a client with the intent to benefit the lawyer or another, and causes serious injury or potentially serious injury to a client; *suspension*, when the lawyer knowingly deceives a client, and causes injury or potential injury to the client; *reprimand*, when the lawyer negligently fails to provide a client with accurate or complete information, and causes injury or potential injury to the client; and, *admonition*, when a lawyer engages in an isolated instance of negligence in failing to provide a client with accurate or complete information, and causes little or no actual or potential injury to a client. *See id.* stds. 4.61-4.64.

The sanctions appropriate for a violation of paragraph (d) depend on the nature of the lawyer's violation. If the violation involves false statements, fraud or misrepresentation, standard 6.1 governs. *See supra* Annotations to Rule 4.1. If the violation involves the abuse of the legal process, standard 6.2 applies. *See supra* Annotations to Rule 6.2. If the violation involves improper communications with individuals in the legal system, standard 6.3 applies. *See supra* Annotations to Rule 3.5.

The sanctions generally appropriate for a violation of paragraphs (e) or (f) are as follows (absent aggravating or mitigating circumstances): *disbarment*, when the lawyer knowingly violates a court rule with the intent to obtain a benefit for the lawyer or another, and causes serious injury or potentially serious injury to a party, or causes serious or potentially serious interference with a legal proceeding; *suspension*, when the lawyer knows that he is violating a court rule, and there is injury or potential injury to a client or a party, or interference or potential interference with a legal proceeding; *reprimand*, when the lawyer negligently fails to comply with a court rule, and causes injury or potential injury to a client or other party, or causes interference or potential interference with a court proceeding; and, *admonition*, when the lawyer engages in an isolated instance of negligence in complying with a court rule, and causes little or no actual or potential injury to a party, or causes little or no actual or potential interference with a legal proceeding. *See* ABA Stds. for Imposing Lawyer Sanctions std. 6.2 (1986) (Abuse of Legal Process); *id.* stds. 6.21-6.24.

The sanctions generally appropriate for a violation of paragraph (g) are as follows (absent aggravating or mitigating circumstances): *disbarment*, when the lawyer knowingly violates a court rule with the intent to obtain a benefit for the lawyer or another, and causes serious injury or potentially serious injury to a party, or causes serious or potentially serious interference with a legal proceeding; *suspension*, when the lawyer knows that he is violating a court rule, and there is injury or potential injury to a client or a party, or interference or potential interference with a legal proceeding; *reprimand*, when the lawyer negligently fails to comply with a court rule, and causes injury or potential injury to a client or other party, or causes interference or potential interference with a court proceeding; and, *admonition*, when the lawyer engages in an isolated instance of negligence in complying with a court rule, and causes little or no actual or potential injury to a party, or causes little or no actual or potential interference with a legal proceeding. *See id.* std. 6.2 (Abuse of Legal Process); *id.* stds. 6.21-6.24.

RULE 8.5. DISCIPLINARY AUTHORITY; CHOICE OF LAW

(a) *Disciplinary Authority.* A lawyer admitted to practice in this jurisdiction is subject to the disciplinary authority of this jurisdiction, regardless of where the lawyer's conduct occurs. A lawyer not admitted in this jurisdiction is also subject to the disciplinary authority of this jurisdiction if the lawyer provides or offers to provide any legal services in this jurisdiction. A lawyer may be subject to the disciplinary authority of both this jurisdiction and another jurisdiction for the same conduct.

(b) *Choice of Law.* In any exercise of the disciplinary authority of this jurisdiction, the rules of professional conduct to be applied shall be as follows:

(1) for conduct in connection with a matter pending before a tribunal, the rules of the jurisdiction in which the tribunal sits, unless the rules of the tribunal provide otherwise; and

(2) for any other conduct, the rules of the jurisdiction in which the lawyer's conduct occurred, or, if the predominant effect of the conduct is in a different jurisdiction, the rules of that jurisdiction shall be applied to the conduct. A lawyer shall not be subject to discipline if the lawyer's conduct conforms to the rules of a jurisdiction in which the lawyer reasonably believes the predominant effect of the lawyer's conduct will occur.

BACKGROUND

The Louisiana Supreme Court adopted this rule on March 8, 2005, and it became effective on April 1, 2005. This rule is identical to ABA Model Rule of Professional Conduct 8.5.

COMMENTS TO ABA MODEL RULE 8.5
Disciplinary Authority

[1] It is longstanding law that the conduct of a lawyer admitted to practice in this jurisdiction is subject to the disciplinary authority of this jurisdiction.

Extension of the disciplinary authority of this jurisdiction to other lawyers who provide or offer to provide legal services in this jurisdiction is for the protection of the citizens of this jurisdiction. Reciprocal enforcement of a jurisdiction's disciplinary findings and sanctions will further advance the purposes of this Rule. See, Rules 6 and 22, ABA Model Rules for Lawyer Disciplinary Enforcement. A lawyer who is subject to the disciplinary authority of this jurisdiction under Rule 8.5(a) appoints an official to be designated by this Court to receive service of process in this jurisdiction. The fact that the lawyer is subject to the disciplinary authority of this jurisdiction may be a factor in determining whether personal jurisdiction may be asserted over the lawyer for civil matters.

Choice of Law

[2] A lawyer may be potentially subject to more than one set of rules of professional conduct which impose different obligations. The lawyer may be licensed to practice in more than one jurisdiction with differing rules, or may be admitted to practice before a particular court with rules that differ from those of the jurisdiction or jurisdictions in which the lawyer is licensed to practice. Additionally, the lawyer's conduct may involve significant contacts with more than one jurisdiction.

[3] Paragraph (b) seeks to resolve such potential conflicts. Its premise is that minimizing conflicts between rules, as well as uncertainty about which rules are applicable, is in the best interest of both clients and the profession (as well as the bodies having authority to regulate the profession). Accordingly, it takes the approach of (i) providing that any particular conduct of a lawyer shall be subject to only one set of rules of professional conduct, (ii) making the determination of which set of rules applies to particular conduct as straightforward as possible, consistent with recognition of appropriate regulatory interests of relevant jurisdictions, and (iii) providing protection from discipline for lawyers who act reasonably in the face of uncertainty.

[4] Paragraph (b)(1) provides that as to a lawyer's conduct relating to a proceeding pending before a tribunal, the lawyer shall be subject only to the rules of the jurisdiction in which the tribunal sits unless the rules of the tribunal, including its choice of law rule, provide otherwise. As to all other conduct, including conduct in anticipation of a proceeding not yet pending before a tribunal, paragraph (b)(2) provides that a lawyer shall be subject to the rules of the jurisdiction in which the lawyer's conduct occurred, or, if the predominant effect of the conduct is in another jurisdiction, the rules of that jurisdiction shall be applied to the conduct. In the case of conduct in anticipation of a proceeding that is likely to be before a tribunal, the predominant effect of such conduct could be where the conduct occurred, where the tribunal sits or in another jurisdiction.

[5] When a lawyer's conduct involves significant contacts with more than one jurisdiction, it may not be clear whether the predominant effect of the lawyer's conduct will occur in a jurisdiction other than the one in which the conduct occurred. So long as the lawyer's conduct conforms to the rules of a jurisdiction in which the lawyer reasonably believes the predominant effect will occur, the lawyer shall not be subject to discipline under this Rule. With respect to conflicts of interest, in determining a lawyer's reasonable belief under paragraph (b)(2), a written agreement between the lawyer and client that reasonably specifies a particular jurisdiction as within the scope of that paragraph may be considered if the agreement was obtained with the client's informed consent confirmed in the agreement.

[6] If two admitting jurisdictions were to proceed against a lawyer for the same conduct, they should, applying this rule, identify the same governing ethics rules. They should take all appropriate steps to see that they do apply the same rule to the same conduct, and in all events should avoid proceeding against a lawyer on the basis of two inconsistent rules.

[7] The choice of law provision applies to lawyers engaged in transnational practice, unless international law, treaties or other agreements between competent regulatory authorities in the affected jurisdictions provide otherwise.

ANNOTATIONS
Generally
Under this rule, a Louisiana lawyer may be disciplined in Louisiana for misconduct that occurs elsewhere. Thus, a lawyer who is practicing law in another state, either because the lawyer is generally admitted to practice there or because he has been admitted *pro hac vice* in connection with a particular matter, may be disciplined in Louisiana for unethical conduct in that jurisdiction.

Conversely, a lawyer who is not licensed to practice in Louisiana is nonetheless subject to disciplinary authority in this state pursuant to Louisiana Rule 8.5, which provides that "[a] lawyer not admitted in this jurisdiction is also subject to the disciplinary authority of this jurisdiction if the lawyer provides or offers to provide any legal services in this jurisdiction." *See In re Nguyen*, 215 So. 3d 668 (La. 2017) (enjoining non-Louisiana lawyer from seeking admission to practice in Louisiana for one year for improper communication with represented person while lawyer was practicing pro hac vice). Indeed, the Louisiana Supreme Court has held that pursuant to its "plenary power to define and regulate the practice of law, we have the right to fashion and impose any sanction which we find is necessary and appropriate to regulate the practice of law and protect the citizens of this state. This power is broad enough to encompass persons not admitted to the bar who attempt to practice law in this state." *See In re Cortigene & Schwartz*, 144 So. 3d 915 (La. 2014).

Disciplinary Sanctions

Given that this rule is jurisdictional in nature, the ABA Standards for Imposing Lawyer Sanctions contain no provisions relating to violations of ABA Model Rule 8.5 ("Disciplinary Authority; Choice of Law").

Professionalism Materials
Professionalism: In General

Over the past three decades[143] members of the bench, bar and legal academy have lamented the decline of professionalism among American lawyers[144]. Among the problems now perceived to plague our profession include[145] that we, as lawyers, have lost an understanding of the practice of law as a "calling."[146] That changes in the economics of the practice of law have transmuted our practice from a profession to a business.[147] That we have lost our way as independent intermediaries and counselors and, in so doing, have become "hired guns," or "Rambos," content merely to do our clients'

---

[143] Excerpted from Dane S. Ciolino, *Redefining Professionalism as Seeking*, 49 Loy. L. Rev. 229, 229-31 (2003).

[144] *See, e.g.,* Warren E. Burger, *The Decline in Professionalism*, 61 Tenn. L. Rev. 1 (1993); *see generally* Mary Ann Glendon, *A Nation Under Lawyers: How the Crisis in the Legal Profession is Transforming American Society* (1994); Anthony T. Kronman, *The Lost Lawyer: Failing Ideals of the Legal Profession* (1993); Sol M. Linowitz & Martin Mayer, *The Betrayed Profession: Lawyering at the End of the Twentieth Century* (1994); *see also* Samuel J. Levine, *Essay, Faith in Legal Professionalism: Believers and Heretics*, 61 Md. L. Rev. 217 (2002); Therese Maynard, *Teaching Professionalism: The Lawyer as Professional*, 34 Ga. L. Rev. 895, 895 n.2 (2000) ("[t]he literature teems with articles that describe, often in rather distressing terms, the crisis within the legal profession today"); Fred C. Zacharias, *Reconciling Professionalism and Client Interests*, 36 Wm. & Mary L. Rev. 1303, 1307 (1995) ("[o]ver the past two decades, hundreds of articles and speeches have focused on the meaning of professionalism, its perceived 'decline,' and steps the bar should take to improve it").

[145] Some also have expressed concerns about the general competency of lawyers and their compliance with disciplinary codes. *See* A.B.A., Final Report and Recommendations of the Task Force on Professional Competence (1983). But this is more a matter of "legal ethics" than "professionalism."

[146] *See* Phoebe A. Haddon, *Education for a Public Calling in the 21st Century*, 69 Wash. L. Rev. 573 (1994).

[147] *See, e.g.,* Wm. Reece Smith, Jr., *Teaching and Learning Professionalism*, 32 Wake Forest L. Rev. 613, 613 (1997); Eleanor W. Myers, *"Simple Truths" About Moral Education*, 45 Am. U.L. Rev. 823, 827 (1996); Norman Bowie, *The Law: From a Profession to a Business*, 47 Vand. L. Rev. 741 (1988).

bidding.[148] And, finally, that the warm, collegial civility and comradery that lawyers once shared (or we think they shared) has been swallowed by an eat-or-be-eaten mentality.[149]

These malignancies, they say, are a cancer on our profession. Lawyers are increasingly disillusioned, clients dissatisfied, and the public disgusted. Because of this crisis, the public perception of lawyers continues to look for a bottom.[150] Where is Atticus Finch when the profession needs him?

In response to these widespread concerns, the profession has waged a multi-frontal crusade to improve professionalism in the practice of law. In addition to forming innumerable committees, the organized bar has conducted symposia[151] adopted civility creeds[152] offered continuing legal education programs,[153] and called upon American law schools to teach professionalism to

---

[148] See Robert F. Cochran, Jr., *Professionalism in the Postmodern Age: Its Death, Attempts at Resuscitation, and Alternate Sources of Virtue*, 14 Notre Dame J.L. Ethics & Pub. Pol'y 305, 311-13 (2000); Margaret Ann Wilkinson, Peter Mercer & Terra Strong, *Mentor, Mercenary or Melding: An Empirical Inquiry into the Role of the Lawyer*, 28 Loy. U. Chi. L.J. 373 (1996); David Luban, *The Noblesse Oblige Tradition in the Practice of Law*, 41 Vand. L. Rev. 717 (1988).

[149] See E. Norman Veasey, *Rambo Be Gone*, 4 Bus. Law Today 12 (Jan/Feb 1995); N. Gregory Smith, *Ethics v. Professionalism and the Louisiana Supreme Court*, 58 La. L. Rev. 539, 541 (1998) (noting that bar journals, legal periodicals and discussions with practitioners "reveal that incivility and unprofessional conduct are far more pervasive than lawyer incompetency or dishonesty.").

[150] See, e.g., Erica Moeser, *Standards, Change, Politics, and the Millennium*, 28 Loy. U. Chi. L.J. 229, 230 (1996).

[151] See, e.g., A.B.A., *Teaching and Learning Professionalism: Symposium Proceedings (1996); A.B.A., Teaching and Learning Professionalism: Report of the Professionalism Committee* (1996).

[152] More than 100 county, city and state bar associations, and many federal courts, have adopted civility codes. See, e.g., Allen K. Harris, *The Professionalism Crisis: The "Z" Words and Other Rambo Tactics*, 53 S.C. L. Rev. 549, 582-83 (2002).

[153] See, e.g., Joryn Jenkins, *Teaching and Learning Professionalism*, Fed. Lawyer, Aug. 1997, at 6 (discussing "The Florida Lawyers Ethics School").

law students.[154] Courts have adopted lawyer–and judge–civility codes and, perhaps most controversially, have implemented mandatory professionalism CLE requirements. For example, the Louisiana Supreme Court in 1997 amended its Rules for Continuing Legal Education[155] to require that every Louisiana lawyer attend at least one hour of professionalism CLE each year.[156] Some of these professionalism codes, creeds and CLE requirements affecting Louisiana lawyers are collected in this section.

Louisiana State Bar Association Code of Professionalism (1992)

My word is my bond. I will never intentionally mislead the court or other counsel. I will not knowingly make statements of fact or law that are untrue.

I will clearly identify for other counsel changes I have made in documents submitted to me.

I will conduct myself with dignity, civility, courtesy and a sense of fair play.

I will not abuse or misuse the law, its procedures or the participants in the judicial process.

I will consult with other counsel whenever scheduling procedures are required and will be cooperative in scheduling discovery, hearings, the testimony of witnesses and in the handling of the entire course of any legal matter.

I will not file or oppose pleadings, conduct discovery or utilize any course of conduct for the purpose of undue delay or harassment of any other counsel or party. I will allow counsel fair opportunity to respond and will grant reasonable requests for extensions of time.

I will not engage in personal attacks on other counsel or the court. I will support my profession's efforts to enforce its disciplinary rules and will not make unfounded allegations of unethical conduct about other counsel.

I will not use the threat of sanctions as a litigation tactic.

---

[154] *See* A.B.A. *Report on Teaching and Learning Professionalism*, supra, at 13-25 ("Law School Professionalism Training").

[155] *See* Smith, *Ethics v. Professionalism*, supra, at 544-47 (discussing the new rule).

[156] Louisiana Supreme Court Order of May 23, 1997. The general reception among practicing, CLE-attending Louisiana lawyers to professionalism CLE has been chilly, at best, and hostile, at worst.

I will cooperate with counsel and the court to reduce the cost of litigation and will readily stipulate to all matters not in dispute.

I will be punctual in my communication with clients, other counsel and the court, and in honoring scheduled appearances.

Following approval by the Louisiana State Bar Association House of Delegates and Board of Governors at the Midyear Meeting, and approval by the Supreme Court of Louisiana on Jan. 10, 1992, the Code of Professionalism was adopted for the membership. The Code originated out of the Professionalism and Quality of Life Committee.

Louisiana Supreme Court Rules Relating to Litigation Conduct in Louisiana Courts (1997)

PREAMBLE

The following standards are designed to encourage us, the judges and lawyers, to meet our obligations to each other, to litigants and to the system of justice, and thereby achieve the twin goals of professionalism and civility, both of which are hallmarks of a learned profession dedicated to public service.

These standards shall not be used as a basis for litigation or sanctions or penalties. Nothing in these standards alters or detracts from existing disciplinary codes or alters the existing standards of conduct against which judicial or lawyer negligence may be determined.

However, these standards should be reviewed and followed by all judges of the State of Louisiana. Copies may be made available to clients to reinforce our obligation to maintain and foster these standards.

JUDGES' DUTIES TO THE COURTS

We will be courteous, respectful, and civil to lawyers, parties, and witnesses. We will maintain control of the proceedings, recognizing that judges have both the obligation and authority to insure that all litigation proceedings are conducted in a civil manner.

We will not employ hostile, demeaning, or humiliating words in opinions or in written or oral communications with lawyers, parties, or witnesses.

We will be punctual in convening all hearings, meetings, and conferences; if delayed, we will notify counsel, if possible.

We will be considerate of time schedules of lawyers, parties, and witnesses in scheduling all hearings, meetings and conferences.

We will make all reasonable efforts to decide promptly all matters presented to us for decision.

We will give the issues in controversy deliberate, impartial, and studied analysis and consideration.

While endeavoring to resolve disputes efficiently, we will be considerate of the time constraints and pressures imposed on lawyers by the exigencies of litigation practice.

We recognize that a lawyer has a right and a duty to present a cause fully and properly, and that a litigant has a right to a fair and impartial hearing. Within the practical limits of time, we will allow lawyers to present proper arguments and to make a complete and accurate record.

We will not impugn the integrity or professionalism of any lawyer on the basis of clients whom or the causes which a lawyer represents.

We will do our best to insure that court personnel act civilly toward lawyers, parties, and witnesses.

We will not adopt procedures that needlessly increase litigation expense.

We will bring to lawyers' attention uncivil conduct which we observe.

We will be courteous, respectful, and civil in opinions, ever mindful that a position articulated by another judge is the result of that judge's earnest effort to interpret the law and the facts correctly.

We will abstain from disparaging personal remarks or criticisms, or sarcastic or demeaning comments about another judge in all written and oral communications.

We will endeavor to work with other judges in an effort to foster a spirit of cooperation in our mutual goal of enhancing the administration of justice.

LAWYERS' DUTIES TO THE COURTS

We will speak and write civilly and respectfully in all communications with the court.

We will be punctual and prepared for all court appearances so that all hearings, conferences, and trials may commence on time; if delayed, we will notify the court and counsel, if possible.

We will be considerate of the time constraints and pressures on the court and court staff inherent in their efforts to administer justice.

We will not engage in any conduct that brings disorder or disruption to the courtroom.

We will advise our clients and witnesses appearing in court of the proper conduct expected and required there and, to the best of our ability, prevent our clients and wit nesses from creating disorder or disruption.

We will not knowingly misrepresent, mischaracterize, misquote, or miscite facts or authorities in any oral or written communication to the court.

We will not engage in ex parte communication on any pending action.

We will attempt to verify the availability of necessary participants and witnesses before dates for hearings or trials are set, or if that is not feasible, immediately after such date has been set so we can promptly notify the court of any likely problems.

We will act and speak civilly to court marshals, clerks, court reporters, secretaries, and law clerks with an awareness that they too, are an integral part of the judicial system.

Practice Resources
Frequently Asked Questions (FAQs)
WHAT SHOULD I THINK ABOUT BEFORE USING SOCIAL MEDIA?

INTRODUCTION

Weblogs and social networking sites (such as Facebook, Twitter and LinkedIn) are increasingly[157] a part of the everyday lives of lawyers as well as the clients, witnesses, opponents and judges with whom they deal. Such on-line services provide lawyers with unprecedented opportunities to market their practices, develop relationships and improve professional competence. Significant perils accompany these opportunities, however. Indeed, the misuse of social media sites has already led to ethical issues for a number of lawyers and judges. Furthermore, several state and local bar associations have issued advisory opinions on lawyer use of social media.[158]

THE BENEFITS

Many lawyers resist changing the way they have always practiced. But none can afford to ignore the benefits of using social media. Blogs and networking sites, including professional networking sites like Avvo, are indispensible marketing tools. Because prospective clients increasingly search for legal services on-line rather than through using traditional media like the Yellow Pages or Martindale-Hubbell, lawyers must have a searchable "presence" on the Internet simply to be found.

Blogs and social media can also help lawyers develop and maintain professional competence. By reading and writing about recent developments in a particular area of the law, social media can be an effective, timely and free source of CLE

---

[157] One blogger has called lawyers' use of social media a "game changer on a grand scale." *See* Nicole Black, Law and Technology Blog, *You Say You Want an Internet Revolution* (Feb. 10, 2009) (http://21stcenturylaw.wordpress.com/2010/02/10/you-say-you-want-an-internet-revolution/) (social media is "changing the world as we know it. Social media is changing the ways in which people communicate, connect, create and collaborate. Participation in social media is growing at an exponential rate and people of all ages are now participating.").

[158] *See, e.g.,* District of Columbia Bar, Ethics Op. 370, *Social Media I: Marketing and Personal Use* (Nov. 2016); District of Columbia Bar, Ethics Op. 371, *Social Media II: Use of Social Media in Providing Legal Services* (Nov. 2016).

for individual lawyers. Moreover, the content published by contributing lawyers can provide valuable and readily-accessible information to the public about the legal profession and the justice system. It may even generate ideas to improve both.

Finally, social networking sites and search engines can help lawyers prepare for their cases. Just as employers often "Google" prospective employees prior to hiring,[159] lawyers can and should mine social media for information about witnesses, clients and opponents to prepare for evidentiary hearings and depositions.[160]

Technological change and social media—like them or not—are undeniable and beneficial aspects of modern law practice. As a result, successful lawyers must adapt their practices accordingly. In so doing, however, they must remain mindful that membership in the social networking community does not come risk free.

THE RISKS

The use of social media by lawyers presents questions and concerns regarding compliance with legal ethics rules. Indeed, concerns about maintaining ethical standards should be expected when any new technology—and particularly communication technology—affects the practice of law.[161] Some of the standards implicated by a lawyer's use of social media are considered below.

A lawyer must provide competent and diligent representation to the lawyer's clients.[162] Social networking threatens a lawyer's competence and diligence because its use can be enormously distracting. It is frighteningly easy to become consumed with visiting social media sites and, as a result, to neglect

---

[159] *See* Stephanie Francis Ward, *BigLaw Associate "Googles" Everyone Before Presenting Job Candidates to Firm*, ABA Journal, Law News Now (Aug. 1, 2009).

[160] *See* Debra C. Weiss, *Social Networking Sites Provide Grist for Lawyers*, ABA Journal, Law News Now (Feb. 20, 2008).

[161] For example, more than ten years ago the ABA Standing Committee on Ethics and Professional Responsibility considered the ethical issues associated with whether lawyers could use email for confidential communications. *See* ABA Formal Opinion 99-413: Protecting the Confidentiality of Unencrypted E-Mail.

[162] *See* ABA Model Rules of Professional Conduct 1.1 ("A lawyer shall provide competent representation to a client. Competent representation requires the legal knowledge, skill, thoroughness and preparation reasonably necessary for the representation."); *id.* r. 1.3 ("A lawyer shall act with reasonable diligence and promptness in representing a client.").

legal matters. Moreover, efforts to "multitask" both social media use and in-office lawyering may significantly reduce the quality of the lawyer's work.[163] Finally, because many social media posts are informal and spontaneous, competence is potentially imperiled when a lawyer provides "off-the-cuff," ill-considered legal advice or information on social networking sites.

A lawyer must maintain the confidentiality of client information.[164] Posting case-related information on social media is easy and immediate—perhaps too easy and too immediate in some cases. Indeed, lawyers have "tweeted" from court[165] and posted confidential client information on blogs[166]. Such tweets and posts are disseminated immediately across the vast Internet to an infinite number of people. Of course, there was a possibility of improper "shop talk" prior to social networking. However, given the broadcast nature of dissemination through social media, the potential for harm from such disclosures is exponentially greater.

A lawyer must not engage in the unauthorized practice of law in a jurisdiction in which the lawyer is unlicensed.[167] While the American Bar Association has taken steps to promote greater nationalization in lawyering, the practice of law in the United States remains largely parochial. A lawyer using social networking certainly has the technological wherewithal on a laptop, or even smartphone,

---

[163] *See* Stanford Report, *Media Multitaskers Pay Mental Price* (Aug. 24, 2009) (http://news.stanford.edu/news/2009/august24/multitask-research-study-082409.html).

[164] *See* ABA Model Rules of Prof'l Conduct r. 1.6(a) ("A lawyer shall not reveal information relating to the representation of a client . . . ."). In addition to a lawyer's obligation to the lawyer's client to refrain from publicly disclosing certain information, a lawyer has an obligation to the public to refrain from making an "extrajudicial statement that the lawyer knows or reasonably should know will be disseminated by means of public communication and will have a substantial likelihood of materially prejudicing an adjudicative proceeding." *See id.* r. 3.6(a).

[165] *See* Robert J. Ambrogi, *More Twittering from the Courtroom,* (Jan. 6, 2009), http://legalblogwatch.typepad.com/legal_blog_watch/2009/01/more-twittering-from-the-courtroom.html.

[166] *See* James M. McCauley, *Blogging and Social Networking for Lawyers: Ethical Pitfalls,* (Jan. 20, 2010), http://ethicsguru.blogspot.com/2010/01/blogging-social-networking-for-lawyers.html.

[167] *See* ABA Model Rules of Prof'l Conduct 5.5(a) ("A lawyer shall not practice law in a jurisdiction in violation of the regulation of the legal profession in that jurisdiction, or assist another in doing so.").

to advise clients throughout the nation and beyond. But any lawyer who takes advantage of these capabilities without an appropriate law license does so at ethical peril.

A lawyer must not make a false or misleading statement to a potential client,[168] to a judge[169] or to a third-person.[170] These content-based restrictions on lawyer speech serve both to protect the public from unfair advantage-taking by a lawyer, and to shield the justice system from improper statements that might affect the reliability of adjudicative proceedings. The use of social media increases the risk not only of making false or misleading statements in the first place, but also of getting caught thereafter.

As to making false statements, the increase in the quantity of communication attendant to social networking directly increases the chance of simply getting something wrong. This is particularly true given that social networking posts are sometimes hastily created, rarely proofread and almost never vetted. Moreover, a lawyer may view Facebook or other networking services as a means to "get dirt" about an opponent (for example, to show that a personal-injury plaintiff is physically active despite a claim of disability). However, to access such information, the lawyer typically needs the opponent to "accept" the lawyer's "friend request"—a request premised on a false pretext or false name. At least one bar association ethics opinion has condemned such lawyer deception as a violation of Rule 8.4(c) (prohibiting conduct involving

---

[168] *See* ABA Model Rules of Professional Conduct 7.1 ("A lawyer shall not make a false or misleading communication about the lawyer or the lawyer's services. A communication is false or misleading if it contains a material misrepresentation of fact or law, or omits a fact necessary to make the statement considered as a whole not materially misleading."); *id.* r. 8.4(c) ("It is professional misconduct for a lawyer to . . . engage in conduct involving dishonesty, fraud, deceit or misrepresentation.")

[169] *See* ABA Model Rules of Professional Conduct 3.3(a)(1) ("A lawyer shall not knowingly . . . make a false statement of fact or law to a tribunal or fail to correct a false statement of material fact or law previously made to the tribunal by the lawyer"); *id.* r. 8.4(c) ("It is professional misconduct for a lawyer to . . . engage in conduct involving dishonesty, fraud, deceit or misrepresentation.").

[170] *See* ABA Model Rules of Professional Conduct 4.1(a) ("In the course of representing a client a lawyer shall not knowingly . . . make a false statement of material fact or law to a third person"); *id.* r. 8.4(c) ("It is professional misconduct for a lawyer to . . . engage in conduct involving dishonesty, fraud, deceit or misrepresentation.").

dishonesty) and Rule 4.1 (prohibiting false statements of material fact to a third person).[171]

As to getting caught, a lawyer's posts, once broadcast, are subject to review and criticism by innumerable ad hoc fact-checkers, other lawyers, opponents, regulators and judges. Indeed, one Texas judge caught a lawyer lying about the reason for requesting a continuance by looking at the lawyer's Facebook status updates "detailing her week of drinking, going out and partying."[172]

A lawyer must not improperly communicate with a represented person,[173] a judge or a juror.[174] These recipient-based restrictions on lawyer speech serve to protect the sanctity of the lawyer-client relationship and the independence of adjudicators by preventing a lawyer from communicating with those over whom the lawyer may exert improper influence. Social media permit a lawyer to have ready access to an audience that may contain represented persons, judges or jurors with whom the lawyer cannot otherwise communicate. For example, the North Carolina Judicial Standards Commission publicly reprimanded a district judge for engaging in ex parte, Facebook communications with a lawyer for one of the parties during an ongoing a domestic matter.[175] While the impropriety of two-way correspondence with a prohibited person should be obvious to most lawyers, the plain language of applicable professional conduct standards is broader than some lawyers may appreciate. These standards prohibit "communications" with represented persons, judges and jurors—including one-way communications from the lawyer to an audience in the public cloud.

---

[171] *See* The Philadelphia Bar Assoc., Prof. Guidance Comm. Op. 2009-02 (Mar. 2009).

[172] *See* Molly McDonough, *Facebooking Judge Catches Lawyer in Lie, Sees Ethical Breaches*, ABA Journal, Law News Now (Jul. 41, 2009).

[173] *See* ABA Model Rules of Prof'l Conduct 4.2 ("In representing a client, a lawyer shall not communicate about the subject of the representation with a person the lawyer knows to be represented by another lawyer in the matter, unless the lawyer has the consent of the other lawyer or is authorized to do so by law or a court order.").

[174] *See* ABA Model Rules of Prof'l Conduct r. 3.5; *id.* r. 3.5(a) ("A lawyer shall not . . . communicate ex parte with such a person during the proceeding unless authorized to do so by law or court order.").

[175] *See In re Judge B. Carlton Terry, Jr.,* Inq. No. 08-234 (Apr. 1, 2009).

A lawyer must not assist a judge in committing a violation of the applicable standards of judicial conduct,[176] or to imply an ability to improperly influence a judge or other public official.[177] Quite obviously, this rule seeks to enlist—or, more accurately, to conscript—lawyers into the service of judicial regulators seeking to preserve the integrity and independence of the judiciary through the enforcement of judicial codes of conduct. This rule effectively prohibits lawyers from "friending" or otherwise communicating with judges whose use of social media in a manner that violates judicial conduct standards. Several judges have run afoul of these standards through the use of social media. A Georgia judge resigned from the bench after using Facebook to initiate an improper relationship with a defendant.[178] A New York judge was transferred after engaging in inappropriate Facebook networking, including the posting of status updates regarding pending matters while on the bench.[179] The Florida Supreme Court Judicial Ethics Advisory Committee has opined that it is unethical for Florida judges to "friend" lawyers on social media sites because "the judge, by so doing, conveys or permits others to convey the impression that they are in a special position to influence the judge."[180]

Each of these ethical risks of lawyer social networking is real. All, however, are manageable.

MANAGING THE PERILS OF SOCIAL MEDIA

To manage the significant risks of using social media, lawyers would perhaps be best advised simply to use common sense. That is, lawyers simply should act reasonably and responsibly while sitting at a keyboard, just as they should act reasonably and responsibly while sitting at counsel table or behind the wheel of an automobile. True. But to tell someone to "use common sense," to "be reasonable," or to "act responsibly" offers little practical help. Rather than

---

[176] See ABA Model Rules of Prof'l Conduct r. 8.4(f) ("It is professional misconduct for a lawyer to . . . knowingly assist a judge or judicial officer in conduct that is a violation of applicable rules of judicial conduct or other law.").

[177] See ABA Model Rules of Prof'l Conduct r. 8.4(e) ("It is professional misconduct for a lawyer to . . . state or imply an ability to influence improperly a government agency or official or to achieve results by means that violate the Rules of Professional Conduct or other law . . . .").

[178] See Debra C. Weiss, *Georgia Judge Resigns After Questions Raised About Facebook Contacts*, ABA Journal, Law News Now (Jan. 7, 2010).

[179] See John M. Annese, *Staten Island Criminal Court Judge to be Transferred to Manhattan After Facebook Postings, Sources Say*, SILive.com (Oct. 15, 2009).

[180] See Fla. Sup. Ct., Jud. Ethics Advisory Comm., Op. No. 2009-20 (Nov. 17, 2009).

taking this approach, this paper concludes with a few simple "dos and don'ts" for lawyers using social media.

Do read and follow the rules of professional conduct applicable in your jurisdiction. Although the rules do not specifically address lawyer social networking issues, they apply to *all* lawyer conduct—irrespective of whether the conduct occurs on the ground or in the cloud. Read them. Follow them.[181]

Don't become consumed with social networking. Do turn it off every now and again. Don't "multitask." Because following Facebook, Twitter, RSS feeds and blogs is fun and feels falsely productive, it can become all-consuming. It's way easier to spend enormous amounts of time staying current with friends and developments using social media than it is to actually work. You are a "competent" and "diligent" lawyer only when you are working. Not when you are friending. Use social media. But use it like alcohol—in moderation.

Do use the confirmation principle. Confirmation is a "technique for preventing unintended actions by requiring verification of the actions before they are performed."[182] Before posting anything on a social media site, confirm that the post is accurate, ethical and professionally appropriate. In other words, before hitting "post" or "send," slow down, proofread, and fact check. While confirmation will slow your workflow, it could save your professional reputation.

Do remember that a lawyer's social media profile that is used only for personal purposes is not subject to lawyer advertising rules. However, a social media profile that a lawyer primarily uses for the purpose of her and her law firm's business is subject to those rules.

Don't lie.

Do police the accuracy of posted information on social media sites that allow for you to curate posts and endorsements. To this end, employ settings that allow review and approval of such information before publication.

Don't give legal advice to anyone on a social networking site, and avoid the inadvertent formation of lawyer-client relationships. Instead, provide only legal information. Distinguishing between "advice" and "information" is sometimes difficult, but here's a start: a post contains "advice" if it applies law to a real issue relevant to an identifiable recipient; in contrast, a post contains

---

[181] Lawyers are good at reading and applying the laws governing their clients. Oddly enough, they are less good at reading and following the rules governing themselves.

[182] *See* WILLIAM LIDWELL, KRITINA HOLDEN & JILL BUTLER, UNIVERSAL PRINCIPLES OF DESIGN at 54 (2009).

"information" if it describes the law in general terms or if it applies the law only to hypothetical issues and persons. To reinforce that you provide only information, place a disclaimer on your site that you only provide information and not advice. Then follow your own disclaimer.

Don't contact a represented person to seek permission to access restricted portions of the person's social media account unless an express authorization has been furnished by the person's lawyer.

Don't reveal confidential information on social media sites. The scope of what is "confidential information" is significantly broader than most lawyers realize. Indeed, under the Model Rules, information is "confidential" if it in any way "relat[es] to the representation of a client."[183] Therefore, post information about clients and cases on social media only when there is "no reasonable likelihood" that a recipient will be able to "ascertain the identity of the client or the situation involved."[184] Better yet, don't post information about clients and cases on social media.[185]

Don't post anything on social media during trial. Pay attention. You're in trial.

Don't communicate with judges and jurors about pending cases. See also the preceding paragraph.

Do supervise nonlawyer employees to assure that their use of social media is consistent with lawyer professional conduct standards.

---

[183] ABA Model Rule of Professional Conduct 1.6(a).

[184] *See id.* r. 1.6 cmt. 4 ("Paragraph (a) prohibits a lawyer from revealing information relating to the representation of a client. This prohibition also applies to disclosures by a lawyer that do not in themselves reveal protected information but could reasonably lead to the discovery of such information by a third person. A lawyer's use of a hypothetical to discuss issues relating to the representation is permissible so long as there is no reasonable likelihood that the listener will be able to ascertain the identity of the client or the situation involved.").

[185] Although it goes without saying, here goes: don't use public social media to communicate with clients about their cases (such as through Facebook wall-to-wall communications or public Twitter posts). Use email.

MAY I UNDERTAKE A LIMITED SCOPE REPRESENTATION?

A Louisiana lawyer may undertake a "limited scope" representation of a client. *See* La. Rules of Prof'l Conduct r. 1.2(c). For example, a lawyer who represents an employee injured on the job may agree to handle a products-liability case against the manufacturer of the machine that caused the injury, but decline to handle the worker's compensation matter against the client's employer. Or, a family lawyer who represents a divorcing spouse may agree to handle a community property partition, but decline to handle a custody dispute. Although permissible, the limitation must be "reasonable under the circumstances," and the client must provide "informed consent." *Id.*

In the matter of *In re Zuber*, 101 So. 3d 29 (La. 2012), the Louisiana Supreme Court considered this rule in the context of an insurance-defense lawyer who agreed to represent the insured—a physician in a medical malpractice case—but who limited the scope of his representation by taking settlement direction only from the insurance company (in accordance with the plain language of the insured's contract of insurance). Under these circumstances, the court suggested the following:

> A prudent lawyer hired by an insurer to defend an insured will communicate with the insured concerning the limits of the representation at the earliest practicable time. For example, basic information concerning the nature of the representation and the insurer's right to control the defense and settlement under the insurance contract reasonably could be incorporated as part of any routine notice to the insured that the lawyer has been retained by the insurer to represent him.

Zuber, 101 So. 3d at 34 (citing ABA Formal Ethics Op. 96-403 (1996)). Thereafter, during the course of the limited scope representation, "the lawyer should make efforts to keep the insured reasonably apprised of developments in the case." *Id.* at 35 (citing *Mitchum v. Hudgens*, 533 So. 2d 194, 202 (Ala. 1988)).

Unfortunately, Zuber did not discuss the limited scope of his representation with his physician client. Fortunately for him, however, the court decided to give him a break: "[G]iven the lack of controlling jurisprudence at the time of respondents' actions in this case and considering the totality of the circumstances, we decline to find clear and convincing evidence of any violation of the Rules of Professional Conduct on their part. Accordingly, we will dismiss the formal charges." *Id.* Future lawyers will not be so lucky:

> [W]e take this opportunity to make it clear to respondents and all members of the bar that limited representation situations are fraught with potential dangers to all parties, as readily illustrated by the instant case. Henceforth, lawyers should be scrupulous in adherence to their obligations under Rule 1.2 to ensure that all clients in such a relationship are fully apprised of the nature of the representation and indicate consent by accepting the defense. Such communications will ensure that the client's rights are protected and minimize any potential for future disagreement over the nature of the representation.

Id. at 35. The takeaway? A limited scope representation is acceptable— if reasonable, and if the client and lawyer go into the representation with eyes wide open.

WHAT ARE THE ETHICAL ISSUES ASSOCIATED WITH LEAVING A LAW FIRM?

There is little guidance and even fewer direct answers in the Louisiana Rules of Professional Conduct. However, several rules, ethics opinions, and other persuasive sources do provide some guidance to Louisiana lawyers who want to depart a law firm. *See, e.g.*, ABA Formal Op. 99-414 (Sep. 1999); Ohio Bd. of Prof'l Conduct, *Ohio Ethics Guide to Switching Law Firms* (Dec. 2017); Restatement (Third) of the Law Governing Lawyers § 9 (2000) ("Law-Practice Organizations—In General"). Set forth below are some basic principles and general considerations for you, the departing lawyer:

- You don't own your clients or their files. Neither does your soon-to-be "old" law firm. Your firm can't impose any restrictions on your ability to "take" clients with you on departure. Indeed, every client has an absolute right to choose a lawyer and to obtain their file. *See* La. Rules of Prof'l Conduct r. 1.16(d).

- The extent to which you can make surreptitious preparations prior to departing is uncertain. On the one hand, the Restatement of Law Governing Lawyers suggests that simply "planning" to depart a firm by making "predeparture arrangements" such as "leasing space, printing a new letterhead, and obtaining financing" is not objectionable. On the other hand, "[t]he departing lawyer generally may not employ firm resources to solicit the client, [and] may not employ nonpublic confidential information of the firm against the interests of the firm in seeking to be retained by a firm client." See Restatement (Third) of the Law Governing Lawyers § 9 cmt. i (2000). Furthermore, the Restatement notes that a departing lawyer may not "misuse firm resources (such as copying files or client lists without permission or unlawfully removing firm property from its premises) or take other action detrimental to the interests of the firm or of clients, aside from whatever detriment may befall the firm due to their departure." *Id.*

- You should inform each client with whom you had "significant personal contacts."[186] If you contact any client of your old firm with whom you did not have a prior professional relationship, your contact may be impermissible solicitation. *See* La. Rules of Prof'l Conduct r. 7.4 ("Direct Contact with Prospective Clients").

- The letter informing each client of your departure must be sent promptly and must not contain any false or misleading statements about you or your old firm. See La. Rules of Prof'l Conduct r. 1.4 (requiring reasonable communication); *id.* r. 7.2(c) ("A lawyer shall not make or permit to be made a false, misleading or deceptive communication about the lawyer, the lawyer's services or the law firm's services.").

- The letter must make it clear to each client that the client has a choice and is neither "stuck" with you nor your former firm. It should inform each client about the status of the client's matter. It should account to each client for any funds held in trust. It should give each client a deadline and a check-the-box selection form to return. It should provide contact information for you and a member of your old firm in case the client has questions. And finally, the letter should establish a default disposition if the client does not respond by the deadline (for example, the letter could inform the client that the file will "go" with you if the client does nothing).

- If you are joining a new law firm, you must evaluate whether any conflicts will exist between the clients that you will bring with you and any existing clients of the new firm. *See* La. Rules of Prof'l Conduct r. 1.7-1.10. If so, you must reevaluate your decision to associate with the firm or to bring a particular client with you. Note that under the Louisiana Rules of Professional Conduct, nonconsensual screening is

---

[186] *See* ABA Formal Op. 99-414 (Sep. 1999). The significance of personal contacts should be judged from the perspective of the client. about your decision to leave, preferably in a joint letter with your "old" firm.

not an option to avoid imputation of conflicts that may arise by joining a new firm. *Compare* La. Rules of Prof'l Conduct r. 1.10 *with* ABA Model Rules of Prof'l Conduct r. 1.10(a)(2).

- Remember that your departing firm will have an interest in being compensated for the work that you performed on each client's file prior to your departure. On contingent-fee cases, that typically means that your old firm will have a quantum meruit claim for the value of services provided on the matter before you left. *See Saucier v. Hayes Dairy Products, Inc.*, 373 So. 2d 102 (La.1979) (a discharged lawyer is generally entitled to recover in quantum meruit for any services provided prior to termination); *see generally* Restatement of Law (Third) Governing Lawyers § 40 (2000). On hourly-fee cases, that typically means that your old firm will have a right to bill your unbilled time to the client.

- Finally, make absolutely sure that no clients or deadlines get lost in the shuffle. Both you and your old firm have a professional obligation to assure that every client is represented competently and diligently notwithstanding your departure. *See* La. Rules of Prof'l Conduct r. 1.1; *id.* r. 1.3.

MAY I SHARE OFFICE SPACE WITH NONLAWYERS?

Technological improvements have allowed lawyers to practice in nontraditional settings. From homes to beaches to shared office suites, lawyers can get more and more work done without secretaries, dictaphones and law libraries. As to shared office suites, choices in Louisiana are ever increasing (Regus Virtual Office and LaunchPad are just two examples).

What ethical issues arise when lawyers take advantage of shared office space? The Louisiana State Bar Association Rules of Professional Conduct Committee addressed these issues in a public advisory opinion entitled "Sharing Office Space with Non-Lawyers." The take away is this: lawyers may share office space with nonlawyers, but must (1) assure confidentiality, professional independence, and (2) must avoid assisting in the unauthorized practice of law, avoid improper business transactions with clients and avoid solicitation and paid referrals.

As to confidentiality, a lawyer must avoid disclosure of confidential information at "leak points" such as shared printers, copiers and fax machines. Lawyers should avoid using shared paper file storage areas (they should probably avoid paper file storage). Lawyers should use great care employing, and then must adequately train, any support staff as to handling confidential information. See Louisiana Rule 5.3.

As to professional independence, a lawyer who exchanges legal services for "free" office space must avoid providing "free" legal services to clients of the landlord/lessor, and must not allow the landlord/lessor to offer "included" legal services to other tenants. Also, the lawyer must not take client- or case-related instructions from the lawyer's landlord/lessor. This conduct also could be construed as assisting the unauthorized practice of law.

As to solicitation and paid referrals, a lawyer must not offer services in-person to other tenants. Moreover, a lawyer must not "kick back" some portion of fees received from clients referred by the landlord/lessor or co-tenants in the space.

Finally, as to engaging in business transactions with clients, a lawyer must be mindful that there are particular hoops through which the lawyer must jump if the lawyer decides to engage in business transactions with any co-tenants or with the landlord/lessor who are also the lawyer's clients. See Louisiana Rule 1.8(a). The term "business transactions" could include loans, service exchanges or partnerships, among other transactions.

Assuming the lawyer is mindful of these issues, office sharing with nonlawyers is permissible.

MAY A LAWYER USE A COMPETITOR'S NAME AS A GOOGLE ADWORD?

The Professional Ethics Committee for the State Bar of Texas has opined that a lawyer *may* use the name of a competing lawyer as a Google AdWord to generate favorable search results. *See* The Prof'l Ethics Cmte. for the State Bar of Tx., Op. No. 661 (July 2016).

Google's AdWords advertising program allows Internet advertisers to purchase keywords that result in favorable and highlighted Google search results. In the opinion of the Texas committee, using another lawyer's name as an AdWord is not "false or misleading" because:

- It does not involve the overt assertion that the advertising lawyer is a partner, shareholder, or associate of the other lawyer.
- A "reasonable person using an internet search engine" would not be misled into thinking that "every search result indicates that a lawyer shown in the list of search results has some type of relationship with the lawyer whose name was used in the search."
- Because of "the general use by all sorts of businesses of names of competing businesses as keywords in search-engine advertising, such

use by Texas lawyers in their advertising is neither dishonest nor fraudulent nor deceitful and does not involve misrepresentation."

In contrast to this Texas opinion, a grievance committee of the North Carolina State Bar censured North Carolina lawyer David J. Turlington in 2013 for engaging in misleading and "dishonest" advertising. *See In re David J. Turlington*, III, No. 13G0121, N.C. Grievance Cmte., Wake County (Nov. 18, 2013). His use of other lawyers' names in a keyword advertising campaign resulted in discipline. Said the committee:

> [Y]ou . . . intentionally add[ed] inappropriate keywords to your Google AdWords advertising campaign; your inappropriate keywords consisted of other individual attorney names (including attorney nicknames), names of law firms, and names of judicial officials. . . . Your intentional inclusion of other attorneys' names and law firms in your keyword advertising campaign is dishonest and therefore violates Rule 8.4(c).

In addition, the committee found that Turlington violated Rule 8.1(c) (prohibiting false statement in disciplinary matters) because he lied to the grievance committee in defending against the allegations by contending that his inclusion of inappropriate keywords was "inadvertent" and the result of a "bulk-purchase of keywords suggested by Google." *Id.*

Likewise, the North Carolina State Bar Association issued an advisory opinion in 2010 that reached the same conclusion as the committee in Turlington:

> It is professional misconduct for a lawyer to engage in conduct involving dishonesty, fraud, deceit, or misrepresentation. Rule 8.4(c). Dishonest conduct includes conduct that shows a lack of fairness or straightforwardness. See In the Matter of Shorter, 570 A.2d 760, 767-68 (DC App. 1990). The intentional purchase of the recognition associated with one lawyer's name to direct consumers to a competing lawyer's website is neither fair nor straightforward. Therefore, it is a violation of Rule 8.4(c) for a lawyer to select another lawyer's name to be used in his own keyword advertising.

N.C. Bar Assoc. Op. 2010-14.

Given these mixed signals, Louisiana lawyers should avoid such Google AdWords practices. Louisiana Rule 7.2 clearly prohibits a lawyer from making "a false, misleading or deceptive communication" about the lawyer, the lawyer's services or the lawyer's firm. Using another lawyer's name to generate preferential search results is an advertising practice that ODC may view as deceptive and misleading.

IS A LAWYER RESPONSIBLE FOR COMMENTS MADE BY OTHERS ON THE LAWYER'S WEBSITE OR SOCIAL MEDIA PAGES?

If your client posts a favorable review or comment about you on a social media platform that you control, must you take it down if it does not comply with the Louisiana Rules of Professional Conduct? A Pennsylvania Bar Association formal opinion addressed this and other issues facing lawyers using social media. *See* Pa. Formal Op. 2014-300 (2014).

Although social media sites like Facebook, LinkedIn, and Twitter are exempt from the filing and review process applicable to most Louisiana advertisements, *see* Rule 7.8(g), a lawyer's postings still must comply with the Louisiana Rules of Professional Conduct. Among others, advertising regulations in Rules 7.2, 7.6(b), and 7.9 are fully applicable. As a result, a lawyer's social media site must include certain required information such as the name of at least one responsible lawyer; the location of all jurisdictions in which the lawyer is licensed to practice; the location of the lawyer's office; and any intent to refer client matters out to another law firm. *See* Rules 7.2, 7.6 and 7.9(c). Moreover, a lawyer's site cannot include any "false" or "misleading" information, *see* Rule 7.2(c)(1)(C), cannot compare the lawyer's services with other lawyers' services (unless the comparison can be factually substantiated), *see* Rule 7.2(c)(1)(G); cannot promise results, and cannot include undisclosed paid endorsements, *see* Rule 7.2(c)(1). Furthermore, the Rules prohibit a lawyer from using the words "specialize," "specialist," "certified," or "expert." *See* Rule 7.2(c)(5).

But what if the you don't post the questionable information, but someone else does? Many social and professional networking sites allow the general public to review, rate or otherwise comment on a lawyer's abilities. For example, LinkedIn allows other members to "endorse" a lawyer for having certain skills. Avvo allows the public to rate a lawyer on a scale of 1-5 for "experience," "industry recognition," and "professional conduct." A lawyer must make reasonable efforts to assure that any such posts by others comply with the Louisiana Rules of Professional Conduct. According to the Pennsylvania Bar Association:

> Although an attorney is not responsible for the content that
> other persons, who are not agents of the attorney, post on
> the attorney's social networking websites, an attorney (1)
> should monitor his or her social networking websites, (2)

has a duty to verify the accuracy of any information posted, and (3) has a duty to remove or correct any inaccurate endorsements. . . . This obligation exists regardless of whether the information was posted by the attorney, by a client, or by a third party. In addition, an attorney may be obligated to remove endorsements or other postings posted on sites that the attorney controls that refer to skills or expertise that the attorney does not possess.

The North Carolina State Bar Association has made similar recommendations. See N.C. Formal Op. 2012-08 (Oct. 26, 2102).

Louisiana lawyers with professional social media sites should heed this advice. Even though your client may tell the virtual world that you're "the best," it is a comparison that cannot be factually substantiated. As a result, it likely violates the rules. Although you may like it and your Facebook friends may "Like" it even more, ODC may not. Take it down.

MAY I ADD AN ARBITRATION CLAUSE TO MY ENGAGEMENT AGREEMENT?

Yes. Most state courts that have considered the enforceability of lawyer-client arbitration clauses have approved them. The issue was an open question in Louisiana, however, until the Louisiana Supreme Court addressed the issue in *Hodges v. Reasonover*, 103 So. 3d 1069 (La. 2012). Noting that an arbitration clause "does not inherently limit or alter either party's substantive rights; it simply provides for an alternative venue for the resolution of disputes," the court held that a "binding arbitration clause between an attorney and client does not violate Rule of Professional Conduct 1.8(h) provided the clause does not limit the attorney's substantive liability, provides for a neutral decision maker, and is otherwise fair and reasonable to the client." *Hodges*, 103 So. 3d at 1076. However, the court imposed a number of "minimum" requirements for enforceable arbitration clauses:

"At a minimum, the attorney must disclose the following legal effects of binding arbitration, assuming they are applicable:

Waiver of the right to a jury trial;

Waiver of the right to an appeal;

Waiver of the right to broad discovery under the Louisiana Code of Civil Procedure and/or Federal Rules of Civil Procedure;

Arbitration may involve substantial upfront costs compared to litigation;

Explicit disclosure of the nature of claims covered by the arbitration clause, such as fee disputes or malpractice claims;

The arbitration clause does not impinge upon the client's right to make a disciplinary complaint to the appropriate authorities;

The client has the opportunity to speak with independent counsel before signing the contract."

See id. at 1077. If a Louisiana lawyer includes these terms in the lawyer's engagement agreement, it will be enforceable.

MUST I REPORT MY OWN MISCONDUCT?

No, but sometimes self-reporting is advisable.

Louisiana Rule 8.3(a) provides that "[a] lawyer who knows that another lawyer has committed a violation of the Rules of Professional Conduct that raises a question as to the lawyer's honesty, trustworthiness or fitness as a lawyer in other respects, shall inform the Office of Disciplinary Counsel."

Self-reporting is not required by Rule 8.3, which pertains only to a violation of the Rules of Professional Conduct by "another" lawyer. Moreover, compelled self-reporting of lawyer misconduct could raise Fifth Amendment issues.

Nevertheless, self-reporting is sometimes the prudent course of action. The Office of Disciplinary Counsel may consider a lawyer's self-report as a "mitigating" factor if disciplinary sanctions are ever imposed after litigation or by consent. The best advice is to consult with counsel experienced in dealing with disciplinary matters before making a final decision to self-report.

MAY I SCAN MY CLOSED FILES AND SHRED THE PAPER?

Yes you can. A 2017 advisory opinion from Nebraska addressed this issue, and concluded that "given the impact of technology on how files can be retained, it is not reasonable or practical to keep physical/paper copies of every client file." *See* Neb. Ethics Adv. Op. for Lawyers No. 17-02 at 3089 (Aug. 2017). Thus, nothing prohibits a lawyer from "keeping a closed client file in electronic form and immediately destroying the physical copy." *Id.* at 3089.

The Louisiana Revised Statutes likewise permit a Louisiana lawyer to maintain copies of past (and present) client records solely in electronic format. After digital imaging, a lawyer may "dispose of the original record," unless the record relates to a claim

or report due to the State of Louisiana. *See* La. Rev. Stat. § 13:3733(A). An electronically-imaged document "shall be deemed to be an original record for all purposes and shall be treated as an original record in all courts or administrative agencies for the purpose of its admissibility in evidence."[187] *See id.* § 13:3733(B).

Prior to making a decision to destroy or to electronically image client documents, a lawyer must make reasonable efforts to assure that the subject documents are eligible for destruction or imaging. The Nebraska opinion advises that a lawyer should consider the following factors in deciding which paper files to destroy:

- the availability and cost of physical and electronic storage space;

- the ease of access to documents;

- the potential need for originals in future litigation; and,

- the need to preserve confidentiality.

Id. at 3092. In most instances, a lawyer need not review each individual document. Rather, the lawyer can simply review broad categories of folders or boxes under consideration for destruction. However, the extent and nature of a lawyer's predestruction review efforts will turn on the nature of the lawyer's practice and the documents in issue.

To avoid any confusion regarding the destruction of closed files, a lawyer should address the issue in the lawyer's client engagement agreement. Here is some recommended language for a paperless lawyer:

> Lawyer will scan and store all Client files in electronic PDF format and destroy all hard-copy (paper) files given to or received by Lawyer immediately after scanning. All files will be stored "in the cloud" using widely-used providers such as SugarSync and Dropbox. Lawyer and Client understand that there are risks to confidentiality associated with this means of data/document storage. Lawyer will store at Lawyer's expense all relevant PDF files relating to Matter for a period of up to five (5) years following termination of Lawyer's representation. Lawyer may thereafter destroy all of Client's files without further notice to Client. Client may

---

[187] The ABA is in accord, advising that lawyer records "may be maintained by electronic, photographic, or other media provided that . . . printed copies can be produced" and that the records are "readily accessible to the lawyer." *See* ABA Model Rules for Client Trust Account Records r. 3 (Aug. 9, 2010).

request in writing that Lawyer make available to Client or the Client's designee any PDF files in Lawyer's possession that have not been destroyed. Within seven (7) days of receipt of such request, Lawyer shall make electronic (not hard-copy) files available for download.

HOW LONG MUST I KEEP THIS FILE?

It depends. In deciding to discard a file, a lawyer should consider the nature of the client, the matter, and the documents. Louisiana Rule 1.15(a) provides as follows:

A lawyer shall hold property of clients or third persons that is in a lawyer's possession in connection with a representation separate from the lawyer's own property. Funds shall be kept in a separate account maintained in a bank or similar institution in the state where the lawyer's office is situated, or elsewhere with the consent of the client or third person. . . . Complete records of such account funds and other property shall be kept by the lawyer and shall be preserved for a period of five years after termination of the representation.

Furthermore, under Louisiana Civil Code Article 3496, "[a]n action by a client against an attorney for the return of papers delivered to him for purposes of a law suit is subject to a liberative prescription of three years. This prescription commences to run from the rendition of a final judgment in the law suit or the termination of the attorney-client relationship."

Given these standards, a good rule of thumb is to keep client files for five (5) years following termination of the matter, unless there is a good reason for maintaining the file for a longer period of time.[188] Such a good reason would exist if the file relates to unprescribed claims, to a minor, or if the file contains promissory notes, wills, trusts or similar "original" documents.

What is included in the "client's file" should be broadly interpreted. According to ABA Formal Opinion 471:

A majority of jurisdictions follow what is referred to as the "entire file" approach. In those jurisdictions, at the termination of a representation, a lawyer must surrender papers and property related to the representation in the lawyer's possession unless the lawyer establishes that a

---

[188]A lawyer clearly has no duty to store *permanently* the files of a former client. *See, e.g.*, Bd. Of Prof'l Resp. of the Sup. Ct. of Tn., Formal Op. 2015-F-160 (Dec. 11, 2015) (citing D.C. Bar Op. 206 (1989); ABA Informal Op. 1384 (1977)).

specific exception applies and that certain papers or property may be properly withheld.

See ABA Formal Op. 471 (Jul. 1, 2015); *see also* Restatement (Third) of the Law Governing Lawyers §46 (2000) ("On request, a lawyer must allow a client or former client to inspect and copy any document possessed by the lawyer relating to the representation, unless substantial grounds exist to refuse.").

MAY I "FRIEND" AN UNREPRESENTED PERSON ON SOCIAL MEDIA TO GATHER INFORMATION TO HELP MY CLIENT?

A June 2013 ethics advisory opinion from the New Hampshire Bar Association Ethics Committee advises against a lawyer "friending" a nonparty witness if the lawyer "omit[s] identifying information" from the request. The committee opined that such an omission "may mislead the witness." *See* New Hampshire Bar Ass'n Ethics Comm. Op. 2012-13/5 (opinion that such conduct would violate Rules 4.1 and 8.4(c)). Ethics opinions from other jurisdictions have given similar full-disclosure advice. *See* Philadelphia Ethics Op. 2009-2 (2009); San Diego County Ethics Op. 2011-2 (2011).

In my view, Louisiana would not require as much disclosure. Louisiana Rule 4.1 prohibits a lawyer from "making a false statement of material fact or law to a third person." Furthermore, in dealing with an "unrepresented person," Louisiana Rule 4.3 provides that a lawyer "shall not state or imply that the lawyer is disinterested," and must make "reasonable efforts" to correct any misunderstanding that the person might have about the "the lawyer's role in a matter." Thus, a Louisiana lawyer must not lie to anyone as to his identity or purpose in making a friend request on social media. Further, the lawyer must make efforts to affirmatively correct any misunderstandings the would-be friend may have about the the lawyer's loyalties. Beyond that, there is no requirement that a lawyer Mirandize a would-be friend in the course of making the friend request.

The takeaway? A Louisiana lawyer may make a friend request to an *unrepresented* person, but the lawyer can't lie or mislead. If the lawyer's would-be friend is confused as to the lawyer's role, the lawyer must correct the confusion. As to the propriety of making such a request to a *represented* person, Rule 4.2 would prohibit any friend requests whatsoever if the friend request relates to a matter on which the would-be friend is represented by counsel.

MAY I ADVISE MY CLIENT TO TAKE DOWN HARMFUL FACEBOOK POSTS AND OTHER SOCIAL-MEDIA CONTENT?

Given the potential harm social media can cause to people's lives and cases, is it appropriate for a lawyer to advise a client to take down an embarrassing or case-imperiling post? An ethics opinion from the New York County Lawyers' Association reached this conclusion:

> An attorney may advise clients to keep their social media privacy settings turned on or maximized and may advise clients as to what should or should not be posted on public and/or private pages, consistent with the principles stated above. Provided that there is no violation of the rules or substantive law pertaining to the preservation and/or spoliation of evidence, an attorney may offer advice as to what may be kept on "private" social media pages, and what may be "taken down" or removed.

See NYCLA Ethics Op. No. 745 (Jul. 2, 2013); *see also* Op. No. 14-1, Professional Ethics of the Florida Bar (Jun. 25, 2015, approved Oct. 16, 2015); N.C. Formal Ethics Opinion 5 (July 25, 2014).

This is good advice. Rule 1.1, which requires a lawyer to be competent, suggests that a lawyer not only can, but should, advise his client about the possible case-related consequences of social-media postings. A client needs to know that the other side may be watching.

Rule 4.1 and Rule 3.3 would prohibit a lawyer from advising a client to post false images or information on a social media site for purposes of manufacturing favorable evidence (for example, by encouraging a personal injury client to post a sad picture of herself in a wheelchair when she was neither sad nor wheelchair-bound).

Note that. Rule 3.4(a) prohibits a lawyer from counseling a person, including a client (1) to engage in spoliation[189] of evidence, (2) to "unlawfully obstruct

---

[189] Under Louisiana law, the term "spoliation of evidence" refers to "an intentional destruction of evidence for purpose of depriving opposing parties of its use." *Pham v. Contico International, Inc.*, 759 So. 2d 880, 882 (La. Ct. App. 5th Cir. 2000) (*citing Hooker v. Super Products Corp.*, 751 So. 2d 889 (La. Ct. App. 5th Cir. 1999); *Kammerer v. Sewerage and Water Board of New Orleans*, 633 So. 2d 1357 (La. Ct. App. 4th Cir. 1994)). The *Pham* court noted that "the tort of spoliation of evidence has its roots in the evidentiary doctrine of

another party's access to evidence," or (3) to "unlawfully alter, destroy or conceal a document or other material having potential evidentiary value." A picture of a personal injury plaintiff jumping on a trampoline *is* a document "having potential evidentiary value" in a case in which the plaintiff claims that she cannot walk. Therefore, a lawyer clearly could not advise the plaintiff to destroy all extant copies of the photograph. But advising a client to remove a photo from Facebook is not advice "to destroy" or "to conceal" it. Such advice is equivalent to advising a client to remove—but not to destroy—an embarrassing picture posted on a billboard. In short, advising a client to take down a Facebook photo and to preserve it for production in the course of discovery[190] should not run afoul of the rules.

MAY I BE DISCIPLINED FOR MY INVESTIGATOR'S QUESTIONABLE CONDUCT?

Perhaps. A lawyer who *knowingly* uses an investigator or other third party to engage in conduct that the rules would forbid the lawyer from engaging in faces the risk of discipline. It is not uncommon for a lawyer to hire an investigator to surreptitiously gather evidence. However, the lawyer must not dispatch the investigator to engage in conduct that would otherwise be unethical for a lawyer. This could occur if the lawyer engages an investigator knowing that the investigator will (1) make a false statement of material fact to a third person, or (2) communicate with a person represented by counsel in the matter in question.

The Kentucky Supreme Court publicly reprimanded a lawyer who, while representing a client in a wrongful termination case, used an investigation firm to interview directly the client's former employer *See Bracher v. Kentucky Bar Ass'n*, No. 2009-SC-000358-KB (Ky. Sep. 9, 2009). In that case, the Kentucky lawyer hired Documented Reference Check, a company that contacted the

---

'adverse presumption,' which allows a jury instruction for the presumption that the destroyed evidence contained information detrimental to the party who destroyed the evidence unless such destruction is adequately explained." *Id.* (*citing Randolph v. General Motors Corp.*, 646 So. 2d 1019 (La. Ct. App. 1st Cir. 1994)).

[190] In contrast, a lawyer who advises a client to take down and destroy digital photographs from a social media site would violate Rule 3.4 and face the risk of severe sanctions. *See* Debra Cassens Weiss, *Lawyer Agrees to Five-Year Suspension for Advising Client to Clean Up His Facebook Photos*, ABA Journal On-Line, Aug. 7, 2013 (http://www.abajournal.com/news/article/lawyer_agrees_to_five-year_suspension_for_advising_client_to_clean_up_his_f).

client's former employer to see what the company had to say about the client. The Kentucky Supreme Court found that in so doing, the lawyer violated Kentucky Rule of Professional Conduct 4.2.

Much the same result could occur in Louisiana. Louisiana Rule 4.1(a) prohibits a lawyer from "knowingly" making "a false statement of material fact or law to a third person." Louisiana Rule 4.2(a) prohibits a lawyer from communicating "about the subject of the representation with . . . a person the lawyer knows to be represented by another lawyer in the matter, unless the lawyer has the consent of the other lawyer or is authorized to do so by law or a court order." Louisiana Rule 8.4(a) prohibits a lawyer from violating or attempt to violate the rules . . . through the acts of another." *See also* La. Rules of Prof'l Conduct r. 5.3.

WHAT DO I DO WITH A MISSING CLIENT'S FUNDS AND FILE?

Under Louisiana Rule 1.15(a): "A lawyer shall hold property of clients or third persons that is in a lawyer's possession in connection with a representation separate from the lawyer's own property. Funds shall be kept in a separate account maintained in a bank or similar institution in the state where the lawyer's office is situated, or elsewhere with the consent of the client or third person."

If a lawyer holds trust funds (or other property) that belong to a client but the client is missing, the lawyer should make reasonable efforts to locate the client. If those efforts are fruitless after approximately five (5) years, the lawyer should consult the office of the State Treasurer as to the disposition of the client's unclaimed property. Additional guidance is available on the LSBA website in a public opinion by the Association's Ethics Advisory Service: LSBA Public Opinion 06-RPCC-009.

MAY I STORE CLIENT FILES IN "THE CLOUD"?

With the deployment of virtually every new law-practice technology come the questions. Is it permissible to use cell phones for client communications? Do professional conduct standards permit lawyers to send documents via fax? Similar questions exist as to lawyers' use of "cloud" service providers, such as on-line document storage vendors (Google Drive, Dropbox and SugarSync), on-line calendaring services (Google Calendar) and total practice management solutions (Clio and Rocket Matter)

The legal ethics issues presented by the use of cloud technology, however, are not materially different from those that arise with regard to more traditional methods of data storage and communication. Irrespective of the technology, a lawyer owes a client the duties of confidentiality and competence.

Furthermore, a lawyer engaging nonlawyer assistants (such as paralegals, secretaries, contractors and vendors) must assure that they act in a manner that is consistent with the professional obligations of a lawyer.

Considering these obligations, a lawyer may store and transmit client data using "the cloud"—if the lawyer takes reasonable precautions to assure that the vendor will maintain the confidentiality and integrity of the data. To assure compliance with these obligations, a lawyer should engage in the following "due diligence" before storing client data on-line:

- Obtain the cloud storage vendor's service agreement. For example, the "terms of service" for Dropbox and SugarSync are posted on those vendors' websites.
- Assure that the service agreement requires the vendor to preserve the confidentiality and security of materials.
- Consider whether the vendor requires password access to the data, and whether the data will be encrypted.
- Consider whether the vendor must inform lawyer of unauthorized access events.
- Investigate how the vendor stores and backs up data, and whether the lawyer will have unrestricted and reliable access to data.
- Investigate how the lawyer can obtain data upon terminating the vendor.
- Become fully competent in the use of the vendor's interface and technology.
- Reevaluate the vendor's contractual obligations and capabilities periodically.
- Respect the client's contrary wishes about cloud storage.
- Save paper copies of wills, notes and other documents when a paper "original" is typically necessary.

Assuming that the lawyer undertakes these reasonable measures, client confidential data can be stored and transmitted in the cloud. All state and local bar association advisory opinions addressing the issue are in accord.

Advisory opinions from bar associations across the country have approved cloud storage of lawyer files, including the following:

- Connecticut Bar Association, Informal Op. 2013-07 (Jun. 19, 2013) (permissible if "lawyers make reasonable efforts to meet their obligations to preserve the confidentiality of client information and to confirm that any third-party service provider is likewise obligated").
- Massachusetts Bar Association, Ethics Op. 12-03 (2012) (lawyer may store electronic files in cloud if lawyer makes "reasonable efforts to assure that the provider's policies and practices are compatible with the lawyer's professional obligation of confidentiality).

428

- New Hampshire Ethics Comm. Advisory Opinion, No. 2012-13/4 (2012) (lawyer may store data in cloud with reasonable due diligence).
- Oregon State Bar Formal Opinion No. 2011-188 (2011) ("Lawyer may store client materials on a third-party server so long as lawyer complies with the duties of competence and confidentiality to reasonably keep the client's information secure within a given situation. To do so, the lawyer must take reasonable steps to ensure that the storage company will reliably secure client data and keep information confidential.").
- Professional Ethics Committee of the Florida Bar Op. 10-2 (2011).
- Pennsylvania Bar Association Committee on Legal Ethics and Professional Responsibility, Formal Opinion No. 2011-200 (2011).
- Iowa Committee on Practice Ethics and Guidelines, Ethics Opinion No. 11-01 (2011) (lawyer may store client data with cloud provider, but must perform due diligence to evaluate whether provider will protect and competently store data).
- New York State Bar Association's Committee on Professional Ethics Op. 842 (2010).
- Vermont, Op. 2010-6 (2010) (lawyer may store client data in cloud with reasonable precautions).
- New Jersey Supreme Court, Advisory Committee on Professional Ethics, Ethics Op. 701 (2006).
- Nevada Bar Association, Standing Comm. on Ethics, Formal Op. No. 33 (2006) (lawyer may store client data in cloud if lawyer competently and reasonably ensures data will be kept secure and confidential).
- Alabama State Bar Association, Ethics Opinion No. 2010-02 (2010) (lawyer may store client data with cloud provider provided the lawyer undertakes reasonable efforts to ensure confidentiality).
- California State Bar Association, Ethics Op. 2010-179 (2010) (cloud storage permitted with reasonable care).
- Maine Board of Bar Overseers, Ethics Op. 194 (2008) (cloud storage permitted with reasonable care).
- Arizona State Bar Association, Ethics Op. 09-04 (2004) (cloud storage permitted with reasonable care).

MAY I CHARGE A "NONREFUNDABLE" FEE?

Yes, but no. The North Dakota Supreme Court recently disciplined a lawyer for refusing to return a $30,000 "nonrefundable" minimum fee in a criminal case after working 26 hours prior to being discharged by the client. *See Disciplinary Bd. v. Hoffman*, No. 20120290 (S.D. Jul. 23,

2013). The court did so using a rule that requires North Dakota lawyers to "refund[] any advance payment of fee or expense that has not been earned or incurred."

While this precise language does not appear in Louisiana's rules, the same principles do. It is permissible for a Louisiana lawyer to charge a general retainer, fixed fee or minimum fee and to place that fee in the lawyer's operating account. However, the lawyer must return such a fee if its continued retention becomes "unreasonable" under the circumstances. See Louisiana Rule 1.5. This would be the case if, for example, the lawyer fails to represent a client diligently and competently, or if a client discharges the lawyer before substantial completion of the work. So, a Louisiana lawyer can charge a "nonrefundable" retainer or minimum fee. But sometimes it must be refunded.

MAY I ENTER INTO AN AGREEMENT RESTRICTING A PERSON'S ABILITY TO REPORT ME TO THE OFFICE OF DISCIPLINARY COUNSEL?

No. A 2017 Illinois disciplinary decision addressed whether it was appropriate for a lawyer to include a "non-disclosure provision" in her engagement agreement. In that provision, the lawyer's client agreed to "refrain from reporting any phase of the representation to any external agency," including disciplinary counsel. *See In re Laura Lee Robinson*, IL Atty. Registration and Disicplinary Comm. No. 2016PR00126 (Aug. 15, 2017). Under the disciplinary standards applicable in Illinois, the answer was pretty clear: Rule 8.4(h) of the of the Illinois Rules of Professional Conduct (2010) states that it is professional misconduct for a lawyer to "enter into an agreement with a client or former client limiting or purporting to limit the right of the client or former client to file or pursue any complaint before the Illinois Attorney Registration and Disciplinary Commission."

Louisiana, however, has no comparable provision in its disciplinary rules. Nevertheless, Louisiana Rule 8.4(d) provides that "[i]t is professional misconduct for a lawyer to . . . [e]ngage in conduct that is prejudicial to the administration of justice." *See* La. Rules of Prof'l Conduct r. 8.4(d). It is virtually certain that the Louisiana Office of Disciplinary Counsel would consider a similar agreement to violate the rules as conduct "prejudicial" to bringing an unethical lawyer to justice.[191]

---

[191] Note also that another lawyer could not participate in the making of such a nondisclosure agreement in the context or a settlement (or otherwise). Louisiana lawyers have an obligation to report serious misconduct by other

DOES AN AFFIRMATIVE DUTY TO AVOID NEGLIGENT DESTRUCTION OF EVIDENCE EXIST IN LOUISIANA?

Louisiana requires parties involved in litigation to avoid the intentional destruction of evidence for the purpose of depriving an opposing party of its use. While it is clear that such a duty exists to avoid the "spoliation of evidence," does a party to litigation have an affirmative duty to preserve evidence from unintentional destruction?

In *Reynolds v. Bordelon*, No. 2014-2362 (La. Jun. 30, 2015), the Louisiana Supreme Court held that Louisiana does not recognize a cause of action for negligent spoliation of evidence. Other remedies exist, however. As to parties to litigation, negligent spoliation can be redressed through the imposition of discovery sanctions and through an adverse evidentiary presumption. As to nonparties to litigation, those who fear destruction can enter into contracts to preserve evidence or seek court orders to preserve evidence.

HOW DO I AVOID DISCIPLINARY COMPLAINTS?

No lawyer wants to receive an envelope from the Office of Disciplinary Counsel containing a complaint. Although the Office dismisses approximately 80% of the complaints it receives, the anguish associated with being accused of misconduct and the time lost gathering old file materials, preparing a written response and submitting to a sworn statement are bruises that remain even after a dismissal. What can you do to avoid the complaint in the first place? Well, you can start by following your mother's good advice not to lie, cheat or steal. Unfortunately though, that's just not enough in today's more complicated regulatory environment. You need to do more, and that more is this.

CHOOSE YOUR CLIENTS CAREFULLY

- If you will be the prospective client's third lawyer, don't become his fourth.
- If the prospective clients wants a loan at the outset, tell him that you're a lawyer not a banker.
- Don't represent friends and family. Really. What you'll lose in friends and Thanksgiving guests that you want, you'll gain in complainants that you don't.

SET REASONABLE EXPECTATIONS EARLY

- Never undertake a representation without a signed engagement agreement. Never.

---

lawyers to the Office of Disciplinary Counsel. *See* La. Rules of Prof'l Conduct r. 8.3(a).

- Let your clients know how and when to contact you and how and when you will get back to them.
- Let your clients know that you have other cases.
- Let your clients know that you are not a pit bull. You are a lawyer.
- Be candid. Talk about the good, the bad and the ugly associated with your clients' cases.

BE DILIGENT

- Don't neglect your cases. Do something. And that "something" that you do—document it in your file. *See* La. Rules of Prof'l Conduct r. 1.3.
- Control your workload. You can do it all until you can't.

BE COMPETENT

- That attractive patent misuse antitrust case your neighbor wants you to take? Pass. You've never even heard of patent misuse. *See id.* r. 1.1.
- Prepare. Meet with those witnesses. Hire that expert. *See supra* "Be Diligent."
- Keep a good, organized file. That pile of papers with yellow sticky notes is not a file. It's a mess.
- Better yet, go paperless. It's not the future anymore.

AVOID CONFLICTS

- In a criminal case: don't represent co-defendants; and, don't communicate with your client's family (even if they are paying you) unless you are specifically authorized by your client to do so. *See id.* r. 1.7.
- In an insurance defense case, determine from the beginning who your client(s) is (are). Is it the insured or the insurance company or both? Once you make this determination, remember it and treat that person like he/it really is your client. *See id.*
- In a plaintiff's personal injury case, be careful representing both the driver and a passenger unless you are sure that the driver is clearly, absolutely, positively not at fault. *See id.*
- In a domestic case, never try and represent the husband and the wife to "paper" the divorce, community partition or custody agreement. *See id.* r. 1.7.
- In a succession, you don't represent "the estate" or "the succession"—there is no such juridical person. Rather, you represent the administrator, executor or heir.
- In a business transaction, you don't represent "the deal" or "the transaction"—you represent a person or persons. Figure out who.

COMMUNICATE

- Return your client's telephone calls, emails and letters. *See id.* r. 1.4. The longer you wait, the angrier they will get. Angry people submit disciplinary complaints. Happy ones don't.
- Do the same with calls, emails and letters from courts and opponents. They get angry too.
- Bury your client in paper. Send him everything.
- Confirm important conversations by email or letter.

AVOID FEE DISPUTES

- Money is the root of all evil. Misunderstandings about money are the root of many disciplinary complaints. Have a written and signed fee agreement that lays out in exhaustive detail how your fee will be computed. If it's an hourly fee, explain that you charge for every email. If it's a contingent fee, explain that you get paid first before expenses are deducted. If it's a flat fee, explain that you get to keep it even if you manage to achieve a great result in just a few hours of time. While we understand these things, many (or most) lay people do not. *See id.* r. 1.5.
- Make people happy about paying your bill. Believe it or not, it's possible with a prompt-pay discount.
- Get an advanced deposit up front. Always. That payment is an emotional and symbolic investment in you. And it may be the only money you ever get. So get it.
- There is no such thing as a "nonrefundable retainer." First, avoid using the sloppy word "retainer" unless you are really being paid just for your general availability to do the client's work (you probably aren't). Usually, what you call a "retainer" is either an advanced deposit or a minimum fee. *See id.* r. 1.5. Second, as to the "nonrefundable" part of "nonrefundable retainer," it's really not. If you take the client's money and don't do substantially all of the promised work, you have to give all or some of it back. That is, you have to R-E-F-U-N-D it. So, it's not nonrefundable. How's that for some double negatives?
- Have your client agree in advance to arbitrate all fee disputes (and all other disputes for that matter). You want your disputes settled by one friendly lawyer—not by twelve angry laymen. And choose the LSBA Fee Arbitration Program. It's inexpensive and efficient.
- If you and your client have a disagreement over what fee you're owed, put the "reasonably" disputed amount in your trust account. Do this even if you have spent it. If necessary, pawn something and put that money in trust. *See id.* r. 1.5(f)(5).

CAREFUL WITH THE TRUST ACCOUNT

- Your trust account is sacred territory. Get one. Put your clients' money into it and nowhere else. Keep your own money out of it. *See id.* r. 1.15.
- Don't overdraw your trust account. *Id.*
- Reconcile your trust account at least monthly.
- Set up notifications for all withdrawals or transfers out of the account.
- Note that there is nothing glib or even marginally witty in this section. When it comes to the trust accounting, everything is damn serious. Seriously.

OBEY THE LAW

- Comply with court orders and rules. *See id.* r. 3.5; *id.* r. 3.4(c). Contempt is not a river in Egypt. It's contempt.
- Avoid sanctions. Fall-back position: promptly pay those sanctions.
- Don't get into a fight in open court, in the hall of the courthouse or at the office Christmas party. *See id.* r. 3.5(d).
- Don't commit murder, aggravated assault, rape, battery, etc. You can find the rest of these "don'ts" conveniently listed in Louisiana Revised Statutes Title 14.
- Don't get that first DWI, but really don't get that second or third one.
- Don't withhold that exculpatory document prosecutors. An eager, young, rebel-with-a-cause will find it during post-conviction and things will get ugly. *See* La. Rules of Prof'l Conduct r. 3.8(d).

TERMINATE YOUR REPRESENTATION GRACEFULLY

- If you are terminated, hand over your client's file. *See id.* r. 1.16(d). Even though it doesn't feel like it, that file belongs to your ex-client and not to you. And don't try to hold the file hostage as ransom for anything. Give it up and walk away.
- Make a copy of your file before you hand it off. Unfortunately, this copy is on your nickel. *See id.*

COOPERATE WITH ODC

- The letter from ODC is unpleasant, but you have to open it. *See id.* r. 8.1(c). Nothing good comes from throwing it away. The only thing at the bottom of the trash basket is a "deemed admitted" proceeding, which is a technical way of saying "you lose."
- Those things in the ODC lawyer's hands? Most of the cards. This is an administrative matter, not a criminal trial. You have rights, but they become relevant only after you have given ODC most everything it wants.
- By "cooperation" I mean only "cooperation"—not pointless surrender. You have no obligation to turn yourself in if you have violated the rules. *See id.* r. 8.3(a) (obligating a lawyer to report violation of "another" lawyer). Stop doing whatever it was you were doing. Now. And fix whatever it is you

broke. But don't dump gasoline on yourself—unless you are going to get caught anyway or some other good can come of it.

WHAT SHOULD I THINK ABOUT WHEN SETTING UP A WEBSITE FOR MY FIRM?

Many Louisiana lawyers have created websites to have an "internet presence" on the World Wide Web. While this is undoubtedly good marketing practice, it can be bad law practice if done sloppily or inattentively. Indeed, Louisiana lawyers have found themselves in trouble for, among other things, failing to supervise web designers and using improper language on a website. To avoid disciplinary problems with a law firm website, consider these dos and don'ts:

- Do realize that the Louisiana Rules of Professional Conduct apply to websites. Although websites are exempt from the filing and review process applicable to most advertisements, see Rule 7.8(g), they still must comply with other advertising rules, including Rules 7.2, 7.6(b), and 7.9.

- Do include the following information on your website: the name of at least one lawyer in the firm; the location of all jurisdictions in which members of the firm are licensed; the location of the firm's office; and any intent to refer client matters out to another law firm. *See* Rules 7.2, 7.6 and 7.9(c).

- Don't include any "false" or "misleading" information on your website. *See* Rule 7.2(c)(1)(C). This prohibition covers not only overtly false information, but also misleading meta tags and hidden text visible to search engines. *See* Florida Bar Advisory Opinion A-12-1 (addressing deceptive search engine optimization techniques).

- Don't promise results, or have an actor portray a client (unless you use a disclaimer), or use a paid endorsement (unless you disclose it), or have an actor portray a lawyer. *See* Rule 7.2(c)(1).

- Don't use the words "specialize," "specialist," "certified," or "expert." Instead, just describe your areas of practice. *See* Rule 7.2(c)(5).

- Don't include fee information unless you also disclose information about costs. See Rule 7.2(c)(6). And if you do decide to include fee information, be prepared to honor it for at least 90 days. *See* Rule 7.2(c)(7).

- Don't allow a lawyer from any other firm to pay for all or part of the website. *See* Rule 7.2(c)(11).

- Do supervise any nonlawyers who help you with the website. *See* Rule 5.3. Remember, it's your site, not theirs.

Finally, do consider submitting your website for review by LSBA Ethics Counsel even though it's not required. Although there is a fee for the service, it is usually worth the modest expense. And it could avoid headaches later.

MUST I HAVE LEGAL MALPRACTICE INSURANCE?

No, the Louisiana Supreme Court does not require Louisiana lawyers to carry malpractice insurance or to disclose whether they do so.

In 2004, the American Bar Association adopted a "Model Rule on Insurance Disclosure." *See* ABA Model Rule on Insurance Disclosure (Aug. 10, 2004). The purpose of the model court rule was to provide potential clients with access to information to make "an informed decision about whether to hire a particular lawyer." *Id.* This model rule requires each licensed lawyer to certify "whether the lawyer is currently covered by professional liability insurance," and "whether the lawyer intends to maintain insurance during the period of time the lawyer is engaged in the private practice of law." The rule exempts any lawyer employed as "a full-time government lawyer" or employed "by an organizational client." *Id.*

Since then, 24 states have adopted an insurance disclosure requirement by mandating disclosure either on bar-registration statements (17 states) or directly to potential clients (7 states); six states have rejected the ABA model rule (Arkansas, Connecticut, Florida, Kentucky, North Carolina, and Texas); and one state requires its lawyers to carry legal malpractice insurance (Oregon). *See* ABA Standing Committee on Client Protection, State Implementation of ABA Model Court Rule on Insurance Disclosure (updated Feb. 10, 2016).

Although Louisiana lawyers are not required to carry malpractice insurance, it is readily available. The Louisiana State Bar Association's endorsed insurance program is administered by Gilsbar (incidentally, the name "Gilsbar" is an acronym that stands for Group Insurance Louisiana State BAR). For more information on this program, visit the LSBA website.

Model Fee Agreements

MODEL LAWYER-CLIENT HOURLY FEE AGREEMENT

1.   *Parties.* This Lawyer-Client Agreement ("Agreement") is entered into by and between Dane S. Ciolino, LLC ("Lawyer"), and _____ ("Client") as of the latest date set forth below. Lawyer is an independent contractor. There are no other parties whatsoever to this Agreement, including, but not limited to, Loyola University New Orleans.

2.   *Scope of Representation.* Client has engaged Lawyer in connection with the following:_____ ("Matter"). Lawyer's representation is in connection with Matter only, unless otherwise agreed in a signed writing.

3.   *Fees and Costs*

   a.   *Costs.* Client will be responsible for all costs. Lawyer, however, may advance such costs. As used herein, the term "Costs," includes, but is not limited to, filing fees, filing boxes and supplies, copying costs, deposition costs, computerized research costs, outsourced document scanning/coding/indexing costs, travel expenses, expert fees, court costs, postage expenses, witness fees, and reasonable interest paid by Lawyer to third-party lenders to cover any cost advances.

   b.   *Hourly Fee for Billable Time*

      i.   *Rates*

         (1)   *Lawyers.* Client agrees to pay Lawyer at Lawyer's regular hourly rate, currently $300.00 per hour, for all Billable Time incurred by lawyers associated with Dane S. Ciolino, LLC, including Dane S. Ciolino.

         (2)   *Paraprofessionals.* Client agrees to pay Lawyer at the hourly rate of $75.00 per hour for all Billable Time incurred by paraprofessionals associated with Dane S. Ciolino, LLC (including law clerks, paralegals, research assistants and investigators). Paraprofessional Billable Time includes, among other things, time incurred scanning and electronically indexing documents.

      ii.   *Billable Time.* Billable Time includes all time spent on the Matter, including, but not limited to, the following: legal research; drafting/reading email, letters, pleadings and documents; telephone calls; consultations and conferences with Client, witnesses, court personnel and other persons; settlement negotiations; pretrial preparation; fact investigation;

reviewing materials; travel time; and, court appearances. All Billable Time will be rounded up to the nearest one-tenth of an hour.

   iii. *Bills.* Lawyer will bill Client either upon written request by Client or periodically at Lawyer's discretion. All bills are due and payable by Client upon receipt. If a bill is not paid within thirty (30) days of receipt, simple interest of 1% per month (or portion thereof) shall be charged by Lawyer calculated from the date due and payable.

   iv. *Not a Contingent Fee.* Client's obligation to pay Fees and Costs is not contingent on the outcome of the Matter and must be paid by Client irrespective of the results obtained.

   v. *Advanced Deposit.*

   (1) *Generally.* Upon request by Lawyer, Client will pay Lawyer an advanced deposit for Fees and Costs. Upon receipt, Lawyer will place the advanced deposit in Lawyer's client trust account and credit it toward the final payment in this matter or, at the discretion of Lawyer, toward interim periodic invoices. Lawyer may apply all or part of any advanced deposit toward interim periodic invoices without further authorization from or notice to Client. Any part of the deposit not used at the conclusion of the case (after all Costs and Fees have been paid) shall be refunded to Client. Lawyer shall fully account for all funds held in trust at the conclusion of the Matter and Lawyer will not provide interim accountings unless requested in writing by Client. Any advanced deposit is neither the total fee in this Matter nor an estimate of the total fee. Client's failure to pay an advance deposit upon request shall constitute good cause for Lawyer to terminate this agreement and to withdraw from any further representation of Client.

   (2) *Initial Advanced Deposit.* Client will pay lawyer an Initial Advanced Deposit of $_____.

   vi. *No Guarantees Regarding Total Fees and Costs.* Lawyer has made no promises or guarantees whatsoever as to the total Fees and Costs of the Matter.

  4. *Arbitration of All Lawyer-Client Disputes.*

   a. *Arbitrable Disputes.* Any dispute, controversy or claim that may arise between Lawyer and Client shall be resolved by arbitration. Furthermore, any award rendered by any arbitrator(s) may be entered in any court having jurisdiction thereof, including but not limited to Civil District Court for the Parish of Orleans. Among other disputes, the parties hereby agree to arbitrate the following:

   i. *Disputes Regarding Fees, Costs and Other Compensation Due to Lawyer.* All disputes relating to Costs, Fees, compensation or remuneration to Lawyer, including but not limited to, disputes arising under the law of contract, unjust enrichment, restitution and/or quantum meruit shall be resolved by arbitration administered by the Louisiana State Bar Association ("LSBA") Program of Arbitration of Legal Fee Disputes.

ii.   *All Other Disputes.* All other disputes, including but not limited to, those arising under the law of tort, contract, restitution and/or legal malpractice shall be resolved by arbitration administered by the American Arbitration Association ("AAA") in New Orleans, Louisiana under the Commercial Arbitration Rules, Expedited Procedures effective at the time of the dispute.

b.   *Miscellaneous Arbitration Provisions.*

i.   *Responsibility for Costs and Fees of Arbitration.* The nonprevailing party shall pay all Costs incurred by the prevailing party. In addition, the nonprevailing party shall pay the prevailing party for all billable time incurred in connection with arbitration and with enforcement of any arbitration award, whether such billable time is incurred by Lawyer acting on his own behalf or by a lawyer or a law firm retained by the prevailing Lawyer or Client. The applicable rate for billable time shall be the same as set forth above. See supra Billable Time.

ii.   *Informed Consent to Arbitration.* Arbitration proceedings are ways to resolve disputes without use of the court system. Lawyer and Client understand that in agreeing to arbitrate, they are expressly waiving their right to file any lawsuit in court, to broad discovery under the applicable rules of procedure, to a trial by a judge or a jury and to appeal. These are important rights that should not be given up without careful consideration. Arbitration may be more expensive than litigation and often involves substantial up-front costs. Lawyer and Client understand that this paragraph does not prospectively limit Lawyer's liability to Client in any way, nor does it impinge upon Client's right to make a disciplinary complaint to the appropriate authorities. Client is advised of the desirability of seeking and is given a reasonable opportunity to seek the advice of independent legal counsel regarding this arbitration provision. Client is further advised to review the detailed procedures and costs associated with arbitration at the LSBA and AAA websites. To provide these opportunities, this paragraph shall not be effective until 21 days after signing. If Client does not wish this paragraph to become effective, Client shall within this 21-day period provide written notice to Lawyer via certified United States mail, return-receipt requested.

5.   *Retention, Delivery and Destruction of Files.* Lawyer will scan and store all Client files in electronic PDF format and destroy all hard-copy

(paper) files given to or received by Lawyer immediately after scanning. All files will be stored "in the cloud" using widely-used providers such as SugarSync and Dropbox. Lawyer and Client understand that there are risks to confidentiality associated with this means of data/document storage. Lawyer will store at Lawyer's expense all relevant PDF files relating to Matter for a period of up to one (1) year following termination of Lawyer's representation. Lawyer may thereafter destroy all of Client's files without further notice to Client. In addition, Lawyer will store all relevant PDF files relating to property of Client that Lawyer has held in trust for a period of five (5) years and may thereafter destroy same without further notice to Client. Client may request in writing that Lawyer make available to Client or the Client's designee any PDF files in Lawyer's possession that have not been destroyed. Within seven (7) days of receipt of such request, Lawyer shall make electronic (not hard-copy) files available for download.

6.   *Communication.* Lawyer and Client will communicate with one another using unencrypted email and cellular telephones. Both understand that there are risks to confidentiality associated with these means of communication.

7.   *No Guarantee.* Client acknowledges that Lawyer has made no guarantee regarding the disposition of any phase of this case. During the course of representation, Lawyer may provide Client with his candid advice and professional predictions regarding how the Matter may be resolved by a jury or other finder of fact. In so doing, Lawyer makes no guarantee regarding the outcome.

8.   *Governing Law.* This agreement shall be governed by the law of the State of Louisiana.

9.   *Complete Agreement, Amendment and Severability.* This is the complete agreement between Lawyer and Client with regard to matters addressed herein. Any changes or amendments to this Agreement and any future agreement(s) as to Costs and/or Fees owed under this Agreement must be set forth in a writing signed by the parties in order to be effective. There are no oral agreements of any kind relating to Lawyer's representation of Client. If any portion of this Agreement, or any portion of any paragraph of this Agreement, is declared invalid, the remaining portions shall be given full effect.

10.   *Electronic Signatures and Copies.* Lawyer and Client agree that a digital signature shall be effective to prove assent to the terms of this Agreement. Furthermore, Lawyer and Client agree that the terms of this Agreement may be proved through an electronic facsimile, including a scanned electronic copy in Portable Document Format ("PDF") or other digital format,

and that no "original" hard-copy document shall be retained by Lawyer to prove the terms of this Agreement.

11.   *Notices.* All notices shall be provided to the parties at the addresses or email addresses set forth below.

12.   *Commencement; Effective Date.* Lawyer will not begin work on Matter, has not been retained by the Client, and is under no duty to represent the Client until Lawyer has signed the Agreement and returned it to Client. Unless otherwise provided herein (i.e., arbitration clause), this Agreement is effective as of the date of Lawyer's signature. However, if Client engages Lawyer, Client is responsible for any authorized Billable Time and Costs incurred by Lawyer prior to the effective date.

13.   *Consultation and Informed Consent.* By signing below, Client acknowledges that Client has had the opportunity to discuss the terms of each paragraph of this Agreement with Lawyer.

14.   *Applicability of Louisiana Rules of Professional Conduct.* Lawyer and Client understand that Lawyer is bound by all provisions of the Louisiana Rules of Professional Conduct ("Rules"). Any obligation arising under this Agreement that conflicts with Lawyer's obligations under the Rules shall have no effect.

Signed (either manually or digitally) as of the dates set forth below.

_____

Lawyer
Dane S. Ciolino for
Dane S. Ciolino, LLC
Tel.: (504) 975-3263
Email: dane@daneciolino.com

Date Signed: _____

_____

Client

Date Signed: _____

MODEL LAWYER-CLIENT CONTINGENT FEE AGREEMENT

1.   *Parties.* This Lawyer-Client Contingent-Fee Agreement ("Agreement") is entered into by and between Dane S. Ciolino, LLC ("Lawyer"), and _____ ("Client") as of the latest date set forth below. Lawyer is an independent contractor. There are no other parties whatsoever to this Agreement, including, but not limited to, Loyola University New Orleans.

2.   *Scope of Representation.* Client has engaged Lawyer in connection with _____("Matter"). Lawyer's representation is in connection with Matter only, unless otherwise agreed in a signed writing.

3.   *Fees and Costs*

    a.   *Costs.* Client will be responsible for all costs. Lawyer, however, may advance such costs. As used herein, the term "Costs," includes, but is not limited to, filing fees, filing boxes and supplies, copying costs, deposition costs, computerized research costs, outsourced document scanning/coding/indexing costs, travel expenses, expert fees, court costs, postage expenses, witness fees, and reasonable interest paid by Lawyer to third-party lenders to cover any cost advances.

    b.   *Contingent Fee.* Lawyer will handle this matter on a contingent-fee basis. Lawyer's fee will be 40% of any gross recovery, prior to the deduction of Costs, upon substantial completion of the Matter, and/or upon interim receipt of sums prior to substantial completion.

        i.   *Illustration.* To illustrate, if the gross amount recovered from the defendant(s) in this matter totals $10,000.00, Lawyer's fee would be $4,000.00. In addition, Client will be responsible for any Costs and expenses, including those advanced by Lawyer. If the case is tried and Client recovers nothing, Client will owe no attorney's fees, but will remain responsible for any incurred Costs.

        ii.   *Discharge Prior to Completion.* If Client should choose to discharge Lawyer prior to substantial completion of the work on the Matter, Client will remain responsible for all Costs. In addition, Client shall pay Lawyer the value of the benefit conferred on the Client by Lawyer's work. Any such claim by Lawyer shall be an arbitrable dispute, *see infra* ("Arbitrable Disputes"). Lawyer shall have a security interest, lien and privilege on any property received, paid or to be paid to Client in connection with Matter to secure Lawyer's claim.

          iii.   *Billing.* Since Lawyer is handling this case on a contingent fee basis, Lawyer will bill Client for fees only upon receipt of funds. At such time, Lawyer will provide Client with a bill and disbursement statement outlining Client's recovery, Lawyer's fees, and any Costs and expenses advanced by the Lawyer.

          iv.   *No Guarantees Regarding Total Fees and Costs.* Lawyer has made no promises or guarantees whatsoever as to the total Fees and Costs of the Matter.

    4.   *Arbitration of All Lawyer-Client Disputes.*

        a.   *Arbitrable Disputes.* Any dispute, controversy or claim that may arise between Lawyer and Client shall be resolved by arbitration. Furthermore, any award rendered by any arbitrator(s) may be entered in any court having jurisdiction thereof, including but not limited to Civil District Court for the Parish of Orleans. Among other disputes, the parties hereby agree to arbitrate the following:

          i.   *Disputes Regarding Fees, Costs and Other Compensation Due to Lawyer.* All disputes relating to Costs, Fees, compensation or remuneration to Lawyer, including but not limited to, disputes arising under the law of contract, unjust enrichment, restitution and/or quantum meruit shall be resolved by arbitration administered by the Louisiana State Bar Association ("LSBA") Program of Arbitration of Legal Fee Disputes.

          ii.   *All Other Disputes.* All other disputes, including but not limited to, those arising under the law of tort, contract, restitution and/or legal malpractice shall be resolved by arbitration administered by the American Arbitration Association ("AAA") in New Orleans, Louisiana under the Commercial Arbitration Rules, Expedited Procedures effective at the time of the dispute.

        b.   *Miscellaneous Arbitration Provisions.*

          i.   *Responsibility for Costs and Fees of Arbitration.* The nonprevailing party shall pay all Costs incurred by the prevailing party. In addition, the nonprevailing party shall pay the prevailing party for all billable time incurred in connection with arbitration and with enforcement of any arbitration award, whether such billable time is incurred by Lawyer acting on his own behalf or by a lawyer or a law firm retained by the prevailing Lawyer or Client. The applicable rate for billable time shall be the same as set forth above. See supra Billable Time.

          ii.   *Informed Consent to Arbitration.* Arbitration proceedings are ways to resolve disputes without use of the court system.

Lawyer and Client understand that in agreeing to arbitrate, they are expressly waiving their right to file any lawsuit in court, to broad discovery under the applicable rules of procedure, to a trial by a judge or a jury and to appeal. These are important rights that should not be given up without careful consideration. Arbitration may be more expensive than litigation and often involves substantial up-front costs. Lawyer and Client understand that this paragraph does not prospectively limit Lawyer's liability to Client in any way, nor does it impinge upon Client's right to make a disciplinary complaint to the appropriate authorities. Client is advised of the desirability of seeking and is given a reasonable opportunity to seek the advice of independent legal counsel regarding this arbitration provision. Client is further advised to review the detailed procedures and costs associated with arbitration at the LSBA and AAA websites. To provide these opportunities, this paragraph shall not be effective until 21 days after signing. If Client does not wish this paragraph to become effective, Client shall within this 21-day period provide written notice to Lawyer via certified United States mail, return-receipt requested.

5. *Retention, Delivery and Destruction of Files.* Lawyer will scan and store all Client files in electronic PDF format and destroy all hard-copy (paper) files given to or received by Lawyer immediately after scanning. All files will be stored "in the cloud" using widely-used providers such as SugarSync and Dropbox. Lawyer and Client understand that there are risks to confidentiality associated with this means of data/document storage. Lawyer will store at Lawyer's expense all relevant PDF files relating to Matter for a period of up to one (1) year following termination of Lawyer's representation. Lawyer may thereafter destroy all of Client's files without further notice to Client. In addition, Lawyer will store all relevant PDF files relating to property of Client that Lawyer has held in trust for a period of five (5) years and may thereafter destroy same without further notice to Client. Client may request in writing that Lawyer make available to Client or the Client's designee any PDF files in Lawyer's possession that have not been destroyed. Within seven (7) days of receipt of such request, Lawyer shall make electronic (not hard-copy) files available for download.

6. *Communication.* Lawyer and Client will communicate with one another using unencrypted email and cellular telephones. Both understand that there are risks to confidentiality associated with these means of communication.

7. *No Guarantee.* Client acknowledges that Lawyer has made no guarantee regarding the disposition of any phase of this case. During the course of representation, Lawyer may provide Client with his candid advice and professional predictions regarding how the Matter may be resolved by a jury or

other finder of fact. In so doing, Lawyer makes no guarantee regarding the outcome.

8.   *Governing Law.* This agreement shall be governed by the law of the State of Louisiana.

9   *Complete Agreement, Amendment and Severability.* This is the complete agreement between Lawyer and Client with regard to matters addressed herein. Any changes or amendments to this Agreement and any future agreement(s) as to Costs and/or Fees owed under this Agreement must be set forth in a writing signed by the parties in order to be effective. There are no oral agreements of any kind relating to Lawyer's representation of Client. If any portion of this Agreement, or any portion of any paragraph of this Agreement, is declared invalid, the remaining portions shall be given full effect.

10.   *Electronic Signatures and Copies.* Lawyer and Client agree that a digital signature shall be effective to prove assent to the terms of this Agreement. Furthermore, Lawyer and Client agree that the terms of this Agreement may be proved through an electronic facsimile, including a scanned electronic copy in Portable Document Format ("PDF") or other digital format, and that no "original" hard-copy document shall be retained by Lawyer to prove the terms of this Agreement.

11.   *Notices.* All notices shall be provided to the parties at the addresses or email addresses set forth below.

12.   *Commencement; Effective Date.* Lawyer will not begin work on Matter, has not been retained by the Client, and is under no duty to represent the Client until Lawyer has signed the Agreement and returned it to Client. Unless otherwise provided herein (i.e., arbitration clause), this Agreement is effective as of the date of Lawyer's signature. However, if Client engages Lawyer, Client is responsible for any authorized Billable Time and Costs incurred by Lawyer prior to the effective date.

13.   *Consultation and Informed Consent.* By signing below, Client acknowledges that Client has had the opportunity to discuss the terms of each paragraph of this Agreement with Lawyer.

14.   *Applicability of Louisiana Rules of Professional Conduct.* Lawyer and Client understand that Lawyer is bound by all provisions of the Louisiana Rules of Professional Conduct ("Rules"). Any obligation arising under this Agreement that conflicts with Lawyer's obligations under the Rules shall have no effect.

Signed (either manually or digitally) as of the dates set forth below.

_____
Lawyer
Dane S. Ciolino for
Dane S. Ciolino, LLC
Tel.: (504) 975-3263
Email: dane@daneciolino.com

Date Signed: _____

_____
Client

Date Signed: _____

Index

27203488R00252

Made in the USA
Columbia, SC
24 September 2018